OCCASIONAL SERIES NO 1

ROMANS AND THE LEGACY OF ST PAUL

Historical, Theological, and Social Perspectives

Peter G. Bolt and James R. Harrison (Editors)

SCD Press
2019

Romans and the Legacy of St Paul
Historical, Theological, and Social Perspectives
(Occasional Series No 1)
Edited by Peter G. Bolt and James R. Harrison

© SCD Press and Contributors 2019

SCD Press
PO Box 1882
Macquarie Park NSW 2113
scdpress@scd.edu.au

ISBN-13: 978-1-925730-11-1 (Paperback)
ISBN-13: 978-1-925730-12-8 (E-book)

Cover design and typesetting by Lankshear Design.

OCCASIONAL SERIES NO 1

ROMANS AND THE LEGACY OF ST PAUL

Historical, Theological, and Social Perspectives

Peter G. Bolt and James R. Harrison (Editors)

SCD Press
2019

Occasional Series:

1. Peter G. Bolt & James R. Harrison (eds.), *Romans and the Legacy of St Paul. Historical, Theological, and Social Perspectives* (Macquarie Park, NSW: SCD Press, 2019).

AUTHOR PROFILES

Associate Professor Peter G. Bolt

Peter G. Bolt is the Academic Director of the Sydney College of Divinity, and the Director of the SCD Centre for Gospels & Acts Research and the Editor of *Journal of Gospels and Acts Research*. A graduate of Moore College, Australian College of Theology, Macquarie University, and King's College London, he is a New Testament scholar with research interests in the Gospels and Acts, Biblical Theology, magic and demonology, eschatology, the earliest Christian missionary movement, and the intersection between the New Testament and the Graeco-Roman world.

He has published *Jesus' Defeat of Death. Persuading Mark's Early Readers* (Cambridge, 2003, 2008); *The Cross from a Distance. Atonement in Mark's Gospel* (IVP, 2004); (with Sharon Beekmann), *Silencing Satan: A Handbook of Biblical Demonology* (Wipf & Stock, 2011); and the popular-level *Living With the Underworld* (Matthias Media, 2007); and *A Light Shining in Our Darkness. Reading Matthew Today* (Acorn Press, 2014). He has also edited several volumes, including (with L. Ball) *Wondering About God Together. Research-Led Learning & Teaching in Theology* (SCD Press, 2018); *Listen to Him: Reading and Preaching Emmanuel in Matthew* (Latimer, 2015); *Christ's Victory over Evil: Biblical Theology and Pastoral Ministry* (IVP, 2009).

Emeritus Professor Brendan Byrne, SJ

Brendan Byrne, SJ, taught New Testament for over three decades at Jesuit Theological College, Parkville, Victoria. While the chief focus of his academic research has been upon the Letters of Paul, especially Romans, he has also published works for wider audiences on the four Gospels, including *The Hospitality of God* (on Luke; revised ed. 2015), *Life Abounding* (on John; 2014). *Freedom in the Spirit: An Ignatian Retreat with St. Paul* appeared in 2016. A member of the Pontifical Biblical Commission (Rome) 1990-96, he is a Fellow of the Australian Academy of the Humanities and Professor Emeritus of the University of Divinity (Melbourne). Besides academic teaching and writing he regularly gives workshops to clergy, teachers and parish communities across Australia.

Dr Alan H. Cadwallader

Alan H. Cadwallader is a Research Fellow at the Centre for Public and Contextual Theology in Canberra. He has been involved in education and research for over three decades. Anything involving the mix of human culture and faith attracts his interest. He especially enjoys the dirt of ancient artefacts, the dust of old manuscripts and the excitement of new discoveries. Recent monographs have been *Beyond the Word of a Woman* (ATF, 2008), *Fragments of Colossae* (ATF, 2015), *The Politics of the Revised Version* (T&T Clark, 2019). He has edited a number of volumes on the interface of early Christianity, ancient culture and contemporary issues: *Pieces of Ease and Grace* (ATF, 2013), *Where the Wild Ox Roams* (Sheffield Phoenix, 2013), and *Stones, Bones and the Sacred* (SBL, 2016). He is currently completing an Earth Bible commentary on Mark's Gospel (T&T Clark) and a new monograph on Colossae and the letter to the Colossians (Eerdmans).

Dr Michele A. Connolly

Michele A. Connolly rsj lectures in Biblical Studies at the Catholic Institute of Sydney, a member Institute of the Sydney College of Divinity. She is Discipline Coordinator for Biblical Studies for the SCD and sits on its Academic Board. She studied theology at Yarra Theological Union Melbourne, and in the USA, graduating in 2008 with the PhD from GTU, Berkeley, CA. Michele's principal area of interest is the Gospel of Mark. In 2018 her doctoral thesis was published by T&T Clark, under the title, *Disorderly Women and the Order of God: An Australian Feminist Reading of the Gospel of Mark*. Michele has taught in Sydney since the 90s at CTU, Hunter's Hill and since 2001 at Catholic Institute of Sydney, Strathfield. Michele speaks regularly at seminars and conferences on the role of Scripture in Christian life.

Stephen D. Gilmour

Stephen D. Gilmour holds an M.Th. in Pauline theology from the Australian College of Theology (Ridley College, Melbourne). He has also completed a B.D. and M.A. (Theology) from Moore College, Sydney. He is an ordained minister in the Anglican church of Sydney, and is currently involved in parish ministry in South West Sydney. His research interests focus on the apostle Paul, and in particular how he conceives of salvation in his letter to the Romans.

Dr Louise Gosbell

Dr Louise Gosbell is a lecturer in New Testament at Mary Andrews College in Sydney and completed her PhD at Macquarie University in 2015. Louise's PhD thesis on disability and the gospels was published with Mohr Siebeck in 2018. Louise is currently working on the overlap of biblical studies and sensory studies in the gospel of John. Louise is involved in a range of different ministry areas with people with disability including being on the overseeing committee for Jesus Club, a ministry to adults with an intellectual disability, and overseeing the Deaf ministry at her church in Sydney.

Professor James R. Harrison

James R. Harrison, FAHA, studied Ancient History at Macquarie University and graduated from the doctoral program in 1997. Professor Harrison is the Research Director at the Sydney College of Divinity. His first monograph was *Paul's Language of Grace in Its Graeco-Roman Context* (Mohr Siebeck, 2003). Recent monographs include *Paul and the Imperial Authorities at Thessalonica and Rome* (Mohr Siebeck, 2011), *Paul and the Ancient Celebrity Circuit: The Cross and Moral Transformation* (Mohr Siebeck, 2019), and *Reading Romans with Roman Eyes: Studies in Paul's Social Perspective* (Fortress, 2019). He is the chief editor of *New Documents Illustrating the History of Early Christianity Vols. 11-15* and is co-editor with Professor L. L. Welborn (Fordham, New York) of the SBL Press series, *The First Urban Churches Vols 1-11* (vol. 5 forthcoming, 2019). He is also editor of E. A. Judge, *The Conflict of Cultures: The Legacy of Paul's Thought Today* (Eugene: Cascade, 2019). His research interests include the historical Jesus, the apostle Paul, the Graeco-Roman world and Second Temple Judaism, and the material remains of eastern Mediterranean cities, with a focus on their archaeology, epigraphy, numismatics, and iconography.

David Hughes

David Hughes is a postgraduate theology student in Canberra with passionate interests in land studies, radical theology, and postmodern hermeneutics. When not studying, David will most often be found in the garden or watching Tottenham Hotspur play (at foolish hours in the morning).

Dr Jin Heung Kim

Jin Heung (Jethro) Kim was born in Busan, South Korea. He studied 'Western History' for 6 years at Seoul National University (B.A.) and post-graduate courses. Then he studied theology at Korea Theological Seminary (M.Div.) and he specialized in Reformation History at Theologische Universiteit van de Gereformeerde Kerken (vrijgemaakt) in Kampen, the Netherlands for 7 years (Drs. and Th.D). 9 years pastoral and teaching work for Presbyterian churches and theological seminaries in South Korea, now he teaches Church History and Systematic Theology at Korean School of Theology in SCD from 2014. He has published (in Korean): *Peter Martyr Vermigli: A Theological Biography* (Busan: Korea Institute for Reformed Studies, 2018); *Survey on Luther's Early Thought in his 95 Theses and the Heidelberg Theses* (Seoul: Sungyak Press, 2017); *Presbyterian Faith according to the Reformed Catechisms: WLC, WSC, HC* (Seoul: Bread of Life, 2017); *Analogia Fidei: Christian Faith according to the Westminster Shorter Catechism* (Seoul: Pamtree, 2011, 2013); and (in English) *Scripturae et Patrum Testimoniis: The Function of the Church Fathers and the Medievals in Peter Martyr Vermigli's Two Eucharistic Treatises: Tractatio and Dialogus* (Apeldoorn: Instituut voor Reformatieonderzoek, 2009)

Dr Peter R. Laughlin

Peter R Laughlin (BEng, BTh(Hon), PhD(ACU)) joined the Australian College of Ministries, a member institution of SCD, as Dean of the Alliance Institute for Mission and Head of Theology in 2017. Prior to this he was the Director of the Alliance College of Australia in Canberra. His research interests include the intersection between historical Jesus studies and atonement, divine justice, theodicy, human well-being, pneumatology and theological method. His major work *Jesus and the Cross: Necessity, Meaning and Atonement* (Pickwick Publications, 2014) was published in the *Princeton Theological Monograph Series* and he has recently contributed to the edited work *Wellbeing, Personal Wholeness and the Social Fabric* (Cambridge Scholars Press, 2017). He serves as the chair of the International Commission for Theological Education for the Alliance World Fellowship and is also published in areas relating to the Christian and Missionary Alliance, most recently contributing to *Advancing the Gospel* (Forthcoming Pickwick Publications, 2019).

Dr Peter Orr

Peter Orr is lecturer in New Testament at Moore College (Sydney, Australia). His doctoral work was undertaken at Durham University where he examined Paul's understanding of the location of Christ. He is author of *Christ Absent and Present: A Pauline Christology* (Mohr Siebeck, 2014) and *Exalted Above the Heavens: The Risen and Ascended Christ* (IVP, 2018).

Professor Mark Reasoner

Mark Reasoner graduated from The University of Chicago with a Ph.D. in New Testament and Early Christian Literature in 1990. He is Professor of Biblical Theology at Marian University, in Indianapolis, Indiana. His first monograph was *The Strong and the Weak: Romans 14:1–15:13 in Context* (Cambridge University Press, 1999). Other books include: *Romans in Full Circle: A History of Interpretation* (Westminster John Knox, 2005); *Documents and Images for the Study of Paul* (with Neil Elliott, Fortress 2011); *Roman Imperial Texts: A Sourcebook* (Fortress, 2013); *The Abingdon Introduction to the Bible: Understanding Jewish and Christian Scriptures* (with Joel Kaminsky and Joel Lohr, Abingdon, 2014); *The Letters of Paul: An Introduction*, 2nd ed. (with Charles Puskas, Michael Glazier, 2014). His research interests include the New Testament letters of Romans and 1 Corinthians and the cultural worlds of the New Testament.

Murray Smith

Murray Smith serves as Lecturer in Biblical Theology and Exegesis at Christ College, Sydney. He holds an MA in Reformation History (University of Sydney), an MA in Early Christian and Jewish Studies (Macquarie University), and an MDiv (Australian College of Theology). His PhD thesis (Macquarie University) examines 'Jesus and the Final Coming of God' in the Gospels. Murray has published several articles on the New Testament and related early Christian literature, including Paul and his letters.

Dr Stephen Spence

Stephen Spence, Associate Academic Dean of Academies Australasia Polytechnic, provides academic leadership and direction for all academic programs within AAPoly. In terms of his academic studies in theology, Dr Spence has graduated with degrees from Fuller Theological Seminary (PhD Theology), the Australian College of Theology (MA Theology), and Asbury Theological Seminary (Master of Divinity). Before his current position, he served as Provost of Tabor in Adelaide, South Australia. Previous roles within Tabor (2007–2018) included Deputy Principal (Academic), Vice President of Education and Research, Dean of Theology and Social Sciences, and Head of School of Ministry, Theology, and Culture. Before his time at Tabor, he served as Principal of Burleigh College, South Australia, (2001–2006) and as lecturer in New Testament and Theology (1997–2000). His areas of research include Teaching for Adult Learning, The Learning Organisation, Pauline Studies, and Historical Jesus Studies. Publishing in the areas of theology and educations, he is well known in Romans studies for his monograph *The Parting of the Ways: The Roman Church as a Case Study* (Leuven/Dudley: Peeters, 2004).

CONTENTS

INTRODUCTION 1

Chapter 1   James R. Harrison, *Romans and the Western Intellectual Tradition: From Church to Society and Back Again* 3

PART 1   **On First Hearing Romans Read Aloud in Neronian Rome: Theological and Historical Reverberations** 17

Chapter 2   Brendan Byrne, SJ, *The Apocalyptic Motif of the Last Judgement: The Essential Horizon of Paul's Argument in Romans* 19

Chapter 3   Brendan Byrne, SJ, *Justification and Last Judgment in Romans: The Place of Chapters 5–8* 51

Chapter 4   Mark Reasoner, *Paul's Letter against the Roman Gods* 71

Chapter 5   Mark Reasoner, *Hope against Hope in Paul's Scriptures and in Rome* 91

PART 2   **Romans and the Challenge of Exegesis: Reading and Being Read by the Epistle** 107

Chapter 6   Stephen Gilmour, *Justification from Sin: An Examination of Romans 6:7* 109

Chapter 7	David Hughes, *The Love Tax: Paul's Neighbourliness in Romans 13:1–7* 133
Chapter 8	Peter Orr, *The Intercession of Christ in Romans 8:34* 157
Chapter 9	Murray Smith, *God's Righteousness, Christ's Faithfulness and 'Justification by Faith Alone'* 181
Chapter 10	Stephen Spence, *Personal Obedience (and Sin) in the New Age of Faith: Rehearing Romans 14:23b* 255

PART 3	**Romans and the Challenge of Theology: From Text to Society** 279
Chapter 11	Louise Gosbell, *A Disability Reading of Paul's Use of the 'Body of Christ' Metaphor in Romans 12:3–8 and 1 Corinthians 12:12–31* 281
Chapter 12	James R. Harrison, *Paul's Legacy in Romans and the Confession Inscriptions of Asia Minor: The Difficulty of Moving Beyond Divine Justice to Mercy in Antiquity* 337

PART 4	**Ancient Epistles and the Puzzling Particularity of Romans** 389
Chapter 13	Peter Bolt, *Untangling the Pauline Handshakes: Who is Greeting Whom in Romans 16?* 391
Chapter 14	Alan Cadwallader, *Phoebe in and around Romans: The Weight of Marginal Reception* 429

PART 5	The Theological, Social and Philosophical Legacy of Romans: From Augustine to Agamben 453
Chapter 15	Peter G. Bolt, James R. Harrison and Peter Laughlin, *The Legacy of Paul's Epistle to the Romans: From Augustine to Agamben* 455
Chapter 16	Jin Heung Kim, *Locus on Justification in Vermigli's Commentary on Romans* 519
PART 6	A Personal Reflection on the Legacy of Romans 547
Chapter 17	Michele Connolly, *On First Looking into Paul's Romans and Why Roman Catholics Need to Do It More* 549

INTRODUCTION

CHAPTER 1

Romans and the Western Intellectual Tradition: From Church to Society and Back Again

James R. Harrison

In 2017 and 2019 two significant landmarks of the legacy of Paul's epistle to the Romans in the western intellectual tradition were celebrated. Both highlight how Romans has remained at the centre of theological, ecclesiastical, social and political discourse over the centuries. First, Martin Luther's preparation of his lectures on Romans at the Saxon University of Wittenburg, commencing in Easter 1515 and concluding in the summer semester of 1516, paved the way for his posting the "Ninety-five Theses on the Power of Indulgences" on the door of the Castle Church in Wittenburg in October 31 1517.[1] Some 500 years later, the Protestant world celebrated the legacy of the Reformation, spawned by Luther's exegetical engagement with Romans and his rediscovery of "justification by faith" as the leitmotiv of the Christian life. The celebration was marked by (a) conferences on the Reformation around the world; (b) an avalanche of academic publications; (c) a Kirchentag (or church convention) in Berlin in May 2017, gathering 100,000 people; (d) an open-air service on 28 May in Wittenberg; (e) tours to Reformation sites across Europe, involving not only Wittenberg

---

1   Luther, *Lectures on Romans* (Pauck).

but also Geneva (John Calvin), Zurich (Huldrych Zwingli), and Strasbourg (Martin Bucer), among many other events. However, before this, on 31 October 2016, the Lutheran World Federation and the Roman Catholic Church had held an ecumenical celebration together in Lund, Sweden, a fruition of many prior ecclesiastical conversations culminating in the 1999 Lutheran-Catholic Joint Declaration on the Doctrine of Justification. The movement from conflict to communion had already begun on both sides of the theological and ecclesiastical divide, notwithstanding the differences that still remain.[2]

However, the decisiveness of the first Roman reaction to Luther's ninety-five theses in 1518, arising out of his exegesis of Romans, underscores how theologically penetrating, culturally acute, and comprehensive in scope Luther's critique of Medieval Catholicism had been.[3] His denunciation is stinging. According to Luther, pope and bishop 'compete with each other in the traffic of relics', 'carefully observing the show of piety', without any sign of mutual submission.[4] Speaking of the sixteenth century, Luther opines that 'the secular as well as the spiritual lords are guilty of pride, dissoluteness, adultery, and still worse sorts of thievery', disregarding God and perpetrating unjust wars.[5] The pope and the higher clergy show extravagant liberality in indulgences for the 'temporal support of that church', with the result that the people of God are diverted from the true worship of God because the religious authorities lack genuine care for the salvation of souls.[6] The secular princes had endowed the churches with rich properties and its leaders with special privileges, causing the laity to hate the clerics.[7] Bishops and abbots

---

2   See the collection of essays in Aune, *Rereading Paul Together*. See too Sobolewski, *Roman Catholic Perception of Luther*. On the movement from conflict to communion that Lutherans and Catholics have pursued for more than the last fifty years, with their respective changing perceptions of the Reformation, see Dieter, 'Ecumenical Commemoration'.
3   See Wicks, 'Roman Reactions'. On how the theses-posting defined subsequent Lutheran memory, self-perception, and the process of reinterpretation in subsequent generations, see Dixon, 'Luther's Ninety-Five Theses'.
4   Luther, *Lectures on Romans*, 368.
5   Luther, *Lectures on Romans*, 37–38.
6   Luther, *Lectures on Romans*, 292. For Philip Melanchthon on the power of the papacy, the abuse of masses, masses, and the worship of the saints, see idem, *Commentary on Romans*, 245–46. On the superstition of statuary devoted to Mary, see ibid., 81.
7   Luther, *Lectures on Romans*, 360–61.

elevate incompetent people to the pulpit,[8] whereas the worldly bishop of Brandenburg ('the burghers') had entered into a dispute with the city council of Wittenberg ('the councillors').[9] The pomp of the ecclesiastical vestments and the prayer service rituals had become so lavish that 'faith and love decline proportionately, and greed, pride and vainglory are being fostered'.[10] The Scholastic theologians are ignorant of the true nature of sin an divine forgiveness, still attributing towards the soul some inclination toward the good.[11]

It might be argued, with Steven Surrency,[12] that Luther's debates in his *Lectures on Romans* were 'intra-confessional', merely articulating 'how scripture should be read, how God's sovereignty should be understood, and how Augustine should be received'.[13] Furthermore, Surrency posits that Luther's call for an end to various abuses were 'run-of-the-mill' in his ecclesiastical context. His reforms were similar to the reform agenda of Giles of Viterbo, an Augustinian bishop and cardinal.[14] Giles, faced with the disintegration of piety, called for the reform of the cult of the saints, a termination of the sale of relics, and a reinvigoration of priestly ministry.[15] Admittedly, in discussing Luther's *Lectures on Romans*, we have to allow the early theology of Luther, encapsulated in his initial lectures, the opportunity to flower into the full richness of

---

8 Luther, *Lectures on Romans*, 355; similarly, ibid, 362–63.
9 Luther, *Lectures on Romans*, 405 n. 3. Note, too, the notorious case of the kidnap of a daughter of a Strasbourg citizen by the canon of St Thomas, who avoided punishment by appealing to the Curia at Rome over against the three members of the City Council Strasbourg (ibid., 363 n. 11). Luther also pillories the feuds between Duke George of Saxony and Count Edzard of East Frisia (ibid., 328).
10 Luther, *Lectures on Romans*, 384–85.
11 Luther, *Lectures on Romans*, 129–30. On Dun Scotus, see ibid., 388–89. For a more positive evaluation of the Scholastic theologians on Luther's part, see ibid., 152. For Melanchthon on Scholastic theology, see idem, *Commentary on Romans*, 55–58. For discussion of Melanchthon's commentary on Romans, see Campbell, *The Deliverance of God*, 258–60.
12 Surrency, *A Gadamerian Analysis*, 113.
13 Surrency, *A Gadamerian Analysis*, 113.
14 Surrency, *A Gadamerian Analysis*, 113: 'Luther's critique of the excesses and extravagances of the Catholic hierarchy offered hope for the renewal and purification of the Roman Catholic ecclesial structures of the time'.
15 Surrency, *A Gadamerian* Analysis, 128.

its later expression,[16] as well as to situate his view of justification within the much earlier theological contribution of Augustine.[17] But, in the context of the narrow aperture of 1513–1518, we can legitimately say that the 'self-accusing faith' of 1513–1516 had developed by 1518 into a full-fledged fiducial faith based upon the promise of righteousness secured through Christ's atoning work of the cross.[18] The interplay in Romans 3:4 between the believer's trust in God's righteous words and its indissoluble connection to his gift of grace—consisting in the status of being declared righteous by God—is explained thus:

> The passive and active justification of God and faith or trust in him are one and the same. For when we acknowledge his words as righteous, he gives himself to us, and because of this gift, he recognises us as righteous, i.e. he justifies us. And we do not justify his words, until we believe that they are righteous.[19]

---

16 Surrency, *A Gadamerian Analysis*, 113: 'In 1515, when Luther lectured on Romans, he was not yet proposing a radically new conception of justification, ecclesial government, or sacramental practices—though some important novelties are evident'. See the excellent chronological coverage of Wicks, 'Justification and Faith'. See also Campbell, *The Deliverance of God*, 250–58, 264–70; Barclay, *Paul and the Gift*, 97–116. Seifrid's fine book on justification (*Justification by Faith*), like many other modern accounts, commences with the modern era of William Wrede and Albert Schweitzer. Such accounts bypass the contributions of Augustine, Luther, Melanchthon, Calvin, and Vermigli, among others, as either 'pre-critical' or, more fundamentally, not informed by the nuanced understanding of Second Temple Judaism afforded through a 'New Perspective' lens. However, the Church Fathers and Reformers have much to teach Romans exegetes. On the Church Fathers, see Gorday, *Principles of Patristic Exegesis*; Roukema, *The Diversity of Laws*; Bray, *Romans*; Patte & TeSelle, *Engaging Augustine*; Gaca & Welborn, *Early Patristic Readings*; Reasoner, *Romans in Full Circle*; Patte & Vihoc, *Greek Patristic and Eastern Orthodox Interpretations*. On the value of Patristic Interpretation of the Scriptures, see Childers, 'Reading the Bible with Old Friends'; Decock, 'On the Value of Pre-modern Interpretation'.
17 Fitzmyer, *Romans*, 259–62.
18 Luther, *Lectures on Romans*, 18–19, 75, 78, 122–23, 146–47, 151, 189, 278–79, 290, 332, 400–402.
19 Luther, *Lectures on Romans*, 78. Additionally, see ibid., 131: '... the righteousness of God is imputed to believers without works ... And so (the saints) were first reckoned as righteous on account of the yearning of their faith, and only afterward also their works were accepted and approved'. Here it is clearly through the *instrumentality* of faith that righteousness is secured for believers and not through faith as a work. In saying that Luther occasionally subscribes to a 'conditional' and 'contractual' view of salvation, Campbell, *The Deliverance of God*, 254, assigns a 'meritorious' nuance to Luther's understanding of faith in some instances, requiring divine requital, as opposed to what is, in my view, Luther's instrumental view of faith. For the decisive three-fold break that Luther made with his early understanding of justification (1513–1514) in his Romans lectures of 1515–1516, see McGrath, Iustitia Dei: *A History*, 193.

Moreover, in contrast to late medieval university theology, Luther's theology of the cross[20] stood on contrast to the Thomist emphasis upon the interrelation of all things under divine wisdom, or the Scotist and Ockhamist accent on divine freedom in a contingent universe.[21] The very strong polemical and ecclesiastical reaction of the Roman church to Luther's radical theology, as expressed in the Romans lectures and in the ninety-five theses, was not without reason. Luther had placed the individual at the centre of God's cruciform love through justifying faith, as opposed to the medieval church and its personnel being the dispenser of divine forgiveness. The rise of the individual over against the ecclesiastical hierarchy in the West had begun.

Second, five centuries after the first edition of Luther's commentary, Karl Barth's celebrated commentary on Romans (*Der Römerbrief*), written during World War I from the summer of 1916 to August 1918, was submitted to the publishers in late 1918. The volume was published in August 2019.[22] The centennial anniversary of Barth's volume on Romans is currently being celebrated in 2019.[23] However, at the time, only 1000 copies of the first edition were printed and a mere 300 were sold. Barth greeted the appearance of second edition of *Der Römerbrief* with considerable relief, being happy to let the first edition 'disappear from the scene'.[24] The appearance of the new edition allowed Barth to address 'the chief weakness' of the book which, in his view, had

---

20 Luther, *Lectures on Romans*, 271: 'The wounds of Christ, "the clefts in the rock", are safe enough for us'. Additionally, ibid., 263: 'For he really and truly offered himself for us to eternal damnation to God the Father ... Because he loved God in this way, God at once raised him from death and hell and thus devoured hell'.
21 Wicks, 'Justification and Faith', 28.
22 On the circumstances of the first edition of Barth's *Römerbrief*, never translated into English, see Brazier, 'Barth's First Commentary on Romans (1919)', 387–88.
23 Two examples of the centennial celebration of Barth's *Römerbrief* will suffice. The 2019 Annual Karl Barth Conference, held at Princeton Theological Seminary, explored the theme of 'The Finality of the Gospel: Karl Barth and the Tasks of Eschatology'. The theme not only honours Barth's death fifty years before (1968) but also it celebrates the centenary of the publication of his *Römerbrief*. Prior to this conference, in 2017 in Adelaide, South Australia, the Karl Barth Study Group of the ANZATS conference chose the theme of 'Reading Romans with Barth' with a view to highlighting the coming centenary of the commentary. The current volume of essays originated from the 2016 Sydney College of Divinity Annual Conference, which celebrated both impending anniversaries in Romans studies.
24 Barth, *The Epistle to the Romans*, 2.

gone unnoticed by his critics[25] and also to rebut charges that he was an enemy of historical criticism,[26] among other issues aired in the reviews of his book. Barth's confidence in the second edition was entirely justified. Barth's completely rewritten second edition, published in 1922, brought about a seismic shift in the modern theologies of the late nineteenth and early twentieth century, though again not without criticism, but this time with the result that *Der Römerbrief* rapidly reached its sixth edition by 1928.[27]

In *Der Römerbrief* Barth struck out against the confidence of nineteenth century neo-Protestant Liberalism in the progress of modernity.[28] At the turn of the twentieth century, modern theologians such as Friedrich Schliermacher had been deeply influenced by the philosophy of Immanuel Kant and G. W. F. Hegel, as well as by the evolutionary theory of Charles Darwin.[29] Prior to World War I, there was a sense on the European continent that 'the whole enterprise of culture and history' exemplified 'the operation of that human spirit which is also the divine Spirit.'[30] Consequently, there was a strong belief in 'man's innate capacity for apprehending the infinite as a kind of religious *a priori* on which whole theories of religion and of the religious nature of a national culture could be built.'[31] Instead Barth enunciated a radical "No" to human achievement. He criticised the human veneration of science and technology, noting that despite its much-vaunted progress, its effects had also led to the social chaos and mass destruction of World

---

25 Barth, *The Epistle to the Romans*, 3
26 Barth, *The Epistle to the Romans*, 6.
27 See Barth, *The Epistle to the Romans*, 1–26, for the individual prefaces to each edition. For an excellent discussion of the prefaces to the first and second editions, see Dreyer, 'Karl Barth's *Römerbrief*, 10–13.
28 On modernity, see Dreyer, 'Karl Barth's *Römerbrief*, 3–5.
29 On neo-Protestant Liberalism, see Dreyer, 'Karl Barth's *Römerbrief*, 5–9. Schleiermacher, *The Christian Faith*, 366–67, argued that the power of Christ's God-consciousness brought about an increasing perfection in humanity as it assimilated the human consciousness of sin to itself. This communication of the God-consciousness on the part of Christ the Redeemer to humanity is what Scheiermacher perceived divine grace to be (*ibid.*, 262–64).
30 Barbour, 'Biblical Classics', 264.
31 Barbour, 'Biblical Classics', 264.

War I.[32] Consider Barth's sweeping denunciation of early 20th century European "civilisation" in the following extract from *Der Römerbrief*:

> Christianity does not set its mind on *high things*. It is uneasy when it hears men speaking loudly and with confidence about 'creative evolution'; when it marks their plans for perfecting the development of pure and applied science, of art, of morals and of religion, of physical and spiritual health, of welfare and of well-being. Christianity is unhappy when men boast of the glories of marriage and of family life, of Church and State, and of Society. Christianity does not busy itself to support and underpin those main 'ideals' by which men are deeply moved —individualism, collectivism, nationalism, internationalism, humanitarianism, ecclesiasticism. Christianity is unmoved by Nordic enthusiasm or by devotion to Western Culture, by the visions of Youth or by the solid and mature wisdom of middle age. Christianity sees no clear distinction between concrete and abstract idealism. It observes with a certain coldness the cult of both 'Nature' and 'Civilisation', of both Romanticism and Realism. It watches with some discomfort the building of these eminent towers, and its comments always tend to slow down this busy activity, for it detects therein the menace of idolatry.[33]

Furthermore, Barth asserted that true knowledge of God was only possible because he had revealed himself in Christ:

> The scandal of the historical revelation of Christ criss-crosses every form of rationalism. God is not 'inevitable reasonableness'. His eternity is not a constant factor which we can affirm

---

32 For Barth's sobering evaluation of war, see *The Epistle to the Romans*, 467–68. On war, peace and revolution (especially in the early 1920s context), see Clough, *Ethics in Krisis*, 48–60, 126–54. Dreyer, 'Karl Barth's *Römerbrief*', 4–5, writes regarding the dramatic change that World War I made to European optimism at the beginning of the 20th century: 'Optimism was replaced by fear, by the knowledge that science and technology not only facilitated the progress and well-being of humanity, but also the devastation of society and destruction of humanity. This realisation brought about a major crisis in European society ... Barth started his journey as a theologian with misery and poverty all around him. Millions of people died and Europe was laid to ruin. Barth was convinced that the Bible had something to say about that'.
33 Barth, *The Epistle to the Romans*, 463–63 (original emphasis).

safely and directly and non-paradoxically, as though it were a series of universal ideas—such as the idea of God, of Christ, and of Mediation. His omnipotence has not the necessity of a logical mathematical function. God is Personality: He is One, Unique, and Particular—and therefore He is eternal and omnipotent. To Him the historical Jesus bears witness ... that is to say, the particularity of God is illuminated by His existentiality ... we encounter in Jesus the scandal of an eternal revelation of that which Abraham and Plato had indeed already seen.[34]

The triumph of grace in Christ, Barth reminds us, had changed everything, even in our darkest hours.[35] As Barth observes, 'Grace is and remains always the Power of God ([Rom] 1:16), the promise of a new man, of a new nature, of a new world: it is the promise of the Kingdom of God'.[36] Finally, Barth graphically captures the existential crisis that he faced in writing his lectures on Romans during World War I with a striking metaphor. He compared his encounter with the text of Romans to reaching out for the hand-rail in a dark church but, after mistakenly seizing the bell-rope, he nevertheless rang out its message loudly in the chaos of post-war Germany.[37]

We have seen from Luther's *Lectures on Romans* and Barth's *Römerbrief* that the legacy of Romans embraced more than just a reforming pietism or was the precursor of the introspective conscience of the West, as Krister Stendahl has famously argued.[38] Instead the legacy of the epistle to the Romans, as outlined by its Reformation and Neo-Orthodox interpreters, exposed the spiritual bankruptcy of the church, the theological and moral compromise of its leaders with the surrounding culture, and its indebtedness to the patronage of the politically powerful and wealthy elites. But their critique of the fallen church and

---

34 Barth, *The Epistle to the Romans*, 276–77.
35 Barth, *The Epistle to the Romans*, 102–03, 211–13. See also Berkouwer, *The Triumph of Grace*. For an insightful discussion of grace in Barth's *Römerbrief*, see Barclay, *Paul and the Gift*, 130–35.
36 Barth, *The Epistle to the Romans*, 203. On the hermeneutical principles underlying Barth's *Römerbrief*, see Burnett, *Karl Barth's Theological Exegesis*.
37 Barth, *Christliche Dogmatik*, ix.
38 Stendahl, 'The Apostle Paul'.

their summons for a return to Paul's gospel of grace moved well beyond the church and engaged the dominant idolatries of their society. They called Christ's church to be a light on the hill and the salt of the earth once again for the sake of the truth of the gospel and because of the hopeless plight of humanity without Christ. John M. G. Barclay alerts us to the paradoxical dynamism of Paul's thought, cogently reminding us that its impact is to be seen as much outside the church as within it:

> Paul's legacy is like a slow-burning firework. Explosive at the start, with huge flashes of illumination, it seems to die down for a while, in a steady rate of lesser activity, before exploding again, unpredictably, in a huge rush of power and light, then quietly fizzing again, before another moment of raw energy and danger.[39]

But, unexpectedly, the legacy of Romans has come full circle in the western intellectual tradition, moving in this instance from modern secular society back to the foundational documents of the first-century New Testament church, with a special focus on the message of Romans in contemporary European context. Modern French and Italian philosophers have discovered in the epistle to the Romans the ideological resources for them to grapple with the threat that hangs over the present moment and also to challenge the reigning models of liberal democracy and secular power with new social and political constructs.[40] While the fuse lit by the epistle to the Romans continues to burn quietly in the lives of believers in the first quarter of the 21st century, we await expectantly the next explosion of its raw energy, in the expectation that the shock waves of divine grace generated will reverberate from a revitalised church back to society again with transformative effects.

Contributions to and Structure of the Volume

This book, arising from the papers delivered at 2016 Sydney College of Divinity Annual Conference, explores in an ecumenical context the

---

39 Barclay, 'Paul and the Philosophers', 171.
40 See Chapter 15 in this volume.

legacy of Romans from a variety of perspectives (ecumenical, historical, exegetical, social, and philosophical). After the introduction to the volume, the theological and social impact of the letter upon the original audience in Neronian Rome is examined in Part 1, exploring the imperial and Jewish apocalyptic context. In Part 2 a series of traditional exegetical studies look afresh at well-explored themes of Romans in the history of the epistle's interpretation: justification, judgement, the intercession of Christ, the bête noir of Romans' interpretation (Rom 13:1–7), and the role of obedience. Part 3 examines the social legacy of Romans for non able-bodied people in the twenty-first century and, in an historical case study, the impact of Romans for Lydian-Phrygian readers in Asia Minor familiar with the confession inscriptions of the Second Sophistic period (second to third century A.D.). Part 4 confronts a problem for modern Romans readers in assessing its legacy: the thorny issue of its particularity. The extensive list of greetings in Romans 16 is looked at from Paul's missionary intentions. The marginal additions adorning the text of Romans in the original New Testament manuscripts are explored for any revelations regarding the activity of Phoebe of Cenchrea as the bearer and reader of the letter. Part 5 locates Romans in a broad sweep of interpretation spanning select Romans exegetes across the ages (Augustine, Luther, Calvin, Barth) and also the modern European philosophers (Taubes Agamben, Badiou). Several concluding suggestions will be made regarding the abiding legacy of Romans for twenty-first century readers in its Neronian context. Also, in a study of another Reformed scholar, Peter Martyr Vermigli's exposition of predestination in Romans is investigated. Last, in Part 6, a contemporary female Gospels scholar presents a personal reflection on what it was like for her as a Roman Catholic to grapple seriously for the first time with the feared 'Protestant epistle', discovering that it spoke to her in an equally transformative way in the present as it had to believers of every generation and faith tradition in the past.

This volume of essays draws together Australian and American scholars from Catholic and Protestant faith traditions in a tribute to the enduring impact of the epistle to the Romans in the lives of believers and in the western intellectual tradition more generally. The breadth of treatment here of the major themes of Romans in diverse contexts across the ages highlights for the reader the real difference that the epistle to the Romans has made to our civilisation and, consequently, its indelible legacy.

Bibliography

Aune, David E. — *Rereading Paul Together: Protestant and Catholic Perspectives on Justification* (Grand Rapids: Baker Academic, 2006).

Barbour, R. S. — 'Biblical Classics: X. Karl Barth: The Epistle to the Romans', *The Expository Times* 90.9 (1979), 264–68.

Barclay, J. M. G. — 'Paul and the Philosophers: Alain Badiou and the Event', *New Blackfriars* 91.1032 (2010), 171–84.

Barclay, J. M. G. — *Paul and the Gift* (Grand Rapids: Eerdmans, 2015).

Barth, Karl — *The Epistle to the Romans*, 6th ed. (Oxford: Oxford University Press, 1968).

Barth, Karl — *Christliche Dogmatik* (Munchen, Kaiser Verlag, 1927).

Berkouwer, G. C. — *The Triumph of Grace in the Theology of Karl Barth* (Grand Rapids: Eerdmans, 1956).

Bray, Gerald — *Ancient Christian Commentary on Scripture. New Testament VI: Romans* (London & New York: Routledge, 1998).

Brazier, Paul — 'Barth's First Commentary on Romans (1919): An Exercise in Apophatic Theology', *International Journal of Systematic Theology* 6.4 (2004), 387–403.

Burnett, Richard E. — *Karl Barth's Theological Exegesis: The Hermeneutical Principles of the Römerbrief Period* (WUNT II 145; Tübingen: Mohr Siebeck, 2001).

Campbell, Douglas A. — *The Deliverance of God: An Apocalyptic Rereading of Justification in Paul* (Grand Rapids: Eerdmans, 2009).

Childers, J. — 'Reading the Bible with Old Friends: The Value of Patristic Bible Interpretations for Ministry', *Restoration Quarterly* 45 (2003), 69–89.

Clough, David L. *Ethics in Krisis: The Significance of Römerbrief for Karl Barth's Ethics* (Unpublished PhD diss., Yale University, 2000).

Decock, P. B. 'On the Value of Pre-modern Interpretation of Scripture for Contemporary Biblical Studies', *Neotestamentica* 39 (2005), 57–74.

Dieter, Theodor 'The Ecumenical Commemoration of the 500th Anniversary of the Reformation in Western Europe', *International Journal for the Study of the Christian Church* 17.1 (2017), 11–25.

Dixon, C. Scott 'Luther's Ninety-Five Theses and the Origins of the Reformation Narrative', *The English Historical Review* 132.556 (2017), 533–69.

Dreyer, Wim A. 'Karl Barth's *Römerbrief*: A Turning Point in Protestant Theology', *Studia Historiae Ecclesiasticae* 43.3 (2017), 1–15.

Fitzmyer, Joseph A. *Romans: A New Translation with Introduction and Commentary* (London: Geoffrey Chapman, 1992).

Gaca, Kathy L., & L. L. Welborn *Early Patristic Readings of Romans* (London & New York: T&T Clark, 2005).

Gorday, Peter. *Principles of Patristic Exegesis: Romans 9–11 in Origen, John Chrysostom, and Augustine* (New York and Toronto: Edwin Mellen, 1983).

McGrath, Alister E. Iustitia Dei: *A History of the Christian Doctrine of Justification.* (Cambridge: Cambridge University Press, 1998 Second Edition).

Melanchthon, P. *Commentary on Romans* (St Louis: Concordia Publishing House, 1992).

Patte, Daniel, & Eugene TeSelle. *Engaging Augustine on Romans: Self, Context and Theology in Interpretation* (Harrisburg: Trinity Press International, 2002).

Patte, Daniel, & Vasile Vihoc *Greek Patristic and Eastern Orthodox Interpretations of Romans* (London & New York: T&T Clark, 2013).

Pauck, Wilhelm, (tr. & ed.) *Luther: Lectures on Romans* (Philadelphia: The Westminster Press, 1961).

Reasoner, Mark	*Romans in Full Circle: A History of Interpretation* (Louisville: Westminster John Press, 2005).
Roukema, R.	*The Diversity of Laws in Origen's Commentary on Romans* (Amsterdam: Free University Press, 1988).
Schleiermacher, F.	*The Christian Faith* (Edinburgh: T&T Clark, 1928).
Seifrid, Mark A.	*Justification by Faith: The Origin and Development of a Central Pauline Theme* (NovT Supp 68; Leiden/New York/Koln: E. J. Brill, 1992).
Sobolewski, Gregory L.	*Roman Catholic Perception of Luther in the Twentieth Century: Magisterial Positions and Their Ecumenical Significance* (Unpublished PhD thesis, Marquette University, 1993).
Stendahl, Krister	'The Apostle Paul and the Introspective Conscience of the West', *Harvard Theological Review* 56 (1963), 199–215.
Surrency, Steven	*A Gadamerian Analysis of Roman Catholic Hermeneutics: A Diachronic Analysis of Interpretations of Romans 1:17–2:17* (Unpublished PhD thesis, University of South Florida, 2015).
Wicks, Jared	'Justification and Faith in Luther's Theology', *Theological Studies* 44 (1983), 3–29.
Wicks, Jared	'Roman Reactions to Luther: The First Year (1518)', *The Catholic Historical Review* 69.4 (1983), 521–62.

PART 1

On First Hearing Romans Read Aloud in Neronian Rome: Theological and Historical Reverberations

CHAPTER 2

The Apocalyptic Motif of the last judgement: the essential horizon of Paul's argument in Romans

Brendan Byrne, SJ

In Acts 17, the author, whom I am happy to call 'Luke', has Paul conclude his speech before the audience at the Areopagus in Athens with the following exhortation:

> [29] Since we are God's offspring, we ought not to think that the deity is like gold, or silver, or stone, an image formed by the art and imagination of mortals. [30] While God has overlooked the times of human ignorance, now he commands all people everywhere to repent, [31] because he has fixed a day on which he will have the world judged in righteousness by a man whom he has appointed, and of this he has given assurance to all by raising him from the dead.

Setting aside the question of historicity—that is, whether Paul actually appeared before the Areopagus and spoke in these terms—the evidence of his letters, notably 1 Thessalonians and Romans, suggests that this conclusion to the speech closely reflects what he would have said when addressing a Gentile audience. More specifically, I believe that the motif of the last judgement—'the day', according to Acts 17:31—is never far from consciousness in Romans. It hangs over the entire letter from beginning to end and should be taken as a controlling element in interpretation. When this eschatological perspective falls from view, assessment of the meaning of terms endlessly debated in Pauline scholarship—justification, righteousness, salvation, gospel, etc.—goes astray. To put the matter more positively, the motif of the last judgement is an essential element of the apocalyptic horizon against which the entire economy of salvation according to Paul must be understood.

My discussion of Romans in this chapter proceeds along the following lines:

1. The recognition of Paul's world view as essentially apocalyptic;
2. Characteristics of Jewish apocalyptic in the Second Temple era;
3. Renewed interest in the significance of the last judgement in Paul;
4. Assessing 'Justification'/'Righteousness';
5. The last judgement in Romans as a whole.

In Chapter 3, I will deal more specifically with Romans 5–8 in light of the significance of the judgement in Paul's apocalyptic perspective.

1. The Apocalyptic World View of Paul

'The apocalyptic world view is the fundamental carrier of Paul's thought'. So wrote J. Christiaan Beker in a classic study (1980) that gave fresh impetus, in the closing decades of the last century, to the locating of Paul within the Jewish apocalyptic tradition.[1] Of course, behind Beker stood Ernst Käsemann, who, in a more general reclaiming of the apocalyptic world view in New Testament studies, famously described apocalyptic as 'the mother of all Christian theology'.[2] Behind Käsemann

---

1   Beker, *Paul the Apostle*, 181.
2   Käsemann, 'The Beginnings of Christian Theology', 102; reasserted in the following essay, 'Primitive Christian Apocalyptic', 137. Käsemann was, of course, locating that 'beginning' in the early post-Easter community.

himself stood a tradition stemming from Albert Schweitzer[3] and, more remotely, Richard Kabisch (1868–1914), who insisted that Paul's theology must not be explained directly from the Old Testament but from the world-view more immediately surrounding him, a world-view thoroughly imbued with eschatological expectation.[4]

Rudolf Bultmann accepted the thoroughly apocalyptic cast of Paul's thought but, in the interests of contemporary proclamation, sought to separate out the essential core gospel, interpreted in an existentialist sense, from its mythological expression.[5] Reacting to this side-lining of apocalyptic in Paul, Käsemann rejected the existentialist-individualism of Bultmann's anthropological approach. Focus upon realised eschatology neglects the 'eschatological reservation' whereby apocalyptic protects Paul's theology from collapsing into the Hellenistic 'enthusiasm' against which the apostle had to battle, especially in Corinth.[6]

Following in the line of Käsemann, J. C. Beker insisted upon the apocalyptic texture of Paul's thought as he explored the dialectic between its 'coherent core' and its 'contingent expression'.[7] The 'coherent core' is a symbolic structure representing a Christian modification of the apocalyptic language of Judaism, a modification stemming from the centrality of the death and resurrection of Christ.[8] This event led to both the 'softening' and the intensifying in Paul of the apocalyptic dualism between the present age and the age to come; the latter is already interpenetrating the former without lessening the sense of imminence of the judgement and the ultimate cosmic triumph of God.[9]

In the 1990's J. Louis Martyn initiated a whole new direction in regard to the apocalyptic cast of Paul's thought. Working especially

---

3   Schweitzer, *The Mysticism of Paul the Apostle*.
4   Kabisch, *Die Eschatologie des Paulus*, 10. Kabisch referred far more frequently to 'eschatology' than to 'apocalyptic'.
5   See Bultmann, *Kerygma and Myth*, 1.1–16.
6   See Käsemann, 'Primitive Christian Apocalyptic', 131–37. As the classic illustration of Paul's debt to the apocalyptic tradition, Käsemann pointed (pp.133–34) to 1 Cor 15:20–28, where Christ *must* continue to reign before ultimately surrendering the ultimate lordship of the universe to God.
7   Beker, *Paul the Apostle*, 11; also *Paul's Apocalyptic Gospel*, especially Chapter 3, 'The Apocalyptic Character of Paul's Gospel' (pp. 29–53).
8   Beker, *Paul the Apostle*, 15–16.
9   Beker, *Paul's Apocalyptic Gospel*, 40.

from Galatians, Martyn insisted upon the radical dualism of the two ages, greatly lessening the sense of a linear progression of salvation.[10] The Christ event is a divine 'invasion', which is itself an 'apocalypse', involving, in epistemological fashion, a totally new way of seeing God, Christ (see 2 Cor 5:16) and reality as a whole.[11]

Martyn's radical view of Paul as an apocalyptic thinker has been taken up by a number of scholars, notably his doctoral students Martinus de Boer and Beverley Gaventa. Central to de Boer's work is the discernment of 'two tracks' in Jewish apocalyptic literature: a 'cosmological apocalyptic track' and a 'forensic apocalyptic track'.[12] De Boer sees the latter pattern predominating in Romans 1–5, while the former emerges in Romans 6–8 (with 5:12–21 constituting a bridge passage where the two patterns interpenetrate to some degree).[13]

The tendency initiated by Martyn has reached its most extreme form in the work of Douglas Campbell. In a monumental re-reading of Paul, with a debt also to Sanders, Campbell finds in Romans 1–4 an apocalyptic soteriological schema of markedly punitive forensic nature ('Justification theory') which Paul attributes to a Jewish Christian teacher. Paul seeks first to refute and then to replace the views of this teacher with a participatory, relational, and christocentric schema to be found in Romans 5–8.[14]

The extreme form of the apocalyptic interpretation of Paul seen in Campbell has not commanded general acceptance.[15] Likewise, the distinction between a 'cosmological apocalyptic track' and a 'forensic apocalyptic track', promoted by de Boer and taken up enthusiastically by Martyn, has been challenged as not borne out in the letters, including the flow of the argument across Romans 1–8.[16] More generally, the tendency flowing from Martyn to find in Paul a rigid break

---

10 Martyn, *Galatians*, 22, 37–39, 97–105.
11 Martyn, 'Epistemology'.
12 See de Boer, *The Defeat of Death*; 'Paul and Jewish Apocalyptic Eschatology'; 'Paul and Apocalyptic Eschatology', esp. 358–66; 'Paul's Mythologizing Program in Romans 5–8'.
13 See de Boer, 'Paul and Apocalyptic Eschatology', 564–65.
14 Campbell, *The Deliverance of God*.
15 See in particular the devastating review article of Matlock, 'Zeal for Paul'.
16 See Shaw, 'Apocalyptic or Covenant', esp. 163–68; also Wright, *Paul and His Recent Interpreters*, 160–67; Davies, *Paul among the Apocalypses?*, 186–93.

in continuity with the prophetic promises of salvation has provoked a strong reaction in the name of a more 'covenantal' approach to his theology. Thus N. T. Wright has devoted a substantial section ('Part 2: Re-enter "Apocalyptic"') of his recent survey of Pauline scholarship to a critical review of the apocalyptic interpretation of Paul from Käsemann to Campbell, with particular focus upon the tendency initiated by Martyn.[17] Wright in fact is disinclined to apply the term 'apocalyptic' to Paul in general, insisting that it has become so loosely applied as to be virtually meaningless and that features considered essential characteristics of apocalypticism, for example the motif of the 'two ages', are simply characteristic of Second Temple Judaism more widely considered.[18]

One may share the reservations voiced by Wright and others concerning the erosion, in the name of apocalyptic, of any sense of continuity with the era of promise while retaining, nonetheless, the category of 'apocalyptic' as essential to an understanding of Paul. The key thing is to be clear about what one means by the term and to remain close to the Jewish texts in which its features have traditionally been found.

2. Characteristics of Apocalyptic in the Second Temple Era

In a field where multiple attempts to 'define' Apocalyptic are on offer, Paul D. Hanson has introduced a clarifying set of distinctions,[19] which may be indicated (with some summarising revision as follows): 1. '*apocalypse*': a particular literary genre incorporating 'the revelation of future events by God through the mediation of an angel to a human servant';[20] 2. '*apocalyptic eschatology*': a religious perspective that can be viewed as a development out of prophetic eschatology when God's final saving acts

---

17 Wright, *Paul and His Recent Interpreters*, 135–218.
18 Wright, *Paul and His Recent Interpreters*, 138–40. For an earlier dismissal of apocalyptic as a viable category, see Glasson, 'What is Apocalyptic?'.
19 Hanson, 'Apocalypse, genre', and 'Apocalypticism'; see also Sturm, 'Defining the Word "Apocalyptic"', 35; de Boer, 'Paul and Apocalyptic Eschatology', 347–49; 'Apocalyptic as God's Eschatological Activity', 45–53; Knibb, 'Apocalypticism and Messianism', 409–12.
20 See Hanson, 'Apocalypse' (*IDBSupp*), 29b. For a widely accepted definition of this category see Collins, *Apocalypse*, 9; later expanded by Adela Yarbro Collins, 'Introduction: Early Christian Apocalypticism', in *Early Christian* Apocalypticism, 1–11, here p.7; for the full definition see Collins, 'Apocalypses and Apocalypticism', 283.

came to be conceived not as the fulfilment of promises within political structures and historical events but as a deliverance out of the present order into a new transformed order;[21] 3. *'apocalypticism'*: a symbolic universe in which a socio-religious movement, under extreme pressure, deals with alienation by codifying its identity and interpretation of reality through recourse to apocalyptic eschatology.[22] Rather than describing 'apocalypticism' immediately as 'a symbolic universe', I would propose that it be described as a socio-religious phenomenon or movement (*eine soziale Bewegung*[23]) wherein a group, under extreme pressure, deals with alienation by codifying its identity and interpretation of reality within a symbolic universe marked by apocalyptic eschatology.[24]

The great variety of literature manifesting apocalyptic eschatology makes an attempt to offer a synthetic description of such eschatology hazardous in the extreme.[25] No one document will contain all the features that might be considered characteristic of apocalyptic eschatology and even features that appear with some frequency will display considerable divergence among themselves. Nonetheless, with this caveat, it is appropriate to list aspects that may be regarded as characteristic. Most recent listings take as point of departure that given by Philipp Vielhauer (1964) under five headings:

1. *Dualism, expressed especially in the doctrine of the two ages*: the present age, considered temporary, characterised by evil; the age to come, transcendent and imperishable, to be ushered in by a divine intervention, in which the present age will be judged and destroyed preparatory to the establishment of God's eternal rule.

2. *Pessimism concerning the present age*, which is marked by moral and physical degeneration, often attributed to the domination of Satan and

---

21 Hanson, *IDBSupp*, 29b–30a.
22 Hanson, *IDBSupp*, 30–31.
23 See Cuvillier, 'Das apokalyptische Denken', 2, who provides a threefold distinction of *'Apokalyptik'* as follows: 1. Eine literarische Gattung; 2. Eine soziale Bewegung; 3. Eine Ideologie. The categories would seem to correspond more or less to Hanson's classification, with inversion of the latter's categories 2 and 3.
24 See further, D'Angelo & Matter, 'Apocalypticism'; Aune, 'Apocalypticism'.
25 See Matlock, *Unveiling the Apocalyptic Paul*. Behind Matlock, there is Rowland, *The Open Heaven*, insisting that 'apocalyptic' be reserved for a type of literature more specifically tied to 'revelation' vouchsafed to particular individuals.

other evil angelic powers. This domination is often portrayed as coming to a climax: a cosmic battle in which God and the agents aligned with God will triumph, ushering in a new age, radically discontinuous with the old.

3. *Universalism and individualism.* While the temporal horizon reaches from the creation to the final dissolution of the present world, the spatial horizon is cosmic in scope, including not only the earth but heaven and the underworld as well. Likewise, with the whole of humankind in view, privileges or liabilities accruing form national belonging (e.g., to Israel or Gentile nations) give way to individual responsibility before God, with each person's righteousness or the contrary destined to be assessed at the judgement.

4. *Determinism and Imminent Expectation.* All has been predetermined by God, according to a pre-existent plan, unfolding according to fixed periods, the discernment of which is open to calculation or is the subject of privileged revelation. Such discernment communicates the sense of belonging to the final epoch, a conviction that the moment of divine intervention and rescue (salvation) is imminent.

5. *Lack of Uniformity*, a significant example of which is the variation in the conception of a 'Saviour-figure' (God, angels, Davidic Messiah, transcendent Son of Man; etc.).[26]

Many scholars in the area consider the last judgement—the dividing factor between the two ages—to be an essential feature of apocalyptic eschatology. For D. S. Russell, 'The doctrine of the last judgement is the most characteristic doctrine of Jewish apocalyptic'.[27] John J. Collins sees 'the belief in the judgement of the dead' as 'a distinctive novelty' of apocalyptic literature compared to the prophetic tradition.[28]

---

26 Vielhauer, 'Apocalyptic', 587–94 ('The World of Ideas'). For a more detailed list of characteristics see Aune, 'Apocalypticism', 27.
27 Russell, *The Method and Message of Jewish Apocalyptic*, 380.
28 Collins, 'Apocalypses', 1.283. D'Angelo & Matter, 'Apocalypticism', 40, list 'judgment' as 'first' among the religious ideas and imagery that characterise apocalyptic literature.

3. Renewed interest in the significance of the last judgement in Paul

Along with the apocalyptic cast of Paul's theology, the significance more specifically of the last judgement has also found renewed appreciation. Outstanding in this connection has been the work of Christian Stettler. Following a study on the last judgement in the prophetic writings of Israel,[29] Stettler has devoted a monograph to the topic in Paul: *Das Endgericht bei Paulus: Framesemantische und exegetische Studien zur paulinischen Eschatologie und Soteriologie* (2017).[30] While acknowledging that explicit references to the last judgement in Paul are comparatively rare, Stettler has brought fresh sophistication to the enquiry by appeal to the concept of 'frames' in Cognitive Semantics.[31] A frame is a vast system of knowledge, in various cognitive categories, that is presupposed and implied in all human communication. Without such a background of understanding, communciation whether in word or written text is impossible. So, for example, when an estate agent begins a conversation with me about a new residence that I am seeking, presupposed between us is a vast field of knowledge associated with the concept of 'house': architectural features, furniture and fittings, location, closeness to amenities, comfort and well-being, 'at homeness', family, ownership, renting, mortgage, etc. Only a small selection of these aspects will appear in our communication but they are all there to be drawn upon as the conversation goes in particular directions. As applied to the interpretation of biblical texts, 'frame' theory requires that the meaning and significance of a concept such as 'last judgement' in Paul not be restricted to its comparatively infrequent appearance and function in particular contexts and to the divergent images of the judgement that emerge in such contexts. Rather, what appears particular contexts is to be seen as various expressions of a unified body of 'encyclopedic' knowledge about the judgement shared by Paul and his audience.

---

29 Stettler, *Das letze Gericht*.
30 Stettler, *Das Endgericht*. On the last judgment in Paul, see also Barclay, 'Believers'; Bull, '"Wir werden alle vor den Richterstuhl Gottes gestellt warden"'; Hogan, 'Apocalyptic Eschatology'; McFadden, *Judgment according to Works*; Prothro, *Both Judge and Justifier*; Stanley, *Four Views on the Role of Works at the Final Judgment*; Synofzik, *Die Gerichts- und Vergeltungsaussagen*; VanLandingham, *Judgment and Justification*; Yinger, *Paul, Judaism, and Judgment*.
31 Stettler, *Endgericht*, 98–120.

Stettler's work, as the title suggests, considers the motif of the last judgement across the entire range of Paul's letters. Necessarily, he does give attention early in the work to two passages in Romans (2:6–16 and 14:10c) where reference to judgement is explicit.[32] My approach here will be different in that I propose to move fairly swiftly across the entire range of the letter, in an attempt to show that, aside from these two passages, the last judgement remains the essential horizon of the letter as a whole. As previously indicated, Chapter 3 will give detailed consideration to the second major block of the letter, Romans 5–8, in this respect.

4. Justification/Righteousness

Among the few studies that, until recently, had been devoted to the topic of the last judgement in Paul, let alone specifically in Romans, a 1976 article by Karl P. Donfried stands out, 'Justification and Last Judgement in Paul'.[33] In the course of the article Donfried wrote:

> Only when one has come to terms with justification can one understand the proper importance of last judgement and its relationship to justification.[34]

My sense is that the case is exactly the other way round: namely, that one can only appreciate Paul's understanding of justification in light of seeing the last judgement as the essential horizon of the entire work.[35]

That said, it is necessary, I believe at this point, to lay my cards on the table in regard to the fraught topic of 'justification'—or, more completely, to the word group 'justification'/'justify'/'righteousness'/'make righteous', which of course are cognate in Greek in a way that they are not in English. In the biblical background to Paul the LXX regularly

---

32 Stettler, *Endgericht*, 58–60, 61–68.
33 Donfried, 'Justification and Last Judgment'.
34 Donfried, 'Justification and Last Judgment', 92, 99.
35 See Snodgrass, 'Justification by Grace', 82 ('..., Paul's judgment teaching must be seen as the presupposition of his justification teaching'), also p.86; Stettler, *Endgericht*, 246. Earlier, Bultmann, *Theology of the New Testament*, 1.272–73. This is contrary to the thesis of VanLandingham, *Judgment and Justification*, 17, who argues that justification may be rigorously separated from the last judgment.

employs *dikaiosynē* to translate the Hebrew *sedeq/sedeqah*. This Hebrew word group is currently understood in two rather divergent ways: 1. as indicating 'behaviour or living according to a norm or standard', on the one hand; 2. as 'faithfulness within a relationship'. The former reflects an understanding of *dikaiosynē* reaching back to the to the ancient Greeks,[36] especially Aristotle, and continues through the sense of 'justice' in the Western tradition.[37] Understood with reference to the deity, 'God's righteousness' in this connection would refer to the divine commitment always to act in accordance with the 'norm' of God's being: as Creator, ruler, and judge of the universe, God seeks constantly to restore its order.[38]

Building upon tendencies already apparent in German interpretation to see a predominantly salvific note in the biblical concept, Hermann Cremer at the turn of the twentieth century promoted a view of God's righteousness in Paul that reflected the understanding of *sedeq/sedeqah* as 'faithfulness within a relationship' (*Verhältnisbegriff*).[39] The relationship particularly in view was the covenant (or kingship) relationship whereby God consistently came to the rescue of Israel, lending an essentially salvific note to the exercise of the divine righteousness—salvific, that is, for Israel, while destructive in regard to her enemies and oppressors.[40]

This essentially salvific view of the divine righteousness set in train by Cremer has become a strong current in Pauline scholarship, most notably as adopted by Käsemann and his school (Peter Stuhlmacher and Christian Müller[41]) and remains a significant feature in the tendencies gathered together under the rubric of the New Perspective on Paul.[42]

It is by no means certain, however, that *dikaiosynē* as used by Paul,

---

36 See LSJ, 429, s.v. '*dikaios*': 'observant of custom or rule'; 'observant of duty to gods and men'; BDAG 246, s.v. '*dikaios*': 'be in accordance with high standards of rectitude'; Schrenk, '*dikaios*', 2.182: 'one who fulfils obligations'; 'one who observes legal norms'.
37 'The quality or condition of being righteous; conformity of life or conduct to the requirements of the divine or moral law', *Shorter Oxford English Dictionary* s.v. 'righteousness', p. 1737.
38 See Seifrid, 'Righteousness Language', 420–22, 425, appealing to the work of Old Testament scholar Schmid on the *sedeq* word group: *Gerechtigkeitsbegriff*; earlier, Scullion, 'Righteousness (OT)', especially the concluding summary pp. 735–36.
39 Cremer, *Die paulinische Rechtfertigungslehre*, 34.
40 Cremer, *Die paulinische Rechtfertigungslehre*, 37, 38.
41 Stuhlmacher, *Gerechtigkeit Gottes*; Müller, *Gottes Gerechtigkeit*.
42 For a sustained critical exposition of Cremer's view and its continuance in biblical studies down to the present, see Irons, *The Righteousness of God*, 29–60; see also Seifrid, 'Righteousness Language', 414–42.

especially with reference to the divine righteousness ('righteousness of God'), has incorporated from the Hebrew *sedeq/sedeqah* a specifically fresh 'biblical' meaning in this salvific direction beyond the otherwise prevalent sense of conformity to a norm. In a doctoral dissertation now published (2015) as *The Righteousness of God: A Lexical Examination of the Covenant-Faithfulness Interpretation*,[43] Charles Lee Irons has subjected the usage of 'righteousness' language in the biblical and post-biblical Jewish literature (notably *sedeq/sedeqah* in the Hebrew and *dikaiosynē* in Greek) to a thorough critical review, employing a more sophisticated linguistic methodology than earlier studies. He concludes that the comparatively frequent references to the divine exercise of righteousness in a salvific sense, notably in Second Isaiah and the Psalms, represents a *subset* of the divine distributive justice, whereby God is faithful to the covenant relationship, punishing Israel's enemies while working to purify and restore the nation.[44] Fidelity to the covenant relationship is not, then, of the essence of divine righteousness but a significant *particular instance* of it.

Fidelity within a relationship can be seen as an instance of righteousness in the traditional sense of conformity to a norm in that two parties in a relationship have expectations in regard to each other on the basis of a generally accepted (but mostly left unstated) principle that relationships require loyalty and faithfulness.[45] Thus one party will adjudge another with whom they are in relationship as 'righteous'—that is, they will 'justify' (or not justify) the other party—in the light of the conformity or non-conformity, as the case may be, of their conduct with that principle. The acknowledgment does not 'make' the person righteous

---

43 See previous note.
44 Irons finds in the literature reviewed basically three categories of righteousness usage: 1. Legal (forensic); 2. Ethical (including 'righteousness before God'); 3. 'Correctness'. The first two categories, in almost equal measure, make up over 80% of the instances in the Hebrew Bible. The pattern continues in the later literature though with an increasing usage in regard to the divine distributive justice. Contrary to what has been maintained by Cremer and others in his suite, there are instances where the divine righteousness does have a punitive sense in regard to Israel. On the other hand, Irons seems to push his case against the salvific sense somewhat too exclusively.
45 'Righteousness' or the judgment that a person or behaviour is 'righteous' (*dikaios*) involves a 'triangular' pattern in this sense: (1) a *law* or *norm* or *principle*, which may remain implicit rather than consciously appealed to, (2) a *person* (or behaviour) that is the *subject of assessment* on the part of (3) *another party*, divine or human, that assesses and declares whether the person (or conduct) is righteous or unrighteous in light of the accepted norm. See Irons, *Righeousness of God*, 162–63.

but declares the person to be such on the basis of their pre-existing behaviour or disposition. It is the behaviour that 'makes' the person righteous, not the positive assessment—just as a negative assessment or verdict does not 'make' the party assessed evil or lawbreaking but, again, acknowledges that the party is unrighteous on the basis of behaviour lacking conformity to the operative norm.[46]

There are no particular grounds for departing from this pattern when considering the various instances of 'righteousness' (*dikaiosynē*) in Paul, though obviously such consideration will require careful attention to the specific contexts in which the term appears. What must be recognised is the *intrinsic link* between righteousness and being 'found righteous'—'justified'—on the basis of one's righteous behaviour and hence qualified to share the divine gift of 'life', whether that be enhanced life in the present or 'eternal life' in a world to come. This principle that righteousness leads to life, along with its corresponding contrary that unrighteousness leads to death, is one Paul shared with the entire Jewish biblical and post-biblical apocalyptic tradition.[47] It is central to his understanding of righteousness within the horizon of the last judgement.

Whether justification is to be understood as 'forensic' depends on whether or not it is used with reference to a legal or, more strictly, a law-court situation, a reference that, as Irons has made clear, it does frequently have in the Old Testament and also later Jewish literature. Such a forensic context does not necessarily exclude an essentially salvific note, especially if, as in most cases, God is instituting judgement against Israel's enemies rather than Israel herself. Since the offer of justification that Paul proposes in the gospel is essentially in view of the last judgement it is appropriate to describe his understanding of justification as 'forensic' since that judgement is portrayed as a final great assize (see Rom 8:31–39). 'Forensic' righteousness in this sense, however, should

---

46 'Just as the action of condemnation does not make one guilty, neither does the action of justification make one righteous. Both instead are a declaration that someone is either guilty or righteous', McFadden, *Judgment*, 123–24.
47 See Lev 18:5; Deut 5:33; 30:15–20; Jer 23:5–6; 33:15–16; Ezek 18:9, 21–28; 33:10–13; Ps 37:29; 140:13; Wis 1:15; 5:1–5, 15; 15:3; *1 Enoch* 1:1–9; 5:6–7 (Greek); 39:4–8; 58:2–3; 62:13–16; 91:12–13; 94–104 passim; *Pss. Sol.* 9:5; 12:6; 14:1–10; 15:6–13; *Bib. Ant.* 51:5; *Sib. Or.* 5: 269–70; *T. Naph.* 8:3; *4 Ezra* 8:33–36, 51–62; 9:7–13; *2 Apoc. Bar.* 44:2–15; 51:1–16; 1QpHab 8:1–3.

not be played off against 'ethical' righteousness as though the two were incompatible. On the contrary, the forensic declaration in which justification consists rests upon an assessment that the one being justified is ethically righteous.

If such be the case, what then are we to make of Paul's contention that God 'justifies the ungodly' (Rom 4:5), that is, the unrighteous? My understanding is that Paul can countenance this paradoxical divine behaviour only and entirely christologically. In response to his obedient death (Phil 2:8; Rom 5:19) God 'justifies' the sinless Christ (2 Cor 5:21), a vindication seen in his resurrection and exaltation to the lordship of the universe (Phil 2:9–11).[48] The ungodly find justification in that 'in Christ', through faith and baptism, they have died with him (Rom 6:3–4, 6–7; see 2 Cor 5:14) and, having so paid the penalty for sin in that death, they are gathered up into the justification accruing to his obedience (Rom 4:25).[49] They are not justified precisely as 'ungodly' at the moment of justification. They are justified as those who were ungodly until the moment of their entry into Christ. This is not a legal fiction. It is a forensic understanding of justification in which the forensic and the ethical co-exist in perfect harmony in Paul's essentially christological understanding of justification.[50]

One still sees assertions that justification appears in Paul's writings as one image, a forensic image, chosen amongst others to illustrate God's work in Christ and its effects—almost with the sense that it was not a necessary image but simply one conveniently at hand. I have picked up this impression from the redoubtable Joseph Fitzmyer on the Catholic side,[51] but also from James D. G. Dunn, on the Protestant, who, in con-

---

48 On the resurrection as God's justification of Christ, see Hooker, 'Interchange and Atonement', 39–41; Wright, 'Romans', 504; Bird, *Saving* Righteousness, 40–59.
49 See Stettler, *Endgericht*, 138, 250–51.
50 Here the distinction made by Westerholm between 'ordinary' and 'extraordinary' righteousness (dubbed 'dikaiosness' by Westerholm) is helpful; see *Perspectives Old and New*, 273–84; 'The Righteousness of the Law'; *Justification Reconsidered*, 67.
51 E.g., Fitzmyer: 'The image most frequently used by Paul to express an effect of the Christ-event is "justification". ...It is an image drawn from Paul's Jewish background, being an OT image expressive of a relationship between God and human beings... But it denotes a societal or judicial relationship, either ethical or forensic (i.e. related to law courts; see Deut 25:1; cf. Gen 18:25)' (*NJBC* 1397a [§82:68]). See much earlier, Dodd, *Romans*, 76: 'When he says, they are justified for nothing by His grace, the idea uppermost in his mind is that of deliverance. But as he is stating it in legal, forensic terms, deliverance takes the form of an acquittal in court'.

nection with the 'crucial transition' from lostness to salvation speaks of the 'wide variety of metaphors' that Paul draws on 'to describe it' (salvation), and continues: 'Paul draws on metaphors from the customs of his time', and heading the list is the 'legal metaphor' 'Justification'.[52] I would not fault Dunn for his claim that Paul was compelled to draw upon a variety of metaphors to express as fully as possible a reality which defied a simple description. He is right to say 'it would be a mistake to take any one of Paul's metaphors and to exalt it into some primary or normative status so that all others must be fitted into its mould'.[53] Nonetheless, one wonders whether in Dunn's view a hint of arbitrariness hovers around Paul's choice of the legal-forensic term, which has, above all since the Reformation, become the central focus of Pauline interpretation.

Justification/righteousness, then, should not be drawn too far away from the forensic setting of the last judgement motif. It does not refer in some extended sense to membership in the people of God[54]—though such membership, in the case of converts from the Gentile world, may well be a happy result of being justified.[55] To set the term adrift from its forensic moorings is—if I may mix the metaphor—to muddy the waters. It is not a particularly attractive aspect of Pauline theology. Law courts, after all, are places to keep out of as far as one can. There is much truth in all the brickbats that Douglas Campbell throws at it in the form of what he dubs 'Justification Theory'—though I think his attribution of it to a deity imagined by the Jewish teacher who he finds to be the principal speaker in Romans 1–4 is severely misguided.[56] But nor is justification, as Albert Schweitzer famously dubbed it, a 'subsidiary crater' on the Pauline landscape. In theology at least it remains an active volcano.

5. The Last Judgement in Romans as a whole

I began this Chapter citing Luke's presentation of Paul's speech before the Areopagus. In so doing I did not mean to suggest that Paul

---

52 Dunn, *The Theology of Paul*, 328. See also Stettler, *Endgericht*, 169–70.
53 Dunn, *Theology of Paul*, 332.
54 So, e.g., Wright, *Climax*, 150.
55 Against such broadenings of justification see Westerholm, *Justification Reconsidered*, 13.
56 See my review of *The Deliverance of God*, 101–4.

proclaimed anything like Romans to his hearers in Athens. There is a great deal in the letter—especially concerning the law of Moses and the fate of Israel—that would have been of scant interest in that context. Much more illuminating in that respect is Paul's own recall of his original preaching in nearby Thessalonica:

> 1 Thess 1:9. For the people of those regions report about us what kind of welcome we had among you, and how you turned to God from idols, to serve a living and true God, ¹⁰ and to wait for his Son from heaven, whom he raised from the dead—Jesus, who rescues us from the wrath that is coming.

We note the references to conversion ('turning') from idols, to awaiting God's Son from heaven, whom he raised from the dead (resurrection), and to the 'rescue from the wrath that is coming' (v. 10).[57] Taking into account the description of Paul's disgust at the idolatry patent in Athens immediately prior to his address to the Areopagus (17:16), this recall of his initial preaching in his earliest letter coheres remarkably well with the refutation of idolatry and summons to conversion in the speech recorded in Acts.[58]

Romans, of course, as already noted, contains a great deal that Paul would not have included when first commending the gospel to interested Gentiles. However, the letter is fundamentally an exposition of the gospel. In the introduction (1:15) Paul explains that it has long been his desire to 'preach the gospel to you in Rome'.[59] Paul hardly needs to preach the gospel to the Roman community as if they were not already converted. Nor, do I think that he writes to Rome primarily to address issues in the community there. His intention is to give an accurate account of the gospel that he preaches so as to counter any false views about it which he plausibly suspects are circulating to his disadvantage among the believers in Rome. Before he appears in person in Rome, Paul writes to 'put the record straight', so to speak, in order that the happy and supportive stay among the community that he outlines towards the end of chapter 15

---

57 On 1 Thessalonians as providing indication of Paul's basic summons to the gospel see Westerholm, *Justification Reconsidered*, 5–7.
58 See Stettler, *Endgericht*, 171.
59 Preferring the reading *hymin* against the Western variant *en hymin*.

(see vv. 24, 29, 32) may be realised in practice.[60] Thus his ambition to embark upon fresh missionary work in the West, in Spain, will not be jeopardised but, he may hope, will find support in every way.[61]

Paul addresses the community as Gentile believers (1:5-7). Yet there is also outstanding preoccupation in the body of the letter with Jewish concerns: the status of the law of Moses and the fate of that majority of the Jewish people that has not come to faith in Christ as Israel's Messiah. To this audience of Gentile believers, many of whom had doubtless become proselytes in the full sense and observed the requirements of the law, Paul has to explain why he does not require such observance in the case of his own Gentile converts—and why the imposition of such a requirement would in fact run counter to the gospel as he understands and proclaims it. And he has to make clear that, contrary to an impression that knowledge of his letter to the Galatians may have given, he is not at all indifferent to the fate of Israel, 'his brethren according to the flesh' (9:3; see 10:1; 11:1).

In dealing with these concerns, Paul's exposition of the gospel in Romans displays many characteristics of apocalyptic: a sense of divine sovereignty; a cosmic viewpoint; the motif of the two ages; preoccupation with evil; malign spiritual powers behind suffering; and so forth. Not least among them is the motif of human accountability at the judgement. In Romans, as in all his writings, Paul works within the apocalyptic framework that sees the entire world headed, with some degree of imminence, to appearing before a divine assize at which evil— and evil-doers—will finally be dealt with and the faithful vindicated and rewarded as Christ reclaims the universe for the rule of God (see Phil 2:9-11; 1 Cor 15:24-28).

We run into the motif of the judgement very early in Romans—in what is generally agreed to be Paul's statement of theme in 1:16-17:

> [16] For I am not ashamed of the gospel; it is the power of God for salvation to everyone who has faith, to the Jew first and also to the Greek. [17] For in it the righteousness of God is revealed

---

60 See further my commentary on the letter, Byrne, *Romans*, 8-19.
61 The significance of the projected Spanish mission has found renewed emphasis in recent studies; notably in the major commentary of Jewett, *Romans*, 44, 74-80; see also Holloway, 'Commendatio aliqua sui', 358-60.

through faith for faith; as it is written, '*The one who is righteous by faith will live*'.

As my previous remarks concerning 'righteousness' will have made clear, I do not believe that it is appropriate to find in the concept of 'God's righteousness' (*dikaiosynē theou*) in itself 'saving' overtones drawn from the Old Testament background, especially Second Isaiah. Nor do I think that Käsemann and those who have followed his lead have done Pauline interpretation a great service by speaking of God's righteousness in terms of 'power'.[62] Käsemann may have been right to draw attention to a subjective sense in which the phrase *dikaiosynē theou* sometimes appears: God's own righteousness. But in Paul's thematic statement 'power' (*dynamis*) pertains to the gospel not to righteousness. The gospel is powerful because it reveals God's righteousness to believers and that revelation becomes for them a means to salvation. In what way the gospel reveals God's righteousness is not presently disclosed in Romans. For that we have to wait for restatement of the theme with specific reference to Christ's death in 3:21–26. Already, though, Paul's angry complaint to the Galatians lets us know what is involved:

> 3:1 You foolish Galatians! Who has bewitched you? It was before your eyes that Jesus Christ was publicly exhibited as crucified! ² The only thing I want to learn from you is this: Did you receive the Spirit by doing the works of the law or by believing what you heard?

The proclamation of the gospel involved a description of the crucifixion and an explanation of that as a revelation of God's righteousness. With the assistance of the Spirit this became for believers a 'power ... leading to salvation' (Rom 1:16).

'Salvation', too, should not be over-generalised and loaded with all the blessings of the messianic age. As Paul uses it, 'salvation'/being 'saved', is very much tied to being saved from 'the wrath', the divine wrath that will be a negative, destructive force at the judgement (5:9; 1 Thess 1:10; 5:9).

---

62 Käsemann, 'The "Righteousness of God" in Paul'.

Understanding salvation in this sense accounts for the otherwise difficult to explain causal (see *gar*) transition to the parallel 'revelation of God's wrath from heaven' (1:18). Humankind *needs* to be 'saved' because the divine wrath is abroad. It is in fact already being 'revealed', as Paul is immediately at pains to shown in the passage that follows.

The formally structured account of the revelation of God's wrath in 1:18–32 need not detain us long.[63] Closely adhering to a conventional pattern seen in parallels such as the Hellenistic Book of Wisdom, the text attributes the provocation of divine wrath to human lapse into idolatry—the refusal to glorify or give thanks to the Creator, whose unseen presence and power was plainly knowable because revealed in the created world (1:19–20). Human spurning of God in this way has then led to God's 'giving them up' (vv. 24, 26, 28) to the dishonouring of the human body in all kinds of deviant behaviour, which is the actual and present manifestation of the divine wrath. The passage concludes with the enumeration of all manner of other vices that have ensued, culminating in the assertion that they knew that all who did such things were worthy of death (vv. 29–32).

Needless to labour the point that with evocation of God's wrath—not simply as something for the future but as already manifested—and in the climactic indication of the penalty, we are very much in the forensic context of the last judgement. And surely not far at all from the content, if not the tone, of Paul's speech in Athens.

The forensic context emerges explicitly at the beginning of chapter 2. Paul rounds on the one he calls 'the Judger' and accuses the one who sits in judgement of this wrongdoing as 'doing the same' (2:1).

> [3] Do you imagine, whoever you are, that when you judge those who do such things and yet do them yourself, you will escape the judgement (*krima*) of God? [4] Or do you despise the riches of his kindness and forbearance and patience? Do you not realise that God's kindness is meant to lead you to repentance? [5] But by your hard and impenitent heart you are storing up wrath (*orgē*)

---

63 For the careful construction of this analysis of the Gentile world's ruinous lapse into idolatry and parallels in Hellenistic Jewish literature, especially the Wisdom of Solomon, especially chapters 13–14, see my *Romans*, 64–65.

for yourself on the day of wrath (*en hēmera orgēs*), when God's righteous judgement will be revealed.

This leads immediately into an unmistakable formulation on Paul's part, first positively and then negatively, of the principle of judgement according to works:

> ⁶ For he will repay according to each one's deeds: ⁷ to those who by patiently doing good seek for glory and honor and immortality, he will give eternal life; ⁸ while for those who are self-seeking and who obey not the truth but wickedness, there will be wrath and fury.
> ⁹ There will be anguish and distress for everyone who does evil, the Jew first and also the Greek, ¹⁰ but glory and honor and peace for everyone who does good, the Jew first and also the Greek.
> ¹¹ For God shows no partiality.
> ¹² All who have sinned apart from the law will also perish apart from the law, and all who have sinned under the law will be judged (*krithēsontai*) by the law. ¹³ For it is not the hearers of the law who are righteous (*dikaioi*) in God's sight, but the doers of the law who will be justified (*dikaiōthēsontai*).

Paul is, of course, subtly shifting the accusation to take in the Jewish world as well as the Gentile, relativising the value of possessing the law. Possession will not count on the day of judgement if one has not practised what the law commands. Paul even takes this relativisation of the law further by claiming that Gentiles, who do not possess the law can still do what the law commands through the 'work' of the law written on their hearts (vv. 14–15).[64]

While there are so many things that could be discussed here, I would point out how unambiguously the references to being 'righteous' (*dikaioi*) and being found 'justified' (*dikaiōthēsontai*) in v. 13 have to do with how one is 'found' by God to be at the last judgement. Secondly, at the end of this section (v. 16) there is the curious allusion when Paul refers to:

---

64 On the issues of these verses see my *Romans*, 90–94.

the day when, according to my gospel, God, through Jesus
Christ, will judge the secret thoughts of all.

The phrase, 'according to my gospel' inescapably implies that Paul's proclamation of the gospel involved, as in Acts 17:30–31, a reference to the day of judgement.

The eschatological horizon recedes for a time in Paul's explicit indictment of a Jewish teacher who, on the basis of knowledge of the law, claims to be an instructor of others (2:17–24). It returns in the following passage, 2:24–29, where Paul completes his relativisation of the value of possessing the torah with a similar relativisation of the value of circumcision. As in the case of the law, circumcision is of value only if one 'keeps (the requirements of) the law' (v. 25; see v. 13). Moreover, if the uncircumcised person keeps the requirements of the law, the lack of circumcision will be reckoned (*logisthēsetai*)—that is, by God at the judgement—as circumcision (v. 26),[65] and the person who keeps the law in a state of 'uncircumcision' (*akrobystia*) will judge (*krinei*) the one (literally, 'you') who, despite (possession of) the written code and circumcision is a transgressor of the law (v. 27).[66] The future tenses in each case point to the judgement. Likewise, in the concluding statements about the 'real Jew' (vv. 28–29), the 'praise' that comes 'not from human beings but from God' (v. 29c) must refer to the divine eschatological assessment.

Reference to the judgement emerges explicitly again in the diatribal passage, 3:1–8, designed to counter the objection that inclusion of Jews in the universal lack of righteousness impugns God's own faithfulness and righteousness. A citation of (LXX) Ps 50:6cd in v. 4b ensures that God *must* be 'justified' and 'victorious' in his judging. It is simply unthinkable (*mē genoito* [v. 6a]) that God could be unjust in inflicting the wrath (v. 5b).[67]

---

65 The statement is formulated as a question expecting the answer 'Yes' in the original.
66 I am now less tentative than before (see my *Romans*, 104) in seeing 'the one who keeps the requirements of the law in a state of uncircumcision' (v. 26) and 'the hidden Jew' who has a circumcision of heart wrought by the Spirit (v. 29), as references to Gentile *believers* who will have a 'delegated' role in the last judgment; see Stettler, *Endgericht*, 256.
67 The future *nikēseis* in the quotation reflects an eschatological reference. That the final judgment is in view throughout Rom 3:1–8, see McFadden, *Judgment*, 68–82—though curiously McFadden, following Käsemann, considers this passage to be 'a digression in the larger argument of the letter' (p.63). It serves the key function of raising the issue of God's own righteousness to which Rom 3:21–26 is the response; see my *Romans*, 107–8.

The universal scale of human sinfulness is then extensively confirmed through the witness of Scripture in vv. 9–19, building at last to the conclusion:

> For 'no human being will be justified in his sight' by deeds prescribed by the law, for through the law comes knowledge of sin (v. 20).

Paul's primary intent throughout Rom 1:18–3:20 has been the negative one of excluding any means of attaining the righteousness required at the judgement other than that of faith (1:16–17). Playing fast and loose, not for the last time in the letter (see 3:31; 7:23; 8:2), with the slippery meaning of the Greek word *nomos*,[68] he has argued that the law, far from providing a way of gaining a favourable verdict (through righteousness) at the judgement, serves on the contrary as a witness for the prosecution. With the way of the law blocked, the only viable alternative human response is that of faith: belief in the revelation of God's righteousness in the Christ event, as revealed in the gospel (3:21–26, 27–28; see 1:16–17).

Let us be clear. The principle that the eschatological judgement will be on the basis of behaviour ('works') emerges, to my mind, unambiguously from the preceding extended prophetic accusation (1:18–3:20). I agree with Klyne Snodgrass that we cannot explain it away on any other basis.[69] What is looming over the entire human race at this point in Romans (3:20) is a negative judgement because of factual human sinning—a universal state of affairs that Paul presupposes and later will indicate as initiated by Adam (5:12). The gospel's proclamation of the availability of justification by grace through faith does not overtake or

---

[68] Especially noteworthy in this connection is the use of *nomos* in multiple meanings in 7:23; see my article, 'The Problem of *Nomos*', esp. 295.

[69] Snodgrass, 'Justification by Grace'. Snodgrass lists others Pauline passages in which the motif of judgment according to works occurs 'without any suggestion that it causes any difficulty': Rom 14:10–12; 1 Cor 3:13–15; 2 Cor 5:10; 9:6; 11:15; Gal 6:7; and Col 3:25; Eph 6:8; 1 Tim 5:24–25; 2 Tim 4:14 (p. 74). Snodgrass ultimately resolves the tension between Romans 2 and Rom 3:20 by relating the phrase 'works of the law' to 'the sphere of' 'works righteousness', 'works done in the flesh', 'a striving after the law on one's own', that 'cannot be seen as the fulfilment of the law or as an equivalent to the various phrases in chapter 2' (p. 84). This echoes the Bultmannian 'hard Lutheran' approach to 'works of the law' in Paul. The article, of course, predates the publication of the Qumran document 4QMMT.

eliminate that principle but in fact sits 'within it'.[70]

With great rhetorical effect, then, resuming the earlier statement of theme (1:16–17), Paul proclaims the eleventh-hour divine rescue from the fate that hangs over the entire race through the revelation of God's righteousness in Christ, 3:21–26. It is not possible within the compass of this chapter to discuss this densely theological passage in any detail. I can only indicate a few matters more strictly relevant to the present enquiry.

First of all, in the context of the threat of condemnation hanging over the human race in view of the universal lack of the righteousness required for acquittal at the judgement, God has made righteousness available to human beings on the basis of faith. God has does so in the person of Christ and specifically in his death—more specifically still, in the love and obedience displayed in his death. Christ, as divine Son (though not explicitly named as such here; but see Rom 1:4; 8:3–4, 31), comes 'from the side of God' ('*God* put him forward ...'[v. 25]) in a display of divine righteousness (faithfulness to humanity as Creator [3:29–30]). At the same time, however, Christ, as 'Latter day (Second) Adam' (see 1 Cor 15:45), represents humanity. His 'obedience unto death' (Phil 2:8; see Rom 5:19), functioning as *hilastērion*,[71] is sufficient to overcome the vast mass of human disobedience, both past ('in the time of God's patience' [Rom 3:26a]) and present ('at the present time' [v. 26b]), and so bring about the righteous status required for justification at the judgement. Human beings—who 'have all sinned and lack the glory of God' (3:23; see Gen 1:26–28; Ps 8:5–8)—can access that righteous status by 'entering' through faith and baptism into the lineage of the Latter-day

---

70 See Wilckens, *Der Brief an die Römer*, 1.145–46, here 145: 'Die Offenbarung der Gerechtigkeit Gottes (3:21ff) ist mißverstanden, wenn man sie als eine neue Heilssetzung Gottes auffaßt, in der die Rechtfertigung des Täters als Prinzip aufgehoben und durch den Glauben als neues, dem aktiven Handeln entgegengesetztes Prinzip rein passive Sich-Beschenken-Lassens ersetzt worden wäre... Das paulinische Evangelium ist in seinem Kern keineswegs Werk-feindlich'; see also Yinger, *Paul, Judaism, and Judgment*, 175–78; Westerholm, *Justification Reconsidered*, 9–10.

71 It is impossible to discuss this controversial term here. I am understanding it as a portrayal of Christ's death in sacrificial terms with the effect in regard of removing the divine wrath against human sin; see further my *Romans*, 126–27, 132–33. I would, however, now give more weight to the *hilask-* stem's meaning in secular Greek and hence incline more to the propitiatory rather than the expiatory sense, while stressing the emphasis upon the divine initiative in Paul (Rom 3:24; 8:3; 2 Cor 5:18–21).

Adam and so come, by pure grace, to have the required righteousness. This is what Paul indicates somewhat later, at the end of chapter 4, when, understanding Christ's resurrection as the outward indication of his personal 'justification' (see above), he writes:

> [24] ... It (that is, righteousness) will be reckoned to us who believe in him who raised Jesus our Lord from the dead, [25] who was handed over to death for our trespasses *and was raised for our justification.*

Christ 'was raised for our justification' in a final, causal sense: that is, with our justification in view.[72]

In this connection, then, it is necessary to think of 'the righteousness of God' in three continuous ways: first, as God's own righteousness, displayed in the sending of the Son, in the face of total unrighteousness on the human side; secondly, as the righteousness of Christ, following his obedience unto death; finally, as the righteousness of believers in so far as they participate in the righteousness of Christ (see 2 Cor 5:21). This is what the rather tortuous syntax of Rom 3:25–26 is trying to express: that what God has done in Christ is both an expression of God's own righteousness *and* (see v. 26c) the enabling of human beings to acquire through faith and participation in Christ the righteousness required to find salvation from the wrath at the judgement.

Again I would emphasise that righteousness and the cognate (in Greek) process of justification can be understood in their proper forensic sense without further theological 'loading'. The forensic sense comes, not from an image chosen by Paul but because of the apocalyptic background with which he was working. This sense continues into the short passage with which chapter 3 concludes, 3:27–31, where Paul draws the conclusion at which he has been driving so far: in view of the universality of human sinfulness, on the one hand, and in view of God's action in Christ, on the other, one route to justification at the judgement has been excluded—that of doing the works of the law. For both Jews and Gentiles alike, only one alternative path is available—that of faith.

---

72 See Wolter, *Der Brief an die Römer*, 312–13, who helpfully notes the congruence of the warning in 1 Cor 15:17 with Rom 4:25b.

Paul reinforces this conclusion with an appeal to Scripture (Rom 4:1–25), choosing Scripture's presentation of Abraham, not as an arbitrary example, but as the figure in whom God's dealing both Israel and humanity as a whole in the messianic age were both foreshadowed and announced.[73]

Despite what has been recently maintained—especially by Martin de Boer and Douglas Campbell—it is not the case that the forensic categories yield in the following chapters (5–8) of the letter to the participationist categories to which Schweitzer so famously called attention. I deal with this section of the letter in greater detail in Chapter 3. My contention will be that 'righteousness' and 'justification' retain the same sense in this area of the letter as in the opening four chapters.

In terms, however, of the overall picture being sketched in this chapter, let me just draw attention to the places in Romans 5–8 where the apocalyptic motif of the judgement comes to the fore again. Aside from reference to being 'saved from the wrath' in 5:9, most striking, surely, is the opening of chapter 8: 'There is now no condemnation ...' (8:1). The condemnation (*katakrima*) in question must be that associated with the last judgement. Above all, there is the evocation in 8:31–39 of what would appear to be the actual scene of the coming judgement itself.

The primary concern with 'salvation' in Romans (1:16) ensures that the thought of the judgement never recedes from view. This is certainly the case in the third major section of Romans (chapters 9–11), concerned with the eschatological fate of that majority of Israel that has not come to faith in the crucified Messiah and the attitude that believers of Gentile origin should take to that ongoing rejection. Paul draws a very long bow in this section before finally formulating the hope for the salvation of 'all Israel' disclosed to him as a 'mystery' (11:25–32). On the way, however, there is the difficult anacolouthon that concludes the image of the potter and the clay in 9:22–23 ('vessels of wrath, ripe for destruction' [v. 22b]) and the whole preoccupation with the 'salvation' of this Israel that begins with the renewed expression of Paul's

---

73 In Paul's totally christological reading of Scripture, the 'ungodly' Abraham was justified by faith (Rom 4:5) proleptically in virtue of the sacrificial death of Christ; see Stettler, *Endgericht*, 250, citing (n. 344) Douglas Carson: 'Paul's assertions in Romans 4 presuppose his detailed account of Christ's cross-work in Romans 3:21–26'.

anguish at the beginning of chapter 10 and turns in a more hopeful direction around 11:13–14: Paul's expression of 'magnifying his ministry' in the hope, through the operation of 'jealousy', of 'saving some'. This concludes with the hope that, after the full number of the Gentiles has come in, 'all Israel will be saved' (11:26), when, according to God's covenant with them, God 'takes away their sins' (v. 27), a clear forensic statement at this late stage in the letter.[74]

In the fourth paranetic section (12:1–15:13), Paul warns against repaying evil with evil (12:17–21). Vengeance is to be left to the wrath of God—clearly to be unleashed at the judgement. The nearness of 'our salvation' is the basis of the exhortation in 13:11–14.

Finally, in Rom 14:1–12 Paul makes extensive play on the motif of judgement in the context of a plea for tolerance in the matter of diet and feast day observance. As servants of Christ, believers must refrain from judging (that is, condemning) each other, since, precisely as servants, each is accountable only to the Lord.[75] As in 2 Cor 5:10, Paul points out that 'all of us will have to stand before the judgement seat (*bēma*) of God' (Rom 14:10c).[76]

Conclusion

I have been suggesting that the apocalyptic motif of the judgement overhangs the entire exposition in Romans. It never really drops away because salvation through the power of the gospel is the overriding theme of Romans (1:16–17) and salvation is first and foremost salvation from the endtime wrath of God (1:18). I have also argued that this pervasive reference to judgement requires that references to justification and the cognate sense of human beings being found righteous in God's sight be understood in a thoroughly forensic sense, not as an image from

---

74 On the 'mystery' of Israel's ultimate salvation as conceived by Paul here see my *Romans*, 348–56.
75 It could be that Paul has in mind here a preliminary accountability to Christ before the final great judgment—one that is perhaps not so final or severe, as the similar passage with respect to ministerial accountability in 1 Cor 3:12–15; 4:4–5 might also suggest. On the different ways in which judgment appears in Paul, see Barclay, 'Believers', 195–96.
76 Paul sees no essential difference between accountability to God or to Christ; see Dunn, *Romans 9–16*, 809; Jewett, *Romans*, 851.

the law court freely chosen but as a 'compulsory' element of the apocalyptic horizon of thought operative throughout the letter. Chapter 3 pursues the motif of righteousness and justification more specifically within the section making up chapters 5–8. By linking justification specially to the last judgement I hope to show the absolutely central role that these chapters play in the letter, something that many interpreters have had difficulty explaining over the years.

A final comment of a more theological nature. Is it possible to hold together the principle that judgement will be according to one's works and that justification will be through God's grace and, on the human side, through faith, within the one unitary understanding of God? I believe that it is possible. The God who will judge according to works is the God who, in the face of the universal prevalence of sin, has provided through the gift of the Son a way for human beings to be found righteous at the judgement with a righteousness made available in Christ. The tortured formula in Rom 3:21–26 is designed precisely to hold these two truths together within a unified vision of the action of God. The crucial requirement for avoiding condemnation and finding (eternal) life at the judgement is to be found 'in Christ' (8:1). Hence the great necessity to proclaim the gospel that 'leads to salvation' (1:16) for those who respond in faith and find thereby freedom from sin and justification in him. 'Outside' of Christ, so to speak, there can only be judgement according to one's works. Paul does not seem to have been a universalist in regard to salvation. I cannot see how he would have found the responsibility to proclaim the gospel so pressing if he were (1 Cor 9:16).[77] And Romans 5–8, as I hope Chapter 3 will show, is designed to explain how this hope is maintained in the present time leading up to the judgement.

---

77 Israel, of course, remains a special case, but I am not convinced that the vision deployed in the latter half of Romans 11 entirely removes the sense of judgment according to works in her case as well, always presupposing, however, that she will be given a second chance to respond to Christ and have her sins removed and so find salvation, when the full number of the Gentiles has 'come in' (11:25–27).

Bibliography

Aune, David E.   'Apocalypticism', in G. F. Hawthorne & R. P. Martin (eds.), *Dictionary of Paul and His Letters* (Downers Grove, IL: Intervarsity, 1993), 25–35.

Barclay, J. M. G.   'Believers and the "Last Judgment" in Paul: Rethinking Grace and Recompense', in H.-J. Eckstein, C. Landmesser, & H. Lichtenberger (eds.), *Eschatologie–Eschatology* (Tübingen: Mohr Siebeck, 2011), 195–208.

Beker, J. Christiaan   *Paul's Apocalyptic Gospel: The Coming Triumph of God* (Philadelphia: Fortress, 1982).

Beker, J. Christiaan   *Paul the Apostle: the Triumph of God in Life and Thought* (Philadelphia: Fortress, 1980).

Bird, Michael J.   *Saving Righteousness: Studies on Paul, Justification and the New Perspective* (Milton Keynes: Paternoster, 2007).

de Boer, Martinus C.   *The Defeat of Death: Apocalyptic Eschatology in 1 Corinthians 15 and Romans 5* (JSNTSuppl 22; Sheffield: JSOT Press, 1988).

de Boer, Martinus C.   'Paul and Jewish Apocalyptic Eschatology', in Joel Marcus & Marion L. Soards (eds.), *Apocalyptic and the New Testament. Essays in Honor of J. Louis Martyn* (JSNTSup 24; Sheffield: JSOT Press, 1989), 169–90.

de Boer, Martinus C.   'Paul and Apocalyptic Eschatology', in John J. Collins (ed.), *The Encyclopedia of Apocalypticism. Vol 1: The Origins of Apocalypticism in Judaism and Christianity* (New York: Continuum, 1999), 345–83.

de Boer, Martinus C.   'Paul's Mythologizing Program in Romans 5–8', in Beverly Roberts Gaventa (ed.), *Apocalyptic Paul: Cosmos and Anthropos in Romans 5–8* (Waco, TX: Baylor University, 2013), 1–20.

de Boer, Martinus C.   'Apocalyptic as God's Eschatological Activity in Paul's Theology', in Ben C. Blackwell, John K Goodrich, & Jason Maston (eds.), *Paul and the Apocalyptic Imagination* (Minneapolis, MN: Fortress, 2016), 45–63.

Bull, Klaus-Michael "'Wir werden alle vor den Richterstuhl Gottes gestellt warden" (Rom 14,10): Zur Funktion des Motivs vom Endgericht in den Argumentationen des Römerbriefs', in Michael Becker & Markus Öhler (eds.), *Apokalyptik als Herausforderung neutestamentlicher Theologie* (WUNT 2/214; Tübingen: Mohr Siebeck, 2006), 125–43.

Bultmann, Rudolph *Kerygma and Myth* (2 vols.; New York: Harper & Row, 1961, 2nd ed.).

Bultmann, Rudolph *Theology of the New Testament* (2 vols.; London: SCM, 1952, 1955).

Byrne, Brendan 'Review of Douglas Campbell, *The Deliverance of God*', *Pacifica* 24.1 (February 2011), 101–104.

Byrne, Brendan *Romans* (SP 6; Collegeville, MN; Glazier, 1996).

Byrne, Brendan 'The Problem of *Nomos* and the Relationship with Judaism in Romans', *Catholic Biblical Quarterly* 62.3 (2000), 294–309.

Campbell, Douglas A. *The Deliverance of God: An Apocalyptic Rereading of Justification in Paul* (Grand Rapids, MI, & Cambridge, UK: Eerdmans, 2009).

Collins, Adela Yarbro (ed.) *Early Christian Apocalypticism: Genre and Social Setting, Semeia 36.* (Missoula, MT: Scholars, 1986).

Collins, John J. *Apocalypse: The Morphology of a Genre, Semeia 14* (Missoula, MT: Scholars, 1979).

Collins, John J. 'Apocalypses and Apocalypticism: Early Jewish Apocalypticism', in David Noel Freedman (ed.), *Anchor Bible Dictionary* (5 vols.; New York: Doubleday, 1992), 1.282–288.

Cremer, H. *Die paulinische Rechtfertigungslehre im Zusammenhange ihrer geschichtlichen Voraussetzungen* (Gütersloh: Bertelsmann, 1900 2nd ed.).

Cuvillier, Elian 'Das apokalyptische Denken im Neuen Testament', *Zeitschrift für Neues Testament* 22 (2008), 2–12.

D'Angelo, M. R. & E. A. Matter, 'Apocalypticism', in John H. Hayes (ed.), *Dictionary of Biblical Interpretation* (2 vols.; Nashville, TN: Abingdon, 1999), 1.40–44.

Davies, J. P.	*Paul among the Apocalypses? An Evaluation of 'Apocalyptic' Paul in the Context of Jewish and Christian Apocalyptic Literature* (New York: Bloomsbury, 2016).
Dodd, C. H.	*The Epistle of Paul to the Romans* (London: Hodder & Stoughton, 1932; repr. Collins-Fontana, 1968).
Donfried, Karl P.	'Justification and Last Judgment in Paul', *Zeitschrift für die neutestamentliche Wissenschaft* 67 (1976), 90–110.
Dunn, J. D. G.	*The Theology of Paul the Apostle* (Grand Rapids, MI: Eerdmans, 1998).
Dunn, J. D. G.	*Romans 9–16* (WBC 38b; Dallas, TX: Word Books, 1988).
Fitzmyer, J.A.	'Romans', in R.E. Brown, J.A. Fitzmyer, & R.E. Murphy (eds.), *New Jerome Bible Commentary* (London: G. Chapman, 1989; Pearson, 1999 3rd ed.).
Glasson, T. F.	'What is Apocalyptic?'. *New Testament Studies* 27 (1980), 93–105.
Hanson, Paul D.	'Apocalypse, genre' and 'Apocalypticism', in Keith Krimm et al. (eds.), *International Dictionary of the Bible Supplementary Volume* (Nashville: Abingdon, 1976), 27–28, 28–34.
Hanson, Paul D.	*The Dawn of Apocalyptic* (Revised edition; Philadelphia: Fortress, 1979).
Hogan, Katrina Martin	'The Apocalyptic Eschatology of Romans: Creation, Judgment, Resurrection, and Glory', in Ben E. Reynolds & L. T. Stuckenbruch (eds.), *The Jewish Apocalyptic Tradition and the Shaping of the New Testament* (Minneapolis: Fortress, 2017), 155–74.
Holloway, Paul A	'Commendatio aliqua sui: Reading Romans with Pierre Bourdieu', *Early Christianity* 2 (2011), 356–83.
Hooker, Morna D.	'Interchange and Atonement', *Essays on Paul* (Cambridge: Cambridge University Press, 1990; repr. Eugene, OR: Wipf & Stock, 2008), 26–41. Originally published in JTS 22 (1971), 349–61.
Irons, Charles Lee	*The Righteousness of God: A Lexical Examination of the Covenant-Faithfulness Interpretation* (WUNT 2/386; Tübingen: Mohr Siebeck, 2015).
Jewett, Robert	*Romans* (Hermeneia; Minneapolis: Fortress, 2007).

Kabisch, Richard	*Die Eschatologie des Paulus in ihren Zusammenhängen mit dem Gesamtbegriff des Paulinismus* (Göttingen: Vanhoeck & Ruprecht, 1893).
Käsemann, Ernst	'The Beginnings of Christian Theology', *New Testament Questions of Today* (Philadelphia: Fortress, 1969), 82–107.
Käsemann, Ernst	'On the Subject of Primitive Christian Apocalyptic', *New Testament Questions of Today*, 108–37.
Käsemann, Ernst	'The "Righteousness of God" in Paul', *New Testament Questions of Today*, 168–82.
Knibb, Michael A.	'Apocalypticism and Messianism', in Timothy H. Lim & John J. Collins (eds.), *The Oxford Handbook of the Dead Sea Scrolls* (Oxford: Oxford University, 2010), 403–32.
McFadden, Kevin W.	*Judgment according to Works in Romans: The Meaning and Function of Divine Judgment in Paul's Most Important Letter* (Minneapolis: Fortress, 2013).
Martyn, J. Louis	*Galatians: A New Translation with Introduction and Commentary* (Hermeneia; New York: Doubleday, 1997).
Martyn, J. Louis	'Epistemology at the Turn of the Ages', *Theological Issues in the Letters of Paul* (Nashville: Abingdon, 1997), 89–110.
Matlock, R. Barry	*Unveiling the Apocalyptic Paul: Paul's Interpreters and the Rhetoric of Criticism* (JSNTSup 127; Sheffield: Sheffield Academic, 1996).
Matlock, R. Barry	'Zeal for Paul but Not According to Knowledge: Douglas Campbell's War on "Justification Theory"', *Journal for the Study of the New Testament* 34.2 (2011), 115–49.
Müller, Christian	*Gottes Gerechtigkeit und Gottes Volk: Eine Untersuchung zu Römer 9–11* (Göttingen: Vandenhoeck & Ruprecht, 1964).
Prothro, James B.	*Both Judge and Justifier: Biblical Legal Language and the Act of Justifying in Paul* (WUNT 2/461; Tübingen: Mohr Siebeck, 2018).
Rowland, Christopher C.	*The Open Heaven: A Study of Apocalyptic in Judaism and Early Christianity* (New York: Crossroad, 1982).
Russell, D. S.	*The Method and Message of Jewish Apocalyptic: 200 BD–AD 100* (London: SCM, 1964; repr. 1980).

Schmid, H. H. *Gerechtigkeitsbegriff als Weltordnung: Hintergrund und Geschichte des alttestamentlichen Gerechtigkeitsbegriffes* (BHT 40; Tübingen: Mohr Siebeck, 1968).

Schrenk, G. 'δίκη, δίκαιος, δικαιοσύνη, δικαιόω, δικαίωμα, δικαίωσις, δικαιοκρισία', *TDNT*, II:182–224.

Schweitzer, Albert *The Mysticism of Paul the Apostle* (London: A&C Black, 1931).

Scullion, J. J. 'Righteousness (OT)', in David Noel Freedman (ed.), *Anchor Bible Dictionary* (5 vols.; New York: Doubleday, 1992), 5.724–36.

Seifrid, Mark A. 'Righteousness Language in the Hebrew Scriptures and Early Judaism', in D. A. Carson, Peter T. O'Brien, & Mark A. Seifrid (eds.), *Justification and Variegated Nomism: Volume 1: The Complexities of Second Temple Judaism* (Tübingen: Mohr Siebeck; Grand Rapids: Baker Academic, 2001), 414–42.

Shaw, David A. 'Apocalyptic or Covenant: Perspectives on Paul or Antinomies at War?', *Journal for the Study of the New Testament* 36.2 (2013), 155–71.

Snodgrass, Klyne R. 'Justification by Grace – to the Doers: An Analysis of the Place of Romans 2 in the Theology of Paul', *New Testament Studies* 32.1 (1986), 72–93.

Stanley, Alan (ed.) *Four Views on the Role of Works at the Final Judgment* (Contributors: Robert N. Wilkin; Thomas R. Schreiner; James D. G. Dunn; Michael P. Barber). (Grand Rapids, MI: Zondervan, 2013).

Stettler, Christian *Das letze Gericht: Studien zur Endgerichterwartung von den Schriftpropheten bis Jesus* (WUNT 2/299; Tübingen: Mohr Siebeck, 2011).

Stettler, Christian *Das Endgericht bei Paulus: Framesemantische und exegetische Studien zur paulinischen Eschatologie und Soteriologie* (WUNT 371; Tübingen: Mohr Sieback, 2017).

Stuhlmacher, Peter *Gerechtigkeit Gottes bei Paulus* (Göttingen: Vandenhoeck & Ruprecht, 1966 2nd ed.).

Sturm, Richard E.   'Defining the Word "Apocalyptic": A Problem in Biblical Criticism', in Joel Marcus & Marion L. Soards (ed.), *Apocalyptic and the New Testament. Essays in Honor of J. Louis Martyn* (JSNTSup 24; Sheffield: JSOT Press, 1989), 17-48.

Synofzik, E.   *Die Gerichts- und Vergeltungsaussagen bei Paulus* (Göttingen: Vandenhoeck & Ruprecht, 1977).

VanLandingham, Chris   *Judgment and Justification in Early Judaism and the Apostle Paul* (Peabody, MA: Hendrickson, 2006).

Vielhauer, Philipp   'Apocalyptic', in *New Testament Apochrypha* (ET ed. R. McL. Wilson of *Neutestamentliche Apokryphen in deutscher Übersetzung* [Tübingen: Mohr, 1964], edited by E. Hennecke and W. Schneemelcher). (London: SCM, 1965), 2.581-607.

Westerholm, Stephen   *Perspectives Old and New on Paul: The Lutheran Paul and His Critics* (Grand Rapids, MI: Eerdmans; Cambridge, UK: 2004).

Westerholm, Stephen   'The Righteousness of the Law and the Righteousness of Faith in Romans', *Interpretation* 58.3 (2004), 253-64.

Westerholm, Stephen   *Justification Reconsidered: Rethinking a Pauline Theme* (Grand Rapids, MI: Eerdmans, 2013).

Wilckens, Ulrich   *Der Brief an die Römer* (EKK 6; 3 vols. Neukirchen-Vluyn: Neukirchener Verlag, 1978-92).

Wolter, Michael   *Der Brief an die Römer: Teilband 1: Röm 1-8* (EKK VI/1; Neukirchen-Vluyn: Patmos, 2014).

Wright, N. T.   *The Climax of the Covenant* (Edinburgh: T&T Clark, 1991).

Wright, N. T.   *Paul and His Recent Interpreters: Some Contemporary Debates* (Minneapolis: Fortress, 2015).

Wright, N. T.   'The Letter to the Romans', in L. E. Keck (ed.), *New Interpreters Bible Volume X* (Nashville: Abingdon, 2002), 423-770.

Yinger, Keith L.   *Paul, Judaism, and Judgment according to Deeds* (SNTSMS 105; Cambridge: Cambridge University Press, 1999).

CHAPTER 3

Justification and last judgement in Romans: The place of chapters 5–8

Brendan Byrne, SJ

In Chapter 2 of this volume, I argued that reference to the apocalyptic motif of the last judgement, both explicit and implicit, is pervasive throughout Paul's Letter to Rome and is the controlling feature for the motif of 'justification' that is prominent in the early chapters but not lacking in later ones. I further argued that 'salvation'—the principal fruit of the power of the gospel, according to the opening statement of theme (1:16–17) —is also directly related to the judgement. It is first and foremost salvation from the wrath destined, according to the apocalyptic perspective, to be unleashed upon evil-doers following the judgement (see 5:9; Gal 1:4; 1 Thess 1:10; 5:9). I further argued that the principle of 'justification according to one's works', formulated unambiguously in Rom 2:6–13, remains in force throughout the letter and is not in any way overridden or set aside through God's saving action in Christ. As formulated especially in the resumption of the theme of the letter in 3:21–26, God has found a way, *within* this principle rather than against or aside from it, to bring believers into the righteousness of Christ as Latter-day Adam (1 Cor 15:45), so that the threat of condemnation at the judgement is removed from them and the path to sharing the risen life of the new Adam opened up.

This present Chapter discusses more specifically the role of chapters 5–8, the second of the four substantial blocks that make up the body of Paul's letter to Rome (1:16 [18]–4:25; 5:1–8:39; 9:1–11:36; 12:1–15:13), within this forensic apocalyptic perspective. I shall argue that, within the continuing horizon of the last judgement and the requirement of living out the righteousness graciously bestowed by God on believers, this section Romans 5–8 provides the essential basis for the hope of salvation proclaimed in the gospel (1:16–17).

1. Accounting for Romans 5–8

Determining the role of Romans 5–8 within the letter is not a new issue. It has long been observed that notable features of the preceding section—the theme of righteousness by faith, concern for Israel, and copious recourse to Scripture—recede from view, to surface once again in chapters 9–11. A surgical excision of 5:1–8:39 from the body of the letter could leave a smoother flow of argument. Moreover, ever since N. A. Dahl, in an influential study,[1] pointed out the extent to which 5:1–11 and 8:1–39 constitute an inclusion, it is now more customary to see a caesura between 4:25 and 5:1 and so regard chapters 5–8 as a unified block.[2]

In 1976 Robin Scroggs proposed that chapters 5–8 constitute a homily, composed prior to the writing of the letter, that Paul saw fit to insert at this point.[3] It seems to me quite likely that Paul did incorporate into his letter material that he had composed or at least thought out earlier.[4] Whatever be its origin, however, the section is firmly incorporated within the letter, forming part of the total rhetorical composition Paul intended. We have to make sense of the letter in its present form, as a unified rhetorical composition.

---

1   Dahl, 'Two Notes on Romans 5', 37–38.
2   For an excellent discussion of the reasons for seeing the beginning of the second section at 5:1, see Moo, *Romans*, 290–95; see further Fitzmyer, *Romans*, 96–98; Beker, *Paul the Apostle*, 83–85. Wilckens, *Der Brief an die Römer*, is a noteworthy exception: see Vol. 1 [*Röm 1–5*], 286–88, now followed by his successor in the same series: Wolter, *Der Brief an die Römer*, 70–71. Dunn, *Romans 1–8*, 242–44, regards chapter 5 as a 'bridging' chapter.
3   Scrogg, 'Paul as Rhetorician'.
4   For example, Rom 6:15–23, while arguing on a different basis, hardly advances the argument of 6:1–14. Both blocks may have originated as independent homilies, Paul seeing fit to include them in Romans side by side, as it were.

A couple of decades ago Frank Thielman sought to lessen the appearance of discontinuity with what precedes and follows by arguing that Israel is by no means absent from chapters 5–8.[5] Though citation of scripture is rare, the Deuteronomistic view of the story of Israel, where Israel consistently breaks the covenant agreements, receives punishment for its sins in the shape of exile, yet can look forward to restoration at God's hand, shapes Paul's interpretation of the situation of believers in this section.[6] Subsequently, Sylvia Keesmat made a similar proposal in regard to the Exodus tradition.[7]

In critical reaction to interpretations along these lines, Charles Cousar, to my mind, stated the essential issue:

> The issue is not whether Paul draws on the language and texts of the Old Testament (that is a given) but whether there is a discernible line of continuity between Israel's story in the past and the death and resurrection of Christ or whether the apocalyptic character of God's disclosure in Christ precipitates an irreparable rupture in the story that makes any smooth notion of continuity difficult to discern.[8]

Cousar plumps firmly for the latter alternative, stressing the apocalyptic cast of Paul's thought, particularly in relation to the onset of the law and the 'two-age' eschatological schema which forms the background to the understanding of the life of believers in this section. Towards the end he remarks: 'The apocalyptic presentation of Christ provides the essential lens through which God, Israel, and the church are viewed'.[9]

2. Rom 6:1–8:13: the Ethical 'Inner Core' of Romans 5–8

While broadly in sympathy with the nuanced stress upon discontinuity proposed by Cousar, I think there is considerably more to be said,

---

5 Thielman, 'The Story of Israel'.
6 Thielman, 'The Story of Israel', 194–95.
7 Keesmaat, *Paul and His Story*.
8 Cousar, 'Continuity and Discontinuity', 196.
9 Cousar, 'Continuity and Discontinuity', 210.

particularly in relation to the 'inner core' of Romans 5–8, namely, 6:1–8:13. Whereas in the opening and concluding sections of chapters 5–8 (5:1–21 and 8:14–39) the theme of 'hope' prevails, this extended central section is shot through with a concern for how believers ought live.[10] In fact, the entire section in many places takes on a distinctly parenetic tone—which is surprising granted that the truly parenetic part of the letter begins at 12:1. Most interpreters argue that the stress upon the overwhelming force of God's grace in 5:12–21 prompts Paul to introduce an ethical section, making clear that grace by no means implies licence to sin. In this connection, John Barclay in his recent work *Paul and the Gift*, distinguishing the variety of ways in which the divine gift of grace is 'perfected' in biblical thought, remarks: 'The divine gift in Christ was *unconditioned* (based on no prior conditions) but it is not unconditional (carrying no subsequent demands)'.[11] What Barclay terms 'the *incongruous* gift' (incongruous, that is, as given to the totally unworthy) is strongly obliging in that it requires a response of a transformed life of obedience to God (italics in both cases original).

This is reasonable enough. But it does not account sufficiently for the introduction and extended treatment of the topic of the law in chapter 7, spilling over to some extent to chapter 8. The section making up 7:7–25 is widely regarded as offering an 'apology' or 'defence' of the law.[12] But why such defence of the law should be offered precisely here—and not, as would seem more appropriate, at the end of chapter 3 (see 3:31!) or at 4:15—remains unexplained. An adequate account of the place of Romans 5–8 within the letter as a whole must explain the role of this inner parenetic section, including the discussion of encounter with (7:7–13) and life under (7:14–25) the law.

---

10 I once termed it 'an ethical excursus' ('Living Out the Righteousness of God', 558). However, far from an 'excursus', I now view the section as an essential element in the running argument of the letter.
11 Barclay, *Paul and the Gift*, 500.
12 As constantly maintained by Dunn: see *Romans 1–8*, 376; *The Theology of Paul the Apostle*, 157–58, 472. In the concluding essay, 'In Search of Common Ground', in the collection edited by him, *Paul and the Mosaic Law*, 309–34, Dunn reports that, 'It was agreed that Rom. 7 was intended by Paul as a defence of the law, but the Symposium was unable to develop that point of consensus very far' (p. 322).

2.1. *Living in the 'Overlap' of the Ages*

In moving towards such an account it is useful to remember James Dunn's helpful characterisation of the eschatological situation of believers in the present era as one of living in the 'overlap' of the 'ages', the old and the new.[13] As far as relations with God go, through justification (see Rom 5:1) believers have been rescued from the old age and, as attested by the gift of the Spirit (5:5), enjoy the 'peace with God' associated with the new. Bodily, however, their existence is still anchored in the conditions of the old, and in their bodies they experience its onslaught in the shape of suffering, temptation, and death.

Romans 5–8 addresses this complex eschatological situation in which believers find themselves. The justification they have received is indeed the eschatological justification. The righteousness they have in Christ is the righteousness required at the great eschatological judgement. Though that judgement is still outstanding (the triumphant concluding section, 8:31–39, evokes it; see below), for those 'in Christ' there should be no prospect of condemnation (8:1, 31–35). Their passports to eternal life are already stamped, as it were, 'righteous'. Thus the physical realities of the present time—especially suffering and the prospect of death—cannot be interpreted as threatening the prospect of full salvation.[14] Only sin, sufficiently grave to lead to exclusion from being 'in Christ' can do that.[15] The God, who in faithfulness to sinful humanity and in an extreme display of costly love (the giving up of the Son: 5:6–10; 8:32) has brought believers from being 'enemies' to being reconciled (5:10), can most certainly be trusted, especially now that it is a question not of enemies but of friends (reconciled), to bring them through to the full salvation. This is the essential 'a fortiori' (*pollō mallon*) logic that is the engine of Paul's argument for hope in 5:1–21 and 8:31–39.[16]

---

13   Dunn, *Theology of Paul*, 464, 495.
14   See Geniusz, *Romans 8:18–30*, 286.
15   On the problem of sin in the Christian community see Stettler, *Das Endgericht bei Paulus*, 241, 262–72.
16   The phrase *pollō mallon* occurs four times in Romans 5 (see also v 10, 15, 17) and is implicit in 8:32 (see also 2 Cor 3:11; Phil 2:12; Rom 11:12, 24 [*posō mallon* in both cases]). It corresponds to the logical device called *qal wāḥōmer* (lit. 'light and heavy') in rabbinic literature; see SB 3.223–26.

'Hope', then, is the overall theme of the entire section. It had actually been anticipated—though this is not often noted—towards the end of chapter 4, where Paul's analysis of the inner structure of Abraham's faith (vv. 17b–21) lays stress upon the persevering aspect of his believing. Abraham had not only to put his faith in God's promise that he would have a son and heir. He had also to hang on in hope until that promise was fulfilled (vv. 18–20). In this sense the patriarch models Christian hope as much as he models—as 'father' of all believers (v. 18)—Christian faith. In the context of the 'deadness' (*nenekrōmenon*) of his own reproductive faculty and that also (*nekrōsis*) of Sarah's womb (v. 19) Abraham believed and hoped in a God who could bring life out of 'death' (v. 17b) and so honour the promise to give him a son and heir. Just so, Christians not only believe that God raised Jesus from the dead but see that past act of power as a guarantee of the hope that God will overcome their own mortality in resurrection. What is stated in their regard in Rom 4:23–25 receives a fuller complement in 8:9–11.[17] In this sense, the theme central to Romans 5–8 emerges naturally and inevitably from that of 'faith' in Rom 1:16–4:25.

2.2. *Two Key Aspects of Paul's Argument*

Right interpretation of Paul's case for hope in Romans 5–8 depends, to my mind, on appreciation of two considerations above all—one an essential presupposition of Paul's argument, the other a feature of his preferred rhetoric.

The first is the axiom, pervasive in apocalyptic Judaism and already mentioned in Chapter 2, that 'life', that is, 'eternal life', flows from being found righteous by God at the coming judgement,[18] a truth Paul sums up succinctly in Rom 8:10c: 'the Spirit (means) *life because of*

---

17 So also in 1 Cor 15:12–18 Paul argues for the resurrection of (dead) believers on the basis of the necessary connection between their eschatological 'fate' and that of (the already raised) Christ; see also 2 Cor 4:13–14.
18 For copious references illustrative of this axiom in biblical and post-biblical Jewish literature, see Chapter 2 in this volume, n.47.

righteousness'.[19] The axiom underlies other expressions in Paul such as *eis dikaiōsin zōēs* in Rom 5:18 and *kai hē charis basileusēi dia dikaiōsynēs eis zōēn aiōnion* in 5:21. In this sense, for Paul the apocalyptic thinker, righteousness is always eschatological righteousness, the righteousness that will be required at the judgement. Within the ambit of this principle, Paul's argument for hope in Romans 5–8 rests essentially upon the truth that through God's gracious act in Christ (3:21–26) believers *have* been graced with the required righteousness *and can* and *must continue to retain that status* in the 'overlap of the ages' era leading up to the final judgement.[20] Salvation is not a second benefit simply additional to righteousness. Paul saw an intrinsic link between the two on the basis of the axiom formulated above.[21] To acknowledge that Paul sees an intrinsic connection between behaviour and the gaining of eternal life is not to introduce a doctrine of merits in the sense that human action somehow earns eternal life apart from the grace of God. For Paul any good action of believers is entirely the product of the Spirit, which has replaced sin as indwelling power (Rom 8:4, 9–11).[22] The essential argument in Romans 5–8 is that, despite the conditions of the present time (suffering and the prospect of death), there is hope of salvation (eternal life) because believers have been found and will be found to be righteous at the judgement.[23]

Thus Paul must argue for both the necessity (hence the parenetic tone) and the *possibility* (hence the argumentative mode; see below) of living, in the time leading up to the judgement, within the verdict of

---

19 For further discussion of interpretive issues in this verse, see my commentary *Romans*, 240–41, 245; see further, my article, 'Living Out the Righteousness of God', 579.
20 Recall the statements along similar lines by Barclay cited at n.11 above.
21 See further my *Romans*, 58, 240–41. Dunn acknowledges that the principle that righteousness leads to salvation is 'characteristically Jewish' (*Romans 1–8*, 258). See also, Lichtenberger, 'Das Tora-Verständnis. Citing (p. 9) a Münster lecture given by Daniel R. Schwartz in 1992, Lichtenberger remarks: 'Auch wenn der belastete Ausdruck "Werkgerechtigkeit" mit gutem Grund im Begriff ist, aus dem Vokabular der neutestamentlichen Wissenschaft zu verschwinden, so bleibt doch die Frage, ob ihr alter Irrtum nicht weniger in der *Wahrnehmung* als vielmehr in der *Bewertung* traditionell jüdischer Vorstellungun von Toragehorsam, Verdienst und Lohn gelegen haben könnte' (p. 10; italics original).
22 See Stettler, *Endgericht*, 257.
23 The oscillation in Paul between past and future with respect to justification can be seen by comparing the firm aorist *dikaiōthentes* in 5:1 and the future reference of *dikaioi katastathēsontai* in 5:19 (see also Gal 5:5: ... *elpida dikaiosynēs apekdechometha*).

righteousness (justification) graciously bestowed by God through the redemptive work of Christ (5:1). This is an essential element of the 'thesis' of Romans (1:16–17): the gospel is the power of God leading to salvation, for every believer, *because* in/through it the (required) righteousness ('the righteousness of God'[24]) becomes available to believers. Hence Rom 6:1–8:13, the 'ethical' inner core of chapters 5–8, is no digression but an essential plank in the argument. Righteousness is a status that believers must live out in their bodily life in a process of 'sanctification' (*hagiasmos* [6:19, 22]), the 'end' or 'goal' (*telos*) of which is 'eternal life' (v. 22).

A second feature required for proper interpretation of Romans 5–8 concerns Paul's mode of argument—specifically, his widely attested predilection for affirming the positive by prefacing it with a formulation (and often a firm rejection; see 6:1) of the countervailing negative. It is part of the antithetical nature of his rhetoric and appears constantly in his writing, sometimes in short statements,[25] sometimes in extended developments.

The most notable examples of the latter feature in Romans 5–8 are, firstly, the reiterated 'Adam-Christ' contrast/comparison formulated in 5:12–21 and, secondly, as I shall argue, the transition across 7:7–8:13 from life under the law to life in the Spirit. Paul introduces the figure of Adam in 5:12–21 and indicates his agency in the onset of sin leading to death for the human race not because he is interested in Adam as such but to set him up as a foil over against which to assert all the more effectively the countervailing positive influence of Christ in regard to righteousness leading to life. Paul employs a Jewish tradition about Adam, with which he presumes his readers are familiar, in order drive home his argument for hope.[26] The basis is that the universal legacy of sin and death unleashed by Adam has been more than matched by a solidarity

---

24 I take the phrase 'righteousness of God', here and in 3:21–26, to refer equally both to God's own (subjective) righteousness and the righteousness graciously 'reckoned' to believers by God in Christ. This bi-polarity is an essential aspect of Paul's argument; see further my commentary *Romans*, 123–24.
25 E.g.: '... it is not a spirit of slavery that you have received—[something to drive you] back again to fear. But you have received a Spirit of divine filiation in which we cry out, "Abba, Father"' (Rom 8:15); see further Rom 3:27; 4:13; 6:17; 6:19–20; 7:5–6; 8:9, 8:12; Gal 3:2; etc.
26 On the 'Adam' tradition see my *Romans*, 174–75.

in righteousness leading to life made available to human beings through God's grace operating in Christ (5:17). In Christ God has opened up a possibility for righteousness that Adam closed, a closure universally ratified by subsequent human sinning (5:12d).[27] Hope prevails, however, because this negative ratification of Adam's sin can be overcome in human lives by a God-given possibility of righteous living in Christ.

3. From Slavery under the Law to Freedom in the Spirit

Just as Adam appears in Rom 5:12–21 to provide a negative foil over against which to assert more powerfully the sure prospect of eternal life in Christ, the same obtains with respect to the contrasting depictions of life under the law and life in the Spirit across 7:7–8:13. Paul leads up to this dramatic comparison/contrast by kick-starting his ethical section (6:1–8:13) with a vigorous dismissal (6:1) of the suggestion that the prevailing power of God's grace (5:20b) could lead to a return to a life of sin. Baptism 'into' Christ, and specifically into his atoning death (3:24–25; 4:25a) and resurrection (4:25b), has ensured that believers have been freed both from the guilt (6:7)[28] and the continuing power of sin; they are 'dead' to sin and are—or ought be—'living to God', as Christ lives to God (v. 11), in a new life of righteousness in their present bodily existence (vv. 12–13).

After an anticipatory shot at the law (6:15), Paul pursues the exhortation with aid of an extended 'slavery' image (6:15–23).[29] Adopting a more systematic tack he points to outcomes: freedom from slavery

---

27 In the process of sin leading to death there is a dual 'causality' expressed in Rom 5:12: a causality set in train by Adam's sin and a causality set in train by subsequent human sinning (*pantes hēmarton*). A sense of Adam's instrumentality is vital for the comparison with Christ, but, like the author of 2 *Apoc. Bar*54: 15–19, Paul will not surrender human responsibility: therefore, 'all have sinned' (see also 3:9, 23). The two aspects must be held together. I interpret the much-discussed *eph' hō* phrase as an intensive causal expression: '... for this very reason that'. In other words, Paul is actuallyunderlining the intrinsic link between sinning and death, the counterpoise to the intrinsic link between righteousness and life; on this see my *Romans*, 183.
28 There is no good reason to exclude the instance of *dikaioō* here from its normal Pauline sense; see Cranfield, *Romans*, 1.310–1; Kruse, *Romans*, 264.
29 The image is anomalous is that, contrary to Paul's usage elsewhere, he speaks of slavery in both positive (v. 18) and negative (v. 19b) connection. He explains this usage in v. 19a; see my *Romans*, 206.

to sin, ensures a service of righteousness (v. 18), the 'fruit' of which is moral transformation—'sanctification' (*eis hagiasmon* [v. 19c])[30]—the end (*telos*) of which is the gift of 'eternal life' (v. 22; v. 23). Paul's avoidance on the positive side of the language of 'wages' that features in the contrastive negative statement (v. 23a), along with his careful selection of terms ('fruit' [*karpos*] and, finally [(v. 23b]), 'gracious gift' (*charisma*), preserves the intrinsic link between righteous living and the gaining of eternal life while avoiding any sense of human works earning that final outcome aside from the grace of Christ.

Any such suggestion is further scotched by the marital image Paul introduces in 7:1–4. At this point the Mosaic Law is explicitly in view. As a married woman is free to marry another man should her first husband die, so the baptismal death to the law that believers have undergone 'through the body of Christ',[31] has given them the freedom to contract a new union with him as risen Lord. Within the continuing image, this union with the risen Lord is fruitful in the way marital union is most obviously fruitful: namely, in the production of offspring, the offspring in this case being the good works of believers in the present time leading up to the judgement.

Paul rounds off the short pericope with, once again, a contrast between the negative situation that prevailed under the regime of the law (v. 5) and that which now obtains. The service under 'the oldness of the letter' (*palaiotēti grammatos*) has been replaced by a service in 'the newness of the Spirit' (*kainotēti pneumatos* [v. 6]). The transition from the influence of Christ as risen Lord (v. 4) to that of the Spirit (v. 5) is understandable in the light of 1 Cor 15:45 where Paul describes 'the latter day Adam' as 'life-giving Spirit' (*pneuma zōopoioun*). As I shall argue shortly in connection with Rom 8:9–11, the risen Lord is *life-giving* Spirit in virtue of the fact that union with him enables believers to live out the righteousness required for entry into eternal life following the judgement.

---

30 While the primary sense of 'the holy' is not necessarily ethical goodness but closeness to the deity, in the biblical tradition an ethical tone inevitably enters in: closeness to the God of Israel demands transformation. In Rom 6:19 the sense of moral transformation in *hagiasmos* is assured by the contrastive parallel with *anomia* ('lawlessness'); see Fitzmyer, *Romans*, 451.

31 On the exegetical choices posed by this clause see my *Romans*, 211, 214–15.

The two statements in vv. 5–6—the first negative, dealing with the past; the second positive dealing with the present—anticipate in a programmatic way the extended contrast that now follows between life under the law (7:7–25) and life in the Spirit (8:1–11).[32] As such they already signal that the two passages, especially 7:14–25 and 8:1–11, are to be read in close connection, with the former, in Paul's characteristic way, serving as a negative foil highlighting the hope emanating from life in the Spirit.

The essential contrast in the sequence as a whole revolves around the factor that is determining human behavior in either situation: whether it be sin, exacerbated by the law, or the Spirit. The law is not *in itself* a negative factor. Though, as noted above, Paul's primary concern here is not here to present an 'apology' for the law, he is careful to disentangle it from sin (7:7), dubbing it in fact as 'holy and just and good' (v. 12). The problem is that the law's arrival on the scene had the effect of exciting in human beings 'all kinds of (self-seeking) desire' (v. 8), leading to the death-dealing virulence of sin (vv. 7–13).

In the following passage, 7:14–25, a representative 'I' describes the ethical plight created for it once the law has in this way brought about the dominance of sin, the enslavement to sin in human 'fleshly' (*sarkinos*) existence (v. 14).[33] In three parallel waves (vv. 14–17; vv. 18–20; vv. 21–23) rising to a crescendo (v. 24) the 'I' pleads its rational agreement and will to do good in obedience to the law's commands, while all along the controlling indwelling power of sin is frustrating that will and leading to evil. Noteworthy is the reiterated refrain, 'sin dwelling within me', that rounds off each 'wave' of the 'I's' lament (v. 17; v. 20b; v. 23b).[34] This triple reference to the fatal *oikein* of sin as indwelling power will be matched in 8:9–11 by a triple reference to a life-giving *oikein* of the Spirit (v. 9; v. 11 [twice]), closely linked to or in fact identified with the impact of Christ as risen Lord (v. 10). The contrastive

---

32 See my *Romans*, 213; Kruse, *Romans*, 294; Wolter, *Römer*, 1.417.
33 On the identity of the 'I', the situation described (whether aside from/before conversion to Christ or an aspect of Christian life), and the rhetorical nature of the passage as a whole, see my *Romans*, 225–27. Along with most recent interpreters, for reasons indicated there, I take the passage as referring to the 'pre-Christian' situation.
34 The 'indwelling of sin' formula in v. 23b is somewhat different from the earlier two but the sense is the same.

parallel created by these reiterated references to the indwelling power ensures that the ethical *possibility*—to fulfil the righteous requirement of the law (8:4)—described in 8:9–11 must be read as a response to the ethical *impossibility* depicted so graphically in 7:14–25.

What has brought about the new possibility of righteous living is the divine intervention in Christ (8:3–4): the sending of the Son, which, in the face of the law's impotence to deal with the weakness of the flesh, has dealt with sin—condemned sin in the flesh—and, for those 'in Christ', released the power of the Spirit as the new factor shaping human behavior (v. 2; v. 4).

> 8:1 There is now no condemnation for those in Christ Jesus. 2 For the law of the Spirit of life in Christ Jesus has set you[35] free from the law of sin and death. 3 For what the law could not do, in that it ws weak because of the flesh, God (has done): sending his Son in the likeness of flesh dominated by sin and as a sacrifice for sin, he condemned sin in the flesh, 4 in order that the righteous requirement of the law might be fulfilled in us, who walk now, not according to the flesh but according to the Spirit.

It is not possible here to go into the many details of exegetical interest in this densely theological 'sending' statement. Let me simply note a few matters relevant to the particular aim of this essay. First the opening assertion, 'There is now no condemnation for those in Christ Jesus', clearly responds to the piteous cry of the 'I' in v. 24a, 'Who will deliver me from the body of this death?'. The death foreseen by the 'I' would be eternal death following condemnation at the impending judgement. The inevitability of that prospect has been lifted (*ouden ... nun katakrima*) for those 'in Christ Jesus' (v. 1)—those, that is, who through faith and baptism have been transferred from 'the body of this death' (the Adamic solidarity) to the 'body of Christ' (6:3–11; 7:4; see Gal 3:27; 1 Cor 12:13).

---

35 In v. 2 the better attested second person singular reading (*se*) goes along with understanding this sequence as a *response* to the plight described in 7:14–25.

The goal or outcome (*hina* [v. 4]) of the divine intervention has been 'the fulfilment of the righteous requirement of the law (*to dikaiōma tou nomou*) in us', who 'walk now, not according to the flesh but according to the Spirit'. 'Walk' is 'Bible-speak' for human living in the sight of God. God has created the possibility for believers to live out the righteousness that the law required but could not bring about—as depicted in the previous section.[36] Of crucial importance in this connection is the passive formulation of the fulfilment, *plērōthēi*. This 'divine passive' wards off any sense of human achievement aside from the grace of God. The possibility of living righteously is the product of the influence of the Spirit within us, the 'fruit' of the marital union between believers and the risen Lord as expressed earlier in 7:4b.

Let us also not fail to note how strongly Paul maintains an ethical tone in the sentences following the 'sending' statement 8:5–11 (13):

> 8:5 For those who live according to the flesh set their minds on the things of the flesh, but those who live according to the Spirit set their minds on the things of the Spirit. ⁶ To set the mind on the flesh is death, but to set the mind on the Spirit is life and peace. ⁷ For this reason the mind that is set on the flesh is hostile to God; it does not submit to God's law—indeed it cannot, ⁸ and those who are in the flesh cannot please God.
>
> ⁹ But you are not in the flesh; you are in the Spirit, since the Spirit of God dwells in you. Anyone who does not have the Spirit of Christ does not belong to him. ¹⁰ But if Christ is in you, though the body is dead because of sin, the Spirit is life because of righteousness. ¹¹ If the Spirit of him who raised Jesus from the dead dwells in you, he who raised Christ from the dead will give life to your mortal bodies also through his Spirit that dwells in you.

The law is not dismissed. Its demands, at least in terms of the values that it enshrines, must continue to be lived out in righteousness. Otherwise, one will not be 'pleasing God' (v. 8) but reverting to a situation of

---

[36] On the understanding of *dikaiōma* in the sense of the righteousness required in general by the law (rather than a specific precept) see my *Romans*, 243–44.

pre-reconciliation 'hostility' to God (5:10–11), the outcome of which will be (eternal) death (v. 6a).

Remarkable in vv. 9–11 is the way in which Paul rings the changes in the description of the indwelling (*oikein*) power. In v. 9b it is 'the Spirit of God', in v. 9c 'the Spirit of Christ', in v. 10 simply 'Christ', in v 11a 'the Spirit of the One who raised Jesus from the dead', in v. 11b '(God's) Spirit dwelling within you'. Clearly, Paul saw little difference in *functional* terms between the influence of the risen Christ and the Spirit of God. We have here simply a more elaborated instance of his statement in 1 Cor 15:45 that 'the Last Adam' (= Christ) became a 'life-giving Spirit' (*pneuma zōopoioun* [1 Cor 15:45]).[37]

By the same token, 8:1–11 as a whole makes clear how the risen Lord functions as 'life-giving Spirit'. The effect of the Spirit on those in Christ is not like that of pumping air into a rubber tube. The Spirit is life-giving via the creation in believers of the capacity to live out the righteousness required for gaining eternal life at the last judgement. The principle that Paul shared with the wider biblical and post-biblical Jewish tradition—that righteousness leads to life—is fully operative here and, as we have already noted, is summed up neatly in the lapidary expression: 'the Spirit (means) life because of righteousness' (v. 10c). The new ethical possibility for believers is thus the essential middle term between the gift of the Spirit and the gaining of life.

Having described the new possibility created by the divine action, Paul rounds off the 'ethical' sequence that began at 6:1 with an admonition of striking severity, 8:12–13:

> 12 So then, brothers and sisters, we are debtors, not to the flesh, to live according to the flesh—13 for if you live according to the flesh, you will die; but if by the Spirit you put to death the deeds of the body, you will live.

Following the positive note of the immediately preceding sentences (vv. 9–11), the stress on avoiding the negative rather than embracing the positive is surprising. We might have expected the exclusion of being 'debtors to the flesh' (v. 12b) to be balanced by a counter affirmation

---

37 See my article, 'Living Out the Righteousness of God', 570–81.

of 'indebtedness to the Spirit'. But this latter indebtedness is merely implied in the reference to the Spirit in v. 13b and even then it comes in the negative guise of 'putting to death the deeds of the body'.[38] The strength and severity of this final warning about the need for to live righteously as a basis for obtaining eschatological life: 'You will live' (v. 13c) further underlines the essential link between these two factors presupposed throughout Romans 5–8 as a whole.

Here we tread upon sensitive areas in regard to Protestant and Catholic interpretation of Paul. My sense is that the Catholic requirement for an intrinsic link between a life of continuing righteousness and the obtaining of salvation can be maintained alongside the Protestant concern for preservation of the divine initiative provided that full weight is given to the passive, *plērōthē* in Rom 8:4. The righteousness that believers are called to live out is entirely the product of the Spirit within them, and ultimately goes back—in a Trinitarian sense—to God's redemptive act in Christ (8:3–4). Salvation at the judgement is not simply an added gift. It stems from divine acknowledgment of the righteousness that believers have lived out in the pattern of their lives under the influence of the Spirit.[39]

---

38 One might have expected here 'deeds of the *flesh*' rather than 'of the body' (cf. Gal 5:19). Paul may have used 'body' because, as in the similar warning in Rom 6:12–13, he was thinking of concrete acts of wrongdoing that are necessarily performed in the body, which, being mortal (v. 10b, v. 11), is anchored in the present age and subject to its onslaughts.

39 Yinger, *Paul, Judaism, and Judgement*, 194–95, n. 151, sees a coherence between my thought and his in this area, with two reservations: I 'seem to want to subordinate the forensic (or participationist) categories to the ethical' and I appear not to have given sufficient weight to the aorist passive, *dikaiōthentes*, in 5:1. In regard to the first, I do not do see it as a matter of subordinating the one to the other but of according due weight to both categories in that the one (the ethical) leads essentially to the other (the forensic). In regard to Yinger's second reservation, we should note that Paul speaks of justification in no less than three time references (past [e.g., Rom 5:1]; present [e.g., Rom 3:24]; future [e.g., Rom 5:19; see also Gal 5:5). Within the scope of this chapter, I cannot discuss the issue raised thereby but hope to do some in a forthcoming monograph. I would not, however, now speak of a 'new righteousness' (as in 'Living Out the Righteousness of God', 569, 570, 580), since it is all a matter of preserving and living out the one gift of righteousness stemming from union with Christ. Likewise, John Barclay, alluding, in connection with Rom 8:10c, to 'Protestant anxieties' lest righteousness be taken as a condition of eternal life, maintains that 'if righteousness is itself the product of the miraculous new life, there is no difficulty in seeing it also as the means to the continuation and perfection of that life in the Spirit (cf. 5:21; 6:22–23; Gal 6:8)', citing my interpretation with apparent approval (*Paul and the Gift*, 502, n. 15). I suspect that Paul was less nervous about divine-human synergism than his Protestant interpreters down the ages.

As many have recognised,[40] what Paul portrays here is simply the fulfilment of the divine pledge recorded in Jer 31:33 to place 'the law within them' and the similar pledge with regard to the Spirit in Ezek 36:26. Paul's reference to the liberating 'law of the Spirit' in Rom 8:2, along with similar allusions in Rom 2:28–29 and 2 Cor 3:3, 6, suggests that, taking these two prophetic texts in close connection, he saw them as indicating a divine promise to create the possibility for righteous living in the messianic age, a promise fulfilled in Christ. The perspective, then, is wholly scriptural and in this sense wholly 'within Israel'—so it is true, as Thielman has insisted, albeit on different grounds, that Israel never really fades from view throughout this section of Romans.

4. Hope Despite the Sufferings of the Present Time: 8:14–39

The assurance 'you will live' (*zēsesthe*)—'live', that is, in the eschatological sense of gaining eternal life—reintroduces the theme of hope that is Paul's overriding concern in the entire section, Romans 5–8. As at the beginning, 5:1–11, the theme returns explicitly in confrontation with that of suffering. Suffering must not be interpreted as an indication of divine disfavour. On the contrary, the suffering that believers undergo precisely as believers, is suffering in union with Christ (8:17, 35–39). It is a suffering that is bound up, on a cosmic scale, with the birthpangs of a new creation coming to be, as Paul outlines in a passage pointing to the 'groaning' of the non-human created world (8:19–22). Just as the old era is coming to judgement, a new creation is coming into being—a new creation in which human beings, through their union with Christ, can play successfully the role marked out for them according to the original design of the Creator (Gen 1:26–28; Ps 8:3–4), a divine design now inexorably unfolding, as Paul indicates in the 'step-like' sequence in 8:29–30. Thus the 'inheritance of the earth', originally bequeathed to Adam, lost by him, and then promised to Abraham (4:13–22), comes

---

40 See Deidun, *New Covenant Morality*, 36–38; Hays, *Echoes of Scripture*, 127–31; Hafemann, *Paul, Moses and the History of Israel*, 162–73; Dunn, *Theology of Paul*, 644–45; see further my *Romans*, 239–40.

to full realisation in Christ (8:17).[41] Hence Paul can evoke with such confidence the prospect of the judgement in 8:31–39.[42] The evocation picks up and develops the assurance stated at the beginning of the chapter that 'there is now no condemnation for those in Christ Jesus' (8:1).

At first sight there may appear to be a tension between the insistence upon the need to live righteously as a condition for obtaining eternal life (8:5–13) and the confident assurance of the certainty of 'acquittal' (see *theos ho dikaiōn* [v. 33b]) in 8:31–39, an assurance emanating with equal force from the description of the inexorable unfolding of the divine plan for the elect in 8:29–30 (see *toutous kai edikaiōsen* [v. 30b]).[43] The tension recedes, however, when one grasps that 8:31–39, in line with the theme of hope in the face of suffering that is resumed in 8:17, has primarily to do with how the sufferings of the present time are to be interpreted. Are they an indication of divine displeasure? Or, on the contrary, are they an indication, not of separation from the love of God or of Christ, but of intimate union with Christ (see 8:17d) and with his 'cause' (see *heneka sou* [v. 36b]), and hence a guarantee that, having shared his suffering, believers will also share his glory (see 8:17, 18, 19, 21; 30)?[44]

Thus 8:31–39 is not concerned with righteous living. It simply presumes it, not eroding in any degree the severe warning expressed in 8:12–13 nor undermining the essential connection between righteousness and the gaining of eternal life that underpins the case for hope argued in Romans 5–8 as a whole. The divine, eternal design to justify and glorify the elect on the pattern of the risen humanity of Christ (8:29–30) stands behind but does not eliminate the requirement that they live righteously in the time leading up to the final judgement. Those

---

41 This is a very short summary of the extended commentary I provide on Rom 8:14–30 in my *Romans*, 247–74. See also a more recent article, Byrne, 'A Pauline Complement to *Laudato Si*', esp. 320–25.
42 For the widely held view that Rom 8:31–39 represents an evocation of the last judgement see Barrett, *Romans*, 173; Dunn, *Romans 1–8*, 499, 500, 502–3; Wright 'Romans', 613; Moo, *Romans*, 538, 541–42; or else that it evokes a law court scene in a more general sense: Fitzmyer, *Romans*; Cranfield, *Romans*, 1.438. Against this, see Jewett, *Romans*, 539; Wolter, *Römer*, 1.544.
43 On this see my *Romans*, 267–70.
44 See Gieniusz, *Romans 8:18–30*, 126, 130–33—though, curiously, Gieniusz does not carry his enquiry beyond 8:30 into 8:31–39, despite the continuing focus upon suffering in this latter passage.

who do so can, in the face of the sufferings that they currently endure, be confident that the divine 'acquittal' so boldly asserted in 8:33 will be theirs at that time, realizing the eternal design of God in their regard.

Conclusion

I have argued that Romans 5–8 and specifically its ethical central core, Rom 6:1–8:13, can be regarded as wholly integral to Romans as a whole in the light of the overriding prospect of the last judgment and the conviction, prevalent in biblical and post-biblical Judaism as a whole, that righteousness is essential to the obtaining of a favourable verdict at that final assize. This is what Paul sets out in his opening thematic statement (1:16–17): that the gospel is the power of God leading to salvation for all believers because in it the divine righteousness is made available on the basis of faith. In the face of universal lack of righteousness on the human side, God has intervened in Christ to bring about the required state of righteousness and ensure the possibility of its preservation in Christ for the time leading up to the judgement. Within this perspective Romans 5–8 has an essential place in the overall argument of the letter.

Bibliography

Barclay, John M. G.   *Paul and the Gift* (Grand Rapids, MI, & Cambridge, UK: Eerdmans, 2016).

Barrett, C. K.   *The Epistle to the Romans* (BNTC; London: Black, 1962, repr. 1971).

Beker, J. Christiaan   *Paul the Apostle: the Triumph of God in Life and Thought* (Philadelphia: Fortress, 1980).

Byrne, Brendan   *Romans* (SP 6; Collegeville, MN; Glazier, 1996).

Byrne, Brendan   'Living Out the Righteousness of God: The Contribution of Rom 6:1–8:13 to an Understanding of Paul's Ethical Presuppositions', *Catholic Biblical Quarterly* 43.4 (1981), 557–81.

Byrne, Brendan	'The Problem of *Nomos* and the Relationship with Judaism in Romans', *Catholic Biblical Quarterly* 62.3 (2000), 294–309.
Byrne, Brendan	'A Pauline Complement to *Laudato Si*', *Theological Studies* 77.2 (2016), 308–27.
Cranfield, C. E. B.	*A Critical and Exegetical Commentary on the Epistle to the Romans* (ICC; 2 vols.; Edinburgh: Clark, 1975, 1979).
Cousar, Charles	'Continuity and Discontinuity: Reflections on Romans 5–8 (In Conversation with Frank Thielman)', in D. M. Hay & E. E. Johnson (eds.), *Pauline Theology. Volume 3: Romans* (Minneapolis, MN: Fortress, 1995), 196–210.
Dahl, Neils A	'Two Notes on Romans 5', *Studia Theologica* 5 (1951), 37–48.
Deidun, T. J.	*New Covenant Morality in Paul* (AnBib 89; Rome: Biblical Institute Press, 1981).
Dunn, J. D. G.	*The Theology of Paul the Apostle* (Grand Rapids, MI: Eerdmans, 1998).
Dunn, J. D. G.	*Romans 1–8* (WBC 38; Dallas, TX: Word Books, 1988).
Dunn, J. D. G.	'In Search of Common Ground', in J. D. G. Dunn (ed.), *Paul and the Mosaic Law* (Grand Rapids, MI, & Cambridge, UK: Eerdmans, 2001), 309–34.
Fitzmyer, J. A.	*Romans* (AB 33: New York: Doubleday, 1993).
Geniusz, Andrzej	*Romans 8:18–30: 'Suffering Does Not Thwart the Future Glory'* (Atlanta, GA: Scholars Press, 1999).
Hafemann, S. J.	*Paul, Moses and the History of Israel: The Letter/Spirit Contrast and the Argument from Scripture in 2 Corinthians 3* (WUNT 81; Tübingen: Mohr Siebeck, 1995).
Hays, R. B.	*Echoes of Scripture in the Letters of Paul* (New Haven, CT: Yale University Press, 1989).
Jewett, Robert	*Romans* (Hermeneia; Minneapolis: Fortress, 2007).
Keesmaat, Sylvia C.	*Paul and His Story: (Re)Interpreting the Exodus Tradition* (Sheffield: Sheffield Academic Press, 1999).
Kruse, Colin J.	*Paul's Letter to the Romans* (Grand Rapids, MI, & Cambridge, UK: Eerdmans, 2012).

Lichtenberger, H.   'Das Tora-Verständnis im Judentum zur Zeit Paulus', in J. D. G. Dunn (ed.), *Paul and the Mosaic Law* (Grand Rapids, MI; Cambridge, UK: Eerdmans, 2001), 7–23.

Moo, Douglas   *The Epistle to the Romans* (NICNT; Grand Rapids, MI: Eerdmans, 1996).

Scroggs, Robin   'Paul as Rhetorician: Two Homilies in Romans 1–11', in R. G. Hamerton-Kelly & R. Scroggs (eds.), *Jews, Greeks and Christians: Religious Cultures in Late Antiquity: Essays in Honor of William David Davies* (SJLA 21; Leiden: Brill, 1976), 271–98.

Stettler, Christian   *Das Endgericht bei Paulus: Framesemantische und exegetische Studien zur paulinischen Eschatologie und Soteriologie* (WUNT 371; Tübingen: Mohr Sieback, 2017).

Thielman, Frank   'The Story of Israel and the Theology of Romans 5–8', in D. M. Hay & E. E. Johnson (eds.), *Pauline Theology. Volume 3: Romans* (Minneapolis, MN: Fortress, 1995), 169–95.

VanLandingham, Chris   *Judgment and Justification in Early Judaism and the Apostle Paul* (Peabody, MA: Hendrickson, 2006).

Wilckens, Ulrich   *Der Brief an die Römer* (EKK 6; 3 vols. Neukirchen-Vluyn: Neukirchener Verlag, 1978–92).

Wolter, Michael   *Der Brief an die Römer: Teilband 1: Röm 1–8* (EKK VI/1; Neukirchen-Vluyn: Patmos, 2014).

Wright, N. T.   'The Letter to the Romans', in L. E. Keck (ed.), *New Interpreters Bible Volume X* (Nashville: Abingdon, 2002), 423–770.

Yinger, Keith L.   *Paul, Judaism, and Judgment according to Deeds* (SNTSMS 105; Cambridge: Cambridge University Press, 1999).

CHAPTER 4

Paul's Letter against the Roman Gods[1]

Mark Reasoner

'So it is my purpose to preach the gospel to you also who are at Rome', Paul says in a significant but underrated sentence of his letter opening (1:15). When this purpose is considered in light of the political and religious landscape in Rome, Paul's emphases on faith, hope, peace, and salvation found in the letter to the Romans in this letter begin to appear in a new light.

The political life of the Roman Republic included the tendency to deify basic virtues. Cult would then spring up around these virtues. This essay begins to consider how the Roman audiences to whom Paul was writing would have heard his letter in light of its reference to the virtues of *fides* (faith), *iustitia* (righteousness or justice), *pax* (peace), *salus publica* (safety or welfare of the people), and *concordia* (social harmony). Paul's purpose to preach the gospel—a word used in political discourse for news such as an emperor's birth or a Roman conquest—in Rome, would in itself imply significant redefinition and realignment of Roman values, in light of the God of Israel's revelation in Christ. And because Paul was

---

1   This paper was first read at the Sydney College of Divinity, on September 30, 2016. To Jim Harrison, who invited me to speak at the Sydney College of Divinity and with his wife Elisabeth hosted me while in Australia, and to all those who offered suggestions after this paper, including Professor E. A. Judge, I remain indebted and thankful. A version of the paper was later offered at the Catholic Biblical Association's annual meeting at the Catholic University of America in Washington, DC on August 6, 2017. To those who commented on it there, my sincere thanks.

writing to the Romans, his gospel as described in this letter is inevitably shaped by Roman expectations of the divinely sustained world.

Victoria

The gospel of the Roman state begins with *victoria* or victory, on which all the other benefits, worshiped as deified virtues depend. By contrast, Paul portrays victory as a communal benefit, a pattern of life for believers who have enjoyed the benefits flowing from God's grace or the love of Christ, which will help them survive threats of displacement and exile.[2]

> Who will separate us from the love of Christ? Tribulation or distress or persecution or famine or nakedness or danger or sword? Just as it is written, 'For your sake we are being put to death all day long. We are considered as sheep for slaughter', No, but in all these circumstances we overwhelmingly conquer through the one who loved us. For I am convinced that neither death nor life nor angels nor rulers nor things present nor things to come nor powers nor height nor depth nor any other created thing will be able to separate us from the love of God that is in Christ Jesus our Lord.[3]

Here at the end of Romans 8, a chapter in which Paul directly contradicts the propaganda of the Roman Empire, Paul writes that 'we overwhelmingly conquer' or more literally, we *hyper-conquer* (ὑπερνικῶμεν). Propagandists under both Augustus and under Nero, the reigning emperor when Paul wrote Romans, had spun these emperors' reigns as returns to a golden age.[4] Paul by contrast says in Romans 8 that creation is subjected to futility and actually enslaved. Despite the ubiquitous 'son of god' caption for emperors' portraits on the Roman coins that Paul and his audience used, Paul insists that believers in Christ were predestined to be conformed to the image of God's Son, who will be the

---

2 On Paul's strategic use of Psalm 44 within Rom 8, see Stewart, 'The Cry of Victory'.
3 Rom 8:35–39; all translations from the New Testament in this essay are mine.
4 Propagandists under Augustus included Virgil and Horace; those under Nero included Calpurnius Siculus.

firstborn among many brothers (8:29).

But why the language of conquering here? Why not the language of survival or deliverance? Perhaps because in the set of Roman virtues to whom the Roman state paid cult, *victoria* was the beginning virtue. As you can see from the quotation from J. Rufus Fears below, once *victoria* was in place other significant virtues, which the Roman state had also deified, were guaranteed. When *victoria* was achieved, then *pax* (peace), *salus publica* (safety and welfare of the people), *concordia* (social harmony) and *fides* (faith or loyalty) would also be in existence. The deified virtue of *victoria* was the key virtue in the Roman state. It was linked to Jupiter Optimus Maximus, but worshipped in its own right as divine.

> Like its imperial predecessors in the Near East and Egypt, the empire of Rome was a universal one, with pretensions to ruling the *oikoumene*; and, as in the Near East and Egypt, the political mythology of oecumenical empire came to be enshrined in and expressed through the figure of the monarch, based upon an image of the emperor as the visible embodiment of cosmic order, in his person and by his deeds ensuring the continuity of civilized existence. By his triumphant actions the emperor ensured for the world those blessed conditions explicit in such abstractions as Pax, Concordia, Libertas, Abundantia, Spes, Securitas, Iustitia, Clementia, Felicitas, and Aequitas. Together these imperial virtues, which play such a major role in imperial propaganda, proclaim the gospel of the imperial golden age. As a composite they evoke an image of the social order which perhaps most closely corresponds to the Egyptian conception of *Ma'at*. Quite literally the emperor is a savior who has brought mankind to an earthly paradise ...
>
> In this system of imperial virtues Victoria Augusta is the linchpin. This was as true under Constantine as under Augustus ... whatever virtues are commemorated, Victory is almost inevitably present; Victoria Augusta continued its Augustan role as the guarantor of all other imperial benefits. This is nowhere seen more clearly than in the intimate association of Pax and Victoria. Hence on the triumphal arches of Nero the triumphant emperor

is escorted by the figures of Pax and Victoria. Pax, encompassing the central themes of Securitas, Salus, Concordia, and Libertas, can only exist under the assurance of imperial victory.[5]

Here is a possible schematic of how the deified virtues are related. The lower the virtue is in this chart, the more theologically all-encompassing and foundational it is. The higher virtues on the chart derive from the virtues below them. The weakness of this chart is that the cult of virtues was not a systematized cult in the Principate. Specific virtues were deified and cult paid to them when there was perceived need for those virtues. So my attempt at configuring the virtues cannot encompass all that the Romans intended when paying cult to them. But this attempt is worthwhile, in that it has the potential to help us understand how the letter of Romans was heard by some of its first audiences, the house churches in mid-first century Rome.

The Roman Principate's Deified Virtues

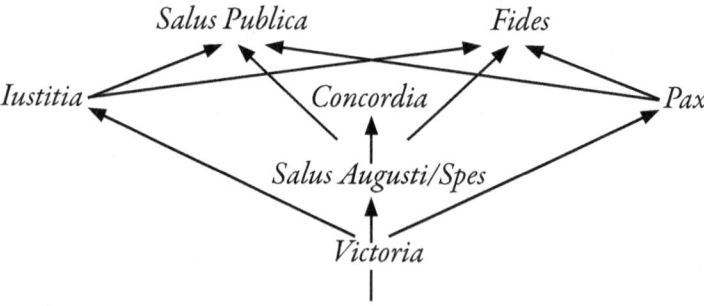

In the Republic, *victoria* was associated with the Roman people, their god Jupiter, and the personification of the Roman people in the goddess Roma. But in the Principate, *victoria* became linked instead to the emperor.[6] Fears thinks it is significant that in the *Res Gestae*, Augustus begins by narrating his early military victories. These legitimate what was otherwise an illegitimate wresting of authority from the Roman senate.

---

5   Fears, 'The Theology of Victory at Rome', 812–13.
6   Fears, 'The Cult of Jupiter and Roman Imperial Ideology', 61.

Like the Athenians in the Melian Dialogue, the rightness, the *iustitia*, of Augustus' rule was established by his military victories, his actualization of the deified virtue of *victoria* for his people.

In contrast, Paul says in Romans that God's *iustitia*, God's justice, is revealed from faith to faith. Romans readers for two millennia have been wondering if that means from God's faithfulness to human faith, from the faith as seen in the Old Testament to the faith as seen in the New Testament, or from Christ's faithfulness to human faith. It is best to understand 'from faith to faith' as meaning that God's justice arises out of the faithfulness of God the Father and his Son Jesus, and evokes a response of faithfulness in humanity.[7]

Here is a schematic of how in Romans Paul reconfigures the Roman state's deified virtues. Of course Paul redefines some of these virtues, in light of his Scriptures and his encounter with the risen Christ.

Paul's Architecture of Virtues

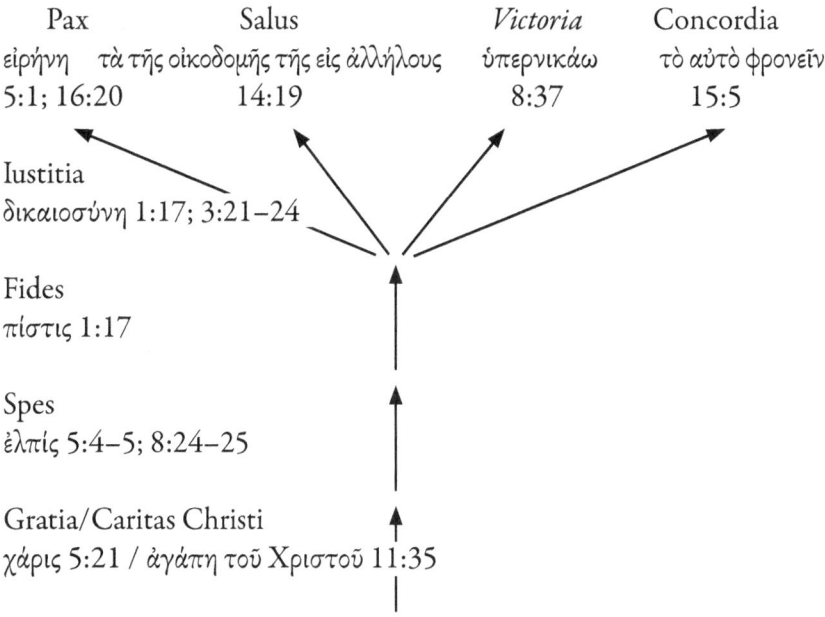

---

7   See the discussion in Gignac, *L'épître aux Romains*, 97–99.

Iustitia

The Greeks had deified δίκη, and in addition to the Roman-deified virtue of *iustitia*, the Romans had also designated a specific function of Mars the god of war that was responsible for working vengeance on people—Mars Ultor, a title ascribed to Mars during the reign of Augustus.[8] Paul counsels against taking personal vengeance and goes on to state that government is allowed to exercise God's rightful function of vengeance (12:19; 13:4), an idea that one accustomed to the Roman gods would understand. The fact that both Greeks and Romans had identified a specific god who would bring about the power or virtue of justice/righteousness constitutes one argument for the inclusion of the subjective genitive reading of δικαιοσύνη θεοῦ. If Paul is at all aware of how the Greeks and Romans theologically grounded their ideas of justice, it is probable that he was willing to allow his letter's hearers to hear in δικαιοσύνη θεοῦ the power to effect justice that remains with God, a power that results in justice for God's people on the earth. Thus δικαιοσύνη θεοῦ cannot be limited to a condition that God grants to believers. It always remains *God's* power.

Paul says that God's righteousness is revealed, and he also describes how this righteousness that is revealed from faith is *in* or *of* Jesus Christ for all who believe. In the Romans state, *iustitia*, or justice/righteousness, was specifically located in the emperor or the state, including some of its military leaders. The first Roman coin with *iustitia* as its theme was minted around 22 CE, a *dupondius* with a portrait of Livia, the wife of Augustus on it. One possibility is that this coin was minted to celebrate the tenth anniversary of the start of the cult of *iustitia*, which occurred when Tiberius returned from Rome in 12 CE after a victorious campaign.[9]

Elliott helpfully shows how Paul's idea of righteousness/justice is not simply the Romans' deified *iustitia* with Christ replacing what Roman propaganda credited to a Roman emperor. After commenting on parallels others have drawn between Roman pictures of decline followed by the propaganda announcing a return to a golden age, Elliott references the last part of Romans 1 as follows: 'What none of these supposed

---

8   Rose & Scheid, 'Mars', 929.
9   Lichocka, *Justitia sur monnaies imperials romaines*, 107, 109; Lott, 'An Augustan Sculpture of August Justice', 266.

parallels provide, however, is the notion that is the very engine of Paul's argument here: that outrageous and destructive sexual indulgence and, ultimately, the utter depravity described in 1:28–32 are evident to all as God's punishment on idolaters'.[10]

But the justice or righteousness spoken of in Romans is what the believer possesses. It is not limited to God or to the emperor or the state. Paul's writes in 14:17 that 'the kingdom of God does not consist in food and drink, but in righteousness and peace and joy in the Holy Spirit'. This fits with the pattern we have observed so far, that Paul is somewhat topsy-turvey in his use of terms from the Roman cult of virtues. I mean that he takes terms that the Romans place at or near the very foundation of their architecture of virtues, such as *victoria* or *iustitia*, and locates them as operative and energizing principles in the end-result, day-to-day life of the believer.

Pax

In the Roman cult of virtues, *victoria* by Rome also led to *pax* or peace. This peace was achieved at a heavy cost. Tacitus famously quoted the British chief Calgacus who complains:

> Robbers of the world, having by their universal plunder exhausted the land, they rifle the deep. If the enemy be rich, they are rapacious; if he be poor, they lust for dominion; neither the east nor the west has been able to satisfy them. Alone among men they covet with equal eagerness poverty and riches. To robbery, slaughter, plunder, they give the lying name of empire; they make a wasteland and call it peace.[11]

The Roman people were interested in maintaining a situation in which they were at peace with the gods, the so called *pax deorum*. The Roman state also cultivated the peace it achieved by conquering others and

---

10   Elliott, *The Arrogance of Nations*, 78.
11   Tacitus, *Agricola* 30. Translation from http://www.thelatinlibrary.com/imperialism/readings/agricola.html, accessed on September 28, 2016. I changed the word 'solitude' to 'wasteland' in the closing phrase here: *ubi solitudinem faciunt, pacem appellant*.

claiming that they established peace in a given region.

For Paul, the peace with God seems to be a result of God's justice, as we see in Romans 5:1—'being justified on the basis of faith, we have peace with God through our Lord Jesus Christ'. An outward peace, that is, whole and healthy relationships with others, is also in view in the two peace benedictions in Romans, at 15:33 and 16:20.

First Objection: a category mistake?

Perhaps you are thinking that this essay is wrongly conceived. Paul's gospel sought to bring the Gentiles out of their paganism, to worship the one true God. Why then are we studying this paganism? Paul's gospel seems so different from the amorphous amalgam of deities in the Roman religious cult.

But the cult of virtues considered here was firmly embedded in the way first century Romans understood their lives in this world. To understand how Paul, who lived in the Roman world of the early Principate and wrote to people living in Rome, we must consider the resonance of these key terms in Romans for its first hearers. Fears writes:

> Thus, the worship of Virtues was neither political charade nor literary allegory. Nor was it an alien form grafted onto the structure of traditional Roman religion. The cult of Virtues represents a characteristic statement of Roman paganism and its peculiar conception of the divine. For the Roman, benefits conferred—*utilitates*—provided the clearest proof of the existence of gods; man's knowledge of divine power could be drawn from no better source than the certain evidence of benefits received from the gods. The corollary of this was a functional conception of divinity; individual divine entities were recognized from the fact of their performance of a specific and characteristic function.[12]

---

12 Fears, 'The Cult of Virtues and Roman Imperial Ideology', 837. Fears' comment on 'their performance of a specific and characteristic function' fits with E. A. Judge's remark to me, after this paper was read at the Sydney College of Divinity on September 30, 2016 that the virtues were worshiped as need arose, and not as much on a consistent, daily basis.

The need for proper worship of God in order to survive God's anger (1:18) is a very Roman idea. Livy 22.57 describes a time in the Hannibalic War when the Roman people knew that they were under the gods' wrath. They vowed a temple to the virtue *mens*—intelligence—knowing that worshiping the god who provided this virtue would be the most probable way for their leaders to gain the intelligence needed to turn the current of the war. In an analogous way, Paul argues that the world is under God's wrath because people do not recognize the creator God as the creator of the world, nor worship him as creator God. The improper worship places them under God's wrath and leads them to be handed over to an unfit mind. The answer is to give themselves to God as living sacrifices, i.e., no longer worshiping creatures but worshiping the creator God directly. This will allow their minds to be renewed (1:18–28; 12:1–2). The practical results of the worship of the gods—*utilitates*—or virtues, shows itself in Romans in Paul's language that God is immanent in the world and thus knowable to humans (1:19–21), and more significantly, that God demonstrates and extends his grace and love through Christ for us (5:8; 8:31–39).

Fides

The *fides* or loyalty that the Roman Republic showed to those peoples or city-states with whom it made treaties was a highly touted quality. So *fides* was definitely used in political discourse to connote how Rome cultivated asymmetric relations of loyalty with conquered or pacified peoples. The following narrative in 1 Maccabees, which describes Judas Maccabeus' high regard for the Romans and his desire to enter into a treaty with them, illustrates the potential appeal of the Romans' *fides* in foreign policy for vulnerable people:

> Now Judas heard of the fame of the Romans, that they were very strong and were well-disposed toward all who made an alliance with them, that they pledged friendship to those who came to them, [2] and that they were very strong ...
> [17] So Judas chose Eupolemus son of John son of Accos, and Jason son of Eleazar, and sent them to Rome to establish

friendship and alliance,[18] and to free themselves from the yoke; for they saw that the kingdom of the Greeks was completely enslaving Israel. [19] They went to Rome, a very long journey; and they entered the senate chamber and spoke as follows: [20] 'Judas, who is also called Maccabeus, and his brothers and the people of the Jews have sent us to you to establish alliance and peace with you, so that we may be enrolled as your allies and friends'. [21] The proposal pleased them, [22] and this is a copy of the letter that they wrote in reply, on bronze tablets, and sent to Jerusalem to remain with them there as a memorial of peace and alliance:

[23] 'May all go well with the Romans and with the nation of the Jews at sea and on land forever, and may sword and enemy be far from them.[24] If war comes first to Rome or to any of their allies in all their dominion, [25] the nation of the Jews shall act as their allies wholeheartedly, as the occasion may indicate to them. [26] To the enemy that makes war they shall not give or supply grain, arms, money, or ships, just as Rome has decided; and they shall keep their obligations without receiving any return. [27] In the same way, if war comes first to the nation of the Jews, the Romans shall willingly act as their allies, as the occasion may indicate to them.'[13]

In hindsight, there is some irony in this description, for eventually, the Romans would turn out to be in the same category as the Seleucids and those Jews loyal to them who are portrayed so negatively in the first chapter of 1 Maccabees. This can be seen in Pompey's capture of Jerusalem and entrance into the temple, Pontius Pilate's insensitive attitude to Jewish concerns, and finally the Empire's aggression in the First and Second Jewish Revolts.

Fides later came to be used in personal relationships as well, including the patron to client relationship. Not only the 'from faith to faith' phrase in 1:17, but also the 'through the faith of Jesus Christ' phrase of 3:2 and the 'on the basis of the faith of Jesus' phrase in 3:26 all include

---

13 1 Macc 8:1–2a, 17–27, RSV.

the possibility of a mutual loyalty that is a personal, patron-client relationship between God or God's Messiah Jesus and a human.

Morgan summarizes the use of '*pistis/fides*' terms in family settings in the early Principate as 'a mixture of mutual trust and loyalty and the recognition and pursuit of shared interests'.[14] She cites examples of the *pistis/fides* bond between mother and son and between husbands and wives.[15] In her chapter, '*Pistis* and *Fides* in Graeco-Roman Religiosity', Morgan notes that the deified virtue of *pistis/fides* 'is constantly portrayed as benevolent. She has a symbiotic relationship with *ops* (plenty, wealth, or power), and *concordia*'.[16] Roman coins with the deified virtue of *fides* on them show that the Roman government looked to *fides* as a guarantor of the prosperity of every dimension of its world, from farming to governmental affairs, in wartime and in peacetime. Valerius Maximus portrays *fides* as offering well-being to all of humanity.[17] Morgan does not dwell long on the deified virtue of *fides* with its distinct cult in Rome, but she is very sensitive to the dynamic of *pistis/fides* in Hellenistic and Roman cult: 'One might not inappropriately identify an economy of *pistis/fides* in Greek and Roman religious thinking of this period, circulating through the divine and human spheres, from the gods to human beings and back again'.[18] When she turns to examine πίστις in Romans, Morgan notes how Paul uses πίστις in apposition to obedience. On the ὑπακοὴ πίστεως of Rom 1:5, Morgan contends that Paul holds that 'the *pistis* into which he brings gentiles is, like his own, a relationship of slavish obedience to Christ'.[19]

A consideration of the Roman cult of *fides* can lead us to some significant insight for the exegesis of Romans. Because *fides* is worshipped as the god who instantiates loyalty within Roman society and between conquered peoples and the Romans, it is probable that the Romans

---

14 Morgan, *Roman Faith and Christian Faith*, 45.
15 Morgan, *Roman Faith and Christian Faith*, 46–49, citing Dionysius of Halicarnassus 8.33.1–4; 8.39.1 – 54.1 for the filial bond, and Val. Max. 6.7; Ovid, *Fasti* 2.815; Ach. Tat. 6.16.3; *CIL* 6.11195 for the marital bond.
16 Morgan, *Roman Faith and Christian Faith*, 129, citing Cic. *Rab. Post.* 4, *Att.* 11.1.2; Horace, *Carm.* 1.35.21 and Freyburger, *Fides*, 299–306.
17 Morgan, *Roman Faith and Christian Faith*, 130, citing Val. Max. 6.6.
18 Morgan, *Roman Faith and Christian Faith*, 142.
19 Morgan, *Roman Faith and Christian Faith*, 282–83.

would have heard the 'faith of Jesus Christ' in 3:22 and the 'faith of Jesus' in 3:26 as including the idea of Jesus' faithfulness. Even if you are never going to consider *fides* in its context of Roman political discourse, I hope you at least take from this essay a sense of how often Paul uses 'faith' in this letter and reflect on its uses. Its uses in Romans do not all have clear precedents in the Old Testament. Especially significant are the measure of faith (12:3) and the analogy or proportion of faith in 12:6, as well as the description of believers with very sensitive consciences as those who are 'weak in faith' (14:1) as opposed to the 'strong' (15:1). Also fruitful for our study of Romans is the way that *fides* might figure in our understanding of 14:23b—'whatever is not of faith is sin'. It is easy, based on only the preceding verse, to think that this only relates to living according to one's personal conscience. But if one keeps looking at the flow of the whole paragraph, we see that how one relates to people is significant in 14:19–21. So 'whatever is not of faith is sin' does not mean 'I can only do what I think is permissible', but rather, 'I can only do what contributes positively to others' faith' or 'I can only live in loyal solidarity with fellow-believers'.

Salus

In the discourse of the Principate, once *pax* had been achieved, the *salus publica* or welfare of the people could be actualized. The Romans had deified the virtue *salus*, which first signified a people's welfare and safety, in the context of their war against the Samnites. In 311 B.C.E., a vow was made that Rome would build a temple to *salus*, if *salus* aided them in their war. This temple was then built and dedicated in 302 B.C.E. It is thought that the Roman virtue of *salus* is related to the virtue deified by the Greeks, *soteria*, though in the second century B.C.E., *salus* also became associated with the Greek virtue *hygeia*, or health.[20] Hygeia ranked first among Asklepios' children, and her cult was absorbed by the Romans into the cult of *salus* by 180 B.C.E.[21] By the late Republic, *salus* would also be invoked for a dictator and then of

---

20 Linderski, '*Salus*', 1350.
21 Stafford, '"Without You No One Is Happy"', 127, 134, citing Livy 40.37.1–3.

course for the emperor. The emperor's health in the Principate came to mean health for the whole world.

Fears mentions *salus* in his discussion of an *aureus* minted in 41 C.E. by Claudius. Under the inscription *PACI AUGUSTAE* ('to the peace of Augustus'), a goddess representing *pax*, with the angelic wings of *victoria* on her back, holds a caduceus representing *concordia* and *felicitas*. The caduceus is pointed at the head of the snake at her feet. Fears identifies the snake as a symbol of *salus*.[22] If this is the case, then Paul's benediction in Rom 16:20 might be a response to the iconography of this coin and in other propaganda related to Claudius' full possession of the deified virutes. We may then gloss Paul's benediction as follows: May the true God of peace, not the Augustan *pax* worshipped in Rome, crush under your feet the enemy (*satan*) who opposes the true God, since the Roman vision of welfare (*salus*) is too enmeshed in the worship of no-gods to portray true health and goodness.

The Romans made adaptations in the cult related to *soteria*. In the public event known as the *augurium salutis*, augurs asked the gods if the civil leaders might pray for the well-being of the Roman people. This ritual was reinstated during the reign of Augustus.[23] There are no clues that Paul was thinking of the *augurium salutis* when he wrote that he prayed for his people's salvation (Rom 10:1). It is more likely that Paul is reacting to the texts in which God tells Jeremiah not to pray for the people's salvation, than it is that Paul is offering his response to the *augurium salutis*.[24]

It is noteworthy that Rome deified *salus* in the context of war. By contrast, Paul in Romans uses the idea of salvation in the sense of a moral rescue that restores a person into a fitting and whole relationship with the Creator (Rom 1:16–21; 5:5–9; 8:18–25). In this letter, unlike his other letters, Paul tells us some specific things about *soteria*, a Greek synonym of *salus*. We learn that we will be saved, in Romans 5:9, as if it is a future event and not always an immediate possession. We also learn

---

22 Fears, 'Cult of Virtues', 893–94 on the coin which no. 28 of plate VI in his article, BMC I, 165; discussed also in Reasoner, 'Paul's God of Peace', 24.
23 Linderski, '*augurium salutis*', 214, citing *ILS* 9337; Cicero, *Div*. 1.105; Cass. Dio 37.24–25, 51; 20.5
24 Jer 7:16; 11:14; 14:11–12; Reasoner, 'The Redemptive Inversions of Jeremiah in Romans 9–11', 391–92.

that we are saved in hope (8:24), an expression we will have occasion to return to examine in Chapter 5 in this volume. I wonder if something like the *salus publica*, the general well-being, might have come into some hearers of this letter when they heard Paul say in Romans 12:17 to 'have regard for what is good in the sight of all people'. But this language of salvation prompts a second objection to the direction of this essay. If we live in the hope of the salvation that Christ brings (5:5–9), and grow spiritually by reading Scripture, why cannot we simply read Scripture on our own, without considering the Roman cult of virtues?

Second Objection: If Scripture is meant to be read by all believers, why speak about the Roman cult of virtues when reading Romans?

This objection begins from a premise with which I agree. It is not necessary to study Roman politics and the gods that supported the Roman state to understand Scripture. Neither scholars nor pastors should ever use knowledge of biblical languages or of the world behind the text to make themselves into an elite priesthood of trained Scripture scholars who read and interpret Scripture in such a way that those untrained in Scripture studies are no longer motivated to read Scripture on their own. All who can take and read Scripture or who can hear it with understanding should definitely continue to encounter and engage with Scripture themselves.

But next, let us remember that all human discourse, including the language of our Scriptures, comes embedded in human culture. In most cases, an acquaintance with distinctive ideas in a culture's worldview or unique behaviors in a given culture helps one understand the language and lives of those in that culture. Because all human discourse is embedded in culture, there are semantic depths to human discourse that are not reached at a first reading by someone outside the writer's culture.

Also, let us acknowledge the weakness of our flesh, as Paul might say. We can easily get bored, distracted, or forget elements in the human discourse in which we participate each day. A fellow graduate student of mine, who had earlier studied music at the Julliard School, told me that one of his teachers there used to say, 'Try to listen to this piece of music as though you are hearing it for the first time'. There are of course different strategies for trying to listen to a family member or friend, or read a familiar text, as though we are encountering this person or text for the first time. One way to do so for Romans is to listen as though we are in Rome, in one of the house churches, there, perhaps in the house church of Prisca and Aquila, hearing this letter read to us by the *grammaticus* of Phoebe, the educated slave she has brought along to keep record of her expenditures and to read aloud the letter Paul asked her to bring to the various house churches of Rome. We hear about faith, peace, social harmony and we hear that we overwhelmingly conquer through the one who loved us. Some of these words would resonate with their use on coins and in announcements engraved on the monuments or sign areas of the early Empire. Paul had ministered in the Roman colony of Philippi, the Roman provincial center of Thessalonica, and was writing this letter from the Roman colony of Corinth. Of course Paul does not mean exactly the same thing when he uses *pistis* (faith) as the Romans meant when they used the terms *pistis* in the Greek-speaking areas, or *fides* at home. But looking at these qualities in light of how they functioned in Roman state discourse helps us look more closely at how the first audience of Romans heard the terms for these qualities and related them to each other.

Hard evidence for reading Romans in light of the deified virtues comes from the specific appellations for God that are only found in Romans, such as 'God of patience and encouragement' (15:5), 'God of hope' (15:13), and 'God of peace', which while found elsewhere, does appear twice in Romans (15:33; 16:20; 1 Thess 5:23; Heb 13:20; 2 Thess 3:16—'Lord of peace'). We don't know why these terms for God appear in this letter, but a strong possibility is that they represent Paul's response to a society that he knew offered cult by building temples, offering sacrifices and minting coins, all in worship of deified virtues. We turn now to the virtue of *concordia,* another virtue in Roman cult that may be significant for a deeper understanding of the practical sections of Paul's letter to the Roman house churches.

Concordia

In our survey of the Roman cult of virtues so far, we have leap-frogged over *concordia*, a deified virtue especially invoked when the harmony of the Roman people was in jeopardy. Thus, in the year he was consul, Cicero offered cult to *concordia* when trying to persuade certain of the *equites* to be less ambitious and offensive to the Senate. *Concordia* thus in 63 B.C.E. was not conceived by Cicero as social harmony for all those living in Rome; it was instead limited to the orders of senators and knights.[25]

On the first day of his tenure as consul in 7 B.C.E., Tiberius Claudius Nero, later known as the emperor Tiberius, began to restore the temple of *concordia*. It was completed about seventeen years later and dedicated on January 16, 10 C.E., the *Aedes Concordiae Augustae*.[26] The restoration and consecration of the temple at this time 'seems to symbolize a new meaning for *concordia*, the Roman Empire's unity'.[27] Only about twenty years after the temple of *concordia*'s dedication, the Senate intentionally met within it on the day they sentenced someone perceived as an archenemy of the state, Sejanus.[28]

Various directions in the 'Let love be without pretense' paragraph of Romans 12 seem to include specific behaviors that would be labeled as learning outcomes for *concordia*, such as 'think the same among one another', 'do not think proudly but associate with the lowly', or 'do not repay evil for evil' (12:16–17a). Paul includes a *concordia* idea in his benediction at 15:5–6 with its idea of glorifying the God and Father of our Lord Jesus Christ in unison, after being granted by the God of patience and encouragement to think the same, according to Christ Jesus.

It is easy for me, as for other New Testament students who are not classically trained, to be enthused about possible parallels between language or ideas in the New Testament and very similar language or ideas in the Jewish, Hellenistic and Roman worlds behind the text, to enter

---

25   Levick, 'Concordia at Rome', 222, noting that the basic image on coin reverses that celebrate *concordia* is a handshake, or two clasped hands.
26   Ehrenberg & Jones, *Documents Illustrating the Reigns of Augustus and Tiberius*, 45.
27   Levick, 'Concordia at Rome', 224.
28   Levick, 'Concordia at Rome', 225.

into a sort of fever of parallelomania.²⁹ But we need to find the differences, to find what is distinctive in the discourse of our Scripture. In Romans 8, it seems that all the benefits God offers to his people begin with grace. Romans 8:32 asks, 'He who did not spare his own son, but gave him up for us all, how will he not also with him grace us (χαρίσεται) with all things?' Similarly the 'love of God which is in Christ Jesus our Lord' at the end of 8:39 seems to be synonymous with this grace. Grace and love were not deified virtues in Rome. Yes, the Romans world used the language of grace, as James Harrison's book on grace shows so well.³⁰ The place of grace in the architecture of virtues is different in Paul's letter to the Romans than it is in the Roman world. Also, does any Roman emperor give a son to die on behalf of others? The connotation of grace is qualitatively different between Roman discourse and the discourse in Paul's letters. But there is an overlap, and the overlap and verbal assonance help us to focus and hear more closely what Paul is saying. Paul has already shown in Romans 6 that grace does not mean we continue living in sin; it actually means that grace defeats sin, so that we can as those under grace present our bodies as instruments of righteousness for God. *Sola gratia*—only by God's grace—is the central and abiding theme of the Reformation that all Christians must always carefully preserve.³¹ Grace or the love of Christ was not a deified virtue in Roman state theology, but it is the foundational idea, as you can see in the diagram called 'Paul's Architecture of Virtues' (p.75 above). Besides the end of Romans 8, consider also 5:8 in context, 'But God displays his own love for us, that while we were still sinners, Christ died for us', Love between people is especially emphasized in Romans chapters 12–15, but this builds on the love of God for humanity in chapters 5 and 8. Though Roman theology as represented in Virgil's *Aeneid* values Venus the goddess of love, there is no deified virtue for love in the Principate. Here as well, our look at Romans in the context of Roman political discourse calls our attention back to Scripture and helps us call others to focus on grace and love as the beginning point for what this letter is telling us about God.

29 Sandmel, 'Parallelomania', 1–13.
30 Harrison, *Paul's Language of Grace*.
31 See Bouyer, *The Spirit and Forms of Protestantism*, 61–78.

Conclusion

Let us review and compare the Roman cult of virtues with the architecture of virtues that Paul constructs in Romans. We have already noted that virtues that are foundational in the Roman cult of virtues, such as the all-important virtues of *victoria* or *iustitia*, occur in Paul's letter as qualities or energy that is dynamic on the level of the individual believer and this believer's relationships. Another feature that we see is that certain of the Roman virtues are closely linked to Christ; they are christologically refracted. For example, *fides*, a quality of the Roman state and later a quality that could be operative in patron-client relationships in Roman life, is closely associated with Christ, as the famous genitives in 3:22, 26 indicate. Whether πίστις Χριστοῦ is translated 'faith of Christ' or 'faith in Christ', in either case faith is seen through the lens of Christ. Paul's understanding of *concordia* is also christologically oriented, as Paul calls believers to think the same according to Christ (15:5). We might be tempted to say that Paul's reference to 'the God of peace' in the blessings of 15:33 and 16:20 is simply God the Father, perhaps a reference to the Old Testament idea that the God of Israel is the one who brings justice and peace (LXX Isa 9:5b–6; 32:17; 45:7–8; 60:17). But Paul's idea of peace shows signs of his own development of the idea, in response to what Christ has done and to Roman political discourse. In 5:1 Paul writes that 'we have peace with God through our Lord Jesus Christ'. In the other letters where Paul uses the phrase God of peace, he does so in the context of allusions to a Roman slogan or understanding of peace (1 Thess 5:3, 23; Phil 4:4–9). It seems that Paul wants to allude to the Romans' understanding of the deified virtue of peace in order to clarify how it is rather the God of Israel who truly brings peace.

As mentioned earlier in this essay, the Romans worshipped their gods for very practical reasons—they perceived that their gods could bring specific, assessable qualities and conditions to the Roman people. And it is this insight that provides a key to our reading of Romans. When Paul uses terms that designated deified virtues, Paul's first audience—the house churches of Rome—would have shared Paul's expectation that the grace, hope, faith, righteousness, peace and salvation announced by Paul's gospel were immanent virtues, necessary for flourishing here on earth.

Bibliography

Bouyer, L. — *The Spirit and Forms of Protestantism* (A.V. Littledale, transl.; London: Harvill Press, 1956; reprint. Princeton, NJ: Scepter, n.d.).

Ehrenberg, V., & A.H.M. Jones (eds.) — *Documents Illustrating the Reigns of Augustus and Tiberius* (Oxford: Clarendon, 1976, second edition).

Elliott, N. — *The Arrogance of Nations: Reading Romans in the Shadow of Empire* (Minneapolis: Fortress, 2008).

Fears, J.R. — 'The Cult of Jupiter and Roman Imperial Ideology', in W. Haase (ed.), *Aufstieg und Niedergang der römischen Welt 2.17.1. Religion: Heidentum: Römische Götterkulte, Orientalische Kulte in der römischen Welt* (Berlin: de Gruyter, 1981), 3–141.

Fears, J.R. — 'The Theology of Victory at Rome: Approaches and Problem', in W. Haase (ed.), *Aufstieg und Niedergang der römischen Welt 2.17.2. Religion: Heidentum: Römische Götterkulte, Orientalische Kulte in der römischen Welt* (Berlin: de Gruyter, 1981), 736–826.

Fears, J.R. — 'The Cult of Virtues and Roman Imperial Ideology', in W. Haase (ed.), *Aufstieg und Niedergang der römischen Welt 2.17.2. Religion: Heidentum: Römische Götterkulte, Orientalische Kulte in der römischen Welt* (Berlin: de Gruyter, 1981), 827–948.

Freyburger, G. — *Fides: étude sémantique et religieuse depuis les origines jusqu'à l'époque Augustéenne* (Paris: Société d'Édition Les Belles Lettres, 2009, second edition).

Gignac, A, — *L'épître aux Romains* (CBNT 6; Paris: Cerf, 2014).

Harrison, J.R. — *Paul's Language of Grace in Its Graeco-Roman Context* (WUNT 2.172; Tübingen: Mohr Siebeck, 2003).

Levick, B. — 'Concordia at Rome', in R.A.G. Carson & C.M. Kraay (eds.), *Scripta Nummaria Romana: Essays Presented to Humphrey Sutherland* (London: Spink and Son, 1978), 217–33.

Lichocka, B. — *Justitia sur monnaies imperials romaines* (Zsolt Kiss, transl.; Warsaw: Editions Scientifiques de Pologne, 1974).

Linderski, J.	'*augurium salutis*', in S. Hornblower & A. Spawforth (eds.), *Oxford Classical Dictionary* (Oxford & New York: Oxford University Press, 1996, third edition), 214.
Linderski, J.	'*Salus*', in S. Hornblower & A. Spawforth (eds.), *Oxford Classical Dictionary* (Oxford & New York: Oxford University Press, 1996, third edition), 1350.
Lott, J.B.	'An Augustan Sculpture of August Justice', *Zeitschrift für Papyrologie und Epigraphik* 113 (1996), 263–70.
Morgan, T.	*Roman Faith and Christian Faith:* Pistis *and* Fides *in the Early Roman Empire and Early Churches* (Oxford: Oxford University Press, 2015).
Reasoner, M.	'Paul's God of Peace in Canonical and Political Perspectives', in T.R. Blanton IV, R.M. Calhoun & C.K. Rothschild (eds.), *The History of Religions School Today: Essays on the New Testament and Related Ancient Mediterranean Texts* (WUNT 340; Tübingen: Mohr Siebeck, 2014), 13–26.
Reasoner, M.	'The Redemptive Inversions of Jeremiah in Romans 9–11', *Biblica* 95 (2014), 388–404.
Rose, H.J., & J. Scheid	'Mars', in S. Hornblower & A. Spawforth (eds.), *Oxford Classical Dictionary* (Oxford & New York: Oxford University Press, 1996, third edition), 929.
Sandmel, S.	'Parallelomania', *Journal of Biblical Literature* 81 (1962), 1–13.
Stafford, E.	'"Without You No One Is Happy": The Cult of Health in Ancient Greece', in H. King (ed.), *Health in Antiquity* (London: Routledge, 2005), 120–35.
Stewart, T.	'The Cry of Victory: A Cruciform Reading of Psalm 44:22 in Romans 8:36'. *Journal for the Study of Paul and His Letters* 3 (2013), 25–45.

CHAPTER 5

Hope against Hope in Paul's Scriptures and in Rome[1]

Mark Reasoner

Hope is an underrated idea in Romans. Paul's hope language in Romans comes right out of his Scripture reading, and it also resonates with the political and literary uses of the idea of hope in the worlds in which Paul lived.

Let us begin at the end of Paul's argument in Romans, and consider Romans 15:7–13. A disproportionate amount of attention is paid to the first 17 verses of this letter, in relation to the conclusion of Paul's argument, which comes here. In many instances in what is written, endings are as or more important than beginnings. So let us begin by considering the ending of Paul's argument.[2]

Paul asks his readers to accept or welcome one another, just as Christ has accepted them for the glory of God. He then describes Christ as a minister to the circumcision and to the nations. As servant of the circumcision, Christ fulfills the truthfulness of God by delivering on the promises made to the Jews' ancestors. As servant in regard to the nations, Christ instantiates God's mercy, so that these nations will

---

1 This paper was first read at the Sydney College of Divinity, on October 1, 2016. To Jim Harrison, who invited me to speak at the Sydney College of Divinity and with his wife Elisabeth hosted me while in Australia, and to all those who offered suggestions after this paper, I remain indebted and thankful.
2 For a reading of the whole letter of Romans that begins with a chapter on Phoebe (16:1–3) and reads "backwards" to chapter 1, see McKnight, *Reading Romans Backwards*.

glorify God (15:7–9a).³ Then Paul offers the last of his Tanak proofs that are more common in Romans than in his other letters. Here in 15:9–12, Paul quotes from Psalms, Deuteronomy, Psalms and Isaiah, to describe how Israel and the nations are viewed as praising God together in the eschaton. The eschatological vision in this Scripture proof, in a way analogous to Jacob's 'Gather round and I must show you what will happen in the latter days' (Gen 49:1), provides an eschatological portrait that is designed to influence how people must conduct themselves in relation to one another.

It is possible that Paul assumes that Christ is speaking in the quotation of LXX Ps 17:50 in Rom 15:9, along the lines of how he tells us in 15:3 that Christ speaks the words of LXX Ps 68:10.⁴ The final text in the catena, LXX Isa 11:10 in Rom 15:12, is very Christological in its reference to 'the root of Jesse'. When we examine the text in Isaiah, we see that Isaiah's sentence continues past what Paul quotes. Indeed, Paul has cut the text short by concluding with 'in him the nations will hope'. Notice that the Masoretic Text (MT) of Isa 11:10 leads to a translation such as we find in the New Revised Standard Version: 'On that day the root of Jesse shall stand as a signal to the peoples; the nations shall inquire of him, and his dwelling shall be glorious'. The LXX has changed 'inquire' (דרש in the MT here) to 'hope', perhaps because of how the nations 'wait' or 'hope' in Isa 42:4 (יחל) and 51:5.⁵ Notice also that the text of Isa 11:10, whether in the MT or in the LXX, goes past the verb in question to say that 'his habitation will be glorious' (MT) or one of 'honor' (LXX).

But Paul cuts short the verse to end his quotation with ἐλπιοῦσιν, 'they will hope'. Why is this? 'Glory' is mentioned earlier in Romans, and it would to include the phrase, 'his habitation will be glorious', though perhaps Paul, relying on the LXX, saw only τιμή (honor) in the

---

3   See Wagner, 'The Christ, Servant of Jew and Gentile', who translates these verses as: 'For I say that the Christ has become a servant of the circumcision on behalf of the truthfulness of God, in order to confirm the promises made to the patriarchs and [a servant] with respect to the Gentiles on behalf of the mercy [of God] in order to glorify God' (pp. 481–82).
4   Wagner adopts this position on 15:9 in 'The Christ, Servant of Jew and Gentile', 475–76, following R. B. Hays's similar move in regard to Rom 15:3 (in which Christ prays LXX Ps 68:10) in 'Christ Prays the Psalms'.
5   Wagner, *Heralds of the Good News*, 319 n. 46.

final phrase of Isa 11:10, and didn't want to include it. There is another possibility however, which is that Paul understands the common pairing in his Scriptures of the idea of not being ashamed with living in hope.

Hope and Avoiding Shame in Paul's Scriptures

'Not being ashamed' is a repeated theme in Romans (1:16; 9:33; 10:11; see also 5:5). The latter two instances represent Paul's quotation of LXX Isa 28:16, which comes in Isaiah in the context of God's answer to people who have false hopes in what will not save (LXX Isa 28:10,13,15,17–19). So 'not being ashamed' can be linked to being freed from false hopes. This is related to trusting in God and not placing one's hope in lesser things, as we see in the context (LXX Ps 43:7) of Paul's quotation of LXX Ps 43:23 in Rom 8:36.

Hope in a positive sense is also linked to 'not being ashamed' in such LXX texts as Isa 51:5–7 (μὴ φοβεῖσθε ὀνειδισμόν, 'do not fear reproach', for μὴ καταισχυνθείην, 'let me not be ashamed'); Pss 21:5–6; 30:2; 70:1; Sir 2:9–10. The following table offers these texts as found in Paul's Scriptures, the LXX. I have italicised phrases for hoping and not being ashamed in the translation column, in order to show how expressions of hope and pleas for avoiding shame commonly occur together.

Hope and Avoidance of Shame in Paul's Scriptures

LXX	Author's translation
Isa 51:5–7	**Isa 51:5–7**
⁵ἐγγίζει ταχὺ ἡ δικαιοσύνη μου, καὶ ἐξελεύσεται ὡς φῶς τὸ σωτήριόν μου, καὶ εἰς τὸν βραχίονά μου ἔθνη ἐλπιοῦσιν· ἐμὲ νῆσοι ὑπομενοῦσιν καὶ εἰς τὸν βραχίονά μου ἐλπιοῦσιν.	⁵My justice approaches quickly, and my salvation will come forth as light, and in my arm the nations *will hope*; islands await me, and in my arm they *will hope*.
⁶ἄρατε εἰς τὸν οὐρανὸν τοὺς ὀφθαλμοὺς ὑμῶν καὶ ἐμβλέψατε εἰς τὴν γῆν κάτω, ὅτι ὁ οὐρανὸς ὡς καπνὸς ἐστερεώθη, ἡ δὲ γῆ ὡς ἱμάτιον παλαιωθήσεται, οἱ δὲ κατοικοῦντες τὴν γῆν ὥσπερ ταῦτα ἀποθανοῦνται, τὸ δὲ σωτήριόν μου εἰς τὸν αἰῶνα ἔσται, ἡ δὲ δικαιοσύνη μου οὐ μὴ ἐκλίπῃ.	⁶Raise your eyes toward heaven, and consider the earth below; for heaven will be taken away as smoke, and the earth will grow old as clothing (does), and those who inhabit it will die as these; but my salvation will be forever, and my justice will not fail.
⁷ἀκούσατέ μου, οἱ εἰδότες κρίσιν, λαός μου, οὗ ὁ νόμος μου ἐν τῇ καρδίᾳ ὑμῶν· ἡ φοβεῖσθε ὀνειδισμὸν ἀνθρώπων καὶ τῷ φαυλισμῷ αὐτῶν μὴ ἡττᾶσθε.	⁷Hear me, you who know judgment, my people, in whose heart is my law; *do not fear people's reproach*, and *do not be overcome by their contempt*.
Ps 21:5–6	**Ps 21:5–6**
⁵ἐπὶ σοὶ ἤλπισαν οἱ πατέρες ἡμῶν, ἤλπισαν, καὶ ἐρρύσω αὐτούς·	⁵In you our fathers hoped, they hoped, and you strengthened them:
⁶πρὸς σὲ ἐκέκραξαν καὶ ἐσώθησαν, ἐπὶ σοὶ ἤλπισαν καὶ οὐ κατῃσχύνθησαν.	⁶to you they cried and were saved, in you they hoped and were not ashamed.
Ps 30:2	**Ps 30:2**
²Ἐπὶ σοί, κύριε, ἤλπισα, μὴ καταισχυνθείην εἰς τὸν αἰῶνα· ἐν τῇ δικαιοσύνῃ σου ῥῦσαί με καὶ ἐξελοῦ με.	²In you, Lord, I hoped, may I never be ashamed: in your justice rescue me and go with me.

Psalm 70:1b–2	Psalm 71:1b–2
¹ᵇ ὁ θεός, ἐπὶ σοὶ ἤλπισα, μὴ καταισχυνθείην εἰς τὸν αἰῶνα. ²ἐν τῇ δικαιοσύνῃ σου ῥῦσαί με καὶ ἐξελοῦ με, κλῖνον πρός με τὸ οὖς σου καὶ σῶσόν με.	¹ O God, in you I hoped; let me never be put to shame. ² in your justice rescue me and go with me; direct your ear to me and save me.
Sirach 2:9–10a	**Sirach 2:9–10a**
⁹οἱ φοβούμενοι κύριον, ἐλπίσατε εἰς ἀγαθὰ καὶ εἰς εὐφροσύνην αἰῶνος καὶ ἔλεος. ¹⁰ἐμβλέψατε εἰς ἀρχαίας γενεὰς καὶ ἴδετε· τίς ἐνεπίστευσεν κυρίῳ καὶ κατῃσχύνθη;	⁹You who fear the Lord, hope for good things, and for eternal happiness and mercy. ¹⁰Consider ancient generations and observe: who trusted in the Lord and was disappointed?

There is therefore a critical mass of texts in Paul's Scriptures that associate hoping in the LORD with not being ashamed. And this is what Paul makes explicit at 5:5, ἡ δὲ ἐλπὶς οὐ καταισχύνει—'hope maketh not ashamed' as the KJV tells us. The association between hope and not being ashamed is the best explanation for why Paul cuts short his quotation of Isa 11:10, the last text in his grand Tanak proof in 15:9–12. The argument of the letter begins with Paul saying he is not ashamed (1:16) and it ends with a benediction asking that the God of hope fill the readers so that they overflow in hope (15:13), following a catena of Scripture texts, whose last text is cut short so that it ends with the verb 'hope'. The one who is divinely graced so as not to be ashamed (1:16–17) is the one who is hoping in Messiah, as Paul indicates by quoting LXX Isa 11:10 and concluding with a blessing of hope (15:12–13).

The association of not being ashamed with hope also indicates that hope is thus more present in Romans than readers of the letter first see. If we add to our hope texts in chapters 5, 8 and 15 the references to not being ashamed (1:16; 5:5; 9:33; 10:11), the scriptural corollary to hoping, the connections to hope in the letter to the Romans are almost doubled. Since hope recurs throughout the letter, it is a more significant idea in this letter than is usually thought.

Spes (Hope) in the Roman Cult of Virtues

To appreciate more how Paul nuances and explains hope in this letter to the Romans, it will be useful now for us to consider how hope or *spes*, as the Romans called it, figured in their culture. Early in the Republic, a private temple to hope was built, called *Spes vetus* ('Old Hope') which was built in 477 B.C.E. Then in 258 B.C.E., A. Attilius Calatinus built a temple that served as a shrine in the public cult paid to *spes*. There are descriptions of this temple being destroyed in both 218 and 31 B.C.E., and evidence that the temple was rebuilt both times, so that the worship of *spes* could continue.[6]

The anniversary of the day on which Augustus assumed the toga of manhood, October 18, became observed in the state cult as a day to pray for hope and youth—*supplicatio spei et iuventuti*.[7] Clark's attempt to trace how hope is related to other deified Roman virtues may be slightly different from my diagram in the preceding chapter, but it nevertheless shows how closely related *spes* was viewed to victory and salvation. Here is what Clark says:

> Victory and Salvation: Plautus' reference to Spes, Salus, Victoria in *Mercator* 867 implies that Hope was conceptually related to the two deities. The juxtaposition suggests that Spes represents the first step toward salvation and final victory. Some scholars have maintained that the temple in the forum Holitorium was originally founded as a fulfillment of a vow for victory over the Carthaginians and for national salvation.[8]

The connection between *spes* and *victoria* is also seen in that cult was paid to both virtues on August 1 in an early calendar.[9] In the Roman configuration of virtues, *spes* was also connected to *fortuna* (material benefits or good fortune) and *ops* (wealth). This ties in to a characteristic that you may already have recognized, that in Roman devotion to *spes*, it is regarded as a deity that helps bring material, earthy benefits. A second

---

6   Clark, 'Spes in the Imperial Cult', 81.
7   Clark, 'Spes in the Imperial Cult', 82, citing *CIL* 10.8375.
8   Clark, 'Spes in the Imperial Cult', 81.
9   Clark, 'Spes in the Imperial Cult', 81–82.

characteristic of the Roman virtue of hope is that it became closely linked to the presence of an heir to the emperor. The emperor Claudius celebrated the deified virtue of hope when he fathered an heir, Tiberius Claudius Germanicus, born in the first year of his reign. He therefore minted a coin in that year—41 C.E.—inscribed with *spes*. Clark treats this as the way that Roman cult normally valued the virtue of hope.[10] The most common epithet for hope on the coins in the Western Empire is *SPES AVGVSTA* or 'the Augustan hope'. Of the accession year coin issue for *spes Augusta*, Fears writes, 'Spes invoked the hope of mankind, newly awakened and focused upon the imperial savior'.[11] It was not only Claudius who linked hope with progeny. After Poppaea gave birth in 63 C.E. to the daughter she and Nero had conceived, the Arval Brethren sacrificed to *felicitas* (or perhaps *fecunditas*; happiness or fertility) *salus publica* (public welfare), and *spes*.[12] In the year 70 C.E., Vespasian issued a *sestertius* that has the goddess *spes* presenting a flower to the emperor and his sons Titus and Domitian.[13] Clark cautions against linking *spes* only with imperial heirs; he writes that sometimes *spes* was simply linked to youth in general.[14]

The Virtue of Hope in Romans

Let us now go back to Romans and examine the hope texts, checking to see how they compare with the use of hope in the state discourse of the imperial cult as a step toward appreciating and hearing these texts as they might have been heard by the believers who heard Paul's letter read to them, not long after it arrived in Rome, perhaps in the winter or spring of 56 C.E.

Hope is introduced in a description of Abraham's faith (4:18). The phrase 'in hope against hope', is an apt way of expressing a tenacious anticipation of what others refuse to envision. It captures well the

---

10 Clark, 'Images and Concepts of Hope in the Imperial Cult'.
11 Fears, 'The Cult of Virtues and Roman Imperial Ideology', 893–94.
12 Fears, 'The Cult of Virtues', 895, citing *Acta Frat. Arv.* Henzen, 85.
13 Clark, 'Spes in the Early Imperial Cult', 83. He identifies the coins as RIC 64 for the Claudius coin and RIC 396 for the Vespasian coin.
14 Clark, 'Spes in the Early Imperial Cult', 83.

idea that the human experience continually involves negotiating and readjusting our hopes. Hope seems to be the context or the fuel for Abraham's faith, according to Rom 4:18. Or as James Ware explains the Pauline triad of virtues: though faith is kept separate from hope and love in Paul's descriptions, faith 'is always *accompanied* by hope and love'.[15] Thus the first mention of hope in Romans is linked with believing, as is the last mention of hope in the benediction of 15:13.

This close association between hope and faith by Paul in Romans is continued by the Paulinist who wrote Hebrews. After defining faith in Hebrews 11:1 as 'the assurance of things hoped for' (NRSV), we get our first extant commentary on Romans 4:18 in Hebrews 11:8–19. The hope that nourished the faith of Abraham seems to be captured in various verbs in this section of Hebrews: 'he went, not knowing where he was going' (11:8); 'sojourned in the land of promise as a foreigner living in tents' (11:9); 'he awaited a city with foundations whose builder and architect is God' (11:10); 'not receiving the promises but seeing them from afar and greeting and confessing that they are strangers and sojourners on the earth' (11:13).

Back in Paul's letter to the Romans, after the reference to Abraham believing in 'hope against hope' (Rom 4:18), we encounter the phrase 'we boast in hope of the glory of God', a boast that results from gaining an entrance into grace (5:2). But Paul is not content simply to say that we hope to participate in or experience God's glory. He backs up and offers another way that hope is formed in us, as a final result of the tribulations, endurance, and proven character that we experience while living as those made righteous, who experience God's peace (5:1, 3–4). Paul does not leave hope as the last virtue, however. 'Hope does not put to shame, because the love of God is poured out in our hearts through the Holy Spirit who is given to us'. While modern interpreters tend to read this as a subjective genitive, early interpreters, such as Origen and Augustine read this as an objective genitive—that hope is connected to our love for God. Origen does say that even if one understands it to be a subjective genitive, God's love for us, this directly enables us to love God, so that the subjective and objective senses of the phrase are both

---

15 Ware, *Paul's Theology in Context*, 123.

there. Aquinas treats this phrase in the *Summa* as an objective genitive, but in his commentary says that it can be either.[16] Brendan Byrne takes the phrase to mean the transforming work that happens in the new age inaugurated by Christ.[17] In light of the following context in which it is clear that God's love is in view (5:8), it is best to side with those who regard the subjective genitive as the primary sense of 'love of God' in 5:5. Paul is saying that hope will be confirmed by God's love that is poured out in our hearts.

This section of Romans was also influential for John Calvin who was writing his Romans commentary at the same time as he was writing and editing the 1539 edition of his *Institutes*. Rom 5:4–5 becomes for Calvin, perhaps influenced by Melanchthon's 1535 edition of the *Loci Communes*, a text that clearly calls Christians to take up their cross and follow Christ. Calvin also ties the idea that 'affliction promotes salvation' to Romans 5:3 in his *Institutes* at 3.8.6. It is worth noting that Calvin 'understands the goal of afflictions as training in patience so that Christians will trust in God's power and strengthen their hope'.[18] So far we can see that several key commentators on Romans 5 find there a call for Christians to live their lives permeated by hope, a hope that paradoxically is to spring up and overflow even in adversity. In Rom 5:4 Paul writes: '... endurance [results in] proven character, and proven character [results in] hope' (ἡ δὲ ὑπομονὴ δοκιμήν, ἡ δὲ δοκιμὴ ἐλπίδα). Endurance thus leads to hope, according to Paul.[19] We can observe that in general the use of hope in Romans is consistent with how Teresa Morgan relates it to faith: 'As a means of enabling and fortifying societies, trust is widely seen as diachronic, forward-looking, and hopeful'.[20]

Longenecker translates 4:18 as: 'Against all hope, Abraham in hope believed and so became the father of many nations'.[21] And Fitzmyer

---

16 See Wilken, '*Fides Caritate Formata*', 1090 (comparison of modern and ancient exegesis; Augustine); 1094 (Aquinas, *Summa theologiae* II–III q. 23 a. 2); 1099 (Origen).
17 Byrne, *Romans*, 167.
18 Sytsma, 'The Exegetical Context of Calvin's Loci on the Christian Life', 265 (1539 Institutes and Romans commentary written in same year); 273 (all other information and quotations).
19 The verb ἐλπίζω is juxtaposed with ὑπομονή in Rom 8:25. In Rom 12:12a–b the verb ὑπομονέω follows the noun ἔλπις. And in 1 Cor 13:7c–d, ὑπομονέω immediately follows ἐλπίζω. Commentators' exegesis of Rom 4:18 also show how hope and faith are related.
20 Morgan, *Roman Faith and Christian Faith*, 16 (see also 22).
21 Longenecker, *The Epistle to the Romans*, 519.

writes on 4:18—'Faith is not some inner sanctimoniousness in contrast to external deeds; it is an unwavering reliance on God's promise, which issues in hope.'[22]

The glory of God in view when we hope, according to Paul (5:2), must be that dimension of existence that we have lost as a result of sin (3:23). The hope Paul has in mind for his readers therefore includes the anticipation of a return to the existence that God meant for humanity—a restored image of God, a deeper participation in God's splendor.

At the same time, the references to hope must carry an edge against the Roman cult of *spes* (hope). In the assertion of 5:1 that 'we have peace with God through our Lord Jesus Christ', Gignac rightly sees an attack against the imperial propaganda of Rome.[23] The references to hope that follow in 5:2, 4–5, a hope that is based on what God will accomplish and not on the imperial agenda or the emperor himself, thus form a second riposte against Rome.

Longenecker finds all of 5:1–4 encapsulated in the word 'hope' in Paul's phrase 'Hope does not disappoint' (5:5), the last explicit reference to hope in this chapter. Because Paul has just said that endurance leads through perseverance to hope, Longenecker is wrong to gloss 'hope' in 5:5 as 'this [message of] hope.'[24] It is not the message, it is the virtue or disposition of hope itself that Paul describes.

In what immediately follows the references to hope at the beginning of chapter 5, Paul describes how God shows love for us by sending Christ to die for us. This is followed by two uses of the future passive, 'we will be saved' in 5:9–10. Here as in 1 Corinthians 9:27, Paul does not view his or our salvation as completed immediately. Salvation is what God eventually brings, as we endure in hope, through the afflictions of this life. Salvation for Paul in Romans is much more earth-focused and open-eyed to the testing and difficulties of life, than most Western characterizations of salvation drawn from Romans have been.[25]

---

22 Fitzmyer, *Romans*, 386–87.
23 Gignac, *L'épître aux Romains*, 215.
24 Longenecker, *Epistle to the Romans*, 561.
25 Here I agree with Peter Oakes that the recipients of Paul's letter would view 'salvation' in a down-to-earth way, looking for deliverance from various forms of economic and social subservience in which they found themselves (*Reading Romans in Pompeii*, 130–49). See also Reasoner, 'The Salvation of Israel in Romans 9–11'.

In Romans 8, Paul counters the Roman propaganda that the Empire was bringing a golden age to the world with the description of the world as subjected to futility and in the slavery of corruption (8:20–21). The only answer he sees to this futility and corruption is a release from the slavery leading to a glorious existence, and adoption that will mean the redemption of our bodies (8:21–23). He then offers a phenomenology of Christian existence in 8:24–25. The phrase, 'hope that is seen is not hope' and the question 'For who hopes for what he sees?' both seem to be aimed at a tendency for some to hope in what they already have.[26] Paul's possible target may be the convention in Roman discourse to link *spes* with someone already in view, as in the celebration of *spes* after an heir of Claudius was born. Paul, as well as his follower who wrote Hebrews, remain adamant that hope is a disposition of trusting anticipation when there is no material evidence. This emphasis fits with the 'in hope against hope he believed' phrase applied to Abraham in 4:18, the description of Abraham and Sarah in 4:19, and with the description of Abraham and others dying without seeing promises completely fulfilled in Hebrews 11:13–16. But it may also be a comment against—at least it would sound very different from—the way the Roman state celebrated and worshiped its deified virtue of hope. Yes, this could simply be Paul's admission that we do not yet see the renewal of creation for which we hope. But in light of the unusual 'God of hope' in the benediction of 15:13 and the similar pattern of these hope references in Romans to Paul's peace references in 1 Thessalonians 5, a good case can be made that Paul deconstructs the deified virtue of *spes* in Rom 8:24–25 and 15:13 in ways analogous to how he has deconstructed *pax* in 1 Thessalonians 5:3, 23 (see also Rom 16:20).[27]

The phrase 'saved in hope' in 8:24 also deserves comment. This is the only place in Romans where the verb 'save' is inflected in a past tense, but of course its significance is qualified by the word 'hope'. Gignac

---

26 Longenecker states that the observation and question in Rom 8:24b–c do nothing to help us understand 8:24a, and that nothing would be lost if 8:24b–c were omitted. He understands the observation and question in 8:24b–c as a rhetorical move to lighten the intensity of statements between which it is sandwiched, Rom 8:24a, 25, *Epistle to the Romans*, 728. This is selling Paul short: Paul is saying something profound about hope in every clause of 8:24–25.

27 See Reasoner, 'Paul's God of Peace in Canonical and Political Perspectives', 17–19 (on 1 Thess 5:23) and 23–25 (on Rom 16:20).

suggests that the 'already/not yet' eschatological orientation is here in Paul's diction and grammar. But without a preposition, it is difficult to decide if the dative 'hope' is instrumental or modal.[28] I think it best to take it as modal, since when other texts in Romans are considered together, Christ is emphasized as the means of salvation (1:16–17; 3:22–26; 5:9–11; 11:26–27).

For too long much of the Romans discourse has viewed salvation as merely a commercial transaction or a chemical reaction that can be accomplished immediately. Here in chapter 8, with its descriptions of expecting God to bring a transformation to this world that is subjected to futility and in bondage to slavery, waiting for the redemption of our bodies, being saved in hope, it is clear that Paul, as in 5:8–10, views salvation as a process. Paul is echoing in chapter 8 what we have already seen in chapter 5: 'Here is how you are saved—you continue to hope in the grace God provides in Christ as you endure through all the afflictions and trials of this life—you are saved by hope'.

With the directives 'rejoicing in hope, enduring in affliction', 12:12 again has the association of endurance and hope that is evident in 5:4. Paul thus seems locked in to the idea that believers' endurance through affliction and opposition is to be accompanied by hope. The same connections are seen in 15:4, this time linked with Christians' reading of Scripture: 'For whatever was written beforehand was written for our instruction, that through endurance and the encouragement of the Scriptures we might have hope'. So there are three texts in this letter, Romans 5:4; 12:12 and 15:4, which link endurance with hope. Two of these texts specifically picture endurance maintained in afflictions (5:3-4; 12:12).

The quotation of Isaiah 11:10a in Romans 15:12 in the final, most significant spot in this composite quotation, inserts a reference to the nations hoping in the root of Jesse. This is a Messianic text if ever there was one. It increases the possibility that in 8:24 Paul is indeed critiquing Roman state discourse about hoping in an heir to the emperor, for here he leaves the reader with the prophecy of the nations hoping in the root of Jesse. It is as if Paul is saying: 'The nations wrongly hope for an heir

---

28   Gignac, *L'épître aux Romains*, 324.

to the *princeps*, the first man, among the Roman people. But we know that in the end, the nations will be hoping in the root of Jesse, who is Jesus the Christ'.

Concluding Implications and Summary of Paul's Emphasis on Hope in Romans

The repeated idea of hope in the context of endurance through afflictions must be significant for Paul and his implied audience, but this can be overlooked if readers think that all they need to know in Romans is that grace received in faith results in salvation, understood as life in heaven. But Paul actually connects hope in his readers' present experience to salvation, for as we saw in chapter 8, he says 'we are saved by hope'. In other words, Paul views salvation as a process that includes our hopeful endurance through the trials of this life.

The plural subjects of ἐλπίς and plural number of ἐλπίζω in 5:2; 8:24–25 confirm Benedict XVI's point that the hope to which Christians are called is always primarily a communal hope.[29] This is seen in how the reference to endurance and the Scriptures leading to hope in 15:4 follows immediately on Paul's call for the strong to bear with the weaknesses of the weak (15:1–2). And the communal nature of hope is also seen in the hope benediction of 15:13, which uses the plural pronouns for 'you' and presupposes that 'joy and peace in believing' and the 'overflow of hope' all occur in the community who are gathered, as in the preceding quotation of Scripture in which the nations join with Israel in praise of God. Hope is therefore not an individual's anticipation of self-fulfillment or self-actualization, but an anticipation, within the community of the faithful, that God will renew and transform this earth that is subjected to futility, enslaved to corruption, and that God will redeem our bodies, which are still weak, prone to distraction because of the weakness of the flesh. Paul thus advocates for an alternative community to the Roman Empire, the called ones who hope in Christ and are not disappointed.

---

29 *Spei Salvi*, 13–15. See also Rom 15:13b.

Paul is not simply correcting the Roman state's object of 'hope', i.e., imperial heirs or material wealth that could be seen. Paul corrects the phenomenology of hope when he insists in 8:24 that hope that is seen, as in the *spes* that is celebrated or worshipped when an imperial heir is born, is not true hope. Instead, those who are fellow heirs with Christ hope in a more radical way, for they hope for the renewal of all creation and their transformation into the glory of the children of God, worshipping the 'root of Jesse' in community with others, though the world recognizes no evidence for this hope (8:17–21; 15:12).

Hope is therefore a key idea in Romans. In Romans 4:18 in its context, Abraham the model of faith is presented as an example of living in hope. In Romans 5–8, Paul's main point is that one who lives on the basis of Jesus' faith lives in hope. Included here is Paul's significant statement, 'we are saved by hope', a phrase Paul wants his audience to remember when he describes how God saves us, completely by grace, through the afflictions of this life. After returning to the connection between hope and enduring affliction in 12:12 and 15:4, Paul presents a picture of the nations hoping in Messiah and asks that the God of hope provide joy and peace in believing, so that his audience can overflow in hope. The benediction ends with overflowing in hope, as if this is an end in itself. Is there more? We know from earlier in the letter that there is more. Hope does not disappoint, because the divine love is poured out in the hearts of those who endure through afflictions, hoping in God.

Bibliography

Byrne, B.	*Romans* (Sacra Pagina 6; Collegeville: Liturgical, 1996).
Clark, M.E.	'Images and Concepts of Hope in the Imperial Cult', in H.R. Kent (ed.), *SBL Seminar Papers 1982* (Chico: Scholars, 1982), 39–43.
Clark, M.E.	'Spes in the Imperial Cult: "The Hope of Augustus"', *Numen* 30 (1983), 80–105.

Fears, J.R.	'The Cult of Virtues and Roman Imperial Ideology', in W. Haase (ed.), *Aufstieg und Niedergang der römischen Welt* 2.17.2. *Religion: Heidentum: Römische Götterkulte, Orientalische Kulte in der römischen Welt* (Berlin: de Gruyter, 1981), 827–948.
Fitzmyer, J.	*Romans: A New Translation with Introduction and Commentary* (Anchor Bible 33; New York: Doubleday, 1993).
Gignac, A.	*L'épître aux Romains* (CBNT 6; Paris: Cerf, 2014).
Hays, R.B.	'Christ Prays the Psalms: Paul's Use of an Early Christian Exegetical Convention', in A.J. Malherbe & W.A. Meeks (ed.), *The Future of Christology* (Minneapolis: Fortress, 1993), 122–36.
Longenecker, R.N.	*The Epistle to the Romans: A Commentary on the Greek Text* (NIGTC; Grand Rapids: Eerdmans, 2016).
McKnight, S.	*Reading Romans Backwards: A Gospel of Peace in the Midst of Empire* (Waco: Baylor University Press, 2019).
Morgan, T.	*Roman Faith and Christian Faith:* Pistis *and* Fides *in the Early Roman Empire and Early Churches* (Oxford: Oxford University Press, 2015).
Oakes, P.	*Reading Romans in Pompeii: Paul's Letter at Ground Level* (Grand Rapids: Eerdmans, 2009).
Reasoner, M.	'The Salvation of Israel in Romans 9–11', in G.A. Anderson & J.S. Kaminsky (eds.), *The Call of Abraham: Essays on the Election of Israel in Honor of Jon D. Levenson* (Notre Dame: University of Notre Dame Press, 2013), 256–79.
Reasoner, M.	'Paul's God of Peace in Canonical and Political Perspectives', in T. R. Blanton IV, R. M. Calhoun & C.K. Rothschild (eds.), *The History of Religions School Today: Essays on the New Testament and Related Ancient Mediterranean Texts* (WUNT 340; Tübingen: Mohr Siebeck, 2014), 13–26.
Sytsma, D.G.	'The Exegetical Context of Calvin's Loci on the Christian Life', *Calvin Theological Journal* 45 (2010), 256–79.
Wagner, J.R.	'The Christ, Servant of Jew and Gentile: A Fresh Approach to Romans 15:8–9', *Journal of Biblical Literature* 116.3 (1997), 473–85.

Wagner, J.R.	*Heralds of the Good News: Isaiah and Paul 'in Concert' in the Letter to the Romans* (NovTSup 101; Leiden: Brill, 2002).
Ware, J.P.	*Paul's Theology in Context: Creation, Incarnation, Covenant and Kingdom* (Grand Rapids: Eerdmans, 2019).
Wilken, R.	'*Fides Caritate Formata*: Faith Formed by Love', *Nova et Vetera* 9 (2011), 1089–1100.

PART 2

Romans and the Challenge of Exegesis: Reading and Being Read by the Epistle

CHAPTER 6

Justification from Sin: An Examination of Romans 6:7

Stephen Gilmour

Interpreters of Paul are divided over whether Paul's language of δικαιόω is covenantal, apocalyptic, relational or judicial, and whether 'justify' or 'rectify' makes the better translation choice. But at the centre of such debates is the much older question of whether δικαιόω is judicial,[1] transformative,[2] or both.[3] Increasingly scholars are adopting the both-and position, no doubt in part motivated by ecumenical concerns between Catholics and Protestants. But this reading of Paul is not without exegetical precedent either. An important piece of the exegetical evidence is Rom. 6:7. This verse says: 'For the one who has died is justified from sin'. However, most translations render the verb δικαιόω as 'freed' or

---

1 Bultmann, *Theology of the New Testament*, 271–76; Cranfield, *Commentary on the Epistle to the Romans*, I.98, 284–86, 311; Schreiner, *Paul, Apostle of God's Glory in Christ*, 206–09 (in his earlier Romans commentary, Schreiner claimed it was both judicial and transformative; Schreiner, *Romans*, 63–71; Westerholm, *Perspectives Old And New On Paul*, 261–96; Moo, *The Epistle to the Romans*, 86–87; Wright, *Paul and the Faithfulness of God*, 958; Murray, *The Epistle to the Romans*, 113–116.
2 Wrede, *Paul*, 130–32; Sanders, *Paul: The Apostle's Life, Letters and Thought*, 506, 568, 638, 722.
3 Sanders, *Paul and Palestinian Judaism*, 495; Campbell, *The Deliverance of God*, 658–65; Dunn, *Romans 1–8*, 40–42; Dunn, *The Theology of Paul the Apostle*, 340–46; Fitzmyer, *Romans*, 105–107, 116–119; Schweitzer, *The Mysticism of Paul*, 220–26; Schnelle, *Apostle Paul*, 320–21; Keck, *Romans*, 34–37, 141; Beker, *Paul The Apostle*, 262; Käsemann, *Commentary on Romans*, 24, 154–56, 177, 224; Käsemann, *New Testament Questions ForToday*, 176–77; Gorman, *Apostle of the Crucified Lord*, 138, 347–80; Stuhlmacher, *Paul's Letter to the Romans*, 61–65; Stuhlmacher, *Revisiting Paul's Doctrine of Justification*, 66–68; Jüngel, *Justification*, 204–24; Jewett, *Romans*, 280–81; Byrne, *Romans*, 123–26.

'set free'. Thus this verse seems to indicate that there is a transformative aspect to justification in Paul, and many interpreters consider this verse important evidence for that view.[4] This essay examines Rom. 6:7 to consider what kind of evidence it provides concerning the nature of justification, i.e. whether it is transformative or not.

There are three broad issues that need to be resolved in order to understand correctly Rom. 6:7, each of which we will consider in turn. First, who is 'the one who has died'? Second, what impact does the preposition ἀπό have on the meaning of the verb δικαιόω? Third, what does τῆς ἁμαρτίας refer to in this context? However, before turning to these questions, it will be helpful to further consider the importance of Rom. 6:7 in determining what Paul meant by δικαιόω in Romans.

The Importance of Rom. 6:7 for Justification in Romans

Paul's densest discussion of justification in Romans occurs from 3:21 to the end of chapter 5. Prior to this, the verb occurs in a very Jewish context in Rom. 2:13 where it is clearly a judicial declaration of not guilty; it also occurs by way of a quotation from Ps. 51:4 (LXX 50:6) in Rom 3:4 and is declarative in this context as well. But Rom. 3:21–5:21 is the crux of Paul's discussion of this concept, and the word group occurs 29 times in these verses. But consider what Paul says afterwards in Rom. 6:1: 'What then shall we say? Will we remain in sin so that grace may abound?' Such a question would seem unlikely, if δικαιόω signaled more than just a judicial declaration. As Michael Bird has said:

> If justification includes both declaring righteous and making righteous it renders virtually incomprehensible the charge of antinomianism leveled against Paul in Rom. 3.7–8 and 6.1–2.

---

4 Bird, *The Saving Righteousness of God*, 17–18, makes this point, and provides the following list of citations: Stuhlmacher, *Gerechtigkeit Gottes bei Paulus*, 75–76; Stuhlmacher, *Paul's Letter to the Romans*, 92; Schreiner, *Romans*, 319; Garlington, 'Imputation or Union with Christ?', 59–77; Byrne, *Romans*, 194, 202. Campbell, *The Deliverance of God*, 663; *The Quest for Paul's Gospel*, 215, interprets δικαιόω as being forensic-liberative, and likewise considers Rom. 6:7 important evidence for his view.

This charge would not have arisen if it were well known that justification includes both declaring and making righteous.[5]

The implication of this question in 6:1 is that Paul's first usage of δικαιόω in 2:13 dominates Paul's discussion to the end of chapter 5. It would seem that if Paul held to a view of justification that was both declarative and transformative, Rom. 6:7 is the place where this would be introduced. A number of scholars, most recently Douglas Campbell, have noted that within scholarship Romans 1–4 appears to be the stronghold of the judicial declarative view, while in Romans 5–8 it is participatory and transformative.[6] Campbell has his own solution to this, which is beyond the scope of this essay. But his observation confirms that in Romans 1–5, justification is declarative. If Paul is to develop δικαιόω beyond its declarative meaning, surely it must begin in Rom. 6:7? We will now turn to our three questions concerning this verse to see what impact it has on interpreting justification in Paul.

1. Who is 'the one who has died'?

The first question to be answered is the question of the subject of the verb. Who does the phrase ὁ ἀποθανών actually refer to? There are three main options amongst interpreters.

The first is the view that this is a general statement about how death frees or acquits people from sin, possibly finding its roots in Rabbinic writings (*b. Shabb.* 151b; *Sifre Num.* §112 commenting on Num. 15:31).[7] In this case, it refers to nobody in particular, but is a proverbial statement

---

5   Bird, *The Saving Righteousness of God*, 18. While Paul is certainly dealing with the charge that he is antinomian in 3:7–8, it is possible that he is responding to an antinomian in Romans 6 rather than to this charge. Nevertheless, if δικαιόω is both declarative and transformative, then there is no sense in having this chapter, since the case has already been made for why moral δικαιοσύνη is necessary: God has transformed them to be this kind of people.
6   Campbell, *The Deliverance of God*, 183–84. Or as Ziesler, *The Meaning of Righteousness*, 6, has put it: 'some have argued that in Romans 1–5, Paul deals with God's righteousness as conferring a new status, and in 6–8 he deals with it as energizing man and leading to a new life'.
7   Sanders, *Paul and Palestinian Judaism*, 159; Dunn, *Romans 1–8*, 320–21; Moo, *The Epistle to the Romans*, 377 n.132; Calvin, *Commentary on Romans*, 194–95; Bruce, *Romans*, 143; Jewett, *Romans*, 404; Longenecker, *The Epistle to the Romans*, 606; Byrne, *Romans*, 192; Hill, *Greek Words and Hebrew Meanings*, 142 n.1; Seifrid, *Christ, our Righteousness*, 72–73.

that explains (γάρ) why those who have died to sin should no longer live as slaves to it (Rom. 6:6). However, some scholars have criticized this approach. Cranfield contends that Rom. 6:7 cannot refer to a general principle of the Rabbis: 'In the sense that 'death pays all debts' this principle is valid only in relation to a human court: it is certain that Paul did not think that a man's death atoned for his sins in relation to God, or that a dead man was no longer accountable to God for his sins'.[8] Likewise Schreiner says: 'This explanation fails to comport with Pauline theology. Paul did not believe that by dying people were automatically freed from sin. Instead, he argued that sin reigned in death (Rom. 5:21)'.[9] While this view is not as improbable as these criticisms suggest, what will become evident throughout this essay is that this view is not correct. Paul does not understand δεδικαίωται ἀπὸ τῆς ἁμαρτίας as occurring through 'dying' but as a subsequent result of it.[10] Such an analysis is confirmed by the use of the aorist tense-form for the participle ὁ ἀποθανών, indicating by its perfective aspect 'action that is antecedent to its leading verb'.[11]

The second view is that this is a statement specifically about Jesus, whose death has freed or acquitted him from sin.[12] Having stated that those who have died with Christ should no longer live as slaves to sin (Rom. 6:6), verse 7 then grounds this (γάρ) in what Christ's death achieved. Verse 7 is not directly addressing what believers receive through Christ's death, but more specifically what Jesus' death meant for himself. However, some scholars have criticised this view. Schreiner says that 'the context does not prepare us for a switch of subject from the believer in verse 6 to Christ in verse 7'.[13] Likewise Fitzmyer notes

---

8   Cranfield, *Romans 1–8*, 310–11. Wright endorses this view in 'The Letter to the Romans', 540.
9   Schreiner, *Romans*, 318–19.
10 Despite his agreement with the next sentence, this is *contra* Porter, *Verbal Aspect*, 270, 300. Campbell, *The Deliverance of God*, 826, has made the suggestion that δεδικαίωται ἀπὸ τῆς ἁμαρτίας is the equivalent to Christ's resurrection. While Paul has associated δικαιόω with Christ's death (5:9) and with forgiveness of sins (3:24; 4:1–12), it is not certain that he has ever done so with Christ's resurrection (in light of μέλλει in 4:24, it would seem future δικαίωσις at the judgment is in view in 4:25). Given the natural reading of 6:7 is that δικαιόω is an effect of Christ's death, and that Paul is consistent in that δικαιοσύνη results in life (1:17; 4:13; 5:9–10, 17, 21; 8:1–12), it would seem unlikely that Campbell is correct.
11 Campbell, *Basics of Verbal Aspect*, 94; Porter, *Idioms of the Greek New Testament*, 188.
12 Campbell, *The Deliverance of God*, 825–27; Scroggs, 'Romans 6:7', 106.
13 Schreiner, *Romans*, 319.

that this view 'renders v. 10 somewhat tautologous'.¹⁴ Käsemann is particularly strong in his dismissal of this view: 'It is completely fantastic to interpret ἀποθανών christologically and hence to conjecture that we have an exposition of Ps. 87:5 LXX'.¹⁵

These criticisms seem essentially right. It would be unlikely that Rom. 6:7 refers to Jesus because Paul has labored throughout 6:1–6 to demonstrate that believers have died in him. Throughout these verses, as well as in verse 8, believers form the subject of every indicative and subjunctive verb except one in Rom. 6:4, where Christ is the subject of the *protasis* in a comparison. There is no explicit signal that Paul is changing the subject between verses 6 and 7 or between verses 7 and 8. Rather, throughout this whole section, Paul is developing the concept that believers have died in Christ. Thus it would seem improbable that Paul would suddenly switch from laboring this point, to making a statement about what Christ's death did for himself in Rom. 6:7, without at least an acknowledgement of this switch or even a subsequent re-appropriation of that benefit for the believer in the next verse. But in verse 8 Paul is still focusing on the believer, in union with Christ. It would seem more likely that Rom. 6:7 is providing the grounds or warrant (γάρ) for why participation in Christ's death should mean that the believer no longer serves sin in verse 6, than that Paul abruptly changes the subject between verses 6 and 7 and then again between verses 7 and 8.

The final view claims that ὁ ἀποθανών refers to believers who have participated in Christ's death on the cross.¹⁶ This is perhaps the more common view amongst interpreters, and is most likely the correct one: it makes the best sense of the context; it does not create an abrupt change in subject between verses 6 and 7 and again between verses 7 and 8; and finally it fits with Paul's other statements and theology throughout Romans. It is the most likely interpretation of the phrase 'the one who has died'.

---

14 Fitzmyer, *Romans*, 437.
15 Käsemann, *Commentary on Romans*, 170.
16 Tobin, *Paul's Rhetoric In Its Contexts*, 195–96; Murray, *The Epistle to the Romans*, 222; Wright, 'The Letter to the Romans', 540; Leithart, 'Justification as Verdict and Deliverance', 68; Kertelge, 'δικαιόω', 1.331; Sanders, *Paul*, 638; Keck, *Romans*, 161; Ziesler, *The Meaning of Righteousness in Paul*, 200; Morris, *The Epistle to the Romans*, 252. Käsemann, *Commentary on Romans*, 170, and Stuhlmacher, *Paul's Letter to the Romans*, 92, think Rom. 6:7 derives from a Jewish saying, but has been adapted by Paul for this view.

2. What is the impact of the preposition ἀπό on the meaning of the verb δικαιόω?

Having decided that this verse refers to believers in their participation in Jesus, the second question concerns the meaning of the verb δικαιόω, and in particular, the way that the preposition ἀπό affects the precise connotation of this word. There are two common views.

The first view claims that this phrase is a judicial declaration of acquittal.[17] This is the view that appears to dominate Paul's discussion in Romans 1–5, and thus, this view maintains continuity with what Paul has said so far. The reason why many have disagreed with it is that they cannot see how it fits with the context of Rom. 6:1–6, with its focus on freedom from sin. However, some have argued against this. C. Clifton Black II says: 'My own opinion is that 6:7 is quite comprehensible when taken juridically: the old self has died and has been destroyed (6:6) and thus is acquitted, because the once-deserved guilty verdict cannot now be passed'.[18] Likewise C. E. B. Cranfield explains that 'to state this fact is indeed to confirm v. 6; for it is the fact that God has justified us that is the firm basis of that new freedom to resist the bondage of sin in our practical living'.[19]

Closely related to this is another view that this phrase is a judicial declaration of release or deliverance.[20] John Murray explains:

> 'Justified from sin' will have to bear the forensic meaning in view of the forensic import of the word 'justify'. But since the context deals with deliverance from the power of sin the thought is, no doubt, that of being 'quit' of sin. The decisive breach with the reigning power of sin is viewed after the analogy of the kind of dismissal which a judge gives when an arraigned person is justified.[21]

---

17 Cranfield, *Romans 1–8*, 311; Black II, 'Pauline Perspectives on Death in Romans 5–8', 423; Scroggs, 'Romans 6:7', 104–05, 108; Ziesler, *The Meaning of Righteousness in Paul*, 200–01; Hill, *Greek Words and Hebrew Meanings*, 142.
18 Black, 'Pauline Perspectives on Death in Romans 5–8', 423.
19 Cranfield, *Romans 1–8*, 311.
20 Murray, *The Epistle to the Romans*, 222; Porter, *The Letter to the Romans*, 135; Campbell, *The Deliverance of God*, 825–26; Seifrid, *Christ, our Righteousness*, 72–73.
21 Murray, *The Epistle to the Romans*, 222.

As this quotation makes clear, the fundamental difference between these two kinds of judicial declaration is the interpretation of τῆς ἁμαρτίας, and so it will be necessary to wait until the third question before it is possible to differentiate between them.

The second view claims that this phrase expresses the setting free of a person.[22] This view is by far the more common amongst interpreters of Paul. Further, as the editor of Calvin's Commentaries says in note 188:

> The verb, δεδικαίωται, 'is', or has been 'justified', has been considered by the early and most of the later commentators in the sense of being freed or delivered. This is the view, among others, of Chrysostom, Basil, Œcumenius, Beza, Pareus, Hammond, Grotius, Doddridge and Macknight. But it must be added, that it is a meaning of which there is no other clear instance in the New Testament, though the verb occurs often.[23]

Hence this view enjoys both ancient and modern support on the grounds of its compatibility with Rom. 6:1–6, despite the discontinuity it creates with Romans 1–5.

Despite the preference by many for the second view, there are good reasons for holding either. It will be useful to consider how prepositions function with respect to the verb δικαιόω before considering what impact ἀπό might have upon it. Throughout the Septuagint, Apocrypha, Pseudepigrapha, Philo, Josephus, and the NT, a number of prepositions

---

22   Tobin, *Paul's Rhetoric In Its Contexts*, 195–96; Stuhlmacher, *Paul's Letter to the Romans*, 92; Keck, *Romans*, 163; Moo, *The Epistle to the Romans*, 377; Bruce, *Romans*, 143; Calvin, *Commentary on Romans*, 194–195; Leithart, 'Justification As Verdict And Deliverance', 68, 72; Jewett, *Romans*, 404–05; Longenecker, *The Epistles to the Romans*, 606; Kertelge, 'δικαιόω', 1.331; Sanders, *Paul*, 638; Byrne, *Romans*, 192; Garlington, 'Imputation or Union with Christ?', 66–70; Käsemann, *Commentary on Romans*, 170. Dunn, *Romans 1–8*, 320–321, and Wright, 'The Letter to the Romans', 540, consider 'to be declared free' a better translation, but functionally speak of it as if it means to be set free. Fitzmyer, *Romans*, 347, 436–37, and Schreiner, *Romans*, 319, both think it expresses a transfer in status from sin to righteousness, such that both acquittal and transformation has taken place, although it should be noted that Schreiner has since changed his views on justification.

23   Calvin, *Commentary on Romans*, 194.

are used to modify δικαιόω.[24] These may be categorized in the following way:

- Three prepositions are used to introduce the judge(s) before whom an acquittal occurs: ἐνώπιόν + gen. (Ps. 142:2; Lk. 16:15; Rom. 3:20), ἔναντι + gen. (Sir. 7:5), and παρά + dat. (Gal. 3:11).
- Three prepositions are used to convey the reason (often broadly speaking) for the judgment: διά + acc. (Philo, *Somniis* 1.212; *Moysis* 1.243), χάριν + gen. (Philo, *Specialibus* 3.180), and ἕνεκεν/ἕνεκα + gen. (Exod. 23:7; Philo, *Moysis* 2.211).
- Three prepositions are used to convey the means by which an acquittal is to be sought: ἐν + dat. (Ps. 50:6; Mic. 6:11; Ezek. 16:51; Acts 13:38; Rom. 3:4; 5:9; 1Cor. 4:4; 6:11; Gal. 2:17; 3:11; 5:4; 1Tim. 3:16), ἐκ + gen. (Matt. 12:37; Rom. 4:2; 5:1; Gal. 2:16; 3:8, 24; James 2:21, 24–25) and ἀπό + gen. (Matt. 11:19).
- Two prepositions are used to convey the evidential basis upon which an acquittal is based: κατά + acc. (1 Kings 8:32; 2 Chron. 6:23; Philo, *Hypothetica* 6.5) and ἐπί + dat. (Josephus, *Antiquities* 17.206).
- Two prepositions are used to convey agency: ἀπό + gen. (Is. 45:25; Lk. 7:35; see also Thucydides' *History of the Peloponnesian War* 1.141) and ὑπό + gen. (Philo, *Migrat* 95; *Fuga*, 69; *Somniis* 2.132).
- Three prepositions are used to make a comparison between two parties, which in the LXX translate the Hebrew particle of comparison min: ἀπό + gen. (Jer. 3:11), ὑπέρ + acc. (Ezek. 16:52), and παρά + acc. (Lk 18:14).[25]
- Finally, the preposition ἐν + dat. can indicate the sphere in which a person is vindicated (Ps. Sol. 2:15; 8:7, 23; 9:2; Philo, *1Qgenesis* 3.20) and, by contrast, the preposition ἀπό + gen. indicates the

---

24 Many of these references have been corroborated by Cosgrove, 'Justification in Paul', 657–58. It should be noted that Cosgrove appears too rigid in his application of his observations to Paul, and that context should remain the determining factor in deciding the function of a preposition. Nevertheless, his observations are illuminating.

25 Such translations of the Hebrew are awkward because of the verb, which in Greek would normally be in the comparative form δικαιότερον, as it is in Demosthenes *Orat. Pro Phormione* 42: καὶ δικαιότερον τόνδ' ἀπὸ τῶν αὑτοῦ λῃτουργεῖν ὑμῖν.

charge(s) against which an acquittal is made (Sir. 26:29; T. Sim 6:1; Acts 13:38).²⁶

While there are a number of categories that involve the preposition ἀπό, the final is the more likely candidate for Rom. 6:7, where the preposition indicates the charge(s) against which an acquittal is made. It will be useful to consider the three passages from this category in further detail.

2.1 The Wisdom of Ben Sira 26:29

The Wisdom of Ben Sira is a book of proverbs originally written in Hebrew but translated into Greek. The Greek version has much better manuscript evidence than the Hebrew, and appears to be a word-for-word translation of the Hebrew, often representing 'the poetic form of the verses as much as possible'.²⁷ The verb δικαιόω occurs 11 times throughout Sirach,²⁸ but only once with the preposition ἀπό. This proverb in Sirach 26:29 says: 'A merchant will scarcely be delivered from wrongdoing, and a retailer will not be innocent (οὐ **δικαιωθήσεται**) of sin (ἀπὸ ἁμαρτίας)'. As this translation from the *New English Translation of the Septuagint* suggests, the verb δικαιόω when combined with ἀπό involves a declaration of innocence with respect to sin. This proverb falls within a collection of proverbs concerning wealth (26:29–27:3). These proverbs warn that those who seek wealth will quickly fall into sin (27:1–2), and that only the fear of the Lord can protect them from

---

26 Gathercole, 'The Justification of Wisdom', 476–88, has argued that Matt. 11:19/Lk. 7:35 belong to this final category on the basis of its usage in these other passages, along with other factors as well. While his proposal is intriguing, for both passages it would seem a look at the broader context would indicate that the more traditional readings reflected above are correct. For example, in Matthew 11, John the Baptist questions Jesus about his identity and is given a response in terms of what Jesus has been doing (vv.1–6). Next Jesus questions the crowds about John the Baptist and then gives them the answer based upon John's actions (vv.7–11). Finally, Jesus states that there are people who take the kingdom of heaven by force (v.12), before highlighting the hypocrisy of this generation in their assessments of Jesus and John (vv.13–19a). Thus it would seem deeds are the means by which wisdom is vindicated, where Jesus/John are to be understood as the representatives of wisdom (Nolland, *The Gospel of Matthew*, 464).
27 Wright, 'To The Reader of Sirach', 718.
28 Sirach 1:22; 7:5; 9:12; 10:29; 13:22; 18:2, 22; 23:11; 26:29; 31:5; 42:2.

this fate (27:3). Thus in 26:29, it seems improbable that a merchant can escape from the entanglement of such wrongdoing, but impossible for a retailer to be declared innocent of sin.[29] While δικαιόω is parallel to a verb meaning 'to release' or 'set free', the two verbs express related yet different ideas that are teased out in the subsequent proverbs.[30] The basic premise that they both share is that wealth allures those who seek it into sin.[31] Thus the preposition ἀπό in Sirach 26:29 does not indicate a transformative understanding of δικαιόω, since this would render this second part of the proverb redundant. Rather, it presents the charge against which a declaration of innocence will not be made. Further, the declarative use of δικαιόω is consistently utilized throughout Sirach, never referring to someone being 'made righteous' or 'freed', but consistently to concepts such as 'vindication', 'acquittal', or being 'deemed righteous'.[32]

2.2 The Testament of Simeon 6:1

Within the pseudepigraphical writing *The Testament of Simeon*, the patriarch gives his final words to his children (1:1–2).[33] Simeon recounts his plot to kill Joseph due to jealousy (2:6–7), and his subsequent anger against Judah for selling Joseph to the Ishmaelites (2:9). The purpose of this is so that Simeon might appeal to his children not to follow his own sins of jealousy and anger (2:14–3:3), but instead to be full of compassion and mercy as Joseph was towards his brothers (4:4–7).[34]

---

29 A very similar proverb occurs in Sirach 31:5: 'He who loves gold will not be justified (οὐ δικαιωθήσεται), and he who pursues profits will be led astray by them' (NETS).
30 Concerning the view that the two verbs should be considered virtually synonymous, Ziesler, *The Meaning of Righteousness in Paul*, 74 n.2, says: 'If we reject this view, it is not only because of the verb's prevailing meaning, but also because "from sin" makes better sense when the verb is taken forensically'.
31 Crenshaw, 'Sirach', 768.
32 Hill, *Greek Words and Hebrew Meanings*, 110.
33 This pseudepigraphical work follows the vein of Genesis 49 where Jacob gives his last words to his twelve sons; see Kee, 'Testaments of the Twelve Patriarchs', 775. Concerning dating, see pp. 777–78.
34 This theme in varying forms is common across all the testaments of the twelve patriarchs; Kee, 'Testaments of the Twelve Patriarchs', 775.

Further, he calls them to abstain from fornication on account of what is written about them in the writing of Enoch: 'your sons will be ruined in sexual immorality, along with you' (5:3–4). As part of this appeal, Simeon says in 6:1: 'Look, I have foretold you all things, so that I might be acquitted from the sin (δικαιωθῶ ἀπὸ τῆς ἁμαρτίας) of your souls'.[35] In this verse, τῆς ἁμαρτίας cannot refer to the sins that Simeon himself committed, and that he recounts in this writing, since there is no suggestion throughout that his children participated in these sins. Further, in T. Sim. 2:13 he describes how he found forgiveness from the Lord through repentance, weeping, and prayer, and in T. Sim. 3:4 he claims that deliverance from envy comes through the fear of God, which he experienced for two years after his envy of Joseph. Given that the sins he seeks to be justified from belong to his children (τῶν ψυχῶν ὑμῶν), it makes better sense if Simeon is seeking to find acquittal from culpability concerning the sins that they alone commit. This meaning is reinforced by the first half of 6:1, which says that Simeon has forewarned his children of everything. He is not trying to find deliverance from their sins but to ensure he himself is above reproach in having warned them concerning the folly of sin. By detailing his own sins and then calling his children not to follow, Simeon intends to ensure he isn't guilty of complicity. However, T. Sim. 6:2–3 could be construed to suggest that more is meant than mere acquittal. It says that if his children do remove sin from amongst them, then 'my [Simeon's] bones will bloom in Israel like a rose and my flesh in Jacob as a lily' whilst 'the seed of Canaan will be destroyed'. But this is not suggesting that if Simeon's children no longer sin then Simeon himself will be helped.[36] Rather as 6:7–7:3 goes on to make clear, this will precipitate the salvation by God of the tribe of Simeon through Judah and Levi. Simeon is pictured as receiving joy from this (6:7), but this does not imply that Simeon himself is somehow caught up in the sins of his children. Therefore 6:1 is a second instance of δικαιόω with the proposition ἀπό referring to a

---

35 Both Charlesworth, *Old Testament Pseudepigrapha*, and Evans and Zacharias, *Old Testament Pseudepigrapha*, translate the phrase in terms of a judicial acquittal. Charlesworth says: 'I might be exonerated with regard to your sin'. Evans says: 'I may be acquitted of the sins of your soul'.

36 The imagery of 6:2 is most likely adopted from the prophetic and wisdom traditions, including Isa 35:1, Song 2:1, and especially Hos 14:5–7. In this last passage, the fragrance of Lebanon is specifically mentioned. Kee, 'Testaments of the Twelve Patriarchs', 787.

judicial declaration, where ἀπό introduces the charge against which a declaration is to be made.

2.3 Acts 13:38

Acts 13 details the first missionary journey of Paul and Barnabas where they travel first to Cyprus and then throughout Asia Minor establishing new churches. In verse 14 it says that Paul and his companions landed in Antioch in Pisidia, having arrived there from Perga in Pamphylia. That Sabbath they went to the synagogue and Paul gave a speech at the request of the local synagogue officials, which Luke narrates from verses 16–41. In this speech, Paul sums up Israel's history from Egypt to King David (vv.16–23), before jumping ahead to John the Baptist (vv.24–25). This survey is crafted to illustrate that Jesus is the king from David's line promised to come (v.25). Paul then turns to Jesus, speaking of his rejection by Jerusalem and her leaders, his death on the cross, subsequent resurrection, and his post-resurrection appearances (vv.26–32). Lastly Paul gives a string of quotations that illustrate that this all occurred by the plan of God (vv.33–37), before making the following claim in v.38:

> Let it be known to you, brothers, that through this man it is proclaimed to you the forgiveness of sins, all of which it is not possible to be justified (δικαιωθῆναι) from in the law of Moses.

It is not immediately clear whether δικαιωθῆναι here means to be set free or to be acquitted. Some commentators claim it means 'to be set free' precisely on its similarity to Rom. 6:7.[37] However, a number of factors work against this. First, the only context in which the Mosaic Law itself speaks of δικαιόω is the forensic context where a declaration that someone is 'in the right' is given (Gen. 38:26; 44:16; Ex. 23:7; Deut. 25:1). Thus the Mosaic Law points to such a reading. Second, the author deliberately chooses two different words—ἄφεσις and δικαιωθῆναι—in Acts 13:38, which suggests that there should be a nuance of meaning between

---

37 Petersen, *The Acts of the Apostles*, 394; Barrett, *Acts 1–17*, 650. Keener, *Acts*, 2074–90, claims it is both 'to be set free' and 'to be acquitted'.

them. Paul seems to be saying that of every sin a person might be found guilty of when judged by the standard of the law (as noted above, ἐν conveys means), all of them can be forgiven through Jesus Christ. Thus while ἄφεσις might mean release from sins, δικαιωθῆναι is the result of this forgiveness rather than a synonym for it. This is similar to how Paul relates these two concepts in Rom. 4:1–12, where Abraham's δικαιοσύνη is related to the forgiveness spoken about by David in Psalm 32.[38] Third, it is important to note that Paul is speaking of the anarthrous, plural 'sins' (ἁμαρτιῶν), which is more likely to refer to sinful moral actions than to sin as an enslaving power. Thus Paul is proclaiming that Jesus can release believers from every sin of which a person would otherwise be found guilty by the law.[39] Acts 13:38 is a third instance of δικαιόω with the proposition ἀπό referring to a judicial declaration, where ἀπό introduces the charges against which a declaration (in this case) cannot be made.

Before drawing a conclusion on the meaning of δικαιόω with the preposition ἀπό in Rom. 6:7, it will be helpful to sum up the evidence evinced so far. What has been discovered is that: (1) The preposition ἀπό does not clarify the meaning of the verb δικαιόω, but introduces the charge(s) against which an acquittal is being made. In such contexts it functions as the obverse to the preposition ἐν, which introduces the sphere in which a person is vindicated. Thus it should be expected that δικαιόω involves a judicial declaration in Rom. 6:7, much as it does in Romans 1–5. (2) In all of the three passages that are relevant to Rom. 6:7, it has been established that the verb δικαιόω refers to a judicial declaration and not to a transformation where someone is 'freed from sin' or 'made righteous'. (3) Of all the passages surveyed above in the analysis of how prepositions function with the verb δικαιόω, only one passage did not lend itself to a declarative meaning: Isa. 45:25. On the basis of 45:24, it would seem this passage concerns being 'made righteous'. (4) It has been argued that Paul's use of δικαιόω in Romans 1–5 conveys the sense of a judicial declaration, with that section being dominated by how this verb is used in Rom. 2:13. Further, the closest parallel to Rom. 6:7 in the whole of Romans is Rom. 5:9. This verse also associates

---

38 Moo, *The Epistle to the Romans*, 266; Longenecker, *Romans*, 501–02.
39 Fitzmyer, *The Acts of the Apostles*, 518–19; Polhill, *Acts*, 305; Bruce, *The Book of Acts*, 262–63; Ziesler, *The Meaning of Righteousness*, 130.

Christ's death with the believers' justification, and few scholars would dispute that Rom. 5:9 is consistent with how the verb is used in the remainder of Romans 1–5. Thus this parallel suggests that 6:7 should be interpreted in a similar way.

However, Don Garlington has argued that δικαιόω in 6:7 must express 'to be set free' because the phrase ἀπὸ τῆς ἁμαρτίας also occurs in 6:18, 22 with the verb ἐλευθερόω.[40] But surely Paul can make two different points about sin that both utilize this same expression. While δικαιόω in 6:7 is a perfect indicative verb, ἐλευθερόω in 6:18, 22 are aorist participles, and so the overlap really is limited to the same preposition and the same articular noun τῆς ἁμαρτίας, which occurs thirteen times in various cases across Romans 6 alone. Since Paul wrote vv.1–14 and 15–23 to answer questions that are interrelated but not identical, the evidence is a bit thin when it comes to equating these two ideas. More likely, Paul is expressing by the verb δικαιόω in 6:7 a judicial declaration of acquittal or deliverance, and the preposition ἀπό introduces the charges or plaintiff against which this declaration is made.

3. What does τῆς ἁμαρτίας refer to in this context?

This brings us to the final question. Given that this verse refers to believers and involves a judicial verdict concerning them, the final question concerns the meaning of τῆς ἁμαρτίας. There are two common views concerning what this refers to.

The first view conceives of sin as a power that has dominion over the individual, and to which they are slaves.[41] This view finds support in the previous verse, where we are told that those who are crucified with Jesus should no longer serve sin (Rom. 6:6). It also finds support in the singular form of the noun 'sin', and in the presence of the article.

---

40 Garlington, 'Imputation or Union with Christ?', 68–69. Sanders, *Paul and Palestinian Judaism*, 472, also takes this view.

41 Campbell, *The Deliverance of God*, 826; Tobin, *Paul's Rhetoric In Its Contexts*, 195–96; Murray, *The Epistle to the Romans*, 222; Moo, *The Epistle to the Romans*, 377; Wright, 'The Letter to the Romans', 540; Cranfield, *Romans 1–8*, 311; Leithart, 'Justification As Verdict And Deliverance', 72; Keck, *Romans*, 161; Sanders, *Paul*, 638; Morris, *The Epistle to the Romans*, 252; Käsemann, *Commentary on Romans*, 170.

The second view conceives of sin as moral actions done in the body.[42] This view also finds support in the previous verse, where we are told that those who are crucified with Christ have abolished the body of sin (Rom. 6:6). Dunn notes that what is striking about the phrase 'the body of sin' in Rom. 6:6 is how the closest parallel to such talk is 'the body in debt to sin' in the Wisdom of Solomon 1:4 (c.f. Sir 18:22). Hence 'the body of sin' in verse 6, or its truncated form 'the sin' in verse 7, denotes sinful actions done in the body.[43]

Some interpreters contend that Paul has both views in mind. As Stuhlmacher says: 'Jesus' death of atonement sets one free from sin and from the compulsion to have to sin'.[44] Given that it is possible to find either interpretation in Rom. 6:6, it therefore may be possible that the complete idea of sin as both sinful moral actions and an enslaving power are in view in the next verse.

However, the evidence suggests that the first view is correct. Paul wrote Rom. 6:1–14 to answer the question of whether believers should remain in sin's domain (v.1), while Rom. 6:15–23 answers the question of whether believers should commit sinful moral actions (v.15). Given that 5:20 claims that where ἡ ἁμαρτία increased, grace super-abounded, it would seem the verb ἐπιμένωμεν in 6:1 is referring to this place where sin increases, i.e. sin's domain.[45] Thus how could ἡ ἁμαρτία refer to sin's oppression in 6:1 but sinful moral actions in 6:7? Further, throughout Romans 5–8, ἡ ἁμαρτία is personified as an oppressive power: 'it "reigns" (5:20; cf. 6:13, 14), can be "obeyed" (6:16–17), pays wages (6:23), seizes opportunity (7:8, 11), "deceives", and "kills" (7:11, 13)'. Thus as Moo concludes: Paul 'personifies sin, picturing it as a power that holds sway in the world outside Christ, bringing disaster and death on all humanity'.[46] And while Schreiner is correct to claim that we must

---

42 Dunn, *Romans 1–8*, 320; Bruce, *Romans*, 143; Black, 'Pauline Perspectives on Death in Romans 5–8', 423; Scroggs, 'Romans 6:7', 107; Byrne, *Romans*, 192.
43 Dunn, *Romans 1–8*, 321.
44 Stuhlmacher, *Paul's Letter to the Romans*, 92. This view was earlier articulated by Calvin, *Commentary on Romans*, 194–95.
45 Moo, *The Epistle to the Romans*, 355–56; Schreiner, *Romans*, 304; Tobin, *Paul's Rhetoric in Its Contexts*, 182–83; Keck, *Romans*, 157–58; Murray, *The Epistle to the Romans*, 213; Longenecker, *The Epistle to the Romans*, 610–11; Jewett, *Romans*, 394–95; Wright, 'The Letter to the Romans', 537.
46 Moo, *The Epistle to the Romans*, 319.

not separate 'sin' as oppressor from 'sin' as sinful moral actions,[47] nevertheless sin's oppressive demands over people's lives are in the forefront in vv.1–14. In Rom. 6:6, Paul says that the old self under sin's dominion has been crucified with Christ so that the 'body of sin' might be nullified (BDAG: καταργηθῇ). The phrase 'the body of sin' is not so different in meaning from 'the old self' in the first part of the verse in that both refer to the whole person and not some aspect of them.[48] But Paul intentionally focuses on the mortal body, the embodied self, which commits such acts of disobedience.[49] In Rom. 3:10–18, Paul characterizes people's mind, throat, tongue, lips, mouth, feet and eyes as ruled by sin. In Rom. 7:14–15, he claims that those under sin do not do what they want to do, but instead do what they hate, while in v.17 he says that it is not the person who does such things, but sin dwelling in them.[50] In all these passages, there is a focus on sin ruling the body so that it obeys sin's demands. In other words, the body is the instrument of sin. But by crucifying the old person, this instrument of sin has been nullified, such that the new person should no longer obey sin's demands (μηκέτι δουλεύειν ἡμᾶς τῇ ἁμαρτίᾳ).[51] Thus ἡ ἁμαρτία can be best understood in Rom. 6:7 as an oppressive power that contends against the believer and makes demands upon them.

Paul's point in 6:7 is that 'the one who has died' has been judicially declared free from sin's oppression. This is why the believer should no longer serve sin. It is because they have received a declaration of release from all the demands sin might hold over them. Rom. 6:7 does not claim that they have been set free from sin's slavery, but neither does it say that they have been acquitted from sin's guilt. It is a judicial declaration that someone is 'in the right' with respect to demands being

---

47 Schreiner, *Romans*, 304.
48 Fitzmyer, *Romans*, 436; Tobin, *Paul's Rhetoric In Its Contexts*, 195; Keck, *Romans*, 162–63; Jewett, *Romans*, 403–04; Cranfield, *Romans 1–8*, 308–09; Byrne, *Romans*, 191, 196–97; Bruce, *Romans*, 142–43; Moo, *The Epistle to the Romans*, 373–76.
49 Morris, *The Epistle to the Romans*, 251–52; Dunn, *Romans 1–8*, 319–20; Murray, *The Epistle to the Romans*, 220–21; Schreiner, *Romans*, 316.
50 Moo, *The Epistle to the Romans*, 453–58; Longenecker, *The Epistle to the Romans*, 659–64; Jewett, *Romans*, 460–67; Wright, 'The Letter to the Romans', 565–67; Fitzmyer, *Romans*, 465, 473–75; Keck, *Romans*, 180, 186–89; Tobin, *Paul's Rhetoric In Its Contexts*, 241–42; Schreiner, *Romans*, 373–74, 390.
51 Porter, *The Letter to the Romans*, 134.

made against them by an adversary: demands in this case of ownership and the requirement for obedience in the form of sinful actions. This explains why Paul can claim believers to be free from sin (Rom. 6:18, 22), and yet still exhort them to flee from it (Rom. 6:11–13, 19). God has declared his people judicially absolved from the requirement to obey sin, and yet this requires believers to live in light of this new reality.

In Luke 18:1–8, Jesus tells the story about a poor and vulnerable widow who is being oppressed by an adversary, and in verse 3 it says she kept coming to the judge to plead for justice.[52] In her plea, the widow uses the closely related verb Ἐκδίκησόν to convey her desire to be legally freed from the unjust demands this adversary was making upon her.[53] She also uses the preposition ἀπό to introduce her opponent, against whom she wishes the corrupt judge to declare her 'in the right'. This woman's plea is not dissimilar to what Paul proclaims has happened in Rom. 6:7. His point is that those who have participated in the death of Jesus are declared 'in the right' from the demands made by 'sin'. They are declared legally free from this oppressive adversary. As Adolf Schlatter said:

> Sin makes its demand upon the sinner; to practice it means to succumb to it, to be mastered by it and to obtain his destiny from it. This was already expressed by the comparison of the dependence upon sin with the condition of a slave; the master controls the slave. But because of his death, every demand of sin upon the individual has ceased [...] every legal demand has been settled; everything that the other party could rightfully claim has been accorded to it.[54]

Before concluding, there is one final issue to resolve. While the debate continues over the perfect tense-form, both Constantine Campbell and Stanley Porter accept that it conveys the most 'marked' aspect, whatever aspect that is (either imperfective or stative).[55] As Porter says: 'The stative (perfect/pluperfect) aspect is more heavily weighted, and to

---

52 Green, *The Gospel of Luke*, 639–40; Stein, *Luke*, 444; Morris, *Luke*, 280.
53 This observation was kindly pointed out to me by David Starling.
54 Schlatter, *Romans*, 143.
55 Campbell, *Basics of Verbal Aspect in Biblical Greek*, 103–04; Porter, *Verbal Aspect*, 245–51.

use it in opposition to the perfective (aorist) and imperfective (present/imperfect) aspects implies the greatest semantic significance'.[56] The implication for Rom. 6:7 is that the perfect tense-form is marking for emphasis the new information being given (the language of 'emphasis' for Rom. 6:7 is Porter's).[57] At one level, the nature of this new information has already been explored: Rom. 6:7 provides the grounds for why the believer should no longer live as slaves to sin. However, there is another reason for why Rom. 6:7 provides new information of significance, and this is because of its development of the concept of δικαιόω from Romans 1–5. This development can best be illustrated through a comparison between Rom. 5:9 and 6:7. Both verses consider Jesus' death, and the meaning of that event for those who participate in it through faith. But whilst in Rom. 5:9, the subsequent result of 'dying' is acquittal from sins (v.8; cf. Rom. 4:1–12; 5:15–17), in Rom. 6:7 it means being declared 'in the right' in the face of sin's oppressive demands for obedience. In other words, the consequent of dying with Christ in both verses is a judicial declaration and neither conveys the process of being set free or of being transformed. But while in 5:9 it is acquittal from sin's guilt, in 6:7 it is vindication from sin's oppression. Thus it would seem Paul uses the perfect tense-form to mark this development in his use of this key term.

This chapter has argued that δικαιόω in Rom. 6:7 concerns the judicial declaration of release that a believer receives on the basis of participation in Jesus' death on the cross. This judicial declaration is not transformative, and so doesn't make them righteous or set them free from sin. Rather it exonerates them from the demands being made by an oppressive adversary. This adversary is sin personified, who seeks to rule over the believer through having them obey its evil demands. But through participation in Jesus' death, the old self is crucified and the body ruled by sin is nullified, such that the believer should no longer serve sin (6:6). Rom. 6:7 thus provides the warrant for Paul's claim that believers should no longer serve sin, and it does so by claiming that God has judicially declared them free from sin's demands. It provides

---

56 Porter, *Idioms of the Greek New Testament*, 22.
57 Porter, *Verbal Aspect*, 90; Porter, *Idioms of the Greek New Testament*, 22.

the bridge between the believer's death to sin, and the call that believers no longer obey it.

Concerning the broader question of the contribution that Rom. 6:7 makes to the understanding of justification in Paul, this verse does remain in continuity with chapters 1–5 in that they both concern a judicial declaration by a judge that the believer is 'in the right'. However, it also constitutes a development because in chapters 1–5 this declaration concerns the guilt of sin whereas in Rom. 6:7 it concerns the demands of sin. Thus for Paul, δικαιόω is more than just an acquittal from sin's guilt; it is also a vindication in the face of sin's oppression as well.

Bibliography

Barrett, C.K.	*Acts 1–14* (ICC; 2 vols. Edinburgh: T&T Clark, 1994).
Beker, J.C.	*Paul The Apostle: The Triumph of God in Life and Thought* (Philadelphia: Fortress Press, 1980).
Black II, C.C.	'Pauline Perspectives on Death in Romans 5–8', *Journal of Biblical Literature* 103.3 (1984), 413–33.
Bruce, F.F.	*Romans: An Introduction and Commentary* (TNTC; Downers Grove: InterVarsity Press, 1985 2nd ed.).
Bruce, F.F.	*The Book of Acts* (NICNT; Grand Rapids: Eerdmans, 1988 revised).
Bultmann, R.K.	*Theology of the New Testament* (K. Grobel, transl.; Waco: Baylor University Press, 2007).
Byrne, B.J.	*Romans* (Sacra Pagina; Collegeville, Minnesota: Liturgical Press, 1996).
Calvin, J.	*Commentary on Romans* (John Owen, transl.; Grand Rapids: Christian Classics Ethereal Library, 1847).
Campbell, C.R.	*Basics of Verbal Aspect in Biblical Greek* (Grand Rapids: Zondervan, 2008).
Campbell, D.A.	*The Deliverance of God: An Apocalyptic Rereading of Justification in Paul* (Grand Rapids: Eerdmans, 2009).
Campbell, D.A.	*The Quest for Paul's Gospel: A Suggested Strategy* (JSNTSup; London: T&T Clark, 2005).

Charlesworth, J.H. (ed.) *Old Testament Pseudepigrapha* (2 vols.; Peabody: Hendrickson, 2010).

Cosgrove, C.H. 'Justification in Paul: A Linguistic and Theological Reflection', *Journal of Biblical Literature* 106.4 (1987), 653-70.

Cranfield, C.E.B. *A Critical and Exegetical Commentary on the Epistle to the Romans:* Volume 1. (ICC; 2 vols.; London: T&T Clark, 2004).

Crenshaw, J.L. 'Sirach', *The New Interpreter's Bible: A Commentary in Twelve Volumes,* Vol. 5: *Proverbs–Sirach* (Nashville: Abingdon Press, 1997).

Dunn, J.D.G. *Romans 1-8* (WBC; Waco: Word Books, 1988).

Dunn, J.D.G. *The Theology of Paul the Apostle* (Grand Rapids: Eerdmans, 1997).

Evans, C.A., & H.D. Zacharias *Old Testament Pseudepigrapha: Greek and English* (Grand Rapids: Eerdmans, 2015).

Fitzmyer, J.A. *Romans: A New Translation with Introduction and Commentary* (The Anchor Bible; New York: Doubleday, 1993).

Gathercole, S.J. 'The Justification of Wisdom (Matt 11.19b/Luke 7:35)', *New Testament Studies* 49.4 (2003), 476-88.

Garlington, D. 'Imputation or Union with Christ? A Response to John Piper', *Reformation & Revival Journal* 12.4 (2003), 45-113.

Gorman, M.J. *Apostle of the Crucified Lord: A Theological Introduction to Paul and His Letters* (Grand Rapids: Eerdmans, 2003).

Green, J.B. *The Gospel of Luke* (NICNT; Grand Rapids: Eerdmans, 1997).

Hill, D. *Greek Words and Hebrew Meanings: Studies in the Semantics of Soteriological Terms* (SNTSMS; Cambridge: Cambridge University Press, 1967).

Jewett, R. *Romans: A Commentary* (Hermeneia; E.J. Epp, ed.; Minneapolis: Fortress Press, 2007).

Jüngel, E. *Justification: The Heart of the Christian Faith* (J.F. Cayzer, transl.; Edinburgh: T&T Clark, 2001).

Käsemann, E. *Commentary on Romans* (G.W. Bromiley, transl. & ed.; Grand Rapids: Eerdmans, 1980).

Käsemann, E.	*New Testament Questions for Today* (London: SCM, 1969).
Keck, L.E.	Romans (ANTC; Nashville: Abingdon Press, 2005).
Kee, H.C.	'Testaments of the Twelve Patriarchs: A New Translation and Introduction', in J.H. Charlesworth (ed.), *The Old Testament Pseudepigrapha* Volume 1: *Apocalyptic Literature and Testaments* (The Anchor Yale Bible Reference Library; New Haven & London: Yale University Press, 1983).
Keener, C.S.	*Acts: An Exegetical Commentary—Acts 3:1–14:28* (4 vols.; Grand Rapids: Baker Academic, 2013).
Leithart, P.J.	'Justification as Verdict and Deliverance: A Biblical Perspective', *Pro Ecclesia* 16.1 (2007), 56–72.
Longenecker, R.N.	*The Epistles to the Romans: A Commentary on the Greek Text* (NIGTC; Grand Rapids: Eerdmans, 2016).
Moo, D.J.	*The Epistle to the Romans* (NICNT; Grand Rapids: Eerdmans, 1996).
Morris, L.	*Luke: An Introduction and Commentary* (TNTC; Downers Grove: InterVarsity Press, 1988).
Morris, L.	*The Epistle to the Romans* (PNTC; Grand Rapids: Eerdmans, 1988).
Murray, J.	*The Epistle to the Romans: The English text with Introduction, Exposition and Notes* (NICNT; Grand Rapids: Eerdmans, 1968).
Nolland, J.	*The Gospel of Matthew: A Commentary on the Greek Text* (NIGTC; Grand Rapids: Eerdmans, 2005).
Petersen, D.G.	*The Acts of the Apostles* (PNTC; Grand Rapids: Eerdmans, 2009).
Polhill, J.B.	*Acts* (New American Commentary; Nashville: Broadman Press, 1992).
Porter, S.E.	*Idioms of the Greek New Testament* (Biblical Languages, Greek; Sheffield: JSOT Press, 1994, 2nd ed.).
Porter, S.E.	*The Letter to the Romans: A Linguistic and Literary Commentary* (New Testament Monographs; Sheffield: Sheffield Phoenix, 2015).

Porter, S.E.	*Verbal Aspect in the Greek of the New Testament with Reference to Tense and Mood* (Studies in Biblical Greek; New York: Peter Lang, 1989).
Sanders, E.P.	*Paul and Palestinian Judaism* (London: SCM, 1977).
Sanders, E.P.	*Paul: The Apostle's Life, Letters and Thought* (Minneapolis: Fortress Press, 2016).
Schlatter, A.	*Romans: The Righteousness of God* (S.S. Schatzmann, transl.; Peabody, Massachusetts: Hendrickson Publishers, 1995).
Schnelle, U.	*Apostle Paul: His Life and Theology* (M.E. Boring, transl.; Grand Rapids: Baker Academic, 2005).
Schreiner, T.R.	*Paul, Apostle of God's Glory in Christ: A Pauline Theology* (Downers Grove: IVP, 2001).
Schreiner, T.R.	*Romans* (Baker Exegetical Commentary on the New Testament; Grand Rapids: Baker Books, 1998).
Schweitzer, A.	*The Mysticism of Paul the Apostle* (London: A&C Black, 1953 2nd ed.).
Scroggs, R.	'Romans 6:7: Ho gar apothanōn dedikaiōtai apo tēs hamartias', *New Testament Studies* 10.1 (1963), 104–08.
Seifrid, M.A.	*Christ, our Righteousness: Paul's Theology of Justification* (New Studies in Biblical Theology; Leicester: Apollos, 2000).
Stein, R.H.	*Luke* (New American Commentary; Nashville: Broadman & Holman Publishers, 1992).
Stuhlmacher, P.	*Gerechtigkeit Gottes bei Paulus* (Forschungen zur Religion und Literatur des Alten und Neuen Testaments; Göttingen: Vandenhoeck & Ruprecht, 1965).
Stuhlmacher, P.	*Paul's Letter to the Romans: A Commentary* (Scott Hafeman, transl.; Louisville: Westminster, 1994).
Stuhlmacher, P.	*Revisiting Paul's Doctrine of Justification: A Challenge to the New Perspective* (Downers Grove: InterVarsity Press, 2001).
Tobin, T.H.	*Paul's Rhetoric in Its Contexts: The Argument of Romans* (Peabody: Hendrickson Publishers, 2004).
Westerholm, S.	*Perspectives Old And New On Paul: The 'Lutheran' Paul and His Critics* (Grand Rapids: Eerdmans, 2004).
Wrede, W.	*Paul* (Boston: American Unitarian Association, 1908).

Wright, B.G.	'To The Reader of Sirach', in A. Pietersma (ed.), *A New English Translation of the Septuagint* (New York: Oxford University Press, 2007), 715–19.
Wright, N.T.	*Paul and the Faithfulness of God:* Volume 2. (Christian Origins and the Question of God; Minneapolis: Fortress Press, 2013).
Wright, N.T.	'The Letter to the Romans: Introduction, Commentary, and Reflections', *The New Interpreter's Bible: A Commentary in Twelve Volumes,* Vol. 10: *Acts, Romans, 1 Corinthians* (Nashville: Abingdon Press, 2002), 393–770.
Ziesler, J.A.	*The Meaning of Righteousness in Paul: A Linguistic and Theological Enquiry* (SNTSMS; Cambridge: Cambridge University Press, 1972).

CHAPTER 7

The Love Tax

David Hughes

Tension and awkwardness pervade Romans 13:1–7. It is seemingly an unnecessary addition within Paul's rhetorical argument to the Roman faith communities. According to some, it is disjointed from its textual context and therefore a later interpolation,[1] To others, it is merely a side note, a nod and a wink to the overwhelming presence of the Roman Empire. The passage has provoked an uneasiness within the ever-evolving world of critical biblical scholarship. There is a growing dissatisfaction about the gospel that Paul preached being manipulated in order to endorse—or, at the very least, to undermine—opposition to violent military campaigns in the twenty-first century.

This uneasiness has resulted in numerous works that have claimed to reveal Paul and his gospel to be consistently subversive of the Imperial order in a manner that is consistent with his Jewish heritage.[2] Commentators have variously described the passage as 'submissive',[3] 'pragmatic',[4] 'alien',[5]

---

1 Walker, *Interpolations*, 221–231; Michel, *Der Brief an die Römer*, 312; Kallas, 'Romans XIII.1–7'; Munro, 'Romans 13:1–7'.
2 See Carter, *Roman Empire*; Horsley, *Jesus and Empire*, 1–14, 129–149; Horsley, 'Rhetoric and Empire', 91; Horsley, *Paul and Empire*; Horsley, *In the Shadow of Empire*; Crossan & Reed, *In Search of Paul*.
3 Denova, 'Paul's Letter to the Romans, 13:1–7', 221.
4 Lategan, 'Romans 13:1–7', 259.
5 Käsemann, *Commentary on Romans*, 352.

'ambivalent',[6] 'counter-imperialist',[7] 'ironic',[8] 'subversive',[9] 'responsible',[10] and 'a clear endorsement of the pagan ruling authorities'.[11] At no point, however, do commentators seriously link vv.1–7 with a message of neighbourliness, or a call to love.[12] In his major commentary on Romans, Ernst Käsemann recognises the possibility of a connection between vv.1–7 and the context of love established in 12:9–21 and revisited in 13:8–10. It is clear he sees this as a possibility because he argues so fervently against it. Käsemann's jaundiced position, no doubt deeply shaped by the Second World War and the betrayal of the German people by its own Government, cannot accept any connection between earthly rulers, and ἀγάπη. For Käsemann, the paragraph is an 'alien body in Paul's exhortation'.[13]

Romans 13:1–7 comes at a dramatic point within the letter to the Roman faith-communities whom Paul was eager to meet. Assuming it is an authentic Pauline writing rather than an inclusion by a later editor, it is necessary that the passage be handled by interpreters as an intentional ingredient in Paul's rhetorical strategy.

This chapter suggests that Romans 13:1–7 is not an awkward addition to Paul's letter, nor is it a passage solely committed to the undermining of the Roman Empire for those with ears to hear. Rather, Romans 13:1–7 is placed within Paul's call to love, that is, his exhortation to exhibit neighbourliness to all—even to the representatives of the Empire. To argue this claim, three elements must be examined: firstly, the relationship between ἀγάπη and πλησίον in Romans 13 and within Paul's social context; secondly, the Genesis 14 account of Abraham and

---

6   Marshall, 'Hybridity', 174.
7   Elliott, 'Romans 13:1–7'.
8   Carter, 'Irony of Romans 13', 210.
9   Lim, 'A Double-Voiced Reading of Romans 13:1–7', 1.
10 Constantineanu, 'The Bible and the Public Arena', 153.
11 Cassidy, 'The Politicization of Paul', 384.
12 Despite noting the apparent 'lack of connection' between vv.1–7 and 'its immediate context', Cranfield, *Romans*, 2.651, notes that the maintenance of the state 'can be regarded as part of one's debt of love to one's neighbour', although this is all he makes of the point. Seemingly, the only connection that N. T. Wright makes between Rom 12 and 13:1–7 is the theme of godly judgement awaiting the ruling class. However, he does emphasise ἀγάπη, though not specifically in reference to 13:1–7; *Paul and the Faithfulness of God*, 1115–6, 1302–04.
13 Käsemann, *Romans*, 352. Like Käsemann, Moo, *Romans*, 790–791, sees little evidence of 'any connection in subject matter'.

Melchizedek—which I suggest is the inspiration for Paul's argument in Romans 13 text; and finally, a brief introduction to the significance of self-sufficiency in the ancient world and why Paul mentions it in Romans 13:8.

Paul's Primary Question

Paul is seeking to answer a land-focused question in Romans 13:1–7, that is, 'how are we to live in this land, one ruled by our oppressors?'.[14] For a diaspora Jew, such a question was pertinent within the first-century Roman Empire, i.e. how are we to live in the empire, especially if we have suffered or inherited the loss of connection with 'ancestral land'? Paul's answer is two-fold, and it is not without tension.

Firstly, Paul encourages the community to live as neighbours to their immediate neighbours, but also to act as loving neighbours to those in power. This is especially distilled in and illustrative of the summation in 13:9, 'Love your neighbour (πλησίον) as yourself', and 15:2, 'Let each one be considerate of our neighbour (πλησίον) for the common good, for upbuilding'.[15]

Secondly, whilst acknowledging the power of the 'governing authorities', in the same 'breath' he undermines their status, their authority and their power upon the land when he declares that they have been 'instituted by God'. They are subsidiaries to a higher power. Paul has also denied the emperor, whether the previous emperor or current, the divine status which was commonly attributed—Paul is in a subtle process of reordering the structure of the imperial cosmic order.[16] This reordering places the instituting authority on Paul's God, rather than the deities promoted by the Roman imperial cult. As such, the might of the Roman Empire is not absolute, its authority is not exhaustive,

---

14 Wright, *Paul and the Faithfulness of God*, 1303.
15 My translation.
16 It is worth noting the Jewish protests against the erection of the imperial statue within the Temple of Jerusalem—an event of such magnitude, Paul would have been almost certainly aware of it. Cf. Philo, *Legat.*, 224. See also Noy, "'A Sight Unfit to See'". However, within Rome, the Emperor's divine status was ubiquitous, even if of a slightly different and more subtle accent from that in the East.

and the seat of the emperor is nothing but a servant to the Pauline God (Rom. 13:1, cf. 8:38–39; 11:32—this includes the Empire's officials; 1 Cor. 15:24–26). Paul does not ask for an uprising, nor does he seek or encourage violence—yet he quietly questions the supposed supremacy of the most powerful empire in the world. But with ἀγάπη love at the forefront of his theological cosmology, Paul continues to acknowledge its place in creation.

While Romans 13 is therefore an inappropriate prooftext to justify ignorant submission to a violent empire, it is also a perfect demonstration of how to live in the land in a way that affirms the core identity of the community: as a neighbour to all.

Ἀγάπη and Πλησίον

Paul's use of πλησίον in Romans 13:8 is a direct quote of the Septuagint translation of Leviticus 19:18—καὶ ἀγαπήσεις τὸν πλησίον σου ὡς σεαυτόν. Translated into English as 'neighbour', the πλησίον is the one for whom love or ἀγάπη is enacted. For the translators of Leviticus 19:18, πλησίον is framed in terms of love, the sort of love between YHWH and YHWH's people, and between individual members of YHWH's people—a love best known as ἀγάπη.[17] Πλησίον, therefore, encourages active participation. It is not a passive recognition of similar geographical proximity, but an identity marker for one who receives love. 'Neighbourliness' then becomes the most appropriate theme of Romans 13, as it is the demonstration of the ἀγάπη motivation that has so influenced the text. By appropriating the Levitical language of πλησίον and ἀγάπη, Paul builds on an established tradition of neighbourliness. He dramatically broadens the scope of ἀγάπη away from a narrow, nationalistic frame as previously expressed in other Jewish texts (cf. Jubilees 46:1).[18] It is evident that such narrow definitions were

---

17 Cranfield, *Romans*, 2.677.
18 Livneh, "'Love Your Fellow as Yourself'", who understands the Jubilees reference as an 'allusion' to Leviticus 19:17–18 and as such, is restricted in interpreting 'kinsman' and 'neighbour' to a 'fellow Israelite'. See also Ateek, 'Who Is My Neighbor?', 158: 'Generally speaking, the Leviticus text reflects our common human nature. It expresses our natural inclination to love those who are close to us and not outsiders'.

common in Paul's milieu, simply because he exerts so much effort arguing against Jewish-exclusivism in his letter to the Galatians, exemplified by the radicalness of his acceptance of gentiles *as* gentiles into the faith (cf. Gal. 2). Paul places the language of Leviticus 19 into relationship with the foreign state, which was exactly the tense reality his audience faced. The restricted, nationalistic definition of love for the neighbour becomes a profound motivator for Paul's expansive and inclusive use of ἀγάπη later in his letter to the Romans.

Romans 13:1–7 is flanked by Paul's call to his Roman addressees to be defined by a culture of ἀγάπη—as it relates to πλησίον ('acting as a neighbour').[19] In the verses preceding Romans 13:1–7, Paul details different ways that ἀγάπη can be expressed. Most significantly, Paul encourages the addressees to 'bless those who persecute you, bless and do not curse them' (v.14). From this point until the end of the chapter, Paul provides a brief guide to living in the midst of persecution and suffering: hating evil whilst holding to good (v.9); affection for one another (v.10); showing honour (v.10); refusing to repay evil for evil (v.17); living peaceably with all (v.18).[20] In the verses following Romans 13:1–7, Paul again makes an impassioned plea for an ἀγάπη-centred community by summarising the commandments—no doubt a touchstone of both individual and communal morality for the local Jewish community. Paul summarises them by directly quoting Leviticus 19:18—love your neighbour as yourself.

Romans 12:9–12 opens Paul's appeal for neighbourliness as initially being focused within the faith community. He immediately sets the standard of ἀγάπη within the community, a community that in its diverse ethnicities can access these universal, wisdom-based ethical principles, only to expand ἀγάπη to include all outside of the community. It appears that such a temperament is inevitable, when Paul writes in 12:3, 'I say to everyone among you not to think of yourself more highly than you ought to think', and later in verse 16, 'associate with the

---

19 Paul's synonymous usage is not unparalleled: 'From the very first the word [πλησίον] has an established place in debates on the commandment of love', Friedrich, 'πλησίον', 316. The Hebraist Muraoka lists the primary meaning of πλησίον is as an identity marker for a neighbour. He includes the adverbial usage [near] of the term as his fourth and final meaning; Muraoka, *Greek-English Lexicon*, 565–66.
20 Or, as Esler labels them 'identity descriptors'; *Conflict and Identity*, 21.

lowly'—which is a confronting challenge to Roman ears. Humility, for Paul, begets love, and love begets neighbourliness.

The shift from exclusive neighbourliness to inclusive neighbourliness reveals Paul's parameters of ἀγάπη and the identity of one's neighbour. The issue of neighbourliness is wrestled with in each of the synoptic Gospels (cf. Matt 19:19, 22:39; Mark 12:32–33; Luke 10:27–29).[21] Neighbourliness also arises in the book of James (2:8, 4:12). Questions of neighbourliness are clearly not unique to Paul, but are widespread within the developing faith-communities of the first-century. All of these scriptural references either quote or are a response to Leviticus 19:18, which is exactly the text Paul quotes in Romans 13. Based on his earlier Pharisaical training, Paul has a well-established familiarity with Leviticus (and the Abrahamic traditions; cf. Romans 4, 1 Corinthians 8, Gal. 1:14, Phil. 3:5).[22] Paul's subtle rebuke of the Roman authorities in 13:1 is particularly fascinating. This rebuke, which is his reordering of the imperial cosmic order, calls the reader back to Leviticus 19:17— 'You shall not hate in your heart anyone of your kin; *you shall reprove your neighbour*, or you will incur guilt yourself'.[23] Commentators have argued for a connection between Leviticus 19:17 and Abraham's rebuke of Abimelech in Genesis 21:25—'Abraham complained to Abimelech about a well of water that Abimelech's servants had seized'.[24] Romans 13:1 is Paul's example of wisely rebuking a neighbour and how the members of the Christian communities of Rome can implement this example in their immediate context. He immediately follows this advice with an encouragement for the community to engage in neighbourly acts, that is, the payment of taxes, which he refines in Romans 13:9, quoting Leviticus 19:18, 'Love your neighbour as yourself'. Loving one's neighbour must include the full gamut of the ἀγάπη experience: humility, traditional rebuke, hospitality, forgiveness, neighbourliness, and the payment of taxes, which is the economic reality that grounds the expression of love as an act of neighbourly hospitality. It is purposefully

---

21 Blumell, 'Beware of Bandits!', 7.
22 See also Murphy-O'Connor, *Paul: A Critical Life*, 59–62; Segal, *Paul the Convert*, 26, 230.
23 Emphasis mine.
24 Milgrom, *Leviticus 17–22*, 1648; Wenham, *Leviticus*, 268. See also the Qumranite text: 1QS 5:25– 6:1 (cf. *T. Gad* 6:3–7; Tobit 4:15; Sir. 19:13–17; Philo, *Spec. Leg.* 2:63; Josephus, *Ant.* 1:212, 1:259).

engaging in the fullness of what it is to live within a context of being a religious minority, and deciding unequivocally to be defined by love. Romans 13 then, is not primarily a work of counter-imperial subversiveness, nor is it a blanket statement about submissiveness, but it is a continuation of the Levitical notion of neighbourliness, modelled by Abraham (on which see below) and fundamental to the developing Christian faith.

The concept of neighbourliness that Paul raises was not foreign to his Roman audience. The language of 'loving your neighbour' certainly resonated with their Graeco-Roman cultural background. Working from the teachings of the Stoic philosopher Hierocles, W. Den Boer comments that, 'The word πλησίον has an important ethical function in the doctrine of concentric circles with man occupying the central place'.[25] Den Boer argues further that the Greek notion of πλησίον did not extend to barbarians or other non-Greeks, since Hierocles' use of the term is specific to citizenship—this is akin to the style of approach found in *Jubilees*.[26] An example of a broader definition of πλησίον is found in *Heauton Timorumenos*, a play by Terence that was first performed in Rome at the Megalesian Games in 163 B.C.E.[27] At one stage in the narrative, the lead character, Menedemus, appears 'concerned about his suffering neighbour, [and] says that, being human, he himself does not regard anything human as foreign; and he acts with accordant care for his fellow'.[28] The driving questions of the play revolve around humanity and neighbourliness, defining the identity of one's neighbour and the way in which one relates to one's neighbour.[29]

One phrase that appears in several classical works is πλησίον τῆς πόλεως ('neighbour of the city').[30] This appears to have been a stock affirmation of someone being a 'good citizen' or a good inhabitant of a region/city—potentially reserved for a notable benefactor. Philo

---

25 Den Boer, *Private Morality*, 62–63. See also Fichtner, 'πλησίον', 312.
26 Den Boer, *Private Morality*, 63–72.
27 Brown, *Terence*, 95.
28 Burnell, 'The Death of Turnus', 195. See also Terence, *Hau.* 75–77.
29 Burnell, 'The Death of Turnus', 199.
30 I am referring to instances when πλησίον τῆς πόλεως is not used in an adverbial way, unlike Diodorus Siculus 13.78.5; see also Reynolds, *Aphrodisias and Rome*, §8.

affirms a couple of people as 'neighbours of everyone and of the city,'[31] and Josephus does similarly.[32] Concepts of neighbourliness could even be connected with political and military alliances, as, for example, in Herodotus' *Histories* 5.66.2.[33] Friendship /alliance /neighbourliness between the emperor and members of the elite class were shown through the wills of the elite. Harry Sidebottom notes that, 'It was a custom to leave something to one's friend (*amici*) in your will. To leave nothing to the emperor was to deny friendship with him.'[34] Such action was politically motivated since 'a declaration that one was not the friend of the emperor was tantamount to a declaration of enmity, which might provoke the mildest of rulers and thus risk confiscation.'[35] This all shows that there are established variations in defining πλησίον that are open to the practical implications of being a neighbour within a Graeco-Roman milieu. It is of the utmost importance that we place Paul within this dynamic context where the definitional parameters of the identity and humanity of a potential neighbour are being thoroughly re-negotiated. Moving beyond stock affirmations, territorial borders, or ethnic criteria, like several of his contemporaries, Paul is in a process of questioning and extending the established definitions.

Ἀγάπη is next used in Romans 13:10: 'Love does no wrong to a neighbour; therefore, love is the fulfilling of the law'.[36] By stating the negative, the positive is argued—love does good to a neighbour. This functions as a call to enact neighbourliness to everyone, including those who are imperial rulers or even oppressors.[37] For Paul, nobody is exempt from ἀγάπη, for neighbourliness must be extended to all (Rom. 13:8–10).[38]

---

31 Philo, *Legat*. 351.
32 Josephus, *AJ*. 1.254.
33 Alliance and friendship also features heavily in 1 Macc. 12. The purposes of giving pledges of all varieties was an act of alliance, friendship, and as far as Paul would interpret: neighbourliness. On this see Kleiner & Buxton, 'Pledges of Empire', especially 59 & 67; cf. Rose, 'The Parthians', 36.
34 Sidebottom, 'Roman Imperialism', 323.
35 Sidebottom, 'Roman Imperialism', 323–24.
36 The Greek translation of Leviticus 19:18 uses the verbal form of ἀγάπη–ἀγαπήσεις, the same is used by Paul in Gal. 5:14.
37 'Here [Paul] explains how one relates to civic and political authorities within the overarching perspective of ἀγάπη,' Esler, *Conflict and Identity*, 332.
38 Note the theological basis that Paul has already provided for this (compare Rom. 3:29–30 and 11:32)

According to Phillip Esler, '[Paul] explains how one relates to civic and political authorities within the overarching perspective of ἀγάπη'.[39] Noting that 'there is... nobody that is not included in "one another"',[40] Cranfield argues that:

> Fulfilment of the law involves not just loving someone other than oneself, but loving *each* man [sic] whom God presents to one as one's neighbour by the circumstance of his being someone whom one *is in a position to* affect for good or ill. The "neighbor" in the NT sense is not someone arbitrarily chosen by us: he is given to us by God.[41]

Cranfield's interpretation of 13:8 confirms Paul's assertion in 13:1 that 'there is no authority except from God'. The authorities, to whom the Roman Christian communities are subject, are instituted by God for the purpose of providing an opportunity for the exercise of neighbourliness on the part of the church. Paul's use of Jewish Scriptural sources demonstrates that he desires to prove his consistency with Mosaic law—Paul is here articulating the significance and relevance of the continuation of the tradition, that is, we live in the land by exhibiting neighbourliness to all.[42]

The evolution that Paul makes in his definition of 'the land' is free from restricted geographical boundaries, and is instead earth-wide. There are even hints that Paul takes this notion one step further into the cosmic realm (cf. Rom. 3:19, Gal. 6:14, Col. 1:15–17). Paul is developing his Jewish inheritance to address the questions raised by Roman imperial realities and the cosmological frame that Rome gave as its authority.

---

39 Esler, *Conflict and Identity*, 332.
40 Cranfield, *Romans*, 2.675; cf. Manson, *Studies in the Gospel and Epistles*, 950.
41 Cranfield, *Romans*, 2.676 (emphasis original).
42 See Esler, *Conflict and Identity*, 333. Ateek, 'Who Is My Neighbour?', 156, describes the opposite of this approach: 'So long as we divide the world and our own communities into friends and enemies, neighbors and strangers, we feel no moral obligation towards those whom we have already designated as outsiders. This distinction between "us" and "them" creates a binary society that shuts the door on viewing the "Other" as a neighbor that deserves to be loved'.

φόρος and τέλος

In order to demonstrate the extent of ἀγάπη in the everyday experience of the community, Paul introduces the payment of taxes as his key example of neighbourliness. 'Pay to all what is due them—taxes (φόρον) to whom taxes are due, revenue (τέλος) to whom revenue is due, respect to whom respect is due, honour to whom honour is due' (Rom. 13:7). Paul uses two terms that refer to specific taxes familiar to his addressees: φόρος and τέλος.[43] Φόρος was the Greek word for the *tributum*, or the 'provincial tax', which was 'a levy placed on people and land that was imposed on everyone in the empire, except Roman citizens living in Roman colonies'.[44] The latter term, τέλος, was the Greek word for *vectigalia*, which were levies on income, goods and services,[45] including the use of public land.[46] Unlike the *tributum*, the *vectigalia* was applicable to Roman citizens. Paul's use of such technical terms shows that he is familiar with the tax system, which is unsurprising considering that he would have encountered it through his trade. Furthermore, the taxation policy had resulted in the build-up of significant tension within Rome.[47] According to Tacitus, 'following persistent demands from the people, who had been accusing the *publicani* of excesses, Nero considered whether he should order the suspension of all indirect taxes and make that his finest gift to the human race' (Tacitus, *Ann.* 13.50–51; cf. Suetonius, *Nero* 10.1). Within a context that passionately promoted the grand benevolence of the emperor, in which even conquest and subjugation were the equivalent of the delivery of a loving gift, that the potential act to relieve the masses of their tax-burden was referred to in such extreme terms is suggestive of the cultural significance of the concept. As for Paul, he commits his focus to taxation because taxation is the point in which an acceptance of the presence and authority of Rome within the land is acknowledged.

---

43   Esler, *Conflict and Identity*, 332–33. For a conflicting perspective of Paul's target, see Nanos, *The Mystery of Romans*, 314–21.
44   Esler, *Conflict and Identity*, 332.
45   Esler, *Conflict and Identity*, 333. See also Dunn, *Romans 9–16*, 766.
46   See Hin, *Demography*, 269.
47   Elliott, 'Romans 13:1–7', 192. See also Philo, *Spec. Leg.* 2:92–95, 3:159–163. Reasoner, *The Weak and the Strong*, 38–39. See also Moo, *Romans*, 792–793.

Whereas Neil Elliott considers that Paul's encouragement to pay taxes is part of a defensive manoeuvre against potential violence in the event that the tension in Rome reached a point where 'tax riots broke out within the city,'[48] Romans 13:1–7 is far more positively motivated. Paul is in a process of crafting 'neighbourliness' as a defining characteristic of the Roman church communities. Paul used φόρος and τέλος as part of his argument to emphasise the necessity for all members of the community, Roman citizen or not, to pay the taxes required of them, for this was a very material demonstration of engaging with their city in a neighbourly way. This demands that none are excluded from the call to neighbourliness. The payment of taxes is neighbourly, an act of πλησίον. The payment of taxes secures the recognition that you are living as a loving neighbour.

Evidently, Paul is attempting to negotiate diaspora realities that the Jesus of the Gospels did not encounter. Most significantly, throughout his letter to the Roman faith-communities, Paul relies upon the example of Abraham, bringing Abrahamic themes into his rhetorical argument with varying degrees of nuance. Paul moves from the intense Abrahamic specifics of chapter 4, into the broad thematic of chapters 11 through 13. As such, when it comes time for Paul to consider the economic demands of neighbourliness, the flow of his Abrahamic inspiration continues. Specifically, this will engage Abraham's tributary tithe to Melchizedek (Gen. 14:20).

After his military victory (Gen. 14:15), Abraham returns to the land and, rather than retaining the spoils of war, Abraham hands over all that had been stolen (Gen. 14:16). Melchizedek, King of Salem, blesses Abraham (Gen. 14:18–20), and in response Abraham makes a further tithe to Melchizedek, giving him 'a tenth of everything' in Abraham's possession. From this point in the narrative, there is no sign of threat against Abraham's movement within the land. The payment of the tithe to Melchizedek signals the conclusion of the preceding violence (14:1–16). The blessing and tithe episode introduced a new degree of peace, freedom, and generosity that had been until then unattainable. Abraham's decision to commit to the tithe payment to his neighbour Melchizedek secured a peaceful existence upon the land which they

---

48 Elliott, 'Romans 13:1–7', 192.

shared. Unlike the author of Hebrews who spiritualises the narrative, Paul takes hold of the Melchizedek episode and borrows the practical elements that most impact his immediate context.

There is nothing in the text that suggests Abraham is 'submitting' to the rule of Melchizedek, particularly since Melchizedek is described as acknowledging Abraham's dependence upon the authority of YHWH (Gen. 14:19–20). Abraham relates to Melchizedek in a manner that encourages neighbourliness between nations.[49] As an act of neighbourliness, the payment of the tithe results in a confirmation of peace, prosperity and progeny for Abraham. Robert Houston Smith comments that regardless of who paid the tithe (whether Melchizedek or Abraham, given the ambiguity of the text), it is clear that the payment confirmed a peaceful future.[50] Melchizedek is regularly associated with righteousness, peace, blessing and promise.

Again reliant upon Abrahamic imagery to bolster his argument as in Romans 4, in chapter 13 Paul appropriates the Genesis 14 concept and places it firmly within the context of imperial Rome—even if the application of tithe as a tax is perhaps an awkward fit. However, it is not unreasonable to argue for a continuation of an Abrahamic influence, already established in Romans 4, rather than the Noahic influence suggested by David Van Drunen.[51]

Nevertheless, Paul encourages the payment of the required tax to the imperial powers as an act of neighbourly love, thereby fulfilling the law (Rom. 13:10). Such action promotes the Kingdom of God to all, and secures a peaceable existence in the land despite the Kingdom of Rome (cf. Rom. 12:18). By acknowledging that the emperor and empire were under the authority of Christ (Rom. 13:1), Paul simultaneously affirms the neighbour, whilst undermining their self-claimed cosmic authority.[52] To act as a neighbour, as far as Paul is concerned, is a fundamental aspect of revealing the Kingdom of God to the world. Robert Jewett

---

49 Habel, *The Land is Mine*, 115–130.
50 Smith, 'Abram and Melchizedek', 134–37. The connection between a tithe and the concept of victory is picked up by Philo, *Congr.* 93, 99. Ellingworth, *Hebrews*, 357, notes that 'righteousness' and 'peace' are strongly associated with Melchizedek. Similarly, Koester, *Hebrews*, 351, links the tithe of Abraham to Melchizedek with 'blessing and promise'.
51 Van Drunen, 'Power to the People'.
52 Jewett, 'Response: Exegetical Support from Romans', 68.

writes that, 'a new empire of inclusion is here seen to be replacing the empire of privilege, power, and domination'.⁵³ Paul's grounding of this Abrahamic notion is (in part) fuelled by pragmatic realism as shown in Romans 13:5: 'Therefore, one must be subject, not only because of wrath but also because of conscience'.⁵⁴ According to Dunn:

> Paul appeals to the moral sensibility of the ancient world ... The counsel would be seen both as socially responsible and as sound common sense (pragmatic). And once again Paul does not separate moral or spiritual obligation from civic responsibility and political reality: civic duty (here subjection to the governing authorities) has the force of moral obligation.⁵⁵

This call to the pragmatic aspects of neighbourliness would have been familiar to Roman ears. Discussions of conscience are scattered throughout Graeco-Roman philosophical traditions and the Stoics, Platonists, and Sophists all engage with the concept in different ways.⁵⁶ In the context of Romans 13, for Paul the conscience acts in a way that encourages neighbourliness towards authorities for the purposes of promoting the historically grounded continuation of the Abrahamic and Levitical principles of 'loving your neighbour'. Such an act goes beyond a purely pragmatic means of avoiding potential conflict, for it is an engagement with the neighbour, despite being the oppressor, whereby they are valued, blessed, and loved. In this way they are included within Paul's expansive, inclusive vision.

53　Jewett, 'Response', 68.
54　The threat of violence at the hand of the empire was never far away.
55　Dunn, *Romans 9–16*, 765–66. Carter, 'Irony of Romans 13', 223, posits an alternative reading of the text: 'the last thing a totalitarian regime wants is a population with a conscience: conscience gets in the way of unquestioning obedience; conscience submits to the authority of God rather than of the state'. However, Carter's reading would twist Paul's message of universal neighbourliness into a quagmire of disguised meaning and, eventually, exclusivity. See further Stein, 'The Argument', 336–40.
56　Atkins, 'Euripides's Orestes', 2; Marietta, 'Conscience in Greek Stoicism'. See also Pierce, *Conscience in the New Testament*, 40–53; and LSJ, sv. συνείδησις.

Genesis 14:23 and Romans 13:8

Immediately following his exchange with Melchizedek, Abraham is offered the reclaimed goods by the king of Sodom (cf. Gen. 14:5–16, 21–24). Rather than accept the lucrative offer, Abraham declines (Gen. 14:23). The text presents two contrasting examples of gift-giving: the first, an offering made by Abraham, the second, an offering refused by Abraham. Some interpret this refusal as an attempt by Abraham to distance himself and his tribe from the morally corrupt people of Sodom.[57] A simpler explanation, however, is that Abraham understands his role upon the land to be a blessing to others within the land, and that the blessing he receives does not come from others, but from YHWH (cf. Gen. 12:2, 24:1).[58] Abraham is careful to avoid the potential situation where he could be in debt to one of his neighbours. There is no way that Abraham, under obligation as a debtor, has the ability to be a blessing, and, therefore, to show neighbourliness to those in the land. In a Roman context, one could argue that the payment of taxes is performed with no other reason but obligation under threat of punishment. However, in Romans 13:8 Paul pushes against this notion. Immediately following his encouragement to his addressees to pay their taxes, so as to be good neighbours to the empire and the local Roman people who were facing the same financial pressures, Paul writes, 'owe no one anything'. On this verse, Cranfield suggests that:

> If then we take εἰ μή in its ordinary sense of 'except', the meaning will be 'Leave no debt outstanding to anyone, except the debt of love to one another'; and the point of the latter part of the sentence will be that the debt of love, unlike those debts which we can pay up fully and be done with, is an unlimited debt which we can never be done with discharging.[59]

It is important to examine the significance of being debt-free in the ancient world, particularly when we approach the never-ending debt of

---

57 Van Wolde, 'Outcry, Knowledge, and Judgement', 71–100; Brodie, *Genesis as Dialogue*, 258–259. See also Philo, *Alleg. Interp.* 3:24, 197; Josephus, *AJ.* 1:179–182.
58 This is similar to the argument in Morschauser, 'Campaigning'.
59 Therefore qualitatively different from the payment of taxes; Cranfield, *Romans*, 2.674.

love that Paul writes about. Αὐτάρκεια, broadly speaking, is to be self-sufficient.[60] It is a notion well-grounded in Graeco-Roman culture.[61] Frederick Brenk writes that αὐτάρκεια 'pervaded virtually all aspects of Greek culture'.[62] Plato, developing his concept of αὐτάρκεια from the myth of Glaukos, states that the 'absolute good' is unachievable without it.[63] Epicurean philosophy contends that αὐτάρκεια produces freedom.[64] This concept was also a regular feature within the writings of the Cynics and the Stoics. For Paul then, to raise thematically the concept of 'owing nothing to anybody' connects strongly in the ancient world with this notion of a self-sufficient, good life. Despite this, Paul takes αὐτάρκεια into new territory. There remains a debt that all must carry and a debt from which they can never be free: the debt of love. As Paul encourages a concept of self-sufficiency that has been a point of vivid discussion in the philosophical, political, and religious world and a notion that is intimately connected with the highest ideals of the ancient world, he immediately pumps the brakes and declares it impossible. To paraphrase: Be free from all debts as much as possible, but never be free from the debt of love to your neighbour—let it be a well that never runs dry—just as Christ's love for all.

Paul's concept of the absolute good denies αὐτάρκεια total control over an individual's or a community's relationship to a neighbour. Love of the neighbour holds a pre-eminent place within Paul's philosophical ethics of self-sufficiency. On Paul's understanding of the dynamics and expansiveness of neighbourliness, it is only in neighbourliness that αὐτάρκεια is expressed and the good life achieved.

On this view, a self-sufficiency (or independence or perhaps even an isolation) that detracts from a relationship with a neighbour is truly an insufficient ingredient of the absolute good and therefore incompatible with the Abrahamic example of neigbourliness.

---

60 Paul echoes this theme in 2 Cor. 9:7–8; cf. 1 Tim. 6:6.
61 Wheeler, 'Note: Self-Sufficiency and the Greek City'; Most, 'The Stranger's Stratagem'. See also LSJ, sv. αὐτάρκεια. Αὐτάρκεια is used throughout the Greek philosophical tradition. Aristotle, *Ethica Nicomachea* 1177a.27; Plato, *Philebus* 67a; Diogenes, *Lives of the Philosophers* 5.63. See also Plutarch, *Comparatio Aristidis et Catonis* 4.2
62 Brenk, 'Sheer Doggedness', 78.
63 Plato, *Philebus*, 67a.7.
64 *Sent. Vat.* 77 (Letter to Menoikeus).

By using πλησίον and ἀγάπη and his thematic use of αὐτάρκεια, concepts familiar to both Jewish and gentile listeners, Paul engages the entire community of the Roman church and calls them beyond mired grumblings about taxation into a new and loving way of thinking: neighbourliness to all, no exceptions.

The Subversiveness of Romans 13:1

Romans 13:1 wears a mask of respect. It appears to be saying one thing, but rather, says something entirely different.[65] It appears to not only justify the existence of the Roman Empire and its conquest narrative, but actually endorse it as being sanctioned by God. It is not far from the statement Josephus attributes to Herod Agrippa II:

> What remains, therefore, is this, that you have recourse to divine assistance; but this is already on the side of the Romans; for it is impossible that so vast an empire should be settled without God's providence. (*BJ.* 2:390)

Readers of Romans 13 should recognise that Paul inherits and takes part in an already established discussion and debate about how Jewish people best ought to negotiate their place within a Roman world. There was no greater power in the world of the first century than that which was held by the Roman Emperor. To many, he was a god among men. To others, he was not merely the leader of the empire, but the father. The emperor was the fulfilment of the imperial values, the literal embodiment of Roman culture, power, and glory. As James Harrison explains:

> The Graeco-Roman writers exalt the ruler as the image of God, the vice-regent of God who is foreknown and commissioned by him, the embodiment of animate law (νόμος ἔμψυχος), the priestly intermediary between his people and the gods, the summation of divine virtue and wisdom, head of the body

---

65 There are even those who suggest that Paul wrote Romans 13 ironically, see Carter, 'Irony of Romans 13', 209–28.

politic, the soul of the *res publica*, and, finally, the world benefactor and the dispenser of mercy.[66]

Paul provides the reader/listener with a revised structure of cosmic authority, one that is profoundly Jewish: God is above all, even the Emperor. This is a challenge to the cosmic structure of the Roman Empire. Paul continues in Romans 13:2 with another challenge to be neighbourly to all: 'whoever resists authority resists what God has appointed, and those who resist will incur judgement' (cf. Lev. 19:17–18). Paul encourages the community to avoid violent reaction to the empire and to instead act as good neighbours—for the governing authorities will eventually be judged by God for their actions—it is only a matter of time. The 'authorities' will be judged, not only for their resistance to God's true authority, but for the violence with which they dominate the land (cf. Rom. 13:4). Paul's warning is in stark contrast to the imperial propaganda concurrent with the writing of this letter, for, with Elliott, Paul's 'reference to the ruler's sword flouted a central theme of Nero's propaganda, according to which the new emperor had ushered in an age of peace without resort to the sword'.[67]

Conclusion

Rather than promoting total complicity with the often abusive authority of governing powers, Romans 13:1–7 encourages a people without power to recognise that God is above all, and, in time, all will answer to God—including those currently in power. This then releases Christians, albeit in small fashion, to operate towards the empire by way of neighbourliness, rather than coercion. It offers the tension of living in peace without selling oneself to Roman ideology.

Hermeneutically, this interpretation of Romans 13 encourages the reader to further broaden the definitional parameters of the identity of our neighbour by revealing a Pauline argument for total inclusivity

---

66 Harrison, *Paul and the Imperial Authorities*, 310. See also Wright, *Paul: Fresh Pespectives*; and Wright, 'Paul's Gospel and Caesar's Empire'.
67 Elliott, 'The Apostle Paul and Empire', 110.

—locally, nationally, and cosmically—opening up a challenging and nuanced discussion about how oppression might be negotiated.

Rather than promoting silent conformity to the rulers as instituted by God, or the demotion of the Emperor from the prime position within imperial propaganda—though this does occur[68]—Romans 13 is Paul's call to the Roman church to follow in the footsteps of the Abrahamic narratives, mandated in Leviticus and expanded by the Jesus tradition, in order to be a good neighbour to all. The payment of taxes is a significant aspect of acting as a πλησίον. Paul argues that the payment of taxes is an opportunity to show neighbourliness to the rulers of the land. It is also an opportunity to partner with neighbouring peoples who are under the same financial burdens and, as such, it is a practical demonstration of being a blessing and not an evil, even to neighbours who persecute (Romans 12:14–21). This is all to answer one important question: 'how are we to live in this land, one ruled by our oppressors?'. Paul's answer is the same as Abraham's: 'with neighbourly love to all'.

---

68 Although this is not Paul's primary objective, it is certainly an important part of his argument.

Bibliography

Ateek, Naim — 'Who Is My Neighbor?', *Interpretation* 62.2 (2008), 156–65.

Atkins, Jed W. — 'Euripedes's Orestes and the Concept of Conscience in Greek Philosophy', *Journal of the History of Ideas* 75.1 (2014), 1–22.

Blumell, Lincoln H. — 'Beware of bandits! Banditry and land travel in the Roman Empire', *Journeys* 8.1–2 (2007), 1–20.

Brenk, Frederick — 'Sheer Doggedness or Love of Neighbor? Motives for Self-Sufficiency in the Cynics and Others', *Illinois Classical Studies* 27/28 (2002–2003), 77–96.

Brodie, Thomas L. — *Genesis as Dialogue: A Literary, Historical, and Theological Commentary* (New York: Oxford University Press, 2001).

Brown, Peter — *Terence: The Comedies* (New York: Oxford University Press, 2006).

Burnell, Peter — 'The Death of Turnus and Roman Morality', *Greece & Rome* 34:2 (1987), 186–200.

Carter, T.L. — 'The Irony of Romans 13', *Novum Testamentum* 46.3 (2004), 209–28.

Carter, Warren — *The Roman Empire and the New Testament: An Essential Guide* (Nashville: Abingdon Press, 2006).

Cassidy, Ron — 'The Politicization of Paul: Romans 13:17 in Recent Discussion', *The Expository Times* 121.8 (2010), 383–89.

Constantineanu, Corneliu — 'The Bible and the Public Arena: A Pauline Model for Christian Engagement in Society with Reference to Romans 13', *KAIROS: Evangelical Journal of Theology* 4.2 (2010), 135–57.

Cranfield, C.E.B. — *Commentary on Romans.* Volume 2: *IX–XVI and Essays* (Edinburgh: T&T Clark, 1979).

Crossan, John Dominic, & Jonathan L. Reed — *In Search of Paul: How Jesus's Apostle Opposed Rome's Empire with God's Kingdom. A New Vision of Paul's Words & World* (New York: HarperCollins, 2004).

Den Boer, W. — *Private Morality in Greece and Rome: Some Historical Aspects* (Leiden: E.J. Brill, 1979).

Denova, Rebecca I. 'Paul's Letter to the Romans, 13:1–7: The Gentile-Christian Response to Civil Authority', *Encounter* 53.3 (1992), 201–229.

Dunn, James D.G. *Romans* (WBC 38; Dallas: Word Books, 1988).

Ellingworth, Paul *The Epistle to the Hebrews: A Commentary on the Greek Text* (Grand Rapids: Eerdmans, 1993).

Elliott, Neil 'The Apostle Paul and Empire', in R.A. Horsley (ed.), *In the Shadow of Empire: Reclaiming the Bible as a History of Faithful Resistance* (Louisville: Westminster John Knox, 2008), 97–116.

Elliott, Neil 'Romans 13:1–7 in the Context of Imperial Propaganda', in Richard A. Horsley (ed.), *Paul and Empire: Religion and Power in Roman Imperial Society* (Harrisburg: Trinity Press International, 1997), 184–204.

Esler, Philip F. *Conflict and Identity in Romans: The Social Setting of Paul's Letter* (Minneapolis: Augsburg Fortress, 2003).

Fichtner, J. 'πλησίον ἀδελφός ἕτερος', *Theological Dictionary of the New Testament*. Volume 6 (G. Kittel & G. Friedrich, eds.; Grand Rapids: Eerdmans, 1968), 311–315.

Friedrich, Gerhard 'πλησίον in the New Testament', *Theological Dictionary of the New Testament*. Volume 6 (G. Kittel & G. Friedrich, eds.; Grand Rapids: Eerdmans, 1968), 316.

Habel, Norman C. *The Land is Mine: Six Biblical Land Ideologies* (Minneapolis: Augsburg Fortress, 1995).

Harrison, James R. *Paul and the Imperial Authorities at Thessalonica and Rome: A Study in the Conflict of Ideology* (WUNT 273; Tübingen: Mohr Siebeck, 2011).

Hin, Saskia *The Demography of Roman Italy: Population Dynamics in an Ancient Conquest Society 21 BCE–14 CE* (New York: Cambridge University Press, 2013).

Horsley, Richard A. 'Jesus and Empire', in Richard A. Horsley (ed.), *In the Shadow of Empire: Reclaiming the Bible as a History of Faithful Resistance* (Louisville: Westminster John Knox Press, 2008), 75–96.

Horsley, Richard A. (ed.), *In the Shadow of Empire: Reclaiming the Bible as a History of Faithful Resistance* (Louisville: Westminster John Knox Press, 2008).

Horsley, Richard A. *Jesus and Empire: The Kingdom of God and the New World Order* (Minneapolis: Augsburg Fortress, 2003).

Horsley, Richard A. 'Rhetoric and Empire—and 1 Corinthians', in Richard A. Horsley (ed.), *Paul and Politics: Ekklesia, Israel, Imperium, Interpretation: Essays in Honor of Krister Stendahl* (Harrisburg: Trinity Press International, 2000), 72–102.

Horsley, Richard A. (ed.) *Paul and Empire: Religion and Power in Roman Imperial Society* (Harrisburg: Trinity Press International, 1997).

Jewett, Robert 'Response: Exegetical Support from Romans and other Letters', in Richard A. Horsley (ed.), *Paul and Politics: Ekklesia, Israel, Imperium, Interpretation: Essays in Honor of Krister Stendahl* (Harrisburg: Trinity Press International, 2000), 58–71.

Kallas, James 'Romans XIII.1–7: An Interpolation', *New Testament Studies* 11 (1964–1965), 365–374.

Käsemann, Ernst *Commentary on Romans* (Grand Rapids: Eerdmans, 1980).

Kleiner, Diana E. E., & Bridget Buxton 'Pledges of Empire: The Ara Pacis and the Donations of Rome', *American Journal of Archaeology* 112.1 (2008), 57–89.

Koester, Craig R. *Hebrews: A New Translation with Introduction and Commentary* (AB 36; New York: Doubleday, 2001).

Lategan, Bernard 'Romans 13:1–7: A Review of Post-1989 Readings', *Scriptura* 110.2 (2012), 259–72.

Lim, Sung U. 'A Double-Voiced Reading of Romans 13:1–7 in Light of the Imperial Cult', *HTS Teologiese Studies / Theological Studies* 71.1 (2015), 1–10.

Livneh, Atar. '"Love Your Fellow as Yourself": The Interpretation of Leviticus 19:17–18 in the Book of Jubilees', *Dead Sea Discoveries* 18 (2011), 173-99.

Manson, T.W. *Studies in the Gospel and Epistles* (M. Black, ed.; Manchester: Manchester University Press, 1962).

Marshall, John W.   'Hybridity and Reading Romans 13', *Journal for the Study of the New Testament* 31.2 (2008), 157–78.

Marietta, Don E., Jr.   'Conscience in Greek Stoicism', *Numen* 17 (1970), 176–87.

Michel, Otto   *Der Brief an die Römer übetsetzt und erklärt* (Göttingen: Vandenhoeck & Ruprecht, 1966).

Milgrom, Jacob   *Leviticus 17–22* (AB 3A; New York: Doubleday, 2000).

Moo, Douglas J.   *The Epistle to the Romans* (NICNT; Grand Rapids: Eerdmans, 1996).

Morschauser, Scott   'Campaigning on Less Than a Shoe-String: An Ancient Egyptian Parallel to Abram's "Oath" in Genesis 13.22–23', *Journal for the Study of the Old Testament* 38.2 (2013), 127–44.

Most, Glenn W.   'The Stranger's Stratagem: Self-Sufficiency in Greek Culture', *Journal of Hellenistic Studies* 109 (1989), 114–33.

Munro, Winsome   'Romans 13:1–7 Apartheid's Last Biblical Refuge', *Biblical Theology Bulletin* 20.4 (1990), 161–68.

Muraoka. T.   *A Greek-English Lexicon of the Septuagint* (Leuven: Peeters, 2009).

Murphy-O'Connor, Jerome   *Paul: A Critical Life* (Oxford: Oxford Paperbacks, 2014).

Nanos, Mark D.   *The Mystery of Romans: The Jewish Context of Paul's Letter* (Minneapolis: Fortress, 1996).

Noy, David   '"A Sight Unfit to See": Jewish Reactions to the Roman Imperial Cult', *Classics Ireland* 8 (2001), 68–83.

Pierce, C.A.   *Conscience in the New Testament* (London: SCM Press, 1955).

Reasoner, Mark   *The Strong and the Weak: Romans 13.1–15.13 in Context* (Cambridge: Cambridge University Press, 1999).

Reynolds, Joyce   *Aphrodisias and Rome* (London: The Society for the Promotion of Roman Studies, 1982).

Rose, Charles Brian   'The Parthians in Augustan Rome', *American Journal of Archaeology* 109.1 (2005), 21–75.

Segal, Alan F.   *Paul the Convert: The Apostolate and Apostasy of Saul the Pharisee* (New Haven: Yale University Press, 1990).

Sidebottom, Harry   'Roman Imperialism: The Changed Outward Trajectory of the Roman Empire', *Historia: Zeitschrift für Alte Geschichte* 54.3 (2005), 315–30.

Smith, Robert Houston   'Abram and Melchizedek (Gen 14:18–20)', *Zeitschrift für die alttestamentliche Wissenschaft* 77.2 (1965), 129–53.

Stein, Robert H.   'The Argument of Romans 13:1–7', *Novum Testamentum* 31.4 (1989), 325–43.

Van Drunen, David   'Power to the People: Revisiting Civil Resistance in Romans 13:1–7 in Light of the Noahic Covenant', *Journal of Law and Religion* 31.1 (2016), 4–18.

Van Wolde, Ellen J.   'Outcry, Knowledge, and Judgement in Genesis 18–19', in Diana Lipton (ed.), *Universalism and Particularism at Sodom and Gomorrah: Essays in Memory of Ron Pirson* (Atlanta: Society of Biblical Literature, 2012), 71–100.

Walker, William O., Jr.   *Interpolations in the Pauline Letters* (London: Sheffield Academic Press, 2001).

Wenham, Gordon J.   *The Book of Leviticus* (NICOT; Grand Rapids: Eerdmans, 1979).

Wheeler, Marcus   'Note: Self-Sufficiency and the Greek City', *Journal of the History of Ideas* 16.3 (1955), 416–20.

Wright, N.T.   *Paul and the Faithfulness of God* (Minneapolis: Fortress Press, 2013).

Wright, N.T.   *Paul: Fresh Perspectives* (London: SPCK, 2005).

Wright, N.T.   'Paul's Gospel and Caesar's Empire,' in Richard A. Horsley (ed.), *Paul and Politics: Ekklesia, Israel, Imperium, Interpretation: Essays in Honor of Krister Stendahl* (Harrisburg: Trinity Press International, 2000), 160–83.

CHAPTER 8

The Intercession of Christ in Romans 8:34[1]

Peter Orr

Although the idea Christ interceding is found only in Romans 8:34 and Hebrews 7:25, the idea has had a doctrinal impact far beyond its textual frequency. However, the precise activity involved has been a matter of debate. Focusing on Romans 8:34, this chapter considers the verb ἐντυγχάνω ('I intercede'), in order to elucidate what activity Paul considers Christ to be engaged in.

In the 3rd and 4th Centuries some used it to 'prove' the inferiority of the Son to the Father.[2] In reaction, others asserted that it was not 'a proof [...] of inferiority' but an accommodation[3] to more clearly show the depth of God's love for us.[4] As such it was understood figuratively *in light of* the Son's relationship to the Father, since, given his equality, he could not 'require to be a suppliant' to intercede for us.[5]

When Arianism, of a kind, was later revived in the anti-Trinitarianism of the late 16th century,[6] similar debates turning on the intercession of Christ emerged. Calvin, for example, argued that 'those err very

---

1 Parts of this paper appear in Orr, *Exalted Above the Heavens*.
2 Tait, *The Heavenly Session*, 149. See also p.153 where he quotes Theodoret on Romans 8:34, 'the heretics say that the Son [makes petition] according to His Deity'.
3 Chrysostom, *Homilies*, 269.
4 Chrysostom, *Homilies,* 270, to 'shew the warmth and vigourousness of His love for us'.
5 Chrysostom, *Homilies,* 269. cf. Gregory Nazianzen, *Faith Gives Fullness*, 272: Christ is not 'a slave who falls prostrate before the Father on our behalf'.
6 See, for example, the discussion in Godbey, 'Socinus and Christ'.

grossly, who imagine that Christ falls on his knees before the Father to pray for us', since this would 'detract from the celestial glory of Christ'.⁷ Calvin understood that Christ's 'death and resurrection stand in the place of eternal intercession, and have the efficacy of a powerful prayer for reconciling and rendering the Father propitious to us'.⁸ Calvin, thus, understands intercession more broadly as mediation and thus as a summary of the entirety of Christ's work.⁹ So, in discussing Romans 8:34, he argues that 'God justifies us by the intercession of Christ'.¹⁰ In contrast, Luther, who predated the anti-Trinitarian controversies, sees Christ's intercession as unqualified prayer on our behalf. The content of this prayer is simply '"Father, I have suffered for this person; I am looking after him"' and as such '[t]his prayer cannot be in vain'.¹¹

In Romans 8:34, what exactly does Paul mean when he describes Christ as interceding for us? Does he understand Christ to be continually praying for us, as Luther, or is his intercession more figurative and metonymy for his death for example, as Calvin?

Word Study

In non-Biblical Greek, the broad semantic range of this word referred to an encounter.¹² Within this range, the word frequently has a verbal communicative focus—often used of making a petition,¹³ either for complaint¹⁴ or advocacy.¹⁵ In a religious context it can mean to 'pray for' someone.¹⁶ Less frequently, the verb can also mean 'to find oneself

---

7   Calvin, '1 John', 2:1.
8   Calvin, 'Romans', 8:34; cf. Calvin, *Institutes*, III.xx.20: 'But we do not imagine that he, kneeling before God, pleads as a suppliant for us; rather, with the apostle we understand he so appears before God's presence that the power of his death avails as an everlasting intercession in our behalf'.
9   Cf. Calvin, *Institutes*, III.xi.16: 'with Christ's righteousness *interceding* and forgiveness of sins accomplished [the believer] is justified' [emphasis added].
10 Calvin, *Institutes*, III.xi.3.
11 Luther, *LW* 30: 236.
12 Examples include Xenophon, *Anabasis*, IV.2.10—used with ὑπέρ; Aristophanes, *Acharnians*, 845; Demosthenes, *Against Medias*, 88; Herodotus I.134; II.70.
13 E.g. Polybius, *The Histories*, IV.76.9
14 Bauernfeind, 'ἐντυγχάνω', 8.243, lists P.Giss., I, 36, 15.
15 E.g. P.Tebt., I, 183.
16 Bauernfeind, 'ἐντυγχάνω', 8.243, lists BGU, I, 246, 12.

somewhere,[17] 'confer',[18] and even 'read'.[19]

In the LXX ἐντυγχάνω can mean 'appeal';[20] 'read'[21]; and 'pray' (Wis. 8:21; 16:28). In Jewish Hellenistic writing, the verb is 'used in various senses for human relations'.[22] So for example: 'to encounter';[23] 'to meet (admit) envoys';[24] 'to approach' someone with a request;[25] 'to pray for';[26] 'to raise a complaint';[27] 'to have an audience with someone'.[28] It can also mean 'to read'.[29] Outside of Romans 8 and Hebrews 7, the verb is used twice in the NT. In Acts 25:24, the Jewish community 'petition' or 'appeal to' Festus, while in Romans 11:2, Elijah 'complains' against Israel.

Though the word can have broader meanings ('read', 'encounter'), by far the most common idea (especially in reference to God) is that of verbal communication. However, although these results would suggest a reference to prayer, the question of a figurative understanding of ἐντυγχάνω in Romans 8:34 remains open. It is complex because not only is it 'difficult to draw a firm line between literal and non-literal uses of language',[30] but also because there are examples of 'Greek words that, while attested in non-biblical literature, appear to be used in a unique fashion by the biblical writers'.[31] Paul could be using ἐντυγχάνω in a figurative sense that may have been clear to their original readers. So, we may have an instance of ellipsis where ἐντυγχάνω was understood to mean 'intercede *by his presence*',[32] or as an umbrella term for a

---

17 E.g. Aristophanes, *Acharnians*, 848; Eur. *Alc.*, 1032.
18 E.g Plutarch, *Lives: Cato the Younger*, XLIX.3—used with ὑπέρ.
19 E.g. Polybius, *Histories*, I.xv.13—here used with ὑπέρ.
20 Daniel 6:13, where it is used to render the *qrv* (to appeal); 1 Macc. 8:32; 10:61, 63, 64; 11:25; 2 Macc. 4:36; 3 Macc. 6:37.
21 2 Macc. 2:25; 6:12; 15:39.
22 Bauernfeind, 'ἐντυγχάνω', 8.243.
23 Josephus, *Wars* 2, 305.
24 Bauernfeind, 'ἐντυγχάνω', 8.243, lists *Epistle of Aresteas*, 174.
25 Josephus, *Wars*, 1, 278, 281, 298; *Ant.*, 12, 18.
26 Philo, *Life of Moses* 1, 173.
27 Josephus, *Antiquities*, 16, 170.
28 Josephus, *Wars* 1, 256.
29 Philo, *Spec. Leg.*, IV, 161—here used with ὑπέρ.
30 Saeed, *Semantics*, 16; cf. Nida & Louw, *Lexical Semantics of the Greek New Testament*, 70.
31 Silva, *Biblical Words*, 75, and the examples discussed, pp. 79–97.
32 E.g. Westcott, *Hebrews*, 231. For a fuller discussion of ellipsis see Silva, *Biblical Words*, 82–83.

wider range of cultic activities.³³ Alternatively, we may have an example of metonymy where ἐντυγχάνω is understood in the broader sense of 'intervenes'.³⁴

Obviously to answer that we need to consider the word more closely in its context in Romans 8:34.

ἐντυγχάνω in Romans 8:34

Towards the end of the chapter Paul reflects on the certainty of God's love for Christian believers, but he then considers the reality of opposition—Satanic or otherwise:

> 8:31 What then shall we say to these things? If God is for us, who can be against us?
>
> Τί οὖν ἐροῦμεν πρὸς ταῦτα; εἰ ὁ θεὸς ὑπὲρ ἡμῶν, τίς καθ᾽ ἡμῶν;

Falling in the last section of that chapter, it matches 5:1–11 in assuring believers that they will, in fact, be glorified.³⁵ The section opens with the familiar τί οὖν ἐροῦμεν ('What then shall we say?') which Paul has used already in Romans to progress the argument.³⁶ Here the question is qualified by πρὸς ταῦτα ('in view of these things').³⁷ Given the repetition of themes found in 5:1–11 in 8:31–39, it would seem best to see 'these things' as referring to what Paul has taught in the entire preceding section of the letter.

As such, Paul's summary of Romans 5–8 is expressed simply as ὁ θεὸς ὑπὲρ ἡμῶν ('God [is] for us'). This echoes the language in 5:6–8 where **ὑπέρ** is used four times—each time referring to or illustrating Christ's death and perhaps suggests that Paul's emphasis here is 'not a concept of God but the saving act centred in the death of Jesus'.³⁸ As part of a

---

33 Spicq, *L'Épître aux Hébreux*, 1:69.
34 Kurianal, *Jesus Our High Priest*, 136; Torrance, *Space, Time and Resurrection*, 116. For a fuller discussion of metonymy, see Silva, *Biblical Words*, 83–84.
35 See the discussion on structure in Moo, *Romans*, 290–94.
36 In exact form in 4:1; 6:1; 7:7 and later in 9:14; 9:30. See also 3:1 τί οὖν.
37 πρός has been understood as 'about' or 'in view of', e.g. Moule, *An Idiom Book*, 63, but the latter seems to suit better given that Paul is about to unpack the implications of 'these things'.
38 Käsemann, *Romans*, 247, quoted in Jewett, *Romans*, 536.

conditional sentence this summary statement repeats the lesser to the greater argument Paul has already employed in chapter 5—if God is now reconciled to us, how can anyone else stand against us.

This lesser to the greater rhetoric is expanded in the following verse

> ³² He who did not spare his own Son but gave him up for us all, how will he not also with him graciously give us all things?

> ὅς γε τοῦ ἰδίου υἱοῦ οὐκ ἐφείσατο ἀλλ᾽ ὑπὲρ ἡμῶν πάντων παρέδωκεν αὐτόν, πῶς οὐχὶ καὶ σὺν αὐτῷ τὰ πάντα ἡμῖν χαρίσεται;

God's gracious activity in the past in the giving of his own Son gives confidence of his future 'easier' action of giving all things needed. The scope of τὰ πάντα has been understood as either the broad idea of sharing in God's sovereignty over the universe (Dunn, Jewett),[39] or the narrower idea of everything that we need to secure our final salvation (Cranfield, Moo).[40] Perhaps we do not need to decide since the former presumes the latter. However, on balance, it would seem that given the parallel with 5:1–11, and in light of 5:9–10, the idea of everything that believers need to secure our final salvation is especially in focus. This, I think, may help us later when we focus in on the scope of Christ's intercession.

The punctuation of vv.33–34 has long been disputed. Moo lists five of the most common ways that the clauses can be related[41] and argues that the most likely arrangement is to read the two verses as each containing a question and an answer as in the NASB: '33 Who will bring a charge against God's elect? God is the one who justifies; 34 who is the one who condemns? Christ Jesus is [...] for us'.[42] This means that the questions in the passage all start with interrogative pronouns and this 'maintains the vivid question-answer style used throughout the paragraph'.[43] Moo further argues that θεὸς ὁ δικαιῶν and τίς ὁ κατακρινῶν belong together and as such the latter should not be seen as a 'fresh, independent question but a "follow-up"' on the discussion in v.33 on

---

39 Dunn, *Romans 1–8*, 502; Jewett, *Romans,* 538.
40 So e.g. Moo, *Romans,* 541; Cranfield, *Romans I–VIII,* 437.
41 Moo, *Romans,* 541 n. 27.
42 See Wright, 'The Letter to the Romans', 461.
43 Moo, *Romans,* 541 n. 28.

the basis 'that "condemn" and "justify" are natural contrasts'.[44] In other words, the question in v.34 should be seen as 'an additional rhetorical response to the statement in v.33b'.[45] Similarly Cranfield sees θεὸς ὁ δικαιῶν and τίς ὁ κατακρινῶν belonging closely together and furnishing the answer to the question of who will bring charges against God's elect with the sense of it is 'God who justifies, who can condemn?'.[46] However, Talbert suggests that vv.31–34 break down into: a transitional question (v.31a) followed by three rhetorical questions (v.31b, v.33a, v.34a). There is not a great deal of difference between these two views, but perhaps Talbert's is to be preferred as it allows each of the interrogative pronouns to have the same force.

How then should the answers to each of Paul's questions be read? It could be that he answers each with an implied 'No One!' and then gives supporting evidence (v.32, v.33b, v.34b).[47] Alternatively, it could be that each is answered with a rhetorical question. This is certainly the case in v.32, but v.33b ('God who justifies?') and v34b ('Christ Jesus who died [...]?') could also function as rhetorical questions. Thus each answer would have the same force, pointing out the good that God and Christ have done, and so the *absurdity* of thinking they could oppose us. We will note the relevance of this in our discussion of Christ's intercession in v.34, seeing it not so much a *direct* answer to τίς ὁ κατακρινῶν (and thus having to be understood *entirely* in juridical categories), but rather part of the general description of Christ thus showing the inappropriateness of considering him as the answer.

On this reading, Paul asks three (separate but related) questions and answers each rhetorically. 'If God is for us, who can be against us?' (v.31b); 'He who did not spare his own Son but gave him up for us all, how will he not also with him graciously give us all things?' (v.32). 'Who will bring a charge against God's elect?' (v.33a); 'God who justifies?' (v.33b). 'Who is the one who condemns?' (v.34a); 'Christ who died [...]?' (v.34b).

---

44   Moo, *Romans*, 542.
45   Moo, *Romans*, 542.
46   This is a summary of Cranfield, *Romans I–VIII*, 437–38.
47   Talbert, *Romans*, 226.

⁣³³ Who shall bring any charge against God's elect? God who justifies?

³⁴ Who is to condemn? Christ Jesus the one who died—more than that, who was raised—who is at the right hand of God, who indeed is interceding for us?

³³ τίς ἐγκαλέσει κατὰ ἐκλεκτῶν θεοῦ; θεὸς ὁ δικαιῶν;
³⁴ τίς ὁ κατακρινῶν; Χριστὸς Ἰησοῦς ὁ ἀποθανών, μᾶλλον δὲ ἐγερθείς, ὃς καί ἐστιν ἐν δεξιᾷ τοῦ θεοῦ, ὃς καὶ ἐντυγχάνει ὑπὲρ ἡμῶν;

The question raised in v.33, then, is 'who will bring a charge against God's elect?' It is generally agreed that ἐγκαλέσει is a forensic term.[48] While the verb is future, rather than seeing a focus on the final judgment,[49] 'the context of present opposition and persecution in the last half of this chapter' perhaps leans us towards seeing the charges as 'the constant opposition of opponents throughout history'.[50] As such, although Satan is included in the list of those who condemn and oppose Christians, we do not need to see him specifically in mind.[51] Those that have charges brought against them are described as the ἐκλεκτῶν θεοῦ ('chosen by God').[52] This section seems to be an echo of Isaiah 50:8–9 and as such Paul may be implying that 'just as God will vindicate the servant, so too the heavenly court will clear believers'.[53]

The absurdity of the charge is answered by the rhetorical 'God who justifies' with the immediate repetition of θεός increas[ing] the emphasis on it'.[54] Dunn has argued that the present tense of the participle (ὁ δικαιῶν) is an indication that justification is an on-going event.[55] However, the broader use of justification in Paul would indicate that

---

48 BDAG; Moo, *Romans,* 541; Schreiner, *Romans,* 462; Dunn, *Romans 1–8,* 502; Cranfield, *Romans I–VIII,* 438; cf. Acts 19:38, 40; 23:29; 26:2, 7, and in the LXX particularly Prov.19:5; Zech 1:4; Wis. 12:12; Sir. 46:19.
49 Moo, *Romans,* 541; Schreiner, *Romans,* 462; Dunn, *Romans 1–8,* 502.
50 Osborne, *Romans,* 426, following Calvin. As such Käsemann, *Romans,* 248, sees the future as logical.
51 So Dunn, *Romans 1–8,* 502; Käsemann, *Romans,* 248; contra Cranfield, *Romans I–VIII,* 438 n.3.
52 ἐκλεκτῶν θεοῦ is a genitive of agency. See Wallace, *Greek Grammar Beyond the Basics,* 126.
53 Schreiner, *Romans,* 461.
54 Dunn, *Romans 1–8,* 503.
55 Dunn, *Romans 1–8,* 503.

justification is a 'verdict rendered at the moment of conversion'.[56] Secondly, the emphasis is not so much the activity—but rather a description of God as the one who justifies.

Paul continues with another question at the start of v.34—who will condemn? κατακρινῶν is most likely a future. However, this future tense form would reflect the 'hypothetical question-and-answer'[57] form rather than referring to the future eschatological judgment. Again the absurdity of the charge is answered by the rhetorical 'Christ?' who is then described in an ascending series of terms.[58] Christ died—and more than that was raised.

Paul continues his description of Christ as ὅς καί ἐστιν ἐν δεξιᾷ τοῦ θεοῦ, ὅς καί ἐντυγχάνει ὑπὲρ ἡμῶν. The first clause, ὅς καί ἐστιν ἐν δεξιᾷ τοῦ θεοῦ ('who is at the right hand of God'), is generally recognised to be an allusion to Psalm 110[LXX 109]:1.[59] However, a number of questions are raised by this phrase. For a start, it needs to be recognised that there is a difference in form from that in the LXX—ἐκ δεξιῶν μου. It is possible that Paul is referring to a different Greek text or rendering the Hebrew directly.[60] Perhaps a rendering of the Hebrew may reflect a contemporary stylistic preference,[61] as might be suggested by the fact that in Hebrews whenever the author alludes to the Psalm he uses ἐν δεξιᾷ (1:3; 8:1; 10:12; 12:2), while in his direct quote in 1:13 he uses ἐκ δεξιῶν.[62] However, on balance, given that almost the exact same form of the allusion in Romans 8:34 is found in 1 Peter 3:22 (ὅς ἐστιν ἐν δεξιᾷ τοῦ θεοῦ), it is more likely that Paul is referring to an existing Christological formulation.[63] This does not, however, rule out a conscious reference to the psalm. As Hay argues, since Paul quotes the Psalm in 1 Cor 15.25, he is probably conscious of alluding to it in Rom 8:34.[64] However, the

---

56 Moo, *Romans*, 542 n. 32.
57 Porter, *Verbal Aspect in the Greek of the New Testament*, 418.
58 Cranfield, *Romans I–VIII*, 438–39.
59 So e.g. Jewett, *Romans*, 542; Cranfield, *Romans I–VIII*, 439; Schreiner, *Romans*, 463; Käsemann, *Romans*, 248 [240]; Moo, *Romans*, 542.
60 לִימִינִי
61 Hay, *Glory at the Right Hand*, 37.
62 Hay, *Glory at the Right Hand*, 35.
63 Cf. Col 3:1: Χριστός ἐστιν ἐν δεξιᾷ τοῦ θεοῦ. Hay, *Glory at the Right Hand*, 40. See also Eskola, *Messiah and the Throne*, 185; Hengel, *Studies in Early Christology*, 142–143.
64 Hay, *Glory at the Right Hand*, 43 n. 31.

question remains concerning how much of the Psalm actually informs Paul's use here. The main issue to consider is the relationship of this clause to the one following, i.e. between Christ being seated at God's right hand and his intercession. Is Paul, in alluding to Psalm 110:1, also alluding to Psalm 110:4 and hence seeing Christ's intercession as that of a priest-king in the order of Melchizidek? Or is the reference to Psalm 110:1 a reference to his identity as Messiah and his intercession a function of that office?

A radical proposal is offered by Hay in his *Glory at the Right Hand*. In considering the link between Christ's position at God's right hand and his intercession, Hay argues that Paul's use of Psalm 110:1 here is mainly an expression of Christ's *honour* and it is this honour which 'guarantees the hope of his followers'.[65] Hay raises a further question—the time of this intercession. He argues that it 'seems to be' that of the eschatological judgment.[66] This fits with the fact that 'Rom 8.31–39 is primarily concerned with the future'.[67] Also, having surveyed the references to Psalm 110:1 in the NT, Hay argues it is 'a serious mistake to claim that early Christian references to Psalm 110:1*b regularly* express convictions about Christ reigning as a royal lord in the present era'.[68] Although this is the case in Eph 1:20, this is not the norm. Hence, 'while 8.34 says nothing to deny that Christ is now at God's right hand, its driving concern is with the future eschatological acquittal of believers'.[69] However, this view cannot be sustained. Eskola, for example, has pointed out that it is not just Eph 1:20 where Christ's exaltation is tied to his *present* rule. In 1 Cor 15:25 Christ reigns 'until he has put all his enemies under his feet'.[70] Christ's reign has commenced with his resurrection. Further, the context of this passage may contain things yet in the future (e.g. v.38 'death') but specifically mentions 'life', 'the present' (v.38 ἐνεστῶτα).

If we do see this intercession as present and related to Christ's present rule—what is the nature of that relationship? Fay sees a reference to Psalm 110:1 alone and argues that it is purely this throne room setting

---

65 Hay, *Glory at the Right Hand*, 60.
66 Hay, *Glory at the Right Hand*, 131.
67 Hay, *Glory at the Right Hand*, 59.
68 Hay, *Glory at the Right Hand*, 91, emphasis added.
69 Hay, *Glory at the Right Hand*, 60.
70 Eskola, *Messiah and the Throne*, 183.

that informs the use of the intercession motif. Jesus 'continues to intercede for [his people] as vice-regent'.[71] He notes that Paul does not appeal to the metaphor of the high priest anywhere else in Romans.[72] Moo, on the other hand, argues that Christ is 'acting as our High Priest'.[73] Similarly, Eskola argues that Paul is using this priestly motif as a 'counterpoint' to the judicial discourse.[74] Hengel also argues 'on the basis of the unique connection between resurrection, sitting at the right hand and intercession other than in Hebrews' that the reference to intercession here is dependent on the reference to the priesthood of Melchizedek in Psalm 110:4.[75] He argues that the parallel in Hebrews 7:25 makes this assumption probable.

This priestly connection might support a figurative understanding of intercession i.e. it is functioning as an umbrella term for a range of priestly activities rather than a specific reference to on-going prayer.

However, two features I think suggest that what is in view is not a metonymic understanding of intercession, but that Paul envisages on-going prayer on the part of Christ. First, an allusion to Isaiah 53:12 and second, the parallel reference to the intercession of the Spirit earlier in the chapter.

Possible Allusion to Isaiah 53:12

Very few commentators have seen a significant link between Christ's intercession in Romans 8:34 and that of the Suffering Servant in Isaiah 53:12.[76] For instance, neither of the two recent studies on Paul's use

---

71 Fay, 'Was Paul a Trinitarian?', 340.
72 Fay, 'Was Paul a Trinitarian?', 340–41.
73 Moo, *Romans*, 543, who does not make reference to Psalm 110:4. See also, for very different reasons, Eskola, *Messiah and the Throne*, 185–86.
74 Eskola, *Messiah and the Throne*, 186
75 Hengel, *Studies in Early Christology*, 159.
76 None of the following refer to it: Achtemeier, *Romans*; Barrett, *Romans*; Barth, *Romans*; Black, *Romans*; Byrne, *Romans*; Calvin, 'Commentary on Romans'; Dodd, *Romans*; Fitzmyer, *Romans*; Godet, *Romans*; Haldane, *Romans*; Jewett, *Romans*; Käsemann, *Romans*; Keck, *Romans*; Leenhardt, *Romans*; Lloyd-Jones, *Romans*; Moo, *Romans*; Morris, *Romans*; Nygren, *Romans*; Osborne, *Romans*; Sanday & Headlam, *Romans*; Schlatter, *Romans*; Stott, *Romans*; Talbert, *Romans*; Ziesler, *Romans*.

of Isaiah in Romans raise the possibility of a link.[77] Bruce, Cranfield, Dunn and Peterson do note the possibility of an allusion or echo to Isaiah 53:12 but no-one that I have found develops the link.[78]

There are a number of reasons that might suggest that Paul, in fact, did not intend any allusion to be made with Isaiah at this point. The conclusion of Isa 53 is rendered וְלַפֹּשְׁעִים יַפְגִּיעַ by the MT. The ESV is typical of most English versions in translating this 'and makes intercession for the transgressors'. However, the LXX has καὶ διὰ τὰς ἁμαρτίας αὐτῶν παρεδόθη ('and he was delivered because of their iniquities'). There are good reasons for following the MT and seeing the LXX as a particularly 'free' translation at this point.[79] Certainly the Targum of Isaiah sees the idea of intercession as key to Isaiah 53. In this chapter, the Servant is specifically identified as the Messiah, and as well as v.12, intercession is introduced in vv.4, 7 and 11.[80] There is a great deal of re-interpretation that goes into the chapter, with the prosperity of the Messiah as expressed in 52:13 seen as the hermeneutical key. Thus, statements referring to the death and suffering of the Servant are changed to apply to others (Gentiles, the wicked etc.).[81]

However, the question remains as to whether Paul is actually referring to Isaiah 53:12 in Romans 8:34 especially given that there is only a connection of one word—and in a different language.[82]

In both Isaiah 53:12 and Romans 8:34 intercession is positioned climactically. The intercession of the Servant in v.12 is in contrast to the rest of the song when he is silent (cf. Is 53:7) and passive.[83] In fact, he 'does nothing and says nothing but let's everything happen to him'.[84] When he does speak we might expect that he would protest his

---

77 Wagner, *Heralds of the Good News*; and Shum, *Paul's Use of Isaiah in Romans*.
78 Studies on Romans, which make reference to but do not develop the link, are Cranfield, *Romans I–VIII*, 439 n.2; Dunn, *Romans*, 504, who approvingly quotes Kleinknecht, *Der Leidende Gererchtfertigte*, 345; also Murray, *Romans 1–8*, 329; Peterson, *Romans*; Wright, 'The Letter to the Romans', 613. Similarly, for studies on Isaiah, see Goldingay & Payne, *Isaiah 40–55 Volume II*, 330; Young, *Isaiah 40–66*, 359; Zimmerli & Jeremias, *The Servant of God*, 65.
79 Seeligman, Isaiah, 128; 165 n.35; cf. Jobes & Silva, Invitation to the Septuagint, 215.
80 Stenning, *The Targum of Isaiah*, 180, and Chilton, *The Isaiah Targum*, 103–5.
81 Ådna, 'The Servant of Isaiah 53', 189.
82 Although, arguably, 'most early Christian exegesis of the Old Testament was done with reference to the Hebrew text, even when the Greek text was also employed'; Bauckham, *Crucified God*, 50.
83 Groves, 'Atonement in Isaiah 53', 85.
84 Clines, *I, He, We and They*, 64–65.

innocence, but, rather, he intercedes for the guilty. This is surprising and the surprise 'is accented by its position as the final clause in the song'.[85] This climactic accent on intercession in Isaiah 53:12 is matched in Romans 8:34. A number of commentators have recognised the climactic nature of the series with the focus building to intercession.[86] So, the addition of μᾶλλον δέ before ἐγερθείς implies progression as does the καί [...] καί syntax which could be translated as 'not only [...] but also'— who is not only at the right hand of God but also intercedes for us.[87]

In the immediate context of Romans 8 a number of references to Isaiah 53 have been suggested. Paul's contention in v.32 that God did not spare (ἐφείσατο) his own son but gave him up for us all has been linked to Isaiah 53:6 (κύριος παρέδωκεν αὐτὸν ταῖς ἁμαρτίαις ἡμῶν).[88] A further allusion has been noted between Romans 8:31b, 33–34 and Isaiah 50:8–9. As well as the linguistic and syntactical similarities between these two texts,[89] both deal with the inability of anyone to bring charges against those justified by God.[90]

As well as considering possible individual allusions, the cumulative effect must be taken into consideration. Accordingly, it is worth noting the use that Paul makes of Isaiah's prophecy as a whole in Romans. It is estimated that citations from Isaiah 'account for nearly half of Paul's explicit appeals to scripture in Romans'.[91] As Wagner notes, '[n]ot only are Isaiah's words cited more often than those of any other scriptural book, but Isaiah himself appears as a named speaker five times'.[92]

---

85 Groves, 'Atonement in Isaiah 53', 85.
86 Schreiner, Romans, 462; Murray, Romans, 330; Cranfield, Romans I–VIII, 439; Moo, Romans, 542; Osborne, Romans, 227; Jewett, Romans, 541–42.
87 Jewett, Romans, 542. Although we should note our caution about the first kai, above.
88 E.g. Moo, Romans, 540 n.19; Schreiner, Romans, 459; Cranfield, Romans I–VIII, 436; Fitzmyer, Romans, 532.
89 Rom. 8:31–34   εἰ ὁ θεὸς ὑπὲρ ἡμῶν, τίς καθ' ἡμῶν; [...] 33 τίς ἐγκαλέσει κατὰ ἐκλεκτῶν θεοῦ; θεὸς ὁ δικαιῶν· 34 τίς ὁ κατακρινῶν; Χριστὸς [Ἰησοῦς] ὁ ἀποθανών, μᾶλλον δὲ ἐγερθείς,
    Isa. 50:8–9   ὅτι ἐγγίζει ὁ δικαιώσας με τίς ὁ κρινόμενός μοι [...] 9 ἰδοὺ κύριος βοηθεῖ μοι τίς κακώσει με ἰδοὺ πάντες ὑμεῖς ὡς ἱμάτιον [...]
90 Others who see a link here include Schreiner, Romans, 462; Fay, 'Was Paul a Trinitarian?', 334; Dunn, Romans, 503; Jewett, Romans, 541 n.85; cf. Hays, Echoes, 61.
91 Wagner, Heralds, 2. See his footnote and also pp. 342–43 for references to lists of citations. See also the list of allusions in Wilk, Die Bedeutung des Jesajabuches, 445. Neither sees a reference to Isaiah 53:12 in Rom 8:34.
92 Wagner, 'Isaiah in Romans and Galatians', 117, lists 9:27–28; 9:29; 10:16; 10:20–21; 15:12.

Further, arguably a proportionally higher number of citations and allusions seem to be taken from the Servant Songs of Isaiah 40–55—especially in Romans 1–8.[93] Also, Paul does not merely use Isaiah's words as proof-texts for his own ends, but they significantly shape his own understanding of his gospel and mission.[94]

Perhaps the strongest reason, though, for seeing an allusion to Isaiah 53:12 is actually the previous allusion in Romans 8:34 to Psalm 110. In Isaiah 53, because the servant 'poured out his soul to death', God will 'divide him a portion with the many' (v12 ESV). Further, 52:13 which introduces this Servant Song and speaks of the Servant's exaltation (ὑψόω), is best understood as a reflection of what will happen after the suffering described in the chapter.[95] This exaltation may be more than simply receiving the praise of human beings. Bauckham has argued that what is in view is the Servant being exalted to the throne of God on the basis that the language of 52:13 picks up on that of the exaltation of God in 6:1 and 57:15.[96] If this connection holds true, then it would seem that the exaltation of the servant mirrors the very exaltation spoken about in Psalm 110:1. It seems that the early Christians made this connection since Psalm 110:1 is alluded to in combination with both Isaiah 52:13 (Acts 2:33; 5:31) and Isaiah 57:15 (Heb 1:3).[97]

---

93 See Shum, *Paul's Use of Isaiah in Romans*, 202, and Bolt, *The Cross from a Distance*, 150.
94 See Wagner, 'Isaiah in Romans and Galatians', 132.
95 Bauckham, *God Crucified*, 50.
96 Bauckham, *God Crucified*, 49–50. This is true in both the MT and the LXX, as can be seen in the following comparison:

    52:13   ἰδοὺ συνήσει ὁ παῖς μου καὶ ὑψωθήσεται καὶ δοξασθήσεται σφόδρα

    6:1   καὶ ἐγένετο τοῦ ἐνιαυτοῦ οὗ ἀπέθανεν Οζιας ὁ βασιλεὺς εἶδον τὸν κύριον καθήμενον ἐπὶ θρόνου ὑψηλοῦ καὶ ἐπηρμένου καὶ πλήρης ὁ οἶκος τῆς δόξης αὐτοῦ

    57:15   τάδε λέγει κύριος ὁ ὕψιστος ὁ ἐν ὑψηλοῖς κατοικῶν τὸν αἰῶνα ἅγιος ἐν ἁγίοις ὄνομα αὐτῷ κύριος ὕψιστος ἐν ἁγίοις ἀναπαυόμενος καὶ ὀλιγοψύχοις διδοὺς μακροθυμίαν καὶ διδοὺς ζωὴν τοῖς συντετριμμένοις τὴν καρδίαν

97 See the following comparison:

    Isaiah 52:13   ἰδοὺ συνήσει ὁ παῖς μου καὶ ὑψωθήσεται καὶ δοξασθήσεται σφόδρα

    Acts 2:33   τῇ δεξιᾷ οὖν τοῦ θεοῦ ὑψωθείς

    Acts 5:31   τοῦτον ὁ θεὸς ἀρχηγὸν καὶ σωτῆρα ὕψωσεν τῇ δεξιᾷ αὐτοῦ

    Isaiah 57:15   τάδε λέγει κύριος ὁ ὕψιστος ὁ ἐν ὑψηλοῖς κατοικῶν τὸν αἰῶνα ἅγιος ἐν ἁγίοις ὄνομα αὐτῷ κύριος ὕψιστος ἐν ἁγίοις ἀναπαυόμενος καὶ ὀλιγοψύχοις διδοὺς μακροθυμίαν καὶ διδοὺς ζωὴν τοῖς συντετριμμένοις τὴν καρδίαν

So, I think the possibilities of the allusion are significant. We need to consider, then, how Isaiah understand the intercession of the Servant. While some commentators see the normal sense of intercessory prayer on view,[98] a significant number argue that the intercession here 'is accomplished not by prayer per se but rather by suffering'.[99] This 'silent' intercession fits the rest of the chapter where the servant 'does nothing and says nothing but let's everything happen to him'.[100] So, Westermann is adamant that intercession here 'does not mean [...] that he made prayers of intercession for them, but that with his life, his suffering and his death, he took their place and underwent their punishment in their stead'.[101] Is this a case where intercession and sacrifice are merged into one act?

Perhaps, though, a closer examination of the text leans us away from collapsing the Servant's intercession into his sacrificial death. In 53:12 we note that the Servant will be blessed with portion and plunder as a result (תַּחַת אֲשֶׁר)[102] of his pouring out his soul to death (הֶעֱרָה לַמָּוֶת נַפְשׁוֹ), being numbered with the transgressors (וְאֶת־פֹּשְׁעִים נִמְנָה). The actions of the Servant are typically expressed using *qatal* forms but interestingly the final reference to intercession reverts to a *yiqtol* (יַפְגִּיעַ). Can we draw any significance from this change in verb form—particularly regarding whether the Servant intercedes during his humiliation, i.e. even *by* his death or whether he intercedes in his exaltation, that is, as a result of but distinct from his death? Some commentators see no significance in this change and translate the final verb as 'made intercession' suggesting that it happens in parallel with his bearing of sin or even that the Servant interceded by bearing sin.[103] As Koole points out if this final clause is dependent on (תַּחַת אֲשֶׁר) then it would have to be read with the previous *qatals*.[104] However, it may be that this final line is a 'new, independent clause which forms an inclusio with 52:13' and thus is 'a new reference

---

98   E.g. Baltzer, *Deutero-Isaiah*, 427.
99   Ballentine, 'The Prophet as Intercessor', 164 n.12.
100 Clines, *I, He, We and They*, 64–65.
101 Westermann, *Isaiah 40–66*, 269.
102 Cf. Num 25:13; Deut 21:14; 2:29; 28:47; 28:62; 1 Samuel 26:21; 2 Kings 22:17; 2 Chron 21:12; 34:25; Jer 29:19; 50:7.
103 de Waard, *A Handbook on Isaiah*, 197–98; Whybray, *Thanksgiving for a Liberated Prophet*, 71; Westermann, *Isaiah 40–66*, 269; Goldingay & Payne, *Isaiah 40–55*, 330 '[t]he change is then no doubt partly for variation'.
104 Koole, *Isaiah*, 343; cf. Baltzer, *Deutero-Isaiah*, 343.

to the glorification of the Servant'.[105] This reading would explain the differences in the verb forms[106] and fits the climactic nature of this final clause. Finally, this movement mirrors 'the paratactic sentence structure of the second line of v.11 [where] the cause of the Servant's elevation is that he bore the guilt of many'.[107] It would seem, at least possible, that the Servant's intercession is being presented as subsequent to his suffering death, a result even—but still distinct from that death.

If we accept this allusion to Isaiah 53:12, we do not have to view intercession here as a priestly activity—and as such understand it figuratively. The allusion could suggest that what is in view is intercessory prayer offered by Christ as he sits at God's right hand. In both cases we have a climactic series of events culminating with intercession, which follows atoning suffering and death and is possible *because of* that death but is not the same as that death. Rather, as we have argued, intercession is something subsequent to and distinct from atoning death in both cases. Obviously, the structure of Romans 8:34 on its own would point to this with its obvious sense of progression (death—resurrection—exaltation—intercession), but the allusion to Isaiah 53:12 helps confirm the significance of this structure. Christ is being presented as an exalted intercessor who intercedes by praying for his people.

The Intercession of the Spirit in Romans 8:26

Paul opens his treatment of the Spirit's intercession by describing it in terms of helping us in our weakness (συναντιλαμβάνεται τῇ ἀσθενείᾳ ἡμῶν). Specifically, the Spirit helps us in our weakness by interceding for us with groanings (στεναγμοῖς, v.26). The implication is that this groaning of the Spirit will continue until believers are glorified and no longer exist in a state of weakness. Their glory is assured because it is the work of the Spirit that sustains them.

---

105 Koole, *Isaiah*, 428.
106 Koole, *Isaiah*, 343, speaks of something which 'has not been given due attention by most exegetes and translations'. It is important to point out that this is not the only reason for this interpretation, given that the *yiqtol* can, in fact, have a range of nuances including acting as a summary. See Athas & Young, *Elementary Biblical Hebrew*, 71.
107 Koole, *Isaiah*, 343. Baltzer, *Deutero-Isaiah*, 428, also takes the verb as future.

Paul continues by saying that the Spirit helps (συναντιλαμβάνεται) our weaknesses. The following γάρ specifies, or at least exemplifies the weakness with respect to prayer. Paul unpacks this prayer weakness as τὸ [...] τί προσευξώμεθα καθὸ δεῖ οὐκ οἴδαμεν.[108] It is weakness in the realm of ignorance. Our prayers, like everything in creation, have been subject to ματαιότης ('futility' v.20).[109] This ignorance on our part is overcome by the intercession (ὑπερεντυγχάνει) of the Spirit himself (αὐτὸ τὸ πνεῦμα). Our inability to pray is matched by the Spirit's own intercession. Paul then sees the Spirit helping believers by actively praying for them according to the will of God.

The content of the Spirit's prayer is described by Paul as στεναγμοῖς ἀλαλήτοις ('inaudible groanings').[110] This phrase has led some interpreters to suggest that the Spirit's distinct praying is not in view. Rather the Spirit somehow 'inhabits' believers' own prayers. Key to this idea is the contention that στεναγμοῖς ἀλαλήτοις actually refers to glossolalia uttered by believers. This suggestion goes back at least as far as Origen and Chrysostom[111] but was revived in the 20th century by Ernst Käsemann, particularly in his Romans commentary.[112] One of the most recent articulations has been by Fee who argues on the basis that what is in view here is the believer's 'prayer in the Spirit'.[113] However, Paul seems to go out of his way to insist that it is the Spirit who intercedes for us. He uses ἀλλά as a strong contrast to the 'actions' of believers who do

---

108 Moo, *Romans*, 523 n.82: 'the "what-we-are-to-pray-as-it-is-necessary" we do not know'.
109 Obeng, 'The Reconciliation of Rom. 8.26f.', 167.
110 Obeng has surveyed the main applications of στεναγμοῖς ('groanings') in the Greek Bible and has highlighted its use as intense prayer to God. Ex 2:24; Ex 6:5; Psalm 78 (79):11 and Tob 3:1. For the other uses see Gen 3:16; Ex 2:24; John 14:16; Mal 2:13; Obeng, 'The Spirit Intercession Motif in Paul', 362.

This intense prayer is further qualified as ἀλαλήτοις. Translations for this word in this context range from 'ineffable' to 'inaudible' and generally depend on whether the commentator sees the prayer as purely the activity of the Spirit (and hence 'inaudible') or prayer by the believer *by* or *in* the Spirit (and hence audible but 'ineffable' or 'inarticulate'). As Gieniusz, *Romans 8:18–30*, 226 argues, given the intrinsic ambiguity in meaning of this word, it alone cannot determine whether the 'glossolalic' (see below) interpretation of this verse is correct. Though as O'Brien, 'Romans 8:26, 27', 70, notes, the passive form might suggest 'unspoken' rather than 'inexpressible'. As such, the context must determine the meaning of the word. Thus, given our argument below, we should probably render it 'inaudible'.
111 For references, see Gieniusz, *Romans 8:18–30*, 222 n.730.
112 Käsemann, *Romans*, 240–41.
113 Fee, *God's Empowering Presence*, 579–86. Cf. T. Engberg-Pedersen, *Cosmology*, 67.

not know (οὐκ οἴδαμεν) what to pray; he uses the pronoun to emphasise that it is the Spirit himself (αὐτὸ τὸ πνεῦμα)[114] who intercedes; and this intercession is not by the saints but for the saints (ὑπὲρ ἁγίων [v.27]) with inaudible groanings.

The Spirit, then, intercedes by praying to the Father when believers can't or don't know what to pray. What is in view is actual prayer on the part of the Spirit.

Romans 8:34

Both the (albeit only) possible allusion to Isaiah 53:12 and the climactic position of the reference to intercession in the verse suggest that Christ's intercession be distinguished from his sacrificial death. The parallel with the Spirit's intercession further suggests that actual prayer is in view. While Paul can use the same word with different meanings in close context,[115] the fact that ἐντυγχάνω is such a rare word for Paul would count against this. Rather, the clear use in v.26 should act as a control for the more disputed use here.

If we do understand that prayer is in view, can we say anything concerning the content of the prayer? A number of factors push us to see a broad view of the goal of intercession here—that Christ is interceding for all that believers need to persevere. For a start, Christ interceding for us mirrors the fact that God is willing to give us 'all things' (τὰ πάντα v.32). The need for such intercession fits the context of the trials that believers face (v.35). As we have noted, it mirrors the intercession of the Spirit who helps us in our weakness. The perseverance of God's people so that his Son may be 'the first-born among many brothers' (v.29) will not fail because of the intercession of Christ and the Spirit in the face of all our weaknesses.

But within this broad framework of intercession, can we include intercession for our forgiveness? In other words, to put it somewhat crudely, does Paul envisage that every time the believer sins, Christ prays for their forgiveness. Against this is the fact that Paul has spent three

---

114 Gieniusz, *Romans 8:18–30*, 223.
115 E.g. νόμος in 8:1—see Moo, *Romans*, 473–76.

verses stressing how God is 'for us' and how the idea of him bringing any charge against us is absurd. This flows from the fact that he has given his Son up for us (v.32), and that he has justified us (v.33). To posit a wrathful stance towards us that needs to be met by Christ's intercession for forgiveness would go against the grain of these verses.

However, by far the most common goal of intercession in the OT was the aversion of God's wrath, and if we accept the allusion to Isaiah 53:12 we should perhaps note that the Servant intercedes for 'transgressors'. Further, the juridical context of condemnation in these verses, suggests that sin is in view. To fully answer this question would involve a wider study on the nature of on-going forgiveness (e.g. John 13:10; 1 John 1:9) for the Christian. Although there is no condemnation for those in Christ (8:1) and God is 'for us', the wrath of God in some sense remains a future reality (Rom 5:9–10; cf. 2:16). That we will be saved from that wrath is not in doubt given that God has done the 'harder' job of reconciling us (5:9), but that salvation still needs to be realized. In a similar way, then, perhaps Christ's intercession includes an application of the benefits of our forgiveness.

In short, we have argued that Romans 8:34 presents Christ as exalted by God and praying for transgressors. As such he fulfils and surpasses the actions of the OT intercessors—none of whom could guarantee that God's purposes in this way. This intercessory prayer of Christ mirrors both God's desire to give believers all things (v.32) and the Spirit's own intercession for us (vv.26–27) and shows the absurdity of Christ ever condemning us. As such, it highlights the central motif of this chapter that 'there is no condemnation for those who are in Christ Jesus' (v.1).

Bibliography

Achtemeier, Paul J. *Romans* (Atlanta: John Knox Press, 1985).

Ådna, Jostein 'The Servant of Isaiah 53 as Triumphant and Interceding Messiah: The Reception of Isaiah 52:13–53:12 in the Targum of Isaiah with Special Attention to the Concept of the Messiah', in Bernd Janowski & Peter Stuhlmacher (eds.), *The Suffering Servant: Isaiah 53 in Jewish and Christian Sources* (Daniel P. Bailey, transl.; Grand Rapids: Eerdmans, 2004 [1996]), 189–224.

Athas, George, & Ian M. Young *Elementary Biblical Hebrew: An Introductory Grammar* (Beverly Hills, NSW: Ancient Vessel Press, 2007).

Ballentine, Samuel E. 'The Prophet as Intercessor: A Reassessment', *JBL* 103/2 (1984), 161–173.

Baltzer, Klaus *Deutero-Isaiah: A Commentary on Isaiah 40–55* (Margaret Kohl, transl.; Minneapolis: Fortress Press, 2001).

Barrett, C.K. *A Commentary on the Epistle to the Romans* (London: Adam & Charles Black, 1962).

Barth, Karl *The Epistle to the Romans* (Edwyn C. Hoskyns, transl.; Oxford: Oxford University Press, 1933, 6th ed.).

Bauckham, Richard *God Crucified: Monotheism and Christology in the New Testament* (Grand Rapids: Eerdmans, 1998).

Bauernfeind, Otto 'ἐντυγχάνω', in Gerhard Kittel & Gerhard Friedrich (eds.), *Theological Dictionary of the New Testament* (Geoffrey W. Bromiley, transl.; Grand Rapids: Eerdmans, 1972), 8.242–44.

Black, Matthew *Romans* (The New Century Bible Commentary; Grand Rapids: Eerdmans, 1989, 2nd ed.).

Bolt, Peter G. *The Cross from a Distance: Atonement in Mark's Gospel* (Leicester: IVP, 2004).

Byrne, Brendan *Romans* (Sacra Pagina 6; Collegeville, Minnesota: Liturgical Press, 1996).

Calvin, John 'Commentary on 1 John', *The John Calvin Collection on CD-ROM* (John Owen, transl.; Ages Software Version 1.0. 1998 [1555]).

Calvin, John — 'Commentary on Romans', *The John Calvin Collection on CD-ROM* (John Owen, transl.; Ages Software Version 1.0. 1998 [1539]).

Calvin, John — *Institutes of the Christian Religion* (LCC 20–21; John T. McNeill, ed.; Ford Lewis Battles, transl.; 2 vols.; Philadelphia: Westminster, 1960 [1559]).

Chilton, Bruce D. — *The Isaiah Targum: Introduction, Translation, Apparatus and Notes* (The Aramaic Bible, 11; Edinburgh: T&T Clark: 1987).

Chrysostom, John — *The Homilies of S. John Chrysostom, Archbishop of Constantinople, on the Epistle of St. Paul the Apostle to the Romans* (A Library of Fathers of the Holy Catholic Church Anterior to the Division of the East and West, 7; J.B. Morris, transl.; London: J.G.F & J. Rivington, 1841).

Clines, David J.A. — *I, He, We and They: A Literary Approach to Isaiah 53* (Sheffield: Department of Biblical Studies, University of Sheffield, 1976).

Cranfield, C.E.B. — *A Critical and Exegetical Commentary on the Epistle to the Romans: Volume I: Introduction and Commentary on Romans I–VIII* (ICC; Edinburgh: T&T Clark, 1975).

de Waard, Jan — *A Handbook on Isaiah* (Winona Lake, Ind.: Eisenbrauns, 1997).

Dodd, C.H. — *The Epistle of Paul to the Romans* (London: Hodder & Stoughton, 1932).

Dunn, James D.G. — *Romans 1–8* (WBC 38A; Dallas: Word, 1988).

Engberg-Pedersen, T. — *Cosmology and Self in the Apostle Paul: The Material Spirit* (Oxford: Oxford University Press, 2010).

Eskola, Timo — *Messiah and the Throne: Jewish Merkabah Mysticism and Early Christian Exaltation Discourse* (WUNT II 142; Tübingen: Mohr Siebeck, 2001).

Fay, Ron C. — 'Was Paul a Trinitarian? A Look at Romans 8', in Stanley E. Porter (ed.), *Paul and His Theology. Pauline Studies: Volume 3* (Leiden: Brill, 2006), 327–45.

Fee, Gordon D. — *God's Empowering Presence: The Holy Spirit in the Letters of Paul* (Peabody: Hendrickson, 1994).

Fitzmyer, Joseph A. *Romans: A New Translation with Introduction and Commentary* (AB 33; New York: Doubleday, 1993).

Gieniusz, A. *Romans 8:18–30: Suffering Does Not Thwart the Future Glory* (Atlanta: Scholars Press, 1999).

Godbey, John C. 'Socinus and Christ', in Róbert Dán & Antal Pirnát (eds.), *Antitrinitarianism in the Second Half of the 16th Century* (Leiden: Brill, 1982), 57–65.

Godet, Frederick *Commentary on Romans* (Grand Rapids: Kregel, 1977 [1883]).

Goldingay, John, & David Payne *A Critical and Exegetical Commentary on Isaiah 40–55 Volume II* (London: T&T Clark, 2006).

Groves, J. Alan H. 'Atonement in Isaiah 53', in Charles E. Hill & Frank A. James III (eds.), *The Glory of the Atonement: Essays in Honor of Roger Nicole* (Downers Grove: IVP, 2004), 61–89.

Haldane, R. *Romans* (Edinburgh: Banner of Truth, 1958 [1874]).

Hay, David M. *Glory at the Right Hand: Psalm 110 in Early Christianity* (Nashville: Abingdon Press, 1973).

Hays, Richard B. *Echoes of Scripture in the Letters of Paul* (New Haven: Yale University Press, 1989).

Hengel, Martin *Studies in Early Christology* (Edinburgh: T&T Clark, 1995).

Jewett, Robert *Romans: A Commentary* (Hermeneia; Minneapolis: Fortress Press, 2007).

Jobes, Karen H., & Moises Silva *Invitation to the Septuagint* (Grand Rapids: Baker Academic, 2000).

Käsemann, Ernst *Commentary on Romans* (Geoffrey W. Bromiley, transl.; Grand Rapids: Eerdmans, 1980).

Keck, Leander E. *Romans* (Abingdon New Testament Commentaries; Nashville: Abingdon, 2005).

Kleinknecht, Karl Theodor *Der Leidende Gererchtfertigte: Die Alttestamentlich-Jüdische Tradition vom 'Leidenen Gerechten' und Ihre Rezeption bei Paulus* (WUNT II 13; Tübingen: Mohr Siebeck, 1984).

Koole, Jan L. *Isaiah Part 3 Volume 2: Isaiah 49–55* (Anthony P. Runia, transl.; Leuven: Peeters, 1998).

Kurianal, James — *Jesus Our High Priest: Ps 110,4 as Substructure of Heb 5,1–7,28* (European University Studies 693; Frankfurt: Peter Lang, 2000).

Leenhardt, Franz J. — *The Epistle to the Romans: A Commentary* (Harold Knight, transl.; London: Lutterworth Press, 1961 [1957]).

Lloyd-Jones, D.M. — *Romans: Exposition of Chapter 8:17–39: The Final Perseverance of the Saints* (Edinburgh: Banner of Truth, 1975).

Luther, Martin — *Luther's Works Volume 30: The Catholic Epistles* (Jaroslav Pelikan, ed.; Saint Louis: Concordia Publishing House, 1967 [1527]).

Moo, Douglas J. — *The Epistle to the Romans* (NICNT; Grand Rapids: Eerdmans, 1996)

Morris, Leon — *The Epistle to the Romans* (Grand Rapids: Eerdmans, 1998).

Moule, C.F.D. — *An Idiom Book of New Testament Greek* (Cambridge: Cambridge University Press, 1959).

Murray, John — *The Epistle to the Romans Volume I: Chapters 1–8* (Grand Rapids: Eerdmans, 1958).

Nazianzen, Gregory — *Faith Gives Fullness to Reasoning: The Five Theological Orations of Gregory Nazianzen* (Supplements to Vigiliae Christianae, 12; Lionel Wickham & Frederick Williams, transls.; Leiden: Brill, 1991).

Nida, Eugene A., & Johannes P. Louw — *Lexical Semantics of the Greek New Testament* (SBL Resources for Biblical Study 25; Atlanta: SBL, 1992).

Nygren, A. — *Commentary on Romans* (Carl C. Rasmussen, transl.; Philadelphia: Fortress Press, 1944).

Obeng, E.A. — 'The Reconciliation of Rom. 8.26f. to New Testament Writings and Themes', *Stulos Theological Journal 39* (1986), 165–74.

Obeng, E.A. — 'The Spirit Intercession Motif in Paul', *Expository Times* 95.12 (1984), 360–64.

O'Brien, P.T. — 'Romans 8:26, 27: A Revolutionary Approach to Prayer?', *Reformed Theological Review* 46.3 (1987), 65–73.

Orr, Peter — *Exalted Above the Heavens: The Risen and Ascended Christ* (NSBT 47; Leicester: IVP, 2018).

Osborne, Grant R. *Romans* (IVP New Testament Commentary Series; Leicester: IVP, 2004).

Peterson, D.G. *Commentary on Romans* (BTCP; Nashville: B&H, 2017).

Porter, Stanley *Verbal Aspect in the Greek of the New Testament, with Reference to Tense and Mood* (Studies in Biblical Greek, 1; New York: Peter Lang, 1989).

Saeed, John I. *Semantics* (Oxford: Blackwell, 1997).

Sanday, W., & A.C. Headlam *A Critical and Exegetical Commentary on the Epistle to the Romans* (Edinburgh: T&T Clark, 1902 [1895] 5th Edition).

Schlatter, Adolf *Romans: The Righteousness of God* (Siegfried S. Schatzmann, transl.; Peabody, Mass.: Hendrickson Publishers, 1995 [1935]).

Schreiner, Thomas R. *Romans* (BECNT 6; Grand Rapids: Baker Books, 1998).

Seeligman, Isaac Leo *The Septuagint Version of Isaiah and Cognate Studies* (Forschungen zum Alten Testament 40; Robert Hanhart & Hermann Spiekermann, eds.; Tübingen: Mohr Siebeck, 2004).

Shum, Shiu-Lun *Paul's Use of Isaiah in Romans: A Comparative Study of Paul's Letter to the Romans and the Sibylline and Qumran Sectarian Texts* (WUNT II 156; Tübingen: Mohr Siebeck, 2002).

Silva, Moisés *Biblical Words and Their Meaning: An Introduction to Lexical Semantics* (Grand Rapids: Zondervan, 1994 [1983] 2nd ed.).

Spicq, C. *L'Épître aux Hébreux* (Paris: J. Gabalda, 1952).

Stenning, J.F. *The Targum of Isaiah* (Oxford: Clarendon Press, 1949).

Stott, John R.W. *The Message of Romans* (Leicester: IVP, 1994).

Tait, Arthur James *The Heavenly Session of Our Lord: An Introduction to the History of the Doctrine* (London: R. Scott, 1912).

Talbert, Charles H. *Romans* (Macon: Smyth & Helwys, 2002).

Torrance, T.F. *Space, Time and Resurrection* (Edinburgh: T&T Clark, 1976).

Wagner, J. Ross *Heralds of the Good News: Isaiah and Paul 'In Concert' in the Letter to the Romans* (Leiden: Brill, 2002).

Wagner, J. Ross   'Isaiah in Romans and Galatians', in Steve Moyise & Maarten J.J. Menken (eds.), *Isaiah in the New Testament* (London: T&T Clark, 2005), 117–32.

Wallace, Daniel   *Greek Grammar Beyond the Basics: An Exegetical Syntax of the New Testament* (Grand Rapids: Zondervan, 1996).

Westcott, B.F.   *The Epistle to the Hebrews: The Greek Text with Notes and Essays* (London: Macmillan & Co., 1889).

Westermann, Claus   *Isaiah 40–66: A Commentary* (London: SCM, 1969 [1966]).

Whybray, R.N.   *Thanksgiving for a Liberated Prophet: An Interpretation of Isaiah Chapter 53* (JSOT Sup 4; Sheffield: Department of Biblical Studies, University of Sheffield, 1978).

Wilk, Florian   *Die Bedeutung des Jesajabuches fur Paulus* (Gottingen: Vandenhoeck & Ruprecht, 1998).

Wright, N. T.   'The Letter to the Romans: Introduction, Commentary, and Reflections', in Leander E. Keck (ed.), *The New Interpreter's Bible: A Commentary in Twelve Volumes* (Nashville: Abingdon, 2002), 10.423–770.

Young, Edward J.   *The Book of Isaiah: The English Text with Introduction, Exposition and Notes.* Volume III: *Chapters 40–66* (Grand Rapids: Eerdmans, 1972).

Ziesler, John   *Paul's Letter to the Romans* (London: SCM Press, 1989).

Zimmerli, W., & J. Jeremias   *The Servant of God* (Studies in Biblical Theology, 20; London: SCM, 1957 [1952]).

CHAPTER 9

God's Righteousness, Christ's Faith/fulness, and 'Justification by Faith Alone' (Romans 3:21–26)

Murray Smith

Introduction

Romans 3:21–26 is the *locus classicus* for the Protestant doctrine of 'justification by faith alone'.[1] For five hundred years, since Martin Luther, it has been widely accepted that the apostle Paul's central concern in this passage is to declare God's gift of a new righteous status received through faith in Christ.[2] On this reading, Paul's declaration that 'the righteousness of God has been made known' (3:21: δικαιοσύνη θεοῦ πεφανέρωται) primarily refers to God's gift to sinners of the new righteous status, and Paul's subsequent reference to 'the faith of Jesus Christ' (3:22: πίστεως Ἰησοῦ Χριστοῦ) concerns the believer's trust in Christ as the means by which this righteous status is received.[3] More recently, however, a steady stream of scholars have renewed older arguments that: (i) 'the righteousness of God' (δικαιοσύνη θεοῦ) refers not to a new righteous status but to God's own righteous character and activity (variously understood), and/

---

1 E.g. the prooftexts for the *Westminster Confession of Faith* (WCF) §11 'Of Justification', include Romans 3:22, 24, 25, 26, 27, 28.
2 Luther, *Romans*, 60 on Romans 3:21: '[Paul] does not speak of the righteousness of God, by which God is righteous, but of that with which He clothes a person when He justifies the ungodly'.
3 Recent essays which defend this view, with various important nuances, include: Horton, 'Traditional Reformed View,' esp. 98; Naselli, 'The Righteous God'.

or; (ii) 'through faith of Jesus Christ' (διὰ πίστεως Ἰησοῦ Χριστοῦ) refers not to the believer's faith, but to Jesus Christ's faith/fulness.[4] This exegesis predates the controversial 'New Perspective on Paul', but has been associated with that movement in various (complicated) ways.[5] Perhaps at least partly for this reason, it has been rejected by many seeking to defend the classic Protestant understanding of 'justification by faith alone'.

The issues involved in this discussion are complex. In this chapter, I attempt neither a thorough exegesis of Romans 3:21–26, nor a full account of the doctrine of justification by faith alone. My limited goal, as a card-carrying Protestant—a confessional Presbyterian no less!—is to demonstrate that reading 'the righteousness of God' as *God's righteousness* and 'the faith of Christ' as *Christ's faith/fulness* in Romans 3:21–26 is both exegetically compelling, *and* thoroughly consistent with the rightly cherished Protestant doctrine of 'justification by faith alone'. There is not space here to engage with a number of other closely related exegetical and theological issues. Certainly, some who argue for this reading of 'the righteousness of God' and 'the faith/fulness of Christ' also adopt positions which stand in serious conflict with the common Reformational confession of 'justification by faith alone'. Most prominently, N.T. Wright, for example, argues that Paul's 'justification' language primarily refers to the divine declaration that a person belongs among the covenant people, that Paul does not affirm the imputation of Christ's righteousness to believers, and that the final judgment will be passed 'on the basis of the entire life'.[6] These conclusions, and their theological implications, certainly do constitute a significant revision of the Reformation doctrine of justification itself. They can, however—and I will argue they should—be unbundled from the exegetical discussion about 'the righteousness of God' and 'the faith of Jesus Christ'.

The argument proceeds in three stages. First, I locate Romans 3:21–26 within the purpose and argument of Romans to show how Paul relates

---

4   For the bibliography, see §2.2.1 and §2.2 below.
5   For a review of the 'New Perspective on Paul', see: Smith, 'Paul'.
6   For a brief review of Wright's position, and responses to it to 2013, see: Smith, 'Paul', 19–28. For Wright's most recent contribution, see Wright, *Paul and the Faithfulness of God*, 775–1042, which further advances the same position. Among more recent critical responses to Wright's views on justification, see esp. Schriener, 'Justification'; Vanhoozer, 'Wrighting the Wrongs'; Starling, 'Covenants'; Cowan, 'N.T. Wright'; Horton, Justification, II: 336–46, 374–94.

'the gospel', to 'the righteousness of God' and 'the faith of Christ', as well as to the 'justification' of 'all who believe'. Second, I provide an exegesis of Romans 3:21–26, with particular reference to 'the righteousness of God' (δικαιοσύνη θεοῦ), 'the faith of Christ' (πίστις Χριστοῦ), and 'justification' (δικαιόω). Finally, I bring Paul's teaching in this passage into conversation with the Reformation doctrine of 'justification by faith alone' by means of an analysis of that doctrine in what is arguably its most mature confessional form, namely, the *Westminster Confession of Faith* (WCF §11). My argument throughout is that the primary purpose of Romans 3:21–26 is to demonstrate how *God's righteousness* has been disclosed through *Christ's faith/fulness*, which provides the only grounds for the *free justification* of all who trust in him. Paul's concern in this paragraph is first *theo-centric* and then *anthropological,* first *Christological* and then *soteriological.* While these pairs are inseparable, the order matters. I conclude that while this reading of 'the righteousness of God', and 'the faith of Jesus Christ' in Romans 3:21–26 is at variance with much of the Protestant *exegetical* tradition, it poses no threat to the classic Reformation *doctrine* of justification by faith alone but, on the contrary, it provides for that doctrine a more secure exegetical foundation.

1. The gospel, the righteousness of God, and justification by faith: Romans 3:21–26 in the argument of the letter

Romans is no systematic theology textbook. It does, however, present a sustained theological argument with its own internal logic designed to serve Paul's purpose in sending the letter to Rome. Our first task, then, is to relate Romans 3:21–26 to Paul's purposes in writing the letter, and to situate this crucial passage within the argument of the letter as a whole.

Paul's purpose in writing the letter has been variously understood, but his central concerns are relatively easily established.[7] He writes to introduce himself to the Roman churches, and to lay out his gospel (1:1–6; 10–15; 2:16; 16:25–27), so as to unite the divided Roman churches (14:1–15:13), and win their support for his mission to the

---

7   For a review of proposals regarding Paul's purpose/s, see esp.: Donfried, *Romans Debate*; cf. McDonald & Porter, *Early Christianity*, 455–459.

nations, specifically Spain (15:18–20, 23–28). First and foremost, his purpose is *theological*. He writes to vindicate God and the gospel. In the face of criticism that the gospel welcomed Gentiles, and excluded Jews from the blessings God promised to Israel (3:1–8; 9:1–11:26), Paul demonstrates that what God has done in Christ *is right*: he has been true to his word and—just as he promised—has judged sin, and now justifies sinners from among all the nations, including Jews if they trust in Christ (3:1–8, 21–26; 9:6–7, 14; 11:1–2, 28–32; 15:8–13). This gospel is thoroughly consistent with all that God had spoken through the Law and the Prophets (1:2; 3:21). Second, Paul's purpose is *pastoral*. The expulsion of the Jews from Rome under Claudius (A.D. 49), and their subsequent return (from A.D. 54), seems to have placed Gentile believers in a dominant position in the churches, and exacerbated divisions between Gentile and Jewish believers.[8] In response to these tensions between 'the strong' and 'the weak' (14:1–15:13), Paul emphasizes the deep continuity between the gospel and God's covenant with Israel (1:2; 3:21, 31; 15:8), urges Gentile believers to recognize that their inclusion amongst the ancient people of God is all of grace (11:14–32), and so calls on them to 'bear with the failings of the weak', and to 'welcome each other just as Christ has welcomed you' (15:1–7). Third, and finally, Paul also writes with a *missional* purpose. He writes to win the support of the Roman churches for his mission to the Gentiles in Spain (15:23–28). Given the tensions in the churches precisely over this issue, Paul demonstrates that the universal horizon of God's saving purposes in Christ flows out of God's faithfulness to his promises to Abraham. The mission to the nations is the culmination of God's purposes (1:5; 15:7–13; 16:26); it ought to be the concern of the whole people of God in Christ.[9]

The central theme of the letter is, unsurprisingly, closely related to this threefold purpose. Paul's central concern throughout the letter is to demonstrate that *the gospel reveals God's righteousness for the benefit of all who trust in Christ and for the sake of his own name*. First, 'the gospel'

---

[8] Schreiner, *Romans*, 33–40, provides a concise review of the evidence for a mixed, Gentile-dominant audience.
[9] Cf. Williams, 'The "Righteousness of God"', 248–255.

(τὸ εὐαγγέλιον) is central to Paul's argument in the letter.[10] This is evident from its prominent position in the epistolary frame of the letter (1:1, 9, 15; 15:16, 19; 16:25), from its appearance in the opening programmatic summary (1:16), and from its function at key points in the argument throughout (2:16; 10:15–16; 11:28; 15:16, 19; 16:25). Paul defines his gospel for the Romans in his opening greeting (1:1–6).[11] The gospel he proclaims is: (i) grounded in God (1:1); (ii) sourced in the Scriptures (1:2); (iii) centred on God's 'Son ... Jesus Christ our Lord' (1:3–4); (iv) announced in his appointment, by resurrection, as 'the Son of God in power' (1:3–4), and; (v) orientated to the obedience of 'all the nations' (1:5–6). This short gospel summary is assumed in subsequent references to 'the gospel' and 'gospelling' throughout the letter. It is significant for our purposes in at least three ways. Paul's characterization of the gospel as 'the gospel of God' (εὐαγγέλιον θεοῦ) simultaneously indicates that the gospel is *from God* (source genitive), proclaimed *by God* (subjective genitive), and *about God* (objective genitive).[12] In this context, it is no surprise to find that—first and foremost—the gospel reveals *God's own righteousness* (1:16–17; 3:21–22). Further, Paul's summary of the gospel highlights Jesus' descent from David and enthronement as Lord—the beginning and the end of his earthly career (cf. 2 Tim 2:8). This indicates that Paul's gospel concerns the whole of Christ's career from his incarnation to his enthronement—from his humiliation to his glorification.[13]

---

10 For 'the gospel' as the theme of the letter, see: Moo, *Romans*, 25–28; cf. Hooker, 'Another Look', 54: 'The book's theme is "the gospel (or good news) of God"'.

11 Schreiner, *Romans*, 30, notes that 16:25–27 forms an *inclusio* with 1:1–5 by the repetition of five motifs: (i) 'the gospel' (1:1; 16:25); (ii) fulfillment of the Scriptures (1:2; 16:26); (iii) Paul as herald of the gospel (1:1, 5; 16:25); (iv) the immediate goal of the obedience of faith among the Gentiles (1:5; 16:26); (v) the ultimate goal of God's glory in Christ (1:5; 16:27).

12 Cf. Schreiner, *Romans*, 82 recognises the twofold sense of a genitive of source ('gospel *from* God') and an objective genitive ('gospel *about* God'). Given that Paul immediately explains that God himself promised the gospel beforehand through the prophets (1:2), we also need to reckon with the sense of a subjective genitive ('gospel *revealed* or *proclaimed by* God'). Certainly, there is no need to limit the nuances of the relationship between the head noun and its genitive, unless lexical or syntactical factors demand otherwise. See Zerwick, *Biblical Greek*, 13 §39; Turner, *Grammar*, 210; Wallace, *Greek Grammar*, 121.

13 Vos, 'Paul's Eschatological Concept', 104, helpfully emphasizes that Paul's gospel summary ('descended from David ... declared Son of God in power') is not so much concerned with Christ's two natures (human and divine), as with his two states (humiliation and exaltation); cf. Horton, *Christian Faith*, 704: 'Eschatology, not ontology, is the point of this particular statement of the gospel'. More recently, see the helpfully nuanced analysis along these lines in: Bates, 'Christology'; Johnson, 'Romans 1:3–4'.

It therefore paves the way for his later emphasis on *Christ's life of faith/fulness*, culminating in his death and resurrection, as the manifestation of God's righteousness, and the ground of the believer's justification (3:22–26; 4:25; 5:18–19). Yet further, Paul's gospel summary highlights the deep continuity between all that God revealed beforehand in the Scriptures and his gospel for the Gentiles, and this paves the way for Paul's argument that, far from undermining God's promises to Israel, the gospel brings them to their fulfilment in its announcement of free justification for all who trust in Christ (3:24, 27–31; 4:9–12).

Second, Paul emphasizes that this gospel reveals 'God's righteousness'.[14] 'Righteousness' is certainly a significant theme in Romans: the noun δικαιοσύνη ('righteousness') occurs thirty-four times,[15] the verb δικαιόω ('I justify') fifteen times,[16] the adjective δίκαιος ('righteous') seven times,[17] the noun δικαίωμα ('righteous decree or regulation') five times,[18] the noun δικαίωσις ('justification') twice,[19] and δικαιοκρισία ('righteous/just verdict'), once.[20] The antonyms ἀδικία ('unrighteousness'), and ἄδικος ('unrighteous') are also prominent.[21] The key phrase—δικαιοσύνη θεοῦ—has been the subject of significant debate, which we will need to explore in due course. At this point it is enough to notice that while Paul employs the phrase a total of ten times in his letters, he does so only twice outside Romans (Rom 1:17; 3:5; 3:21, 22, 25, 26; 10:3 (x2); 2 Cor 5:21; Phil 3:9). This already suggests that our interpretation of the phrase needs to be closely guided by its role in the argument of the letter. For this reason, it is important to note the close connections in Romans between 'the gospel' and 'the righteousness of God'. The 'righteousness of God' is not the gospel, but it is revealed in the gospel. Paul announces

---

14 The significance of 'God's righteousness' as an integrating theme in Romans is widely acknowledged. For important discussions, albeit with different understandings of the key terms, see esp. Käsemann, 'Righteousness of God'; Williams, 'Righteousness of God', 241–90; Wright, 'Romans', 395–412; Seifrid, 'Rightousness Language'; Seifrid, 'Paul's Use'; Irons, *The Righteousness of God*; Moo, *Romans*, 82–100.
15 Rom. 1:17; 3:5, 21, 22, 25, 26; 4:3, 5, 6, 9, 11 (x2), 13, 22; 5:17, 21; 6:13, 16, 18, 19, 20; 8:10; 9:30 (x3), 31; 10:3 (x3), 4, 5, 6, 10; 14:17.
16 Rom. 2:13; 3:4, 20, 24, 26, 28, 30; 4:2, 5; 5:1, 9; 6:7; 8:30 (x2), 33.
17 Rom. 1:17; 2:13; 3:10, 26; 5:7, 19; 7:12.
18 Rom. 1:32; 2:26; 5:16, 18; 8:4.
19 Rom. 4:25; 5:18.
20 Rom. 2:5.
21 ἀδικία (x7): Rom 1:18 (x2), 29; 2:8; 3:5; 6:13; 9:14; ἄδικος: Rom 3:5.

this reality in his opening programmatic statement (1:16–17), which then serves to link his opening introduction of the gospel (1:1–6) to the crucial explication of God's righteousness in our passage (3:21–26). The connections from 1:1–6 to 1:16–17 are found in their common references to 'the gospel' rooted in the Scriptures (1:1, 16: τὸ εὐαγγέλιον), and to 'power' (1:4, 16: δύναμις), 'faith' (1:5, 16–17: πίστις / πιστεύω), and 'all the nations' (1:5, 16: πᾶς + ἔθνος / Ἕλλην). The connections from 1:16–17 forward to 3:21–26 are found in 'five points of explicit overlap' which—as D. Campbell writes—together identify Rom 1:17 and 3:21–22 as 'sibling texts, if not twins'. In both texts: (i) δικαιοσύνη θεοῦ is the subject; (ii) δικαιοσύνη θεοῦ is the subject of a verb of revelation; (iii) δικαιοσύνη θεοῦ is expanded by a similar prepositional phrase (ἐκ πίστεως) / διὰ πίστεως); (iv) a purposive εἰς construction using the πιστ- root completes the sentence; (v) the attestation of the Scriptures features prominently. The Scripturally-rooted, Christ-centred, and universally-applicable gospel of 1:1–6 is thus directly connected to 'the righteousness of God' explicated at 3:21–26 via the programmatic summary at 1:16–17. For this reason, it is no surprise to find that, like 1:1–6, the paragraph at 3:21–26 emphasizes the continuity of God's new work with his promises to Israel (3:21), the culmination of God's purposes in Christ (3:22, 24), and the universal implications of God's achievement in him (3:22–24, 27–31).[22] The gospel reveals God's righteousness for the sake of his name and the benefit of all who believe. Indeed, Paul's further references to 'the righteousness of God' underline the way in which the gospel reveals that *what God has done in Christ is right*. To begin with, the gospel reveals that God does right in judging sin, not only the sin of those outside God's covenant with Israel, but also of those within it (1:18–3:21): Paul's 'gospel' declares that God will judge all people (2:16), and this reveals 'God's righteousness' (3:5). In addition, 'the righteousness of God' provides the key to understanding God's dealings with Israel and, especially, the inclusion of the Gentiles within his saving purposes (9:1–11:36). Unbelieving Jews are missing out on the promised blessing not because of any failure on God's part (9:6; 11:1–2), but because of their unbelief (11:20). More pointedly,

---

22 Campbell, 'The Faithfulness of Jesus Christ', 60.

it was because they 'did not submit to God's righteousness' that they have failed to receive the promised blessings (10:3). In welcoming the Gentiles, then, God has done what is right. At the heart of Paul's letter to the Romans, then, is his presentation of the gospel as it reveals the righteousness of God.

Third, the revelation of the righteousness of God in the gospel is for the benefit of all who believe, and for the sake of his own name. This emphasis on 'all those who believe' as the beneficiaries of God's grace in Christ appears repeatedly throughout the letter. Paul frames the entire letter by references to the goal of the gospel—the obedience of faith among 'all the nations' (1:5; 16:25–27; cf. 15:18). Paul frequently speaks of 'the nations' (τὰ ἔθνη 29x), and emphasizes—in a range of ways—the universal horizon of God's saving purposes, and especially the fulfillment of God's promise to Abraham, manifested in the inclusion of the Gentiles amongst God's covenant people (3:22, 31; 4:11–12, 16–17; 10:11–13; 11:11–32; 15:8–29; 16:26). Closely related to this is the theme of 'faith' (πίστις, πιστεύω), which Paul introduces in connection with 'the gospel' and 'the nations' in his opening gospel summary (1:5; cf. 1:8, 12). 'Faith' is further connected to 'the gospel', 'the righteousness of God', and 'all who believe', in the programmatic summary (1:16), and in our crucial passage (3:22–24). These links are further cemented by the repetition of references to 'the gospel' or Jesus' resurrection, 'righteousness', 'faith', and 'the nations' in Paul's appeal to Abraham (3:27–4:25), and at the heart of his discussion about Israel and the nations in Romans 9–11 (esp. 9:30, 10:4, 6, 8–17). Finally, Paul further connects 'the gospel', 'God's righteousness', 'faith', and 'the nations' to his ultimate concern for God's 'name' (ὄνομα) or 'glory' (δόξα).[23] This connect is again established in the letter opening, and confirmed in its conclusion (1:5; 16:25–27). Throughout the body of the letter, Paul repeatedly shows that God's 'name' or 'glory' is his ultimate concern: the essence of sin is the rejection of God's 'glory' (1:23; 3:23); Israel has rejected God's 'glory' and blasphemed his 'name' (2:24; 9:4); God has renewed his 'glory' in Christ, especially his resurrection (6:4); the

---

23 ὄνομα (x5): Rom 1:5; 2:24; 9:17; 10:13; 15:9; δόξα (x16): Rom. 1:23; 2:7, 10; 3:7, 23; 4:20; 5:2; 6:4; 8:18, 21; 9:4, 23; 11:36; 15:7; 16:27.

righteous give God 'glory' (4:20; 11:36); the unity of God's people in Christ is for the 'glory' of God (15:7); God's purpose is that his 'name' might be 'proclaimed in all the earth' as the one who judges and saves (9:17; 10:13; 15:9); sharing in God's 'glory' is the ultimate promise for those who trust in Christ (2:7, 10; 5:2; 8:18, 21; 9:23).[24] Crucially, Paul explicitly connects his 'gospel' as it reveals 'the righteousness of God' (1:16–17) to God's revelation his 'glory' in judgment (3:5–7) and his 'name' as the Lord who saves (10:1–13).

The multiple connections between Paul's 'gospel', 'the righteousness of God', 'faith', 'the nations', and the 'glory' or 'name' of God make it clear that any interpretation of Romans 3:21–26 needs to account for how this crucial paragraph contributes to these mutually interpretive themes within the argument of the letter as a whole. This essay argues that Romans 3:21–26 makes best sense when understood as Paul's most concentrated exposition of how his gospel reveals God's own righteousness, through Jesus' Christ's faith/fulness, for the benefit of all who believe, and for the sake of his own name among the nations.

2. God's righteousness and Christ's faith/fulness in Romans 3:21–26

The marginal note in the Luther Bible famously declared that Romans 3:21–26 is 'the chief point, and the very central place of the Epistle, and of the whole Bible'. There are, of course, other contenders for 'the very central place ... of the whole Bible', but this paragraph certainly plays a crucial role in Romans: it picks up Paul's opening summary of the gospel (Rom 1:1–6), and his programmatic statement of the letter's theme (Rom 1:16–17), and shows how the gospel reveals God's righteousness, for the benefit of all who believe, and for the sake of God's own name. Unsurprisingly, the paragraph is as dense as it is rich, and as difficult as it is significant.[25] The goal, therefore, is not to offer an exhaustive

---

24 This theme is rightly emphasized by Schreiner, *Romans*, 51, 139–43; cf. Grindheim, 'Theology of Glory', who helpfully shows that God's 'glory' in Romans is his 'revelatory presence', rejected by Israel, but renewed in Christ.
25 Horton, 'Traditional Reformed View', 180, lists a 'cluster of difficult questions that have momentous theological implications'.

exegesis, but to show that Paul's teaching is focused on the revelation and vindication of *God's own righteousness*, through *Jesus Christ's faith/fulness*, for the *free justification of all who believe*. Concentrating, therefore, on Paul's language of 'righteousness' (δικαιοσύνη, δικαιόω, δίκαιος) and 'faith' (πίστις, πιστεύω) within the logic of the paragraph as a whole. The final section (§3) turns to the theological implications of this understanding of Romans 3:21–26, and shows that it is not only consistent with the classic Protestant doctrine of 'justification by faith alone', but provides a more thoroughly theological and Christocentric grounding for it.

2.1 *God's righteousness revealed*

First, in Romans 3:21–26 Paul demonstrates that the gospel reveals *God's own righteousness* (cf. 1:17). 'The righteousness of God' *(δικαιοσύνη θεοῦ) is certainly the main subject of the paragraph*. The phrase appears four times in six short verses, always with reference to God (3:21, 22: δικαιοσύνη θεοῦ; 3:25, 26: τῆς δικαιοσύνης αὐτοῦ). It is also the subject of the primary verb, which communicates that 'the righteousness of God' has been 'revealed' *(πεφανέρωται)*. That God himself is the source of this revelation is indicated by the passive voice of the verb (a 'divine passive'). The eschatological nature of the revelation is indicated by the strong contrast between the plight of humanity in sin (3:18–20), and the new revelation in Christ (3:21–22).[26] Its present and ongoing significance is indicated by the verb's perfect tense.[27] Indeed, the central significance of 'righteousness' related to God in this paragraph is further underlined by three further occurrences of words with the δικ- root: God is described, once, by the adjective 'righteous' (3:26: δίκαιος), and

---

26 The contrast between the old age and the new is created by: (i) the temporal marker νυνὶ δὲ ('but now'); (ii) the parallel contrasting expressions 'from works of the law' or 'through the law' (3:20: ἐξ ἔργων νόμου / διὰ ...νόμου) and 'apart from the law' χωρὶς νόμου (3:21); (iii) the dual reference to the 'law' (νόμος) in 3:21: 'the righteousness of God' has been disclosed χωρὶς νόμου ('apart from law'), so that the new revelation marks a decisive break with the old, but also stands in deep continuity with it, 'being witnessed to by the law and the prophets' (μαρτυρουμένη ὑπὸ τοῦ νόμου καὶ τῶν προφητῶν).

27 This holds whether we adopt the 'traditional' understanding of the Greek tense forms, or one which emphasizes the role of verbal aspect. For a brief review, see Campbell, *Advances*, 117–118. Further discussion in Crellin, 'Semantics'.

God functions, twice, as the subject or agent of the cognate verb δικαιόω ('justify'), which appears in participial form and describes, alternatively, God 'who justifies' (3:26), and 'those who are justified' [by God] (3:24).

'The righteousness of God' has been revealed! But what, exactly, does this mean? At very least, 'the righteousness of God' is a definite entity: Paul speaks not of '*a* righteousness' (*contra* NIV84), but of '*the* righteousness of God'.[28] Beyond this, however, there is widespread debate. Two key questions, therefore, must focus our discussion: (i) *how* does the genitive θεοῦ relate to the head noun δικαιοσύνη? (ii) what is the nature of this δικαιοσύνη?

2.1.1 *God's own righteousness*

The genitive 'of God' (θεοῦ) has been understood to refer either to a 'righteousness' people receive from God, or to God's own righteousness (variously understood). The first main option—δικαιοσύνη θεοῦ as a righteousness people receive from God—relies, grammatically speaking, on reading θεοῦ as either: (i) an objective genitive with the sense of 'righteousness *that counts before* God', or; (ii) a genitive of source (origin), giving the meaning 'righteousness *that comes from* God (as a gift)'. In one form or another, this first reading goes back at least to Augustine,[29] received a major impetus from Luther,[30] and Calvin,[31] and has been

---

28 Apollonius' Canon states that in genitive phrases the head noun and the genitive either both have the article, or lack it, and that such constructions are, either way, 'normally definite'; Wallace, *Greek Grammar*, 239–40. Apollonius' Corollary states further that 'when both nouns are anarthrous, both will usually have the same semantic force' (pp.239–40, 250, citing Hedges, *Apollonius' Canon*). In the phrase δικαιοσύνη θεοῦ, 'God' (θεός) is definite, so the whole phrase is definite.
29 Augustine, *The Spirit and the Letter*, 15.9, cited in Bray, *Romans*, 99: 'The righteousness of God is not that by which God is righteous but that with which he clothes man when he justifies the ungodly'.
30 Luther, *Romans*, 60, on Romans 3:21 (cited above n.2); cf. Luther, 'Preface', 336–337: 'the righteousness of God is that by which the righteous lives by a gift of God, namely by faith. And this is the meaning: the righteousness of God is revealed by the gospel, namely, the passive righteousness with which merciful God justifies us by faith'.
31 Calvin, *Romans*, on Romans 3:21: 'It is not certain for what distinct reason he calls that the righteousness of God, which we obtain by faith; whether it be, because it can alone stand before God, or because the Lord in his mercy confers it on us. As both interpretations are suitable, we contend for neither. This righteousness then, which God communicates to man, and accepts alone, and owns as righteousness, has been revealed'. In the *Institutes*, when Calvin discusses God's righteousness, he describes it in terms of God's faithfulness to his promises: 'Righteousness, therefore, refers rather to the truth of the divine promise than to the equity of paying what is due' (*Institutes* §3.18.7).

popular ever since, especially among Protestants scholars generally, and Lutherans in particular.[32] This reading was popularized, in two very different contexts, by Luther's 1545 German Bible, which translates δικαιοσύνη θεοῦ as an objective genitive—*die Gerechtigkeit, die vor Gott gilt* ('the righteousness which counts before God'),[33] and the NIV84, which renders δικαιοσύνη θεοῦ as a source genitive—'*a* righteousness *from* God' (italics added).

In contrast, the second main option—δικαιοσύνη θεοῦ as God's own righteousness—relies on reading the genitive θεοῦ as either: (i) an adjectival, possessive genitive, referring to an aspect of God's own character; or, (ii) a verbal, subjective genitive, referring to God's righteous acts.[34] This reading also claims ancient precedent in Ambrosiaster,[35] finds some limited acknowledgment amongst early Reformed interpreters,[36] and has recently gained increasing support amongst a range of scholars,[37] especially among a number who understand God's righteousness as his 'covenant faithfulness'.[38] The shift in scholarly opinion towards this reading is partially reflected in the NIV11, which now renders δικαιοσύνη θεοῦ as 'the righteousness of God' (except at 3:22), and so allows for this reading, without necessarily supporting it (cf. NRSV; ESV; CSB).

---

32 Bultmann, *Theology*, 1.285; Bornkamm, *Paul*, 138; Conzelmann, *Outline*, 218–220; Cranfield, *Romans*, 1.96–99; Carson, 'Atonement', 124–125; Irons, *The Righteousness of God*, 311–118; Schreiner, *Romans*, 125–142.
33 Cf. Tyndale's translation (1526): 'the rightewesnes no dout which is good before God'.
34 This verbal subjective genitive reading is predicated on the often unstated, but perfectly valid, assumption that δικαιοσύνη may be taken as an 'action noun' (verbal noun). Wallace, *Greek Grammar*, 112, defines a verbal genitive construction as one in which 'the head noun has a verb as a cognate'. In this case, the head noun δικαιοσύνη has the cognate verb δικαιόω.
35 Ambrosiaster, *Commentary on Paul's Epistles*, cited in Bray, *Romans*, 99: 'the righteousness of God is all about God's divinity ... the righteousness of God appears to be mercy because it has its origin in the promise, and when God's promise is fulfilled it is called "the righteousness of God". For it is righteousness when what is promised has been delivered'.
36 E.g. Gouge & Gataker, *Westminster Annotations*, on Romans 1:17: 'righteousness of God: Of Christ given to us by God, and received by faith'. The divines also note, however, that it is called 'righteousness of God ... because it is the accomplishment of all his promises; for so is the righteousness of God sometimes taken for his faithfulness and mercy, Rom. 3.26'.
37 Barrett, *Romans*, 29; Kümmel, *Theology*, 198; Fitzmyer, *Romans*, 262.
38 Williams, 'Righteousness of God', 285; Hays, 'Justification', 3.1129; Wright, 'Letter to the Romans', 398–340; Wright, *Justification. God's Plan*, 63; Wright, 'Justification: Yesterday', 56; Wright, *Paul and the Faithfulness of God*, 796, 804, 928; Wright, 'Translating δικαιοσύνη'; Bird, *Saving Righteousness*, 15–16.

A variant of this position, attempting to mediate the debate, argues, following the influential work of E. Käsemann, that δικαιοσύνη θεοῦ operates as both a subjective genitive and a genitive of source, denoting both active God's saving power, and the gift of righteousness created by that power.[39] Most recently, R. N. Longenecker, D. Moo, and F. Thielman have all independently argued, with various different nuances, that God's righteousness is simultaneously an attribute to God's character (possessive genitive), God's saving activity (subjective genitive), and the righteous status granted to believers (source genitive).[40]

Despite strong arguments on all sides, reading δικαιοσύνη θεοῦ as a possessive/subjective genitive best accounts for the evidence: 'The righteousness of God' is God's own righteous character and actions.'[41] Specifically, I will argue below, 'the righteousness of God' is his fidelity to his own name, his commitment to do what is right, especially in his covenant with creation and with Israel, which involves both judging sin and saving his people. Paul declared that this righteousness of God has been eschatologically enacted and embodied in Christ. At this point, it is enough to establish that Paul speaks of God's own righteousness. Four considerations are decisive.

First, the Scriptures of Israel, which undoubtedly shaped Paul's theological understanding more than any other source, consistently speak of 'the righteousness of God' as an aspect of God's own character and actions. The precise phrase צדקת אלהים / δικαιοσύνη θεοῦ does not occur in the OT. There are, however, a number of close parallels, and these overwhelmingly refer not to a status that God confers on his people, but to God himself. The Scriptures: (i) describe the LORD by the

---

39 Käsemann, 'Righteousness of God', 167–193; Beker, *Paul*, 262–264; Dunn, *Romans 1–8*, 41–42; Stuhlmacher, *Romans*, 61–65; Jewett, *Romans*, 141–142; Campbell, *Deliverance*, 677–704; Grieb, 'Righteousness of God', 65–78; Schnabel, *an die Römer*, 174–181.
40 Longenecker, *Romans*, 175 (cf. pp.168–175); Moo, *Romans*, 241 (cf. pp.73–100, 241–246); Theilman, *Romans*, 203 (cf. pp.81–93, 202–205). Also: Naselli, 'Righteous God', 217, argues that '*God's attribute of being righteous* is the fundamental concept' and that in Romans 'that entails both *God's gift of a righteous status* ... and *God's activity of saving*'. He considers that '*God's gift of a righteous status* is most prominent in Romans' (italics original).
41 The fine distinctions between the possessive genitive and subjective genitive readings should not be pressed too hard. Given the close connection between character and actions in Jewish thought, it is quite likely that Paul intended both connotations.

adjective 'righteous' (צדיק / δίκαιος);⁴² (ii) use a noun phrase to speak of 'the righteousness of the LORD', or (in the plural) the 'righteous deeds of the LORD' (צדקת יהוה / δικαιοσύνη + κύριος);⁴³ (iii) employ possessive pronouns to report God's self-reference to 'my righteousness' (צדקי / ἡ δικαιοσύνη μου),⁴⁴ to address him by referring to 'your righteousness' (צדקתך / ἡ δικαιοσύνη σου),⁴⁵ or to speak in the third person of 'his righteousness' (צדקתו / ἡ δικαιοσύνη αὐτοῦ);⁴⁶ (iv) attribute righteousness to the LORD God in other ways.⁴⁷

The closest OT parallels to Paul's declaration that 'the righteousness of God has been revealed' (1:17: δικαιοσύνη θεοῦ ... ἀποκαλύπτεται; 3:21: δικαιοσύνη θεοῦ πεφανέρωται) are found in the psalms and Isaiah: (i) Psalm 98 declares that 'the LORD has made known his salvation; he has revealed his righteousness (גלה צדקתו / ἀπεκάλυψεν τὴν δικαιοσύνην αὐτοῦ) in the sight of the nations' (Ps 98:2 [LXX 97:2]). Here the context makes clear that it is God's 'marvelous' actions in history, bringing

---

42 E.g. Deut 32:4; 2 Chron 12:6; Ezra 9:15; Neh 9:8, 33; Pss 11:7; 116:5; 145:17 [LXX 10:7; 114:5; 144:17]; Isa 45:21; Lam. 1:18; Dan 9:14; Zeph 3:5; Zech 9:9 (?); cf. 4 Ezra 10:15–16: 'bear bravely the troubles that have come upon you. For if you acknowledge the decree of God to be righteous, you will receive your son back in due time'; 14:32: 'because he is a righteous judge, in due time he took from you what he had given'; 2 Bar. 44:4: 'he whom we serve is righteous and that our Creator is impartial'; 78:5: 'so that you may consider the judgment of him who decreed it against you to be righteous'.

43 E.g. Deut 33:21; Judg 5:11; 1 Sam 12:7; Mic 6:5; Cf. 1QS 10:23: 'For thanksgiving shall I open my mouth, the righteousness of God (צדקות אל; [pl. = the righteous acts?]) shall my tongue recount always'; 10:24–25: 'Counselled by wisdom, I shall recount knowledge ...conforming to the righteousness of God (לצדקת אל [sg. = God's righteous character revealed in the law/ wisdom?]); 1QS 11:11–12: 'As for me, if I stumble, God's loving-kindness forever shall save me. If through sin of the flesh I fall, my justification (משפטי) will be by the righteousness of God (בצדקת אל) which endures for all time'; 1QM 4:6: 'When they go to battle they shall write on their banners, "The truth of God", "The Righteousness of God" (צדק אל), "The glory of God", "The justice of God"'.

44 Isa 46:13: 51:5, 6, 8; 56:1.

45 Pss 5:9 [ET 5:8]; 31:2 [LXX 30:2; ET 31:1]; 35:24, 28 [LXX 34:24, 28]; 36:7, 11 [LXX 35:7, 11; ET 36:6, 10]; 37:6 [LXX: 36:6]; 51:16 [LXX: 50:16; ET 51:14]; 71:2, 16, 19 [LXX 70:2, 16, 19]; 88:13 [LXX 87:13; ET: 88:12]; 89:17 [LXX 88:17; ET 89:16]; 119:40, 142, 160 LXX; 143:1, 11; 145:7 [LXX 118:40, 142, 160; 142:1, 11; 144:7]; Dan 9:16; Cf. 4 Ezra 8:36: 'For in this, O Lord, your righteousness and goodness will be declared, when you are merciful to those who have no store of good works'; Ps. Sol. 2:15: 'I will justify you, O God, in uprightness of heart. For in your judgments is your righteousness (ὅτι ἐν τοῖς κρίμασίν σου ἡ δικαιοσύνη σου), O God'.

46 Pss 7:18 [ET 7:17]; 22:32 [LXX 21:32; ET 22:31]; 50:6; 97:6; 98:2; 103:17; 111:3 [LXX 49:6; 96:6; 97:2; 102:17; 110:3]; Isa 42:21; 59:16 [MT only].

47 E.g. Pss 89:15 [LXX 88:15; ET 89:14]; 97:2 [LXX 96:2]; Isa 41:10; Dan 9:7, 9 LXX; cf. Wis. 5:17–18, 20: 'the Lord ... will put on righteousness as a breastplate' (ἐνδύσεται θώρακα δικαιοσύνην) ... and creation will join with him to fight against his frenzied foes'.

salvation to his people, which have revealed his righteousness; (ii) Isaiah 56 has the LORD himself declare that 'soon my salvation will come and my righteousness be revealed' (Isa 56:1: וצדקתי להגלות / καὶ τὸ ἔλεός μου ἀποκαλυφθῆναι), where the LXX employs the verb ἀποκαλύπτω, but translates 'righteousness' with 'mercy (τὸ ἔλεός μου ἀποκαλυφθῆναι). Here again, God's righteousness will be revealed when he acts to save his people. In OT and the early Jewish literature, then, what the LORD reveals as his righteousness is his *own character and actions*.

Crucially, and by contrast, there is no clear precedent in the Scriptures or the early Jewish literature for 'the righteousness of God' referring to a righteous status that God might grant to his people. The LORD himself *is* the righteousness of his people;[48] he *credits them* with righteousness;[49] he *clothes them* with righteousness;[50] he *works* righteousness for them.[51] In none of these constructions, however, do the Scriptures speak of 'the righteousness of God'. All of the closest biblical and early Jewish antecedents for Paul's phrase refer to God's own character or actions.

Second, and crucially, Paul's use of the phrase 'righteousness of God' (δικαιοσύνη θεοῦ) in Romans is consistent with this biblical and early Jewish pattern (1:17; 3:5, 21, 22, 25, 26; 10:3 (x2)): δικαιοσύνη θεοῦ refers to God's own character and actions. This is certainly clear in Romans 3:5, where the apostle lays out a series of contrasts between Israel and God: Israel's 'faithlessness' contrasts with God's 'faithfulness' (3:3); Israel's 'lies' contrast with God's 'truth' (3:4, 7); 'our unrighteousness'

---

48 Ps 4:2 [ET 4:1]: 'O God of my righteousness' (אלהי צדקי / ὁ θεὸς τῆς δικαιοσύνης μου); Isa 45:24: 'Only in the LORD ... are righteousness and strength' (אך ביהוה לי אמר צדקות ועז); Jer 23:6; 33:16: 'The LORD is our righteousness' (יהוה צדקנו); 1QS 10:11: 'To God shall I say, "O, my Righteousness" (לאל אומר צדקי)'.
49 Gen 15:6: ויחשבה לו צדקה / καὶ ἐλογίσθη αὐτῷ εἰς δικαιοσύνην; Ps 106:31: ותחשב לו לצדקה / καὶ ἐλογίσθη αὐτῷ εἰς δικαιοσύνην.
50 E.g. (i) Isaiah 61:10: 'he has clothed me with the garments of salvation; he has covered me with the robe of righteousness' (מעיל צדקה יעטני). The righteousness is, however, not said to be God's (*contra* NIV 'his righteousness'), and the LXX, at any rate, translates צדקה with εὐφροσύνης ('joy, merriment') rather than δικαιοσύνη; (ii) Ps 132:9 [LXX 131:9]: 'Let your priests be clothed with righteousness (ילבשו צדק / ἐνδύσονται δικαιοσύνην)'; but again, the righteousness is not said to be God's (*contra* NIV 'your righteousness').
51 E.g. (i) Ps. 72:1 [LXX 71:1] has the prayer 'give to the king your justice, O God, and your righteousness (וצדקתך /) to the royal son'. The context makes clear that this is not a righteous status, but the ability to execute justice (74:1–4); (ii) Ps. 103:6 [LXX102:6]) affirms that 'the LORD works righteousness and justice for all who are oppressed'. This also concerns God working out right outcomes for the oppressed, rather than granting them a righteous status.

(ἡ ἀδικία ἡμῶν) contrasts with 'God's righteousness' (θεοῦ δικαιοσύνην) (3:5). Even those who argue that 'the righteousness of God' elsewhere refers to a righteous status which God gives to believers recognize that in 3:5 the phrase refers to an aspect of God's own character.[52] Similarly, in Romans 3:25-26, Paul affirms—twice—that God's ultimate purpose in putting Jesus forward as a 'place of atonement' (ἱλαστήριον) was to demonstrate his own righteousness (3:25: ὃν προέθετο ὁ θεὸς … εἰς ἔνδειξιν τῆς δικαιοσύνης αὐτοῦ; 3:26: πρὸς τὴν ἔνδειξιν τῆς δικαιοσύνης αὐτοῦ). Again, there is no question here that the righteousness in view is God's own righteousness, demonstrated through Jesus' death on the cross.

In the more disputed passages (Rom 1:17; 3:21-22 and 10:3), Paul's verbs encourage the recognition that God's righteousness is an attribute of God himself, climactically revealed in Christ. In both Romans 1:17 and 3:21-22, 'the righteousness of God' (δικαιοσύνη θεοῦ) is the subject of a verb of revelation (1:17: ἀποκαλύπτεται; 3:21: πεφανέρωται). Throughout the Scriptures, God can and does reveal more than himself, but God's own name, will, and works are at the very centre of his revelation. Given that 'the righteousness of God' is revealed in the gospel—the very climax of God's work in the world—we are right to expect that this revelation relates very closely to God's own character. In the context of Paul's argument from Romans 1:18-3:20, which begins with the announcement of 'God's wrath … being revealed from heaven' (1:18: Ἀποκαλύπτεται γὰρ ὀργὴ θεοῦ ἀπ' οὐρανοῦ), it is unlikely that Paul now speaks of a new human status being revealed. On the contrary, it makes good sense to say that, alongside his wrath against sin, God has now revealed—in Christ, and especially in his death—God's own commitment to bring relief for sinners in the face of that wrath, while also judging with their sin (3:24-26). Similarly, in Romans 10:3, Paul speaks of many Jews 'being ignorant of the righteousness of God' (ἀγνοοῦντες …. τὴν τοῦ θεοῦ δικαιοσύνην) so that 'they did not submit to God's righteousness' (τῇ δικαιοσύνῃ τοῦ θεοῦ οὐχ ὑπετάγησαν). The verbal ideas of 'being ignorant' and failing to 'submit' sit uncomfortably with 'the righteousness of God' as a righteous status granted to believers. They makes good sense, however, if 'the righteousness of God' is

---

52 E.g. Moo, *Romans*, 198-199; Schreiner, *Romans*, 278-80.

God's own righteousness, revealed in Christ.

Third, the understanding of δικαιοσύνη θεοῦ as God's own righteousness is further supported by the observation that in Romans 1–3 Paul sets the phrase in parallel with a number of other genitive constructions, all of which clearly refer to God's own character and actions. Most immediately, Paul sandwiches 'the righteousness of God' (1:17: δικαιοσύνη θεοῦ) between 'the power of God' (1:16: δύναμις ... θεοῦ), and 'the wrath of God' (1:18: ὀργὴ θεοῦ), both of which are clearly subjective genitives referring to *God's* power and *God's* wrath, which strongly suggests that Paul also speaks of *God's* righteousness.[53] In the wider context, Paul employs a number of parallel phrases, all of which are best taken as subjective genitives: the 'goodness of God' (2:4: χρηστὸν τοῦ θεοῦ),[54] 'the righteous judgment of God' (2:5: δικαιοκρισίας τοῦ θεοῦ), 'the faithfulness of God' (3:3: τὴν πίστιν τοῦ θεοῦ), 'the truth of God' (3:7: ἡ ἀλήθεια τοῦ θεοῦ; cf. 15:8), and 'the forbearance of God' (3:26: ἐν τῇ ἀνοχῇ τοῦ θεοῦ). These parallels further support the conclusion that 'the righteousness of God' refers to an aspect of God's own character which has been climactically revealed in Christ.

Fourth, the use of the phrase 'the righteousness of God' (δικαιοσύνη θεοῦ) elsewhere in the NT (Matt 6:33; Jas 1:20; 2 Pet 1:1), as well as by Paul in his other letters (2 Cor 5:21; Phil 3:9) is also arguably consistent with this reading. The three references outside Paul all quite clearly refer to an attribute of God's character, on the basis of which Christians have been saved (2 Pet 1:1), or which they are to emulate in their lives (Jas 1:2), and to 'seek' in the world (Matt 6:33). Amongst Paul's letters, 2 Corinthians 5:21 affirms that Christ became sin 'so that we might become the righteousness of God in him' (ἵνα ἡμεῖς γενώμεθα δικαιοσύνη θεοῦ ἐν αὐτῷ), which is certainly capable of being read as a reference to God's own righteousness.[55] The verb 'might become' (γενώμεθα) sits

---

53 Jewett, *Romans*, 142.
54 Note here also Paul's use genitive pronoun, with God as its antecedent, to refer to God's 'kindness, forbearances, and patience' (2:4: τῆς χρηστότητος αὐτοῦ καὶ τῆς ἀνοχῆς καὶ τῆς μακροθυμίας).
55 Cf. Hooker, 'On Becoming the Righteousness of God', provides a well-worked example of this kind of approach. Her construal of 'the righteousness of God' relies too heavily on Käsemann's understanding of God's righteousness as his saving power. Nevertheless, Hooker points up the inadequacies of reading δικαιοσύνη θεοῦ in 2 Corinthians 5:21 as a reference to a righteous status granted to believers.

uncomfortably with the idea of a forensic declaration, which is rightly associated with Paul's teaching on justification by faith (see §2.3). Paul's logic, rather, seems to be that Christ so fully bore the sin of his people that, since they are 'in him', God's own righteousness—God's commitment to do what is right, which he has worked out in Christ—is now manifested in them. Philippians 3:9 may, at first glance, seem to be an exception to this understanding of δικαιοσύνη θεοῦ, since in that text Paul does indeed refer to 'the righteousness *from* God' (τὴν ἐκ θεοῦ δικαιοσύνην). The preposition ἐκ certainly requires a reference to something which *comes from* God. But this is precisely the point: Philippians 3:9 is not a true parallel. That text is distinguished from Paul's nine references to God's own righteousness (δικαιοσύνη θεοῦ) in two ways: (i) τὴν ἐκ θεοῦ δικαιοσύνην is goverened by the participle ἔχων ('having'), which Paul nowhere else associates with δικαιοσύνη θεοῦ, and indicates that Paul here speaks of something that people might possess; (ii) the prepositional phrase 'from God' (ἐκ θεοῦ), which Paul also does not employ in any of the other δικαιοσύνη θεοῦ texts, indicates that Paul now speaks of a righteousness which has God as its source. These syntactical distinctions make it clear that in Philippians 3:9 Paul does not speak of God's own righteousness, but the grant of righteousness *from* God, *possessed* by those who trust in Christ, which the apostle elsewhere describes by recourse to the verb δικαιόω ('justify'; see §2.3 below).

By δικαιοσύνη θεοῦ, then, Paul intends God's own righteous character and actions. In keeping with the Scriptures everywhere, Paul's references in Romans 3:21–22 and 25–26 to 'the righteousness of God' refer to an aspect of God's own character, now revealed most fully in his actions in Christ, rather than to the righteous status believers receive by his grace.

2.1.2 *God's righteousness as God's commitment to his own name*

But there is a second question: what kind of character and actions are envisaged by the noun δικαιοσύνη? In the Scriptures, God's 'righteousness' (צדקה / צדק/ δικαιοσύνη) *is his fundamental commitment to do what is right, by acting consistently with his own character, especially in his covenant relationship with creation, with Israel, and through Israel for the nations*. From the beginning, the LORD is described as 'righteous'

(צדיק / δίκαιος) in an eternal and absolute sense: Moses declares that 'the LORD *is* righteous' (Deut 32:4: יהוה צדיק / ὁ ... κύριος δίκαιος); the psalmist concurs that 'his righteousness endures forever' (Ps 111:3: וצדקתו עמדת לעד / LXX 110:3: ἡ δικαιοσύνη αὐτοῦ μένει εἰς τὸν αἰῶνα τοῦ αἰῶνος); he confesse to God, 'righteousness and justice are the foundation of your throne' (Ps 89:15 [ET 89:14]: צדק ומשפט מכון כסאך / LXX 88:15: δικαιοσύνη καὶ κρίμα ἑτοιμασία τοῦ θρόνου σου), and he praises God, 'your righteousness is righteous forever' (Ps 119: 142: צדקתך צדק לעולם / ἡ δικαιοσύνη σου δικαιοσύνη εἰς τὸν αἰῶνα). In a range of other ways, the Scriptures reveal that God's righteousness is a fundamental aspect of his character: God's righteousness means that 'his work is perfect' and 'all his ways are justice', that he is 'a God of faithfulness' and 'without iniquity' (ESV), that 'he does no wrong' (NIV).[56]

God's commitment to do what is right, of course, cannot be conceived as God conforming to an absolute moral norm which stands above or outside him. Given who he is, God's commitment to do what is right can be nothing other than his utter fidelity to the norms created by his own character. God's righteousness is his commitment to act in consistency with his own 'name'. In Psalm 31, David appeals to the LORD, 'deliver me in your righteousness' (בצדקתך / ἐν τῇ δικαιοσύνῃ σου), and closely follows this with 'for the sake of your name (למען שמך / ἕνεκεν τοῦ ὀνόματός σου) lead and guide me' (Ps 31:2, 4 [LXX 30:2, 4; ET 31:1, 3]. Psalm 89, likewise, sets God's 'name' and God's 'righteousness' in parallel when it declares 'blessed are the people ... who exult in your name (בשמך / ἐν τῷ ὀνόματί σου) all the day and in your righteousness (ובצדקתך / ἐν τῇ δικαιοσύνῃ σου) are exalted' (Ps 89:16–17 [LXX: 88:17; ET 89:15–16]). In the same way, again, in Psalm 143, David appeals to God, 'for the sake of your name, LORD (למען שמך יהוה / ἕνεκα τοῦ ὀνόματός σου, κύριε), preserve my life, and in your righteousness (בצדקתך / ἐν τῇ δικαιοσύνῃ σου), bring me out of trouble' (Ps 143:11 [LXX 142:11]). The prophet Daniel, likewise, sets God's 'name' (שם / ὄνομα), his 'righteousness' (הצדקה / ἡ δικαιοσύνη), and his 'righteous acts' (צדקתך / τὴν δικαιοσύνην σου) in parallel as he acknowledges

---

56 Deut 32:4; Isa 45:21; Pss 11:7; 50:6 [LXX 10:7; 49:6]; 89:15 [LXX 88:15; ET 89:14]; 97:2, 6; 116:5 [LXX 96:2, 6; 114:5]; 119:137, 142, 160; 145:17 [LXX 118:137, 142, 160; 144:17]; Zeph 3:5.

Judah's sin, and appeals for God to save his people (Dan 9:15–16, 18–19).[57] These parallels reveal that God's righteousness is, most fundamentally, his commitment to act in accordance with his own name.

God's self-revelation of this 'name'—his very character—to Moses is foundational to God's self-revelation in the OT and, indeed, the whole of the Scriptures. The LORD declared his 'name' to Moses as 'the LORD, the LORD, the compassionate and gracious God, slow to anger, abounding in love and faithfulness, maintaining love to thousands, and forgiving wickedness, rebellion, and sin, but who will by no means clear the guilty' (Exod 34:5–7 with 3:14–15). This oft-repeated description of God's character simultaneously draws attention to God's grace and justice, his mercy and his wrath.[58] God's righteousness involves, above all, his fidelity to *this* name. From the human point of view, and in the outworking of redemptive history, the divine attributes revealed in the 'name' stand in significant tension with each other.[59] God's grace and justice are not antithetical since, in biblical thought, 'justice is above all the way in which the grace and love of God are maintained and made to triumph'.[60] Nevertheless, the question of *how* the LORD can be faithful to his 'name', simultaneously 'gracious and merciful', *and* 'not clearing the guilty' is one of the fundamental tensions of the biblical narrative. In this context, Paul's opening declaration that the gospel *reveals* God's righteousness (Rom 1:17) promises that the gospel will reconcile this tension, and simultaneously reveal both God's justice and his grace, both his wrath against sin, and his mercy towards sinners.

This recognition that God's righteousness is his fidelity to his own character provides the necessary foundation for an integrated account

---

57 Schreiner, *Romans*, 139–143 also recognizes these associations between God's 'name' and 'righteousness'. He holds that God's righteousness in Romans 1:17 and 3:21–22 is his gift of righteousness to his people, and argues God's 'desire to glorify his name' provides the fundamental reason why God grants the gift of righteousness to his people. The relationship between God's name and his righteousness is, however, even more fundamental.
58 Num 14:18; Deut 4:31; 5:9–10; 7:9–10; Pss 25:6–10; 30:5; 33:5; 40:10; 78:38; 86:3–5, 15; 103:8–9; 105:8; 111:4; 145:8; Neh 9:17, 31–32; Isa 30:18–19; Jer 30:11; 32:18; Dan 9:4; Joel 2:13; Jon 4:2; Mic 7:18–20; Nah 1:2–3.
59 The Christian tradition rightly affirms, however, that within God himself, that is, within the divine 'simplicity', God's attributes exist in perfect unity. See esp. Aquinas, §I.3; Bavinck, *Reformed Dogmatics*, 2.§196–97 (pp. 170–77).
60 Bavinck, *Reformed Dogmatics*, 2.228.

of God's righteousness in relation to the world. Modern scholarship has often set creational, covenantal, and forensic understandings of God's righteousness in opposition to each other. Properly understood, however, they belong together.

First, when considered in relation to the world, God's righteousness is a *creational* category. God's commitment to act in accordance with his own character naturally includes his commitment to act rightly towards his creation. It is no surprise, then, that God's righteousness has a cosmic dimension. In numerous texts, especially in the Psalms, God's righteousness expresses his commitment to set things right in all the world.[61] To this extent, H.H. Schmid was correct to place biblical 'righteousness' language on the broad canvas of the order of creation.[62] God's commitment to do what is right includes his determination to 'secure the good and beneficial order of creation'.[63]

Second, however, God's righteousness is a *covenantal* category. This is in no way opposed to the first category and is, indeed, already implied by it. God's utter transcendence as Creator means that the only way creatures may have any fruitful relationship with him is if he voluntarily condescends, making himself available to them.[64] God's covenant with Adam, and through him with the entire creation, means that all of God's relationships with his creatures are covenantal from the start.[65] Thus, although the creational and the covenantal emphases of biblical 'righteousness' language have sometimes been played off against each other,[66] any dichotomy drawn between them is a false one. God's covenant with creation is foundational, and the Scriptures consistently present God's covenant with Israel as the means by which he intends to

---

61 Pss 9:9 [ET 9:8]; 36:7; 48:11; 65:6 [LXX 35:7; 47:11; 64:6; ET 36:6; 48:10; 65:5]; 96:13 [LXX 95:13]; 98:2, 9 [LXX 97:2, 9].
62 Schmid, *Gerechtigkeit*.
63 Seifrid, 'Righteousness Language', 426.
64 Cf. WCF §7.1 citing Isa 40:13–17; Job 9:32–33; 1 Sam 2:25; Pss 113:5–6; 100:2–3; Job 22:2–3; 35:7–8; Luke 17:10; Acts 17:24–25.
65 See esp. Gen 1:28; 2:16–17; 6:18; 9:8–17; Isa. 24:5; Hos 2:18; 6:7; Jer 33:19–22 (cf. 31:35–36). For a classic discussion of God's covenant with Adam / creation, see: Bavinck, *Reformed Dogmatics*, 2.§ 294-296 (pp.564-571). For recent defences of an original creation covenant, albeit with various emphases, see: Vogels, *God's Universal Covenant*, ch. 1; Merrill, 'Covenant'; Bartholomew, 'Covenant', 28–30; Niehaus, *God at Sinai*, 143–159; cf. Niehaus, 'Covenant', 231–33; Gentry, 'Kingdom', 28–29; Gentry & Wellum, *Kingdom*, 147–222; Dumbrell, *Covenant and Creation* (2013), 1–58; Ward, *God and Adam*, 12–25.
66 E.g. Seifrid, 'Righteousness Language', 425–429; Bird, 'Progressive Reformed View', 141–142.

'set things right' in the entire creation. For this reason, it is no surprise that righteousness language appears not only in the context of God's covenant with creation, but also in close connection with his covenants with Abraham, Israel, and David.[67] To this extent, the 'covenant faithfulness' view of God's righteousness, first advanced by H. Cremer and most recently developed by N.T. Wright, is correct: 'righteousness' in the Hebrew Scriptures is commonly 'a concept of relationship', denoting right behaviour in relationship, and especially within God's covenant with Israel.[68] More specifically, this reading is certainly correct that *God's righteousness is manifested in* his faithfulness to his covenant promises, and in his saving actions on their behalf, and ultimately through them for all the nations and the whole of creation.[69] The 'covenant faithfulness' view is limited, however, by its tendency to *reduce* God's righteousness to his covenant faithfulness and, in some accounts, to reduce this even further to his fidelity to his *gracious* promises over against his commitment to punish sin.[70] Although 'God's righteousness' cannot be simply equated with his 'covenant faithfulness', it certainly includes it.

Third, God's righteousness is a *forensic* category. Again, this must not be set in opposition to 'God's righteousness' as a creational and covenantal category, for the simple reason that all of God's covenants in Scripture are fundamentally legal arrangements. God's covenants confirm and secure his relationship with his world and his people, and provide the terms under which the relationship is conducted. It is no surprise, then, that God demonstrates his righteousness by governing the world, establishing his righteous law, and judging justly.[71] In particular, God's righteousness

---

67 E.g. Gen 15:6, 18: 'righteousness' and 'covenant'; Num 25:12: God's 'covenant' with Phinehas = Ps 106:31 [LXX 105:31]: God reckoned Phinehas 'righteous'; Neh 9:8; Ps 143:1 [LXX 142:1]. It is also significant that the LXX sometimes translates חסד ('steadfast love' / 'loving-kindness') with δικαιοσύνη ('righteousness'): e.g. Gen 19:19; 20:13; 21:23; 24:27; 32:10.
68 Cremer, *Rechtfertigungslehre*, 53. For Wright's works, see n.38 above.
69 Dumbrell, *Covenant and Creation* (1984), 87: '(Israel) will provide, under the direct divine rule which the covenant contemplates, the paradigm of the theocratic rule which is to be the biblical aim for the whole world'; cf. Wright, *Justification*, 154: 'God's righteousness is God's own righteousness ... His faithfulness to the covenant, to Israel, and beyond that again to the whole of creation'.
70 For a critique of the 'covenant faithfulness' reading of 'God's righteousness', see esp. Irons, *Righteousness of God*; cf. Irons, 'Is "Righteousness" a Relational Concept'.
71 Exod 9:27; 2 Chron 12:6; Job 34:17; Pss. 7:12; 9:5, 9 [ET 7:11; 9:4, 8]; 51:6 [LXX 50:6; ET 51:4]; 89:15 [LXX 88:15; ET 89:14]; 96:13; 97:2; 98:9; 119:7, 62, 106, 137–38, 142, 160, 164; 129:4 [LXX 95:13; 96:2; 97:9; 118:7, 62, 106, 137–38, 142, 160, 164; 128:4]; Isa 45:23; Jer 11:20; 12:1; Lam 1:18; Dan 9:14; Neh 9:33; Zeph 3:5.

(צדקה / δικαιοσύνη) is the basis for his judgment upon the idolatrous nations, and especially on faithless Israel. Precisely because God's covenants with creation, Israel, and David all included the promise of curses for disobedience (Gen 2:16–17; Lev 26:1–46; Deut 27–30; 2 Sam 7:14), God is repeatedly described as 'righteous' when he brings wrath upon the nations, and judgment on his faithless people.[72] At the same time, in all of the biblical covenants, God's promise to punish sin is set within the content of his univocal and unconditional promise to bless (Gen 1:28; 12:1–3; 2 Sam 7:12–13, 15). God's 'righteousness' is, therefore also—especially—revealed when he rescues his people and punishes his enemies (e.g. Exod 9:27; Deut 33:21; Judg 5:11; 1 Sam. 12:7; Dan. 9:16; Mic. 6:5). The psalmists regularly celebrate God's righteousness as the source of blessing, and invoke God's righteousness as the grounds on which they seek deliverance.[73] The same dynamic is evident in the prophets, especially in Isaiah 40–66, where God's 'righteousness' (צדקה / δικαιοσύνη) is presented as the ground of Israel's hope for deliverance, and is closely associated with his salvation (תשועה; LXX: σωτηρία),[74] as well as with other descriptions of God's gracious deliverance of his people.[75] God's commitment to do what is right—his righteousness—includes both judging sin and vindicating the righteous, both executing the curses, and bringing the blessings, of the covenant.[76]

---

72   2 Chron. 12:6; Isa. 5:16; 10:22; 28:17; 51:5; 59:16–19; Lam 1:18; Dan 9:7, 9 LXX, 14; Ezra 9:15; Neh 9:33; cf. Ps. Sol. 2:15: 'I will justify you, O God, in uprightness of heart. For in your judgments is your righteousness (ὅτι ἐν τοῖς κρίμασίν σου ἡ δικαιοσύνη σου), O God'; Wis. 5:17–18, 20: 'the Lord … will put on righteousness as a breastplate (ἐνδύσεται θώρακα δικαιοσύνην) … and creation will join with him to fight against his frenzied foes'; 4 Ezra 10:15–16: 'bear bravely the troubles that have come upon you. For if you acknowledge the decree of God to be righteous, you will receive your son back in due time'; 14:32: 'because he is a righteous judge, in due time he took from you what he had given'; 2 Bar. 44:4: 'he whom we serve is righteous and that our Creator is impartial'; 78:5: 'so that you may consider the judgment of him who decreed it against you to be righteous'.
73   Pss 31:2 [LXX 30:2; ET 31:1]; 35:24, 27–28 [LXX 34:24, 27–28]; 71:2 [LXX 70:2]; 85:11–14 [LXX 84:11–14; ET 85:1–13]; 119:123, 40; 143:1, 11 [LXX 118:123, 40; 142:1, 11]; cf. Dan 9:16.
74   Isa 45:8; 46:13; 51:4–5, 6, 8; 56:1; 59:16–18; 63:1; cf. Pss 65:6; 71:15–19; 98:2 [LXX 64:6; 70:15–19; 97:2].
75   See nn.43, 45.
76   Cf. Bavinck, *Reformed Dogmatics 2* §206 (p. 222): 'He is righteous and all his judgments are righteous (Ps. 119:137; 129:4); the punishment of the wicked is often ascribed to God's righteousness (Exod. 6:5; 7:4; Ps. 7:11; 9:4–8; 28:4; 62:12; 73; 96:10, 13; 2 Chron. 12:5–7; Neh. 9:33; Lam. 1:18; Isa. 5:16; 10:22; Dan. 9:14; Rom. 2:5; 2 Thess. 1:5–10). It is also true, however, that the punishment of the wicked is usually inferred from God's wrath, and that the righteousness of God especially comes to the fore in Scripture as the principle of salvation for God's people'.

This forensic aspect of God's righteousness is not, however, the Graeco-Roman concept of distributive justice (*iustitia distributiva*), which is 'too formal and abstract to describe Israel's thought'.[77] At least partly due to the Vulgate's translation of the δικαιοσύνη by the Latin *iustitia*, the medieval church came to understand of 'the righteousness of God' in this way as 'the divine attribute by which God rewards man according to his just deserts'.[78] As Martin Luther rightly saw, this understanding of 'the righteousness of God' cannot account for the way in which Paul connects it to 'the gospel' and 'salvation' in Romans 1:17.[79] As just demonstrated, however, Paul's usage in Romans 1:17 is consistent with the Scriptures generally, which present 'the righteousness of God' as not only standing behind his judgment of sin, but also—especially—energizing his saving acts on behalf of his people.[80] In biblical usage, then, God's righteousness is God's fidelity to his own name, his commitment to act in accordance with his own character, and therefore his commitment to keep his covenant promise to bless his people and, indeed, humanity as a whole, while also judging sin. It is this righteousness that, according to Paul, God has more fully revealed in the gospel.

2.1.3 *God's righteousness in Romans*

In Romans, Paul's declarations regarding God's righteousness share these same emphases: 'God's righteousness' is his commitment to act in accordance with his own name—to do what is right—and therefore to both judge sin, and bring salvation, for Israel, the nations and, indeed, the whole creation. This holistic understanding of God's righteousness seems required by the way in which Paul introduces the theme of the *whole* of the letter by affirming that the gospel—God's climactic work in Christ—reveals God's righteousness (1:16–17). This

---

77 Horton, *Christian Faith*, 269, n.20.
78 McGrath, *Iustitia Dei* (1998), 52–53.
79 Luther, 'Preface', 336–337: 'For I hated that word 'righteousness of God', which, according to the use and custom of all the teachers, I had been taught to understand philosophically regarding the formal or active righteousness, as they call it, with which God is righteous and punishes the unrighteous sinner'.
80 Cf. Bird, *Saving Righteousness*, 15: in the Scriptures of Israel 'the righteousness of God ... is the character of God embodied and enacted in his saving actions which means vindication (for Israel and the righteous) and condemnation (for the pagan world and the wicked)'.

opening statement already encourages us to see that God's righteousness in Romans cannot be equated with the righteous status that God undoubtedly gants to those who trust in Christ. Indeed, this holistic understanding of God's righteousness is the only way to make sense of all of Paul's references to δικαιοσύνη θεοῦ. By contrast, those who seek to understand 'God's righteousness' as his gift of righteousness are forced to posit a distinction between God's 'saving righteousness' (1:17; 3:21–22; 10:3) and his 'judging righteousness' (3:5, 25–26).[81] But Paul makes no such distinction. The revelation of 'God's righteousness' in the gospel (1:16–17) introduces all of the apostle's teaching regarding not only justification, but also the transformation of God's people in Chirst and their eschatological hope (Rom 5–8), the place of Israel and the Gentiles in God's purposes (Rom 9–11), the life of the church in the world (Rom 12–15).[82]

Certainly, 'God's righteousness' (δικαιοσύνη θεοῦ) is the source of his judgment of sinful humanity, including faithless Israel. In Romans 2 Paul warns those who are 'storing up wrath' for themselves on the 'day of wrath, when God's righteous judgment (δικαιοκρισίας τοῦ θεοῦ) will be revealed' (2:5). He then announces that 'God, through Jesus Christ, will judge the secret thoughts of all' (2:16). This judgment—which clearly includes even the covenant people—is, Paul says, 'according to my gospel', the same gospel that at 1:16–17 is said to reveal 'the righteousness of God' (δικαιοσύνη θεοῦ). Thus God's judgment on sin is rooted in 'the righteousness of God'. Likewise, in Romans 3, in the section dealing with the place of Israel in God's purposes, Paul makes it clear that God's wrath against his covenant people is an expression of his righteousness: God will be justified (δικαιωθῇς) in bringing judgment against his

---

81 E.g. Schreiner, *Romans*, 126–43, 319–45, repeatedly uses these categories. He does acknowledge that 'the saving righteousness and judging righteousness of God find their resolution, as 3:21–26 illustrates, in the gospel' (p.158). They are, however, on Schreiner's reading, essential different things: 'God's judging righteousness' is his activity in judging sin, while 'God's saving righteousness' is his gift of a righteous status to believers.

82 Cf. Bird, 'Progressive Reformed View', 141, on Romans 1:16–17: 'the "righteousness of God" is *not* justification by faith. There is indeed a gift of a righteous status from God (see Rom. 5:17; Phil. 3:9), but the righteousness of God introduces the entire package of salvation in all of Romans (not just Romans 1–4) including justification, redemption, sacrifice, forgiveness of sins, covenant membership, reconciliation, the gift of the Holy Spirit, power for a new obedience, union with Christ, freedom from sin and eschatological vindication'.

people (3:4 citing Ps. 51:6 [LXX50:6; ET 51:4]); he is certainly not 'unrighteous' (ἄδικος) in bringing wrath upon them (3:5).[83] In this sense, the 'unrighteousness' (ἀδικία) of the covenant people serves to confirm 'the righteousness of God' (θεοῦ δικαιοσύνην). So also again in Romans 3:25–26, Paul emphasizes by repetition that God put Jesus forward (προέθετο) 'for a demonstration of his righteousness' (3:25: εἰς ἔνδειξιν τῆς δικαιοσύνης αὐτοῦ; 3:26: πρὸς τὴν ἔνδειξιν τῆς δικαιοσύνης αὐτοῦ). This demonstration was needed because 'of the overlooking of the former sins' (3:25: διὰ τὴν πάρεσιν τῶν προγεγονότων ἁμαρτημάτων). God has now demonstrated his righteous, Paul emphasizes, by judging sin in the death of Christ. Thus, as in the Scriptures of Israel, so in Romans 2–3, 'God's righteousness' entails his commitment to judge sin.

At the same time, and emphatically, God's righteousness is the source of the salvation made available in the gospel. At Romans 1:16 Paul declares that 'the gospel' is 'the power of God for salvation (σωτηρία) to everyone who believes'. This salvation is closely associated with God's covenant with Israel, since it is 'for the Jew first', but it also has a universal scope, since it is 'also for the Greek'. Crucially, Paul grounds this salvation in 'the righteousness of God' (δικαιοσύνη θεοῦ), which the gospel reveals (1:17). In combining the language of God's righteousness (δικαιοσύνη θεοῦ), revealed (ἀποκαλύπτεται), 'for salvation' (εἰς σωτηρίαν) of 'all who believe' (παντὶ τῷ πιστεύοντι), including 'the Greek' (Ἕλληνι), Paul unmistakably alludes to Ps 98:2 [LXX 97:2]: 'The Lord has made known his salvation (τὸ σωτήριον αὐτοῦ); he has revealed (ἀπεκάλυψεν) his righteousness (τὴν δικαιοσύνην αὐτοῦ) in the sight of the nations (ἐναντίον τῶν ἐθνῶν)'. This promise, Paul declares, is now being fulfilled in what God has done in Christ, and through the proclamation of the gospel about him in all the world. Romans 3:21–26 repeats and expands this same emphasis on God's righteousness as the source of God's work in Christ, which secures a universally-applicable salvation. Now, Paul explains, the revelation of 'God's righteousness'

---

83 Williams, 'Righteousness of God', 266–267, argues that τὰ λόγια τοῦ θεοῦ at 3:2, 4 refers to God's promise to bless the nations through Abraham. While this reading is attractive, the emphasis in 3:1–8 on God's just wrath on his faithless people suggests that τὰ λόγια τοῦ θεοῦ entrusted to the Jews should be understood more broadly to mean 'God's covenant with Israel' which included both the promise of blessing (for Israel and through them the nations) and the promise of curse on disobedience.

(δικαιοσύνη θεοῦ) is the source of the 'justification' of all—both Jews and Gentiles—who believe (3:22, 24). God's righteousness, then, manifested in the gospel of Jesus Christ, is the source of a universally applicable salvation. Indeed, in the broader argument of Romans this salvation, rooted as it is in 'the righteousness of God' (δικαιοσύνη θεοῦ) extends even to the non-human creation, since the eschatological 'revelation' (τὴν ἀποκάλυψιν) of the 'sons of God'—that is, their resurrection—will ultimately mean the end of the curse on the earth, and the liberation of the cosmos from its 'bondage to decay' (8:18–25; cf. Isa 24:5).[84]

The 'the righteousness of God', then, both in the Scriptures of Israel and in Paul's letter to the Romans, is his fidelity to his own name—his commitment to do what is right—especially in his covenant with the creation, with Israel, and through Israel for the world. It therefore finds expression both in his condemnation of sin (in Israel and the nations), and his achievement of a salvation of universal scope. This is ultimately why 'the gospel' reveals 'the righteousness of God': in Christ, and especially in his death on the cross, God has simultaneously condemned sin (3:25; 8:3), and saved sinners; he has shown himself to be both 'righteous' (δίκαιον) and 'the righteousifier (δικαιοῦντα) of the one who is of the faith of Jesus' (3:26).

2.2 *Christ's faith/fulness*

God's righteousness, Paul says in 3:22, has been revealed διὰ πίστεως Ἰησοῦ Χριστοῦ ('through the faith of Jesus Christ').[85] God's revelation of his righteousness has occurred in Jesus Christ. That much is clear. Nevertheless, as for 'the righteousness of God', the phrase 'the faith of Jesus Christ' is the subject of significant and ongoing

---

84 It is significant that Rom 8:18–25 links the ultimate liberation of creation (8:21: ἐλευθερωθήσεται) to human salvation (8:24: ἐσώθημεν) via the repetition of the key term hope (ἐλπίς) at 8:21 and 24. Since human salvation is rooted in 'the righteousness of God' revealed in 'the gospel' (1:16–17), the clear implication is that this cosmic liberation has the same source. See here: J. Moo, 'Romans 8.19–22'.
85 The repetition of δικαιοσύνη θεοῦ at the beginning of 3:22 indicates that it remains the subject of the sentence, and πεφανέρωται remains the main verb.

debate.[86] In particular, there is significant disagreement about both the lexical import of the head noun πίστις ('faith' or 'faithfulness'), and the function of the genitive Ἰησοῦ Χριστοῦ ('of Jesus Christ').

On the one hand, the dominant view in the reception history of the text reads πίστεως as 'trust' and Ἰησοῦ Χριστοῦ as the object of that trust (objective genitive): 'faith *in* Jesus Christ'. In support of this reading, it is possible to find statements in theologians as significant as Athanasius and Augustine to the effect that Christ, being God, could not have exercised faith.[87] Aquinas mounts a positive dogmatic argument to this effect.[88] Certainly, the Reformation and post-Reformation exegetical tradition strongly supports reading Paul's numerous references to πίστις Χριστοῦ as references to Christian faith *in* Christ,[89] and this view continues to receive support from the majority of commentators.[90] This reading was cemented for Protestant interpretation by Luther's German translation, *den Glauben an Jesum Christum* (1522), and is represented in all the major modern English translations (NRSV, ESV, NIV, CSB), as well as the most recent edition of the Lutherbibel (2017).

On the other hand, it is possible to read πίστεως as 'faith expressed in faithfulness', and Ἰησοῦ Χριστοῦ as a designation of the one who execised that faith/fulness (subjective genitive): the 'faith/fulness *exercised by* Jesus Christ' or 'Jesus Christ's faith/fulness'. At the level of

---

86 For a major collection of essays, see Bird & Sprinkle, *Faith of Jesus Christ*. For recent reviews of the debate, see Easter, 'The Pistis Christou Debate'; Kugler, 'ΠΙΣΤΙΣ ΧΡΙΣΤΟΥ'. Significant recent contributions include: Moo, *Galatians*, 38–48; McFadden, 'Does Πίστις Mean "Faith(fulness)"'; Schliesser, '"Christ-Faith"'; Hooker, 'Another Look'. Downs & Lappenga, *Faithfulness of the Risen Christ*. A major new study is also promised: Gupta, *Paul and the Language of Faith*.

87 Athanasius, *Orationes contra Arianos* §2.6.9 argues that πιστόν at Hebrews 3:2 must refer to Christ as the *object* of faith and not as the one exercising faith/fullness. Augustine, *On the Spirit and the Letter*, § 15, commenting on πίστις Χριστοῦ at Romans 3:22, argues that Paul cannot mean 'the faith with which he [Jesus] himself believes', since faith is a quality of man.

88 Aquinas, *Summa Theologiae* §3a, q.7, a.3 argues from Hebrews 11:1 that 'where divine reality is not hidden there is no point in faith. But from the moment of conception Christ had the full vision of the very being of God ... Therefore he could not have had faith'.

89 E.g. Gouge and Gataker, *Westminster Annotations* on Rom 3:22: 'Gr. Tec. *In Jesus Christ*. Which we yield to Jesus Christ, or which faith resteth upon him'.

90 E.g. Murray, *Romans*, 370–371; Cranfield, *Romans* 1.203; cf. Cranfield, 'On the πίστις Χριστοῦ Question'; Hultrgren, 'The Pistis Christou Formulations'; Dunn, *Romans 1–8*, 166–167; cf. Dunn, 'Once More'; Silva, 'Faith versus Works', 227–34; Jewett, *Romans*, 278; Keener, *Romans*, 57–58; Schreiner, *Romans*, 127–49, 323–28; Moo, *Romans*, 73–100, 241–46; Thielman, *Romans*, 81–93, 202–205.

theology, the mainstream of orthodox Christology rightly refuses to allow Christ's divine nature to overwhelm his human nature. Christ, being fully human, exercised real faith and faithfulness. Thus, against Aquinas' objection (just noted), M. Allen has recently demonstrated that whether or not Paul affirms Christ's faith by the phrase πίστις Χριστοῦ, 'the Christ's faith coheres with and is, in fact, a necessary implication of orthodox Christology and the soteriology of the magisterial Reformation'.[91] In terms of the exegetical tradition, the subjective genitive reading may or may not be able to claim ancient precedent; this is itself a matter of debate.[92] The view was advocated by a strong minority of scholars in the nineteenth and twentieth centuries,[93] received a major impetus from Richard Hays 1983 monograph *The Faith of Jesus Christ*,[94] and is adopted in a significant number of more recent works.[95] In terms of the translations, the Vulgate's rendering *fides Iesu Christi* retained the ambiguity of Paul's original,[96] and this tendency persisted in Erasmus' Latin translation, and in Tyndale's English translation as 'the faith of Christ' (1526), which was followed by the KJV (1611). Modern translations have tended to remove the ambiguity in favour of the believer's faith in Christ, but the NRSV and NIV11 translation notes acknowledge 'faithfulness of Jesus Christ' as an alternative. A variation on this view holds that the phrase is deliberately ambiguous and that, at least in some of its instances, Paul intended to evoke both Christ's faith and our

---

91 Allen, *The Christ's Faith*, 2.
92 For arguments that some of the Fathers read Paul as referring to Christ's faith, see: Wallis, *The Faith of Jesus Christ*; Bird & Whitenton, 'Faithfulness of Jesus Christ'. To the contrary, see: Harrisville, 'ΠΙΣΤΙΣ ΧΡΙΣΤΟΥ'; Silva, 'Faith Versus Works', 227–229; Elliott, 'Πίστις Χριστοῦ'. Cf. Matlock, 'Saving Faith', 87, who argues that when the Fathers do offer explicit comment on πίστις Χριστοῦ in Paul, they tend to favour the objective genitive reading.
93 Haussleiter, *Der Glaube Jesu Christi*, 109–145; Kittel, 'Πίστις Ἰησοῦ Χριστοῦ'; Barth, *Romans*, in loc.; Hebert, '"Faithfulness"'; Torrance, 'One Aspect'; Valloton, *Le Christ*; Longenecker, *Paul*, 149–152; Howard, 'Notes', and '"Faith of Christ"'; Robinson, '"Faith of Jesus Christ"'; Williams, 'Righteousness of God', 272–278, and 'Again Pistis Christou'.
94 Hays, *Faith of Jesus Christ*; cf. Hays, 'ΠΙΣΤΙΣ'.
95 Johnson, 'Romans 3:21–26'; Hooker, 'ΠΙΣΤΙΣ ΧΡΙΣΤΟΥ', and 'Another Look', suggesting that 'the phrase refers primarily to the faith/faithfulness of Christ, but that this is also something shared by those who are "in Christ"'; Wallace, *Greek Grammar*, 115–116; Wright, 'Romans', 469–470, *Paul and the Faithfulness of God*, 836–842; Longenecker, *Romans*, 409–413.
96 Howard, 'Faith of Christ', 461.

faith in him.⁹⁷ Or, pushing the interpretation even further, yet others argue for a 'third view' on the question, contending—primarily on the basis of Galatians 3:23–26—that πίστις Χριστοῦ for Paul is 'not an individual disposition or character (either Christ's or that of the believer), but rather ... an eschatological event'.⁹⁸

In engaging this debate it is important to recognise that it is possible to make too much of its theological significance.⁹⁹ In particular: (i) both the objective and subjective readings are compatible with orthodox Christian theology; (ii) Paul certainly affirms the perfection of Christ's trusting obedience to the Father, whether he does so with this phrase or not (esp. Rom 5:18–19; 2 Cor 5:21; Phil. 2:6–8), and; (iii) Paul also certainly emphasizes the necessity of human faith *in* Christ as the only instrument of justification, not least in Romans 3:22: 'to all who believe'. Nevertheless, as M. Hooker notes, as we approach this question, 'we are locked firmly into the so-called hermeneutical circle': our theology will inevitably influence our exegesis, and our exegesis will, in turn, not be insignificant for our theology.¹⁰⁰ Our exegetical conclusions will to some extent colour our theological construction of the doctrine of justification by faith, providing more or less exegetical support either for Christ's perfect obedience as the objective ground of justification, or for human faith as its instrument.

Eight considerations tip the scales in favour of the view that Paul's phrase πίστεως Ἰησοῦ Χριστοῦ (3:22) refers to Jesus Christ's faith/fulness to God, rather than human faith in him. First, lexicographically, the semantic range of πίστις includes not only 'faith' (= 'trust' or 'belief') but also 'faithfulness'. In the LXX, πίστις regularly translates

---

97 For varieties of this view, see: Williams, 'Again Pistis Christou', 445–446, on Rom 3:26 (otherwise Williams sees Paul using πιστεύω and πίστις for the believer's faith, and πίστις Χριστοῦ for Christ's faith [pp.444, 447]); Hooker, 'ΠΙΣΤΙΣ ΧΡΙΣΤΟΥ', 341, concludes that πίστις Χριστοῦ refers both to Christ's faith/fulness and 'the answering faith of believers, who claim that faith as their own'; Hooker, 'Another Look', 46–62; Hays, *The Faith of Jesus Christ (2002)*, 172, 203 on Galatians 3:7, 24; Longenecker, *Triumph*, 103–104, on Gal 3:23; Downs, 'Faith(fullness)', 144–45 on 2 Tim 3:15; Morgan, *Roman Faith*, 271, n.39.
98 Schliesser, '"Christ-Faith"'; cf. Sprinkle, 'πίστις Χριστοῦ'.
99 Cf. Matlock, 'Detheologizing'.
100 Hooker, 'Another Look', 47; Cf. Myers, 'From Faithfulness', 291: 'The πίστις Χριστοῦ debate involves a conflict over the fundamental shape of Paul's theology'; Hunn, 'Debating', 26: 'It is theology, not grammar, that continues to drive the debate'.

the Hebrew nouns אמונה and אמת and carries the sense of 'steadfastness', 'trustworthiness', or 'faithfulness'.[101] Examples where πίστις means 'trust' are not entirely lacking, but they are certainly rare.[102] The adjective πιστός similarly translates אמן (usually nifal) and means 'trustworthy' or 'faithful' and the cognate verb πιστεύω, by contrast, regularly translates אמן (usually hifil), and consistently means 'trust' or 'belief'.[103] In the NT, where the language of faith is particularly prominent, the senses of the verb πιστεύω ('I believe', 'I trust'),[104] and the adjective πιστός ('faithful') remain constant.[105] The noun πίστις takes on the 'active' meaning of 'trust' far more commonly than in the LXX, but still often enough means 'faithfulness'.[106] Taking all this into account, T. Morgan's major recent study has confirmed that not only in the LXX, but also in the Graeco-Roman world of the first century, and—in an even more heightened form—in the early Christian texts, the Greek πίστις and the Latin *fides*, with their associated word groups, are primarily used to describe *relationships of trust* which create community, and therefore involve notions of both trust and fidelity.[107]

---

101 E.g. Deut 32:20; 1 Sam 26:23; 2 Kgs 12:16; 22:7; 2 Chron 31:12, 15, 18; 34:12; Ps 32:4 [MT 33:4]; Prov 3:3; 12:17, 22; 14:22; 15:27a; Hos 2:2 [ET 2:20]; Jer 5:1, 3; 7:27; 35:9 [MT 28:9]; 39:41 [MT 32:41]; cf. Wisd 3:14; Sir 1:27; 15:15; 40:12; 45:4; 46:15; Ps. Sol. 8:28; 17:40. See: Lust, Eynikel & Hauspie, *Greek-English Lexicon*, loc. cit.; Koehler & Baumgartner, *HALOT*, 1.62–63.
102 Jer 9:2 [ET 9:3] (?); Sir 22:23; 27:16.
103 Koehler & Baumgartner, *HALOT*, 1: 63–64; Lust, Eynikel & Hauspie, *Greek-English Lexicon*, loc. cit..
104 BDAG, 816–818, lists five definitions, the first three of which cover the last majority of occurrences and reflect the sense of trusting, or trusting in, or entrusting.
105 BDAG, 820–21, lists: (i) 'pertaining to being worthy of belief or trust' (glosses: *trustworthy, faithful, dependable, inspiring trust/faith*); (ii) 'pertaining to being trusting' (glosses: *trusting, cherishing faith/trust*). The majority of NT occurrences carry the first meaning.
106 πίστις occurs 243x in the GNT. BDAG, 818–20, provide three definitions: (i) 'that which evokes trust and faith' (glosses: *faithfulness, reliability, fidelity, commitment, assurance, oath, troth, proof, pledge*); (ii) 'state of believing on the basis of the reliability of the one trusted' (glosses: *trust, confidence, faith*); (iii) 'that which is believed' (glosses: *body of faith / belief / teaching*). Although 'faithfulness' is listed first, 'faith' / 'trust' has by far the larger number of examples. A cursory survey through the NT occurrences reveals that this accurately reflects the NT usage.
107 Morgan, *Roman Faith*, 14, 281. For reviews of Morgan's work, with a particular critique of her tendency to subordinate propositional content of 'faith' to relational concerns, see: Watson, 'Roman Faith'; Seifrid, 'Roman Faith'. Note also here Bates, *Salvation by Allegiance*, who proposes 'allegiance' as the most appropriate translation for πίστις. For an extended review, see Timmins, 'A Faith Unlike Abraham's'.

Paul certainly employs πίστις (142x) with both senses. On the one hand, the majority of Paul's references to πίστις have this sense of 'trust'. In Romans 4, for example, Paul's references to Abraham's πίστις rely on Genesis 15:6 (4:3: Ἐπίστευσεν δὲ Ἀβραὰμ τῷ θεῷ), are regularly coupled with the verb πιστεύω, and clearly refer to Abraham's trust in God's promises (4:5, 9, 11, 12, 13, 16–17, 18–19, 20, 24). Abraham's trust certainly issued in faithfulness, but Paul describes that in other closely related terms (4:12: τοῖς στοιχοῦσιν τοῖς ἴχνεσιν τῆς ... πίστεως τοῦ πατρὸς ἡμῶν Ἀβραάμ [*to those who walk in the footsteps of* the faith of our Father Abraham']). On the other hand, Paul also employs πίστις to describe human 'faithfulness' in a good number of texts (Tit 2:10; Gal 5:22; 2 Thess 1:4; 1 Tim 1:4 (?); 2:7; 4:12; 5:12; 6:11; 2 Tim 2:22; 3:10). In Romans 3, Paul's reference to τὴν πίστιν τοῦ θεοῦ surely means neither 'faith in God', nor 'God's faith', but 'God's faithfulness' (3:3). Lexicographically, then, πίστις in Paul's phrase πίστεως Ἰησοῦ Χριστοῦ could refer either to 'faith' or to 'faithfulness' or—given the close connection between trust and obedience in biblical thought generally, and in Romans in particular—to both 'faith' and 'faithfulness' at the same time, what we might call 'trusting obedience'.

For this reason, a number of scholars have argued that the sharp linguistic distinction in English translation between 'faith' and 'faithfulness' is unwarranted, and it has become common to gloss the term as 'faith/fulness'.[108] Against some looser applications of this approach, K.W. McFadden has successfully shown that Paul can, and often does, disambiguate πίστις by context; πίστις means 'trust' when it is used 'interchangeably or in parallel with the verb πιστεύω', and when it has an object indicated by a preposition;[109] it means 'faithfulness' in Christian virtue lists, and in descriptions of character. Nevertheless, McFadden claims too much when he concludes that 'πίστις does not mean both "faith" and "faithfulness" at the same time in Paul'.[110] That Paul *often* disambiguates the term does not mean he *always* does so, for it remains

---

108 See esp. Robinson, 'Faith of Jesus Christ', 76; Hooker, 'ΠΙΣΤΙΣ ΧΡΙΣΤΟΥ', 339–340; Campbell, 'Romans 1:17', 281; Hays, *The Faith of Jesus Christ (2002)*, 140, 151–52, 161, 203, 295; Downing, 'Ambiguity'; Wright, *Paul and the Faithfulness of God*, 968, 1471.
109 McFadden, '"Faith(fullness)"'; cf. earlier protests along similar lines by: Barr, *Semantics*, 204; Matlock, 'Detheologizing', 5–6; '"Even the Demons Believe"', 316.
110 McFadden, 'Faith(fulness)' in Paul?', 270.

a distinct possibility that in some contexts Paul deliberately works with the inherent polysemy of the term. Indeed, in biblical thought generally, and in Paul in particular, while 'faith' and 'faithfulness' are distinct, they are inseparable; trust in God is the root of faithful living; faithful living is the inevitable fruit of trust in God.[111] The goal of Paul's apostolic calling was, after all, 'the obedience of faith (ὑπακοὴν πίστεως) among all the nations' (1:5; 16:26).[112] Moreover, such a deliberate polysemous use of πίστις would seem to be particularly appropriate when Christ is the subject of the verbal idea in the noun. In Paul's theology, as across the NT, Christ is an utterly unique figure—both fully human, *and* participating in the divine identity, both capable of exercising 'faith' in God, *and* alone utterly 'faithful' to God. Thus, despite McFadden's protest, 'faith/fulness' may well be a helpful gloss for πίστις, especially in the phrase πίστεως Ἰησοῦ Χριστοῦ.

Second, on grammatical grounds, it is more likely that the genitive phrase 'faith of Jesus Christ' (πίστεως Ἰησοῦ Χριστοῦ) has subjective force. To be sure, the genitive can indicate the object of faith. This is certainly the case in Mark 11:22 (Ἔχετε πίστιν Θεοῦ), and quite probably also in other texts with a personal object in the genitive (Acts 3:16; Jas 2:1; Rev 2:13; 14:12), or an impersonal object in the genitive (Col 2:12; 2 Thess 2:13).[113] Extra-biblical examples of πίστις with the objective genitive are also available.[114] Paul's usage, however, is consistent. The only other times that Paul speaks of πίστις followed by the genitive of a noun denoting a person, the genitive is subjective: 'the faithfulness of God' (3:3: τὴν πίστιν τοῦ θεοῦ), is set in contrast with the 'faithlessness' (ἀπιστία) of the Jews, and must refer to *God's* faithfulness (subjective genitive), not faith *in* God (objective genitive);[115] and the 'faith of Abraham' (4:12: τῆς ...

---

111 E.g. Rom 10:16; Gal 5:6; 1 Thess 1:3; 1 Tim 1:5; cf. Heb 11:4, 7, 8–9, 17–18, 23–31, 33–38; Jas 2:14–26.
112 The meaning of the phrase ὑπακοὴν πίστεως is disputed, but it is best read as a subjective genitive ('the obedience *exercised by* faith') or a source genitive ('the obedience which comes from faith'), rather than an epexegtical genitive ('the obedience *which consists in* faith'). For discussion, with arguments to this effect, see esp.: Longenecker, *Romans*, 79–82; Schreiner, *Romans*, 80–82.
113 Wallace, *Greek Grammar*, 116.
114 See Matlock, 'Detheologizing', 19, n.59. The point holds even if some of Matlock's examples are capable of a subjective reading.
115 ESV, NRSV, NASB render 'faithfulness of God'; NIV11 'God's faithfulness'.

πίστεως τοῦ πατρὸς ἡμῶν Ἀβραάμ; 4:16: ἐκ πίστεως Ἀβραάμ), must refer to *Abraham's* faith (subjective genitive), not faith *in* Abraham (objective genitive).[116] In a further twenty texts, Paul uses πίστις + genitive of a person referred to by a pronoun, and all of these also refer to the faith or faithfulness of the person, and never present the individual as the object of faith.[117] Romans 3:3 and 4:12, 16, however, are particularly decisive: they are Paul's only uses of the πίστις + genitive of a noun denoting a person (apart from the disputed phrase), and they occur in the immediate context. This must surely strengthen the case for πίστεως Ἰησοῦ Χριστοῦ as a reference to Christ's faith/fulness.

Third, the possibility that 'faith of Jesus Christ' (πίστεως Ἰησοῦ Χριστοῦ) refers to Christ's faith/fulness is strengthened by Paul's Christological appeal to Habakkuk 2:4 in the crucial introduction to his argument regarding faith (1:17), and its expansion in 3:22. In the opening programmatic statement (1:16–17), Paul's citation of Habakkuk 2:4 serves to ground his affirmation that 'the righteousness of God' is revealed ἐκ πίστεως εἰς πίστιν ('from faith to faith'). This may mean, as the NIV renders the phrase, 'by faith from first to last'.[118] The Greek idiom, 'from (ἐκ) X to (εἰς) X', however, does not seem to have been used to mean 'emphatically X'. It often communicates, rather, progression from one period of time to another, or from one person to another.[119] While some commentators have entertained the former idea (from the faith of the Old Testament to the faith of the New),[120] Paul's speaks of 'the righteousness of God' being (climactically) revealed 'from faith'; the first 'faith' is somehow instrumental in the new revelation. Most likely, then, the reference is first to Christ's faith/fulness (ἐκ πίστεως) and then to the human faith which responds to him (εἰς πίστιν). Indeed, all three elements of the citation are best understood

---

116 Cf. Williams, 'Righteousness of God', 273–274.
117 Rom 1:8, 12; 4:5; 1 Cor 2:5; 15:14, 17; 2 Cor 1:24; 10:15; Phil 2:17; Col 1:4; 2:5; 1 Thess 1:8; 3:2, 5, 7, 10; 2 Thess 1:3, 4; 2 Tim 2:18; Phil 6.
118 Cranfield, *Romans*, 1.99–100, argues the phrase is a rhetorical way of saying 'completely by faith'; Moo, *Romans*, 76: 'the combination is rhetorical and is intended to emphasize that faith and "nothing but faith" can put us into right relationship with God'; so also Keener, *Romans*, 29–30.
119 For examples in the Greek literature, with discussion, see: Quarles, '"From Faith to Faith"'.
120 Calvin, *Romans*, loc. cit. considers the view that Paul intends 'an implied comparison between the Old and the New Testament ... more refined than well-founded'. He suggests, rather, that 'from faith to faith' means 'the daily progress that is made by every one of the faithful'.

as speaking primarily of Christ: the designation 'the Righteous One' (Ὁ δίκαιος), the reference to 'by faith/fulness' (ἐκ πίστεως), and the promise that 'he will live' (ζήσεται). This needs to be briefly unpacked.

(i) The designation 'the Righteous One' (ὁ δίκαιος) most likely refers to Christ.[121] In Habakkuk 2:4, the masculine singular צדיק may be read as a generic singular (NIV: 'the righteous person'), but it is also capable of being read as a reference to a *particular* individual. This sense is strengthened by the LXX which translates the noun with the definite article 'the righteous (one)' (ὁ δίκαιος). The prophets certainly apply the adjective 'righteous' (צדיק / δίκαιος) and the noun 'righteousness' (צדק / δικαιοσύνη) to the promised eschatological redeemer,[122] and—at least partly on this basis—the designation 'the Righteous One' was certainly used as a title for the eschatological redeemer in at least some early Jewish texts (1 En. 38:2; 53:6; 91:10 (?)). Crucially, according to Luke, Paul himself spoke of Christ as 'the Righteous One' (Acts 22:14 [quoting Ananias]). It has sometimes been urged that there is 'no evidence that anyone in antiquity interpreted Habakkuk 2:4 as a reference to the Messiah'.[123] This may well be the case but, while a Jewish antecedent or parallel would strengthen the case that Paul read the prophecy in this way, it is not unusual for Paul and the other apostles to pioneer a christological exegesis of texts not otherwise applied to the Messiah (e.g. Rom 10:13 with Joel 3:5 [ET 2:32]; 1 Cor 8:4–6 with Deut 6:4; Phil 2:1011 with Isa 45:23). There is not space to defend it here, but a Christological reading of Habakkuk 2:4 also makes good sense of Paul's appeal to the prophecy in Galatians

---

121 For fuller defence of this reading, see: Campbell, 'Faithfulness', 65–66; Johnson, *Reading Romans*, 28; Keck, *Romans*, 54; Heliso, *Pistis*; Young, 'Romans 1.1–5'; Jipp, *Christ is King*, 253–57.
122 Isa 11:4-5; 53:11; Jer 23:5-6; Zech 9:9 (?).
123 Thielman, *Romans*, 205; citing Watson, 'By Faith (of Christ)', 155–59.

3:11.[124] At any rate, Paul is not the only ancient interpreter to read Habakkuk 2:4 as a prophecy of Christ: Hebrews 10:37–38 also cites Habakkuk 2:3–4 LXX (with Isaiah 26:20 LXX) to speak of Christ as 'the Coming One' (ὁ ἐρχόμενος), and 'my Righteous One' (ὁ ... δίκαιός μου).[125]

(ii) Paul's reference to 'by faith/fulness' (ἐκ πίστεως) also makes good sense as a designation of Christ's faith/fulness. Habakkuk's original prophecy certainly means more than bare 'trust' or 'belief', and includes reference to 'his faithfulness' (Hab 2:4b: אמונתו).[126] In the Hebrew Scriptures, the key term אמונה consistently carries the sense of an active fidelity, and nowhere unambiguously means 'trust' (correctly NIV11).[127] Of course, given the inseparability of faith and faithfulness in biblical thought the distinction ought not to be pressed too sharply.[128] The faithfulness Habakkuk envisages must arise—as always in biblical thought—from trust in the LORD, specifically, in God's promise of deliverance, granted to the prophet in the vision. Nevertheless, the prophecy makes best sense as an affirmation of the consistent teaching of the Scriptures that those who trust

---

124 So Howard, *Paul*, 63–64; Matera, *Galatians*, 119; de Boer, *Galatians*, 202–204. Others see a reference to both Christ's faith/fulness and human faith: Martyn, *Galatians*, 314; Hays, *The Faith of Jesus Christ* (2002), 138–141; de Roo, *Works*, 206–207. In rejecting this view, Moo, *Galatians*, 206, makes two arguments: (i) πίστις (and the cognate πιστεύω ...) has referred to human faith thus far in Gal. 2–3', and (ii) 'Hab. 2:4b almost certainly also refers to human faith/faithfulness'. The first of these is hotly disputed. The second fails to see that in Paul's christological exegesis the prophet's promise of life to human faith/fulness finds its fulfilment in Christ, the truly human one.
125 The Christological reference is made clear by: (i) the earlier prophecy that 'Christ ... will appear a second time' (Heb 9:28); (ii) Hebrews' addition of the definite article to read ὁ ἐρχόμενος (Heb 10:37).
126 The masculine singular suffix ו on אמונתו refers not to the faithfulness of the vision, or of God, but of 'the righteous one' (צדיק). For a review of these options, with arguments for this view, see esp. Hunn, 'Habakkuk'.
127 Koehler & Baumgartner, *HALOT*, 1.62–63, also recognise the meanings 'steadfastness', 'honesty', 'official duty', 'conscientious', and 'security', but not 'faith' / 'trust'; cf. Scott, 'New Approach', 337. Against this Hunn, 'Habakkuk', 227, argues that in its context אמונה 'does not require action because Yahweh himself will bring salvation. It only requires faith in the certainty of the vision'. But this asserts a false dichotomy.
128 Cf. Silva, *Interpreting Galatians*, 165: אמונה means '"steadiness, faithfulness"—thus implying obedience to the law', but also stresses that for Habakkuk as for Paul, 'there was no such dichotomy between faith and faithfulness'. See already: Lightfoot, *Galatians*, 154–155.

God, and so obey him ('the faithful'), will 'live'.[129] Certainly, the Qumran commentary on Habakkuk interprets the prophet's reference to 'faithfulness' as obedience to God's law, together with trust in the community's founder (1QpHab 8:1–3).[130] The rabbinic tradition, likewise, understood Habakkuk 2:4 as a summary of the whole law, which implies a reference to faith/fulness[131] The tragedy, as Paul shows so emphatically in Romans 1:18–3:20, is that no-one—not even anyone amongst the covenant people—has been truly 'faithful' to God. Paul underlines this failure at the crucial point of his argument in Romans 3:1–5 by employing the antonym ἀπιστία to speak of the Jews' 'faith/lessness' (3:3: ἡ ἀπιστία αὐτῶν).[132] In this context, Paul's opening citation of Habakkuk 2:4 appears as a prophetic announcement of 'the gospel'; the apostle appeals to it, primarily, as a prophetic affirmation of *Christ's faith/fulness*. While all people, Israel included, have been 'unfaithful' to God and so die, the 'good news'—announced beforehand by Habakkuk—is that Christ, 'the Righteous One', has been 'faithful', and so 'lives'! This reading is entirely in keeping with the original intent of the prophecy, which calls on 'the righteous' remnant amongst the Jews to trust and obey the LORD and so live. It declares that this faith/ful response has been offered by Christ, the true Israelite, the only faithful one.

---

129 Gen 2:9, 17; Lev 18:5; Deut 30:15–20; Ezek 20:11, 13; Rom 10:5; Gal 3:12.
130 1QpHab 8:1–3: 'this concerns all those who observe the Law in the House of Judah, whom God will deliver from the House of Judgement because of their suffering and because of their faith in the Teacher of Righteousness'.
131 *Mid. Ps.* 17A.25 and *b.*Mak 24a both report that David summarised the law in eleven principles (Ps 15), Isaiah in six (Isa 33:14–16), Micah in three (Mic 6:8), Isaiah elsewhere in two (Isa 56:1), Amos in one (Amos 5:4), and Habakkuk also in one (Hab 2:4).
132 ἡ ἀπιστία is usually translated 'faithlessness' (ESV) or 'unfaithfulness' (NIV11). Cf. BDAG, 103 §2. Alternatively, Cranfield, *Romans*, 1.180 translates ἡ ἀπιστία as 'unbelief', largely on the basis of its wider NT usage. This text actually seems to be a good candidate for a polysemous use of ἀπιστία as 'faith/lessness'. In the context, Paul states that the Jews 'were entrusted (ἐπιστεύθησαν) with the oracles of God' (3:2), but also stresses their lawless living (2:17–24; 3:5–20); taken together, this implies that their failure took the form of *failing to trust* God's 'oracles', expressed in a *failure to live* in accordance with his law.

(iii) The promise 'he will live' (ζήσεται) also makes good sense if applied, first and foremost, to Christ himself. Paul's opening paragraph in Romans (1:1–5) makes clear that 'the gospel' was 'promised beforehand (προεπηγγείλατο) through his prophets (τῶν προφητῶν αὐτοῦ) in the Holy Scriptures (ἐν γραφαῖς ἁγίαις)' (1:2). This reference to the prophetic Scriptures surely includes Habakkuk 2:4, the very first prophetic text Paul explicitly cites in the letter (1:17: καθὼς γέγραπται). It is significant, then, that Habakkuk's prophecy declares that 'the Righteous One by his faith/fulness *will live*' and so appears as a prophecy of 'the gospel' of God's 'Son', the faith/ful one, and his 'resurrection from the dead' (ἐξ ἀναστάσεως νεκρῶν) (1:3–4).[133] Certainly, Paul elsewhere presents Christ's perfect obedience as the meritorious cause of his resurrection / exaltation (Phil 2:9: διό).[134] In Romans itself, Jesus' perfect obedience, even to the point of death—his faith/fulness—together with his subsequent resurrection, is at the heart of Paul's gospel, and closely connected with 'righteousness' (1:3–4; 4:25; 5:9–10, 18–19; 8:10–11).

In his crucial opening programmatic statement (1:16–17), then, Paul already suggestively characterises Christ as 'the Righteous One' who 'by faith/fulness will live'.

This conclusion, in turn, suggests that in Romans 3:22 Paul refers to 'the faith/fulness of Jesus Christ'. Given Paul's regular habit of introducing key ideas in pithy phrases which he later elaborates and expands, 1:17 is well understood as a condensed and cryptic version of the argument developed in 3:21–22.[135] 'From faith' (1:17: ἐκ πίστεως) corresponds to 'through faith of Jesus Christ' (3:22: διὰ πίστεως Ἰησοῦ Χριστοῦ), and 'to/for faith' (1:17: εἰς πίστιν) is expanded by 'to all who believe' (3:22: εἰς πάντας τοὺς πιστεύοντας). The difference in the prepositions (1:17:

---

133 Williams, 'Righteousness of God', 256.
134 Cf. Bavinck, *Reformed Dogmatics* 3, §399, p.434: 'Scripture ... over and over ... presents the state of humiliation as the way and the means by which alone Christ can attain his exaltation (Isa. 53:10–12; Matt. 23:12; Luke 24:26; John 10:17; 17:4–5; Phil. 2:9; Heb. 2:10; 12:2). The preposition διό (therefore) in Philippians 2:9 refers not to the order and logic but specifically to the meritorious cause of the exaltation. *Because* Christ humbled himself so deeply, *therefore* God has so highly exalted him'. The whole discussion (pp.433–36) is important.
135 For the connections between Rom 1:17 and 3:21–22, see §1 above.

ἐκ πίστεως; 3:22: διὰ πίστεως) is adequately explained by the immediate influence of Habakkuk 2:4 LXX at 1:17 (ἐκ πίστεως).[136] Thus, Paul's cryptic phrase in 1:17 ('from faith to faith'), expanded in 3:22 means: 'the gospel reveals God's righteousness *through* Christ's faith/fulness (1:17: ἐκ πίστεώς; 3:22: διὰ πίστεως Ἰησοῦ Χριστοῦ) *to* human faith (1:17: εἰς πίστιν; 3:22: εἰς πάντας τοὺς πιστεύοντας)'.[137] Once this connection is made it is not hard to see the same pattern of thought (admittedly without recourse to the πιστ- root) in Paul's later affirmation that Jesus' 'one act of righteousness' (ἑνὸς δικαιώματος) and 'obedience' (διὰ τῆς ὑπακοῆς) resulted in 'the justification of life' (εἰς δικαίωσιν ζωῆς) of those who belong to him (5:18–19). On the basis of his faith/fulness— his trusting obedience even to the point of death—God vindicated / raised Christ, 'the Righteous One', and this provides the basis for the vindication / justification / life of those who trust in him.[138]

Fourth, Paul's theological syntax in Romans 3:21–22 also supports the subjective reading of διὰ πίστεως Ἰησοῦ Χριστοῦ. Paul affirms that 'God's righteousness has been *revealed* ... *through* faith of Jesus Christ' (3:21–22). The verb πεφανέρωται is decisive: it is hard to see how *God's* righteousness could be *revealed* through *human* faith in Christ.[139] More likely, Paul intends that God has revealed his *own* righteousness through what *he* has done in the Messiah. M. Hooker states it well:

---

136 Certainly, ἐκ and διά can both readily indicate agency. See: BDAG, 224–25 § 3, 4: ἐκ with pp.296–97 §3d–f: διά.
137 Alternatively, ἐκ πίστεως at Romans 1:17 could perhaps be a reference to *God's* faithfulness. So: Barth, *Romans*, 41; Dunn, *Romans 1–8*, 43–44; Wright, 'Romans', 425; Hooker, 'Another Look', 55. This reading may be strengthened by the observation that Habakkuk 2:4 LXX[B] adds the genitive personal pronoun μου, which may be read in the subjective sense of 'from my faithfulness' (ἐκ πίστεώς μου). There are, however, four reasons why this cannot be considered determinative for Paul's meaning in Romans 1:17: (i) the possessive pronoun is lacking in the MT; (ii) Habakkuk 2:4 LXX[A] attaches the genitive personal pronoun to ὁ δίκαιός to read 'my righteous one' (ὁ δίκαιός μου; cf. Heb 10:38); (iii) even in LXX[B] the genitive could be read in other ways as an objective genitive ('faithfulness *to me*'), or a source genitive ('faithfulness *granted by* me'); (iv) Paul's citation lacks the pronoun (also Gal 3:11).
138 Cf. Wright, *Justification*, 83.
139 Cf. Robinson, 'Faith of Jesus Christ', 80; Campbell, *Rhetoric*, 63–64; Hays, 'What is at Stake?', 721. To ease this difficulty, the NIV84 supplements Paul's verb 'manifested' / 'revealed' (πεφανέρωται) with a second verb 'come', so that Romans 3:22 reads 'this righteousness of God *comes* through faith in Jesus Christ'. The NIV11 strikingly omits the repetition of θεοῦ at 3:22 and supplies the verb 'given' to read 'this righteousness *is given* through faith in Jesus Christ'. Such emendations of Paul's language are hard to justify when a satisfactory explanation of his Greek is close to hand.

We expect Paul to tell us here *how* God's righteousness is revealed, and this phrase seems to provide the explanation. From the summary of the gospel in 1:2–4, and those still to come in 4:24–5, and 5:6–11, the answer is plain: he has acted *in Christ*. This suggests that Paul is referring here to Christ's own πίστις, rather than that of believers. God's righteousness is revealed *through Christ himself*, not in our response *to* him.[140]

Moreover, the perfect tense-form of the controlling verb πεφανέρωται ('has been revealed') probably confirms this sense. On the traditional understanding of the perfect, the verb here indicates a past divine revelation with ongoing effects; it points to what God *has revealed* in Christ, rather than an ongoing revelation, which would seem to be required by a reference to human faith. Romans 1:17, to be sure, employs the present passive to affirm that God's righteousness 'is being revealed' (ἀποκαλύπτεται) 'in the gospel', but this difference is well explained by the context: while 1:17 affirms the ongoing revelation of God's righteousness in the proclamation of the gospel, 3:21 speaks of the past revelation of God's righteousness in Christ himself, with its ongoing effects and consequences (NRSV, NIV, ESV, CSB).[141] But however we understand the verbal tense forms, the point here holds: it is *God's righteousness* that has been revealed, and we rightly expect that his righteousness is revealed in something *God has done*.

Fifth, the whole phrase 'through faith/fulness of Jesus Christ for all who believe' provides a balanced statement connecting Christ's faith/fulness to the human faith which responds to him. If διὰ πίστεως Ἰησοῦ Χριστοῦ means 'through faith *in* Christ', then 'for all who believe' (εἰς πάντας τοὺς πιστεύοντας) repeats a very similar thought (cf. Gal 3:22). It is too much to say that this reading would make the latter phrase

---

140 Hooker, 'Another Look', 58–59. Schreiner, *Romans*, 325, 328, recognises the force of this argument, and attempts to counter it by arguing that 'God's righteousness has two dimensions', namely, 'God's work in history that was manifested in the atoning work of Jesus Christ', and 'the righteousness of God .... subjectively appropriated by faith'. The response fails because 'the righteousness of God' in Romans 3:21–26 refers to *God's* righteousness revealed in Christ.

141 i.e. πεφανέρωται is an extensive or consummative perfect (Wallace, *Greek Grammar*, 577). The semantic force of the perfect remains a matter of debate, with some recent discussion arguing that the Greek perfect encodes aspect rather than time at the semantic level. For a brief review, see Campbell, *Advances*, 117–118. Further discussion in Crellin, 'Semantics'.

redundant.¹⁴² Paul *could* be repeating for emphasis, with a slightly different focus, first on the object of faith ('Jesus Christ') and then on the universality of access to Christ by faith ('*all* who believe'). More likely, however, Paul deliberately distinguishes between Christ's faith, which he refers to with the noun πίστις + Χριστοῦ, and Christian faith *in* Christ, which he refers to by use of the substantive participle 'those who believe' (τοὺς πιστεύοντας). It is true that Paul nowhere makes Jesus the subject of the verb 'believe' (πιστεύω).¹⁴³ This, however, may be part of the point: there is a qualitative difference between Christ's perfect faith/fulness, and faltering human faith in him.

Sixth, two parallel διά / ἐκ + genitive expressions later in the paragraph (3:25, 26) further support the subjective genitive reading of διὰ πίστεως Ἰησοῦ Χριστοῦ (3:22).

(i) At 3:25 Paul explains that God put Jesus forward (προέθετο) as a 'place of atonement' (ἱλαστήριον) 'through [the] faith/fulness, in/by his blood' (διὰ [τῆς] πίστεως ἐν τῷ αὐτοῦ αἵματι). Most major English translations interpret the prepositional phrase διὰ [τῆς] πίστεως at 3:25 as an objective genitive, referring to human faith, and further interpret the parallel prepositional phrase ἐν τῷ αὐτοῦ αἵματι as the object of that human faith (Luther, Tyndale, KJV; NIV84). Recent English translations often supply a verb (or two!) or an additional noun to support this interpretation. Thus NRSV: 'by his blood *effective* through faith'; ESV: 'by his blood *to be received* by faith'; NIV11: 'through *the shedding of* his blood—*to be received* by faith'; CSB: 'in his blood, *received* through faith'. Paul, however, nowhere else calls for faith in Christ's 'blood', or in any other object. He consistently calls, rather, for faith in God (4:3, 17, 24; 9:33; 10:11; Gal 3:6, 22; 1 Thess 1:8; Titus 3:8), or Christ (3:26; Gal 2:16; Phil 3:9; 1 Tim 1:16), or God's word (Rom 10:16), or God's power (1 Cor 2:5; Col 2:12), or a particular conviction (Rom 10:9; 14:2; 1 Cor 11:18; 1 Thess 4:14; 2 Tim 1:12), or a testimony about something (2 Thess 1:10; 2:11;

---

142 For a critique of the argument from redundancy see Matlock, 'Rhetoric: Galatians'.
143 Moo, *Romans*, 246 considers this decisive; cf. Schreiner, *Romans*, 328.

2:12–13).[144] But Paul never calls for faith in Christ's 'cross', or 'empty tomb', or 'blood'. A more straightforward reading of the Greek, therefore, which is also more consistent with Paul's theological syntax, sees the two prepositional phrases standing in apposition to each other: 'a sacrifice of atonement through the faith/fulness (διὰ [τῆς] πίστεως), by his blood (ἐν τῷ αὐτοῦ αἵματι)'. The repetition of 'through the faith/fulness' (διὰ [τῆς] πίστεως), especially if the anaphoric article is original, suggests a reference back to 'the faith/fulness of Jesus Christ' (3:22), which is then further explained by the added phrase 'by his blood' (ἐν τῷ αὐτοῦ αἵματι).[145] Paul speaks, then, not of faith *in* Christ, but of Christ's faith/fulness *even to the point of death*. He presents Christ's death—referred to metonymically by 'his blood' (τῷ αὐτοῦ αἵματι)—as the culmination of his trusting obedience.[146] Moreover, as Longenecker notes, Paul sandwiches this reference to 'the faith/fulness' (διὰ [τῆς] πίστεως) between references to Christ's atoning work (προέθετο ὁ θεὸς ἱλαστήριον) and 'his blood' (ἐν τῷ αὐτοῦ αἵματι), which further suggests a sustained reference to what Christ has done, rather than to Christian faith in him.[147] Certainly, this fits well within the developing argument of the letter, where it is Christ's trusting obedience, even to the point of death, that secures justification for God's people. Romans 5:9 again affirms that the believer's justification has come 'by his blood' (ἐν τῷ αἵματι αὐτοῦ), and 5:18–19 emphasizes that justification comes 'through the obedience' (διὰ τῆς ὑπακοῆς) of Christ. These later parallels tend to confirm that it is the ground of justification (Christ's faith/fulness to the point

---

144 Cf. Thielman, *Romans*, 208.
145 The textual evidence for and against the originality of the article is inconclusive. The external evidence slightly favours originality: the article is present 𝔓⁴⁰ᵛⁱᵈ, B, Ψ, C³, D², a number of minuscules, and the Byzantine text; it is absent in ℵ C* D* F G; the whole phrase is omitted in A, but this is most likely accidental (cf. Metzger, *Textual Commentary*, 449). Internal considerations also slightly favour the authenticity of the article: it is conceivable that the article was added to produce an anaphoric reference back to 3:22; more likely, however, give the anaphoric use of the article at 3:30, 31, the article is original.
146 Cf. Johnson, 'Faith of Jesus', 79–80; Hooker, 'Another Look', 60.
147 Longenecker, 'Πίστις in Romans 3.25'.

of death), rather than the instrument of justification (human faith), which Paul signals by the phrase 'faith of Jesus Christ'.

(ii) At 3:26 Paul states that God justifies 'the one of the faith of Jesus' (τὸν ἐκ πίστεως Ἰησοῦ). This phrase is also often understood as reference to human faith, with the preposition ἐκ being rendered by the English preposition 'in': 'those who have faith *in* Jesus' (ESV; NRSV; NIV; cf. Lutherbible2017: *der da ist aus dem Glauben an Jesus*). The prepositioin ἐκ ('of' / 'from' / 'out of'), however, usually denotes source or origin, and is not used elsewhere to denote the object of a verb or a verbal noun.[148] More specifically, in relation to 'faith' (πίστις), Paul habitually employs other prepositions to indicate the object of faith, but nowhere unambiguously uses ἐκ in this way.[149] The construction ἐκ + πίστεως + noun denoting a person occurs in only three other texts in Paul: Galatians 2:16 and 3:22 also have Χριστοῦ / Ἰησοῦ Χριστοῦ as the final noun; Romans 4:16 has Ἀβραάμ in the final position. This last text provides a particularly exact and illuminating parallel. In both Romans 3:26 and 4:16 Paul: (a) employs the generic article ('the one who');[150] (b) has the construction ἐκ + πίστεως; (c) speaks of the 'faith of' an individual by a simple reference to their personal name (3:26: Ἰησοῦ; 4:16: Ἀβραάμ). 'The one who is of the faith of Jesus' (3:26) parallels exactly 'the one who is of the faith of Abraham' (4:16). Indeed, the parallel is particularly striking given Paul's unusual reference to 'the faith of Jesus'—without his customary addition of the title 'Christ' or 'Lord'—which is, for that reason, highly suggestive of Jesus' own personal exercise of faith/fulness.[151] The latter text, regarding Abraham, clearly refers not to 'the one who *has faith in* Abraham', but to

---

148 BDAG, 295–97.
149 (i) ἐπί: Rom 4:5, 24; 9:33 and 10:11 (cf. Isa 28:16); 1 Tim 1:16; (ii) ἐν: 1 Cor 2:5; Gal 3:26; Eph 1:13, 15; Col 1:4; 1 Tim 1:14; 3:13; 2 Tim 1:13; 3:15; (iii) εἰς: Rom 10:14; Gal 2:16; Phil 1:29; Col 2:5; (iv). πρός: 1 Thess 1:8; Philem 5.
150 Wallace, *Greek Grammar*, 227–230.
151 Paul refers to 'Jesus' by name 212x. On only 15 occasions does he have Jesus' name without the titular 'Christ', or 'Lord': Rom 8:11; 1 Cor 12:3a; 2 Cor 4:5b; 2 Cor 4:10–11 (4x), 14b; 2 Cor 11:4; Gal 6:17; Eph 4:21; Phil 2:10; 1 Thess 1:10; 4:14 (2x).

the one for whom Abraham's faith is, in some sense, the source and pattern of their own.¹⁵² This strongly suggests that, in like manner, 'the one who is of the faith/fulness of Jesus' (3:26 τὸν ἐκ πίστεως Ἰησοῦ) refers to the Christian believer, for whom Jesus' faith/fulness is the source and pattern of their own.¹⁵³ This conclusion, of course, does not necessarily require that Abraham's faith and Jesus' faith/fulness are the source of the Christian believer's faith in exactly the same way: the Christian believer's faith is *like* Abraham's, but *grounded in* Jesus' faith/fulness. Nevertheless, the parallel is significant, and tends to confirm that Paul intends to refer to Jesus' own faith/fulness.

The parallel phrases in Romans 3:25 and 3:26 thus further underline Paul's emphasis throughout the paragraph on Jesus' faith/fulness as the means by which God has revealed his righteousness, and so confirm that in Romans 3:22, the apostle speaks of 'the faith/fulness of Jesus Christ'.

Seventh, Paul's emphasis on Christ's faith/fulness in Romans 3:21–26 is consistent with his teaching elsewhere. Specifically, Paul's four other references to πίστις Ἰησοῦ Χριστοῦ / πίστις Χριστοῦ all make good sense when Ἰησοῦ Χριστοῦ is taken as a subjective genitive (Gal 2:16 [2x]; 3:22, Phil 3:9).¹⁵⁴

> (i) Galatians 2:16: Paul declares that we are justified 'through faith of Christ' (διὰ πίστεως Ἰησοῦ Χριστοῦ) and 'from faith of Christ' (ἐκ πίστεως Χριστοῦ), twice employing the noun 'faith' (πίστις) with the genitive of 'Jesus Christ' / 'Christ'. He distinguishes this, syntactically, from having 'believed into Christ' (εἰς Χριστὸν Ἰησοῦν ἐπιστεύσαμεν), which employs the verb πιστεύω with the preposition εἰς. It seems that Paul distinguishes between two distinct but related realities: Christ's

---

152 NRSV: 'those who share the faith of Abraham'; ESV: 'the one who shares the faith of Abraham'; Lutherbibel2017: 'die aus Abrahams Glauben leben'.
153 Cf. Johnson, 'Faith of Jesus', 80; Wright, 'Romans', 474; Hooker, 'Another Look', 60.
154 Galatians 2:20 and Ephesians 3:12 are also important for the discussion, and may further support Paul's emphasis on Christ's faith/fulness. I pass over them here because Paul's constructions are slightly different in those texts.

faith/fulness as the ground of justification, and believing in Christ as its instrument.[155]

(ii) Galatians 3:22: Paul seems to deliberately distinguish between 'Christ's faith/fulness' and human faith in him, in the same way he does at Romans 3:22 and 26, by referring to first to Christ's faith/fulness (ἐκ πίστεως Ἰησοῦ Χριστοῦ), and then to human faith in Christ (substantival particle: τοῖς πιστεύουσιν). This is confirmed by the argument which follows (Gal 3:22–25), where Paul makes a redemptive-historical distinction between the time of the law and the time of faith.[156] In this context, he sets the coming of Christ in parallel with the 'coming' of 'faith' (3:23: Πρὸ τοῦ δὲ ἐλθεῖν τὴν πίστιν), or the 'revelation' of 'faith' (3:23: εἰς τὴν μέλλουσαν πίστιν ἀποκαλυφθῆναι); since Christ has come, so 'faith has come' (3:25: ἐλθούσης δὲ τῆς πίστεως). Paul surely cannot mean that saints under the old covenant did not exercise faith in God, or in the promised Messiah, since earlier in the same passage he cites Genesis 15:6 to speak of how 'Abraham believed God' (Gal 3:6: Ἀβραὰμ ἐπίστευσεν τῷ θεῷ; cf. Rom 4:3, 5–8). It is possible that Paul speaks of the arrival of faith 'not in an absolute, but in a comparative sense',[157] or of the arrival of 'faith in its christological shape',[158] but Paul's distinction is sharper than this. Galatians 3:22–25 speaks not of the fuller revelation of the faith principle, but of the 'coming' of Christ, the faith/ful one.

---

155 Williams, 'Righteousness of God', 273.
156 See esp. Caneday, *Curse*, 185–186, 190–198, and 'Faithfulness of Jesus Christ', 185–205; Hays, 'Galatians', 269–70. Schreiner, *Romans*, 328, n.20 recognises the force of the argument, and accepts that 'the redemptive-historical element is certainly present in the text'. Nevertheless, he attempts to counter this argument by suggesting that 'Personal faith in Christ has now become a reality because of the shift in redemptive history … The redemptive-historical work of Christ has created the possibility and actuality of personal faith'. There is no doubt that personal faith is a significant theme in Galatians 3, but surely Paul's appeal to Abraham demonstrates that 'personal faith' is not new with the new covenant.
157 Calvin, *Galatians*, on Galatians 3:23: 'The doctrine of faith, in short, is attested by Moses and all the prophets: but, as faith was not then clearly manifested, so the time of *faith* is an appellation here given, not in an absolute, but in a comparative sense, to the time of the New Testament'.
158 Moo, *Galatians*, 242.

(iii) Philippians 3:9: Paul speaks of having 'the righteousness of God' ... 'through the faith/fulness of Christ' (διὰ πίστεως Χριστοῦ), which is 'upon the faith' (ἐπὶ τῇ πίστει). Again, good arguments can be made on both sides,[159] but the syntactical distinction between πίστις + genitive personal noun (Χριστοῦ) and the preposition phrase ἐπί + πίστις is best taken as indicating two distinct but closely related realities, Christ's faith/fulness and faith in him.[160]

The recognition of Paul's emphasis on Christ's faith/fulness in Romans 3:22, then, is in keeping with his use of the phrase πίστις Χριστοῦ elsewhere. The syntactical distinction between 'Christ's faith/fulness' and the Christian's faith in him seems to have been a well-established distinction in Paul's customary locutions.

Finally, reading πίστις Χριστοῦ as a reference to Christ's trusting obedience to his Father is consistent with the broader sweep of biblical revelation, where trusting obedience is demanded of all of God's covenant partners, from Adam, through to Noah, Abraham, Israel, and David.[161] In the context of the universal failure of humanity in Adam to trust and obey, the Gospels, and the other NT texts, consistently present Jesus as the true Adam, true Israel, and true David—the Spirit-dependent,[162] prayerful,[163] faithful,[164] and fully obedient Son of God.[165] The subjective genitive reading of πίστις Χριστοῦ is thus consistent with the portrait of

---

159 For a recent review, slightly favouring the objective genitive, see: Hellerman, *Philippians*, 186–187.
160 Cf. O'Brien, *Philippians*, 399–400.
161 Adam: Gen 2:16–17; Noah: Gen 9:1, 7; Abraham: Gen 17:1–17; 18:17–19; 22:16–18; 26:5; Israel: Exod 19:4–6; Lev 18:5; 26:1–46; Deut 30:15–20; Neh 9:29; 2 Chron 7:14; 33:8; Isa 48:18–19; David: 2 Sam 7:8–16; 1 Kgs 2:2–4; 3:14; 6:12; 8:25; 9:4–6; 1 Chron 22:12–13; 28:7–9; 2 Chron 6:16; 7:17–22; Pss 89:31–33 [LXX 88:31–33; ET 89:30–32]; 132:12 [LXX 131:12]; Jer 17:19–25; 22:4–5.
162 Matt 3:16 // Mark 1:10 // Luke 3:22; Matt 4:1 // Mark 1:12 // Luke 4:1; Matt 1:18, 20; 12:18, 28; Luke 1:35; 4:14, 18; 10:21; John 1:32–33; 3:34; Acts 10:38; Rom 1:4; 8:11; 1 Tim 3:16; Heb 9:14.
163 Matt 26:36–46 // Mark 14:32–42 // Luke 22:39–46; Mark 1:35; 6:46; 9:29; Matt 14:23; 19:13; Luke 3:21; 5:16; 6:12; 9:18, 28–29; 10:21; 11:1; 22:32; 23:46; John 12:27–28; 17:1–26; Heb 5:7.
164 Heb 2:17–18; 3:2; 4:15–16; 5:7–10; 1 Pet 2:21–23; Rev 1:5; 3:14; 19:11.
165 Matt 4:1–11 // Luke 4:1–13; John 4:34; 5:19–20, 30; 6:38; 7:18; 8:46; 10:17–18; 15:10; 2 Cor 5:21; Phil 2:8; Heb 7:26 10:5–10; 1 Pet 2:22; 1 John 3:5. For the Gospels, see discussion in Crowe, *Obedient Son*, and *The Last Adam*.

Christ's perfect trusting obedience across the NT and, more specifically, with Paul's emphasis in Romans, and throughout his letters, on Christ's perfect obedience as the true Adam (5:12–21; cf. Phil 2:8), the son of David (1:3), and the true Son of God (1:3–4, 9; 5:10; 8:3–4, 29, 32).[166] Indeed, this redemptive historical logic is evident in Romans 3 itself, where Paul contrasts Israel's 'unfaithfulness' (3:3: ἡ ἀπιστία αὐτῶν) with Christ's faith/fulness (3:22) and so presents Jesus as the true Israel.[167]

The subjective genitive reading, moreover, creates a theologically precise and well-balanced presentation in which 'the righteousness of God' (source) is manifested through 'the faith/fulness of Jesus Christ' (agent) for the benefit of 'all who believe' (beneficiaries). This reading thus maintains a very Pauline balance between God's grace as the source of salvation, Christ's trusting obedience even to the point of death as the objective ground of justification, and human faith as the required subjective response.[168]

For these eight reasons, it is most likely that by the phrase διὰ πίστεως Ἰησοῦ Χριστοῦ Paul intends to emphasise Jesus' own faith/fulness—his perfect trusting obedience to the Father, which culminated in his death on the cross—rather than human faith in Christ. To be sure, Paul goes on immediately to speak of human faith as the instrument of justification (3:22b). His intention in 3:22a, however, is to indicate Christ's own trusting obedience as simultaneously the means by which God's righteousness has been disclosed, and the only grounds for the justification of those who believe. This emphasis, in turn, provides the resolution to the tension of the two aspects of God's righteousness noted above: through the faithful death of the Messiah God has found a way simultaneously to judge sin, and to extend blessing to all who believe both in Israel, and among all the nations.

2.3 Free justification for all who believe

To Paul's emphasis on God's righteousness as the source of justification, and Christ's faithfulness as the ground of justification, a third emphasis

---

166 For this theme in Romans, see: Kirk, 'Appointed Son(s)'; Kim, 'Jesus the Son of God'; Hooker, 'Another Look', 60–62; Bird, *Jesus the Eternal Son*, 11–23.
167 Cf. Wright, *Paul and the Faithfulness of God*, 836–842.
168 Cf. Williams, 'Righteousness of God', 275; Hooker, 'ΠΙΣΤΙΣ ΧΡΙΣΤΟΥ', 337.

must be added, namely, human faith as the instrument of justification. In the face of universal sin, it is thus 'all those who believe' (3:22: πάντας τοὺς πιστεύοντας) who are 'justified freely by his grace' (3:24: δικαιούμενοι δωρεὰν τῇ αὐτοῦ χάριτι). Both the nature of this justification, and the import of Paul's emphasis on 'faith' require brief explanation.

2.3.1 Justification

Paul declares that God 'justifies' those who trust in Christ. The verb δικαιόω ('I justify') appears twice in this short paragraph. At 3:24 Paul employs the present passive participle to affirm that 'all' who believe 'are justified by his grace as a gift' (δικαιούμενοι δωρεὰν τῇ αὐτοῦ χάριτι). At 3:26 he employs the present active participle δικαιοῦντα, with God as subject, to speak of God as 'he who justifies' (NRSV; NIV11) or 'the justifier' (ESV). The contrast between the passive and the active participles serves to emphasize God as the source of human justification. The additional phrase, 'freely by his grace' (δωρεὰν τῇ αὐτοῦ χάριτι) underscores the entirely gratuituous nature of this justification: it comes freely from God, by his unmerited favour, as a gift.

The meaning of 'justification', however, has been the subject of a long running debate. The Vulgate's translation of δικαιόω with the verb *iustifico* ('to *make* righteous') and, especially, Augustine's understanding of 'justification' as including moral transformation, lead to an understanding of 'justification' in the medieval Church as being 'synonymous with the entire process of salvation'.[169] At the level of confessional theology, this remains the focus of the continuing division between Roman Catholic and Protestant understandings of justification.[170] The *Joint Declaration on the Doctrine of Justification* (2000) represents some

---

169 Horton, *Justification*, I: 90. For the influence of Augustine, see esp. McGrath, *Iustitia Dei* (2005), I: 12–16; Wright, 'Justificaiton in Augustine'.
170 Compare: *The Catechism of the Catholic Church*, 492, citing the Council of Trent (1574): 'justification is not only the remission of sins, *but also the sanctification and renewal of the interior man*' (italics added). Contrast: WCF 11:1: 'Those whom God effectually calls, He also freely justifies; *not by infusing righteousness into them*, but by pardoning their sins, and by accounting and accepting their persons as righteous; *not for any thing wrought in them, or done by them*, but for Christ's sake alone; *nor by imputing faith itself, the act of believing, or any other evangelical obedience to them, as their righteousness*; but by imputing the obedience and satisfaction of Christ unto them' (italics added).

advance in mutual understanding, but is certainly not yet the resolution of these differences.[171] Nevertheless, among biblical scholars, a strong consensus—which includes those working within Roman Catholic, 'Traditional Protestant', and 'New Perspective' approaches—recognises that biblical 'justification' language is forensic language;[172] 'justification' is the language of the courtroom.[173]

In the OT, the verb צדק in the hifil stem is regularly translated in the LXX by δικαιόω, and is clearly a forensic term.[174] In particular, the Scriptures repeatedly employ the verb in judicial contexts, sometimes with God as judge (Exod 23:7; 1 Kgs 8:32; 2 Chron 6:23; Ps 82:3 [LXX 81:3]), sometimes with a human judge (Deut 25:1; Isa 5:23; Job 27:5), but always with the sense of 'declare righteous'. In a number of these texts an antithetical construction contrasts 'vindicating' (צדק / δικαιόω) the righteous with 'condemning' the guilty (Deut 25:1; Prov 17:15; 1 Kgs 8:32; 2 Chron 6:23; Isa 5:23). Most important are two texts which speak of future justification before God: (i) the psalmist acknowledges universal human sin: 'no-one living will be declared righteous (יצדק / δικαιωθήσεται) before you' (Ps 143:2 [LXX 142:2]); (ii) Isaiah, however, declares that because the LORD is 'a righteous God and a Saviour' (Isa 45:21), 'all the offspring of Israel will be justified (יצדקו / δικαιωθήσονται) by the LORD' (Isa 45:25), and even extends this promise 'to all the ends of the earth' (Isa 45:22).

In the NT, the verb δικαιόω, like its Hebrew antecedent, is also a forensic and declarative term, with the primary sense of 'declare righteous'

---

171 *Joint Declaration on the Doctrine of Justification*. For a brief but judicious analysis, see: Horton, *Christian Faith*, 622–627.
172 For representative discussions see, for example: Roman Catholic scholars: Fitzmyer, 'Romans', 241–44; 'Traditional Protestant' scholars: Moo, *Romans (1996)* 227–228; Horton, 'Traditional Reformed View', 91–92; 'New Perspective' scholars: Sanders, *Paul and Palestinian Judaism*, 198–199; Wright, *Justification* 69–71; Dunn, 'New Perspective Response', 118.
173 For a concise summary of the evidence, see Bird, *Saving Righteousness*, 17–18. For extended discussion, see Moo, *Romans*, 82–100: 'Excursus: 'Righteousness Language in Paul'.
174 Koehler & Baumgartner, *HALOT*, 1003, offers ten definitions across five verbal stems, all of which are clearly forensic; cf. Lust, Eynikel, and Hauspie, *Greek-English Lexicon*, loc. cit. gives the primary sense in the LXX as: '*to pronounce and treat as righteous, to justify, to vindicate, to acquit*'.

or 'vindicate'.¹⁷⁵ Certainly, the promise that God will 'justify' (δικαιόω) those who trust in Christ is a significant theme in Paul's letters, especially Romans and Galatians, and Paul consistently uses the verb δικαιόω in a forensic and declarative sense.¹⁷⁶ In Romans, Paul envisages the divine courtroom, and makes the judicial metaphor explicit when he couples δικαιόω with the language of 'judgment' (3:4: κρίνω; cf. 1 Cor 4:4), and bringing 'charges' (8:33: ἐγκαλέω).¹⁷⁷ This judicial metaphor is, however, not employed by Paul to evoke just any court-room scene: the verdict he has on view is that given by God the Judge in the courtroom of the final day. This eschatological reference point is indicated both by Paul's use of the future forms of the verb (2:13; 3.20, 30; cf. Gal 2:16), and by his insistence that justification concerns a person's standing 'before God' or 'in his sight' (3:20: ἐνώπιον αὐτοῦ; 4:2: πρὸς θεόν; Gal 3:11: παρὰ τῷ θεῷ). It is striking, therefore, that in both references to 'justification' in Romans 3:21–26 Paul employs present participles (3:24: δικαιούμενοι; 3:26: δικαιοῦντα), dependent on a present indicative (3:23–24: ὑστεροῦνται) and an aorist indicative (3:25–26: προέθετο), to affirm that this 'justification' is a reality enjoyed by believers 'in the present time' (3:26: ἐν τῷ νῦν καιρῷ). This is confirmed in Romans 5:1–11, where Paul summarizes his argument so far, and employs the aorist participle to indicate a sequence in which the believer's present 'peace with God' is predicated upon their prior justification: 'Therefore, since *we have been justified* (δικαιωθέντες) by faith, *we have peace* (ἔχομεν) with

---

175 δικαιόω occurs 39x in the GNT. BAGD, 249, offers the primary definition (§2): 'to render a favorable verdict' (gloss: *vindicate*). The other three definitions either do not occur in the NT (§1), or are far less common: §3: 'to cause someone to be released from personal or institutional claims that are no longer to be considered pertinent or valid' (gloss: *make free/pure*) is suggested only for Acts 13:38; Rom 6:7; 1 Cor 6:11; §4: 'to demonstrate to be morally right' (gloss: *prove to be right*) only for Rom 3:4 and 1 Tim 3:16.
176 Rom 2:13; 3:4, 20, 24, 26, 28, 30; 4:2, 5; 5:1, 9; 6:7; 8:30, 33; 1 Cor 4:4; 6:11; Gal 2:16–17; 3:8, 11, 24; 5:4; 1 Tim 3:16; Titus 3:7.
177 Romans 6:7 is the only possible exception in Romans to a forensic reading of δικαιόω. Paul states that 'whoever has died has been justified from sin' (δεδικαίωται ἀπὸ τῆς ἁμαρτίας). This verse has been used as evidence that Paul understood justification in terms of moral transformation as well as judicial verdict. Against this, however: (i) δικαιόω + ἀπό may be idiomatic for 'freed from' (cf. Acts 13:38–39) or 'vindicated from' (Matt 11:19 / Luke 7:35); (ii) if δικαιόω for Paul meant both 'declare righteous' and 'make morally righteous', the charge of antinomianism against him is incomprehensible (cf. 3:7–8; 6:1–2). [Ed. note: see further Chapter 6 in this volume]

God through our Lord Jesus Christ' (5:1);[178] 'Since, therefore, *we have now been justified* (δικαιωθέντες νῦν) by his blood, much more shall we be saved by him from the wrath of God' (5:9). The remarkable announcement of the gospel is that, in Christ, the verdict of the final day has been brought forward into the present.[179] Thus, for Paul, δικαιόω denotes God's eschatological judicial declaration that a person is righteous, rather than a process by which someone is made morally righteous. Paul is certainly concerned with moral transformation, but he does not use justification language to speak about it. For Paul, rather, 'justification' is the positive verdict of the final day, announced already in the present for those who are in Christ.

The basis for this present verdict, of course, is the faith/fulness of Christ, culminating in his death and resurrection. Paul declares that for those who trust in Christ, the eschatological verdict of the final day of judgment has been brought into the present, because—in Christ's death and resurrection—*the final judgment itself* has been brought into the present. God's present justification of sinners is possible, that is, because the final judgment of their sin *has already taken place*: through 'the redemption that is in Christ Jesus' (3:24: διὰ τῆς ἀπολυτρώσεως τῆς ἐν Χριστῷ Ἰησοῦ), whom 'God put forward as a place of atonement' (ὃν προέθετο ὁ θεὸς ἱλαστήριον), and especially 'by his blood' (3:25; 5:9: ἐν τῷ αὐτοῦ αἵματι), God has 'shown his righteousness' (3:25-26). The meaning of the crucial term ἱλαστήριον (3:25) has been a matter of dispute. The key to its interpretation, however, is the recognition that the 'mercy seat' (כפרת) of the tabernacle is consistently translated in the LXX by this term.[180] For this reason—as was already recognised by Luther and Tyndale—Paul almost certainly refers, metaphorically, to the 'mercy

---

178 The textual issue is difficult. The external evidence favours the subjunctive ἔχωμεν ('let us have peace with God'). The internal evidence, however, is decisive: Paul's argument up to this point strongly leads us to expect an indicative. For detailed discussion, see esp. Moo, *Romans*, 323, n. 26; Thielman, *Romans*, 264.
179 Moo, *Romans (1996)*, 228: 'This judicial verdict, for which one had to wait until the last judgment according to Jewish theology, is according to Paul rendered the moment a person believes. The act of justification is therefore properly "eschatological", as the ultimate verdict regarding a person's standing with God is brought back into our present reality'.
180 Exod 25:17-22; 31:7; 35:12; 37:6-9; Lev 16:2, 13-15; Num 7:89; cf. Heb 9:5.

seat' or the 'atonement cover' of the Ark of the Covenant,[181] and thus presents Christ, in his death on the cross, as the 'place' where heaven and earth meet as God and his people are reconciled by sacrifice.[182] The RSV, following the influential arguments of C.H. Dodd, translated ἱλαστήριον as 'expiation', giving the sense that Jesus' death 'made amends' or 'reparation' for human sin.[183] Against this, L. Morris, among others, demonstrated that, within Paul's argument, ἱλαστήριον includes the idea of 'turning aside God's wrath' or 'propitiation' (ESV).[184] The term itself does not *mean* 'propitiation', but there can be no doubt that, within Paul's theology of the cross in Romans, God turned aside his own wrath through Jesus' death. God's wrath (ὀργή) is opposed to sin throughout the whole letter, and Jesus' death is the means by which the problem of sin is dealt with (1:18; 2:5, 8; 3:5; 4:15; 5:9). There should be no doubt, therefore, that Paul understood Christ's death on the cross as the 'place' where God, in the person of his Son (1:3), took upon himself the full force of his own wrath against sin, and so provided, in Christ's faithful sacrifice (3:22, 24), a demonstration of his righteousness (3:25–26), the basis for the free justification of all who believe (3:24) and, indeed, the full 'redemption' of his people (3:24).[185] As Paul makes clear in Romans 8:1–4, by his repetition of the language of condemnation, God has 'condemned sin' (κατέκρινεν τὴν ἁμαρτίαν) in the flesh of his Son (8:3),

---

181 Weiß, 'Christus Jesus', shows that etymologically, the stem ἱλασ- refers to appeasement or conciliation, and the suffix -τήριον refers to the location in which, or the instrument by which, something is accomplished.
182 See esp. Bailey, 'Jesus as the Mercy Seat', summarizing the author's PhD dissertation; cf. now Thielman, *Romans*, 209–11.
183 Dodd, 'ΙΛΑΣΚΕΣΘΑΙ'.
184 Morris, *Apostolic Preaching*, 144–213.
185 'Redemption' (ἀπολύτρωσις) in Paul is a broader category than 'justification', and full discussion is beyond our scope here. The metaphor of 'redemption' is drawn from the marketplace and refers to the liberation of a slave by the payment of a price (BGAD, 117). In the NT, ἀπολύτρωσις and related words commonly refer to God's rescue of sinners through Christ (Luke 21:28; Rom 8:23; 1 Cor 1:30; Eph 1:7, 14; 4:30; Col 1:14; Heb 9:15; cf. Matt 20:28 // Mark 10:45: λύτρον; Luke 24:21; Tit 2:14; 1 Pet 1:18: λυτρόω). In the wider biblical context, the language of 'redemption' evokes the great redemption wrought by God on the part of his people when he rescued them from slavery in Egypt. These echoes are almost certainly to be heard in Romans, where Paul emphasises the great cost of the 'redemption' bought through Jesus' death, and declares that God has now worked an even greater redemption through his Son, setting his people free from their slavery to sin (3:9; 6:17–18, 22; 8:12–17, 20–23). This 'redemption' will reach its final manifestation in the 'redemption of our bodies' (τὴν ἀπολύτρωσιν τοῦ σώματος ἡμῶν) at the end (8:23).

so that 'there is therefore now no condemnation' (8:1: Οὐδὲν ἄρα νῦν κατάκριμα) for those who are in Christ Jesus'. Moreover, in Jesus' resurrection, the final vindication has also already taken place: thus, Paul can declare that 'he was raised for our justification' (4:25: ἠγέρθη διὰ τὴν δικαίωσιν ἡμῶν).[186]

All of this is confirmed by the important parallel between God's 'forbearance' (ἀνοχή) in Romans 2:4 and 3:26: Paul speaks, in the first text, of God's 'forebearance' (ἀνοχή) *in the present* as he bears with sin until 'God's righteous judgment will be revealed' (ἀποκαλύψεως δικαιοκρισίας τοῦ θεοῦ) *on the final 'day of wrath'* (ἐν ἡμέρᾳ ὀργῆς) (2:4–5); he speaks, in the latter text, of God's 'forebearance' (ἀνοχή) *in the past* as he bore with sin until the execution of his righteous judgment against sin *in Jesus' death on the cross* (3:25–26).[187] J. Linebaugh states it well: 'Justification is not a separate verdict from the one God will speak at the final judgment, nor is it only 'an anticipation of the final verdict'. Justification is the final verdict—a forensic word from the future spoken in the enactment of God's eschatological judgment that is the 'now' of Jesus' death (and resurrection; cf. Rom 4:25)'.[188]

2.3.2 *Faith*

The free justification promised in the gospel comes 'to all who believe' (εἰς πάντας τοὺς πιστεύοντας) in Christ. Paul has, as we have seen, already presented Jesus' own faith/fulness—and especially is sin-bearing, wrath-placating death—as the grounds upon which those who trust in him might be declared righteous. Jesus Christ's own 'faith/fulness' (διὰ πίστεως Ἰησοῦ Χριστοῦ) secures the justification of sinners who believe. There is, however, no doubt that Paul couples his emphasis on Christ's faith/fulness to death with an equal and answering emphasis on the 'faith' of those who come to him. Indeed, Romans 3:21–26 provides the foundation for the agument Paul mounts in Romans 4, that God's righteousness is revealed through Christ for the benefit of any and all

---

186 For extended discussion here, see: Bird, 'Justified by Christ's Resurrection'; cf. Horton, *Justification*, II: 195–280.
187 Linebaugh, 'Righteousness Revealed', 228–30.
188 'Righteousness Revealed', 231–32.

who, like Abraham, who 'believe God'. The transition in Paul's focus is indicated by the occurrence of the verb πιστεύω: this verb occurs only once in the active voice in Romans 1:1–3:20, in the opening programmatic statement (1:16);[189] it is reintroduced in Romans 3:22, in the midst of the dense paragraph which is our focus, but occurs only once in the substantival participle 'those who believe' (τοὺς πιστεύοντας); the verb then becomes the focal point, however—even the dominant verb—in Romans 4, where it occurs five times (4:3, 5, 11, 17, 18, 24) in Paul's extended interpretation of Genesis 15:6.[190] In this verbal form, πιστεύω clearly refers to human trust in God.

Paul clearly distinguishes this 'trust in Christ' from 'works of the law' (3:20, 28: ἔργων νόμου), since his declaration of the righteousness of God, revealed in Christ, is sandwiched between two references to this crucial phrase. There has, unsurprisingly, also been significant debate in recent years over whether Paul's polemic here is aimed at Jewish legalism and merit-righteousness—human moral effort designed to earn God's favour (the so-called 'Old Perspective')—or Jewish presumption and ethnocentrism—trust in the exclusive 'badges' of covenant membership in Israel (so 'the New Perspective'). The debates here again are complex, and there is not space here to enter them in any detail.[191] It is enough to notice that the heart of the issue is whether Paul is primarily concerned to contrast two types of human response to God ('trusting' vs 'trying'), or to contrast two stages in salvation history ('the law' vs 'Christ'). Romans 3:21–26, read in its immediate context, however, suggests that this is almost certainly a false dichotomy. On the one hand, Paul is deeply concerned with the standing of sinners before God, and the fundamental question for Paul is whether a person might be 'justified before him' (3:20: δικαιωθήσεται ... ἐνώπιον αὐτοῦ). Paul emphasizes, likewise, that justification comes 'freely by his grace' (3:24: δωρεὰν τῇ αὐτοῦ χάριτι) which clearly discounts any idea of earning justification by merit, a point further underlined by the example

---

189 Romans 3:2 has the aorist passive ἐπιστεύθησαν with the sense 'entrusted'.
190 Dunn, 'New Perspective View', 197, overstates the case when he says that the subjective genitive reading of πίστις Χριστοῦ 'diminishes or sidetracks' that which Paul highlights, namely, the need for human faith.
191 For a review, with bibliography to 2013, see Smith, 'Paul', 23–24. Since 2013, the most important contribution is Barclay, *Paul and the Gift*, ch. 15.

of Abraham 'not working but trusting him who justifies the ungodly' (4:5: τῷ δὲ μὴ ἐργαζομένῳ πιστεύοντι δὲ ἐπὶ τὸν δικαιοῦντα τὸν ἀσεβῆ). This is the burden of the traditional Reformation understanding, and it is clearly supported by Paul's teaching here. 'Faith' is a fundamental disposition of trust in God and his gracious provision n Christ. The 'works of the law' which Paul rejects as any basis of a person's standing before God are not merely the 'covenant markers' of membership in Israel, but any and all human effort designed to put God in one's debt.[192] On the other hand, Paul is also deeply concerned with the inclusion of the Gentiles in the one new covenant people of God. At 3:21 he emphasizes that 'the righteousness of God', which provides the source for the believer's justification, has been revealed χωρὶς νόμου ('apart from law'), and the repetition of πᾶς at 3:22-23 (all who believe/all have sinned) is surely to be read with a sharp polemical edge against those who might exclude Gentiles from sharing in the blessings promised to Abraham. Certainly, that is exactly where Paul takes the argument in 3:29, where the pointed question—'Is God the God of Jews only? Is he not the God of Gentiles also?'—serves to underscore the point that God will justify *all* who believe. And again, the example of Abraham in chapter 4 is significant, since Abraham's faith was counted to him as righteousness (4:9: Ἐλογίσθη τῷ Ἀβραὰμ ἡ πίστις εἰς δικαιοσύνην) *before* he was circumcised, that is, while he was still a Gentile.

In sum, Paul's insistence that 'all those who believe' are 'justified freely by his grace' primarily refers to the right standing before God of all who trust in Christ, but also includes—as an important and necessary corollary—their inclusion amongst God's covenant people. The irony here, as S. Chester has recently shown, is that these two 'perspectives'— distorted in both popular Protestantism and the extremes of the 'New Perspective' reaction to it—were actually already well-integrated in the best of Reformation-era exegesis.[193] The Reformers, that is, already recognized that Paul's argument emphasizes, *first*, that there is no question of justification being earned by moral effort, *and also* that there is no ground for boasting in Jewish (or other human) distinctives. Since the

---

192 Cf. Schreiner, *Romans*, 301–308, who offers an excellent nuanced discussion of this question, with recent bibliography.
193 Chester, *Reading Paul*.

gospel reveals God's righteousness, through Christ's faith/fulness, it comes to all 'without distinction' (3:22: οὐ γάρ ἐστιν διαστολή), that is, to whoever will trust in Christ.

3. Theological synthesis: Paul's gospel and the doctrine of justification by faith alone

Paul's logic in Romans 3:21–26 leads to three exegetical conclusions. In Romans 3:21–26: (i) δικαιοσύνη θεοῦ is *God's own righteousness*, that is, his commitment to act in accordance with his own character, and therefore to judge sin while also graciously justifying sinners, both in Israel, and among the nations, for the sake of his own name; (ii) πίστις Χριστοῦ is *Christ's faith/fulness*, his trusting obedience towards God the Father, ultimately expressed in his sacrificial death, in which he bore God's righteous wrath against sin; (iii) 'justification' (δικαιόω) is God's eschatological, judicial, vindication of his people, announced in the present upon those who trust in Christ. The first and second of these exegetical conclusions differ quite significantly from the mainstream Protestant *exegetical* tradition. Nevertheless, the foregoing exegesis actually serves to strengthen the central insights of the common Reformation doctrine of 'justification by faith alone'. A thorough analysis of the Reformation traditions on these questions is, of course, well beyond the scope of this paper. I therefore adopt what is arguably the most mature of the Reformation-era Confessions, the *Westminster Confession of Faith*, as a kind of brief case study, and demonstrate the way in which the foregoing exegesis is not only consistent with its affirmations, but actually provides a more secure exegetical grounding for some of them.

First, the recognition that the gospel reveals *God's own righteousness*—his commitment to act in accordance with his own character, and so simultaneously judge sin and justify his people—is thoroughly in keeping with the WCF's affirmation of God's character. WCF 2.1 famously declares God's character as the God who is 'most loving, gracious, merciful, long-suffering, abundant in goodness and truth, forgiving iniquity, transgression, and sin; the rewarder of them that diligently seek Him; and withal, most just, and terrible in His judgments, hating all sin, and who will by no means clear the guilty'. This affirmation, of course, merely repeats and preserves the biblical 'tension' between God's grace and God's justice, God's mercy and God's wrath. In this context, the Confession's chapter on 'Justification' (WCF 11) shows how God's work in Christ's resolves this tension—or, rather, how God's work in Christ reveals the true unity of God's grace and justice. WCF 11.3 affirms that Christ 'by His obedience and death' has 'made full satisfaction to his Father's justice' in relation to his people's sins. It adds, however, that since Christ was 'given by the Father for them, and his obedience and satisfaction accepted in their stead' so that 'their justification is only of free grace'. It therefore concludes that, through Christ, 'both the exact justice, and the rich grace of God' are 'glorified in the justification of sinners'. Unsurprisingly, Romans 3:26 is among the prooftexts for this last affirmation—a verse which, as we have seen, affirms that God's own righteousness is revealed in his righteous justification of sinners. Far from there being any conflict between the Reformed doctrine of justification, and an exegesis of Romans 3:21–26 which affirms that 'the gospel reveals God's own righteousness', the two—to borrow a phrase from elsewhere in the Confession—'do sweetly comply' with each other (WCF 19.7).

Second, the recognition that Paul emphasizes *Christ's faith/fulness* is the grounds of the believer's justification is also fuly consistent with the WCF's doctrine of justification. The Confession's famous 'covenant theology' emphasizes that God's covenantal relationship with human beings always demands 'perfect obedience' on the part of God's people. It famously affirms a 'Covenant of Works' with Adam, and explicates this covenant in terms of the 'life promised to Adam; and in him to his posterity', as well as the 'condition of perfect and personal obedience' (WCF 7.2; cf. 19.1). This demand for perfect obedience on the part of God's human covenant partners continues in the Confession's 'Covenant of Grace' (WCF 7.3), with the crucial distinction that, in the person of his incarnate Son, God himself undertakes to provide the necessary obedience, offered in Christ on behalf of his people. Thus, in its majestic statement on the work of Christ (WCF 8), the Confession states that 'the Lord Jesus, by His perfect obedience, and sacrifice of Himself ... has fully satisfied the justice of His Father' (WCF 8.5; cf.

8.4). This emphasis on Christ's perfect obedience continues in the Confession's chapter on 'Justification', where Christ's 'obedience and satisfaction', or 'obedience and death', are mentioned three times (WCF 11.1, 3 (x2)). The Confession, moreover, emphasizes Christ's death as the culmination of his obedience and the ground of the believer's justification (WCF 11.3), while also affirming, following Paul, the crucial role of Christ's resurrection, who did 'rise again for their justification' (WCF 11.4; citing Rom 4:25).

To be sure, the Confession nowhere explicitly attributes 'faith' in the sense of 'trust' to Christ. It emphasizs, rather, Christ's perfect 'obedience'. Nevertheless, the Confession strongly implies that Christ exercised faith by drawing an unmistakable parallel between Christ's true and full humanity, and that of those who belong to him. With regard to *Christ's* obedience, the Confession explicitly affirms: (i) Christ's true and full humanity (WCF 8.2); (ii) his anointing by the Spirit (WCF 8.3), and; (iii) his 'perfect obedience, and sacrifice of Himself' enabled by the same Spirit (WCF 8.5). With regard to *Christian* obedience, the Confession explicitly affirms that: (i) true faith is the gift of God's Holy Spirit (WCF 7.3; 14.1); (ii) true faith inevitably produces the fruit of obedience (WCF 11.2); and (iii) true obedience has trust in God as its necessary root (WCF 16.2). Thus, as M. Allen has shown, with regard to the Reformed tradition as a whole, while 'affirmations that Christ exercised faith have been scant or lean', Reformed covenant theology nevertheless 'emphasizes the humanity of Christ *in a manner which provides a hospitable dogmatic environment for the doctrine of Christ's faith*, especially under the rubric of the active obedience of Christ'.[194] It is, therefore, thoroughly consistent with the doctrine of the Westminster Confession to attribute Spirit-enabled trusting obedience to Christ, as the necessary root of his perfect obedience and offering up of himself to God, as a sacrifice of atonement for his people. Indeed, anything less would undermine the Confession's affirmation of Christ's full humanity.

In this context, it is no surprise to find that the Reformed tradition as a whole does indeed affirm that Christ exercised faith. Calvin's *Institutes*

---

194 Allen, *Christ's Faith*, 154 (italics added); the whole discussion is relevant (pp.154–164).

provide strong indications that Christ exercised faith,[195] and his commentary on Hebrews explicitly affirms as much.[196] F. Turretin explicitly asks the question 'did Christ have faith and hope?' and answers in the affirmative (citing Matt 27:46; Acts 2:26; Heb 2:17; 3:2), while also carefully distinguishing between ordinary human faith in the mercy of God, which was not required of Christ, and Christ's prefect trust in God's goodness.[197] H. Bavinck, similarly, discusses the question and affirms that 'faith for Christ was not, as it is for us, trust in the grace and mercy of God, for this feature is something faith only obtained as a result of the state of sin in which we find ourselves'. Nevertheless, 'By nature, faith for Adam and Christ was nothing other than the act of clinging to the word and promises of God, a holding on to the Invisible One. And that is what Jesus did as well' (citing Matt 27:46; Heb 2:17–18; 3:2).[198] The discussion in John Owen is especially significant. He shows that Christ's full divinity, and the unity of the two natures in the one person of Christ, in no way obviated the need for the Spirit's enabling of his human nature for the whole work of redemption, from his incarnation to his glorification.[199] In particular, in a manner very similar to that outlined by the Westminster Confession, Owen demonstrates in some detail that the Holy Spirit enabled Christ's *'faith* and *trust in God* which, with fervent prayers, cries, and supplications, he now acted on God and his promises, both with respect unto himself and to the covenant which he was sealing with his blood' (citing Heb 2:13; Matt 27:43 [46?]; John 17).[200] Indeed, Owen argues that Christ's sacrifice was effective in reconciling us to the Father only because, by faith, he 'voluntarily and freely offered up himself a sacrifice unto God'.[201] Thus,

---

195 Allen, 'Calvin's Christ'.
196 Calvin, *Hebrews*, 28, on Hebrews 2:13, says of Christ: '... if He had not been a man subject to human needs, He would have no need of such faith. Since He depends on the help of God, His condition is therefore the same as ours'.
197 Turretin, *Institutes,* Vol. 2 QXII §V.–VI. (p.348)
198 Cf. Bavinck, *Reformed Dogmatics 3* §372 (p.312). Cf. Allen, *Christ's Faith*, 103: 'faith may be predicated of Jesus. Such faith cannot be strictly identical to the faith sinners place in him for justification, insofar as Jesus is neither a sinner nor in need of justification by means of another's representation. Given these covenantal differences, the faith of Jesus will best be considered alongside that faith exercised in the pre-lapsarian situation'.
199 Owen, *Pneumatologia*, §3–4 (pp.159–88).
200 Owen, *Pneumatologia*, §4 p.179.
201 Owen, *Pneumatologia*, §4 p.179 (also p.180).

as Allen has shown at length, 'the faith of the Christ coheres with both orthodox Christology and Reformation soteriology and, thus, need not be feared by those within the Reformed tradition'.[202] This conclusion, of course, does not itself resolve the exegetical debate. It does, however, create the dogmatic space within which those who wish to affirm classic Reformed doctrine are also able to weigh merits of the exegetical case without prejudice.

Conclusion

The Protestant exegetical tradition relating to Romans 3:21–26 emphasizes: (i) God's grace as the source of the believer's justification; (ii) the nature of justification as a judicial verdict, by which God grants to sinners a new righteous status, on the basis of Christ's death; (iii) faith—trust in Christ—as the sole instrument through which God's grace of justification is received. The argument advanced here in no way opposes any of these traditional emphases and, indeed, affirms that they are all clearly evident in Romans 3:21–26. Nevertheless, the apostle's emphasis in this crucial paragraph is first *theological* and *Christo-centric*: he affirms, first and foremost, that the gospel reveals and vindicates *God's own righteousness*, manifested in *Christ's trusting obedience* to the Father, even to the point of death, and that this work of Christ provides the only ground for the justification of all who believe. Indeed, far from posing a threat to the long-cherished Reformed doctrine of justification by faith alone, this understanding of Paul's argument in Romans 3 provides it with deeper roots. For if the gospel reveals *God's own righteousness*, it reveals nothing less than God's commitment to act in accordance with his own name, the name which declares that he is 'the LORD, the LORD, gracious and compassionate, abounding in steadfast love and faithfulness'. On this reading, Paul's affirmation that justification comes from God's free grace is not limited to the brief statement in Romans 3:24 ('by his grace as a gift'), but deeply anchored in the very name of God. In the same way, if the gospel reveals that God's righteousness has

---

202 Allen, *Christ's Faith*, 4.

been manifested in *Christ's faith/fulness*, 'the blood' which provides the ground for the sinner's justification is no arbitrary sacrifice, but the culmination of the perfect trusting obedience of the true Adam, the son of David, whose sacrifice of himself fully satisfies God's justice precisely because it was the one and only sacrifice offered in perfect faith.

Bibliography

Allen, R.M.	*The Christ's Faith: A Dogmatic Account* (London: T & T Clark, 2009).
Allen, R.M.	'Calvin's Christ: A Dogmatic Matrix for Discussion of Christ's Human Nature', *IJST* 9.4 (2007), 382–397.
Aquinas, T.	*Summa Theologica* (New York: Benziger Brothers, 1947).
Bailey, D.P.	'Jesus as the Mercy Seat: The Semantics and Theology of Paul's Use of Hilasterion in Romans 3:25', *TynBul* 51 (2000), 155–158.
Barclay, J.M.G.	*Paul and the Gift* (Grand Rapids: Eerdmans, 2015).
Barr, J.	*The Semantics of Biblical Language* (London: Oxford University Press, 1961).
Barrett, C.K.	*A Commentary on the Epistle to the Romans* (BNTC; London: A. & C. Black, 1957).
Barrett, J.P.	'Biblical Judgements and Theological Concepts: Toward a Defence of Imputed Righteousness', *SBET* 32.2 (2014), 152–169.
Barth, K.	*The Epistle to the Romans* (E.C. Hoskyns, transl.; London: Oxford University Press, 1933).
Bartholomew, G.	'Covenant and Creation: Covenant Overload or Covenantal Deconstruction', *CTJ* 30 (1995), 11–33.
Bates, M.W.	*Salvation by Allegiance Alone: Rethinking Faith, Works, and the Gospel of Jesus the King* (Grand Rapids: Baker Academic, 2017).
Bates, M.W.	'A Christology of Incarnation and Enthronement: Romans 1.3–4 as Unified, Nonadoptionist, and Nonconciliatory', *CBQ* 77 (2015), 107–127.

Bauer, W., F.W. Danker, W.F. Arndt, & F.W. Gingrich   *A Greek-English Lexicon of the New Testament and Other Early Christian Literature* (Chicago: University of Chicago Press, 2000 3rd ed.).

Bavinck, H.   *Reformed Dogmatics: Vol. 2 – God and Creation* (Grand Rapids: Baker Academic, 2004).

Bavinck, H.   *Reformed Dogmatics: Vol. 3 – Sin and Salvation in Christ* (Grand Rapids: Baker Academic, 2006).

Beker, J.C.   *Paul the Apostle: the Triumph of God in Life and Thought* (Philadelphia: Fortress, 1980).

Bird, M.F.   *Jesus the Eternal Son: Answering Adoptionist Christology* (Grand Rapids: Eerdmans, 2017).

Bird, M.F.   'Progressive Reformed View', in J.K. Beilby & P. R. Eddy (eds.), *Justification: Five Views* (Downers Grove: IVP, 2011), 131–157.

Bird, M.F.   *The Saving Righteousness of God: Studies on Paul, Justification and the New Perspective* (Milton Keynes: Paternoster, 2006).

Bird, M.F.   'Justified by Christ's Resurrection: A Neglected Aspect of Paul's Doctrine of Justification', *SBET* 22.1 (2004), 72–91.

Bird, M.F., & P.M. Sprinkle (eds.)   *The Faith of Jesus Christ: Exegetical, Biblical and Theological Studies* (Milton Keynes: Paternoster, 2009).

Bird, M.F., & M.R. Whitenton,   'The Faithfulness of Jesus Christ in Hippolytus's De Christo et Antichristo: Overlooked Patristic Evidence in the Πίστις Χριστοῦ Debate', *NTS* 55.4 (2009), 552–562.

Bornkamm, G.   *Paul* (D.M.G. Stalker, ed.; London: Hodder & Stoughton, 1971).

Bray, G.L. (ed.)   *Romans* (Ancient Christian Commentary on Scripture, vol. 6; Downers Grove: IVP, 1998).

Bultmann, R.   *Theology of the New Testament* (K. Grobel, transl.; 2 vols.; New York: Charles Scribners' Sons, 1951), vol. 1.

Calvin, J.   *The Epistles of Paul the Apostle to the Galatians, Ephesians, Philippians and Colossians* (CC; Grand Rapids: Eerdmans, 1965).

Calvin, J.   *The Epistle of Paul the Apostle to the Hebrews and the First and Second Epistles of St. Peter* (CC; Grand Rapids: Eerdmans, 1963).

Calvin, J.	*The Epistles of Paul the Apostle to the Romans and the Thessalonians* (CC; Edinburgh: St. Andrews Press, 1961).
Campbell, C.R.	*Advances in the Study of Greek: New Insights for Reading the New Testament* (Grand Rapids: Zondervan, 2015).
Campbell, D.A.	*The Deliverance of God: An Apocalyptic Rereading of Justification in Paul* (Grand Rapids: Eerdmans, 2009).
Campbell, D.A.	'The Faithfulness of Jesus Christ in Romans 3.22', in M.F. Bird & P.M. Sprinkle (eds.), *The Faith of Jesus Christ: Exegetical, Biblical and Theological Studies* (Milton Keynes: Paternoster, 2009), 57–72.
Campbell, D.A.	'Romans 1:17: A Crux Interpretum for the ΠΙΣΤΙΣ ΧΡΙΣΤΟΥ Debate', *JBL* 113 (1994), 265–285.
Campbell, D.A.	*The Rhetoric of Righteousness in Romans 3:21–26* (JSNTSup 65; Sheffield: JSOT, 1992).
Caneday, A.B.	'The Faithfulness of Jesus Christ as a Theme in Galatians', in M.F. Bird & P.M. Sprinkle (eds.), *The Faith of Jesus Christ: Exegetical, Biblical and Theological Studies* (Milton Keynes: Paternoster, 2009), 185–205.
Caneday, A.B.	*The Curse of the Law and the Cross: Works of the Law and Faith in Galatians 3:1–14* (Ann Arbor, MI: University Microfilms International, 1992).
Carson, D.A.	'Atonement in Romans 3:21–26: "God Presented Him as a Propitiation"', in C.E. Hill & F.A. James (eds.), *The Glory of the Atonement—Biblical, Historical and Practical Perspectives: Essays in Honour of Roger Nicole* (Downers Grove: IVP, 2004), 119–139.
Carson, D.A.	'The Vindication of Imputation: On Fields of Discourse and Semantic Fields', in M. Husbands & D.J. Treier (eds.), *Justification: What's at Stake in the Current Debates* (Downers Grove: IVP, 2004), 46–78.
Chester, S.J.	*Reading Paul with the Reformers: Reconciling Old and New Perspectives* (Grand Rapids: Eerdmans, 2017).
Conzelmann, H.	*An Outline of the Theology of the New Testament*)New Testament Library; London: SCM, 1969).

Cowan, J.A.	'N.T. Wright and Justification Revisited: A Contrarian Perspective', in J.A. Dunne & E. Lewellen (eds.), *One God, One People, One Future: Essays In Honour Of N. T. Wright* (London: SPCK, 2018), 440–465.
Cranfield, C.E.B.	'On the πίστις Χριστοῦ Question', in *On Romans and Other New Testament Essays* (Edinburgh: T&T Clark, 1998), 81–97.
Cranfield, C.E.B.	*A Critical and Exegetical Commentary on the Epistle to the Romans* (2 vols.; Edinburgh: T&T Clark, 1975–1979 6th ed.).
Crellin, R.	'The Semantics of the Perfect in the Greek of the New Testament', in S.E. Runge & C.J. Fresch (eds.), *The Greek Verb Revisited: A Fresh Approach to Biblical Exegesis* (Bellingham: Lexham, 2016), 430-457.
Cremer, H.	*Die paulinische Rechtfertigungslehre im Zusammenhange ihrer geschichtlichen Voraussetzungen* (Gütersloh: Bertelsmann, 1900 2nd ed.).
Crowe, B.D.	*The Last Adam: A Theology of the Obedient Life of Jesus in the Gospels* (Grand Rapids: Baker, 2017).
Crowe, B.D.	*The Obedient Son: Deuteronomy and Christology in the Gospel of Matthew* (BZNW 188; Berlin: De Gruyter, 2012).
de Boer, M.C.	*Galatians: A Commentary* (NTL; Louisville: Westminster John Knox, 2011).
de Roo, J.C.R.	*Works of the Law at Qumran and in Paul* (New Testament Monographs; Sheffield: Sheffield Phoenix, 2007).
Dodd, C.H.	'ΙΛΑΣΚΕΣΘΑΙ, its Cognates, Derivatives, and Synonyms in the Septuagint', *JTS* 32 (1931), 352–360.
Donfried, K.P.	*The Romans Debate* (Peabody: Hendrickson, 1991 Rev. and exp. ed.).
Downing, F.G.	'Ambiguity, Ancient Semantics, and Faith', *NTS* 56.1 (2010), 139–162.
Downs, D.J., & B.J. Lappenga,	*The Faithfulness of the Risen Christ: Pistis and the Exalted Lord in the Pauline Letters* (Waco: Baylor University Press, 2019).
Downs, D.J.	'Faith(fulness) of Christ Jesus in 2 Timothy 3.15', *JBL* 131.1 (2012), 143–160.

Dumbrell, W.J.	*Covenant and Creation: An Old Testament Covenant Theology* (Milton Keynes: Paternoster, 2013 rev. ed.).
Dumbrell, W.J.	*Covenant and Creation: A Theology of the Old Testament Covenants* (London: Paternoster, 1984).
Dunn, J.D.G.	'New Perspective Response [to Traditional Reformed View]', in J.K. Beilby & P. R. Eddy (eds.), *Justification: Five Views* (Downers Grove: IVP, 2011), 117–122.
Dunn, J.D.G.	'New Perspective View', in J.K. Beilby & P. R. Eddy (eds.), *Justification: Five Views* (Downers Grove: IVP, 2011), 176–201.
Dunn, J.D.G.	'Once More, ΠΙΣΤΙΣ ΧΡΙΣΤΟΥ', *SBL 1991 Seminar Papers* (1991), 730–744.
Dunn, J.D.G.	*Romans 1–8* (WBC; Dallas: Word, 1988).
Easter, M.C.	'The Pistis Christou Debate: Main Arguments and Responses in Summary', *CBR* 9.1 (2010), 33–47.
Elliott, M.W.	'Πίστις Χριστοῦ in the Church Fathers and Beyond', in M.F. Bird & P.M. Sprinkle (eds.), *The Faith of Jesus Christ: Exegetical, Biblical and Theological Studies* (Milton Keynes: Paternoster, 2009), 277–289.
Fesko, J.V.	*Death in Adam, Life in Christ: The Doctrine of Imputation* (Reformed Exegetical Doctrinal Studies; Ross-Shire: Mentor, 2016).
Fitzmyer, J.A.	'The Letter to the Romans', in R.E. Brown, J.A. Fitzmyer & R.E. Murphy (eds.), *The New Jerome Biblical Commentary* (London: Geoffrey Chapman, 1995), 291–331.
Fitzmyer, J.A.	*Romans: A New Translation with Introduction and Commentary* (AB 33; New York: Doubleday, 1993).
Kittel, G.	'Πίστις Ἰησοῦ Χριστοῦ bei Paulus', *TSK* 79 (1906), 419–436.
Gentry, P.J.	'Kingdom Through Covenant: Humanity as Divine Image', *SBJT* 12.1 (2008), 16–42.
Gentry, P.J., & S.J. Wellum	*Kingdom through Covenant: A Biblical-Theological Understanding of the Covenants* (Wheaton: Crossway, 2012).
Gouge, W., & T. Gataker	*The Westminster Annotations and Commentary on the Whole Bible* (London: Evan Tyler, 1657).

Grieb, A.K.	'The Righteousness of God in Romans', in L. Sumney (ed.), *Reading Paul's Letter to the Romans* (Resources for Biblical Study; Atlanta: Society of Biblical Literature, 2012), 65-78.
Grindheim, S.	'A Theology of Glory: Paul's Use of Δόξα Terminology in Romans', *JBL* 136.2 (2017), 451-65.
Gupta, N.K.	*Paul and the Language of Faith* (Grand Rapids: Eerdmans, forthcoming [2020]).
Harrisville, R.A., III	'ΠΙΣΤΙΣ ΧΡΙΣΤΟΥ: Witness of the Fathers', *Novum Testamentum* 36 (1994), 233-241.
Haussleiter, J.	*Der Glaube Jesu Christi und der christliche Glaube: Ein Beitrag zur Eklärung des Römerbriefe* (NKZ; Erlangen: Deichert, 1891).
Hays, R.B.	'The Letter to the Galatians: Introduction, Commentary, and Reflections', in L.E. Keck (ed.), *New Interpreter's Bible* Vol. 11: *Second Corinthians to Philemon* (Nashville: Abingdon, 2000), 181-348.
Hays, R.B.	*The Faith of Jesus Christ: An Investigation of the Narrative Substructure of Galatians 3:1-4:11* (SBLDS; Chico: Scholars Press, 1983). Republished as: *The Faith of Jesus Christ: The Narrative Substructure of Galatians 3:1-4:11* (The Biblical Resource Series; Grand Rapids: Eerdmans, 2002 2nd ed.).
Hays, R.B.	'Justification', in *Anchor Bible Dictionary* (D.N. Freedman, ed.; New York: Doubleday, 1992), 3.1129-1133.
Hays, R.B.	'ΠΙΣΤΙΣ and Pauline Christology: What is at Stake?', *SBL 1991 Seminar Papers* (Atlanta: Scholars, 1991), 714-729.
Hedges, D.W.	*Apollonius' Canon and Anarthrous Constructions in Pauline Literature: An Hypothesis* (Winona Lake, IN: Grace Theological Seminary, 1983).
Heliso, D.	*Pistis and the Righteous One: A Study of Romans 1:17 against the Background of Scripture and Second Temple Jewish Literature* (WUNT II 35; Tübingen: Mohr Siebeck, 2007).
Hellerman, J.H.	*Philippians* (EGGNT; Nashville: Broadman & Holman, 2015).
Hebert, A.G.	"'Faithfulness' and 'Faith'", *Theology* 58.5 (1955), 373-379.
Hooker, M.D.	'Another Look at πίστις Χριστοῦ', *SJT* 69 (2016), 46-62.

Hooker, M.D.	'On Becoming the Righteousness of God: Another Look at 2 Cor 5:21', *NovT* 50 (2008), 358–375.
Hooker, M.D.	'ΠΙΣΤΙΣ ΧΡΙΣΤΟΥ', *NTS* 35 (1989), 321–342.
Horton, M.S.	*Justification* (NSD; 2 vols.; Grand Rapids: Zondervan, 2018).
Horton, M.S.	*The Christian Faith: A Systematic Theology for Pilgrims on the Way* (Grand Rapids: Zondervan, 2011).
Horton, M.S.	'Traditional Reformed View', in J.K. Beilby & P. R. Eddy (eds.), *Justification: Five Views* (Downers Grove: IVP, 2011), 83–111.
Howard, G.E.	*Paul: Crisis in Galatia; A Study in Early Christian Theology* (SNTSMS 35; Cambridge: Cambridge University Press, 1979).
Howard, G.E.	'The 'Faith of Christ'', *ExpT* 85 (1973–74), 212–215.
Howard, G.E.	'Notes and Observations on the 'Faith of Christ'', *HTR* 60 (1967), 459–465.
Hultgren, A.	'The Pistis Christou Formulations in Paul', *NovT* 22 (1980), 248–263.
Hunn, D.	'Debating the Faithfulness of Jesus Christ in Twentieth-Century Scholarship', in M.F. Bird & P.M. Sprinkle (eds.), *The Faith of Jesus Christ: Exegetical, Biblical and Theological Studies* (Milton Keynes: Paternoster, 2009), 15–32.
Hunn, D.	'Habakkuk 2.4b in its Context: How Far Off Was Paul?', *JSOT* 34.2 (2009), 219–239.
Irons, C.L.	*The Righteousness of God: A Lexical Examination of the Covenant-faithfulness Interpretation* (WUNT II 386; Tübingen: Mohr Siebeck, 2015).
Irons, C.L.	'Is "Righteousness" a relational concept in the Hebrew Bible?', in R.A. Taylor & C.E. Morrison (eds.), *Reflections on Lexicography: Explorations in Ancient Syriac, Hebrew, and Greek Sources* (Perspectives on Linguistics and Ancient Languages; Piscataway, N.J.: Gorgias Press, 2014), 135–145.
Jewett, R.	*Romans: A Commentary* (Hermeneia; Minneapolis: Fortress, 2007).

Jipp, J.W.	*Christ is King: Paul's Royal Ideology* (Minneapolis: Fortress, 2015).
Johnson, L.T.	*Reading Romans: A Literary and Theological Commentary* (Reading the New Testament; New York: Crossroad, 1997).
Johnson, L.T.	'Romans 3:21–26 and the Faith of Jesus', *CBQ* 44 (1982), 77–90.
Johnson, N.C.	'Romans 1:3–4: Beyond Antithetical Parallelism', *JBL* 136.2 (2017), 467–490.
Käsemann, E.	'The Righteousness of God in Paul', *New Testament Questions of Today* (London: SCM, 1969), 168–82.
Keck, L.E.	*Romans* (ANTC; Nashville: Abingdon Press, 2005).
Keener, C.S.	*Romans* (NCCS; Eugene: Cascade, 2009).
Kim, S.	'Jesus the Son of God as the Gospel (1 Thess 1:9–10 and Rom 1:3–4)', in M.F. Bird & J. Maston (eds.), *Earliest Christian History: History, Literature and Theology. Essays from the Tyndale Fellowship in Honour of Martin Hengel* (Tübingen: Mohr Siebeck, 2012), 117–141.
Kirk, J.R.D.	'Appointed Son(s), An Exegetical Note on Romans 1:4 and 8:29', *BBR* 14 (2004), 241–242.
Koehler, L., & W. Baumgartner	*The Hebrew and Aramaic Lexicon of the Old Testament* (M.E.J. Richardson, transl.; Leiden: Brill, 2000).
Kugler, C.	'ΠΙΣΤΙΣ ΧΡΙΣΤΟΥ: The Current State of Play and the Key Arguments', *CBR* 14 (2016), 244–255.
Kümmel, W.G.	*The Theology of the New Testament according to its Major Witnesses: Jesus-Paul-John* (Nashville: Abingdon, 1973).
Lightfoot, J.B.	*Saint Paul's Epistle to the Galatians: A Revised Text with Introduction, Notes and Dissertations* (London: Macmillan, 1884 8th ed.).
Linebaugh, J.A.	'Righteousness Revealed: The Death of Christ as the Definition of the Righteousness of God in Romans 3.21–26', in B.C. Blackwell, J.K. Goodrich & J. Maston (eds.), *Paul and the Apocalyptic Imagination* (Minneapolis: Fortress, 2016), 219–238.
Longenecker, B.W.	*The Triumph of Abraham's God: The Transformation of Identity in Galatians* (Nashville: Abingdon Press, 1998).

Longenecker, B.W. 'Πίστις in Romans 3.25: Neglected Evidence for the 'Faithfulness of Christ'?'. *NTS* 39 (1993), 478–480.

Longenecker, R.N. *The Epistle to the Romans: A Commentary on the Greek Text* (NIGTC; Grand Rapids: Eerdmans, 2016).

Longenecker, R.N. *Paul, Apostle of Liberty* (Grand Rapids: Baker, 1964).

Lust, J., E. Eynikel, & K. Hauspie   *A Greek-English Lexicon of the Septuagint* (Stuttgart: Deutsche Bibelgesellschaft, 2003 2nd ed.).

Luther, M. 'Preface to the Complete Edition of Luther's Latin Writings', in *Luther's Works Vol 34: Career of the Reformer IV* (H.T. Lehmann & L.W. Spitz, eds.; St Louis: Concordia, 1960), 323–338.

Luther, M. *Commentary on the Epistle to the Romans* (Grand Rapids: Zondervan, 1954).

Lutheran Federation *Joint Declaration on the Doctrine of Justification: The Lutheran World Federation and the Roman Catholic Church* (Grand Rapids: Eerdmans, 2000).

Martyn, J.L. *Galatians: A New Translation with Introduction and Commentary* (AB; New York: Doubleday, 1997).

Matera, F.J. *Galatians* (Sacra Pagina 9; Collegeville: Liturgical Press, 1992).

Matlock, R.B. 'Saving Faith: The Rhetoric and Semantics of πίστις in Paul', in M.F. Bird & P.M. Sprinkle (eds.), *The Faith of Jesus Christ: Exegetical, Biblical and Theological Studies* (Milton Keynes: Paternoster, 2009), 73–90.

Matlock, R.B. 'The Rhetoric of πίστις in Paul: Galatians 2.16, 3.22, Romans 3.22, and Philippians 3.9', *JSNT* 30.2 (2007), 173–203.

Matlock, R. B. '"Even the Demons Believe': Paul and πίστις Χριστοῦ', *CBQ* 64.2 (2002), 300–318.

Matlock, R.B. 'Detheologizing the πίστις Χριστοῦ Debate: Cautionary Remarks from a Lexical Semantics Perspective', *NovT* 42.1 (2000), 1–23.

McDonald, L.M., & S.E. Porter   *Early Christianity and Its Sacred Literature* (Peabody: Hendrickson, 2000).

McFadden, K.W. 'Does Πίστις Mean 'Faith(fulness)' in Paul?', *TynB* 66.2 (2015), 251–270.

McGrath, A.E.	*Iustitia Dei: A History of the Christian Doctrine of Justification*. Cambridge: Cambridge University Press, 1998 2nd ed., 2005 3rd ed.)
Merrill, E.H.	'Covenant and the Kingdom: Genesis 1–3 as Foundation for Biblical Theology', *CTR* 1.2 (1987), 295–308.
Metzger, B.M.	*A Textual Commentary on the Greek New Testament* (London/New York: United Bible Societies, 1994 2nd ed.).
Moo, D.J.	*The Letter to the Romans* (NICNT; Grand Rapids: Eerdmans, 2018 2nd ed.).
Moo, D.J.	*Galatians* (BECNT; Grand Rapids: Baker Academic, 2013).
Moo, D.J.	*The Epistle to the Romans* (NICNT; Grand Rapids: Eerdmans, 1996).
Moo, J.	'Romans 8.19–22 and Isaiah's Cosmic Covenant', *NTS* 5 (2008), 74–89.
Morgan, T.	*Roman Faith and Christian Faith: Pistis and Fides in the Early Roman Empire and Early Churches* (Oxford: Oxford University Press, 2015).
Morris, L.	*The Apostolic Preaching of the Cross* (Grand Rapids: Eerdmans, 1965).
Murray, J.	*The Epistle to the Romans: the English Text with Introduction, Exposition and Notes* (London: Marshall, Morgan & Scott, 1974).
Myers, B.	'From Faithfulness to Faith in the Theology of Karl Barth', in M.F. Bird & P.M. Sprinkle (eds.), *The Faith of Jesus Christ: Exegetical, Biblical and Theological Studies* (Milton Keynes: Paternoster, 2009), 291–308.
Naselli, A.D.	'The Righteous God Righteously Righteouses the Unrighteous. Justification according to Romans', in M. Barrett (ed.), *The Doctrine on which the Church Stands or Falls: Justification in Biblical, Theological, Historical, and Pastoral Perspective* (Wheaton: Crossway, 2019), 213–238.
Niehaus, J.J.	'Covenant: An Idea in the Mind of God', *JETS* 52.2 (2009), 225–246.
Niehaus, J.J.	*God at Sinai: Covenant and Theophany in the Bible and Ancient Near East* (SOTBT; Carlisle: Paternoster, 1995).

O'Brien, P.T.	*The Epistle to the Philippians: A Commentary on the Greek Text* (NIGTC; Grand Rapids: Eerdmans, 1991).
Owen, J.	*Pneumatologia or A Discourse concerning the Holy Spirit: Wherein an Account is Given of His Name, Nature, Personality, Dispensation, Operations, and Effects; His Whole Work in the Old and New Creation is Explained; the Doctrine concerning It Vindicated from Oppositions and Reproaches* (Works of John Owen; London: Banner of Truth, 1966).
Piper, J.	*The Future of Justification: A Response to N.T. Wright* (Wheaton: Crossway, 2007).
Quarles, C.L.	"'From Faith to Faith': A Fresh Examination of the Prepositional Series in Romans 1:17', *NovT* 45 (2003), 5–13.
Robinson, D.W.B.	"'Faith of Jesus Christ'—A New Testament Debate', *RTR* 29 (1970), 71–81. Now published in E. Loane (ed.), *Donald Robinson. Select Works.* Vol. 3: *Biblical and Liturgical Studies* (Camperdown, NSW: Australian Church Record & Moore College, 2018), 130–144.
Sanders, E.P.	*Paul and Palestinian Judaism: A Comparison of Patterns of Religion* (Philadelphia: Fortress, 1977).
Schliesser, B.	"'Christ-Faith" as an Eschatological Event (Galatians 3.23–26), A "Third View" on Πίστις Χριστοῦ', *JSNT* 38 (2016), 277–300.
Schmid, H.H.	*Gerechtigkeit als Weltordnung: Hintergrund und Geschichte der alttestamentlichen Gerechtigkeitsbegriffes* (Beiträge zur historischen Theologie; Tübingen: Mohr, 1968).
Schnabel, E.J.	*Der Brief des Paulus an die Römer: Kapitel 1–5* (Historisch-theologische Auslegung; Witten: Brockhaus, 2015).
Schreiner, T.R.	*Romans* (BECNT; Grand Rapids: Baker, 2018 2nd ed.).
Schreiner, T.R.	'Justification: The Saving Righteousness of God in Christ', *JETS* 54.1 (2011), 19–34.
Schreiner, T.R.	*Romans* (BECNT; Grand Rapids: Baker, 1998).
Scott, J.M.	'A New Approach to Habakkuk 2:4–5a', *VT* (1985), 330–340.
Seifrid, M.A.	'Roman Faith and Christian Faith', *NTS* 64.2 (2018), 247–255.

Seifrid, M.A.	'Paul's Use of Righteousness Language Against Its Hellenistic Background', in D.A. Carson, P.T. O'Brien & M.A. Seifrid (eds.), *Justification and Variegated Nomism*. Vol. 2: *The Paradoxes of Paul* (Grand Rapids: Baker, 2004), 39–74.
Seifrid, M.A.	'Righteousness Language in the Hebrew Scriptures and Early Judaism', in D.A. Carson, P.T. O'Brien & M.A. Seifrid (eds.), *Justification and Variegated Nomism*. Vol. 1: *The Complexities of Second Temple Judaism* (Grand Rapids: Baker, 2001), 415–442.
Silva, M.	'Faith Versus Works of Law in Galatians', in D.A. Carson, P.T. O'Brien & M.A. Seifrid (eds.), *Justification and Variegated Nomism*. Vol. 2: *The Paradoxes of Paul* (Grand Rapids: Baker, 2004), 217–248.
Silva, M.	*Interpreting Galatians: Explorations in Exegetical Method* (Grand Rapids: Baker Academic, 2001 2nd ed.).
Smith, M.J.	'Paul in the Twenty-First Century', in M. Harding and A. Nobbs (eds.), *All Things to All Cultures: Paul among Jews, Greeks and Romans* (Grand Rapids: Eerdmans, 2013), 1–33.
Sprinkle, P.M.	'πίστις Χριστοῦ as an Eschatological Event', in M.F. Bird & P.M. Sprinkle (eds.), *The Faith of Jesus Christ: Exegetical, Biblical and Theological Studies* (Milton Keynes: Paternoster, 2009), 165–184.
Starling, D.	'Covenants and Courtrooms, Imputation and Imitation: Righteousness and Justification in *Paul and the Faithfulness of God*', *JSPL* 4.1 (2014), 37–48.
Stuhlmacher, P.	*Paul's Letter to the Romans: A Commentary* (S.J. Hafemann, transl.; Louisville: Westminster John Knox, 1994).
Thielman, F.S.	*Romans* (ZECNT; C.E. Arnold, ed.; Grand Rapids: Zondervan, 2018).
Timmins, W.N.	'A Faith Unlike Abraham's: Matthew Bates on Salvation by Allegiance Alone', *JETS* 61.3 (2018), 595–615.
Torrance, T.F.	'One Aspect of the Biblical Conception of Faith', *ExpT* 68 (1957), 111–114.
Turner, N.	*A Grammar of New Testament Greek*. Vol. 3: *Syntax* (Edinburgh: T&T Clark, 1963).

Turretin, F.	*Institutes of Elenctic Theology* (G.M. Giger, transl.; 3 vols.; Phillipsburg: P&R, 1992–1997).
Valloton, P.	*Le Christ et la foi: Etude de théologie biblique* (Geneva: Labor & Fides, 1961).
Vanhoozer, K.J.	'Wrighting the Wrongs of the Reformation? The State of the Union with Christ in St. Paul and Protestant Soteriology', in N. Perrin & R.B. Hays (eds.), *Jesus, Paul, and the People of God: A Theological Dialogue with N.T. Wright* (London: SPCK, 2011), 235–259.
Vatican	*The Catechism of the Catholic Church* (Vatican City: Libreria Editrice Vatican, 1997).
Vogels, W.	*God's Universal Covenant: A Biblical Study* (Ottawa: University of Ottawa Press, 1986 2nd ed.).
Vos, G.	'Paul's Eschatological Concept of the Spirit', *Redemptive History and Biblical Interpretation: The Shorter Writings of Geerhardus Vos* (R.B. Gaffin Jr., ed.; Phillipsburg: P&R, 1980), 91–125.
Wallace, D.B.	*Greek Grammar Beyond the Basics: An Exegetical Syntax of the New Testament* (Grand Rapids: Zondervan, 1996).
Wallis, I.G.	*The Faith of Jesus Christ in Early Christian Traditions* (SNTSMS 84; Cambridge: Cambridge University Press, 1995).
Ward, R.S.	*God and Adam: Reformed Theology and the Creation Covenant* (Lansvale: Tulip Publishing, 2019 rev. ed.).
Watson, F.	'Roman Faith and Christian Faith', *NTS* 64.2 (2018), 243–247.
Watson, F.	'By Faith (of Christ), An Exegetical Dilemma and Its Scriptural Solution', in M.F. Bird & P.M. Sprinkle (eds.), *The Faith of Jesus Christ: Exegetical, Biblical and Theological Studies* (Milton Keynes: Paternoster, 2009), 147–163.
Weiß, A.	'Christus Jesus als Weihegeschenk oder Sühnemal? Anmerkungen zu einer neueren Deutung von *hilasterion* (Röm 3,25) samt einer Liste der epigraphischen Belege', *ZNW* 105.2 (2014), 294–302.
Williams, S.K.	'Again Pistis Christou', *CBQ* 49 (1987), 431–447.

Williams, S.K.	'The 'Righteousness of God' in Romans', *JBL* 99.2 (1980), 241–290.
Wright, D.F.	'Justification in Augustine', in B.L. McCormack (ed.), *Justification in Perspective: Historical Developments and Contemporary Challenges* (Grand Rapids: Baker, 2006), 55–72.
Wright, N.T.	'Translating δικαιοσύνη: A Response', *ExpT* 125.10 (2014), 487–490.
Wright, N.T.	*Paul and the Faithfulness of God* (COQG; Minneapolis: Fortress, 2013).
Wright, N.T.	'Justification: Yesterday, Today and Forever', *JETS* 54.1 (2011), 49–64.
Wright, N.T.	*Justification: God's Plan and Paul's Vision* (London: SPCK, 2009).
Wright, N.T.	'The Letter to the Romans: Introduction, Commentary, and Reflections', in L.E. Keck (ed.), *New Interpreter's Bible* (Nashville: Abingdon, 2002), 393–770.
Young, S.L.	'Romans 1.1–5 and Paul's Christological Use of Hab. 2.4 in Rom. 1.17: An Underutilized Consideration in the Debate', *JSNT* 34 (2012), 277–285.
Zerwick, M.	*Biblical Greek; Illustrated by Examples* (Rome: Scripta Pontificii Instituti Biblici, 1963).

CHAPTER 10

Personal Obedience (and Sin) in the New Age of Faith: Rehearing Romans 14:23b[1]

Stephen Spence

Starting with a Confession

This chapter starts with a confession. I am, and have always been, one of those who would fit within a class of Christians that the Apostle Paul identifies in Romans 14 as 'the strong'—those with the power to welcome or exclude. In my context that means being one of those Christians who are white, male, from a Christian family, educated, middle-class, married (never divorced), heterosexual, and an ordained leader within my church (Baptist). Of course, that is not the confession; that is just who I am. My confession is that I have used my position of power within the church, sometimes overtly but more often inadvertently, to decide for others under what circumstances they could fully belong to a local church. I considered myself both welcoming and helpful—I would welcome anyone into the church with the intent of helping them to mature into the kind of follower of Jesus that I was or, if I couldn't conform them to my way of following Jesus, to at least acknowledge that mine

---

[1] I am thankful to Professor Jim Harrison for the opportunity to present an earlier version of this paper at the Sydney College of Divinity conference, 'Romans and the Legacy of St Paul: Social, Theological, and Pastoral Perspectives' (2016); it has provided me with a forum to go beyond an attempt to merely describe what Paul might have meant when he wrote to the Christians in first–century Rome in order to consider its pastoral implications.

was the better way.² Because this is a confession, I am expressing my sin in a framework that I was unaware of at the time. Even as I was failing to 'welcome those who are weak in faith, but not for the purpose of quarrelling over opinions' (Romans 14:1)³ I would have been able to provide a much more pious description of my behaviour. I am no longer willing, however, to collude with exegetical readings of Romans 14 that either leave Paul's instructions to the church in Rome as focused on now-irrelevant religious practices or as addressing only those issues that we, 'the strong', deem to be adiaphora—those 'matters that are neither required of nor prohibited to believers in Jesus'⁴ and, therefore, can be left to individual consciences to judge their appropriateness.

My training strove against what we deemed to be eisegetical readings by 'others' in favour of a methodology intended to uncover the objective truth within the passage. I am still against treating the text as a literary artefact upon which I can graft my 'reader response'. But I have abandoned the naiveté of believing that differing interpretations are a result of the failure of 'others' to do their exegesis correctly. Instead, I have accepted the common wisdom that 'exegesis without presuppositions is impossible'.⁵ I will not claim, therefore, that the way I now hear Romans 14 address me is solely the result of having arrived at a better exegetical reading of the text. Indeed, I do think that I have arrived at a better exegetical reading of the text, and this chapter will point to some of those observations, but there has been more to it than that. The something more is not the focus of this chapter, but I am sure as you read it you will catch glimpses of the various gospel, theological, and hermeneutical issues that have shaped my attempt to hear faithfully and respond to this important part of Paul's letter to the Christians in Rome.

---

2   In the 1970s and 1980s this included such sins as smoking, any alcohol consumption, cohabitation, and divorce.
3   All English Bible quotations are from the nrsv.
4   Longenecker, *The Epistle to the Romans*, 1001.
5   '[W]hen traditionalist and revisionists [within the Church of Scotland] approach the issue of homosexuality—even with the same explicit questions in mind—they do so with different implicit questions, questions that arise from the differing theological and philosophical presuppositions they hold. These differing presuppositions have arisen from a tension within Scottish theology between the saving love of Jesus Christ on the one hand, and the confessional and scriptural structure that presents and communicates that saving love on the other'; Fraser, 'A Tradition in Crisis', 157.

Some Unasked Exegetical Questions

For each one of us, there is a traditional way to read Romans 14. Whichever ecclesial community provides that traditional reading for us, we will find that there are certain questions we do not ask because, in our tradition, they have been answered (or deemed to be unimportant). Particularly with such an important letter as Romans, the impact of its reception history in forming a community consensus—what can be accepted as settled and what must be established—cannot be underestimated.[6] A text's reception history can lead a reader into certain cognitive biases that blind them to their exegetical presuppositions.[7]

Among the commentators that I read there are certain issues that are so settled they can simply be asserted. In particular, it is agreed that Romans 14 is about adiaphora and not about those weighty matters that many Christians are today clearly wrestling with, such as sexual identity. Richard Longenecker offers such a consensus view in his commentary: Romans 14 concerns 'matters having to do primarily with social background, personal opinion, or personal preference—that is with the so-called *adiaphora*'.[8] But despite this received consensus, I want to ask the following:

- Who decides what is or is not included among the possible '*dialogismōn*' (Romans 14:1) that we are not to pass judgment on?
- Who gets to decide for you and for me what is required or prohibited?
- How did 'judge not' become 'judge—as long as your attitude is acceptable'?
- Who are the 'weak in faith' (*asthenounta tē pistei*) today? Am I certain that I am not causing them to stumble?
- Is it true that 'everything that does not come from faith is sin' (14:23b) and does this imply that 'everything done in faith—seeking to honour God and to give him thanks —is not sin'?

---

6   Knight, '*Wirkungsgeschichte*, Reception History, Reception Theory'.
7   Chalmers, 'The Influences of Cognitive Biases on Biblical Interpretation'.
8   Longenecker, *Romans*, 1001.

Some of My Changing Presuppositions

(i) Now when I read Paul I am trying to hear the coherent narrative from which he writes his contingent applications.[9] In doing so, I assume that it is possible for a consistent coherent narrative to produce inconsistent contingent applications. An apostolic instruction is not always intended to be applicable in a different context. We must reckon with the reality that Paul was accused by his opponents of being inconsistent.[10] He denied it, but that was because, in his mind, what they considered to be contrary applications each came from the same coherent narrative. Yes, he was at times 'under the law' and at other times he was 'outside the law', but he was always driven by the same desire to share the blessings of the gospel to all, and not just the 'all' who were already like him or who were willing to become like him.

> For though I am free with respect to all, I have made myself a slave to all, so that I might win more of them. To the Jews I became as a Jew, in order to win Jews. To those under the law I became as one under the law (though I myself am not under the law) so that I might win those under the law. To those outside the law I became as one outside the law (though I am not free from God's law but am under Christ's law) so that I might win those outside the law. To the weak I became weak, so that I might win the weak. I have become all things to all people, that I might by all means save some. I do it all for the sake of the gospel, so that I may share in its blessings. (1 Cor 9:19–23)

It would be to miss the radicalness of this apostolic practice of inconsistent contingent applications by simply equating Paul's reference to 'Christ's law' with the Torah (the error of early Judaizers) or with the so-called non-ritual parts of the Torah that some equate with 'God's law' (the error of many contemporary Christians).[11]

---

9   Beker, 'Recasting Pauline Theology'.
10 E.g., with reference to 2 Cor 1:12–2:13, Hafemann, 'Corinthians, letters of', 168.
11 This is not just a contemporary view. 'Justin [Martyr] argues that Christians observe the parts of the Mosaic code that are "eternal and fit for every nationality" (*Dial.* 67:10; cf. 93:1–2). For Justin, only particular parts of the Mosaic law function as a type of universal, or natural, law code'; Wendel, 'Torah Obedience and Early Christian Ethical Practices', 186. Some sexual ethics would feature, for many Christians, within this 'universal, or natural, law code'.

Paul advises purposeful, context-informed behavioural choices. The gospel revelation remains consistent, but the application of the gospel changes because contexts change. Many in today's church expect that believing the same gospel will always lead the Church to the same practices. Therefore, for example, the Church must have a single approach to how it responds to followers of Jesus who identify as homosexual or who seek to enter into a same-sex marriage. Too often, in an attempt to create certainty, the Church has resisted diversity of practice by either arguing it away or by excluding it. Yet, what some consider cultural compromise may be an expression of contextual application of the gospel.

I am not arguing that Paul did not consider homosexuality to be a sin; Paul uses homosexuality as an illustration of sin in Romans 1 because among his churches this is unquestioned.[12] I am suggesting that Paul's approach to homosexuality was contingent, representing a (then) Christian response to 'the Roman world's sexual practices' that was consistent with the Jewish critique of pagan culture.[13] And I am asking, is it possible that Paul's coherent theology could reshape legitimate contingent applications beyond Paul's personal practices? Is it a more faithful response to Paul's letters to live shaped by our wrestling with Paul's coherent theology or by trying to repeat his contingent applications?

(ii) Like many, I have found the debates around the New Perspective(s) of Paul to have significantly reframed my understanding of Second Temple Judaism and, therefore, the theological context of Paul's letter to the Romans.[14] Now, when I read Paul, I no longer assume that he

---

12 McKnight, *A Fellowship of Differents*, esp. 123–34. McKnight shows both a sensitivity to Paul's historical cultural context and to contemporary pastoral issues: 'One can argue that Paul's concern was not what is being discussed today—the appropriateness or inappropriateness of same-sex, faithful unions and marriages. Yet even if that is not his central focus, his words in Romans 1 about "unnatural" apply to all same-sex relations'. McKnight argues for a 'third way' that unambiguously welcomes homosexuals into the fellowship of the local church in order to journey with them, as the church journeys with all of its members, towards holiness. We differ in that McKnight seems to expect that the goal of homosexual Christians is always celibacy rather than marriage; 'same-sex marriage might be law [but] that does not make it, for the traditionalist, "right"' (p.254 n.17). Certainly, God calls some homosexuals and some heterosexuals to celibacy but, I am arguing, it is for the Spirit, not the 'traditionalist', to decide what is right for them.
13 McKnight, *A Fellowship of Differents*, 128.
14 E.g., Wright, *The New Testament and the People of God: Christian Origins and the Question of God, 1* and *Jesus and the Victory of God: Christian Origins and the Question of God, 2*.

is battling to establish within the early Church a firm belief in 'salvation by faith alone' against a Jewish emphasis upon 'salvation by works of the Torah'. Judaism has always been a religion of God's grace, which leads to the gracious response of God's people—a response guided by the 'spiritual' Torah (7:14). For the Jews of Paul's time, the Torah 'was the path to life and blessing, and a means of overcoming evil desires and injustice';[15] the means by which God's people knew how to please God through obedient service.

So, when Paul describes his letter as something rather bold (15:15), he is not referring to his advocacy of an idea that is not contested within the church in Rome, 'justification by grace through faith', but rather to what I would describe as 'sanctification by grace through faith'. It is not the importance of faithful allegiance to God that the Romans must learn. What they must learn is the importance of looking to the Holy Spirit for empowering guidance, rather than to the ineffectual Torah (because of the slavery of sin, 7:1–25) if they are to 'know the good, pleasing, perfect will of God' (12:2). This certainty of Paul, that we are now part of the New Creation and that we are children of God who are indwelt by the Spirit of God (8:9–17), leads him to the view that 'those who are led by the Spirit of God are sons of God' (v.14). This is extraordinarily bold in a context in which the Torah was seen as God's ordained way to restrain sin.

Michael Bird concludes, 'Whether it was socially, ethnically, or theologically motivated there were differences of opinion among the Romans congregations about what the role of Torah should have in the life of believers'.[16] For me, these differences of opinion revolved around sanctification (how to live lives pleasing to God) and not justification (how to become one of God's people). There were those in Rome who 'rely on the law' as the basis for their claim to know God's will and to be able to teach it to others (2:17–20).[17] There are those who believe that Paul's teachings will lead to more sinning (6:1). How else, they might reasonably ask, are those converted from paganism to know how to

---

15 Mitchell, 'The New Perspective and the Christian Life', 97.
16 Bird, *Romans*, 463.
17 '[I]n the rhetoric of Romans, Paul the apostle to the Gentiles, confronts another Jew who is also a teacher of gentiles'; Stowers, *A Rereading of Romans*, 149.

serve God if we do not teach them in the ways of Torah? Paul's answer, writ large in Romans, is 'live/walk by the Spirit' and, if you do, 'you will fulfil the righteous requirement of the law' (8:4). It is possible that those who 'walk by the Spirit' will be seen by others as 'sinners' (Gal 2:17), but there is no condemnation for them (8:1).

(iii) Now when I read Paul I am looking for his 'apocalyptic imagination'.[18] The resurrection of Jesus is the watershed moment of creation; the moment when those 'in Adam' become those 'in Christ', a part of the New Creation, indwelt by the Spirit of God.[19]

Romans leads its first hearers through a deep re-visioning of the gospel narrative from the old Adamic Age in which Sin reigns to the new Age of Jesus and the Spirit ruled by grace, in order to call them, as people of the new Age, to an obedience lived not through Torah but through faith. Paul's dichotomy Spirit/Torah in Romans is not primarily about salvation; it is Paul's bold reminder (15:15) that obedience to God means living in the new Age of Faith, not in a pre-Spirit Age, when Torah instructed God's people. In this New Age it is the Spirit who guides, transforms, and enables obedience.

For Paul, those who are 'in Christ' live immediately within the Age of the Spirit. It is their indwelling by, and indwelling of, the Spirit that makes them truly the children of God. To turn aside from the Spirit, even if it is to pursue the guidance of Torah, is to step outside of Christ and his New Creation and to return to enslavement within this present Evil Age.[20]

The Purpose of Paul's Letter to the Romans

There are many proposed reasons for Romans. Michael Bird has provided an overview of them in his recent commentary.[21] But any reason

---

18 E.g. Blackwell, Goodrich, & Maston, *Paul and the Apocalyptic Imagination*.
19 Mitchell, 'The New Perspective and the Christian Life', figure 4.1 (p.82).
20 This theme is also evident in Galatians.
21 Bird, *Romans,* 6–12. He concludes, 'Paul's primary aim is to gather the support of the Roman Christians for his planned journey to Spain ... [and] from the Romans side, Paul's goal is to foster a confederation of ethnically diverse house churches in Rome who constitute the renewed people of God in the new covenant age' (pp.10,11).

identified by scholars that does not focus on Paul's explicit intent must be considered secondary. Accepting that Paul's letters are a substitute for his presence,[22] the most likely reason for Romans is an extension of Paul's personal apostolic mission that is described in the letter's opening and stressed again as the letter is brought to a close.[23]

> we have received grace and apostleship to bring about the obedience of faith among all the Gentiles for the sake of his name, including yourselves who are called to belong to Jesus Christ... (1:5–6)
>
> Nevertheless on some points I have written to you rather boldly by way of reminder, because of the grace given me by God to be a minister of Christ Jesus to the Gentiles in the priestly service of the gospel of God, so that the offering of the Gentiles may be acceptable, sanctified by the Holy Spirit. (15:15–16)

Too much focus has been given to trying to describe the 'what' of Romans, as if theology/doctrine was an object to be studied rather than a way of life to be lived. Paul wrote as an Apostle appointed to 'bring about the obedience of faith among all the nations' (1:5), which leads to the fruit of his ministry becoming an offering, 'sanctified by the Spirit' (15:16). Paul's letter aims to bring about the obedience of faith among the Romans by first teaching them that God's people are the eschatological people of faith who walk by the Spirit, and then by challenging them to life by the Spirit. It is not surprising that within a letter seeking to establish 'the obedience of faith'[24] that Paul should declare 'whatever does not proceed from faith is sin' (14:23).

The recipients of this letter are already holy ones/saints, that is,

---

22 Paul's opening prayer of Thanksgiving for the Romans, 1:8–15, repeatedly stresses his desire to be among them.
23 I explore this in more detail in *The Parting of the* Ways, 262–69.
24 Jewett, *Romans*, 110, argues that *hypakoēn pisteōs* is an adnominal genitive; '*pisteōs* limits the meaning of *hypakoēn*. Whereas there are many forms of obedience, including obedience under the law, Paul here speaks of the special sort of obedience produced by the gospel'. This much analysed Pauline term ('coined by Paul to fit the rhetorical exigency of this letter') is not given enough attention when exploring the reasons for Romans.

God's people.[25] Paul is not seeking to win them to faith; they are already believers/saints. Paul is seeking to ensure that they live within faith, 'For in [the gospel] the righteousness of God is revealed through faith for faith; as it is written, "The one who is righteous will live by faith"' (1:17). They—both Jewish-heritage believers and pagan-heritage believers—must learn to live as saints, 'sanctified by the Holy Spirit' (15:16). Paul's concern is the continuing and ongoing struggle of the Christian life which is overwhelmed by Sin if it seeks the guidance of Torah rather than the enabling guidance of the Spirit (5:12–8:39).

The early church's wrestling with who are the faithful people of God and how are they to live as God's faithful people is the broad context for Romans. Did Gentiles, even though they are saved by faith, have to adopt the guidance of Torah in order to follow Jesus, the Jewish Messiah, and worship Yahweh, the God of Israel? Did Jews, also saved by faith, have to abandon the guidance of Torah practices in order to follow Jesus? Was it possible for God's people to practice different acts of obedience and still remain one people? Robert Jewett reaches a similar conclusion:

> The two related issues that were of great concern to the Christians in Rome: (1) how believers in Jesus are to be guided in their thinking and actions, whether by the commands of the Mosaic law or by ... the guidance given by the Holy Spirit, and (2) how believers in Jesus during this 'present time of salvation history' are to live out their new life in Christ, whether by means of a nomistic lifestyle ... or by a Christ-based response to the Spirit's guidance.[26]

The church continues to wrestle with these questions today, even if the issues cannot be so easily captured in the language of competing Jewish and Gentile identities.

---

25 *'hagioi* ("holy ones") is found sixty-one times in the NT and is always employed [...] with respect to God's holy people, whether translated as "saints", "his holy ones", or "God's holy people"'; Longenecker, *Romans*, 86.
26 Jewett, *Romans*, 1005.

The Weak and the Strong among the Christians in Rome

The *ekklesia* in Rome meets around a meal table.[27] This is too easily forgotten when we speak of 'the church' in Rome. The conflict relating to food is not about the social time following a service, as we might assume if we anachronistically imagine their church to be much like the church we now attend. The conflict relating to food is not a trivial issue but relates to the very presence of the weak among the gathered people of God. If they are made to feel unwelcome at the table, then they are being excluded from the fellowship. And if they are excluded from the fellowship, then they are in danger of being caused to 'stumble' (14:13, 21) and, possibly, be 'destroyed': (14:20; 'it is wrong for you to make others fall', 14:20). The seriousness of this warning to 'the strong' (*oi dunatoi*) cannot be underestimated and reflects a dominical woe,

> If any of you put a stumbling block before one of these little ones who believe in me, it would be better for you if a great millstone were fastened around your neck and you were drowned in the depth of the sea. Woe to the world because of stumbling blocks! Occasions for stumbling are bound to come, but woe to the one by whom the stumbling block comes! (Mt 18:6–7)

Paul is not judging the genuineness of their faith when he identifies them as 'weak in faith'. It is not that the weak are only partially converted, perhaps Jewish followers of Jesus who still choose Judaism over Christianity.[28] The weak and the strong are 'brothers and sisters' (14:10); they are both servants of the Lord (14:4), called to the obedience of faith (1:5). The strong are not more genuinely Christian than the weak. Indeed, in Paul's assessment, the weak are not motivated by a 'sub–Christian' desire to keep Torah, but a fully Christian desire to

---

27 For an imagined narrative description of a church meeting in Rome, see Banks, *Going to Church*.
28 These terms are, of course, anachronistic. I am framing this thought from a perspective that a modern reader might adopt rather than suggesting that this was an option that Paul might have considered.

honour the Lord and to give him thanks (14:6)![29]

Paul is not judging their theological commitment to an essential doctrinal truth, as if 'weak' might equate to a conceded pass on a Doctrines of the Reformation exam. Anthony Thiselton's suggestion that 'in theological terms the 'weak' tended to compromise Christian freedom in Christ' is implausible given Paul's willingness to tolerate their position.[30] Paul is not looking to correct a theological error of the weak; rather, he instructs them to hold their ground (14:22), and he instructs the strong not to dispute with them (14:1). Paul is arguing in this passage for the freedom of the weak to serve Christ in true freedom—free from the judgment of the strong.

Paul is using 'weak' (it is unlikely that they labelled themselves) to capture his concern that they are in danger of being lost to the faith ('do not ... destroy the work of God ... it is wrong for you to make others fall ...', 14:20). 'Weak' describes the strength of their attachment to the body of Christ (the church in Rome) and consequently their attachment to Christ. In contemporary terms we might identify them as 'at risk'; at risk of stumbling and at risk of falling and being destroyed. Weak Christians, unable to find a home within the *ekklesia* of Rome, will either drift back to the synagogues,[31] where Christ is not known, or abandon gathering with others completely. They are unable to reshape the *ekklesia* that they are attending to make it an acceptable home for

---

29 It is argued, e.g., by Horrell, *Solidarity*, 202–203, that '[T]he issue at stake in Rom 14.1–15.13 concerns "the observance or non-observance of the Jewish law", as John Barclay, among others have persuasively shown [...] The motivation for such practice was evidently to ensure that Jewish dietary laws were not violated and to avoid the idolatrous connections of Gentile meat and wine [... Paul is dealing with] a question of difference among Christians who hold different convictions concerning obedience to the Jewish law'. This is implausible given all that Paul has written in Romans up to this point. The issue's provenance may indeed be the Torah, but Paul does not address them as if they as choosing Torah-observance over Spirit-guidance. These are Spirit-filled believers who are acting in honour of the Lord (14:6). They are walking by the same Spirit, even if they are discerning different paths. Their motivation is faith.

30 Thiselton, *Discovering Romans*, 239, also takes 1 Corinthians 8–10 as the background (an interpretive lens) for this passage; this freedom was 'to ignore secondary rules and regulations'. Consider, however, Galatians as evidence of Paul's unwillingness to accept positions that might compromise our freedom in Christ.

31 Most commentators consider the weak to be Jewish-heritage believers, but there is no reason not to consider the weak a mixed group in the same way that the strong, with whom Paul identifies, are a mixed group of Jewish-heritage and pagan-heritage believers. There are possible echoes of the letter to the Hebrews here.

themselves, and they are unable to establish their own *ekklesia*—that is why they are called weak; the strong could achieve either of these two outcomes.³² Their weakness is caused by the possibility of exclusion (inadvertently by being unwelcomed or overtly by being forced into constant disputation) from the *ekklesia* by the strong who—s Paul evidently believes—are insensitive to the real spiritual danger to which they are subjecting the weak by not welcoming them.

Welcome and Judge Not

(i) Paul's explicit instruction to the strong which sets the context for 14:1–15:6 (13) is 'Welcome the weak', the standard of which is the way in which God welcomes them (14:4) and Christ has accepted us (15:7). The evidence that this welcoming is truly accepting is that it will not be 'for the purpose of quarrelling over opinions' (14:1) and it will not involve passing judgement on those whom 'God has welcomed' (14:3).

Paul is prioritising unity in worship over conformity in practices.³³ '[T]he unity of the community is not to be fostered through the adoption of a common stance on this issue of ethical dispute but fostered precisely in the face of this diversity'.³⁴ Indeed, there is no evidence in Romans 14 that Paul is seeking to change anyone's personal judgement concerning abstaining or eating. Romans 14 is not an example of how a church might attempt to reach a consensus over a divisive issue that would result in conformity—in fact, he discourages the disputation that might lead to a consensus. Romans 14 is an example of a church being told to worship together from out of their contentious diversity.

Of course, the strong are not to be considered as somehow acting unreasonably. Their basis for not welcoming the weak is a reasoned judgment of what is just too unacceptable to God for the church in Rome to accept in its practices. What is significant in Paul's first response to this

---

32 I explore this dynamic in more detail in *Parting of the Ways*, where I also consider the likelihood that this dynamic suggests a Roman context for the sermon of Hebrews.
33 'The purpose of Romans is to encourage Jewish and Gentile Christians in Rome [...] to set aside their differences and to worship together', Watson, *Paul, Judaism, and the Gentiles*, 186.
34 Horrell, *Solidarity and Difference*, 205. Jewett, *Romans*, 860, 'it is once again clear that Paul does not want to encourage either side to continue the effort to convert the other'.

is not that he argues that their judgment is unsound but that he argues they have no right to judge the servant of another (14:4)!

(ii) It is fair to say that the Church's reputation for being judgmental is tragic witness to our failure to take to heart Paul's repeated instruction, which must surely be considered as based upon dominical teaching; we are to 'no longer pass judgement upon one another' (14:13; cf. Luke 6:37).

The basis for Paul's instruction is abundantly clear. The weak, upon whom the strong are passing judgment, have been welcomed by God (14:3), are servants of their Lord (14:4), and are their 'brothers and sisters [in Christ]' (14:10). God is the only judge of God's own people; we are all accountable individually only to our Lord (14:10–12).

Despite the continuing re-enforcement of this point, the Reception History of this passage reassures us that Paul was overstating his case. Jewett shows this practice of agreeing with the received wisdom; 'Roetzel argues...that Paul is not attempting to eliminate judgment entirely, but to eliminate 'contemptuous' and 'disdainful' judgment ... Glad goes further ... Judgment among members should continue but in a way that guards against mutual caricature and arrogance'.[35]

Apparently it is acceptable for us to judge one another as long as our attitude is correct. The strong have found a way to hear Paul and to continue on doing what they (we) have being doing all along—judging the servant of another! Judging a brother or sister in Christ is acceptable, our traditions tell us, when the strong are able to speak the very judgment reserved for Jesus against the weak with albeit humble confidence; of course, the strong will only exclude the weak after we have contended with them and found them to be unwilling to recognise in us the voice of their Lord.

It is not unfair, however, for these commentators (and others) to point out that at times Paul was also prepared to pass judgment upon others, and sometimes quite harshly—1 Corinthians 5:3 comes readily to mind. But what concerns me in the commentary on Romans 14 is that there is little evidence of acknowledging the coherent narrative—we are

---

35 Jewett, *Romans*, 857.

each one a servant to our Lord who must answer to him—behind Paul's varying contingent applications of how we deal with one another. Is Paul's treatment of the man whose behaviour shocks even the pagans exceptional or exemplary?[36]

We should be able to agree that the Eucharist is the Lord's table and, therefore, his table, his rules. But can we also agree that it is the role of the Holy Spirit to judge, convict, and lead his people rather than assign this role of policing the rules to a magisterium of the strong?

(iii) Is it possible that Paul is saying that we should only welcome one another if the disputable matter is inconsequential (i.e., adiaphora), but that when a disputable matter is consequential, then this instruction to welcome and not to judge is no longer applicable? Michael Bird, for example, suggests that Paul 'can accept differences of opinion on matters that might be regarded as being of secondary importance. The issues of food, wine, and sacred days are obviously secondary for him.'[37] Paul does suggest such a distinction himself, 'the kingdom of God is not a matter of eating and drinking, but of righteousness, peace, and joy in the Holy Spirit' (14:17).

It is more likely, however, that the distinction between food and righteousness is not to be found in a trivial/consequential or primary/secondary dichotomy but in an old creation/new creation dichotomy, which would be more consistent with Paul's 'apocalyptic imagination'. And, if this is the case, is it not possible that sex, which is not an eternal part of the kingdom of God, belongs with temporal issues such as food

---

36 The 1 Corinthian passage naturally generated discussion when an earlier version of this paper was delivered. I have no answer short enough for an adequate response, but I will make two general observations. The guiding framework for Paul's action is that unbelievers are not to be turned from the gospel because of the shocking behaviour of the church. I would argue that the Church's continuing refusal, for example, to welcome homosexual Christians is currently turning unbelievers from a hearing of the gospel. I am not certain that Paul considers the man within the fellowship who is under his judgment is a true member of the Church—he is evil 'yeast' rather than good 'dough'. Yet I am personally convinced that, to continue with the same example, Christians who identify as homosexual are fellow members of Christ's body.
37 Bird, *Romans*, 468.

and drink as matters about which we should not dispute.[38] Paul clearly valued celibacy over marriage, which he identifies as a concession to control lust (1 Cor 7:8–9), and, perhaps reflecting another dominical saying,[39] declares that the old division of 'male and female' is no longer applicable for those who are in Christ (Gal 2:23). I am not claiming that Paul disregards sexual morality as part of following Jesus; I am suggesting that, for Paul, sex was more likely on the food and drink side of the dichotomy than alongside righteousness, peace, and joy. Righteousness is not a synonym for moral purity in contrast to ritual purity, but to do with 'a right relationship with God'.[40] A brother or sister, who has concluded differently from us about the issue of sexual identity, should not be 'destroyed' or caused 'to fall' by our failure to walk in love (14:15) evidenced by our unwillingness to welcome them.

Even although Horrell unnecessarily limits the application of his insight into Paul's intention,[41] I think he has a good sense of Paul's concern:

> Paul's concern in both 1 Corinthians 8–10 and Romans 14–15 is not primarily to resolve or rule on the substance and specific issues of ethics but rather to argue for the practice of the kind of morality which he sees as essential to the maintenance of community harmony given continuing differences. Other-regard is in this sense precisely a moral value.[42]

---

38   *Contra* Horrell, *Solidarity and Difference*, 186: 'It should be noted, however, that these passages both deal with questions concerning food, which Paul treats differently from sexual morality [… S]exual morality and idolatry are to be shunned, and are dealt with in terms related to the body and its participation in competing unions. Food *per se* does not have the same ethical significance and is thus the focus for the developing of different forms of ethical argument'. Horrell, however, has not seen that 'food and drink' is not the ethical issue for Paul in Romans 14, but the ethical issue is whether the weak are welcomed or not. In this context, 'food and drink' does not contrast with 'sex' as something 'not of the kingdom' or something 'of the kingdom'. Both are not of the kingdom, which is 'righteousness, peace, and joy in the Holy Spirit'.
39   The triple tradition records Jesus' teaching that 'in the resurrection they neither marry nor are given in marriage, but are like angels in heaven' (Mt 22:30).
40   'The triad of 'righteousness and peace and joy', […] is used to describe the new life of Christian congregations 'in [the] Holy Spirit', in which love overcomes social distinctions and barriers', Jewett, *Romans*, 863.
41   See footnote 39.
42   Horrell, *Solidarity and Difference*, 221.

The kingdom of God requires us to see issues through an eternal lens in which people are more significant than temporal practices of eating or abstaining. Our first concern must be, 'do not by your eating destroy your brother for whom Christ died' (14:15).

Based upon the way Paul develops his argument in Romans 14, it is wrong to identify 'disputable matters' as encompassing only the so-called adiaphora. 'Disputable matters' are those behaviours that are practiced with thanksgiving in order to honour God by those who are 'weak', but are considered sinful by those who are 'strong'.

Many may consider 'considered sinful' too soft in this context: is not sin sin? If the strong know something to be a sin, and not just a matter of adiaphora, are they not required to disciple/discipline the weak?

'Everything That Does Not Come from Faith Is Sin' (14:23b)

In the first chapter of Romans, Paul (vv. 18–32) gives an extended reflection on the nature of ungodliness. Drawing from his coherent narrative, he points to the fundamental failure to worship the Creator—to honour him and to give him thanks—as the source of sin.[43] Ungodliness is evidenced in a person's refusal to 'honour God as God or give thanks to him', even 'though they knew him' (1:21). The sinful actions identified in this passage, which includes homosexuality as well as gossip and envy, are a consequence of ungodliness; ungodliness is not a result of accumulating various sins.

It is on this basis that we know Paul considers neither the actions of the weak nor of the strong to be sin. Even although one eats and one abstains they both do so 'in honour of the Lord' and they both 'give thanks to God' (14:6). They can both be said to be 'acting from faith' (14:23); that is, from their position as a faithful servant of God.

The basis for judging sin is no longer the Torah, which for Paul is a part of the old creation, but whether the servant of God is seeking to honour God and to give God thanks. This is the outward evidence of

---

43 The term *hamartia* is not used, but it is implicit. Thiselton, *Discovering Romans*, 83, citing Schlatter, relates '"ungodliness and wickedness" [Romans 1:18] to the two tables of the law, sin against God, and sin against fellow humans'.

the believer's intent to walk in obedience to the Spirit of God.

The maxim in 14:23, 'Everything that does not come from faith is sin', offers a definition of sin that is fitting to Paul's emphasis of living in the New Creation, an Age of Faith[44] and of the Spirit. Despite this, Longenecker dismisses 14:23b in a footnote: it 'probably stemmed from some common Jewish religious aphorism'.[45] Yet the single cited evidence for such an aphorism is from Philo and includes neither '*pistis*' nor '*harmatia*'.[46] Both of these terms, faith and sin, are key Pauline terms and point to the importance of this maxim in understanding how Paul has reasoned his way through the acceptability of the practice of the weak.

Thiselton accepts that the maxim is Pauline, but he is concerned to ensure that it 'should not be abstracted from its context and simply interpreted as if it was a universal or context-free maxim'.[47] It 'depends', he continues, 'on its meaning on its implied contrast. Virtually all commentators agree [Dunn is an exception] that it should not be interpreted out of context'. Thiselton draws upon Cranfield as interpreting this maxim as 'one's confidence that one's faith allows one to do something',[48] in this case that something is the freedom 'to ignore secondary rules and regulations'.[49]

Paul, in my view, does not see the actions of the weak as failing to live in freedom. Rather, he sees their actions as a positive choice to live in service to God. Thiselton's interpretation is too passive for Paul. We are not called to freedom, we are called to obedience. We are freed from the bondage of Sin, but we are set free to become 'slaves of righteousness' (6:18), which is why Paul identifies himself primarily as 'a servant

---

44 *Pistis* in 14:23 should be heard within Paul's apocalyptic dualism in which faith is characteristic of the New Age. Käsemann, *Romans*, 379, argues, 'To translate *pistis* by good conscience (Gaugler; Ridderbos) or even more weakly by conviction (Sanday and Headlam; Lietzmann; Gutjahr; Bardenhewer; Best) is most questionable'. The link to conscience has been made via 1 Cor 8:11ff, 'but one must take seriously that fact that conscience is not mentioned' in Romans 14.
45 Longenecker, *Romans*, 1010 n. 28.
46 Philo *de Abrahamo* 18: 'Whatever is done apart from being mindful of God is unprofitable'. Jewett, *Romans*, 872, regards the Philo citation as the 'only one relevant example [in the quest for parallels to this maxim], so far as I know'.
47 Thiselton, citing Cranfield, *Discovering Romans*, 242.
48 Thiselton, *Discovering Romans*, 243.
49 Thiselton, *Discovering Romans*, 239.

[*doulos*] of Jesus Christ' (1:1). Paul is not arguing that the weak are free to do whatever they want (so long as they feel confident about it). No slave has a right to personal choices. Paul is arguing that they are walking with the Spirit, as is evidenced by their desire to honour God and to give thanks to God (14:6). The root of godlessness (sin) is a failure to honour God and to give him thanks (1:21). Therefore, those children of God who are honouring God and giving him thanks are not sinning—even if we disagree with their choices.

This Pauline maxim in 14:23b is not just a restatement of the summary given in 23a but a coherent theological axiom. 'Everything that does not come from faith is sin' is used by Paul to generate the contingent argument summarised in 14:23a, 'the one who doubts is condemned if he eats, because eating is not from faith'. Here, then, is our guide to following Jesus (serving God, walking by the Spirit) and to Christian ethics: faith. 'The one who is righteous will live by faith' (1:17). They will live neither by a restored Torah, with the inappropriate 'Jewish' parts removed, nor by a Christian Scripture that has been repurposed as Christian Torah,[50] nor by a magisterium of the strong, but they will live by (and in) faith.

Paul's Ethic[51]

We are not simply attempting to find Paul's 'meaning' but, more importantly, we are attempting to hear his challenge to the gate-keepers of the various churches in Australia, that is, those who might be reasonably considered 'the strong'. How are we to ensure that our judgment of our brothers and sisters, which excludes them from finding a place

---

50 McKnight, *The Blue Parakeet*, 206–207, recounts this conversation (from memory) with Professor F. F. Bruce, when he asks, '"Professor Bruce, what do you think of women's ordination?". "I don't think the New Testament talks about ordination", he replied. "What about the silencing passages of Paul on women?", I asked. "I think Paul would roll over in his grave if he knew we were turning his letters into Torah". Wow! I thought. That's a good point to think about. Thereupon I asked a question that he answered in such a way that it reshaped my thinking: "What do you think, then, about women in church ministries?". Professor Bruce's answer was as Pauline as Paul was: "I'm for whatever God's Spirit grants women gifts to do"' (emphasis added).

51 In *Solidarity and Difference*, Horrell gives considered attention to identifying 'a contemporary reading of Paul's ethics' in light of Romans 14–15 (and 1 Corinthians 8–10).

of welcome among God's people, is not placing a 'stumbling block or obstacle' into their path?

In Romans 14, David Horrell argues, Paul 'seeks to legitimate different patterns of ethical conduct and to remove any basis for judgment or criticism. He does so by outlining a form of ethical relativism ... [that we might label] a constructivist realism: things really are such, to the one who reckons them so'.[52] This idea that what is sinful for me might not be sinful for you is a struggle for those who see sin in terms of Torah (or Christian readings of the Scriptures) for which there will be a single judgment for each action. But if we accept that sin is relational, that is, it arises from our failure to follow the Spirit in ways that honour God and give him thanks, then it is possible to accept that the Spirit's call to one servant to eat and for another servant to abstain as God-honouring for both. And, importantly, that it would be a sin for the one called by the Spirit to abstain to instead eat just in order to find welcome among those who are judging them.

This Pauline freedom to follow the Spirit is not a freedom to do as we wish. It is a freedom from the power of Sin and Death, which is enslaving to those in the present Evil Age, in order to serve Jesus in the New Creation as a slave to righteousness (5:12–6:23). It is not a godless relativism, in which individuals decides for themselves how to live, but true sanctification in which we live in obedience to our only Judge. For Paul, godly obedience is not to a code (Torah, or the voice of the Church) but to a Lord. It is 'the obedience of faith' (1:5).

This argument is not an argument for the right of humans to choose

---

52 In *Solidarity and Difference*, 204–5, Horrell argues, however, '[T]here is a question about the limits of Paul's "tolerance". It is clear that in the realm of sexual ethics [...] there is a good deal less room for a diversity of convictions. People may legitimately decide to marry or not to marry, but they may not insist on their right to liaisons with *pornai*, nor on their freedom to divorce' (p.213). Horrell's analysis of Romans 14 is shaped by his reading of 1 Corinthians 8–10, which he suggests is 'widely recognised' as the source ('drawn on and reworked', p.184, 'repeats, rephrases, echoes the arguments of', p.185) of the material in Romans 14. This leads him to focus upon individual convictions and conscience (*syneidēsis*), which he links to Paul's use of faith (*pistis*) in Romans 14. Longenecker, *Romans*, 994, provides a better argument: 'So most commentators today do not understand 14:1–15:13 as a set of exhortations on Christian liberty generated in the apostle's mind by certain circumstances he encountered at Corinth'. Such a viewpoint allows the analysis of Romans 14 to be focused in light of the letter's theological framework (e.g., the Post–Resurrection Age of the Spirit) and so gives appropriate attention to the importance of these believers, even the weak, as being led by the Spirit in their choice to abstain.

their own destiny. It is an argument for believers to live freely under the Lordship of Jesus.[53] This must be the case even if their living freely takes them down a different path of obedience from mine. I am not their judge. I am not arguing for an 'anything goes' ethic, or for an ethic in which my conscience rules my behaviour. I am arguing for a true absolutizing of the Lordship of Jesus. And because Jesus is our Lord, we will not be called to do that which will cause a weak one to stumble and to be lost to the fellowship of believers.

Pastoral Implications: It Gets More Difficult

The charge against Paul of antinomianism, by some within the church in Rome, is justified.[54] Paul will not bring the Torah into the New Age of the Spirit, just because it used to be the God-given way to keep Sin in check. In this New Age of the Spirit, the Age of Faith, there is only one criteria for self-judgment by a Spirit-led child of God: am I walking according to the Spirit? And only our Lord can be allowed to judge us on this.

The fear that Paul's coherent theology will lead to non-Torah conforming behaviour is rational, and it has been demonstrated time after time throughout the story of the Church. But as people of the New Creation we must take the risk of discerning the Spirit together, without the fall back option of the 'gate keepers' ruling for the 'at risks' what it is that the Spirit is calling for them to do. We cannot replace 'discerning the Spirit' by 'judgement by the strong' and then conformity by all others.

Individuals are not left to their own consciences. We are to help each other discern the voice of the Spirit to us. But this help cannot be coercive. The gate keepers cannot use the power of exclusion to impose upon others their understanding of what is sin. We all, weak and strong, gay and straight, must together in fellowship seek to hear what God's

---

53 Fitzmyer, *Romans*, 697, rightly argues, 'The essence of the kingdom does not consist in freedom from such things as dietary regulations, but in the freedom of the Christian to react to the prompting of the Holy Spirit'.
54 Cf. Bird, *Romans*, 97: Paul's 'Torah-free gospel for Gentiles was regarded as promoting antinomianism (see Acts 21:20–21; Rom [3:8,] 6:2)'.

call to obedience looks like for us individually. But each of us must take responsibility for our path of faith obedience. Stanley Porter captures this spiritual requirement:

> [E]ach Christian is responsible for his or her own behaviour. Paul makes clear that each one must be convinced in his or her own mind ... [E]ach Christian is ultimately responsible, not just to other Christians for their behaviour toward one another, but to God. God is the one before whom each Christian stands and who ultimately and finally judges whether each one's behaviour is right or not, and whether such a position is upheld or condemned.[55]

Discerning the Spirit does not mean an abandonment of Scripture, or an abandonment of the voice of the Church. The Spirit speaks faithfully through both these sources. But discerning the Spirit does mean that we first set our mind on the things of the Spirit and then read Scripture from a kingdom perspective of righteousness, peace, and joy in the Holy Spirit. Evidence of this will be our welcoming one another and our making 'every effort to do what leads to peace and to mutual edification' (14:19). The life of faith must be lived within the community of faith.

Closing Thoughts

A concern for the unity of the body of Christ, including the non-conforming Christians who are 'at risk', is a driving value for Paul that he wishes the 'gate keepers' in Rome to adopt. The churches of Jesus cannot be narrower than the Church of Jesus—we are to welcome one another. If someone is a brother or sister in Christ, we must do what we can to ensure that they do not stumble because we have excluded them.

Because this is still a contentious issue within the parts of the Church in Australia to which I belong, it is not possible for me to wrestle with Romans 14 without asking about the welcome offered to believers who

---

55 Porter, *Romans*, 258–9, adding 'the use of the pronouns in this passage depicts judgment as a corporate event in that all must participate without exemption, but an individual event in that each makes an individual account of his or her own actions and behaviour' (p.263).

identify as LGBTIQ+. Although on this matter the major Roman commentators seem to be willing to leave me to my own reflections. I am not convinced that excluding Christians who identify as LGBTIQ+ from the fellowship of the Church is going to strengthen them in their faith and protect them from stumbling. As such, I believe we should allow the Lord to judge those who are his own as we seek to act in accord with what we believe the Spirit is calling us to.

We cannot expect consensus on this. Certainly not in my lifetime! But Paul's goal in writing to the Roman Christians was not consensus, but a genuine welcoming of one another. I am not arguing, for example, that we first decide if divorce or if homosexuality, irrespective of context, is a sin or not a sin. I am arguing that we welcome the divorced, the married, and the single, as well as the straight and the gay into full fellowship within the church so that as one we might together worship the Lord.

It is for those of us who are among the strong to give space within our fellowship to the weak. We must give them an unambiguous welcome and join with them in their, and our, attempts to discern the call of God's Spirit. It would be right to say that Paul believes that the gospel challenges each of us to find our identity first and foremost in Christ, and that all other tribal allegiances whether political, social, or sexual must be subservient to our allegiance to Christ. Because of this it would be completely inappropriate for us to move towards a situation where there is a so-called homosexual church and heterosexual church. God forbid! As Paul elegantly says, God is one (3:30) and we who are his one people must learn to worship together—Jew and Gentile, rich and poor, man and woman, and straight and gay—as one people.

> Welcome one another, therefore, just as Christ has welcomed you, for the glory of God (15:7).

> May the God of steadfastness and encouragement grant you to live in harmony with one another, in accordance with Christ Jesus, so that together you may with one voice glorify the God and Father of our Lord Jesus Christ (15:5–6).

Bibliography

Banks, R. — *Going to Church in the First Century* (Beaumont: Christian Books Publishing House, 1980).

Barclay, J.M.G. — '"Do we undermine the Law?": A Study of Romans 14:1–15:6', in J.D.G. Dunn (ed.), *Pauline Churches and Diaspora Jews* (Grand Rapids: Eerdmans, 2011), 37–59.

Beker, J.C. — 'Recasting Pauline Theology: The Coherence-Contingency Scheme as Interpretive Model', in J.M. Bassler (ed.), *Pauline Theology,* Volume 1: *Thessalonians, Philippians, Galatians, Philemon* (Atlanta: SBL Press, 2003), 15–24.

Bird, M.F. — *Romans* (The Story of God Commentary; Grand Rapids: Zondervan, 2016).

Blackwell, B.C., J.K. Goodrich, & J. Maston (eds.) — *Paul and the Apocalyptic Imagination* (Minneapolis: Fortress, 2016).

Brower, K., & A. Johnson (eds.) — *Holiness and Ecclesiology in the New Testament* (Grand Rapids: Eerdmans, 2007).

Chalmers, A. — 'The Influences of Cognitive Biases on Biblical Interpretation', *Bulletin for Biblical Research* 26.4 (2016), 467–80.

Fitzmyer, J.A. — *Romans: A New Translation and Commentary* (Anchor Bible 33; New York, NY: Doubleday, 1993).

Fraser, L.J. — 'A Tradition in Crisis: Understanding and Repairing Division Over Homosexuality in the Church of Scotland', *Scottish Journal of Theology* 69.2 (2016), 155–70.

Horrell, D.G. — *Solidarity and Difference: A Contemporary Reading of Paul's Ethics* (London: Bloomsbury, 2016, 2nd edition).

Jewett, R. — *Romans: A Commentary* (Hermeneia; Minneapolis: Fortress, 2007).

Käsemann, E. — *Commentary on Romans* (G.W. Bromiley, trans. & ed.; Grand Rapids: Eerdmans, 1980).

Knight, M. — '*Wirkungsgeschichte,* Reception History, Reception Theory', *Journal for the Study of the New Testament* 33.2 (2010), 137–46.

Longenecker, R.N. — *The Epistle to the Romans: A Commentary on the Greek Text* (NIGTC; Grand Rapids: Eerdmans, 2016).

McKnight, S.   *A Fellowship of Differents: Showing the World God's Design for Life Together* (Grand Rapids: Zondervan, 2014).

McKnight, S.   *The Blue Parakeet: Rethinking How You Read the Bible* (Grand Rapids: Zondervan, 2008).

McKnight, S., & J.B. Modica (eds.)   *The Apostle Paul and the Christian Life: Ethical and Missional Implications of the New Perspective* (Grand Rapids: Baker Academic, 2016).

Mitchell, P.   'The New Perspective and the Christian Life: Solus Spiritus', in S. McKnight & J.B. Modica (eds.), *The Apostle Paul and the Christian Life: Ethical and Missional Implications of the New Perspective* (Grand Rapids: Baker Academic, 2016), 71–102.

Porter, S.E.   *The Letter to the Romans: A Linguist and Literary Commentary* (Sheffield: Sheffield Phoenix, 2015).

Spence, S.   *The Parting of the Ways: The Roman Church as a Case Study* (Interdisciplinary Studies in Ancient Culture and Religion, 5; Leuven: Peeters, 2004).

Thiselton, A.C.   *Discovering Romans: Content, Interpretation, Reception* (London: SPCK, 2016).

Wendel, S.J.   'Torah Obedience and Early Christian Ethical Practices', in S.J. Wendel & D.M. Miller (eds.), *Torah Ethics and Early Christian Identity* (Grand Rapids: Eerdmans, 2016), 177–91.

Watson, F.   *Paul, Judaism, and the Gentiles: Beyond the New Perspective* (Grand Rapids: Eerdmans, 2007, rev. & exp.).

PART 3

Romans and the Challenge of Theology: From Text to Society

CHAPTER 11

A Disability Reading of Paul's Use of the 'Body of Christ' Metaphor in Romans 12:3–8 and 1 Corinthians 12:12–31

Louise Gosbell

Introduction

In his letters to the churches in Rome and Corinth, the Apostle Paul outlines his expectations of the *ekklesia* as a place of unity and concord by using the metaphor of the Body of Christ (Romans 12:3–8; 1 Corinthians 12:12–31).[1] In both pericopes, Paul likens the members of the ecclesiastical community of Christ to members of the human body where all the various parts have particular functions and roles to play within the whole. Paul's use of the body as a metaphor for a group of people is not unique. Throughout the Greco-Roman world, the image of a body was employed frequently to represent the members of a collective body, such as a social or political group. The premise of the metaphor is that just as the human body requires all its diverse parts to work together for the greater good of the body, so too the body politic needs to work together with all the various members playing their part. Paul uses the image of the body in a similar way when calling on Christ-followers to strive for unity and for the well-being of the whole body. Thus, Paul's adoption of the body metaphor is one of the

---

1 Rom. 12:5: 'we are one body in Christ' (σῶμά ἐσμεν ἐν Χριστῷ); 1 Cor. 12:27 'body of Christ' (σῶμα Χριστοῦ).

most important and frequently utilised descriptors of the church in his corpus.²

The image of the Body of Christ—the church—existing harmoniously and utilising all of its various parts is often invoked by Christian practitioners and academics alike to encourage unity amongst the diverse members of the church. In particular, the metaphor has garnered much attention from those seeking to promote the inclusion of marginalised people groups into the church. This application equates the 'unpresentable' parts and the 'parts ... that seem to be weaker', described in 1 Corinthians 12, with various marginalised people groups, including first nations peoples, people with HIV and AIDS, refugees and asylum seekers, and transgender people.³ In the same way, the imagery of an inclusive Body of Christ has also struck a chord with theologians and practitioners writing at the intersection of disability and theology. For scholars wishing to promote the inclusion of people with disability in church communities, Paul's vision of the Body of Christ as a place of diversity and inclusion for all people is particularly appealing. Not only does the metaphor encourage all people of differing abilities and gifts to play their part, but even those considered 'weak' and 'unpresentable' are considered 'indispensable' for the adequate functioning of the Body of Christ. While the broader society might overlook and marginalise people with disability, the church should not do likewise. Church communities are thus called upon to seek out marginalised believers so that all members are present and the Body of Christ is whole and functioning at capacity. Without the marginalised, such as people with disability, the church cannot be complete.

The irony that is often missed in such analyses, however, and one that is particular to the discussion of disability, is that in claiming that the Body of Christ cannot function adequately without the presence of people with disability, these writers are essentially labelling the Body of Christ—the church—as incomplete, indeed, 'disabled' because it is

---

2   Rom. 12:3–8; 1 Cor. 12:12–31; Eph. 4:1–16; Col. 1:15–20; cf. Rom. 7:4; 1 Cor. 10:16; 11:29; Eph. 5:23; Col. 3:15.
3   E.g., van Klinken, '"The Body of Christ has Aids"'; Lowe, 'Re-Embracing the Body of Jesus Christ'; Troupe, 'One Body, Many Parts'.

not functioning as it should.⁴ Indeed, some scholars state this explicitly.⁵ Extending this idea to its logical conclusion, these writers contend that people with disability should not be excluded from the church because they have valuable contributions to make, and yet, simultaneously, when the *church* is missing body parts it is deemed 'disabled', and incomplete, a state which for the Body of Christ is considered to be wholly negative and undesirable. The value of a 'disabled' body is thus called into question. Given the propensity for writers to call upon the Body of Christ metaphor as the theological blueprint for the inclusion of people with disability, what can we do with this apparent paradox regarding the 'disabled' Body of Christ? This essay seeks to assess the applicability of the Body of Christ metaphor for ministry with, and outreach to, people with disability, as well as considering what applications, if any, can be drawn from using disability as a lens through which to assess Paul's Body of Christ imagery.

While Paul's metaphor of the Body of Christ appears in four places in the Pauline corpus, this chapter addresses only those which appear in Romans 12 and 1 Corinthians 12.⁶ Although Paul's metaphor of the Body of Christ appears in greater theological detail in 1 Corinthians and will be addressed accordingly throughout this chapter, the historical context and Paul's literary reliance on body politic imagery from the Greco-Roman world is as valid for Romans as it is for 1 Corinthians. For this reason, both of these examples of the Body of Christ imagery are examined throughout the present chapter.

---

4   E.g. Reynolds, *Vulnerable Communion*, 237: 'excluding one member of the body of Christ mars its image'; Yong, *The Bible, Disability and the Church*, 95: 'The health of the body requires the working of its many parts'.
5   E.g. Hedges-Goettl, 'Thinking Theologically about Inclusion', 15: '[f]or the Church to be whole, all must be included' and '[t]he church is disabled when persons with disabilities are not included'.
6   Paul's body imagery also appears in Colossians and Ephesians, but given the difference in presentation of the metaphor in those locations (e.g. the development of Christ as the head of the body), and the doubt surrounding Pauline authorship of these texts, this chapter does not address these occurrences.

Section 1: The Body of Christ in Paul

Paul's Body of Christ metaphor is fundamental to his presentation of the nature of the church.[7] As James D. G. Dunn observes, the image of the Body of Christ is the 'dominant theological image in Pauline ecclesiology'.[8] For this reason, ascertaining the cultural and theological origins of Paul's Body of Christ imagery has been of prime importance in Pauline scholarship. Though the idea is now out of vogue, some scholars see in Paul's imagery a connection to the Gnostic primal man myth.[9] Others see a semantic similarity between the Body of Christ and the sacramental language of the Eucharist in chapter 11 of 1 Corinthians ('this is my body which is for you'; 1 Cor. 11:24; cf., Matt. 26:26; Mark 14:22; Luke 22:19).[10] However, the view that is cited most frequently by Pauline scholars is that Paul's image of the Body of Christ is characteristic of body politic imagery used in Greek and Roman rhetorical sources to encourage unity among the polity.[11] Such unity is often described in terms of a body functioning at full capacity. Speeches which included the body politic imagery—referred to as *homonoia* ('concord') speeches—were commonly used in times of political turmoil to encourage members of the city-state, political, or civic group, to maintain unity by quashing discord and disturbance for the good of the group. In this respect, the image of the body was the most commonly employed *topos* for unity in the ancient world.[12]

1.1 *Origins of the Body of Christ Metaphor in Paul*

One of the most well-known examples of the body politic metaphor, and one that is often presented as fundamental to Paul's use of the Body of Christ imagery is a fable recorded by the Greek fabulist Aesop

---

7   While scholars debate the extent to which Paul's Body of Christ language is metaphorical, it is clearly not literal in either 1 Corinthians 12 or Romans 12; see Judge, 'Demythologising the Church', 577.
8   Dunn, *The Theology of Paul*, 548.
9   E.g. Käsemann, *Leib und Leib Christi*; Bultmann, *New Testament Theology*, 2:151–152.
10 E.g. Rawlinson, 'Corpus Christi'; Conzelmann, *1 Corinthians*.
11 E.g, Martin, *The Corinthian Body*, 38–68; Dunn, *Theology of Paul*, 550; Barrett, *First Corinthians*, 287; Ciampa & Rosner, *First Corinthians*, 597–598; Garland, *1 Corinthians*, 593–594; Witherington, *Conflict and the Community*, 253–54.
12 Mitchell, *Paul and Rhetoric of Reconciliation*, 161.

entitled *The Belly and the Members*. Aesop gives the context of the fable as a time when the common people of Rome had rebelled against the Senate claiming they were ill-treated. As a consequence, an insurrection occurred which saw many people relocate outside of the city. When the dissent was such that the division seemed irreparable, Menenius Agrippa (5th century B.C.E.), a consul of the republic, was sent to the plebians as a negotiator, where, according to Quintilian, 'Menenius Agrippa is said to have reconciled the plebs to the patricians by his fable of the limbs' quarrel with the belly'.[13] Aesop records Menenius Agrippa's speech as follows:

> Long ago when the members of the human body had very strong wills of their own and did not work together as amicably as they do now, they denounced the belly for leading an idle and luxurious life, while they were wholly occupied in supporting it and ministering to its wants and pleasures. At one point, they agreed to cut off the belly's supplies for the future. The hands declared that they would not lift a thing, not even a crust of bread; the mouth that it would not accept any more food for the teeth to chew; the legs that they would no longer carry the belly from place to place, and so on with the others. No sooner did they set their plan of starving the belly into subjections than they all began, one by one, to fail and flag so that the whole body started to pine away. Consequently, the members became convinced that the belly, cumbersome and useless as it seemed to be, also had an important function of its own. In fact, they realized that they were just as dependent on it as it was on them and that if they wanted to keep the body in a healthy state, they would have to work together for the common good of all.[14]

The premise of the fable is that although it *appears* that some members of the body are working harder than others, all members of the body must contribute and play their part otherwise the whole body suffers.

---

13 Quintilian, *Inst.* 5.11.19.
14 Fable 130 on Perry Index, cited here from Zipes, *Aesop's Fables*, 58.

The fundamental idea behind the metaphor is that, as Ruth Isley Hicks has noted, 'as all parts of the human body have their own function and are mutually necessary for its proper performance, so all members of a corporate body are essential for its health and well-being'.[15]

By the first century B.C.E., the body metaphor had become much more developed and the language of polity was much more explicit than the fifth-century B.C.E. text of Aesop. In his mentions of the fable, Cicero (106–43 B.C.E.), for example, uses terms such as 'a body of citizenry (*corpus ciuitatis*)'[16] and the 'body of the state (*ut totum corpus rei publicae curent*)'.[17] Likewise, the fable appears in more detail in Plutarch's first century C.E. *Life of Coriolanus*:

> [Menenius Agrippa] said namely, that all the other members of a man's body once revolted against the belly, and accused it of being the only member to sit idly down in its place and make no contribution to the common welfare, while the rest underwent great hardships and performed great public services only to minister to its appetites; but that the belly laughed at their simplicity in not knowing that it received into itself all the body's nourishment only to send it back again and duly distribute it among the other members. "Such, then", said Agrippa, "is the relation of the senate, my fellow-citizens to you; the matters for deliberation which there receive the necessary attention and disposition bring to you all and severally what is useful and helpful".[18]

What is apparent from both versions of the fable is that the stomach represents the ruling classes while the rest of the members of the body are the general populace. This fable essentially argues that, as Kar Yong Lim states, '(w)hile the ruling elites appeared to be taking from the masses all the time, they were, in fact, essential to the wellbeing of society, a fact that other members of the body failed to recognize'.[19] While

---

15 Hicks, 'The Body Political and the Body Ecclesiastical', 29.
16 Cic., Inv. rhet. 2.168.
17 Off. 1.85. Cicero also uses the phrase 'corpus rei publicae' in Phil. 8.15; Pis. 25.
18 Plutarch, *Life of Coriolanus* 6.3.
19 Lim, *Metaphors and Social Identity Formation*, 169.

there are many different members of the body that contribute to its overall well-being, the most important part is clearly the stomach – the senate ruled by the elites—without which the rest of the body could not survive. The fable thus speaks against the dangers of division and factionalism in the body corporate.

As the body politic imagery became more explicit, so did the references to the impact of divisions and factions in the body, and division and discord in the civic body being depicted as disease, impairment, or disablement in the body. While on occasion disease was seen as something that would come as an external, 'invasive agent',[20] generally, disease was seen as something that came from *within* the body and was the result of imbalances within the various members and organs of the body.[21] Such imbalances must be addressed and brought back into balance, or in the worst of cases, if this was not possible, the offending parts must be removed. Such a view is espoused, for example, by Cicero in his *Philippics* in a discussion regarding the Catiline conspiracy. Cicero writes about his discovery in 63 B.C.E. of a plot devised by Roman aristocrat Lucius Sirgius Cataline to assassinate members of the Roman Senate:

> If something in the body is of the sort to cause harm to the rest, we allow it to be cauterized or cut so that this or that part may perish rather than the whole body. Likewise in the body politic: let whatever is noxious be amputated so that the whole may be saved.[22]

Such views on the health of the body politic were influenced by ancient medical views that the health of the physical body was the result of a balance of all the various bodily elements, for example, humors (the four essences of life: blood, black bile, yellow bile, and phlegm) and states (hot/cold, moist/dry).[23] The Hippocratic *On the Nature of Man*, for example, states: 'Now he enjoys the most perfect health when these

---

20 Martin, *Corinthian Body*, 39; cf. Aelius Aristides, *Oration* 23.31.
21 Hippoc., Aph. 2.20; Morb. 4; Mul. 11; Galen, *San Tuend*. 1.3.
22 Phil. 8.15 (Bailey, LCL). Cicero refers to Cataline and his followers as 'a dangerous contagion (pestis) of the republic' (1.11).
23 Humours: Hippoc., *Nat. Hom.* 5. An earlier version exists in the Hippocratic *On Diseases*, where the four humors are described as phlegm, blood, bile, and water (4.35). States: Hippoc., *Nat. Hom.* 3. For more on both, see Martin, *Corinthian Body*, 29, 32, 159–160, 231.

elements (blood, black bile, yellow bile, and phlegm) are duly proportioned to one another in respect of compounding, power, and bulk, and when they are perfectly mingled'.[24] Imbalance, on the other hand, brought about disease and impairment.

The body politic is often depicted as a body in a state of sickness due to discord or dissension.[25] The Greek rhetorician Aelius Aristides (117–81 C.E.) described discord in the body politic as a disease that was equivalent to the tearing apart of the body or the foolishness of cutting off one's own feet.[26] Plato also employed the image of a city-state that is 'sick' or 'in pain'. In his *Republic*, Plato compared 'a well-run state' with the 'human body in its manner of reacting to the pain and pleasure of one of its parts'.[27] Josephus (37–100 C.E.) likewise used such body imagery, frequently speaking of the disruption of civil order in terms of disease which must be healed lest it threaten the health of the whole body. When writing of the disorder in Judea during the Jewish wars in 70 C.E., Josephus suggests that those Jews who were enacting extreme acts of violence against the Romans, and not just acting defensively, should be removed, because, '[n]ow as it is in a human body, if the principal part be inflamed, all the members are subject to the same distemper'.[28] Plutarch likewise, in relation to threats to the whole body politic, asserted that 'the diseased parts of a body must be repaired by the strong ones; if the whole becomes diseased it cannot repair itself'.[29] The 'strong' members of the body are thus those in positions of power in whom lies the capacity to heal the body. Indeed, the role of the statesman is '(a)lways to instill concord and friendship in those who dwell together with him and to remove strife, discords, and all enmity'.[30]

Because of their strength and power, civic leaders are elsewhere depicted as having the capacity to heal the whole body politic. In

---

24 Hippoc., *Nat Hom.* 4.1–6.
25 For example, Thucydides' use of plague-related language to describe the effects of the Dekeleia on the Athenians (7.27–28). See further, Kosak, 'Polis nosousa'; Brock, 'Sickness in the Body Politic'.
26 Aelius Aristides, *Orat.* 17.9; 23.31; 24.18, 38-39; 26.43.
27 *Resp.* 5.464b; cf. 5.556e.
28 *Jewish Wars* 4.406.
29 Plut., *Praec. Ger. Reip.* 824A.
30 Plut., *Praec. Ger. Reip.* 824D.

speaking of the Catiline conspiracy, Cicero describes himself as someone with the power to heal the sick members of the collective body stating: 'What can be cured, I will cure, by whatever means it may be possible. What must be cut away, I will not suffer to spread, to the ruin of the republic'.[31] A text attributed to the Roman poet Florus, writing at the end of the second century C.E., likewise demonstrates that strong leadership aids in healing the body politic:

> It was, however, a ground for congratulation that, in that great upheaval, the chief power passed into the hands of none other than Octavius Caesar Augustus, who by his wisdom and skill, restored order in the body of empire [*imperii corpus*], everywhere paralyzed and confused, which certainly would never have been able to achieve coherence and harmony unless it had been controlled by the will of a single ruler which formed, as it were, its soul and mind.[32]

As a corollary, poor leadership resulted in the poor health of the body politic. For example, Philo (20–50 C.E.) states that Gaius Caligula 'brought disease to the healthy, crippling to the sound limb and in general death to the living'.[33] Tacitus (56–120 C.E.) likewise refers to the Emperor Domitian as making the empire sick, with his successors (Emperors Nerva and Trajan) having to heal the sick and deformed body of the empire:

> Now at last heart is coming back to us ... Trajan is increasing daily the happiness of the times...Though it is true that from the nature of human infirmity cure operates more slowly than disease, and, as the body itself is slow to grow and quick to decay, so also it is easier to damp men's spirits and their enthusiasm than to revive them ... For the term of fifteen years ... others ... have perished by the Emperor's ferocity.[34]

Just as with the human body, imbalance in the body politic meant the body was not able to function. But also like the human body, wellness

---

31 Cicero, *Against Catiline* 2.5.11 (Yonge).
32 Florus, 2.14.5–6.
33 *Legat.* 107.
34 *Agricola* 3.1–2.

and health could be restored to the body politic through bringing all the elements of the body back into harmony and balance through the governance of good leadership. According to the Greek and Roman rhetoricians utilising *homonoia* speeches, the key to maintaining the good health of the body politic lay with all members of the corporate body, from the leadership right down to the general population, playing their part. Rather than being dissatisfied with their position in the body or its function, all members of the body needed to commit to the role that was accorded to them by nature and submit to the existing body hierarchy.

This hierarchy of the body politic is made apparent through another metaphor used of the citizenry in the ancient world, that of the household. A household is deemed to be existing harmoniously when all the members of the household are playing their part in accordance to the strict hierarchy of the household. While the different members of the household were equally important to the harmonious running of the household, the value afforded to each—whether to the head of the household (*paterfamilias/ oikodespotos*), or to wife, children, slaves— was attributed based strictly on status and power. Harmony could only occur when the appropriate respect and submission was afforded to those above them in the household hierarchy.[35] The head of the household is likewise equated with the head of the body politic. Such an example can be seen in Seneca where he refers to Nero as the head on whom the good health of the body, the empire, depends[36] and asserts that 'we are limbs of a great body'.[37] Indeed, Seneca states that it is not just the good health of the civic body that is reliant on this head but its entire existence: '[f]or a long time now Caesar has been so merged with the commonwealth that the one could not be separated from the other without destroying both: Caesar needs the commonwealth's strength

---

35 E.g., 1 Clement 21:7–8; Dio Chrysostom, *Discourse* 24.24; 38.15; Aelius Aristides, *Oration* 24.7.
36 In the NT period, the Caesar was the head of the body and governed all the parts of the body. For this reason, Seneca writes that 'Good health starts from the head: all else is energetic and alert, or drooping in exhaustion, to the degree that the mind is full of life or enfeebled' (Seneca, *Clem* 2.2.1 [Kaster & Naussbaum]. Cf. 'you are the commonwealth's mind and it is your body' (1.5.1).
37 Seneca, *Ep. Mor.* 95.52; cf. Philo, *Spec. Leg.* 3.131, of the high priest's purpose in offering sacrifice for the nation: 'that every age[-group] and all the parts of the nation may be welded into one and the same family as though it were a single body'.

while the commonwealth needs Caesar as its head'.³⁸

In this respect, the metaphor of the human body as well as that of the household, both served to encourage harmony and concord through the maintenance of the status quo. Nature had placed those with strength and power into the ruling class with those who were weak and of lower status apportioned their appropriate place in the social rankings of the lower class³⁹ and '[t]o deviate from the proscribed duties means to disturb natural order'.⁴⁰ In this respect, the metaphorical images of the civic body represented by a physical body as well as that of the household are ancient attempts to conjure the 'most intimate expression possible of the interdependence of ruler and subject in order to reinforce the social duties of one to another'.⁴¹ The rationale of the 'body politic' imagery is thus clear: 'If the political body is similar to the human physical body, then its members ought to act in harmony for the well-being of the political whole'.⁴² Just as the parts of the human body cannot and do not work independently of each other, so too must all the members of a society function in the same way for the greater good of the whole. For this reason, in *homonoia* speeches aimed at encouraging concord and unity, the language of the body politic was often employed. While interdependence was vital to the functioning of the body, this by no means indicated equality between the members, but such speeches assumed a fixed hierarchy deemed 'natural and necessary for the health and life of the body'.⁴³

---

38 Seneca, *De Clem.* 1.4.3 (Kaster & Nussbaum). cf. Tacitus, *Histories* 1.16. Canavan, *Clothing the Body of Christ*, 122, notes: 'By the time of Tacitus' writing, the term *imperium* clearly has geographical boundaries, parts, and a vast body (corpus)'.
39 The language of weak and strong is also prevalent in *homonoia* speeches, e.g. Dio Chrysostom, *Discourses* 34.16.21. Aelius Aristides clearly acknowledges disputes between the rich and poor but seeks harmony not through a declaration that both parties are equal but that both parties must play their hierarchical role. E.g. *Oration* 24.32–33.
40 Peterlin, 'Stomach, Hands', 69.
41 Judge, 'Demythologising the Church', 581.
42 Peterlin, 'Stomach, Hands', 67.
43 Peterlin, 'Stomach, Hands', 67.

1.2 *The Importance of Body-Related Imagery in the Greco-Roman World: Physiognomy*

In order to be able to understand and assess Paul's use of the body politic metaphor, we must also consider the attitudes towards and values of the human body expressed in the contemporary Greco-Roman literature. Although there are many facets which could be explored here, this discussion will be limited to the pseudo-science known as physiognomics/physiognomy.[44]

The fundamental principle of physiognomy is that there is a relationship between the outward appearance of the body and one's inner character and attributes. Physiognomic ideals 'permeated the Greco-Roman thought world'[45] and were a common feature in a range of different literary genres from the time of Homer into the third century C.E. The correlation between a person's physical appearance and character created 'fixed character types'[46] so that certain physical features were used to describe those who were honourable and virtuous while other sets of features correlated to those who were lacking in honour and virtue. These stereotypes about a person's character did more than simply generalise about a person's nature, they were considered to be an accurate method of revealing a person's value whether positively or negatively.

The Pseudo-Aristotelian *Physiognomics* outlines some of the fundamental principles. A person's character and mental capacity are expressed in one's physical appearance, especially in those parts of the body upon which 'there is the greatest evidence of intelligence', such as 'the eyes, forehead, head, and face; secondly, the region of the breast and shoulders, and lastly that of the legs and feet'.[47] This correlation is because the 'body and soul interact with each other so that each is mainly responsible for the other's affections'.[48] The correlation between one's personality and physical appearance was so strong that any shift in personality would cause a corresponding alteration to one's outward

---

44   See Parsons, *Body and Character*. On disability in the Greek and Roman worlds, see, Gosbell, 'The Poor, the Crippled, the Blind, and the Lame', 44–111; Laes, Goodey, & Rose, *Disabilities in Roman Antiquity*; Rose, *The Staff of Oedipus*.
45   Parsons, *Body and Character*, 17.
46   Harrill, *Slaves in the New Testament*, 37.
47   Pseudo-Arist., *Physiog.* 814b5–8.
48   Pseudo-Arist., *Physiog.* 805a9–10.

appearance and vice versa.⁴⁹ This connection between personality and appearance was so immutable that even if it were possible for 'good things' such as 'honour, wealth and bodily excellences' to be given to a 'foolish' man, such an act would be worthless:

> For the things men fight about and think the greatest, honour and wealth and bodily excellences and pieces of good fortune and powers, are good by nature but may possibly be harmful to some men owing to their characters. If a man is foolish or unjust or profligate he would gain no profit by employing them, any more than an invalid would benefit from using the diet of a man in good health, or a weakling (ἀσθενής) and a cripple (ἀνάπηρος) from the equipment of a healthy man and of a sound one.⁵⁰

The relationship between a person's character and body was so intertwined that incompatibility was simply not possible. It is also significant that the 'foolish man' is not only described as being deprived of 'honour, wealth and bodily excellences', but also paralleled linguistically with the 'invalid', 'weakling', and 'cripple', which reinforces these physiognomic ideals and presents physical disability and foolishness as corresponding entities.⁵¹

In this process of determining character through appearance, the Roman male citizen became the standard norm for expectations of the human body in the ancient world. Such bodies were physically whole and strong, without blemish or impairment. In contrast, bodies that deviated from this norm were bodies that were incomplete and weak in terms of both their physical appearance and their corresponding character. Thus, a set of physical characteristics were also associated with women, slaves, non-Romans, and people with disability, which were composed of language and imagery wholly different from the body of the male Roman citizen.⁵² Such an example can be seen with the depiction of Emperor Caligula in Seneca's *On the Firmness of the Wise Man*.

---

49 Pseudo-Arist., *Physiog.* 805a4–5.
50 Pseudo-Arist., *Eud. Eth.* 1248b.
51 Gosbell, 'The Poor, the Crippled, the Blind, and the Lame', 68.
52 Parsons, *Body and Character*, 25; Harrill, *Slaves in the NT*, 37.

Because the physical description of Caligula would have been understood to reveal his character traits, it would have indicated clearly to the ancient audience that he was someone not deserving of honour:

> a most fruitful source of ridicule, such was the ugliness of his pale face bespeaking his madness, such the wildness of his eyes lurking beneath the brow of an old hag, such the hideousness of his bald head with its sprinkling of beggarly hairs. And he had, besides, a neck overgrown with bristles, spindle shanks, and enormous feet.[53]

The principles of physiognomics were not restricted to individual bodies but could also be used to determine the characteristics of a corporate body or even an entire people group. Roman writers thus lauded the characteristics of the Roman Empire in contrast to those of the surrounding people groups. In the first-century B.C.E., Vitruvius described the Roman Empire as 'the truly perfect territory', saying that 'the races of Italy are the most perfectly constituted in both respects—in bodily form and in mental activity to correspond to their valour', in comparison to other peoples who 'naturally differ in mental and physical conformation and qualities'.[54]

The link between physiognomics and the body politic is made most apparent in visual representations from the Roman Empire. Visual depictions of both Concordia and Fortuna fulfill all the virtuous characteristics described by the physiognomists. Harry O. Maier describes a Pompeiian statue of Livia depicted as Concordia which 'illustrates the union of virtue, ideal form and Augustan rule, and thus portrays in sculptural form the harmony of the civic order'.[55] In addition to this, Michael Squire, in a study on the literary and visual representation of the body politic in the Roman world, contends that 'the idea of the 'body politic' can...be said to have revolutionized the semantics of embodied imagery'. Indeed, Squire suggests that in the Roman period, visual portrayals of the emperors 'came not merely to represent an image of the

---

53 *Constant.* 18.1 (Basore, LCL).
54 Vitruvius, *de Architectura* 6.1.11.
55 Maier, *Picturing Paul in Empire*, 58.

individual ... but also to incorporate within it a materialized idea of an abstract "body politic"'. Squire argues that visual representations of the emperors reveal not only the character of the emperor himself but of the people he rules and represents.[56]

Given the extent to which physiognomic ideals were prevalent in the first century C.E., and the extent to which a whole and functioning physical body was used to represent the body politic in both literary and visual representations in the Roman Empire, it is reasonable to assume that a physiognomically-aware audience would have expected Paul to use the image of a whole and fully-functioning human body as the basis for his metaphor of the Body of Christ. Ancient audiences, knowing the link between character and physical body, would have expected the Body of Christ to be the ideal Greco-Roman body: one that was perfectly balanced, physically whole, and without defect. But is this the kind of body to which Paul envisages the members of the Body of Christ belonging? This question will be addressed in section 2 below.

1.3 *Paul's Use of the Body Politic Imagery in Romans 12 and 1 Corinthians 12*

In Romans 12 and 1 Corinthians 12, Paul calls on the image of a physical body with all its various members working together for the greater good of the body. Like other writers employing the body politic metaphor,[57] Paul uses descriptions of different parts of the body playing their particular roles,[58] conversations between various members of the body,[59] and in particular, the threat of schisms to the body,[60] and the

---

56 Squire, '*Corpus imperii*', 311. 'The corpus of the emperor emerges, we might say, as a literal embodiment—an anthropomorphic personification—of a figurative *corpus imperii*: as "lord of the empire" (*arbiter imperii*), Augustus himself also serves as the "image of the fatherland that flourishes through him" (*patriae per te florentis imago*: Ov. Tr. 5.2.47, 49)' (p.309).
57 Rather than envisioning the church as becoming the literal, physical body of the resurrected Jesus (so Jewett, *Paul's Anthropological Terms*, 303; Käsemann, 'Theological Problem', 102–21), Paul's use of the body imagery is metaphorical and is therefore used in a similar way to other ancient writers who speak of the civic or social body as a human body (so also, Judge, 'Demythologising the Church', 577; cf. Carter, 'Christ's Body', 94–95; Gundry, Sōma *in Biblical Theology*, 228–229; Yorke, *The Church*, 45).
58 E.g., 1 Cor. 12:14; Rom. 12:4.
59 E.g., 1 Cor. 12:15–16.
60 E.g., 1 Cor. 12:25; Rom. 10:12; 16:17.

interdependence of each of the members for the good of the body.[61] In light of these similarities, many scholars argue that Paul must have had *homonoia* speeches in mind as he crafted his image of the Body of Christ for his Roman and Corinthian audiences.[62]

According to Timothy A. Brookins, the scholarly consensus has identified Menenius Agrippa's speech as 'the closest parallel to Paul's body image'.[63] Daniel Lynwood Smith takes this further stating that Paul's allegory of the body does not simply have echoes of Menenius Agrippa's fable but rather that 'Paul here draws on his rhetorical training, reworking and embellishing a version of the fable of the Members and the Belly in order to strengthen his case against factions in Corinth'.[64] But does Paul use his body imagery to parallel the use in other ancient sources or is Paul attempting to create a new alternative expectation of the body for those participating in the Body of Christ?

Some scholars see in Paul's use of the body politic imagery a very similar call to unity as that which is expressed by the Greek and Roman writers. Richard Horsley considers Paul's use of the Body of Christ metaphor a means by which to emphasise that the community of believers in Christ was a new, alternative society standing in stark opposition to the power- and status-obsessed Roman Empire.[65] Likewise, Margaret Mitchell, influenced heavily by the work of Mary Douglas on boundaries and the body,[66] sees Paul's Body of Christ imagery as promoting unity for all the members of the body in a way that parallels directly the Greco-Roman *homonoia* speeches.[67] For Mitchell, unity among all the members of the body of Christ was vital for the effective functioning of this new community and for its ability to be identified as a community separate and unique from the Roman Empire. The focus on the body

---

61 E.g., 1 Cor. 12:7; Rom. 12:5.
62 For example, Mitchell, *Paul and Rhetoric of Reconciliation*, passim; Horsley, '1 Corinthians', 252.
63 Brookins, 'Paul and the Ancient Body Metaphor', 78.
64 Smith, 'Rhetorical Subversion', 150.
65 Horsley, '1 Corinthians', 209, suggests that '[Paul] was building an international political-religious movement' that he himself understood as a 'political assembly ... in pointed juxtaposition and competition with the official city assembly'. According to Yoder, *Body Politics*, passim, even if the church wasn't intentionally anti-imperial, the characteristics of Christian community are automatically at odds with those of the Empire.
66 Douglas, *Purity and Danger, passim*.
67 Mitchell, *Paul and Rhetoric of Reconciliation*, 20–64.

as a bounded-system results in a focus on maintaining boundaries and ensuring that those within this bounded body—in this case, followers of Christ—are to be clearly distinguishable from people outside of this corporate body, that is, the rest of society. For this reason, the boundaries marking who is 'in' and who is 'out' of this bounded community are meant to be clearly evident. For Mitchell, Paul utilised the Body of Christ imagery to help the early church address the question of identity and allegiance for followers of Christ.[68] Thus, Mitchell states that '(t)he metaphor of the body for the social organism in ancient political tests... *is used to combat factionalism* ... That is the same application which Paul makes of his transferred metaphor "the body of Christ".[69]

Other see in Paul's Body of Christ imagery a call to maintain the existing system of hierarchy promoted in the *homonoia* speeches. This view is expressed most clearly by Jerome Neyrey in his work on anthropology and the body in the ancient world, which also relies heavily on the bounded body imagery promoted by Mary Douglas.[70] Neyrey sees Paul describing and affirming a diversity of the members of the body, which is clearly hierarchical in nature affording power and honour to certain members over others:

> The differentiated parts of the body are also ranked. The head is greater than the feet; the eye is more important than the ear; the hand is above the foot. Paul even admits that in the body there are honorable and less honorable parts, presentable and inferior parts, stronger and weaker members (12:22–24). The ranking of the differentiated parts is related to the roles ascribed to the members of the church: 'first there are apostles, second prophets, third teachers, then ... then ... then ...' (12:28b). This, too, is God's doing for "God has appointed" them (12:28b). God has also drawn the *map of the social body*. Even the charismatic gifts can be differentiated and ranked: prophecy over

---

68 E.g. Lee, *Paul, the Stoics, and the Body of Christ*, 105; Mitchell, *Paul and Rhetoric of Reconciliation*, 65-66; Dewey, 'Paul and the Remapping', 133, also argues that the Corinthians were lacking a sense of identity and part of what Paul was doing them was helping to work this out of the Body.
69 Mitchell, *Paul and the Rhetoric of Reconciliation*, 161.
70 Neyrey, *Paul in Other Words*, 104–106.

tongues, and charity over all (12:31; 13:13).[71]

In Neyrey's view, God has ordained a clear hierarchy within the church which is manifested in the distribution of gifts and in each member's position in the body. Neyrey does acknowledge a kind of reversal of honour in the Body of Christ, since those who 'seem weaker' and who are 'unpresentable' are deserving of the greatest honour. However, this redistribution of honour in the Body of Christ does not change the reality that the ecclesiastical body possesses and is governed by a hierarchy which is God-ordained, pre-determined, and must be adhered to.[72]

Neyrey's reading of hierarchy is based on a number of elements in the Body of Christ texts, but is rooted primarily in Paul's enumerated list of gifts in 1 Corinthians 12:28 ('God has placed in the church first of all apostles, second prophets, third teachers, then miracles, then gifts of healing, of helping, of guidance, and of different kinds of tongues'), as well as Paul's directive for the Corinthians to 'seek the greater gifts' (1 Cor. 12:31). Neyrey, among other scholars, considers the enumerated list in 1 Corinthians 12:28 (and its parallels in Rom. 12:6–8; Eph. 4:11–12), as Paul's presentation of a God-given ranking of spiritual gifts in respect to their importance and value in of the early church.[73] In this respect, Leon Morris writing of the gift of prophecy listed in Romans 12 states that 'If anyone is not given that great gift but is given the more humdrum gift of being able to serve in a lowly place, then he should not sigh for what he does not have but use the gift God has given him'.[74]

But is such an interpretation of Paul's body imagery plausible given Paul's criticisms of the Corinthians' elitist attitudes presented throughout 1 Corinthians? Rather than reinforcing the idea of hierarchy that was prevalent in the world around him, Dale Martin contends that Paul employs the same rhetorical techniques and language of the

---

71 Neyrey, *Paul in Other Words*, 139.
72 Neyrey, *Paul in Other Words*, 137.
73 E.g. Bruce, *1 and 2 Corinthians*, 122–23. Barrett, *First Corinthians*, 295, suggests that the first three gifts listed in 1 Corinthians (apostles, prophets, teachers) are the primary objectives of the church and thus all other gifts have to be secondary in comparison. For Garland, *First Corinthians*, 598, the gifts 'appear to be ranked in order of importance'; for Ciampa & Rosner, *First Corinthians*, 609, they are 'not given in absolute order of value, but the first three gifts or offices are clearly ordered and set above the others'; c.f. Murray, *Romans*, 121.
74 Morris, *Romans*, 441.

Greco-Roman *homonoia* texts, but, he reverses the order of priority.[75] In 1 Corinthians 4:1–13, Paul is clearly critical of the Corinthian elites who prized the gifts of 'exultation and visible demonstrative "success"'[76] which prioritised individual edification over the building up of others. In ranking the gifts in 1 Corinthians 12, Paul provides a list which would have inverted the priority of gifts as understood by the members of the Corinthian church. The gifts which seemed unremarkable in the Corinthians church—those of teaching and prophesying—are ranked at the top of Paul's list, while the gift prized most highly by the Corinthians—*glossolalia*—is ranked last.[77] This view is also promoted by Ben Witherington who considers Paul's aim here as 'relativis(ing) the sense of importance and necessity of the weaker, lower status Corinthian Christians ... the "less presentable" members'.[78]

This redistribution of honour as a means of bringing equilibrium gains traction when considered in light of the prevailing theories of bodily health in the first century. But rather than seeking to install a new inverted mode of hierarchy, Paul's aim was to correct the imbalance in the Corinthian church with respect to gifts and status. Medical theories prevalent in the first century espoused the idea that bodily imbalance could be countered by the application of the opposite element or humor. For example, the Hippocratic author of *Aphorisms* states that 'diseases caused by repletion are cured by depletion; those caused by depletion are cured by repletion'.[79] It appears that Paul is likewise promoting this same technique of 'curing' imbalance within the Body of Christ: the imbalance of power and honour in the Corinthian church needed to be 'treated' by the complete reversal of the methods used to attribute honour in this church. It is in the process of offering honour to the 'unpresentable parts' and those not normally attributed honour that balance would be restored to the stratified Corinthian church. It is not that Paul considered the roles of apostles, prophets, and teachers as greater to any other role within the Body of Christ, but rather,

---

75 Martin, *Corinthian Body*, 92–96; cf., Dutch, *The Educated Elite*, 37.
76 Thiselton, *First Corinthians*, 1023.
77 Some scholars see no hierarchy—reversed or otherwise—in the content of 1 Corinthians 12; Lim, *Metaphors and Social Identity Formation*, 161; Yong, *Disability, the Bible and the Church*, 95.
78 Witherington, *Conflict and Community*, 258–9.
79 Hippoc., *Aph.* 2.20; cf. Hippoc., *Mul.* 11.

treating such gifts with greater honour is what would help bring about the balancing out required to redistribute honour to all the gifts within the Body. The fact that gifts are transposed in other lists elsewhere, also supports the view that Paul is not promoting a strict universal hierarchy of gifts, but rather, the order of the gifts listed in 1 Corinthians 12 was tailored to this particular community.

This idea of correcting imbalance fits better with Paul's presentation of himself in emulating the humility of Jesus. Paul's depiction of Jesus throughout his epistles is as the antithesis of the Greco-Roman ideals of power and honour: Jesus demonstrated servitude and humility, sought to give glory to God rather than self, associated with the unclean and the marginalised and was ultimately crucified as a common criminal. As a follower of Jesus, Paul sought to emulate these facets of Jesus' life and ministry with Paul referring to himself as one who is deemed as foolish by the world,[80] the 'scum of the earth',[81] a slave,[82] and garbage.[83] By reserving such epithets for himself and his fellow teachers and apostles, it would be incongruous of Paul then to speak of the Body of Christ as governed by a ranking system that mirrored those used in the broader society, with himself and other apostles in positions of honour and privilege over the rest of the early Christian community. Instead, Paul wishes to remind the Corinthian church that whatever it is they laud and esteem, whatever the worldly values they draw their identity from, these are not the things that are valued by God and they should not be sought after in the Body of Christ.

While the final verse in this section, 1 Corinthians 12:31, has caused much debate among scholars,[84] there is one particular aspect which has a direct bearing on our interpretation of Paul's enumeration of gifts in this chapter: whether Paul's use of the word ζηλοῦτε (zēloute) should be translated as an indicative or imperative. In general, English translations assume ζηλοῦτε (zēloute) is an imperative and thus is to be considered an

---

80 1 Cor. 3:18; 4:10.
81 1 Cor. 4:13.
82 Rom. 1:1; 7:25.
83 1 Cor. 4:13.
84 Scholars also debate whether v.31 belongs at the end of chapter 12 or would be better at the beginning of chapter 13 and how the word 'greater' should be translated.

exhortation to seek, 'strive for', or 'earnestly desire the greater gifts'.[85] But this translation is at odds with the rest of 1 Corinthians 12, in which Paul stresses that it is God alone who allocates gifts to each member of the body. How then can the Corinthians 'strive for' gifts that they do not possess and which have not been gifted to them by God? Instead, Thiselton argues that ζηλοῦτε (zēloute) should be rendered as an indicative and proposes that Paul means something akin to *'do not stop being zealously concerned about the "greatest" gifts,* provided that you follow me in transposing and subverting your understanding of what counts as "the greatest"'.[86] Paul exhorts the Corinthians to focus not on themselves and the betterment of their own gifts, but rather, to utilise their gifts in a way that edifies and glorifies the wider body of the church.

While Paul certainly wrote to the Corinthian church to encourage unity and to exhort the members to avoid schisms,[87] Paul's idea of unity was not one formed through adherence to the accepted hierarchies in the Roman Empire. Paul's vision of unity is tied to being like-minded in Christ and accepting that all members—though each gifted differently—are equally valuable in the Body of Christ. The interdependence of the various members of the Body of Christ is such that 'each member belongs to all the others'[88] and none can think higher or lower of themselves than any other member.

What appears to be the case in both Romans and Corinthians is that the churches were not functioning in a way that was consistent with Paul's presentation of the Body of Christ. In Romans, Paul critiques the way in which the Gentile and Jewish Christians considered their own pathway into the church as superior to the other. The Jewish Christians thus lauded their heritage as the chosen people of God recorded in the Jewish scriptures, while the Gentile Christians considered their direct entrance into the Christian community through the message of Jesus as

---

85   Collins, *First Corinthians*, 471, for example, suggests 'avidly desire'. The argument for the imperative is often based on the fact that both of the two other uses of ζηλοῦτε (*zēloute*) in 1 Corinthians are imperative, including in this same context at 14:1; e.g., Garland, *First Corinthians*, 601. NIV = 'eagerly desire'; NLT, ESV, NASB = 'earnestly desire'; NRSV = 'strive'; HCSB, CEV = 'desire'.
86   Thiselton, *First Corinthians*, 1024; cf. Smit, 'Two Puzzles'.
87   1 Cor 1:10; 12:25.
88   Rom 12:5.

the superior way, with both groups considering the 'others' as the weaker members of the body. In respect to the Corinthian Christians, Paul describes a church which reflected the political and social structures consistent in the ancient world, focusing on people's social rank, the demonstration of the so-called highly-prized gifts, and overlooking the needs of the poor and marginalised.[89] In both cases, Paul encourages the church by reminding them that all members of the Body of Christ are valued irrespective of the status-markers of the broader society around them. Issues such as ethnicity, socio-economic status, social status, and religious heritage were irrelevant within the diversely-gifted Body of Christ where all members are equipped with different but equally-valuable gifts to utilise in service to one another.

Paul's representation of the Body of Christ, then, is markedly different from the body politic imagery expressed in the Stoic writers. Paul is not advocating for a unity of the body that merely accepted the *status quo* of the highly stratified hierarchy of the Empire. Instead, Paul's view of the Body of Christ was as a new kind of corporate body being forged in the name of Jesus, emulating Jesus' servitude and humility. Unlike Plutarch's image of Menenius Agrippa, Paul's call to unity in the Body of Christ envisions a body where all the parts are valued equally for their contribution to the body. And uniquely to Paul, his image of all the various parts working together turns the Roman hierarchical body politic imagery on its head by declaring that in the Body of Christ, those parts which 'seem weaker' are actually 'indispensable' and should be awarded due honour. If anything, Paul's image of the body of Christ in Romans 12 and 1 Corinthians 12 is anti-hierarchy, seeking to quash any other systems at play in the church that might defer to any status based on wealth or social rank. In this respect, the Body of Christ is not one whole in spite of its diversity but because of it.[90]

---

89 Cf. Ciampa & Rosner, *First Corinthians*, 605; Yorke, *The Church*, 71.
90 Dunn, *Romans 9–16*, 725; Edwards, *Romans*, 286–287; Fee, *First* Corinthians, 602 n.12; Judge, 'Demythologising the Church', 582; Peterlin, 'Stomach, Hands', 73.

Section 2: Disability and Body-related Imagery in the Biblical Texts

2.1 *Disability Studies and Biblical Literature*

While the biblical texts are replete with disability-related language—employed both literally and figuratively—for the most part, it is only in the last 15 years of biblical scholarship that there has been any 'sustained interest in critically examining disability within biblical scholarship'.[91] Prior to this, references to disability in the biblical texts were not deemed 'worthy of critical inquiry'[92] in their own right but were considered incidental elements of the text[93] which only serve to emphasise other more prominent issues in the text, for example, Jesus' skill as a healer of physical bodies. The occasional investigations with some interest in issues of disability were limited to attempts to diagnose particular conditions described in the biblical texts. Such 'retrospective diagnoses'[94] attempt to apply modern medical diagnostic methods to ancient descriptions of illness and impairment described in the Bible or other ancient texts. In this way, attempts have been made to 'diagnose' Job's sores, Jacob's blindness, and Paul's 'thorn in the flesh'.[95]

While many postmodern literary techniques—such as post-colonial, feminist, and ecological critical approaches—focus on employing new methodologies and techniques to the biblical texts, this is not the case for disability readings of the biblical texts. Instead, scholars interested in the presentation of disability in the biblical texts utilise the same 'conventions of critical biblical scholarship, including methods of argumentation, standards for acceptable evidence, citations of primary texts in their original languages and relevant secondary scholarship familiar to other scholars trained in biblical studies'.[96] Disability studies, in this respect, is not a new methodological approach or a new form of biblical criticism, but rather, disability studies of the biblical

---

91 Junior & Schipper, 'Disability Studies', 21.
92 Moss & Schipper, 'Introduction', 5.
93 For example, Birch, 'Impairment as a Condition in Biblical Scholarship', 185.
94 Also called retrospective diagnostics. Graumann, 'Monstrous Births and Retrospective Diagnosis'; Leven, 'Retrospective Diagnosis and Ancient Medical History'.
95 See Gosbell, *'The Poor, the Crippled, the Blind, and the Lame'*, 8–9.
96 Moss & Schipper, 'Introduction', 4.

texts employ the same traditional methodologies applied to the biblical texts—exegetical studies, form criticism, redaction criticism, and other critical methods—but these critical approaches are used in such a way as to understand better the references to disability included in the texts rather than gloss over them as merely incidental or metaphorical.[97]

Since 2004, numerous publications have been produced which seek to bring disability theory into dialogue with biblical studies.[98] Scholars interested in this area suggest that by assessing the presence of a 'disabled'[99] body in any ancient text, we can gain a better understanding of the value given to bodies—whether those bodies are 'disabled' or able-bodied —within the specific historical and social milieu of those texts. While assessing references to disability in the bible may yield little in terms of reconstructing the everyday life experiences of people with disability in the ancient world,[100] attempting to understand the way the biblical authors used disability-related language, or indeed, any kind of embodied language, gives us an insight into the way the ancient communities may have interpreted, valued, reflected, or indeed countered, ancient ideals about the physical body, disabled or otherwise.[101]

In this way, the intersection of disability and biblical studies is more than simply assessing isolated references to particular persons described as having some form of disability,[102] but rather, looking more broadly at the way disability is represented through the biblical texts and how integral issues of the body, including the 'disabled' body, are to a broad

---

97 This approach stands in stark contrast to that of Gould, *Practicing Prayer for the Dead*, 67 n.83, who considers the use of 'sickness and disability language' in the Gospels as a 'metaphor for sin' and it 'symbolize(s) the redemption of exiled Israel (not of impaired individuals)'.
98 See the bibliography in Gosbell, *'The Poor, the Crippled, the Blind, and the Lame'.*
99 While many people with disability intentionally used the word 'disabled' to describe themselves, in Australia, we general adhere to a person-first use of disability-related language, especially when referring to the disabilities of others. For example, instead of referring to a 'disabled person' we would use the phrase 'a person with disability' to emphasise that disability is a part of a person but does not describe their whole life. However, when referring generally to disability and not to a specific person, we can still employ the language of a 'disabled' body.
100 E.g., Gosbell, *'The Poor, the Crippled, the Blind, and the Lame'*, 27–30; Moss & Schipper, 'Introduction', 6; Olyan, *Disability in the Hebrew Bible*, 4.
101 Gosbell, *'The Poor, the Crippled, the Blind, and the Lame'*, 27–30; Moss & Schipper, 'Introduction', 6.
102 For example, assessing biblical characters such as those in the Gospels seeking healing from Jesus for various disabilities, Jacob's blindness, Moses' speech impediment, Paul's 'thorn in the flesh', etc.

range of biblical themes.[103] Deborah Creamer thus proposes that it is impossible to address the issue of embodiment at all in the biblical texts unless we also address the issue of disability.[104] This is because the value attributed to a body considered whole or normative can only be understood when examined in light of its corollary, the body deemed to lack wholeness, value or bodily integrity. Through a more deliberate focus on the meaning given to the 'disabled' body in the biblical texts, we can develop more nuanced readings and interpretations of these passages featuring body-related imagery. Not only this, but Nyasha Junior and Jeremy Schipper contend that 'even in texts that do not deal with disability explicitly, the critical study of disability may help us to understand better the cultural expectations for human normalcy reflected in biblical literature'.[105]

Mikeal Parsons' work on physiognomy in Luke-Acts, though strictly speaking not a disability reading, is a helpful example of the kinds of insights that can be yielded from the biblical texts through close attention to language related to the body and embodiment. Parsons has argued convincingly that the writer of Luke-Acts seeks to subvert traditional physiognomic language in favour of new methods of defining character and identity.[106] Where descriptions of people in Luke-Acts feature physical characteristics deemed undesirable, the assumption of ancient audiences would have been that these people were also flawed in their character, for example, the physical description of Zaccheus in Luke 19:1–10. Parsons argues that Luke's description of Zaccheus as 'short in stature' (Luke 19:3) is significant because of the physiognomic ideals regarding a man's height. According to Pseudo-Aristotle, 'These are the marks of a small-minded person. He is small-limbed, small and round, dry, with small eyes and a small face, like a Corinthian or Leucadian'.[107] In contrast, 'greatness of soul' was associated with the commensurate greatness in stature.[108] Parsons also assesses the physical descriptions of the Ethiopian eunuch in Acts 8:26–40 with respect to physiognomic ideals.

103 Raphael, *Biblical Corpora*, 2.
104 Creamer, *Disability and Christian Theology*, 4.
105 Junior & Schipper, 'Disability Studies and the Bible', 33.
106 Parsons, *Body and Character*, *passim*.
107 Pseudo-Arist., *Physiog.* 808a30.
108 Aristotle, *Eth. Nic.* 4.3.1123b7; 4.8.1128a8–13.

Parsons suggests that the Ethiopian eunuch would have been considered by Luke's audience as 'sexually ambiguous, socially ostracized, and morally evil', and yet, 'Luke's response is surely that neither the eunuch's physical condition, nor his place of origin, nor his likeness to a sheared sheep prevents his entrance into the eschatological community'.[109]

Parsons also highlights Paul's subversion of physiognomic ideals in the Pauline corpus.[110] In respect to his own body, Paul repeatedly refers to his own physical imperfections and weaknesses which, from the perspective of ancient rhetoric, would have left Paul vulnerable to his opponents' slurs regarding both physical and moral flaws.[111] Indeed, Paul states this view explicitly in 2 Corinthians 10:10 where, as Martin has noted, Paul's 'critics point to his weakness of body (whether due to illness, disfigurement, or simply constitutional infirmity) as irrefutable evidence of his weakness of character. His letters (strong) do not match his presence or speaking ability (weak)'.[112] Paul's intention in describing his physical body is not merely to have a record of his physiology, but rather, to subvert the ancient ideals of physiognomy and masculinity. Rather than presenting his physical characteristics in a way which would align himself with the symbols of masculinity and strength as would be expected, in 2 Corinthians 10, Paul refutes the invective charged against him not by commending his wisdom, rhetorical skills, or education, but instead, by describing himself in a way that aligns him with the members of the lower classes who were devoid of honour in the ancient world: that of the slave[113] and the fool.[114]

Given the subversion of physiognomic ideals in Luke-Acts, and Paul's use of this subversion in respect to his own body in 1 and 2 Corinthians, to what extent could Paul also be subverting the view of the Body of Christ as one that is meant to be perfect and whole? What is apparent

---

109 Parsons, *Body and Character*, 141.
110 Parsons, *Body and Character*, 48–51. It is interesting to note here the description of Paul given in the apocryphal *Acts of Paul and Thecla* where he is described as 'a man of small stature, with a bald head and crooked legs, in a good state of body, with eyebrows meeting and nose somewhat hooked', 1.237 lines 6–9 (*NTApoc* 2.354).
111 For example, Gal. 4:13–14; 1 Cor. 2:3; 2 Cor. 10:1; 12:7).
112 Martin, *The Corinthian Body*, 55.
113 Rom. 1:1; 1 Cor. 9:19
114 1 Cor. 1–4 cf. Welborn, *Paul, the Fool of Christ, passim.*

from the interpretations of most scholars reading the Pauline Body of Christ imagery in Romans 12 and 1 Corinthians 12 is the assumption that Paul envisions the Body of Christ as a body that is physically whole and perfect. Only when all the members are playing their parts is the Body of Christ whole and complete. If the body is missing members, the result is that the Body of Christ is not functioning as it ought, but is unhealthy, incomplete, or indeed, disabled.

2.2 *The Basis for a Disability Reading of 1 Corinthians 12 and Romans 12*

By virtue of the fact that the metaphor used by Paul in 1 Corinthians 12 and Romans 12 is that of a human body, there are good reasons for assessing Paul's Body of Christ pericopes from a disability perspective. Here we will outline two key areas for consideration which will then be developed further in the following sections (§§2.2.1; 2.2.2). Firstly, we will address the way in which the Body of Christ pericopes in Romans 12 and 1 Corinthians have been interpreted with respect to the body and/or disability-related imagery and, in particular, the interpretations of those scholars writing specifically on issues of disability and biblical studies. Secondly, we will address the way these passages have been interpreted programmatically as a model for inclusive ecclesiastical practice especially in relation to people with disability.

2.2.1 *Disability-related Interpretations of Romans 12 and 1 Corinthians 12*

Commentators on Romans 12 and 1 Corinthians 12 often assume that the basis of Paul's metaphor is the image of a perfect and complete body akin to those featured in the *homonoia* speeches, whereby any failure of members to participate would lead to the compromised functioning of the body. As a result, scholars regularly employ the same kind of dichotomous language of functioning/non-functioning and healthy/unhealthy in relation to the Body of Christ that is used in the Greco-Roman body politic sources. In doing so, these scholars propose that not only is it possible for believers to be left out of the Body of Christ but that in their absence they leave a void which compromises the efficacy and 'proper functioning' of the Body of Christ.[115] Richard Longenecker says that in Romans Paul uses 'the metaphor of a healthy human body'[116] which is the aim for the Body of Christ. Kenneth E. Bailey uses imagery akin to that in the Greco-Roman sources on the body politic stating that '(a)ny disruption of that harmony (in the Body of Christ) is a sign of illness',[117] quoting Archbishop Desmond Tutu who says that 'God has made us in such a way that we need each other...the totally self-sufficient person... is subhuman'.[118] In the language of Tutu, if the Body of Christ does not utilise all its members, the body is 'subhuman' and thus, by extension, severely disabled. J. D. G. Dunn uses similar language stating that '(t)he point is that the body is *one* not despite its diversity, but is *one body* only by virtue of its diversity; without that diversity the body would be a monstrosity'[119]—language implying a body that is grossly 'deformed'.

The dualistic language of healthy/unhealthy or functioning/non-functioning in respect to the Body of Christ is also used regularly in disability readings of 1 Corinthians 12 and Romans 12. For example, Amos Yong contends that people with disability must be included in the church because '[t]he health of the body requires the working of its many parts'.[120] Thomas E. Reynolds likewise asserts the necessity of including people with disability into faith communities stating that 'excluding one member of the body of Christ mars its image ... Christians are less than whole without one another, without the contributions that all make to the household of God'.[121] Barbara J. Hedges-Goettl similarly suggests that '[f]or the Church to be whole, all must be included', even stating explicitly that '[t]he church is disabled when persons with disabilities are not included'.[122]

Even though William C. Gaventa likewise suggests that 'the body is not whole unless all parts are there' and that 'the body is incomplete

---

115 Ciampa & Rosner, *First Corinthians*, 599; Longenecker, *Romans*, 928; George, 'Voices and Visions', 101.
116 Longenecker, *Romans*, 928.
117 Bailey, *Paul Through Mediterranean Eyes*, 343.
118 Tutu, *God Has a Dream*, 25.
119 Dunn, *Romans 9–16*, 725.
120 Yong, *Disability, the Bible and the Church*, P 95.
121 Reynolds, *Vulnerable Communion*, 237.
122 Hedges-Goettl, 'Thinking Theologically About Inclusion', 15.

unless every part is connected', he is one of the few scholars who recognises the paradox of claiming that the Body of Christ is disabled without the presence of people with disability.[123] Gaventa's solution is to suggest that although the Body of Christ is impaired without the inclusion of people with disability, it will nevertheless continue to function:

> The body is really an incredibly wonderful whole. If we take out a piece or part here or there, or a sensory ability, it can still function and flourish. But for the Body of Christ, the whole is blessed and empowered by reconnecting with overlooked, forgotten, pushed away, and discarded parts.[124]

In their *Making a World of Difference: Christian Reflections on Disability*, Roy McCloughry and Wayne Morris also observe this same paradox of calling the Body of Christ 'disabled' without the presence of people with disability. So while McCloughry and Morris state that 'to exclude disabled people is to mar the image of God',[125] they likewise acknowledge that Paul's expectation of the body

> seems to have in mind a non-disabled person's body for the church—a symbol of health and 'perfection' in which every part is working properly. This metaphor is one that aims to include, but the very metaphor itself has the power to exclude.[126]

McCloughry and Morris' statement expresses insightfully the paradox of attempting to apply Paul's Body of Christ imagery to issues of disability and inclusion. Before moving on to consider the implications of this paradox for disability readings of Paul, we will address the way these passages have been interpreted as being programmatic for the inclusion of people with disability into church communities.

---

123 Gaventa, 'Preaching Disability', 239.
124 Gaventa, 'Preaching Disability', 242.
125 McCloughry & Morris, *Making a World of Difference*, 77.
126 McCloughry & Morris, *Making a World of Difference*, 81.

2.2.2 Paul's Body of Christ Imagery as the Basis for Inclusive Ecclesiastical Practice

For many scholars writing at the intersection of disability and biblical studies, Paul's representation of the Body of Christ 'offers the normative biblical portrayal of Christian inclusion'.[127] The basis of this assessment is that the body is described by Paul as an interdependent organism which requires all members to be present and active in order for the body to function effectively. When certain members of the body—whether they are people with disability or other overlooked members of the body—are missing through absence or non-participation, there is a void in the body which results in the church's power and efficacy being compromised and its mission limited, or indeed, 'disabled'. It is this compromise of the activity and reach of the Body of Christ that is used to compel church communities to rethink their current practices to ensure people with disability are present and participating in the Body of Christ through using their God-given gifts.

In contrast to the modern western world which marginalises and excludes people with disability from participation in society, Paul's representation of the Body of Christ is seen as a model of inclusion which highlights that all believers have the potential to contribute meaningfully to the body. Although some able-bodied members might undervalue the gifts of people with disability, the directive of 1 Corinthians 12 is that God has allocated gifts to the members at his discretion and that every person in Christ should be given the opportunity to use their particular gifts in service the rest of the body. If we prevent people with disability from participation in the church, whether through physical, attitudinal, or theological barriers, we disregard God's taxonomy of the church and limit its mission and power. It is not simply enough to have people with disability attending church, but in order to see the church's full impact, we need to ensure that every member of the body is an active participant through encouraging all members to find ways they can use their gifts, however humble these gifts might appear to others.

Proponents of this view consider this message of inclusion

---

127 Brock, 'Theologizing Inclusion', 354, summarising the views of Yong, *Disability, the Bible, and the Church*, 90–95, and Monteith, *Epistles of Inclusion*, 61–93.

particularly relevant for people with disability because of Paul's depiction of the reversal of honour codes in 1 Corinthians 12. According to this passage, the body contains members who are considered weaker than other members of the body. But rather than belittling the meagre contributions of these weaker members, or amputating them from the body as with the Greco-Roman examples of the body politic metaphor, Paul instead declares that the rest of the body is to treat these members with 'greater honour' (1 Cor. 12:24).

For many, Paul's language of 'weakness' finds a parallel with modern societal attitudes towards people with disability. People with disability are often considered weak and treated as though they have no skills they could use for the betterment of broader society. For this reason, many scholars see that Paul's language of weakness, while not specifically addressing issues of disability, can be applied to include this particular kind of weakness. Amos Yong argues that while 'there is no historical-grammatical reason to limit weakness to those with bodily impairments or disabilities ... there is also no a priori reason to exclude such references'. Yong suggests that recognising that the Christian community in Corinth were demonstrating 'attitudes of elitism and superiority'[128] means understanding that Paul was encouraging the Corinthians to resist factionalism and divisions that arise from any kind of social, cultural, or bodily difference. While Paul specifically refers to various forms of division in his letters, sometimes in dualistic language (e.g., male/female, Greek/Jew, slave/free),[129] and other times in terms of factionalism (e.g., 'For when one says, "I follow Paul," and another, "I follow Apollos", are you not mere human beings?' [1 Cor. 3:4]), in both cases Paul exhorts the Christian community to seek peace and unity among themselves. In this way, while Paul does not use the language of able-bodied/disabled in his letters, Yong suggests, that we can assume that an able-bodied/disabled dichotomy would also sit logically with Paul's intention to 'break down the elitist, triumphalistic, and exclusionary attitudes that certain Corinthians had developed vis-à-vis others in the congregation'.[130]

---

128 Yong, *The Bible, Disability and the Church*, 91.
129 Further examples in 1 Corinthians include strong/weak (1:18–29), wise/foolish (8:1–3), sated/hungry (11:18–22).
130 Yong, *The Bible, Disability and the Church*, 91.

At the centre of this interpretation of Paul is a belief that the Body of Christ is weakened by the absence of people with disability and as such, it is the responsibility of church communities to attend to this absence and correct it for the ongoing health and functioning of the whole body. It is thus of prime importance to the church, for their own survival and efficacy, to ensure that people with disability and others who society considers 'weak' should not only be present at church gatherings but also immersed fully into the life of the church. Although it is tempting for some commentators on 1 Corinthians 12, such as David E. Garland, to assert that the gift of 'the weaker, unpresentable members ... [is that they] give others a concrete opportunity to practice love and patience',[131] in light of Paul's description of the body, people with disability are not merely beneficiaries of other's gifts but also have their own gifts which they are to use in service to God's people. For this reason, people with disability must be afforded the opportunity to exercise their God-given gifts, even when those gifts may appear unimpressive in the eyes of other members of the body. Thus, without the presence or the participation of people with disability in church communities, many scholars writing from a disability perspective contend that the Body of Christ, in its current configuration, is incomplete and not functioning at its capacity. In order to ensure the maximum effectiveness of the church, Christian communities need to ensure that the barriers which prevent people with disability from full participation are removed. Until this happens, the church can never be all that God requires of it.

Section 3: New Interpretations—Disability and Paul's Body of Christ Imagery

While applying a disability lens to biblical texts is still a relatively new methodological approach in biblical studies, already these examinations have yielded important theological insights overlooked previously through traditional critical approaches. Focusing attention on the representation of the human body in the biblical texts—whether that body

---

131 Garland, *1 Corinthians*, 597. Garland finds this idea in Moltmann, 'The Knowing of the Other', as cited in Thiselton, *First Corinthians,* 1009; *Contra*, Ciampa & Rosner, *First Corinthians*, 604.

is able-bodied or 'disabled'—gives us insight into ancient views of the body and the value attributed to certain bodies based on their gender, race, physical appearance, age, as well as their physical and intellectual ability/disability. Examining the way in which bodies are depicted in the biblical texts yields greater insight into the extent to which the biblical writers affirmed or subverted existing beliefs about the human body. For the first time, studies have given consideration to the agency of people with various disabilities featured in Jesus' healing ministry rather than interpreting these people only as vehicles for Jesus' divine power to be demonstrated.[132] Mikael Parsons' work on physiognomy in the biblical texts, although not strictly speaking a disability reading, overlaps with the intentions of disability readings in assessing the value of the body as presented in ancient texts. In his study, Parsons highlights the ways in which the writer of Luke-Acts has subverted traditional physiognomic ideals and representations of the body by examining in detail Lukan characters such as the Ethiopian eunuch and Zacchaeus the tax collector. Recent studies on barrenness and infertility in the biblical texts have, for the first time, considered the state of childlessness with a disability lens, which has led Rebecca Raphael to label barrenness and infertility as 'the defining female disability in the Hebrew Bible'.[133] In this respect, disability studies have the potential to enhance traditional approaches to biblical studies by employing body-related imagery to give more nuanced readings.

In the emerging intersection of disability and biblical studies, new readings of Paul's Body of Christ imagery have also been sought. The metaphor of the Body of Christ used by Paul is, by its very nature, a metaphor of a human body which thus lends itself to examination from an embodied and disability perspective. One of the aspects of these passages that has proven most appealing to those scholars interpreting the metaphor from a disability perspective is Paul's depiction in 1 Corinthians 12 of those members who 'appear weaker' than other members of the body. As a consequence of their gifts not being valued or appreciated, Paul says that these members should be afforded greater

---

132   E.g. Lawrence, *Sense and Stigma*, passim.
133   Raphael, *Biblical Corpora*, 57–58.

honour. Assessing the Body of Christ imagery with a disability lens, reveals in Paul's taxonomy of the body a close parallel between the language of the members who 'appear weaker' and the experiences of people with disability in broader society as well as in the church today. Just as with the church at Corinth, contemporary churches may also have a tendency to show greater honour to those members who appear stronger and possess more impressive gifts and, as a consequence, overlook those members who appear weaker. The outcome of this is marginalisation, and sometimes even complete rejection, of people with disability from church communities.[134]

This view suggests that, as a consequence of the marginalisation or complete absence of people with disability from our church communities, the strength and effectiveness of the Body of Christ is compromised. When members are absent or non-participating, a void appears in the fabric of the body which no other members can fill. This void then weakens and disables the body and lessens its capacity to fulfil its mission of edifying all its members. Proponents of this view interpret the gifts as activities of individual members which remain unused when people with disability are not present in the Body of Christ. For many writers working at the intersection of disability and biblical studies, these people with disability are missing out on using their gift in the Christian community, and, as well as the people with disability themselves. The whole body suffers when members are not able to utilise their gifts. The view posits that if church communities were more willing to accept and include people with disability and seek out opportunities for their meaningful contributions to the church, the church would have greater strength and increased capacity to function in the world today.

But is this view an accurate reflection of Paul's body of Christ imagery, in particular, the multi-faceted approach Paul presents of the gifts as activities for service? This final section will attempt to ascertain whether such interpretations are true to the content of Romans 12 and 1 Corinthians 12 with respect to Paul's understanding of the role of gifts and the overall functionality of the Body of Christ.

---

134 E.g. Yong, *The Bible, Disability and the Church*, 83–95.

3.1 Reconsidering the Gifts and Functioning of the Body of Christ from a Disability Perspective

In order to be able to assess the appropriateness of using Paul's Body of Christ imagery as a model for the inclusion of people with disability, we must first determine what Paul means by the members of the body possessing various 'gifts'.

In both Romans 12:6 and 1 Corinthians 12:4, Paul uses the term χάρισμα, to describe the gifts given to the members of the body— or as Dunn describes them, expressions of God's 'gracious giving'.[135] However, given the 'novelty and unusual character'[136] of Paul's usage of the term in 1 Corinthians 12, these spiritual gifts receive two additional descriptors. The second term Paul employs in relation to the gifts is διακονία (v.5), which indicates that these are gifts which are to be used in service to one another. The third term Paul uses to describe these gifts is ἐνέργημα (v.6), which is described in the *Theological Dictionary of the New Testament* as 'efficient power'.[137] In this sense, the gifts are a demonstration, outworking, or display of power —but not human power. They are a demonstration of God's power which is for the benefit (συμφέρω) of the 'common good' (1 Cor. 12:7). This means, there is no concept here of believers possessing a gift that remains dormant or unused, but rather, the power of the gifts only exists in the process of them being used. This is not, as Brian Brock notes, 'merely a potency that might later become activated in order to become efficient. The gifts exist *only* as they are *enacted*'.[138] The gifts are given for use in the community and made manifest through their appropriation in serving and ministering to one another. The purpose of the gifts is to reveal or display (φανέρωσις) the Spirit at work in the community of believers (v.7). Gifts (χάρισμα), then, are given by God and are ministries or services (διακονία) that are to reveal (φανέρωσις) the Spirit at work for the edification and benefit of the whole community and not at all reliant on the individual strengths or skills of the individual members.

Given this combination of descriptors, it becomes apparent that Paul

---

135 Dunn, *The Theology of Paul the Apostle*, 553.
136 Brock, 'Theologizing the Body of Christ', 356.
137 Bertram, 'ἔργον, κτλ', 652–654.
138 Brock, 'Theologizing the Body of Christ', 356. Italics original.

does not consider the gifts as latent abilities that will go to waste if people are marginalised or estranged from the rest of the church community. Paul's metaphor does not present the *ekklesia* as an incomplete jigsaw puzzle with some of the puzzle pieces missing. And yet, by claiming that the Body of Christ is limited, marred, or disabled through the absence of people with disability, or any other marginal groups or individuals, this is exactly what is being claimed. Such an interpretation considers the gifts of each member as a strength or ability which, when combined with the strengths and abilities of all the other members, gives the Body of Christ its strength and usefulness. However, this interpretation misunderstands Paul's presentation of the functioning of the members and their use of gifts.

In the churches in Rome and Corinth, some members were placing a higher value on some gifts over others. Paul writes to correct this view, reminding the churches that the gifts each of the members possesses have been given to each by God and he has arranged each of the members precisely where he desired them to be. No one should over- or under-value either their own gifts or others', because the placement of gifts is wholly outside of each member's governance. It is God alone who allocates gifts and the placement of each of the members within the body. But for Paul, it is not only the distribution of gifts that God controls but also every person's membership in the body. Every person who is *in Christ* is automatically included and participating as a member of the body. For Paul, it was simply not possible for people to be in Christ but existing separately or outside of the rest of the body, just as the eyes and ears cannot exist separately from the rest of a physical body. Paul does not therefore write to encourage the churches to mend the gaps left by non-participating members. Instead, Paul writes to correct the attitudes of the members towards each of the other members in the body. Given that all those who are in Christ are members in the body, and given that it is God who has distributed gifts to all the members as well as their placement, Paul says there is no reason for members to judge the gifts or the placement of any of the members. Paul's focus here is not on whether all members are present in the body, but rather, his focus is wholly on the attitudes and treatment of the members of the body towards one another.

While the language of 'the church' and 'the Body of Christ' is used interchangeably by numerous writers, including those addressing disability in the Pauline texts, we are in fact talking about two very different concepts. For Paul, participation in the Body of Christ is inevitably and inextricably linked with being a follower of Christ. Every member is placed in the body by God's design to bring about his purposes. Every member is contributing and participating by merely being present in the body. No member has the power or ability to exclude others or themselves from participation in this body because 'God has placed the parts in the body, every one of them, just as he wanted them to be' (1 Cor. 12:18). Whether we attend church on Sunday or stay at home, whether we are non-verbal or loquacious, whether we meet face-to-face or communicate virtually via assistive technology, anyone who is in Christ is an active and participatory member of the Body of Christ.

But when writers addressing issues of disability discuss the absence of people with disability from the Body of Christ, what they are actually referring to is the physical manifestations of the church in its localised form. Are people with disability attending Sunday services? Are they serving on prayer, preaching, or meal rosters? Are people with disability leading bible study groups? Are children with special needs included in mainstream kids' church programs? In the case of many local churches, people with disability are absent, or at least invisible, members of the church.

3.2 *The Body of Christ from an Australian Disability Perspective*

In Australia, while extensive research on the number of people with disability attending churches is yet to be done, initial results indicate that 'the Australian church has less than half the proportion of people with a disability compared to the population as a whole (7.7 per cent, compared to 18.5 per cent).'[139] Denominationally, the statistics indicate that 10% of Anglicans and Catholics surveyed identify as having a disability, and the percentages in other denominations decrease from there. The lowest number of people identifying as having a disability was in the

---

139   Forbes & Gale, 'Disability in the Australian Church', 99. Statistics gathered through the 2011 Australian National Church Life Survey.

Pentecostal church, at only 0.3% of people surveyed.[140] Given that the national (and global) statistics indicate that somewhere around 18–20% of the population are living with disability,[141] there is a significant discrepancy between the number of people with disability in broader society and the number of people with disability in church communities. However, while this deficit is problematic and grievous, the motivation for seeking inclusion is not because members with disability are absent and are leaving a void in the Body of Christ, thus limiting the body's efficacy. But rather, this oversight of people with disability and other marginal members of our communities must be addressed because without doing so, we are failing to emulate the interdependence and mutuality modelled for the local churches by Paul's Body of Christ metaphor.

When Paul writes about the Body of Christ, he is not writing about an organism that can be impaired or limited by the non-participation of some members of the body. In this respect, Paul's presentation of the corporate body stands in stark contrast to the body politic as presented in the *homonoia* speeches. The Stoic philosophers presented the corporate body as an organism whose members were interdependent but certainly not equal in status or value. In this model of the body politic, if members failed to complete their assigned duties to the body, that part of the body became weakened or ill, which as a consequence had the potential to infect or weaken the whole body. To keep the body strong, the infected members must be healed, or, in the worst of cases, these members must be amputated in order to prevent the whole body from becoming infected. This model of the corporate body equates membership in the body with active participation in the body. If any member failed to contribute and play their part, they threatened the strength of the body, and as a result, their status as a member of this body could be easily withdrawn and the member removed.

Paul, however, interprets the functioning of the Body of Christ in a vastly different way. Membership in the Body of Christ is not contingent on any member's ability to fulfill their unique role in the body, but rather, membership in this body is simply the natural consequence

---

140 Forbes & Gale, 'Disability in the Australian Church', 99–100.
141 Current Australian statistics indicate that 18.3% of Australians reported living with disability (Australian Bureau of Statistics, 'Disability, Ageing and Carers, Australia',

of being *in Christ*. Participation in this body, then, is not the expected duty or responsibility of the individual members, nor is participation based on the skills or abilities of the individual members, but every member has a role to play and participates in the body precisely because this is the way God designed it to be. As Paul writes in 1 Corinthians 10:16–17: 'Is not the cup of thanksgiving for which we give thanks a participation in the blood of Christ? And is not the bread that we break a participation in the body of Christ? Because there is one loaf, we, who are many, are one body, for we all share the one loaf'.

For Paul, there is no such thing as a non-functioning member and never any threat of a member being 'amputated' as a result of a failure to fulfill their particular duties. The Body of Christ is not a body that is strong because all its members are gifted and fulfilling their duties. In fact, the Body of Christ is made up wholly of broken and weak members that come together in one body in their weakness and limitations which God himself transforms into a demonstration of his power. No member, then, can think more highly of him/herself than any other member because no members have earned their place or position in the body. All the work that happens in the body and through the body is done by God alone working through the weak and faulty human vessels which make up the body's members.

The Body of Christ in Paul's reckoning is not simply a combination of all our individual strengths and talents that could increase if more members, especially those marginalised and overlooked, could also contribute their gifts and abilities to the body. If anything, Paul's vision of the Body of Christ is the complete opposite. We come together in our human weakness and frailty acknowledging our reliance on God and interdependence on the other members of the body. We are interconnected and interwoven and therefore must 'relinquish the status markers that are everything to we competitive and pecking-order attuned humans'.[142] There is simply no room and no necessity for a ranking of members in the Body of Christ because the gifts are distributed just as the Spirit determines (1 Cor. 12:11).

If Paul's presentation of the Body of Christ, then, is one that defies

---

142 Brock, 'Theologizing the Body of Christ', 372.

societal expectations of power, elitism, and hierarchy, this must cause us to reflect upon those members of our church and broader communities who are too often the casualties of this kind of societal stratification. When our idea of being in church is focused only on the skills and talents we interpret as being God-given gifts, and focus on individual contributions to the body, those with apparently less-impressive talents are marginalised and can be seen by others—and potentially by themselves also—to have nothing valuable to contribute to the body (e.g. 'Now if the foot should say, "Because I am not a hand, I do not belong to the body", it would not for that reason stop being part of the body', 1 Cor. 12:15). But when we are prepared to embrace the image of the Body of Christ as a corporate body united in the Spirit through our weaknesses rather than our strengths, there is a complete reframing of what it means to be part of the Body of Christ. There is no need to attempt to rank or stratify roles or gifts amongst ourselves because we are all equally weak and equally limited—even though some members '*appear* weaker'—but we are also equally gifted by the Spirit to enact *charisma* and be vessels for the power of God to be displayed. In recognising that the only power that is demonstrated in the Body of Christ is God's power working through our weaknesses, then we have no choice but to be vulnerable and honest in respect to our individual failings and flaws. We are all—irrespective of our physical or intellectual abilities or disabilities—equal in our position in the body. There are no members who are superior and no members who are inferior in the Body of Christ. But all are called equally to serve as parts of the whole. It is from this position, in recognising our own vulnerability, limitations, and weaknesses, that what Paul saw demonstrated in his own life is likewise demonstrated with respect to the whole Body of Christ: God's power is made perfect in our weakness (2 Cor. 12:9).

Everyone who is in Christ is in the Body of Christ, and this should have a direct impact on the way our individual church communities include and value all the members of the body. Local church communities ought to emulate the inclusive nature of the body by limiting the barriers—physical, attitudinal, or theological—that prevent people with disability from being full participators in the life of the church. A disability reading of Paul's metaphor should emphasise that all members of the Body of Christ possess gifts given by God to demonstrate his grace in community with one another. God's gifts are not restricted to only certain members of the body, but all the members of the body, irrespective of physical or intellectual ability or lack thereof, have the ability to serve the Christian community through using their God-given gifts. As easy as it is to equate the spiritual gifts with natural talents and abilities, this is not the way Paul describes these gifts. Indeed, in doing so, we quantify and rank the gifts in the same way the Corinthian community used their social world to inform the status of individuals and value of the members in their own community. Instead, we are called to follow the model Paul gives of the Body of Christ as the site of interdependence, mutual service, and a valuing of all the members for their contributions to the body.

Section 4: Concluding Reflections

The Body of Christ passages in 1 Corinthians 12:3–8 and Romans 12:12–31 have proven popular with those writers working at the intersection of disability and biblical studies. The reason for this interest is that Paul's metaphors reveal an image of the Body of Christ that is fully inclusive with all the members of the body active and contributing meaningfully by using their gifts in service to the body. These writers express concern that without the participation of people with disability in local congregations, the Body of Christ is not functioning at full capacity as God intended. The absence or non-participation of people with disability, it is argued, results in a deficit in the body which leads to a disabling of the power and function of the Body of Christ. Such theological interpretations thus seek to encourage church communities to include people with disability and other marginal and excluded members for the sake of the whole body and to increase the reach and scope of the church in the world.

Such interpretations of the Body of Christ consider that each person who is in Christ possesses their own unique gifts which lie dormant and unused if members are not active participants in local church communities. Each member's gifts are considered a necessary contribution to the Body of Christ without which the whole body is weakened and thus disabled. However, by claiming that the Body of Christ is limited or 'disabled' without the presence and active participation of people with disability, these writers create an inevitable paradox. While saying that *people* with disability are valuable as they are in their current bodily form, these writers also suggest that the Body of Christ is 'disabled' without the inclusion of people with disability, but this corporate body with disability is *not* acceptable in its current 'disabled' form. It seems contradictory to be suggesting that people with disability are acceptable as they are and do not need to be fixed or healed, while simultaneously saying that the Body of Christ is disabled and must indeed be fixed or healed in order to achieve God's purposes for the church. The 'cure' for fixing the disablement and limitations of the 'disabled' church is presented as local churches and denominations proactively ensuring that people with disability are included and participating in church communities.

Such an interpretation is reliant on the belief that Paul envisions the Body of Christ as an amalgamation of all the combined gifts of the members. Scholars thus assume that the kind of body that Paul envisions the Body of Christ to be is one that is a perfectly balanced, whole, symmetrical body such as those bodies depicted in the other *homonoia* texts from the Greco-Roman world. Like the writers of the *homonoia* texts, Paul too envisions a body with all its members working together for the good of the whole body. However, Paul's presentation of the Body of Christ aims at inverting the existing methods of honouring some members over others as well as emphasising that all members of this body are equally valuable in their contribution to the body. This new vision of the corporate body features some of the traditional characteristics of the body politic imagery, but more significantly, Paul's presentation of the Body of Christ is informed by his understanding of the nature of the Kingdom of God as an example of inverted ideals. Paul refers to the message of the gospel as one that is 'foolish' (e.g. 1 Cor. 1:18, 21) and that God chooses the things the world considers shameful and dishonourable—especially the crucifixion of Jesus—to demonstrate his power and wisdom (1 Cor. 1:27). When Paul gives any consideration to the physical body of Jesus, while it is glorious and resurrected, it also concomitantly crucified and marked.[143] The metaphorical body of which believers are members, must therefore surely be for Paul a body that parallels the literal body of Jesus, which is physically limited and vulnerable and yet still hosting and demonstrating the power of God.

Just with Paul's physical descriptions of himself which subvert the traditional physiognomic ideals of bodily and moral perfection, the description Paul gives of the physical body of Jesus likewise leads us to consider Paul's descriptions of the physical body of Jesus as also interrupting the ancient bodily ideals of physiognomy. Though beaten and broken through his crucifixion, though put to death as a common criminal, Paul sees in these symbols of weakness the ultimate sign of God's power at work. But this is not the authoritarian, oppressive power envisaged by Paul's Stoic contemporaries but a power that resides wholly in humility, mercy, and self-sacrificial love: the power of God made perfect in human weakness (2 Cor. 12:9). This is the case for Paul not only in respect to his own life but is programmatic for God's relationship with the whole Body of Christ. It is not in their collective strengths but in their collective weaknesses that God's power is demonstrated amply through the members of the Body of Christ.

Paul's concern then is not whether people are included in the Body of Christ, because Paul knows that by virtue of being a member of this body, each member participates in the body. But rather, Paul's concern is in respect to the members' own attitudes toward the other members of the body as well as their attempts to remodel the Body of Christ in the likeness of the stratified and hierarchical systems of the outside world. The members of the Body of Christ in Corinth, though equal in status and value, had attempted to recreate the stratified world of the Roman Empire within the local church giving higher rank and value to some positions in the body over others. As a consequence, some members were over-valuing and others under-valuing the placement and function of various members within the body. Paul thus writes to the Corinthians to remind them of the real composition of the Body of Christ and to challenge their attempts at reproducing the existing

---

143 Paul even seems to allude to the marks on Jesus' body as referring to them on his own: 'From now on, let no one cause me trouble, for I bear on my body the marks of Jesus' (Gal. 6:17).

power and honour systems amongst the members of the Body of Christ. In this body, membership is not reliant on individual strength, power, status, or ability but resides wholly in the power and sovereignty of God enacted through the Spirit.

If Paul's emphasis in the Body of Christ passages is not on whether all the members are participating, but rather, is on the attitudes of each of the members towards the others, what, if anything, can we take away from Paul's Body of Christ imagery that might relate to the inclusion of people with disability in church communities? Firstly, Paul suggests that there are members that are being devalued in the church because they 'appear weaker' than other members. Paul contends that the nature of the church means it is a place of equality and interdependence. All the members have been placed together by God in order for them to work together in synchronicity. Modern churches, however, might be like some of the first century churches Paul was addressing, which were fooled by appearances, seeking out the power and strength demonstrated and admired in the Greco-Roman world around them. Paul contends, however, that the workings of the church are not hierarchical and relationships in the body should not in any way reflect the power struggles of the outside world. While some are judged as weaker with less impressive gifts, Paul says this is not actually the case, but rather, all have equally important gifts. But as a result of the lack of honour that is shown to these members considered weaker, Paul seeks to correct the imbalance of honour and status in the Corinthians church by encouraging the members to give greater honour to those members who have been overlooked and marginalised in the church. Paul sees this not as a new model of hierarchy to replace the old, but rather, the method of restoring balance and equilibrium to the unbalanced body.

In many respects, local church communities in the 21st century can also be fooled by focusing on those members who possess the most impressive or desirable gifts for their community. Rather than overlooking and dismissing the gifts of those members who are appear to be weaker due to disability, illness, ageing, non-English speaking backgrounds, poverty, or poor communication skills, Paul contends that all members of the Body of Christ have gifts that God uses to work through each of them. And despite these factors that people assume will limit God's capacity to be at work, in the Body of Christ, where God has placed all the members as he desired, all members, irrespective of intellectual or physical ability or disability are tools for God's Spirit to work for the 'common good' of the body. Our treatment of and attitudes toward people within our local church communities should be reflective of this inclusion giving honour to all members of the body.

Secondly, while numerous authors addressing disability issues consider the Body of Christ an organism whose power and authority is compromised through the absence of people with disability, it has been argued here that this is not the case. The Body of Christ has been put together with all members being interdependent and functioning together to see God's purposes fulfilled. No members of the body have more important roles than others and neither can any members of the body boast in their achievements. All the gifts have been selected and distributed by God to demonstrate his grace. It is not in the combined gifts and strengths of the individual members that makes the church effective, but it is simply God's work demonstrated powerfully through the limitations and weaknesses of all members. While we may judge each other based on appearances and attempt to rank ourselves in comparison to the gifts and abilities of other members, it is God who makes up for the limitations and deficiencies of the members of the body. The image of the body of Christ then is not just one of triumphant victory, but also the image of a body in service to one another in in honest recognition of our strengths and weaknesses. Susanne Rappman thus proposes that far from a symbol of power or strength, 'the church [is] a disabled and bruised community where God is present in shortcomings'.[144]

Reading the Body of Christ imagery from a disability perspective should cause us to reflect on the generosity of God in his distribution of gifts to all members of the body and the way in which the Body of Christ demonstrates the fully inclusive nature of the mission of God. This inclusive model should thus be the blueprint for creating inclusive congregations, not because the power and efficacy of the church is compromised without members with disability, but the reverse: the Body of Christ includes members of all varying abilities and disabilities, those

---

144 Rappmann, 'Disabled Body of Christ', 34.

who are competent in the eyes of the world, and those who are not, and so our local congregations should be a direct reflection and embodiment of this model of inclusion.

Reflecting on the imagery of the Body of Christ from a disability perspective should also cause us to re-shift our focus with respect to those we worship alongside in our Sunday services. Rather than questioning or doubting the giftedness of any member, ourselves included, Brock reminds us that '[t]he gift given by the disabled person, the poor person, the recovering addict, all those of low esteem to the world, emerges only through the spiritual discernment that is utterly certain that there is even in these unexpected places (in the eyes of fallen humanity) a *charisma* to be received'.[145] It should not surprise us then that people with disability are the recipients of God's grace-gifts, but rather, that God condescended to impart any of fallen humanity in their weakness and frailty with any kinds of gifts at all. This is indeed the embodiment of Paul's message of the inclusive Body of Christ.

Conclusion

In this chapter, we have examined Paul's use of the Body of Christ imagery in two locations in the Pauline corpus, that of Romans 12:3–8 and 1 Corinthians 12:12–31. Although the primary focus has been on the longer, more theologically-developed Pauline usage of this imagery in 1 Corinthians 12, the ancient context of the body politic imagery applies as much to Romans 12 as it does to 1 Corinthians 12. While Paul certainly appears to employ the same language and metaphor of the body politic that was attested regularly in *homonoia* texts from the Greco-Roman world, Paul's aim appears to be somewhat different. Rather than seeking to promote unity above all else and the existing hierarchy as the status quo, Paul instead appears to subvert these ideals, preferring to emphasise that the Body of Christ is characterised by diverse members who are all important and valued equally in the body.

In considering the image of the Body of Christ in both Romans 12

---

145 Brock, 'Theologizing Inclusion', 372.

and 1 Corinthians 12, scholars interested in the overlap of disability and biblical studies have focused their attention on the Body of Christ as the site of strength and power. In doing so, the absence and non-participation of certain groups of people, in particular those with disability, is considered problematic and compromising the efficacy of the whole body. However, by reframing the discussion of the Body of Christ as the model through whom the local church is to find its structure and purpose forces us to seek out those with disability not merely to prop up a weakened and failing body, but to represent the fully inclusive nature of the Body of Christ demonstrated through the generosity of God in distributing gifts to all members equally.

Bibliography

Primary Sources

Aelius Aristides	*Orations* (LCL; 4 vols.; C.A. Behr, transl.; London & Cambridge, Mass.: Heinemann & Harvard University Press, 1973; M. Trapp, transl., 2017).
Aesop	*Aesop's Fables* (Jack Zipes, transl.; London & New York: Penguin, 1996).
Aristotle	*Athenian Constitution: Eudemian Ethics. Virtues and Vices* (LCL; H. Rackham, transl.; Cambridge, MA: Harvard University Press, 1935).
Aristotle	*Minor Works: On Colours. On Things Heard. Physiognomics. On Plants. On Marvellous Things Heard. Mechanical Problems. On Indivisible Lines. The Situations and Names of Winds. On Melissus, Xenophanes, Gorgias* (LCL; W.S. Hett, transl.; Cambridge: Harvard University Press, 1936).
Cicero	*Orations: Philippics* (LCL; 2 vols.; D.R. Shackleton Bailey, transl.; Cambridge: Harvard University Press, 2009–2010).
Cicero	*The Orations of Marcus Tullius Cicero* (C.D. Yonge, transl.; London: G. Bell & Sons, 1856).
Dio Chrysostom	*Dio Chrysostom* II. *Discourses 12–30* (LCL; J.H. Cohoon, transl.; Cambridge, Mass.: Harvard University Press, 1939)

Dio Chrysostom	*Dio Chrysostom* III. *Discourses 31–36* (LCL; J.H. Cohoon & H.L. Crosby, transls.; Cambridge, Mass.: Harvard University Press, 1940).
Dio Chrysostom	*Dio Chrysostom* IV. *Discourses 37–60* (LCL; H.L. Crosby, transl.; Cambridge, Mass.: Harvard University Press, 1946).
Florus	*Epitome of Roman History* (LCL 231; E.S. Forster, transl.; Cambridge: Harvard University Press, 1984 [1929]).
Galen	*A Translation of Galen's Hygiene* (*De Sanitate Tuenda*) (Robert Montraville Green, transl.; Springfield: Thomas, 1951).
Hippocrates	(LCL; William H. S. Jones, E. T. Withington, & Paul Potter, transls.; 10 vols.; Cambridge: Harvard University Press, 1923–2012).
Josephus	*The Works of Flavius Josephus* (William Whiston, transl.; Edinburgh: W.P. Nimno, Hay & Mitchell, 1895).
Philo	*Philo* (LCL; Francis H. Colson & G.H. Whitaker, transls.; 10 vols.; Cambridge: Harvard University Press, 1929–1962).
Plato	*Republic, Volume I: Books 1–5* (LCL 237; Christopher Emlyn-Jones, William Preddy, eds. & transls.; Cambridge, MA: Harvard University Press, 2013).
Plutarch	*Lives* (LCL; Bernadotte Perrin, transl.; 11 vols.; Cambridge, MA: Harvard University Press, 1914–1926).
Plutarch	*Moralia. Volume X* (LCL 321; Harold North Fowler, transl.; Cambridge, MA: Harvard University Press, 1936).
Quintilian	*The Instituto oratorio of Quintilian* (LCL; Harold E. Butler, transl.; 4 vols.; Cambridge, MA: Harvard University Press, 1920–1922).
Schneemelcher, Wilhelm	*New Testament Apocrypha Volume 2: Writings Relating to the Apostles: Apocalypses and Related Subjects* (London: Lutterworth, 1965). (=*NTApoc.*)
Seneca	*Moral Essays, Volume I: De Providentia. De Constantia. De Ira. De Clementia* (LCL 214; John W. Basore, transl.; Cambridge, MA: Harvard University Press, 1928).
Seneca	*Lucius Annaeus Seneca Anger, Mercy, Revenge* (Robert A. Kaster & Martha C. Nussbaum, transls.; Chicago: University of Chicago Press, 2010).

Tacitus	*Agricola. Germania. Dialogue on Oratory* (LCL 35; M. Hutton, W. Peterson, transls.; Revised by R. M. Ogilvie, E. H. Warmington, Michael Winterbottom; Cambridge, MA: Harvard University Press, 1914).
Tacitus	*Histories: Books 1–3* (LCL 111; Clifford H. Moore, transl.; Cambridge, MA: Harvard University Press, 1925).
Thucydides	*History of the Peloponnesian War*, Volume IV (LCL 169; C.F. Smith, transl.; Cambridge, MA: Harvard University Press, 1923.
Vitruvius	*On Architecture: Volume II: Books 6–10* (LCL; Frank Granger, transl.; Cambridge, MA: Harvard University Press, 1934).

Secondary Sources

Australian Bureau of Statistics	'Disability, Ageing and Carers, Australia', [2015]. Access: 17 March 2019. https://www.abs.gov.au
Bailey, Kenneth E.	*Paul Through Mediterranean Eyes: Cultural Studies in 1 Corinthians* (Downers Grove: IVP, 2011).
Barrett, C.K.	*First Epistle to the Corinthians* (London: A&C Black, 1992 2nd ed.).
Bertram, Georg	ἔργον, ἐργάζομαι, ἐργάτης, ἐργασία, ἐνεργής, ἐνέργεια, ἐνεργέω, ἐνέργημα, εὐεργεσία, εὐεργετέω, ευεργέτης', in Gerhard Kittel (ed.), *Theological Dictionary of the New Testament* (Geoffrey W. Bromiley, transl.; Grand Rapids: Eerdmans, 1964), 2.635–655.
Birch, Bruce C.	'Impairment as a Condition in Biblical Scholarship: A Response', in Hector Avalos, Sarah J. Melcher, & Jeremy Schipper (eds.), *This Abled Body: Rethinking Disabilities in Biblical Studies* (Semeia Studies 55; Atlanta: SBL, 2007), 185–196.
Brock, Brian	'Theologizing Inclusion: 1 Corinthians 12 and the Politics of the Body of Christ', *Journal of Religion, Disability, and Health* 15.4 (2011), 351–376.
Brock, Roger	'Sickness in the Body Politic', in Valerie M. Hope & Eireann Marshall (eds.), *Death and Disease in the Ancient City* (London: Routledge, 2000), 24–34.

Brookins, Timothy A. 'Paul and the Ancient Body Metaphor: Reassessing Parallels', *Journal for the Study of Paul and His Letters* 6 (2016), 75-98.

Bruce, F.F. *1 and 2 Corinthians* (NCB; Grand Rapids: Eerdmans, 1980).

Bultmann, Rudolf *New Testament Theology* (2 vols.; New York: Scribner, 1951).

Canavan, Rosemary *Clothing the Body of Christ at Colossae: A Visual Construction of Identity* (WUNT II 334; Mohr Siebeck: Tübingen, 2012).

Carter, Timothy L. 'Looking at the Metaphor of Christ's Body in 1 Corinthians 12', in Stanley E. Porter (ed.), *Paul: Jew, Greek, and Roman* (Leiden: Brill, 2008), 93-115.

Ciampa, Roy E., & Brian S. Rosner *First Letter to the Corinthians* (PNTC; Grand Rapids: Eerdmans, 2010).

Clarke Kosak, Jennifer B. *'Polis Nosousa:* Greek Ideas about the City and Disease in the Fifth Century b.c.', in Valerie M. Hope & Eireann Marshall (eds.), *Death and Disease in the Ancient City* (London: Routledge, 2000), 35-54.

Collins, Raymond F. *First Corinthians* (SP 7; Collegeville: Liturgical Press, 1999).

Conzelmann, Hans *1 Corinthians* (Hermeneia; Philadelphia: Fortress Press, 1975).

Creamer, Deborah B. *Disability and Christian Theology: Embodied Limits and Constructive Possibilities* (Oxford: Oxford University Press, 2009).

Dewey, Arthur 'Paul and the Remapping of the Body', *Classical Bulletin* 86.1 (2010), 97-129.

Douglas, Mary *Purity and Danger: An Analysis of Concepts of Pollution and Taboo* (New York: Hammondsworth, 1966).

Dunn, James D. G. *Romans 9-16* (WBC; Dallas: Word, 1988).

Dunn, James D. G. *The Theology of Paul the Apostle* (Grand Rapids: Eerdmans, 1998).

Dutch, Robert *The Educated Elite in 1 Corinthians: Education and Community Conflict in Graeco-Roman Context* (LNTS 271; London: T&T Clark, 2005).

Edwards, James R. *Romans* (NIBC; Peabody: Hendrickson, 1992).

Fee, Gordon D. The First Epistle to the Corinthians (NICNT; Grand Rapids: Eerdmans, 1987).

Forbes, Jason, & Lindsey Gale 'Disability in the Australian Church: Results from the 2011 Church Life Survey', in Andrew Picard & Myk Habets (eds.), *Theology and the Experience of Disability: Interdisciplinary Perspectives from Voices Down Under* (Abingdon: Routledge, 2016), 95–117.

Garland, David E. *1 Corinthians* (BECNT; Grand Rapids: Baker, 2008).

Gaventa, William C. 'Preaching Disability: The Whole of Christ's Body in Word and Practice', *Review and Expositor* 113.2 (2016), 225–242.

George, Samuel 'Voices and Visions from the Margins on Mission and Unity: A Disability-Informed Reading of the Pauline Metaphor of the Church as the Body of Christ', *International Review of Mission* 100.1 (2011), 96–103.

Gosbell, Louise A. *'The Poor, the Crippled, the Blind, and the Lame': Physical and Sensory Disability in the Gospels of the New Testament* (WUNT II 469; Mohr Siebeck: Tübingen, 2018).

Gould, James B. *Practicing Prayer for the Dead: Its Theological Meaning and Spiritual Value* (Eugene: Cascade Books, 2016).

Graumann, Lutz A. 'Monstrous Births and Retrospective Diagnosis: The Case of Hermaphrodites in Antiquity', in Christian Laes, C. F. Goodey, and M. Lynn Rose (eds.), *Disabilities in Roman Antiquity: Disparate Bodies: a capite ad calcem* (Leiden: Brill, 2013), 181–209.

Gundry, Robert H. *Sōma in Biblical Theology: With an Emphasis on Pauline Anthropology* (Cambridge: Cambridge University Press, 1976).

Harrill, J. Albert *Slaves in the New Testament: Literary, Social and Moral Dimensions* (Minneapolis: Fortress, 2006).

Hedges-Goettl, Barbara J. 'Thinking Theologically about Inclusion: Disability, Imago Dei and the Body of Christ', *Journal of Religion, Disability and Health* 6.4 (2002), 7–30.

Hicks, Ruth Ilsley 'The Body Political and the Body Ecclesiastical', *Journal of Bible and Religion* 31.1 (1963), 29-35.

Horsley, Richard A. '1 Corinthians: A Case Study of Paul's Assembly as an Alternative Society', in Richard A. Horsely (ed.), *Paul and Empire: Religion and Power in Roman Imperial Society* (Harrisburg: Bloomsbury Academic, 1997), 206–214.

Jewett, Robert *Paul's Anthropological Terms: A Study of Their Use in Conflict Settings* (Leiden: Brill, 1971).

Judge, E.A. 'Demythologising the Church: What is the Meaning of "the Body of Christ"?', in E.A. Judge, *The First Christians in the Roman World* (James R. Harrison, ed.; WUNT 229; Tübingen: Mohr Siebeck, 2008), 568–585.

Junior, Nyasha, & Jeremy Schipper 'Disability Studies and the Bible', in Steven L. McKenzie & John Kaltner (eds.), *New Meanings for Ancient Texts: Recent Approaches to Biblical Criticisms and Their Applications* (Louisville: Westminster/John Knox, 2013), 21–38.

Käsemann, Ernst *Leib und Leib Christi: Eine Untersuchung zur paulinischen Begrifflichkeit* (Beiträge zur historischen Theologie; Tubingen: Mohr Siebeck, 1933).

Käsemann, Ernst 'The Theological Problem Presented by the Motif of the Body of Christ', in *Perspectives in Paul* (Margaret Kohl, transl.; London: SCM, 1971), 102–121.

Laes, C., C. F. Goodey, & M. Lynn Rose (eds.) *Disabilities in Roman Antiquity: Disparate Bodies;* a capite ad calcem (Leiden: Brill, 2013).

Lawrence, Louise *Sense and Stigma in the Gospels: Depictions of Sensory-Disabled Characters* (Oxford: Oxford University Press, 2013).

Lee, Michelle V. *Paul, the Stoics, and the Body of Christ* (SNTSMS 137; Cambridge: Cambridge University Press, 2006).

Leven, Karl-Heinz. '"At times these ancient facts seem to lie before me like a patient on a hospital bed"—Retrospective Diagnosis and Ancient Medical History', in Herman F.J. Horstmanshoff & Marten Stol (eds.), *Magic and Rationality in Ancient Near Eastern and Graeco-Roman Medicine* (Studies in Ancient Medicine 27; Leiden: Brill, 2004), 369–386.

Lim, Kar Yong *Metaphors and Social Identity Formation in Paul's Letters to the Corinthians* (Eugene: Pickwick Publications, 2017).

Longenecker, Richard N. *The Epistle to the Romans* (NIGTC; Grand Rapids: Eerdmans, 2016).

Lowe, Mary Elise 'Re-Embracing the Body of Jesus Christ: A Queer, Lutheran Theology of the Body of Christ', in Carl-Hennic Grenholm & Göran Gunner (eds.), *Lutheran Identity and Political Theology* (Church of Sweden Research Series volume 9; Eugene: Pickwick, 2014), 117-133.

Maier, Harry O. *Picturing Paul in Empire: Imperial Image, Text and Persuasion in Colossians, Ephesians, and the Pastoral Epistles* (London: Bloomsbury, 2013).

Martin, Dale B. *The Corinthian Body* (New Haven: Yale University Press, 1995).

McCloughry, Roy, & Wayne Morris *Making a World of Difference: Christian Reflections on Disability* (London: SPCK, 2002).

Mitchell, M. Margaret *Paul and Rhetoric of Reconciliation: An Exegetical Investigation of the Language and Composition of 1 Corinthians* (Hermeneutische Untersuchungen zur Theologie 28; Tubingen: Mohr Siebeck, 1991).

Moltmann, Jürgen 'The Knowing of the Other and the Community of the Different', in Jürgen Moltmann (ed.), *God for a Secular Society* (M. Kohl, transl.; London: SCM, 1999), 135–152.

Monteith, Graham *Epistles of Inclusion: St Paul's Inspired Attitudes* (Guildford: Grosvenor House, 2010).

Morris, Leon L. *The Epistle to the Romans* (Grand Rapids: Eerdmans, 1988).

Moss, Candida R., & Jeremy Schipper 'Introduction', in Candida R. Moss & Jeremy Schipper (ed.), *Disability Studies and Biblical Literature* (New York: Palgrave Macmillan, 2011), 1–11.

Murray, John *The Epistle to the Romans* (NTC; Grand Rapids: Eerdmans, 1997).

Neyrey, Jerome H. *Paul in Other Words: A Cultural Reading of his Letters* (Louisville: Westminster, 1990).

Olyan, Saul M. *Disability in the Hebrew Bible: Interpreting Mental and Physical Differences* (Cambridge: Cambridge University Press, 2008).

Parsons, Mikael C. *Body and Character in Luke-Acts: The Subversion of Physiognomy in Early Christianity* (Grand Rapids: Baker, 2006).

Peterlin, Davorin 'Stomach, Hands, Legs, Feet, Eyes, Ears, Mouth, Upper and Lower Teeth, Molars, Eyebrows and Head: The Unity of Christians and the Ancient *Topos* of Body and Members', *Evangelical Journal of Theology* 4.1 (2010), 63–83.

Raphael, Rebecca *Biblical Corpora: Representations of Disability in Hebrew Biblical Literature* (Library of Hebrew Bible/Old Testament Studies 445; London: T&T Clark International, 2008).

Rappmann, Susanne 'The Disabled Body of Christ as a Critical Metaphor—Towards a Theory', *Journal of Religion, Disability and Health* 7.4 (2003), 25–40.

Rawlinson, A.E.J. 'Corpus Christi', in G.K.A. Bell & A. Deissmann (eds.), *Mysterium Christi* (London: Longmans, 1930), 225-244.

Reynolds, Thomas E. *Vulnerable Communion: A Theology of Disability and Hospitality* (Grand Rapids: Brazos Press, 2008).

Rose, Martha L. *The Staff of Oedipus: Transforming Disability in Ancient Greece* (Ann Arbor: University of Michigan Press, 2003).

Smit, J.F.M. 'Two Puzzles: 1 Cor 12:31 and 13:3: Rhetorical Solutions', *New Testament Studies* 39 (1993), 246–264.

Smith, Daniel Lynwood 'Why Paul's Fabulous Body is Missing its Belly: The Rhetorical Subversion of Menenius Agrippa's Fable in 1 Corinthians 12.12-30', *Journal for the Study of the New Testament* 41.2 (2018), 143-160.

Squire, Michael '*Corpus imperii*: Verbal and Visual Figurations of the Roman "body politic"', *Word and Image* 31.3 (2015), 305–330.

Thiselton, Anthony C. *The First Letter to the Corinthians* (NIGTC; Grand Rapids: Eerdmans, 2000).

Troupe, Carol 'One Body, Many Parts: A Reading of 1 Corinthians 12:12-27', *Black Theology* 6 (2008), 32-45.

Tutu, Desmond *God Has a Dream: A Vision of Hope for Our Times* (Reading: Ebury Publishing, 2005).

van Klinken, Adriaan S. '"The Body of Christ has Aids": A Study on the Notion of the Body of Christ in African Theologies Responding to HIV and AIDS', *Missionalia* 36.2-3 (2008), 319-336.

Welborn, L.L. *Paul, the Fool of Christ: A Study of 1 Corinthians 1–4 in the Comic-Philosophic Tradition* (London: T&T Clark, 2005).

Witherington, Ben, III *Conflict and the Community in Corinth: A Socio-Rhetorical Commentary on 1 and 2 Corinthians* (Grand Rapids: Eerdmans, 1994).

Yoder, John Howard *Body Politics: Five Practices of the Christian Community before the Watching World* (Scottdale: Herald Press, 2001).

Yong, Amos *The Bible, Disability and the Church: A New Vision of the People of God* (Grand Rapids: Eerdmans, 2011).

Yorke, Gosnell L.O.R. *The Church as the Body of Christ in the Pauline Corpus* (Lanham: University Press of America, 1991).

CHAPTER 12

Paul's Legacy in Romans and the Confession Inscriptions of Asia Minor: The Difficulty of Moving Beyond Divine Justice to Mercy in Antiquity

James R. Harrison

The Gentile converts of Paul would have inherited from the first-century Graeco-Roman reciprocity system a series of deeply ingrained beliefs about the operation of divine and human grace. In the world-view of the ancients, the principle of *do ut des* ('I give in order that you may give') governed the contract between the gods and their worshippers. A cycle of grace, initiated from the human side, unfolds the dynamics of the relationship. Cultic ritual prepares the ground for the gods' favour; the gods then dispense benefactions; the recipient returns gratitude and exhibits continued reverence in the gods' service; the gods, with consummate fairness, reciprocate the worshipper's piety and offerings with gratitude. Caution, nevertheless, is merited here. The assertion that the requital of obligation is the universal dynamic underlying operations of the reciprocity system requires nuancing in particular instances.[1] The proposition that the gods were never merciful unless they were solicited beforehand by cult or prayer is, as we will see, also not universally true in antiquity. But, overall, the cycle of grace revealed in the honorific inscriptions encapsulates how relationships with the gods worked in antiquity.

However, the inscriptions reveal that serious disruptions to the divine allocation of grace could periodically occur, precipitated by cultic or purity anomalies in the activities of the temples, or by impure individuals in their sacred spaces that provoked the divine wrath. Also the perceived indifference of the gods raised the perplexing issue of theodicy in the writings of the Graeco-Roman philosophers and, more mundanely, in the inscriptional epitaphs of the dead. The mercy of the gods is affirmed in the honorific inscriptions in a variety of thanksgiving contexts, but while the gods can be powerful friends, they can equally be very dangerous enemies. How, then, does one move beyond the demands of divine justice to an experience of divine mercy in the Mediterranean world? And how does this transition work out in social relations?

This chapter will first explore the inscriptional ἴλεως ('mercy') terminology of Asia Minor, prefacing an investigation of disruptions to the mercy of the gods in antiquity and how the ancients reacted to these, focusing in particular on the thorny issue of divine justice. With this background established, it will examine the modern scholarly debate concerning the rise of early Christianity and the Lydian-Phrygian confession inscriptions and the relationships with the gods evinced therein. How does this intersect with the Pauline understanding of divine justice and mercy in the epistle to the Romans articulated a century before the genre of confession inscription flourished in Asia Minor? What

---

1   I am grateful for Dr Alan Cadwallader's comments on a preliminary version of this chapter, acknowledged throughout in the footnotes below. For a nuanced understanding of obligation in the ancient reciprocity system, see Parker, 'Pleasing Thighs'; Konstan, 'The Freedom to Feel Grateful'. More generally on the gods and reciprocity, see Straten, 'Gifts for the Gods'; Bremer, 'The Reciprocity of Giving and Thanksgiving in Greek Worship'; Wildberg, 'Piety as Service, Epiphany as Reciprocity'; Peel, 'Thwarted Expectations of Divine Reciprocity'. For recent collections of essays on gift giving in antiquity, see Satlow, *The Gift in Antiquity*; Carlà & Gori, *Gift Giving*. On χάρις, the gods and reciprocity, see Harrison, *Paul's Language of Grace in Its Graeco-Roman Context*, 53–57, 85–87. Abbreviations for Old and New Testament sources, primary and secondary, conform to Alexander, et al., *SBL Handbook*.

ideological legacy did Paul's teaching leave for the discourse in antiquity regarding justice and mercy, divine and human?

The date range of epigraphic evidence covered is from the III. cent. B.C.—III. cent A.D. Although some of this evidence post-dates the New Testament period by two centuries and is therefore subject to the charge of anachronism as far as the selection of documents, readers are reminded that that the volume in which this essay appears is concerned with the *legacy* of Romans. There is an intrinsic interest in seeing how Paul's gospel of justifying grace in Romans would have been perceived from the viewpoint of second and third century A.D. eastern Mediterranean auditors as much as from the perspective of its original first-century audience in the capital of the Roman Empire.

1. The Mercy of the Gods in Asia Minor: The Inscriptional ἵλεως Terminology

We will confine our investigation of divine mercy to the epigraphic ἵλεως terminology from Asia Minor. Apart from the widespread use of the language of grace (χάρις) for divine beneficence in antiquity,[2] the gods themselves are also depicted as dispensing 'mercy' and being propitious to their worshippers' prayer requests and dedications.[3] The first two examples demonstrate how the propitiousness of the god/gods is delicately balanced against the wrath of the gods. First, a IV cent. B.C. purity regulation from Metropolis threatens the withdrawal of divine mercy from those who violate funeral and sexual purity rites, turn away suppliants at the sanctuary, or act in an unrighteous manner towards the worshippers: 'Whoever does something unrighteous, the Gallesian Mother will not be merciful (εἴλως) towards him'.[4] The converse, however, must be also true: those who abide by the purity regulations will experience divine mercy.

---

2   See Harrison, *Paul's Language of Grace*.
3   The 'mercy' of the gods in antiquity has only been studied primarily from the viewpoint of the ancient philosophers: see Bordt, 'Platon über Gottes Zorn', and Schenk, 'Darstellung und Funktion des Zorns'. However, see also Harris, 'The Idea of Mercy', and Judge, 'The Quest for Mercy'. On the 'pity' of the gods in antiquity, see Konstan, *Pity Transformed*, 109–119.
4   IEph 7.1.3401.

Second, the regulations for a private cult in Philadelphia (I cent. B.C.) details the necessity of a freeborn woman to be sexually chaste, having intimate relations with no other man than her husband, and not participating in the sacrifices, purifications, and mysteries of the cult if she has been unchaste. She is threatened with evil curses if she violates any of these ordinances. But, remarkably, the inscription elaborates that the god does not want to be vengeful but instead merciful and beneficent to the obedient (or πιστός), the category of worshipper that the gods always love in principle:

> For the god does not desire these things to happen at all, nor does he wish it, but he wants obedience. The gods will be gracious ([ἔ]σονται ἵλεως) to those who obey, and always give them all good things, whatever gods give to men whom they love (ὃυς φιλοῦσιν). But should any transgress, they shall hate such people and inflict upon them great punishments.[5]

Here we see the gods' merciful character exalted over against their desire to inflict punishment. This feature is unusual in the honorific inscriptions.

Other Asian inscriptions underscore the propitiousness or graciousness of the gods,[6] but the initiative is routinely with the suppliant, who by his piety and cultic worshipfulness elicits the kindness of the gods. Attalos, a victor in the games of the Asian League and worshipper of the gods, makes a dedication to Saviour Hekatē and torch-bearing Artemis, 'the gracious goddesses' (τὰς εἵλεως θεάς: IvP 3.119 [Pergamum]). Demetrios requests 'great Zeus in heaven' to be gracious to him (εἵλεως μοι: B.C.H 7 [1883], 322, 52 [Malakopea in Cappadocia]). Another suppliant makes the following request (MAMA 8.297 [Ikonion, Lyaconia]): 'I pray to the Saviour gods, both Agdistis and the great mother Boethene and the [...] Apollo and Artemis, (to be) gracious (ἵλεως) and b[enevolent t]o the colony Ikonion'.

In an intriguing inscription, Argeios, son of Phanekritos, erected a

---

5   *SIG*³ 985. For translation, see Barton & Horsley, 'A Hellenistic Cult Group'; Hanges, *Paul, Founder of* Churches, 260-304.
6   For the rare epigraphic occurrence of ἱλάσκομαι in Asia (all oracles), see *SIG*³ 1044 (Halicarnassos); *SEG* 14.655, 15.632, 17.493, 40.1109 (Kaunos); *SEG* 17. 493.

stele on behalf of the health of both his wife and the safety of Phanekritos. He expresses his prayer wish to Apollo Pituaēnos regarding his family thus (TAM 5.2.881 [Thyateira, Lydia: 276/5 B.C.]): 'Therefore may Apollo be always merciful (ἵλεως) to Argeios and his wife and children and brothers'. Unusually, the prayer-wish seems to be made in this instance as a response to the prior beneficence of Apollo in rescuing his father, 'who had been seized by the Galatians'. However, the erection of the stele by the grateful suppliant secures the likelihood of future divine beneficence and enables him to ask boldly for mercy throughout all time (διὰ παντός) towards his family.

In conclusion, the experience of such unsolicited divine beneficence preceding the prayer wish is highly unusual in the epigraphic context of Asia Minor: normally the prior prayer-wish or cultic offering elicits the mercy of the god/s.[7]

2. Reactions to Disruptions of Divine Mercy

Although the gods regularly dispensed favours and mercy to suppliants, as the inscriptions above testify, the relations between the gods and their dependents were fraught with dangers and ambiguities and had to be approached carefully. A particularly valuable inscription in this regard is the dice oracle of Kremna in Central Pisidia, carved on all four sides of a tall rectangular pillar in the centre of the west side of the forum.[8] The fifty-six responses of the oracle are secured in each case by five throws of the dice, the sum of which leads the inquirer to the particular oracle of the god after whom each throw is named.

Most of the oracles dispense a 'prosperity theology', with various qualifications punctuating the promises dispensed to the inquirer. However, occasionally, there are clear limits to the unqualified grace of the god consulted. For example, the favour of Olympian Zeus is only

---

7   However, there are inscriptions and papyri recording offerings or thanksgivings to the god/s as *responses of gratitude* for slave manumissions, dream guidance regarding a mission of benefaction (Grant, *Hellenistic Religions*, 144–145), dream revelations at Epidauros resulting in 43 healings (IG IV² 1 §§121–22), divine rescues (TAM 5.2.881), among others. For the manumission inscriptions with translations, see Meyer, 'The Greek Manumissions Project'.
8   Horsley & Mitchell, *The Inscriptions of Central Pisidia*, §5.

available to those who 'appease Aphrodite and the son of Maia' (A. I; cf. A. XI). Elsewhere, the oracles caution that one has to 'obey the gods and be hopeful' (C. XXXI). But the danger of showing hubris is also strongly underscored a several junctures:

> You are kicking against the goads, you are struggling against the waves that oppose you. You are looking for a fish in the ocean, don't hurry into the matter. It is not profitable for you to force the gods inopportunely.[9]

Or again:

> Throwing seeds and writing letters on the ocean, both are pointless toil and a fruitless task. Since you are a mortal do not force the god, who will do you some harm.[10]

In sum, the grace of the gods cannot be presumed upon: tread warily, the ancients were advised, because the temperament of deities was unpredictable and especially vindictive towards the ritually disobedient.[11] The latter point finds chilling confirmation in the many inscriptions dedicated in antiquity to deities who had previously imposed punishment upon their suppliants.[12] To say this is not denying that there were spontaneous and intensely felt celebrations of the mercy of the gods by grateful suppliants in antiquity, some of which are noted above.[13] But often the mercy was conditional, being somehow dependent on the worthiness of the worshipper.[14]

---

9 Horsley & Mitchell, *The Inscriptions of Central Pisidia*, B. XIV. Similarly, B. XV: 'Don't devise awful thoughts or make prayers against the Daimones'. Once again: 'Don't strive in vain, like the bitch that gave birth to a blind whelp' (B. XXI; cf. C. XXXII).
10 Horsley & Mitchell, *The Inscriptions of Central Pisidia*, C. XLV.
11 Note in this regard the warning in an inscription from Sounion (Attica): 'Anyone who interferes with the god's possessions or is meddlesome, let him incur sin against Men Tyrannos which he certainly cannot expiate'; Horsley, 'Expiation and the Cult of Men', 21.
12 For examples, see Horsley, 'Two Confession Texts'; 'Expiation and the Cult of Men', 27; MacMullen & Lane, *Paganism and Christianity*, §7.10, 104–105.
13 For example, MacMullen & Lane, *Paganism and Christianity*, §7.3.
14 For example, see the dedication to the demi-god Heracles by Lucius Mummius, destroyer of Corinth in 146 b.c., who concludes with this appeal to the god: 'for this and other gifts grant thy blessings to a deserving man' (*CIL* I. 2). For a translation, see Grant, *Ancient Roman Religion*, 230. In this regard, see also the discussion of the Isis aretalogy in Strom, *Reframing Paul*, 118–119.

Another remarkable inscription from North Galatia highlights the plight of parents faced with the demand of reciprocity towards the gods: how do parents return thanks to the gods who had indifferently presided over the death of their three children? The answer is simple: as per the demands of the reciprocity system, one returns 'thanks' to the gods—but, in this case, a 'thankless thanks' (ἄχαρις χάρις). This is the only place where this unique phrase is used in the entire corpus of eastern Mediterranean Greek inscriptions collated by the Packard Humanities Institute.[15] Although the inscription postdates the New Testament period, belonging to the mid third century A.D., it eloquently captures the dilemma of the ancients as they struggled to reconcile the reciprocity system with the arbitrary justice of the gods:

> The fates have seen the place which is always just, and fixed the end of life as our portion. For they have snatched away the finest bloom of beloved youth and we shall no more arrive at the prime (?) of life. This tomb conceals first of all our virgin sister, called Olympias, and then to us, prematurely dead. Theseus was the eldest brother, and my name was Amemptos, a child, younger in age. His cheeks bloomed with a thin down and he was in the flower of youth, like the gods. Theseus died in the winter, then Amemptos in the fourth month, at the beginning of summer. Here may be seen the thankless thank offering (ἄχαρις χάρις) of their wretched parents, a libation on the tomb for their children who died before their wedding day. First virgin Olympias, then Theseus with the unflawed bloom on his cheeks, then a third end took away Amemptos. They lie here as a common family and the tomb has joined their remains together.[16]

---

15 Dr Alan Cadwallader also pointed me to the interesting epigram (MAMA 7.156, restored further at *SEG* 30.1477) that speaks of dying in a 'thankless/graceless era' (ἄχαρις χρόνος).
16 Mitchell, *Regional Epigraphic Catalogues of Asia Minor*, §392.

3. Unleashing the Gods: Approaching Divine Justice in Antiquity

Other than the 'thankless thanks' of our Northern Galatian tombstone above, we still have not gained sufficient insight into the variety of strategies adopted by the ancients in handling the indifferent or vengeful gods of antiquity.[17] A vastly different approach to the issue is found in the inscriptional imprecations against grave desecration, which belong mainly to the third century A.D. of the imperial period.[18] The gods are invoked to act with great vengefulness against those who desecrate funeral monuments, specific crimes against the civic funeral laws, and the alienation of the grave, either by selling it or buying it for anything other than its original purpose.[19] In the view of Strubbe, the imprecations are publically inscribed for all to see at the grave site because of the widespread 'belief in the inefficacy of civil justice', with imprecations becoming a legitimate 'means of deterring and punishing a desecrator whose crime has not been noticed'.[20] Consequently, the more vengeful the divine imprecation invoked, the more likely that justice will be upheld by the gods, irrespective of whether the civil courts are inadequate or the crime of the desecrator has been unobserved by any member of the Hieropolitan public.

A superb example of this tendency is found in the imprecatory inscription of P. Ail. Apollinarios Makedon and his wife (?) Neratia Apollonis on a marble sarcophagus, placed on a large bomos, at Hierapolis in north-west Phrygia.[21] After outlining the fines against those who might interfere with the burial site, the inscription (second half of II. cent. AD), inscribed both on the sarcophagus and the bomos, says:

> The man who does anything against the prescriptions will be liable to fines, and may he not know the pleasure of children and of life, may the earth be not accessible and the sea

---

17 See also the reaction of Cercidas the Cynic to divine theodicy in *P. Oxy.* 8.1082 (Harrison, *Paul's Language of Grace*, 198–199). Additionally, on the fickleness of the gods, see Harris, 'Roman Opinions about the Truthfulness of Dreams'.
18 See Strubbe, ΑΡΑΙ ΕΠΙΤΥΜΒΙΟΙ, xiv.
19 Strubbe, ΑΡΑΙ ΕΠΙΤΥΜΒΙΟΙ, xiii.
20 Strubbe, ΑΡΑΙ ΕΠΙΤΥΜΒΙΟΙ, xiii.
21 Strubbe, ΑΡΑΙ ΕΠΙΤΥΜΒΙΟΙ, §285.

not navigable, but may he die with all sufferings, childless (ἄκτενος) and destitute (ἄβιος) and deformed (πηρός), and may he find after his death the gods of the underworld punishing and enraged (τιμωρούς), both the man who has ordered it to be built or made, and the workman.²²

The unusual savagery of the retributive justice invoked in this particular inscription can be deduced from the fact that among J. Strubbe's collection of 404 imprecations,²³ the words ἄβιος ('destitute') and πηρός (literally, 'disabled in a limb', 'maimed') are only found in this inscription. Furthermore, not only are the gods of the underworld punishing according to the justice of civic prescriptions, with their clearly stipulated fines, but they are also depicted as 'enraged' (τιμωρούς). This heightening of the divine emotions is unusual. From a search of all the inscriptions from the province of Asia,²⁴ the word τιμωρός only occurs in this particular inscription, apart from one other instance where the editor has restored the word along with its accompanying phrase (MDAI[A] 27 [1902], 138, 170: μετὰ [θάνατον ἔχοι τοὺς ὑποχθονίους θεοὺς τιμωρούς]). The composer of our inscription is heightening the ideological stakes by extending the scope and fury of the retributive justice that the underground deities will invoke against those undermining civil justice.

Clearly the Hierapolitan upper middle classes and elites, who articulated their social values by means of their grandiose tombs and carefully composed inscriptions,²⁵ are deliberately magnifying the power and retributive justice of the underground gods. One should also remember in this regard that the priestly Galloi descended to worship the underground deities in the famous Plutonium of Hierapolis.²⁶ We are probably witnessing another case of the city's Second Sophistic enhancement of its indigenous mythic and civic identity by means of its

---

22   Strubbe, APAI EPITYMBIOI, §285 *ll.* 9–12 (=W. Judeich, 'Inschriften', §339).
23   Strubbe, APAI EPITYMBIOI, *passim*.
24   Web search of the Packard Humanities Institute Greek Epigraphy programme, accessed 26/10/2016.
25   Strubbe, APAI EPITYMBIOI, xvi.
26   For the Galloi inscription, see Ritti, *Epigraphic Guide to Hierapolis (Pamukkale)*, §27. On the Ploutonion, see D'Andria, *Cehennem 'Den Cennet'e Hierapolis (Pamukkale)*. Additionally, see Kreitzer, 'The Plutonium of Hierapolis'.

elaborate necropoleis, of which there were three at Hierapolis,[27] along with its famous theatre, Plutonion, and Apolline oracular sites. The gods were powerful, assiduous in their retributive justice, and revelatory at Hierapolis.

In conclusion, before we turn to the confession inscriptions, we have seen that the initiative for divine beneficence mostly comes from the human side, with the favours sought being secured by a correct cultic approach to the deity. This respectful piety placed the god under obligation to reciprocate, though very occasionally the suppliant's piety is offered in response to the god's prior unsolicited beneficence. The mercy of the gods is underscored in the Asian inscriptions, though much less frequently than one would imagine. Moreover, it is a rare occurrence that the gods are more willing to be merciful than to punish. A more frequent occurrence is the vengefulness of the gods, who are sometimes invoked by suppliants to display strong retributive justice where the justice of the civil courts is weak, inconsistent or absent.

What picture of divine justice and mercy emerges from the evidence of the Lydian and Phrygian confession inscriptions? To what extent is the portrait similar or different to that outlined above?

4. Early Christianity and the Confession Inscriptions

At the outset we must realise that several epigraphic genres were employed in Asia Minor to enforce the divine juridical order: this theocratic phenomenon was not the preserve of the confession inscriptions alone.[28] The various genres included protective curses (either placed on

---

27 Strubbe, APAI EPITYMBIOI, 192.
28 For discussion of the confession inscriptions by classical scholars, see Petzl, *Die Beichtinschriften Westkleinasiens*; Chaniotis, 'Illness and Cures in the Greek Propitiatory Inscriptions and Dedications of Lydia and Phrygia'; Ricl, 'The Appeal to Divine Justice in the Lydian Confession–Inscriptions'; *Varinlioğlu*, 'Zeus Orkamaneites and the *Expiatory Inscriptions*'; Gordon, 'Raising a Sceptre'; De Hoz, 'Literacy in Rural Anatolia'; Rostad, *Human Transgression-Divine Retribution*; Rostad, 'The Religious Context of the Lydian Propitiation Inscriptions'; Belayche, 'Du texte à l'image'; Chaniotis, 'Ritual Performances of Divine Justice'; de Hoz, 'The Aretalogical Character of the Maionian "Confession" Inscriptions'; Versnel, *Fluch und Gebet*; Chaniotis, 'Constructing the Fear of Gods'; Cadwallader, 'Bodily Display and Epigraphical Confession at the Sanctuary of Apollo Lairbenos'.

a tomb,[29] inserted as *defixiones* in graves and erected as juridical prayers in sanctuaries,[30] or belonging to the distinctive group of Knidian texts),[31] as well as *Hosios kai Dikaios* dedications,[32] aretalogies,[33] and our confession inscriptions (including, as another subset, the oracular genre).[34] In the case of the confession inscriptions, since the appearance of Petzl's 1994 corpus, the number of texts has swelled to well over 142 publications.[35] Each inscription has been found in the general region of Lydia and Phrygia in Asia Minor, an unusual feature that requires explanation.[36] The date range of the confession inscriptions congregates around A.D. 115–210, with the only first-century texts being a fragmentary inscription datable to A.D. 57/58, itself questionably a confession text,[37] as well as a complete text belonging to A.D. 81/82.[38] The confession inscriptions were inscribed on stone stelae and were erected in sanctuaries. The offenders confessed to a series of 'sins': religious misdemeanours, civic crimes, and personal offences. While the stele was erected voluntarily, as far as we can discern, the prior punishment of the gods invariably precipitated the suppliant to seek atonement with the gods.[39] Release from punishment was only accomplished when the stele was erected. Thus the relentless justice of the gods drove the desire

---

29 Strubbe, '"Cursed Be He That Moves My Bones"'; Strubbe, ΑΡΑΙ ΕΠΙΤΥΜΒΙΟΙ, *passim*.
30 Versnel, 'Beyond Cursing'. At the most fundamental level, Versnel, *Fluch und* Gebet, 4–40, distinguishes between *defixiones* and prayers for justice on the basis that they are found in graves as opposed to sanctuaries.
31 E.g. *I. Knidos* 148 and 150. See Chaniotis, 'Under the Watchful Eyes of the Gods', 6–8, and the literature cited.
32 Ricl, 'Hosios kai Dikaios. Première partie'; 'Hosios kai Dikaios. Seconde partie'; 'Hosios kai Dikaios. Nouvaux monuments'.
33 Belayche, 'Les stèles dites de confession'.
34 For a confession inscriptions with an oracular response from the god, see Petzl, *Die Beichtinschriften Westkleinasiens*, §98. κεκληδονίσϑε με: 'I received the (the following) oracular response'. For dream incubation in the confession inscriptions, see p.106: 'I was much punished by the gods, and in my dreams he stood before me and said that he (?) would take my slave ?? by the feet and take him away'.
35 Chaniotis, 'Constructing the Fear of Gods', 3. For new publications up to 2007, see Chaniotis, 'Ritual Performances of Divine Justice', 116 n.7.
36 For the precise sites, see Chaniotis, 'Constructing the Fear of Gods', 3–4.
37 Rostad, *Human Transgression-Divine Retribution*, 144, argues that the text is possibly an ex-voto inscription.
38 For the dates of the epigraphic corpus in Petzl, *Die Beichtinschriften Westkleinasiens*, in chronological order, see Rostad, *Human Transgression-Divine Retribution*, 142–144.
39 See Chaniotis, 'Under the Watchful Eyes of the Gods', for a useful summary of the transgressions confessed. Also see Arnold, '"I Am Astonished That You Are So Quickly Turning Away!"', 443.

for reconciliation,⁴⁰ which the gods in their mercy granted upon the completion of the right cultic protocols. Finally, although the gods are routinely thanked in this process, fear of the gods continues to drive the morality. As Arnold states:

> The central Anatolian deities maintained a moral code that was not to be trifled with. Although there was no written law in cultic books for the people in the regions ruled by these various gods to read and learn, the steles themselves stood as firm reminders of the kinds of moral offenses that could result in stern punishment from the local gods. Undoubtedly, there was a sensitivity among Anatolian peoples not to overstep these moral boundaries for fear of offending these deities and bringing divine wrath upon themselves.⁴¹

This poses the methodological question as to whether Paul would have had much exposure to the confession inscriptions during his eastern Mediterranean travels, given their specific geographical location in Asia Minor, and their appearance almost entirely after the production of his epistles. But, as Chaniotis notes, the confession genre predates the first-century A.D. by several centuries in the Greek world,⁴² even if its earlier forms do not approximate the later Asia Minor confession texts in their rhetoric and structure. Nor is there any need to attribute the emergence of the Lydian-Phrygian confession inscriptions in the second and third centuries A.D. exclusively to oriental influences,⁴³ for the ideological continuities with the epigraphic traditions of the wider Greek world tell against this. In all probability a blend of Greek and

---

40 On reconciling the gods in the confession inscriptions, see Petzl, *Die Beichtinschriften Westkleinasiens*, §5: 'but now he has reconciled the gods and written down (the events) on a stele and paid for his transgressions'. §112: '[Eut]ykhis (?), whom this story is about (?), has made this stele (?), admitted her guilt and reconciled (the god)'. §6: 'And I have reconciled the gods for the sake of my grand-children and the descendants of my descendants'. §123: '[- - - I reconciled the] Lord with purifications and sacrifices that he should save my body, and with toil he restored me in my body'.
41 Arnold, '"I Am Astonished That You Are So Quickly Turning Away!"', 442–443.
42 See the mid IV cent. b.c. inscription from Epidauros in LiDonnici, *The Epidaurian Miracle Inscriptions*, 121, cited in English translation in Chaniotis, 'Ritual Performances of Divine Justice', 136.
43 Rostad, *Human Transgression-Divine Retribution*, 21–24, 37–39, 241–245.

Lydian-Phrygian indigenous traditions contributes to the emergence of the confession inscription genre in Asia Minor.[44]

These continuities allow us to posit that Paul would have been aware of the 'divine justice' ideology promulgated by the cults throughout the Greek East in their various genres, though he would not have seen the later Lydian-Phrygian confession inscriptions. In my view, Paul formulated his searing denunciation of Gentile idolatry and articulated his bleak portrait of the enslaving power of Sin and Death in Romans partially against this wider ideological backdrop, though several other perspectives, Jewish and Graeco-Roman, also feature in his rhetoric. The apostle hoped that he would engage the futility and misguided nature of the Gentile preoccupation with the divine judicial order by highlighting not only the eschatological vindication of God's justice in the risen and returning Christ, but also the extension of God's unconditioned mercy to sinners in the ἱλαστήριον ('propitiation') of Christ. As we will see, the terminological overlap between Paul's letter to the Romans and the confession inscriptions is intriguing in this regard, as well as its significant omissions by contrast. Possibly this reflects how carefully the apostle couched his language in terms that engaged the 'divine justice' ideology promulgated by the cults in the Greek East, while nevertheless establishing a sharp theological contrast in terms of their respective worldviews. In moving his ministry from the Greek East to the Latin West, Paul necessarily approached the imperial cult and the deities at Rome from his provincial understanding of such phenomena, neither having visited the capital nor having been the founder of the Roman house churches. However, although the apostle viewed Julio-Claudian Rome and its indigenous religious traditions through a *provincial* lens, the apostle theologically subjected the city and its inhabitants to the eschatological judgement of the just Creator of all, with a view to explaining how the wild olive shoot of the Gentile nations could be graciously grafted into covenantal Israel though God's dishonoured and crucified Benefactor.

However, scholars investigating the intersection of the Lydian-Phrygian confession inscriptions with the early Christian literature have

---

44 Rostad, *Human Transgression-Divine Retribution*, 244.

come to quite different conclusions regarding their mutual relationship. Susan Elliott presents a portrait of 'a divine judicial system in which monarchical deities took a direct investigative and enforcing role in the daily lives of their subject worshipers',[45] including Men, Attis and the self-castrated *galloi* priests. Consequently, Elliott situates Paul's polemic in Galatians against its Anatolian backdrop, focusing on Paul's implied critique of the Anatolian mother goddess in Galatians 4:21–31[46] and the polemic against indigenous castration practices in Galatians 3:1–5 and 5:1–6:10.[47] Following in Elliott's wake, Clinton Arnold has focused more closely on the confession inscriptions, arguing that the harsh religious ideology of Anatolia explained why Paul's gospel of grace and freedom at Galatia found such a favourable response.[48] However, when the Jewish-Christian missionaries claimed that Torah obedience, in which circumcision was the litmus test, was a necessary addition to their new faith, the Galatians would have found this entirely comprehensible from an Anatolian perspective. Significantly, as Arnold admits, no confession inscriptions have been found in provincial Galatia.[49] Against this backdrop Arnold makes several intriguing exegetical connections between the confession traditions and Paul's epistle to the Galatians. By contrast, Eckhard Schnabel proposes that the rise of the confession inscriptions is best explained by the local Anatolian priests establishing their own local authority, which, fortuitously, coincided with the rise of Christianity in Asia Minor.[50] Last, H.-J. Klauck argues that the miracles in the confession inscriptions and in the New Testament may have had the element of penance in common, but he denies any idea of mutual influence.[51]

By way of response to these proposals, Schnabel's assessment is justifiably the most cautious and the most likely, though, in my opinion, the emergence of the Lydian-Phrygian confession inscriptions was but

---

45 Elliott, *Cutting too Close for Comfort*, 349; cf. pp.62–88.
46 Elliott, *Cutting Too Close for Comfort*, 258–286.
47 Elliott, *Cutting Too Close for Comfort*, 287–348.
48 Arnold, "'I Am Astonished That You Are So Quickly Turning Away!'", 429–449.
49 Arnold, "'I Am Astonished That You Are So Quickly Turning Away!'", 436; Rostad, *Human Transgression-Divine Retribution*, 31.
50 Schnabel, 'Divine Tyranny and Public Humiliation'.
51 Klauck, 'Die kleinasiatischen Beichtinschriften und das Neue Testament'.

another localised Asian expression of wider Second Sophistic phenomena in the late first and second centuries A.D. Although there are remains of the confession inscriptions in the biblical cities of Hierapolis and Sardis,[52] for example, their presence in Galatia has not so far been proven. Nevertheless, it is legitimate to speak of a 'divine justice' ideology being widespread through the Mediterranean basin in a variety of epigraphic and cultic genres, with which Paul is perhaps interacting to some degree. However, this essay is not anachronistically suggesting that Paul was somehow engaging an earlier and more rudimentary form of the later confession inscriptions from regional Asia Minor. Rather in the discussion of Romans below we are dealing with the *legacy* of Paul's teaching regarding divine justice and mercy, comparing it to the very useful and geographically confined data bank of the confession inscriptions. The purpose is to highlight what is distinctive about Paul's general approach to the ancient propitiatory cults by contrast. So how is the concentration of the confession inscriptions in Lydia and Phrygia in the second and third centuries A.D. to be explained?

As noted, I proposed that this is another case of the Second Sophistic enhancement of indigenous mythic and civic identity at particular localities.[53] The confession inscriptions demonstrate the superior power, wrath, and justice of the Lydian-Phrygian gods in superintending the civic life of their cities and villages through the agency of their local priests, while offering reconciliation to those facing punishment for their personal and cultic sins, to the public praise and acclamation of the gods themselves. Indeed, in several of the confession inscriptions the deities of the actual city are acclaimed or honoured: 'Great are the Nemeseis in Perkos' (or: 'Perkon');[54] 'Polion (dedicates this stele) to Zeus Oreites and Men Axiottenos, who rules Perkos (or: 'Perkon') as a king';[55] 'The gods at Azitta are great'![56] In sum, the confession inscrip-

---

52 Hierapolis: Petzl, *Die Beichtinschriften Westkleinasiens*, §120. Hierapolis area (Dionysoupolis): Petzl, *Die Beichtinschriften Westkleinasiens*, §108. Sardis: I SardBR 7.1, §§95, 96.
53 On the Second Sophistic, see Bowie, 'The Greeks and Their Past in the Second Sophistic'; Bowersock, *Greek Sophists in the Roman Empire*; Anderson, *The Second Sophistic*; Swain, *Hellenism and Empire*; Goldhill, *Being Greek under Rome*; Madsen, *Eager to Be Roman*.
54 Petzl, *Die Beichtinschriften Westkleinasiens*, §7.
55 Petzl, *Die Beichtinschriften Westkleinasiens*, §6.
56 Petzl, *Die Beichtinschriften Westkleinasiens*, §69.

tions reveal how one group of cities in Asia Minor, competing among themselves against the other self-promoting cities in the province of Asia, demonstrated the superiority of their civic and cultic justice by referring to the wrathful punishment and atoning mercy of their superintending deities. It also reinforced the authority of the local priests and established what was the priestly view of a just society. What flourished in the second and third centuries A.D. may have had its glimmerings in the late first century A.D., but the evidence from the first century period is minimal and fragmentary.

Turning now to the picture of relationships with the gods that the confession inscriptions depict, how do they differ from the traditional relations with the gods articulated in the Graeco-Roman reciprocity system, outlined above?

5. Relationships with the Gods in the Confession Inscriptions

The intricate web of relationships between the sinner and the offended god is spelt out in great detail in the confession inscriptions.[57] Frequently there is acknowledgment by the offender that the offence was committed either knowingly or unknowingly/accidentally.[58] In one particularly interesting inscription, two individuals ask how they might atone for the sins they had committed 'knowingly and unknowingly' (ἐξ εἰδότων καὶ μὴ εἰδότων).[59] In the case of the sins of ignorance, one inscription sets out graphically the crisis precipitated by an offender cutting down an oak of Zeus. Immediately, the inscription explains, this unknowing act

---

57 All English translations of the confession texts below are from Chaniotis and Horsley (articles cited below), Buckler & Robinson, *Sardis*, and Rostad, *Human Transgression-Divine Retribution*. Rostad, Appendix B, 284–302, translates 29 inscriptions from Petzl's collection.
58 For unknowing and accidental transgressions, see Petzl, *Die Beichtinschriften Westkleinasiens*, §6: 'When (the circumstances) were hidden for me, and I overstepped the border without permission, the gods punished him (= me)'. A goddess demanded that a new stele be raised when an offender 'unintentionally' (ἀκουσίως) broke it (§78). Note, too, the following inscription: '– – – daughter of Apoll[oni]os through a transgression because she (= I) was accidentally in the (holy) area and I have twice walked through the village in an impure state; unmindful (?)' (§23).
59 Petzl, *Die Beichtinschriften Westkleinasiens*, §38.

mobilises the god's punitive power.⁶⁰ Even though the sin is committed in ignorance, the god regards the act as a serious case of high-handed cultic disbelief deserving prompt punishment. Consequently, the god placed the offender in a deathlike condition.⁶¹ However, the god graciously intervenes to act as a powerful benefactor, resolving the crisis by saving Stratoneikos from great danger. Significantly, this seems to be an unconditioned act on the part of the god to restore cultic peace for the city as much as for the individual involved. The god's soteriological act elicits gratitude from the recipient, with the result that a stele is raised as a testimony to the divine grace given. It is no surprise, therefore, that the inscription begins with a public acclamation of Zeus:

> Great (Μέγας) is Zeus of the Twin Oaks. Stratoneikos son of Euangelos because of ignorance (διὰ τὸ ἀγνοεῖν) cut down one of the oaks belonging to Zeus Didymeites. And the god mobilized his own power (τὴν ἰδίαν δύναμιν) because he (i.e. Stratoneikos) did not believe in him (διὰ τὸ ἀπιστῖν), and placed him - - - in a deathlike condition. He was saved from great danger (σωθεὶς ἐγ μεγάλου κινδύνου) and raised the stele in gratitude (εὐχαριστῶν). I declare that no one shall ever show contempt for his powers (τάς δυνάμις) and cut down an oak. In the year 279, on the 18th of the month Panemos.⁶²

In the case where sins are carried out knowingly, the misdemeanors are listed with relentless precision, including the various sacrifices offered

---

60 Petzl, *Die Beichtinschriften Westkleinasiens*, §9. Exactly the same cultic ignorance (κατὰ ἄγνιαν) regarding the trees of Zeus and Artemis is mentioned in §76: 'I was punished and raised the sign of gratitude (εὐχαριστήριον) after having promised to do so'. See also §9.
61 In another confession inscription where the offender is placed in a 'deathlike condition', Fortune intervenes ('But my Fortune gave hope [ἐλπίδαν]'), with the result that the Nemeseis in Pergos are acclaimed as 'great'. Petzl, *Die Beichtinschriften Westkleinasiens*, §7.
62 Petzl, *Die Beichtinschriften Westkleinasiens*, §10. For further examples of the power of the gods in the confession inscriptions, see §9: 'Great is Zeus founded at the Twin Oaks and his powers (αἱ δυνάμις αὐτοῦ)'. §55: 'Great is Meter who gave birth to Men, great is Meis Uranios, Meis Artemidorou who rules Axiotta and his power (ἡ δύναμις αὐτοῦ). When P(h)osphoros, son of Artemas, a child six years old, was dressed in a garment stained with impurity, the god investigated. A triad took (the transgression) away, and he (i.e. Phosphoros) wrote down the powers (τὰς δυνάμις τοῦ θεοῦ) of the god on a stele. In the year 245 on the 12th of the month Panemos'.

to the god as atonement.[63] The language of ἁμαρτία is predominant throughout in the inscription relating to Theodoros' sexual misdemeanors below:

> In the year 320, on the 12th of the month Panemos. In accordance with the fact that I was instructed by the gods, by Zeus and the great Men Artemidoros: 'I have punished Theodoros on his eyes according to the transgressions (κατὰ τὰς ἁμαρτίας) he committed'. I had intercourse with Trophime, the slave of Haplokomas, wife of Eutykhes, in the *praetorium* (?) (εἰς τὸ πλετώριν). He removed the first transgression (τὴν πρώτην ἁμαρτίαν) with a sheep, a partridge and a mole. The second transgression (Δευτέρα ἁμαρτία): Even though I was a slave of the gods (δοῦλος τῶν θεῶν) in Nonu, I had intercourse with Ariagne, who was unmarried. He removed the transgression with a piglet and a tuna. At the third transgression (Τῇ τρίτῃ ἁμαρτίᾳ) I had intercourse with Arethusa, who was unmarried. He removed the transgression with a hen (or cock), a sparrow and a pigeon; with a *kypros* of a blend of wheat and barley and one *prokhos* of wine. Being pure he gave a *kypros* of wheat to the priests and one *prokhos*. As intercessor (παράκλητον), I took Zeus. (He said): Behold! I hurt his sight because of his deeds, but now he has reconciled the gods (εἰλαζομένου αὐτοῦ τοὺς θεούς) and written down (the events) on a stele and paid for his transgressions (τὰς ἁμαρτίας). Asked by the council (the god proclaimed): I will be merciful (εἴλεος εἰμι), because my stele is raised on the day I appointed. You can open the prison; I will release the convict when one year and ten months has passed.[64]

---

63 On atonement in the confession inscriptions, coupled with the language of praise, see Petzl, *Die Beichtinschriften Westkleinasiens*, §36: 'When the god made his demand, the heirs made atonement praising (εὐλογοῦντες ἀπέδωκαν) (the god). In the year 276, in the month of Peritios. To Men Axeitenos—"She defiled my podium"—praising we make atonement (εὐλογοῦντες ἀποδείδομεν)'.

64 Petzl, *Die Beichtinschriften Westkleinasiens*, §5.

Chaniotis argues that the confessions of Theodoros 'alternate with quotations of oracles given by Zeus, thus creating the impression of a dialogue between the sinner and the god'.[65] The text sounds like the minutes taken in a case presided over by an unidentified "council" (perhaps, as we will see, of priests or village elders?).[66] The case is straightforward enough. Theodoros, who was a temple slave (δοῦλος τῶν θεῶν), should have been committed to sexual abstinence,[67] but he had violated the slave wife of Eutykhes in the *praetorium* (?).[68] The charge of adultery would be much less seriousness than in modern society because it only involves the penetration of a slave's body.[69] What was much more important was the fact that Theodoros had compounded the sin by bringing cultic impurity upon his role as a sacred slave in the temple.[70] Two further sexual sins are confessed. But, as Theodoros obfuscates, his sexual immorality did not matter because he only seduced unmarried women.[71] Nevertheless, Zeus upholds the importance of purity in sexual relationships in cultic matters,[72] not accepting Theodoros' casuistry that he was only deflowering unmarried women, and roundly condemning both his adultery and, as is clearly implied, the abdication of his celibacy as a temple slave. Zeus, therefore, damages the eyesight of Theodoros

---

65 Chaniotis, 'Under the Watchful Eyes of the Gods', 27.
66 Chaniotis, 'Under the Watchful Eyes of the Gods', 27. Petzl, *Die Beichtinschriften Westkleinasiens*, 10, proposes that it represents the actual trial proceedings, with a priest acting out the role of Zeus. Dr Alan Cadwallader has drawn my attention to a 'council of the gods' (σύγκλητος τῶν θεῶν) in another confession inscription (*SEG* 57.1186). This nuance is certainly a possibility in terms of our inscription, but the lack of specification of the 'Council' being 'of the gods', as in *SEG* 57.1186, perhaps points to a human council in this instance, with the priest acting as Zeus.
67 Chaniotis, 'Under the Watchful Eyes of the Gods', 27.
68 For the identification of εἰς τὸ πλετώριν with the praetorium, see Petzl, *Die Beichtinschriften Westkleinasiens*, 9.
69 See Glancy, *Slavery in Early Christianity*.
70 On Greek cultic relations and the importance of ritual purification after sexual activities, see Rostad, *Human Transgression-Divine Retribution*, 109–112.
71 Rostad, *Human Transgression-Divine Retribution*, 198, writes that Theodoros stresses that the two women were unmarried because 'he wants to avoid being accused of having had sex with other men's wives'.
72 Cultic purity rather than the morality of sexual ethics is the issue at hand. Rostad, *Human Transgression-Divine Retribution*, 227, succinctly states: 'With the exception of a few regulations from Asia Minor [e.g. *LSAM* 20], sexual activity ... is not regarded as wrong, provided the pollution is properly dealt with before one enters a shrine'.

as punishment.[73] How is this cultic crisis, which is the primary issue, resolved? Zeus only acts as intercessor for Theodoros after the offender has reconciled the gods by erecting his confession stele, with the god then forgiving him his sins (εἴλεος εἰμι). Significantly, the divine mercy is elicited by the appropriate ritual and the cultic flashpoint has been resolved. As Rostad remarks, Theodoros 'can no longer be accused of breaking the rules surrounding his status as a *hierodoulos*'.[74]

In an inscription from Sardis, a sick man is explicit in linking his ill health to the need of confession of sin in the hope that further mercy might be shown to him:

> I, X, son of Aristoneikos (?), because I had mercy shown to me and committed sin (ἐλεη[θεὶς] καὶ ἁμ[αρτήσας]), have now fallen into ill health, and I acknowledge my sin to Men of Axiotta and engrave the statement on a stele.[75]

What is interesting about this confession inscription is that the man had already experienced divine mercy but had foolishly displayed ingratitude by continuing to sin and not obey the god. Thus divine punishment inexorably followed, necessitating the man's ritualistic confession to Men. The confession inscriptions graphically spotlight the slippery tightrope between divine grace and divine chastisement that the ancients walked in interpreting the unexpected calamities in their personal lives and communities. The prior call of a god to participate in

---

73 Regarding punishment in the eyes, note the confession inscription at Sardis: 'To Artemis Anaitis Ammias, daughter of Matris, erected this because chastised in her eyes – – –' (I SardBR 7.1.95, with the iconographic incision of two eyes under the second line of the text). For discussion, see Robert, *Nouvelles Inscriptions de Sardes*, 27–33. See also the eye in a relief in Petzl, *Die Beichtinschriften Westkleinasiens*, §90. Note, too, the mention other bodily punishments (e.g. buttocks as opposed to eyes) in the confession inscriptions. A confession inscription from the sanctuary of Apollon Labeirnos states (Ozturk & Tanriver, 'Some New Finds from the Sanctuary of Apollon Lairbenos', §2): '... [I was punished] on my buttock. I declare that nobody should disregard (the god), because he will find my stele as a (warning) example (ἐξευπλάριον)'. The stele relief shows a leg to the left of the text. For further examples of 'buttocks' punishments, see Petzl, *Die Beichtinschriften Westkleinasiens*, §§75 (with photograph of the accompanying relief of an upper leg and buttock on the stele) 122. Note the relief of a leg and a pair of breasts in Petzl, *Die Beichtinschriften Westkleinasiens*, §70. I am grateful to Dr Alan Cadwallader for drawing my attention to these 'buttocks' texts in the confession inscriptions.
74 Rostad, *Human Transgression-Divine Retribution*, 198.
75 I SardBR 7. 1.96.

his mystery cult, when ignored by a worshipper, will also eventuate in a long punishment that can only be released by the erection of a confession stele. Once again, to neglect the call of the god to cultic piety, even in private contexts of the mystery cults, not only threatens the individual but ultimately the welfare of community:

> C. Antonius Apellas from Blaundos, having been punished by the god (κολασθεὶς ὑπὸ τοῦ θεοῦ) often and for a long period of time because, although he had been called, he did not want to come and be present at the mystery (τῷ μυστηρίῳ καλούμενον)...[76]

Furthermore, the communal focus of the confession inscriptions is reinforced by their paradigmatic nature. The confession of sin by the offender is set up publicly on the stele to warn others of the foolishness of showing contempt towards the gods, thereby becoming an exemplum of how to re-establish right relations with the offended deity (cf. *supra*, n.75):

> I, Sosandros from Hierapolis, went in to the common altar (?) in an impure state after committing perjury. I was punished. I proclaim that no one shall show contempt for Lairmnos, because he will have my stele as an example (ἔξενπλον).[77]

The confession inscriptions are aretalogical in their nature, magnifying the attributes of the local gods of the city. One potent example from Lydia, north of Ayazviran and dateable to A.D. 57, will suffice. Although the genre of this inscription is clearly identified as a 'eulogy' (εὐλογία) within its text, nevertheless Chaniotis is correct in saying that the inscription has close affinities with the genre of confession inscription.[78] The text unfolds the puzzling circumstances of how the nephew of Glykon and Myrtion were held captive by their nephew, despite their prior help of him. But in ways not specified in the inscription, the god has—in what is clearly an act of unsolicited mercy—freed the couple,

---

76 Petzl, *Die Beichtinschriften Westkleinasiens*, §108.
77 Petzl, *Die Beichtinschriften Westkleinasiens*, §120. See also §106: 'I proclaim that no one shall show contempt for the god Helios Apollon, because he will have the stele as an example'. Additionally, §§111, 112, 121. See also the use of ἐξενπλάριον in supra n.73.
78 Chaniotis, 'Ritual Performances of Divine Justice', 116.

eliciting their effusive praise for his liberating grace:

> Great (Μέγα) is the Mother of Mes Axiottenos.
>
> Glykon, the son of Apollonios, and Myrtion, the wife of Apollonios, (set up)
>
> this praise (εὐλογίαν) for Mes Ouranios and for Mes of Artemidoros who rules
>
> over Axiotta, for their rescue and for that of their children.
>
> For you, Lord, have shown mercy (ἐλέησες), when I was a captive.
>
> Great is your holiness (τὸ ὅσιον)! Great is your justice (τὸ δίκαιον)! Great is your victory (νεικὴ)! Great your punishing power (νεμέσεις)! Great Dodekatheon that has been established in your vicinity!
>
> For the son of my brother Demainetos made me his captive.
>
> For I had neglected my own affairs and helped you, as if you were my own
>
> son. But you locked me in and kept me captive, as if I were a criminal and
>
> not your paternal uncle!
>
> Now, great is Mes, the ruler of Axiotta!
>
> You have given me great satisfaction. I praise you.[79]

What is especially impressive is the explosive exclamation, consisting of accumulating epithets enhancing the stature of the god of the local city of Axiotta ('holiness', 'justice', 'victory', 'punishing power'). Here we are seeing in the mid first-century A.D. the gradual movement towards the Second Sophistic enhancement of indigenous mythic and civic identity at particular localities in the second and third centuries A.D. The divine juridical order of the local villages addressed the injustices suffered or perpetrated by individuals, as well as a threat of contagion to the purity

---

79 *SEG* 53.1344.

of sacred spaces within the local city, by means of cultic atonement.[80] Individuals in the cities in Lydia-Phrygia celebrated the power of their gods in accomplishing these atoning and liberating acts, with the gods maintaining their divine benevolence towards the cities. In this process cultic purity was continuously ensured by the erection of confession inscriptions on the part of the sinful, the ungrateful, and the ritually impure, almost invariably after harsh punishment had been powerfully meted out by the gods, who had intervened to rectify the issue of impurity or justice being overlooked by the individual concerned. Rostad rightly observes that this feature surpassed the normal protocols of the *do ut des* mentality in Asia Minor and the Greece East more generally:

> Paying respect to the gods was after all a central aspect of most cults, and therefore regarded as self-evident. It is surprising to see that it was so strongly emphasised in Lydian religion, and in this respect it is reasonable to claim that there was a significant difference from similar rules found in Greek cultic regulations.[81]

Intriguing, too, is the revelatory role that *angeloi* very occasionally play in the confession inscriptions. In a recent tour-de-force, G. H. R. Horsley and J. M. Luxford have discussed the two Lydian-Phrygian confession inscriptions where *angeloi* of the god Meis/Men appear,[82] rightly dismissing any suggestion that these angelic references might be credited to Jewish influences.[83] In one case, the divine emissary gives instructions about what should happen regarding a stolen cloak: 'So the god gave instructions through an *angelos* (δι' ἀνγέλου) that the cloak be sold and that his powers (τὰς δυνάμεις) be recorded on a stele.'[84] More puzzling, however, are the circumstances and content of the angelic

---

80 For example, see Petzl, *Die Beichtinschriften Westkleinasiens*, §36: 'For Men Labana(s). Elpis showed contempt for Men Labana(s) and being in an impure state she entered his podium and examined the podium and his tablets. When the god made his demand, the heirs made atonement praising (the god). In the year 276, in the month of Peritios. To Men Axeitenos— "She defiled my podium"—praising we make atonement'.
81 Rostad, *Human Transgression-Divine Retribution*, 208.
82 Horsley & Luxford, 'Pagan Angels in Roman Asia Minor', see 145–146, for translations.
83 Horsley and Luxford, 'Pagan Angels in Roman Asia Minor', 147–149.
84 Petzl, *Die Beichtinschriften Westkleinasiens*, §3.

revelation, but the role of the ancestral gods and their divine emissary is plain enough:

> Khryseros and Stratonikos asked the ancestral gods stemming from the things/people they know and the things/people they do not know, just as it was revealed to us by the *angelos* of the god Men Petraeites Axetenos; therefore, I Ammias give thanks on behalf of Dionysias, and we have provided one hundred *denaria* just as the ancestral gods sought.[85]

Finally, we touch on the communal dimension of the Lydian-Phrygian confession inscriptions,[86] an issue worth pursuing given that Paul was intending to establish alternative communities of divine and human grace throughout the eastern and western Mediterranean basin (Rom 12:3–8; 15:18–32; 16:1–23). First, as A. P. Gregory correctly observes,[87] the gods exercised direct control over individuals in their communities. The social order was maintained through their priests, who, as representatives of the gods, held ritual hearings and procedures regarding the sins to be confessed and expiated. This often involved the legal process of 'trial by sceptre', where retribution often involved the payment of reparations to the victim and quantities of produce to the priests.[88] The village elders were also probably involved in the wider legal processes as well. Where there was no legal resolution of culpability through the courts, the next social resort was, as we have seen, to invoke curses or imprecations, leaving it to the gods to avenge. Second, the temple sanctuaries, Gregory argues,[89] also act as 'protectors of the weak or marginal in society', whether it involves the protection of a mother from her son's provocation,[90] protection from unlawful intercourse,[91] or protection of

---

85 Petzl, *Die Beichtinschriften Westkleinasiens*, §38.
86 See the excellent discussion in Gregory, *Village Society in Hellenistic and Roman Asia Minor*, 478–502.
87 Gregory, *Village Society*, 487.
88 Petzl, *Die Beichtinschriften Westkleinasiens*, §§3, 35, 68, 69. For reparations and the offer of produce to the priests, see §§5, 6.
89 Gregory, *Village Society*, 209.
90 Petzl, *Die Beichtinschriften Westkleinasiens*, §47.
91 Petzl, *Die Beichtinschriften Westkleinasiens*, §111.

a son from his mother's damnation.⁹² Third, guilt before the gods, when exposed, not only involved the culpability of the individual but also families were held to be responsible as well, as is evidenced when Asklas and his nephews atoned for the sin of Asklas' father by setting up a stele in honour of Zeus Sabazios.⁹³ Fourth, the range of sins not just confined to cultic violations.⁹⁴ Sins of sexual morality are highlighted, for example, including the social shame occasioned for parents by the sin of their daughter's pre-marital sex.⁹⁵ Further social crimes include theft of a garment,⁹⁶ other offences of sexual indiscretion,⁹⁷ stolen monies and failures to repay debts,⁹⁸ among others. The strong determination of the Lydian-Phrygian priests and the village elders to establish a just society under the auspices of the gods should not be underestimated.⁹⁹

What intersection, then, is there between the divine juridical order of the confession inscriptions with Paul's epistle to the Romans?

6. Justice and Mercy in the Confession Inscriptions and the Epistle to the Romans

This essay has argued that although Paul did not see the Lydian-Phrygian confession inscriptions, he would have been exposed to the 'divine justice' ideology promulgated by the cults in their various epigraphic genres throughout the eastern Mediterranean. Thus in seeking to write to the Roman converts living in the capital, about whom he only knew what he periodically heard from Prisca and Aquila (Rom 16:3) and perhaps, in ways unknown to us, from the other names he greets in Romans 16:3–16. His perceptions of Rome and its culture would therefore have been entirely provincial, never having visited the

---

92 Petzl, *Die Beichtinschriften Westkleinasiens*, §17. I am grateful to Gregory, *Village Society*, 25, for these and the following references.
93 Petzl, *Die Beichtinschriften Westkleinasiens*, §24.
94 E.g. the mockery of the god Men, see Petzl, *Die Beichtinschriften Westkleinasiens*, §17.
95 Petzl, *Die Beichtinschriften Westkleinasiens*, §59.
96 Petzl, *Die Beichtinschriften Westkleinasiens*, §3.
97 Petzl, *Die Beichtinschriften Westkleinasiens*, §18.
98 Petzl, *Die Beichtinschriften Westkleinasiens*, §§38, 46, 58.
99 Dr Alan Cadwallader suspects that 'the very public name–shaming of an inscription was a strong promoter of better behaviour'.

city until his appeal to Caesar led him inexorably to the capital (Acts 28:16–30). Instead he would have gathered a strong sense of the ideology of the capital from the 'mirrors' of its culture in the Roman colonies that he visited (e.g. Pisidian Antioch [Acts 13:14–51], Philippi [16:12–40], Corinth [18:1–18]). This would have been augmented by the ubiquitous imperial cult and the public proclamation of decrees from the Roman ruler and his officials throughout the provinces, as well as snippets of information that he may have heard from businessmen and other travellers going to and returning from Rome.[100] Nonetheless, there would have been a disjunction between Paul's provincial image and the urban reality of the capital. The shock registered by first-time visitors to Rome over the immensity of its urban sprawl and the size and brutality of its spectacles underscores this. Nevertheless, the apostle was able on the basis of the provincial image of Rome to reconstruct imaginatively what the megalopolis was like to some degree in writing pastorally to the Romans. How effectively did the apostle combat those Gentile cults that claimed that the local gods brought about justice in village life where the legal systems were ineffective or had broken down.

6.1. *The Gravity of Paul's Portrait of Sin and Divine Wrath*

First, it is clear that sin is more seriously and graphically depicted in Romans than its counterpart in the confession inscriptions. This is not just a matter of the numerically higher occurrence of *hamartia* terminology in Romans (ἁμαρτία ['sin']: 41 times: ἁμαρτωλός ['sinner']: 4 times; ἁμαρτάνω ['I sin']: 7 times; ἁμάρτημα ['sinful deed']: once) as opposed to the confession inscriptions (ἁμαρτία: 9 times; ἁμαρτάνω: 9 times; ἁμάρτημα: 2 times). Rather it relates to the personified, enslaving, deceitful and corrupting nature of sin—informed by LXX perspectives—as depicted by the apostle in Romans 1, 5 and 8. In Romans 1:18–32, for example, Paul presents an unremittingly bleak prospect for Gentile humanity. Humanity faces the eschatological wrath of God in the present (Rom 1:18) because knowing the truth, humankind suppresses it. The reality of God's echatological judgement never recedes from the forefront of Romans (Rom 1:18; 2:5, 8; 4:15a; 5:9; 9:22;

---

100 See Judge, 'The Roman Base of Paul's Mission', 556, 566.

14:10; cf. 3:9–20, 23). There is no sense here, as is the case with the confession inscriptions, that the Gentiles are 'not knowing' about God's revelation. Rather they know sufficient from creation to be without excuse (1:18b, 20) and their innate knowledge of the Law is seen in the moral reasoning of their conscience (2:12–16). Similarly, the Jews are willfully ignorant (ἀγνοοῦντες) regarding the divine righteousness that is located in Christ as the *telos* of the Law (Rom 10:3–4), tragically thinking that their can pursue their alternative version of rightousness (Rom 9:32; 10:2–3). As far as the present experience of eschatological wrath falling upon the Gentile world, it is seen in God's abandonment of them to (a) enslavement to sexual sin (Rom 1:24–25), (b) the practice of idolatry (1: 26–27), and (c) a debased mind in their thinking (1:28–29).[101] In the process of this single act of condemnation in a threefold expression, any suggestion that sexual sin is only wrong when it threatens issues of cultic purity, noted in Theodorus' confession inscription above, is totally jettisoned. Such deluded and corrupt thinking is an expression of the eschaological wrath in advance.

Further, any hope of cultic reconciliation—which prompts thanksgiving in the confession inscriptions—is savagely debunked in Romans 1:20–24. Creation, not the cult, reveals God's 'everlasting power and divinity' (Rom 1:20b: τε ἀΐδιος αὐτοῦ δύναμις καὶ θειότης). Paul focuses instead on the dishonourable response of the Gentile world to God's natural revelation, drawing upon the semantic domains of honour (ἐδόξασαν) and benefaction (ηὐχαρίστησαν) in order to depict the high-handed sin of human ingratitude (Rom 1:21a). Utilising the LXX traditions that speak of Israel exchanging the divine glory for idolatry (δόξα: Pss 4:2; 106 [LXX 105]:20; Jer 2:11; Hos 4:7; 9:11; 10:5; cf. Sir 49:5), Paul states that Gentile idolaters make the same mistake in the present (Rom 1:23).[102] What is intriguing is that Paul nominates the types of image worshipped by the Gentiles: corruptible man, birds, quadrupeds, and reptiles. Jewish auditors familiar with the Genesis narrative would have spotted Paul's clear allusion to the subjugation of the

---

101 Seifrid, *Christ, Our Righteousness*, 49, rightly speaks of a 'threefold "law of retribution"' in Romans 1:24–29.
102 For full discussion of the Old Testament echoes in Romans 1:21–25, see Beale, *We Become What We Worship*, 204–216.

created order (Gen 1:26b: birds, livestock, creeping things), over which mankind, as the image of God (Gen 1:26a), was commanded to rule as the steward of the created order. In an ironic reversal of the 'dominion' mandate (Gen 1:26, 28), Paul highlights that human beings are subjecting themselves to created beings, including their own species, instead of worshipping the glorious Creator of all.

Paul's wide-ranging use of δύναμις terminology throughout Romans is also of interest, given its presence in the confession inscriptions in relation to the gods (12 occurrences).[103] For Paul, divine power is demonstrated in a variety of ways. The δύναμις of God is revealed in creation (Rom 1:20b), by raising from the dead the Son of God in power (Rom 1:4), by securing believers against all other malevolent powers (8:38), by exercising the power of the gospel unto salvation (1:16), by raising up Pharaoh in order to release Israel (9:17), by wielding wrath as a demonstration of divine power (9:22), and by the Holy Spirit empowering believers in their experience of joy and the miraculous (15:13, 19). Paul's understanding of δύναμις, therefore, stands in clear contrast to the counterfeits of power in the Gentile cults and the Lydian-Phrygian confession inscriptions. What is interesting and differentiating regarding the New Testament understanding of δύναμις, in contrast to the confession inscriptions, is its variety and range of expressions: creational, soteriological, pneumatological, and eccesiological.

There are additional rhetorical strategies on Paul's part that are worth exploring if we are to gauge how Roman auditors might have responded to the graphic portrait of the hypostasised powers of Sin and Death in Romans 5:12–21, as well as the wider panorama of the groaning creation in 8:18–25. In both the Roman and Pauline rhetorical traditions, moral decline is charted from a defining historical event, sullying virtue from that moment onwards and plunging history into moral disarray and creation generally into serious dislocation.[104] In Roman theories of historical degeneration, the year 146 B.C. (i.e. the destruction of Carthage) looms large in the writings of Roman historians and moralists, especially Sallust (86—c. 35 B.C.: *Cat.* 6–13; *BJ* 4.4–8). This was

---

[103] Petzl, *Die Beichtinschriften Westkleinasiens*, §§9, 10, 14 (restored), 35, 47, 54, 55, 59, 62, 68, 69, 79.

[104] For the Jewish background, see Hahne, *The Corruption and Redemption of Creation*.

the date from which the supposedly pristine righteousness of republican society was corrupted.[105] There were, however, other dates of decline proposed among proponents of the theory of historical degeneration. The historian Polybius (c. 200–118 B.C.), for example, nominated the year 168 B.C. as the beginning of Rome's newly acquired 'universal dominion' (Polybius 3.4.6), proposing that after that year moral decline accelerated, though it had already been present in Rome as early as 200 B.C.[106] Paul, by contrast, locates decline from the very beginning of human creation, drawing upon the Genesis 3 tradition and Second Temple Judaism more widely.[107] With the disobedience of the ancestor of the human race, Adam, in Paul's apocalyptic understanding of history, inaugurates the current evil age of Sin and Death (cf. Gal 1:4). Even in the pre-Sinai period, which was characterised by the absence of any knowledge of the Mosaic Law (Rom 5:13–14), Sin and Death nonetheless reigned and ravaged humanity.

As far as the 'knowledge' rhetoric of the confession inscriptions, irrespective of whether we are 'knowing' or 'unknowing', Paul would have agreed that punishment for Sin has been wreaked and continues to be wreaked against human beings. As noted, Death still reigned when the Law was not known in the pre-Mosaic period (Rom 5:14). But even when the Mosaic Law did eventually come, the Law was recruited against its will by the reigning and enslaving powers, Sin and Death, which, in a bold personification of the apostle, had entered the world and were now ranged against humanity (Rom 5:12). Consequently, Sin was aroused by the advent of the Mosaic Law and further empowered by the Law (Rom 7:5, 7–11, 13; 1 Cor 15:56b), which, ironically, was

---

105 See Earl, *The Political Thought of Sallust*; Conley, 'The Stages of Rome's Decline', 379–382; Judge, 'The Roman Theory of Historical Degeneration'; Vasta, *The Crisis of Exemplarity*.
106 Q. Caecilius Metellus was apprehensive about the deleterious effects that Rome's recent victory over Carthage (202 b.c.) would have on the civic virtue of Rome, arguing that decadence had already set in by that time (Valerius Maximus 7.2.3). Miles, *Forbidden Pleasures*, 57, astutely observes regarding this early date: 'If more literary evidence has survived for the fourth and the third centuries b.c., I have little doubt but that similar ideas would have found expression'. By contrast, the annalist Calpurnius Piso dated the onset of Rome's decline to the censorship of M. Messala and C. Cassius in 154 b.c. (Pliny, *HN* 27.244), whereas Livy nominates Manlius Vulso's introduction of Asian wealth in 187 b.c. (Livy 39.6.7) as the turning point in the collapse of morality.
107 See Levison, *Portraits of Adam*.

the agent of true knowledge regarding Sin (Rom 3:20b). Although the Law is holy and just and good (Rom 7:7, 12–14, 16, 22), it was impotent to effect righteousness due to the ravages of the sinful flesh and its self-centred desires (Rom 8:3, 7; cf. Gal 3:21–22).

In sum, both Jewish and Graeco-Roman readers were rhetorically familiar with the notion of hypostatised and personified powers and the tortured history of moral decline.[108] But Paul pushes both traditions to breaking point to show how there is no hope for humanity apart from Christ. He also moves the emphasis away from cultic violations and social sins, the main concern of the confession inscriptions, to the moral accountability of all humanity for eschatological wrath that it would face, the experience of which had begun in the present (Rom 1:18)—itself another Pauline twist to Jewish eschatological perspectives. On the rare occasions where the confession inscriptions acknowledged something more than an individual's culpability for sin before the gods, it was confined to one's immediate family, who, as we have seen, had to seek reconciliation with the gods by erecting the stele on behalf of their sinful relative. Paul, however, speaks of accountability for sin in personal (Rom 5:12b), cosmic (8:19–22), and primordial terms (5:12–21; 16:20).

Another area of divine revelation in the confession inscriptions, which provides noetic solutions to social sins in the Lydian-Phrygian villages, is totally downgraded by Paul: namely, angelic revelation. Indeed, in a calculated swipe against Graeco-Roman and Jewish apocalyptic angelology,[109] Paul asserts that even 'angels' cannot separate us from the love of Christ (Rom 8:38), clearly viewing these particular angels as fallen beings deleterious to humanity. Similarly, in Galatians 1:9, the apostle hypothetically pivots the revelation of 'an angel from heaven' against the true knowledge of the gospel of grace in Christ, the apostle being well aware of Second Temple Judaism traditions about the pre-temporal fall of Satan and his angels (cf. 2 Cor 11:14–15).[110] But,

---

108 See Axtell, *The Deification of Abstract Ideas*; Stafford, *Worshipping Virtues*; Dodson, *The 'Powers' of Personification*; Judge, 'The Roman Theory of Historical Degeneration'; Vasta, *The Crisis of Exemplarity*.
109 On Pauls' angelology, see Harrison, 'In Quest of the Third Heaven', 43–46.
110 See Jenks, *The Origins and Early Development of the Antichrist Myth*.

over against the Lydian-Phrygian confession inscriptions, the Jewish scriptures and traditions, and later Christian apocryphal tradition, Paul does not attribute to the angels any revelatory or judicial role.

We turn now to Paul's depiction of grace and mercy in Romans in comparison to the confession inscriptions.

6.2. Encountering the Grace and Mercy of a Wrathful God

It might be thought that grace was a central part of the depiction of the gods in the confession inscriptions, given the fact that they are better called 'appeasement' or 'reconciliation' inscriptions. The surprise is that 'grace' language is largely absent from the confession inscriptions, with only two texts employing χαρίς ('favour', 'grace').[111] The language of mercy, however, is more frequent in the cultic inscriptions, with ἱλάσκομαι ('I appease', 'I propitiate') appearing 13 times and ἴλεος ('mercy') once.[112] However, the cognate of χαρίς, εὐχαριστέω routinely appears, being employed some 13 times because it captures the human response of gratitude for one's release from divine wrath through cultic appeasement.[113] By contrast, there is an explosion of grace language in Romans: χαρίζομαι ('I forgive'), once (Rom 8:32); χαρίς, 22 times,[114] χάρισμα ('gift'), 6 times.[115] Surprisingly, εὐχαριστία does not appear in Romans, whereas εὐχαριστέω ("I thank") only appears five times.[116] In the case of ἔλεος ('mercy'), there are only three occurrences,[117] but 7 occurrences for ἐλεέω ('I am merciful').[118] It would seem from the statistics above that Romans places much more emphasis on God's demonstration of grace, whereas the confession inscriptions highlight the human reaction of thanksgiving for forgiveness experienced. The theocentric emphasis of Romans is once again born out.[119]

---

111   Petzl, *Die Beichtinschriften Westkleinasiens*, §§ 58, 102.
112   Petzl, *Die Beichtinschriften Westkleinasiens*, §§5, 6, 33, 45, 47, 54, 60, 68, 70, 73, 74, 80, 112.
113   Petzl, *Die Beichtinschriften Westkleinasiens*, §5.
114   Rom 1:5, 7; 3:24; 4:4, 16; 5:2, 15, 17, 20, 21; 6:1, 14, 15, 17; 7:25; 11:5, 6; 12:3. 6; 15:15; 16:20, 24.
115   Rom 1:1; 5:15, 16; 6:23; 11:29; 12:6.
116   Rom 1:8, 21; 7:25; 14:6; 16:4.
117   Rom 9:23; 11:31; 15:9.
118   Rom 9:15, 16, 18; 11:30, 31, 32; 12:8.
119   See Morris, 'The Theme of Romans', 249–263.

How do we see the superiority of grace over against the cultic world of the confession inscriptions? First, when Paul speaks of 'Grace', 'Death' and 'Sin' as reigning powers in Romans 5: 14, 17, 21 (βασιλεύειν), he alludes to the familiar idea of dominions ('ages' or aeons) in Jewish apocalyptic thought.[120] Thus the new age of grace and its gift of righteousness (Rom 5:17b; 21b: βασιλεύειν) has supplanted the present age of Sin and Death (5:14a; 17a; 21a: βασιλεύειν). The eschatological newness of χάρις is underscored by the accompanying language of abundance (Rom 5:15: ἐπερίσσευσεν; 5:17: τὴν περισσείαν; 5:20) and by the death-and-life contrasts (5:12, 14, 17, 21). I have suggested elsewhere that Paul's language of 'overflow' in Romans 5:12–21 came conceptually and terminologically from the Julio-Claudian reign of unparalleled and unrivalled grace.[121] Cilliers Breytenbach, however, has convincingly argued that it is derived from the LXX Psalms, where God's overflowing forgiveness of sinners is effusively enunciated.[122] To illustrate the point by way of a metaphor, the husk of Paul's terminology may well be Graeco-Roman, as I have argued, but, as Breytenbach has decisively shown, its theological and conceptual kernel was Jewish. Either way, God's forgiveness in Christ simply overflowed.

Second, Paul's language of mercy, which he has in common with the confession inscriptions, would have been puzzling for Lydian-Phrygian auditors, given that the confession inscriptions centred upon cultic appeasement and obedience to the gods. For Paul, however, divine mercy (ἔλεος) is covenantal,[123] corresponding to Old Testament *hesed* ('mercy', 'kindness'), the standard Hebrew term for covenantal grace.[124] The apostle's preoccupation with this motif is further demonstrated by the way that he expounds central LXX covenant-renewal texts throughout Romans 9–11 (Exod 32–34 [Rom 9:4–5]; Hosea 2:23 and 1:10 [Rom 9:24–29]; Deut 30:11–14 [Rom 10:6–11]; Isa 59:20–21 and 27:9 [Rom 11:26–27]) from the perspective of their fulfilment in Christ. For

---

120 See Harrison, *Paul's Language of Grace*, 226–234.
121 See Harrison, *Paul's Language of Grace*, 234.
122 Breytenbach, 'CHARIS and ELEOS in Paul's Letter to the Romans', 251–258.
123 The reciprocal relationship between God and Israel emerges when *hesed* is linked to divine grace and the mutual obligations of the covenant or *berit* (e.g. 1 Sam 20:8, 14–18; Ps 89:28; 106:45).
124 Jacob, *Theology of the Old Testament*, 106.

Paul, divine mercy demonstrates God's freedom in pursuing his soteriological purposes, expressing an unwavering commitment to his covenant renewal promises (Rom 3:1–4; 9:6a; 11:1).[125] Faced with the problem of theodicy arising from God's alleged abandonment of his covenantal promises to ethnic Israel (Rom 9:4; 11:1),[126] Paul's exposition of divine mercy in Romans represents an important strut in his argument, countering any suggestion of arbitrariness or indifference on God's part.

In response to critics of 'justification by faith' (Rom 3:8), Paul sets out in Romans 9 what would become a major emphasis in Romans 9–11. All who belong by birth to Israel, Paul argues, are not necessarily members of the 'true' Israel. Drawing upon the 'remnant' theology of the Old Testament,[127] Paul argues that only an elect remnant would inherit the covenantal promises (Rom 9: 6b–9, 27b; 11:3–10). This group of the divinely chosen within ethnic Israel are designated 'vessels of mercy' because they have been prepared beforehand for glory (Rom 9:23: σκεύη ἐλέους). Nevertheless, throughout their long and tortured history, the remainder of disobedient ethnic Israel, called 'the vessels of wrath' (9:22; cf. 9:31–33; 10:3, 21; 11:10, 20a, 23a), have been repeatedly summoned by a patient God to repent (Rom 9:22; 10:21). Indeed, the continued spiritual obduracy of ethnic Israel towards the claims of the gospel in the present age deeply distresses the apostle (Rom 9:1–5; 10:1–4; 11:1).

However, the issue of theodicy reappears with renewed force—in spite of Paul's magisterial response to the issue in Romans 8:31–39—when one tries to reconcile God's gracious election of a remnant with the problem of the present stumbling of ethnic Israel: 'What are we then to say? Is there injustice on God's part?' (Rom 9:14; cf. 9:19). Paul's answer to the charge is to cite LXX Exod 33:19 in Romans 9:15: 'I will have mercy (ἐλεήσω) on whom I have mercy (ἐλεῶ)'. The sovereignty of God's mercy seems at first blush uncompromisingly harsh in its application. But the Old Testament context is important here. Despite Israel's disobedience and infidelity over the golden calf episode (Exodus 32),

---

125   I am indebted here to the argument of Whittle, *Covenant Renewal*, 31–75.
126   Kirk, *Unlocking Romans*, 208, overstates the case when he says regarding Romans that 'Paul's argment is primarily an argument about theodicy, not about soteriology'.
127   See Hasel, *The Remnant*.

Yahweh still chose to 'manifest his mercy, favouring Israel as his chosen people', moving history inexorably towards the arrival of the Messiah.[128] Furthermore, Yahweh would not be dictated to by Moses—perhaps symbolising righteousness by works of the Law[129]—concerning the mode of his divine self-revelation (Exod 33:17–23). That manifestation was also a matter of divine mercy (Rom 9:16b: τοῦ ἐλεῶντος θεοῦ), unable to be influenced by human will or exertion (9:16a), but again finding its culmination in the self-revelation of God in Christ. In sum, there is sovereign freedom in the exercise of God's mercy, but it is always related to God's wider soteriological purposes. God, therefore, does not respond to works in electing the younger Jacob over the older Esau (Rom 9:10–13), a fact supremely demonstrated by the choice of Jacob prior to his birth to belong to Christ's messianic line (Rom 9:4; cf. Matt 1:2; Luke 3:34). Nor, conversely, does God baulk at hardening Pharaoh's heart (Rom 9:17, 18b), preferring to exercise his mercy (9:18a: ἐλεεῖ) on whomever he chooses by releasing Israel from captivity.

With the vistas of divine election and mercy now more clearly focused for his readers, Paul opens up the wider panorama of God's soteriological purposes for Jews and Gentiles in history, emphasising the utter reliability of God in fulfilling his covenantal promises. God has sovereignly hardened the disobedient members of ethnic Israel so that the elect Gentiles, as a wild olive shoot, might be grafted into the olive tree of Israel (Rom 11:17–22). This is not to suggest that God has somehow forgotten the Jews during his incorporation of the elect Gentiles into God's family. God has been continuously calling out the elect remnant of Jews unto salvation in the messianic age, stirring them to soteriological envy by the inclusion of the Gentiles in the olive tree of Israel (Rom 11:7a, 11–16 [possibly v. 31b, infra n. 132]).

But, according to Paul, there is still a further mystery to be revealed (Rom 11:25a). God's mercy tempers the hardening of ethnic Israel that he has sovereignly implemented throughout the messianic age (Rom 9:18, 11:7b): the hardening is only 'a hardening in part' (11:25b) until

---

128 Fitzmyer, *Romans*, 566–567.
129 Byrne, *Romans*, 296.

the fullness of the Gentiles has come in.[130] However, when this temporal unfolding of the progressive stages of salvation has occurred (i.e. Rom 11:11–24[131] God will again act mercifully to disobedient ethnic Israel (i.e. 'all Israel': 11:26a), remembering the Abrahamic covenant extended to Jacob and his ethnic heirs (11:26b, 27a), maintaining thereby the beloved status of the Jews due to the patriarchs and their irrevocable calling (11:28–29). Thus, at the Parousia, the messianic Deliverer will return from heavenly Zion at the eschaton and extend forgiveness, effected solely by the unsolicited grace of the cross, to ethnic Israel (Rom 11:26b–27; cf. 1 Thess 1:10b).[132] Just as the Gentiles had once been disobedient but were shown mercy by God (11:30: ἠλεήθητε), so too the disobedient Jews, temporarily hardened so that mercy might come to the Gentiles (11:31a: ἐλέει]), would themselves '[now] receive mercy (11:31b: ἐλεηθῶσιν)'.[133] In sum, Christ became a servant of the circumcised in order to confirm the patriarchal promises, undermining any suggestion of theodicy by virtue of his cruciform commitment to his Father's will, enabling the Gentiles to praise God fulsomely for his impartial soteriological mercy (Rom 15:8–9: ὑπὲρ ἐλέος, v. 9; cf. 2:10b–11).

---

130 On 4 Ezra 4:35–37 and its applicability to the 'fullness of the Gentiles' (Rom 11:25b; cf. Luke 21:23b–24), see Moo, *Romans*, 719.
131 On the temporal force of οὕτως ('in this way': i.e. an adverb of manner) in Romans 11:26a—not the temporal meaning of 'then' or 'after that' (an adverb of time)—and its relevance for the progressive unfolding of salvation in Romans 11:11–25a, see Moo, *Romans*, 719–720. However, the widespread claim that οὕτως does not have the temporal meaning of 'then' (e.g. Moo, *Romans*, 720; Fitzmyer, *Romans*, 622–623) has recently been rebutted. Van der Horst ('"Only Then Will All Israel Be Saved"') has marshalled sufficient samples from the Greek and Judeo-Greek literature to indicate that a temporal meaning is entirely possible. Nevertheless, the progressive hardening of Israel 'in part', ushering in the Gentiles to salvation while simultaneously provoking Israel to soteriological jealousy (Rom 11:11–24), is better accounted for by the adverb of manner. See Robinson, 'The Salvation of Israel in Romans 9–11'.
132 Contra, Wright, 'Romans', 688–691. For the view that the first coming of Jesus is envisaged in Romans 11:26b as opposed to his parousia, see Voorwinde, 'Rethinking Israel', 43–47.
133 Regarding the disputed textual status of [νῦν] ('now') in Romans 11:31, see Schreiner, *Romans*, 630; also Jewett, *Romans*, 694, argues that νῦν is original as the more difficlut reading, even though it is omitted by some important external witnesses. Dunn, *Romans 9–16*, 677, concludes that a clear-cut decision is unobtainable. However, rather than the presence of νῦν scuttling the interpretation of the future eschatological turning of ethnic Israel to Christ (11:26b–27), outlined above, the νῦν is more 'an expression of imminence', meaning 'now, at any time', as opposed to signifying 'that the event will infallibly take place within a few years'; Moo, *The Epistle to the Romans*, 735. As Schreiner, *Romans*, 628, states: 'Israel's salvation is "now" in the sense that the era of messianic salvation has arrived'.

These divine 'mercies' (Rom 12:1: διὰ τῶν οἰκτιρμῶν), articulated fulsomely in Romans 3:21—11:36, render obsolete the rituals of the Old Testament cult and expose the ineffectuality of the Graeco-Roman propitiatory system,[134] subject as it was to the divine wrath (1:18, 22-23). Instead a 'spiritual worship' (Rom 12:1-2: τὴν λογικὴν λατρείαν) has arrived that is holy and acceptable to God. The bodies of the assembled believers at Rome are presented on the altar as living sacrifices (Rom 12:1), an expression of the newness of resurrection life (6:4), accompanied by the transformative renewal of the believer's mind (12:2: τῇ ἀνακαινώσει τοῦ νοός) and the newness of the Spirit in personal and corporate relationships (7:6b; cf. 14:16b; 15:13, 16b). In sum, the newness of the messianic age of mercy is deftly emphasised throughout Romans. Divine mercy, therefore, is the foundation for the ethical imprint of Christ's resurrection and pneumatic life in the Body of Christ (Rom 6:11-23; 7:6; 8:3-5; 12:1-15:13).[135] Thus, whereas a hierarchical and elitist form of justice was exercised by the priests towards the weak in the Lydian-Phrygian villages, for Paul mercy is exercised in a traditional Jewish manner (cf. Tob 1:3) within the Body of Christ by means of various forms of practical care, including almsgiving, to those in need of help (12:8b: ὁ ἐλεῶν).[136] This includes those inside and outside of the community of believers, and, in a radical twist, friend and enemy equally (12:14-21; cf. Luke 6:27-36 [v. 36: 'Be merciful (οἰκτίρμονες), just as your Father is merciful (οἰκτίρμων)']). The intersection of divine mercy with divine justice forges new pathways for social relations and beneficence in a Graeco-Roman context.

Third, Paul makes it entirely clear that the initiative for reconciliation and atonement comes from God alone. God, for example, puts forward Christ as the atoning ἱλαστήριον ('propitiation') to demonstrate his righteousness (Rom 3:25). By contrast, in the case of the confession inscriptions, the sinner erects his own stele and the god then forgives. Again, unlike the relentlessly punitive gods of the confession

---

134 While Jewett, *Romans*, 727-728, argues that Paul draws upon the technical language of sacrifice from Greek religion in employing παραστῆσαι θυσίαν (Rom 12:1: 'present ... a sacrifice'), it is unlikely that his auditors (at the very least, his Jewish ones) would have exclusively interpreted the imagery against this backdrop.
135 Jewett, *Romans*, 727.
136 Jewett, *Romans*, 753-74.

inscriptions, Paul argues that God had forestalled the full expression of his wrath so that grace in Christ might still be exercised (Rom 2:4; 3:25b). We have also seen that in the confession inscriptions that the texts speak about the sinner 'reconciling the god' by means of the erection of the stele (*supra*, n.40). The absolute reverse is the case in Paul, with God reconciling the 'weak', the 'ungodly' (Rom 5:6. cf. 4:5), and his 'enemies' (Rom 5:10a), as opposed to the 'worthy' in the epigraphic tradition (*supra*, n.14). God justifies the ungodly. The triple use of the aorist passive in Paul's language of reconciliation (Rom 5:10a: κατηλλάγημεν; 5:10b: καταλλαγέντες σωθησόμεθα; 5:11b: τὴν καταλλαγὴν ἐλάβομεν) strips human beings of any contribution to their reconciliation with God, leaving 'no room for misunderstanding as to the completeness and certainty of what God has done'.[137]

Additionally, R. P. Martin makes the telling observation that Paul's use of 'reconciliation' terminology provides 'the picture of a seeking, caring and forgiving God who meets the sinner before he repents is one that has no parallel in Judaism', with the exception of Jesus' parable of the Prodigal Son (Luke 15:11–32). A similar comment may be made in regard to the confession inscriptions. Repentance, symbolised by the erection of the stele, must be made before the god's wrath can be assuaged. For Paul, however, justification in Christ's blood rescues believers from the eschatological divine wrath by God establishing peace with his unrepentant enemies (Rom 5:8; cf. 5:1). This dramatic transition is expressed in the 'forensic-cultic idiom' of Paul's justification and soteriological imagery,[138] but Paul's rhetoric of reconciliation moves the theological argument into the new territory of relational categories based upon indwelling love (Rom 5:5; 13:8–10) and familial status (8:14–18).[139]

Fourth, grace is more than a favour conferred but is also a power unleashed.[140] In Paul's reconfiguration of the Graeco-Roman reciprocity system, Roman believers inherit the role, allocated through divine grace, of meeting the needs of others (Rom 12:8b; cf. 12:6a), exercising

---

137 Martin, Reconciliation, 150.
138 Martin, *Reconciliation*, 153.
139 Martin, *Reconciliation*, 152–153.
140 Schreiner, *Paul*, 246.

mercy (ὁ ἐλεῶν) within the Body of Christ (12:8c; cf. 15:25-27; 16:1-6, 13b), overcoming the enmity of outsiders by exercising practical care towards them (12:20-21; cf. 1 Thess 5:15), and giving to the mission of believers in advancing the gospel in new regions (Rom 15:24). All this is an expression of the debt of love owed to everyone because of the indebtedness of believers to the crucified Christ (Rom 13:8-10; cf. 5:6-8), who now live under the reign of grace (6:14-15) and experience the newness of the Spirit (7:6b; 8:4-5). Moreover, it is an expression of the interdependence of believers in the Body of Christ (12:5b), evincing a radically different understanding of mutuality than the patronal dynamics characterising the ancient reciprocity system, and posing an alternative to the priestly hierarchicalism of Lydian-Phrygian village life. There is nothing comparable to this in the world of the confession inscriptions, even if the priests, under the auspices of the gods, were intending by means of their cultic meticulousness to establish villages where justice dwells.

6.3. Encountering the Justice of God in a Just Community

A comparison of divine 'justice' in the confession inscriptions with Paul's epistle to the Romans turns up something totally unexpected. Given the zealous drive for justice in the Lydian-Phrygian villages, it is very surprising that the confession inscriptions barely use the language of 'justice' and 'righteousness' at all. The adverb, δικαίως ('justly'), occurs only once in the entire corpus.[141] But, tellingly, there is no use of δίκαιος ('just', 'righteous'), the adjective, δικαιοσύνη ('justice', 'righteousness'), the noun, or δικαιόω ('declare righteous'), the verb, in Petzl's entire collection of 124 inscriptions. What is remarkable is the range of 'righteousness' language in Romans: δικαιοσύνη (33 times: 'righteousness', 'justice'); δικαιόω (5 times: 'acquit', 'declare righteous'); δικαίωμα (5 times: 'judgement'; 'just requirement'; 'righteous deed'); δικαίωσις (2 times: 'acquittal'); δικαιοκρισία (once: 'righteous judgement'); δίκαιος (7 times: 'righteous', 'just').[142] How do we explain the stark difference between both traditions?

---

141 Petzl, *Die Beichtinschriften Westkleinasiens*, §58 l.19.
142 Reumann, *Righteousness in the New Testament*, 42.

The answer is that the confession inscriptions are driven by cultic concerns as far as morality, with ethical accountability being viewed within strictly circumscribed ritual and purity agendas. The concern for justice within the Lydian-Phrygian villages is established by the gods punitively intervening, exposing the sin of the offender and provoking them to repent, and by the gods being reconciled when the offender erects the stele. There is no sense that the offender undergoes a change of status with the gods other than moral appeasement (cf. Rom 5:19; 8:14–17, 20–23, 31–35a). With the moral flashpoint resolved for the offender, there is no mention of a continuing ethical transformation within a pneumatically empowered and transforming community (cf. Rom 8:3–5, 13; 12:3–30; 15:16b). No paradigm of continuing conformity to the deity or divine imitation is offered to the forgiven offender (cf. Rom 6:1, 15–16; 8:29; 15:7).

By contrast, Paul's vision for community relations is prefaced by the believer's sacrifice (Rom 12:1) being 'the proper response to God's covenant-making',[143] founded upon the atoning work of the crucified Christ (3:25 [ἱλαστήριον]; 8:3: περὶ ἁμαρτίας).[144] Consequently, because Christ's atonement undergirds the establishment of his community, Paul highlights the Spirit-driven transformation required from the new covenant morality operative in the Body of Christ (Rom 7:6b; 8:1–4,12–13; 12:2 [cf. v. 1: διὰ τῶν οἰκτιρμῶν τοῦ θεοῦ]).[145] There is an eschatological 'newness' here that fulfils and surpasses the Mosaic covenantal categories. For Paul, God's Kingdom is concerned with righteousness, peace, and joy in the Spirit (Rom 14:17). Peace and mutual upbuilding among believers (Rom 14:19; 15:33) and, as far as possible, living peaceably with all in the capital (Rom 12:18b) was the new social dynamic. As M. A. Seifrid comments regarding Romans 12:21, 'Subtly, but unmistakably, Paul reminds his readers of the work of God in Christ by which they have been conquered for the good (see 5:6–8; 8:37). They are now to do the same.'[146]

---

143 Whittle, *Covenant Renewal*, 79–109.
144 On the nuances of ἱλαστήριον and περὶ ἁμαρτίας, suggesting atonement, see Schreiner, *Romans*, 192–194, 403–404.
145 See Deidun, *New Covenant Morality in Paul*, 69–79, 194–202.
146 Seifrid, 'Romans', 681.

The backdrop of Paul's understanding is the Old Testament and intertestamental portrait of the righteousness of God as the Creator, King, and Judge of all (e.g. Exod 9:7; 14:4; Num 16:19; Jdgs 5:11; 1 Sam 12:7; Neh 9:33; Pss 4:1; 17:1; 23:3; 35:5–7; 40:9–10; 51:14, 16; 71:15–16; 72:1–3; 89:14, 16; 98:1–3, 6–9; Isa 8; 40:5; Jer 22:23; Dan 9:24; cf. 2 Esdr 7:114; CD 20.20; 1QS 11.2–15).[147] Consequently, as we have seen, the apostle confronts the dilemma of how a holy and just God can forgive sinners without violating his core identity (Rom 3:4–5, 25b–26), whether that is understood in terms of his covenant loyalty, his righteous character, or saving righteousness.[148] Paul's answer is summed up in the justification of the ungodly (Rom 4:5), which he had personally experienced on the Damascus road (Act 9:1–19; Gal 1:13–24; 1 Cor 15:8–10). But, ultimately, justification by faith had its origins in Jesus' parable about the Pharisee and the Tax-collector (Luke 18:9–14; cf. 15:25–32; Matt 20:1–6) and in his identification with sinners during his ministry. As G. Bornkamm comments, 'Paul's gospel of justification by faith alone matches Jesus' turning to the godless and the lost'.[149]

7. Conclusion

This chapter has asked after the legacy of Romans in antiquity when compared to the later Lydian-Phrygian confession inscriptions. These were studied as important epigraphic examples of the wider ideology of the divine juridical order present in Asia Minor. Paul's strong emphasis on the sovereignty of divine grace challenged the entitlement and civic status of the Lydian-Phrygian priestly elites and village elders, as well as the 'works' ideology underlying the confessional and reconciliatory cults. Crises in the appeasement of divine punishment occurred when the gods intervened and demanded justice to be invoked against errant individuals in the local villages, filling the accused with abject terror.

---

147 See Ziesler, *The Meaning of Righteousness in Paul*, 17–127; Williams, 'The "Righteousness of God" in Romans'; Reumann, *Righteousness in the New Testament*, 12–26; Seifrid, *Christ, Our Righteousness*, 38–45; Bird, *The Saving Righteousness of God* 12–18; Wright, *Justification*, 37–58. Most recently, Irons, *The Righteousness of God*.
148 Reumann, *Righteousness in the New Testament*, 72.
149 Bornkamm, *Paul*, 237.

This could only be resolved by the sinner's erection of a stele, sometimes accompanied by iconography appropriate to the punishment (*supra*, n.73), with gratitude on the part of the sinner reciprocating the divine forgiveness. Paul, however, depicted an even graver situation for humanity as it faced the eschatological wrath of God, which the Gentile world was already experiencing in advance. Both Jew and Gentile were enslaved to the personified 'superpowers' of Sin, Law, and Death. Nevertheless, divine grace had trumped these enemies ranged against humanity once and for all by means of the atoning, propitiatory, and reconciling death of the risen Christ. The transition from being an object of wrath to being δίκαιος in Christ was extraordinary enough, but the reversal in status from being an enemy to being a beloved child in God's family through the indwelling Spirit was equally as remarkable. The accusations of the Lydian-Phrygian gods, and more generally the strictures of the divine judicial order in Asia Minor, had been rendered null and void. Moreover, the overflowing gifts of divine grace poured out upon the Body of Christ established alternative communities of mercy throughout the eastern Mediterranean basin. The mercy of God in Christ moved beyond the socially paralysing demands of justice in the Lydian-Phrygian villages to an ethnically, geographically, and socially diverse movement of forgiveness and compassion towards the outsider and the enemy, as well as familial care for its own internal members. The newness of the Spirit had orchestrated a social novelty within antiquity.

Finally, we should remember the legacy of the epistle to the Romans in relation to the Second Sophistic movement and its attachment to the mythic past and civic identity in Asia Minor during the second and third centuries A.D. As we have seen, the Lydia-Phrygia priests and village elders celebrated the power of their gods in accomplishing these atoning and liberating acts recorded in the confession inscriptions and in the other juridical texts of Asia Minor. This is particularly evident in the A.D. 57 eulogy from Lydia, north of Ayazviran, discussed above. This 'megology' acclaims the god Mes, the ruler of the city of Axiotta, as Μέγα ('Great!') seven times, celebrating the greatness of his holiness, justice, victory and power, whose mercy the erector of the stele had also experienced.[150] What is especially noteworthy in Romans are the two effusive doxologies concluding Paul's exposition of the salvation history of Jew and Gentile (Rom 11:33–36; cf. 9:1–11:32) and the unity of Christ's Spirit-indwelt community (16:25–27; cf. 12.1–16.24). Paul acclaims the eternal God as 'glorious' for revealing the long-hidden mystery of Christ and bringing about the obedience of the Gentiles, for demonstrating his wisdom and knowledge throughout the various stages of salvation history, and for justifying his dependents by a single act of grace as opposed to the continuous repayments of the ancient reciprocity system. God's mercy had met and satisfied all the challenges posed by God's impartial justice for sinful humanity in the face of the imminent eschatological wrath, transforming believers into God's agents of justice and mercy in a broken world, while they waited expectantly for their adoption in the new creation to be gloriously revealed.

---

150 See Chaniotis, 'Megatheism'.

Bibliography

Alexander, P.H., J.F. Kutsko, J.D. Ernest, S. Decker-Lucke, & D.L. Petersen (eds.), *The SBL Handbook of Style for Ancient Near Eastern, Biblical, and Early Christian Studies* (Atlanta: SBL Press, 2014 2nd ed.).

Anderson, G. *The Second Sophistic: A Cultural Phenomenon in the Roman Empire* (London/New York: Routledge, 1993).

Arnold, C.E. '"I Am Astonished That You Are So Quickly Turning Away!" (Gal 1.6): Paul and Anatolian Folk Belief', *NTS* 51 (2005), 429–449.

Axtell, H. *The Deification of Abstract Ideas in Roman Literature and Inscriptions* (Chicago: University of Chicago Press, 1907).

Barton, S.C., & G.H.R. Horsley 'A Hellenistic Cult Group and the New Testament Churches', *JbAC* 24 (1981), 7–41.

Beale, G.K. *We Become What We Worship: A Biblical Theology of Idolatry* (Downers Grove: IVP, 2008).

Belayche, N. 'Les stèles dites de confession: Une religiosité originale dans l'Anatolie impériale?', in L. de Blois, P. Funke, & J. Hahn (eds.), *The Impact of Imperial Rome on Religions, Ritual, and Religious Life in the Roman Empire* (Leiden: Brill, 2006), 66–81.

Belayche, N. 'Du texte à l'image: les reliefs sur les stèles "de confession" d'Anatolie', in S. Estienne, D. Jaillard et C. Pouzadoux (eds.), *Image et religion dans l'antiquité gréco-romain. Actes du Colloque de Rome 11–13 décembre 2003* (Naples: Centre Jean Bérard; École française d'Athènes, 2008), 181–194.

Bird, M.F. *The Saving Righteousness of God: Studies on Paul, Justification and the New Perspective* (Colorado Springs: Paternoster, 2006).

Bordt, M. 'Platon über Gottes Zorn und seine Barmherzigkeit', in R.G. Kratz & H. Spieckermann (eds.), *Divine Wrath and Divine Mercy in the World of Antiquity* (Forschungen zum Alten Testament 2. Reihe 33; Tübingen: Mohr Siebeck, 2008), 143–152.

Bornkamm, G. *Paul* (London: Hodder & Stoughton, 1971).

Bowersock, G.W.G. *Greek Sophists in the Roman Empire* (Oxford: Clarendon Press, 1969).

Bowie, E.L. 'The Greeks and Their Past in the Second Sophistic', *P&P* 46 (1970), 3–41.

Bremer, J.M. 'The Reciprocity of Giving and Thanksgiving in Greek Worship', in C. Gill, N. Postlethwaite & R. Seaford (eds.), *Reciprocity in Ancient Greece* (Oxford: Oxford University Press, 1998), 127–139.

Breytenbach, C. 'CHARIS and ELEOS in Paul's Letter to the Romans', in U. Schnelle (ed.), *The Letter to the Romans* (BETL 226; Leuven: Leuven University Press/Uitgenerij Peeters, 2009), 247–277.

Buckler, W.H., & D.M. Robinson *Sardis. VII, 1: Greek and Latin Inscriptions* (Leiden: Brill, 1932).

Byrne, B. *Romans* (SP 6; Collegeville: Michael Glazier/Liturgical Press, 1996).

Cadwallader, Alan H. 'Bodily Display and Epigraphical Confession at the Sanctuary of Apollo Lairbenos: An Examination of Emotional Responses', *Journal of Epigraphic Studies* 1 (2018), 183–201.

Carlà, F., & M. Gori, (eds.) *Gift Giving and the 'Embedded' Economy in the Ancient World* (Heidelberg: Universitätsverlag Winter, 2014).

Chaniotis, A. 'Constructing the Fear of Gods: Epigraphic Evidence from Sanctuaries of Greece and Asia Minor', in A. Chaniotis (ed.), *Unveiling Emotions: Sources and Methods for the Study of Emotions in the Greek World* (Stuttgart: Steiner Verlag, 2012), 205–234.

Chaniotis, A. 'Megatheism: The Search for the Almighty God and the Competition of Cults', in S. Mitchell and P. van Nuffelen (eds.), *One God: Pagan Monotheism in the Roman Empire* (Cambridge: Cambridge University Press, 2010), 112–140.

Chaniotis, A. 'Ritual Performances of Divine Justice: The Epigraphy of Confession, Atonement, and Exaltation in Roman Asia Minor', in H.M. Cotton, R.G. Hoyland, J.J. Price, & D.J. Wasserstein (eds.), *From Hellenism to Islam: Cultural and Linguistic Change in the Roman Near East* (Cambridge: Cambridge University Press, 2009), 115–153.

Chaniotis, A. 'Illness and Cures in the Greek Propitiatory Inscriptions and Dedications of Lydia and Phrygia', in H.F.J. Horstmanshoff, Ph. J. van der Eijk, & P.H. Schrijvers (eds.), *Ancient Medicine in its Socio-Cultural Context. Papers Read at the Congress Held at Leiden University, 13–15 April 1992*, vol. II (Amsterdam: Rodopi, 1995), 323–344.

Chaniotis, A. 'Under the Watchful Eyes of the Gods: Divine Justice in Hellenistic and Roman Asia Minor', in S. Colvin (ed.), *The Greco-Roman East: Politics, Culture, Society* (Cambridge: Cambridge University Press, 2004), 1–43.

Conley, D.F. 'The Stages of Rome's Decline in Sallust's Historical Theory', *Hermes* 109 (1981), 379–382.

D'Andria, F. *Cehennem 'Den Cennet'e Hierapolis (Pamukkale): Ploutonion. Aziz Philippus 'un Mezari ve Kutsal Alani* (Istanbul: Yayinlari, 2014).

De Hoz, M.P. 'The Aretalogical Character of the Maionian "Confession" Inscriptions', in A.M. Fernández (ed.), *Estudios de Epigrafía Griega. Serie investigación 1,* (La Laguna: Servicio de Publicaciones, Universidad de la Laguna, 2009), 357–367.

De Hoz, M.P. 'Literacy in Rural Anatolia', *ZPE* 155 (2006), 139–144.

Deidun, T.J. *New Covenant Morality in Paul* (Analecta Biblica 89; Rome: Pontificio Istituto Biblico, 2006).

Dodson, J.R. *The 'Powers' of Personification: Rhetorical Purpose in the Book of Wisdom and the Letter to the Romans* (Berlin/New York: Walter de Gruyter, 2008).

Dunn, J.D.G. *Romans 9–16* (Word 38B; Dallas: Word, 1988).

Earl, D.C. *The Political Thought of Sallust* (Cambridge: Cambridge University Press, 1961).

Elliott, Susan *Cutting too Close for Comfort: Paul's Letter to the Galatians in Its Anatolian Cultic Context* (Sheffield: Sheffield Academic Press, 2004).

Fitzmyer, J.A. *Romans: A New Translation with Introduction and Commentary* (AB 33; London: Geoffrey Chapman, 1992).

Glancy, Jennifer A. *Slavery in Early Christianity* (Oxford: Oxford University Press, 2002).

Goldhill, S. (ed.)   *Being Greek under Rome: Cultural Identity, the Second Sophistic and the Development of Empire* (Cambridge: Cambridge University Press, 2001).

Gordon, R.   'Raising a Sceptre: Confession–Narratives from Lydia and Phrygia', *JRA* 17 (2004), 177–196.

Grant, F.C.   *Hellenistic Religions* (Indianapolis: The Library of Liberal Arts, 1953).

Grant, F.C., (ed.)   *Ancient Roman Religion* (New York: Liberal Arts Press, 1957).

Gregory, A.P.   *Village Society in Hellenistic and Roman Asia Minor* (Unpublished PhD, Columbia University, 1997).

Hahne, H.A.   *The Corruption and Redemption of Creation: Nature in Romans 8:19-22 and Jewish Apocalyptic Literature* (London: T&T Clark, 2006).

Hanges, J.C.   *Paul, Founder of Churches: A Study in Light of the Evidence for the Role of 'Founder–Figures' in the Hellenistic–Roman Period* (WUNT 292; Tübingen: Mohr Siebeck, 2012).

Harris, B.F.   'The Idea of Mercy and Its Graeco–Roman Context', in P.T. O'Brien and D.G. Peterson (eds.), *God Who Is Rich in Mercy: Essays Presented to D.B. Knox* (Homebush West: Lancer Books, 1986), 89–105.

Harris, W.V.   'Roman Opinions about the Truthfulness of Dreams', *JRS* 93 (2003), 18–34.

Harrison, J.R.   'In Quest of the Third Heaven: Paul and His Apocalyptic Imitators', *VC* 58.1 (2004), 24–55.

Harrison, J. R.   *Paul's Language of Grace in Its Graeco–Roman Context* (WUNT II 172; Tübingen: Mohr Siebeck, 2003).

Hasel, G.F.   *The Remnant: The History and Theology of the Remnant Idea from Genesis to Isaiah* (Berrien Springs: Andrews University Press, 1974).

Horsley, G.H.R.   'Expiation and the Cult of Men', in G.H.R. Horsley (ed.), *New Documents Illustrating Early Christianity, 3. A Review of the Greek Inscriptions and Papyri published in 1978* (Macquarie University: Ancient History Documentary Research Centre, 1983), §6, 20–31.

Horsley, G.H.R.   'Two Confession Texts from Graeco-Roman Phrygia', G.H.R. Horsley (ed.), *New Documents Illustrating Early Christianity. A Review of the Greek Inscriptions and Papyri published in 1976* (Macquarie University: Ancient History Documentary Research Centre, 1981), §7, 32–33.

Horsley, G.H.R., & Jean M. Luxford,   'Pagan Angels in Roman Asia Minor: Revisiting the Epigraphic Evidence', *Anatolian Studies* 66 (2016), 141–183.

Horsley, G.H.R., & S. Mitchell (eds.),   *The Inscriptions of Central Pisidia, Including Texts from Kremna, Ariassos, Keraia, Hyia, Panemoteichos, the Sanctuary of Apollo Perminoundeis, Sia, Kocaaliler, and the Döşeme Boğazı* (Bonn: Habelt, 2000).

Irons, C.L.   *The Righteousness of God: A Lexical Examination of the Covenant-Faithfulness Interpretation* (WUNT II 386; Tübingen: Mohr Siebeck, 2015).

Jacob, E.   *Theology of the Old Testament* (London: Hodder & Stoughton, 1958 [French: 1955]).

Jenks, C.J.   *The Origins and Early Development of the Antichrist Myth* (Berlin/New York: Walter de Gruyter, 1991).

Jewett, R.   *Romans: A Commentary* (Hermeneia; Minneapolis: Fortress, 2008).

Judeich, W.   'Inschriften', in C. Humann, C. Cichorius, W. Judeich, F. Winter (eds.), *Altertümer von Hierapolis* (Berlin: Druck und Verlag von Georg Reimer, 1898).

Judge, E.A.   'The Roman Theory of Historical Degeneration', in E.A. Judge, *The First Christians in the Roman World: Augustan and New Testament Essays* (WUNT 229; J.R. Harrison, ed.; Tübingen: Mohr Siebeck, 2008), 52–58.

Judge, E.A.   'The Roman Base of Paul's Mission', in E.A. Judge, *The First Christians in the Roman World: Augustan and New Testament Essays* (WUNT 229; J.R. Harrison, ed.; Tübingen: Mohr Siebeck, 2008), 553–567.

Judge, E.A.   'The Quest for Mercy in Late Antiquity', in P.T. O'Brien and D.G. Peterson (eds.), *God Who Is Rich in Mercy: Essays Presented to D.B. Knox* (Homebush West: Lancer Books, 1986), 107–121.

Kirk, J.R.D. *Unlocking Romans Resurrection and the Justification of God* (Grand Rapids: Eerdmans, 2008).

Klauck, H.-J. 'Die kleinasiatischen Beichtinschriften und das Neue Testament', in H. Cancik, H. Lichtenberger, P. Schäfer (eds.), *Geschichte-Tradition-Reflexion. Festschrift für Martin Hengel zum 70. Geburtstag* (3 vols.; Tübingen: Mohr Siebeck, 1996), 3.63-87.

Konstan, D. 'The Freedom to Feel Grateful: The View from Classical Antiquity', in D. Carr (ed.), *Perspectives on Gratitude: An Interdisciplinary Approach* (London and New York: Routledge, 2016), 41-53.

Konstan, D. *Pity Transformed* (London: Duckworth, 2001).

Kreitzer, Larry J. 'The Plutonium of Hierapolis and the Descent of Christ into "The Lowermost Parts of the Earth" (Ephesians 4:9)', *Bib* 79 (1998), 381-393.

Levison, J.R. *Portraits of Adam in Early Judaism from Sirach to 2 Baruch* (JSPSupp 1; Sheffield: Sheffield Academic, 1988).

LiDonnici, L.R. *The Epidaurian Miracle Inscriptions: Text, Translation, and Commentary* (Atlanta: Scholars Press,1995).

MacMullen, R., & E.N. Lane (eds.), *Paganism and Christianity 100-425 CE: A Sourcebook* (Minneapolis: Fortress, 1992).

Madsen, J.M. *Eager to Be Roman: Greek Response to Roman Rule in Pontus and Bithynia* (London: Duckworth, 2009).

Martin, R.P. *Reconciliation: A Study of Paul's Theology* (London: Marshall, Morgan & Scott, 1981).

Meyer, Elizabeth 'The Greek Manumissions Project', at www2.iath.virginia.edu/meyer/home.html, accessed 28.02.2017.

Miles, D.P. *Forbidden Pleasures: Sumptuary Laws and the Ideology of Moral Decline in Ancient Rome* (Unpublished PhD thesis, University College London, 1987).

Mitchell, S. *Regional Epigraphic Catalogues of Asia Minor. The Ankara District: The Inscriptions of North Galatia II* (Oxford: B.A.R., 1982).

Moo, D. *The Epistle to the Romans* (NICNT; Eerdmans: Grand Rapids, 1996).

Morris, L.L.	'The Theme of Romans', in W.W. Gasque & R.P. Martin (eds.), *Apostolic History and the Gospel: Biblical and Historical Essays Presented to F.F. Bruce on His 60th Birthday* (Exeter: Paternoster, 1970), 249–263.
Ozturk, E.A., & C. Tanriver,	'Some New Finds from the Sanctuary of Apollon Lairbenos', *Epigraphica Anatolica* 42 (2009), 87–97.
P.W. van der Horst	'"Only Then Will All Israel Be Saved": A Short Note on the Meaning of καὶ οὕτως in Romans 11:26', *JBL* 119 (2000), 521–525.
Parker, R.	'Pleasing Thighs: Reciprocity in Greek Religion', in C. Gill, N. Postlethwaite & R. Seaford (eds.), *Reciprocity in Ancient Greece* (Oxford: Oxford University Press, 1998), 105–125.
Peel, S.	'Thwarted Expectations of Divine Reciprocity', *Mnemosyne* 69.4 (2016), 551–571.
Petzl, G.	*Die Beichtinschriften Westkleinasiens = Epigraphica Anatolica* 22 (Bonn: Habelt, 1994), 1–143.
Reumann, J.	*Righteousness in the New Testament: 'Justification' in the United States Lutheran–Roman Catholic Dialogue* (Philadelphia/New York: Paulist/Fortress Press, 1982).
Ricl, M.	'Hosios kai Dikaios. Nouvaux monuments', *Epigraphica Anatolica* 20 (1992), 95–100.
Ricl, M.	'Hosios kai Dikaios. Première partie: Catalogue des inscriptions', *Epigraphica Anatolica* 17 (1991), 1–70.
Ricl, M.	'Hosios kai Dikaios. Seconde partie: analyse', *Epigraphica Anatolica* 19 (1992), 71–102.
Ricl, M.	'The Appeal to Divine Justice in the Lydian Confession-Inscriptions', in *Forschungen in Lydien* (Asia Minor Studien 17; E. Schwertheim, ed.; Bonn: Rudolf Habelt, 1995), 67–76.
Ritti, T.	*Epigraphic Guide to Hierapolis (Pamukkale)* (P. Arthur, transl.; Istanbul: Italian Archaeological Mission at Hierapolis, 2006).
Robert, L.	*Nouvelles Inscriptions de Sardes* (Paris: Librairie d'amérique et d'orient, Adrien Maisonneuve, 1964).

Robinson, D.W.B. 'The Salvation of Israel in Romans 9–11', *Reformed Theological Review* 26 (1967), 81–96. Now published in P.G. Bolt & M.D. Thompson (eds.), *Donald Robinson. Select Works. 1: Assembling God's People* (Camperdown, NSW: Australian Church Record & Moore College, 2008), 47–63.

Rostad, A. 'The Religious Context of the Lydian Propitiation Inscriptions', *SO* 81 (2006), 88–108.

Rostad, A. *Human Transgression-Divine Retribution: A Study of Religious Transgressions and Punishments in Greek Cultic Regulations and Lydian–Phrygian Reconciliation Inscriptions* (Unpublished PhD Thesis, University of Bergen, 2006).

Satlow, M.L. (ed.) *The Gift in Antiquity. The Ancient World: Comparative Histories* (Chichester: Wiley–Blackwell, 2013).

Schenk, P. 'Darstellung und Funktion des Zorns der Götter in antiker Epik', in R.G. Kratz & H. Spieckermann (eds.), *Divine Wrath and Divine Mercy in the World of Antiquity* (Forschungen zum Alten Testament 2. Reihe 33; Tübingen: Mohr Siebeck, 2008), 153–175.

Schnabel, E. J. 'Divine Tyranny and Public Humiliation: A Suggestion for the Interpretation of the Lydian and Phrygian Confession Inscriptions', *NovT* 45.2 (2003), 160–188.

Schreiner, T.R. *Paul: Apostle of God's Glory in Christ. A Pauline Theology* (Downers Grove: IVP, 2001).

Schreiner, T.R. *Romans* (ECNT 6; Grand Rapids: Baker, 1998).

Seifrid, M.A. 'Romans', in G. K. Beale & D. A. Carson (eds.), *Commentary on the New Testament Use of the Old Testament* (Grand Rapids, MI: Baker, 2007).

Seifrid, M.A. *Christ, Our Righteousness: Paul's Theology of Justification* (NSBT 9; Leicester: Apollos, 2000).

Stafford, E. *Worshipping Virtues: Personification and the Divine in Ancient Greece* (London: Duckworth/Classical Press of Wales, 2000).

Straten, F.T. 'Gifts for the Gods', in H.S. Versnel (ed.), *Faith, Hope and Worship* (Leiden: Brill, 1981), 65–151.

Strom, M. *Reframing Paul: Conversations in Grace and Community* (Downers Grove: IVP, 2000).

Strubbe, J.H.M. (ed.) ΑΡΑΙ ΕΠΙΤΥΜΒΙΟΙ: *Imprecations against Desecrators of a Grave in the Greek Epitaphs of Asia Minor. A Catalogue* (Bonn: Dr Rudolf Habelt GMBH, 1997).

Strubbe, J.H.M. '"Cursed Be He That Moves My Bones"', in C.A. Faraone & D. Obbink (eds.), *Magika Hiera: Ancient Greek Magic and Religion* (New York/Oxford: Oxford University Press, 1991), 33–59.

Swain, S. *Hellenism and Empire: Language, Classicism, and Power in the Greek World AD 50–250* (Oxford: Clarendon Press, 1996).

Varinlioğlu, E. 'Zeus Orkamaneites and the Expiatory Inscriptions', *Epigraphica Anatolica* 1 (1983), 75–86.

Vasta, M.S. *The Crisis of Exemplarity and the Role of History in Sallust* (Unpublsihed PhD, Indiana University, 2014).

Versnel, H.S. *Fluch und Gebet: Magische Manipulation versus religiöses Flehen? Religionsgeschichtliche und hermeneutische Betrachtungen über antike Fluchtafeln* (Berlin: De Gruyter, 2009).

Versnel, H.S. 'Beyond Cursing: The Appeal to Justice in Judicial Prayers', in C.A. Faraone & D. Obbink (eds.), *Magika Hiera: Ancient Greek Magic and Religion* (New York/Oxford: Oxford University Press, 1991), 60–106.

Voorwinde, S. 'Rethinking Israel: An Exposition of Romans 11:25–27', *Vox Reformata* 68 (2003), 4–48.

Whittle, S. *Covenant Renewal and the Consecration of the Gentiles in Romans* (SNTSMS 161; Cambridge: Cambridge University Press, 2015).

Wildberg, C. 'Piety as Service, Epiphany as Reciprocity: Two Observations on the Religious Meaning of the Gods in Euripides', *Illinois Classical Studies* 24/25 (1999–2000), 235–256.

Williams, S.K. 'The "Righteousness of God" in Romans', *JBL* 99.2 (1980), 241–290.

Wright, N.T. 'Romans', in L.E. Keck (ed.), *The New Interpreter's Bible: A Commentary in Twelve Volumes Vol. X* (Nashville: Abingdon, 2002), 423–770.

Wright, N.T. *Justification: God's Plan and Paul's Vision* (London: SPCK, 2009).

Ziesler, J.A.   *The Meaning of Righteousness in Paul: A Linguistic and Theological Enquiry* (SNTSMS 20; Cambridge: Cambridge University Press, 1972).

PART 4

Ancient Epistles and the Puzzling Particularity of Romans

CHAPTER 13

Untangling the Pauline Handshakes: Who is Greeting Whom in Romans 16?

Peter G. Bolt

1. Introduction: A Hypothesis to be Tested

a. Hypothesis Stated

This essay is in the form of an experiment, testing a hypothesis about the persons listed at the end of the letter to the Romans (16:1–15).[1] The hypothesis can be stated in the form of a question:

> Rather than this long list of people being members of the Roman church(es) being greeted by Paul (as is usually assumed), what if they are a mission team sent from Paul, and the apostle is introducing them and asking the Roman Christians to greet them, as they arrive in Rome with Phoebe and his letter?

---

[1] For a methodological similarity, cf. Robinson, *Redating*, 207, who 'seeks not a conclusive demonstration but a hypothesis that gives the most reasonable explanation for the largest amount of the data', to 'allow it to be tested by the results it yields' (pp.33, 207). Rather than seeking the supposed 'certainty' of foundational truths upon which an edifice can then be constructed, this method examines multiple interlocking elements that may mutually reinforce the truth of a complex historical reality as it emerges from their re-sifting. This article assumes that the final chapter is an integral part of Romans, addressed to the Romans; as does, among others, Mathew, *Women*, 3–4. The suggestion made here actually overcomes the main objections to a Roman audience; as given by, e.g., Llewelyn, '#12. The Development of the Codex', 255 n.27; Edmundson, *Church in Rome*, 21–22.

b. A very strange list

The catalyst for proposing this hypothesis is the oft-recognized strangeness of this list of greetings within the Pauline corpus (and, indeed, the New Testament).

The first strange feature is the number of names listed. Even if not common, other letters survive from the ancient world in which an author greets a long list of recipients.[2] Take for example, the 4th century Christian letter written with atrocious spelling and grammar by Euthalios.[3] Opening with 'many greetings' (πολλὰ χαίριν) to his 'lady mother', followed by a prayer for her 'good health before the Lord God', more than half of the letter is then devoted to opening and closing greetings (17 out of a total of 31 lines), directed to a reasonably lengthy list of people. After briefly dealing with the business, the final greetings all utilize (a form of) the verb used in Romans 16, ἀσπάζομαι:

---

2   For the study of Greek epistolography and its relation to the New Testament, see the survey of scholarship at *NewDocs* 4, #16, pp. 58–63. For comparative data, this article utilises papyri letters found in the *New Documents* series as a sample data set.
    Sometimes the greeting is to a group, whose names are not listed, e.g. *NewDocs* 1, #16: 'greet (ἄσπασαι) all your folk, men and women'; #18: 'I greet (ἀσπάζομε) you and your wife and all yours'; #85: 'I greet (ἀσπάζωμαι) your children–may they be immune from the evil eye'. Letter 'to the beloved brothers', IV/V, unknown in Egypt. *NewDocs* 4, #124, opens with personal greetings, using the first person, to a list of people. It also passes on greetings from another person at the author's end, before closing with further greetings in the first person. See also *NewDocs* 2, 31–32: 'Greet (ἄσ[πασ]αι) all those yours and all those in your house'.
    Rather than providing a list of names, other letters ask the recipient to greet others at their end 'by name', κατ' ὄνομα, e.g. *NewDocs* 3, #1, POxy 3312, l.14: ἀσπάζου πάντας τοὺς |σοὺς κατ' ὄνομα καὶ οἱ <ἐ>μοὶ |16 πάντες σε ἀσπάζονται. 'Greet all your family individually. Just as all mine greet you'; cf. *NewDocs* 3, #52; Cf. 3 John 15, the solitary NT example: ἀσπάζου τοὺς φίλους κατ' ὄνομα. This expression is not frequent even in the papyri, see *NewDocs* 1, #15 p.56, #19, #21 p.66. Cf. *NewDocs* 4, #16: ἄσπασαι πρὸς ὄνομα πάντας τοὺς ὑμᾶς φιλοῦντας πολλά 'Greet warmly by name all those who love you'; *NewDocs* 1, #19: 'Greet as from me (προσαγόρευαι ὡς ἀπ' ἐμοῦ) the *praepositus*, together with all his (family) by name [...] together with all their (families) by name'.
    Examples of lists of names include, e.g. *NewDocs* 2, #20: 'Greet (ἀσπάζου) Sarapias and her mother and Baukalas and all those with you individually (κατ' ὄνομα)'; Diodora to her (?defacto) Valerius Maximus: *NewDocs* 1, #15: begins (l.3) with χαίρειν καὶ ὑγιαίνειν, then ll.9–12 'Greet (ἀσπάζου) Amas, Paulina, Publius, Diodoros, Granias, and Tyche'. Editor notes that 'the extended list of greetings [...] has numerous parallels in the papyri, dated I–IV', and notes the parallel with Rom 16.3–16, p.55. 6/16 lines are given to opening/closing greetings; *NewDocs* 2, #21 No. 5: 'Greet (ἄσπασε) Maximus and his wife, and Sempronius, Kyrillos and Satornilus and Gemellus and Julius and his family, and Helen and her family, and Skythikos and Kopres, Chairemon, Themouthis and her children'; *NewDocs* 3, #2: 'Greet most noble Alexandros, and his Sarapio and Theon and Aristokleia – may the evil eye not touch them! – and Aristokleia's children'.
3   *NewDocs* 1, #84, IV, unknown provenance.

[17] 'I greet you (ἀσπ]άδωμαι ὑμῖν). Nonna sends you many greetings (ἀσπάδεται ... πολλά). Silvane greets (ἀσπάδαιται) you. Annoutis and Theonilla and Ischyrion |[20] greet (ἀσπάδωμαι) you. I greet (ἀσπάδωμαι) Apion, and the overseer and his wife and children. And I, Mikke, greet (ἀσ[π]άδωμαι) the overseer along with his children and his wife. [...] I greet (ἀσπάδωμαι) | my lord father.

Despite such analogies, amongst the New Testament letters Romans 16 is the only case of greetings being extended to a lengthy list of persons.

However, it is not simply the number of names that makes this list stand out. It is the very fact that Paul greets anybody at all. Whereas he quite often concludes his letters by sending greetings from those with him,[4] as in Romans 16:21–23, Paul himself rarely greets groups or individuals. The two possible exceptions in the Pauline corpus are Colossians 4:15 and 2 Timothy 4:19, greeting, respectively, Nympha and the church associated with her house, and Priscilla and Aquila and the household of Onesiphorus[5]—although if the hypothesis discussed here proves valid and can be applied, these may also fall by the wayside.

Even so, these rare examples are vastly overshadowed by the list in Romans 16, which identifies 27 individuals—17 males and 10 females[6]—mostly named and some further elaborated. This is clearly a cameo appearance for 22 of them, for Priscilla and Aquila (v.3) are the only two characters clearly well-known to the NT (Acts 18:2, 18, 26; 1 Cor 16:19; 2 Tim 4:19).[7] Although each case is disputable, several others named here are also likely known from elsewhere in the New Testament: Mary, Rufus and his mother, and Junia.

---

4 Greetings to the recipients of Paul's letters are sent from Paul's side by: the Churches in Asia, Priscilla and Aquila, their household church (1 Cor 16:19); all the brethren (1 Cor 16:20); all the saints (2 Cor 13:13); the brethren with Paul (Phil 4:21b), all the saints, especially those of Caesar's household (Phil 4:22); Aristarchus, Mark, Jesus called Justus, Epaphras, Luke, and Demas (Col 4:10–11, 12, 14); Eubulus, Pudens, Linus, Claudia, and the brethren (2 Tim 4:21); Epaphras, Mark, Aristarchus, Demas, and Luke (Philem 23–24).
5 Paul also passes on generalised greetings to 'all the saints in Christ Jesus' (Phil 4:21a) and to the brethren at Laodicea (Col 4:15).
6 Assuming that Junia is original and female.
7 Sanday & Headlam, *Romans*, 418, note that tracking their movements is very complicated and their presence in this list has been used to throw doubt on the authenticity of this section of the letter, or to say it was addressed to Ephesus not Rome.

Despite her name being one of the two commonest Jewish female names at the time,[8] it is highly probable that Mary (v.6) was well-known as one of the several women by that name in earliest Christianity.[9] Given other associations in this list, and the validity of the hypothesis being tested here, she would most likely be Mary, the mother of James (the younger) and Joseph (Matt 27:56, 61; 28:1; Mark 15:40; 16:1; Luke 24:10), who was the wife of Cl[e]opas, and the sister-in-law of Jesus' own mother (John 19:25),[10] Cleopas being the brother of Joseph, Jesus' earthly father.[11] In the morning of resurrection day, Mary was one of the women who discovered the empty tomb, and in the afternoon, Cleopas famously met the risen Jesus on the road to Emmaus, but was prevented from recognising him at the time (Luke 24:18).[12] Their son Symeon became the leader of the Jerusalem church after James the Lord's brother was murdered in A.D. 62.[13]

8   Judge, '#26. The Names of Jewish Women', 156–7, refers to Ilan, 'Notes': of 247 women using 68 names, the two names (2.9%) Salome and Mariam applied to 119 women (47.7%); and to the expanded list of 402 women in Ilan, *Lexicon*, Part 1, which gives the two names 35.6% share.
9   The New Testament mentions (at least) five: Mary the mother of Jesus; Mary the wife of Cleopas; Mary of Bethany; Mary Magdalene; Mary the mother of John Mark.
10 For discussion, see Bauckham, 'Mary of Clopas', *Gospel Women*, Ch. 6. On p.181: 'The Mary (Μαρία) of Romans 16:6 seems to be someone whose identity could be well known just through the use of this name. If she is a Jewish Christian with the Hebrew name Miriam, rather than a Gentile Christian with the Latin name Maria, then she too may have come from Jerusalem, and could be identified with Mary the Mother of James and Joses, whom the Synoptic evangelists evidently expect to be someone their readers will know by repute (Matt. 27:56, 61; 28:1; Mark 15:40, 47; 16:1; Luke 24:10)'. For examples and discussion of Maria as a Jewish or Roman name, see *NewDocs* 4 #115, concluding that onomastics cannot decide whether this Maria is a Jew or a Roman (p.230). For 'sister in law', see p.209. Bauckham (pp. 209–210) does not identify John's Mary of Clopas with the Synoptic's Mary, mother of James and Joseph, arguing that it would be more likely to have her named after her more famous son Symeon. Robinson, *Redating*, 106–107, solves this problem by suggesting a date for the Gospels prior to A.D. 62, when James was killed and Symeon took over.
11 Eusebius of Caesarea, quoting the 2nd century historian Hegesippus: *H.E.* 3.11; 3.32.6 Clopas 'an uncle of the Lord'; cf. 4.22.4; 3.32.3 Mary, the wife of Clopas, the father of Symeon. Epiphanius, *Panarion* 78.8–9, bishop's list, ?derived from Eusebius, *Chronicle*: 'Symeon, the son of James' uncle, with them—Symeon, the son of Cleopas the brother of Joseph'; 'Symeon was crucified under Trajan'.
12 The variation in spelling is of no consequence—Clopas (in John) being his semitic, and Cleopas (in Luke) (=Cleopatros) his Greek equivalent; see Bauckham, *Gospel Women*, 211; Letronne, 'Sur les noms grecs de Cléopas'.
13 James was put to death by the high priest Ananus, son of the Ananus who appears in the New Testament accounts as Annas (Luke 3:2; John 18:13, 24; Acts 4:6). Due to the resultant outcry, Ananus, despite having held office for only three months, was dismissed by Agrippa II (Josephus, *A.J.* 20.200–203; Eus. *H.E.* 2.23.21–24; Epiphanius, *Panarion* 78.8–9: 'James, who was martyred in Jerusalem by beating with a cudgel, [lived] until the time of Nero'). Bauckham, *Gospel Women*, 209–210; Pixner, *Paths of the Messiah*, Ch. 31.

Mary has apparently already displayed a special concern for the Roman church(es), having 'laboured much for you' (πολλὰ ἐκοπίασεν εἰς ὑμᾶς).

Rufus and his mother (v.13) are probably related to Simon of Cyrene who was forced to carry the cross of Christ (Mark 15:21). It is also entirely possible that Simon of Cyrene is also the Simeon Niger, part of the earliest mission to Antioch (Acts 11:20; 13:1; cf. 4:36, 21:16).[14] If this relationship is seriously considered, rather than simply dismissed,[15] then the event(s) which prompted Paul to designate Rufus' mother as also his own would have occurred very early and in Jerusalem. Presumably Simon has since died, but his family now continue his witness.

Bauckham has made a good argument that Junia (v.7), a female,[16] is the Romanised name adopted by Joanna, known in Herodian and Lukan circles.[17] The wife of the Nabatean, Chuza, the manager of the household of Herod Antipas, the Tetrarch of Galilee, she became part of that circle of female followers of Jesus in Galilee, alongside Mary Magdalene (Luke 8:2–3), who supported Jesus and his disciples out of their own resources and followed him to Jerusalem. Joanna was almost certainly one of Luke's major sources, supplying insight into the household of Herod Antipas (Luke 13:31; 23:7–12, 15; cf. Acts 4:27),[18] and

---

14 Simeon is the LXX way of spelling Simon; as noted by Ilan, *Lexicon*, I.335–336. Finding two other examples of Jews bearing the name in Palestine, and three in the Western diaspora, Ilan notes that Niger is Latin and a nickname; Ilan, *Lexicon*, I.335–336, III.526. If the family tomb has been discovered in the Kidron valley, then there was also a daughter, Sara; see Ossuary 5, Evans, 'Excavating Caiaphas', 338.

15 E.g. Mathew, *Women*, 39, considers it implausible, but offers a confused argument. From 'a mother of mine', she rightly infers (p.111) that this woman helped Paul in a specific situation or regularly at some point. The ossuary of Rufus' brother, Alexander, may have been discovered in the Kidron valley; see Evans, *Jesus and the Ossuaries*, 94–96; and 'Excavating Caiaphas', 338–340.

16 Edmundson, *Church in Rome*, 25 n.25, represents many older commentators, arguing that Junia is 'generally taken as masculine, Junias an abbreviation for Junianus'. Bauckham, *Gospel Women*, 166, however, notes that the case for Junia (fem) has been well made since the 1970s and is now widely accepted; it is not attested as a male name (p.169); but well-attested as a female name (pp.99–100). See also Mathew, *Women*, 97–100; Lampe, 'Junias'.

17 See Bauckham, 'Joanna the Apostle', *Gospel Women*, ch. 5. Mathew, *Women*, 9, trivialises the argument to a 'speculative', 'sound-equivalence theory'. She rightly dismisses Winter's suggested identification with Junia Theodora (*Roman Wives*, 201; cf. Kearsley, '#3. Women'), who could not have been in Christ before Paul (p.101).

18 Wenham, *Easter Enigma*, 50. Although, it should also be noted that the earliest Christian movement had other connections to the Herodian court, such as Manaean (Acts 13:1), who clearly operated in the same circles as Luke (cf. Bauckham, *Gospel Women*, 119)—especially if Luke was Lucius of Cyrene (cf. Acts 13:1); and presumably some of the Herodians (Mark 3:6; 12:13; Matt. 22:16).

first-hand evidence of Jesus' last journey to Jerusalem.[19] Although she was not one of the women who discovered the empty tomb, she stood with those who had done so as they reported the discovery to the larger group (Luke 24:10).[20]

Alongside these individuals, Paul mentions five groups of people generically:

1. the church associated with the household of Priscilla and Aquila (v.5, τὴν κατ' οἶκον αὐτῶν ἐκκλησίαν);
2. those who are out of the people of Aristobulus (v.10b, τοὺς ἐκ τῶν Ἀριστοβούλου);
3. those out of the people of Narcissus, who are in the Lord (v.11b, τοὺς ἐκ τῶν Ναρκίσσου τοὺς ὄντας ἐν κυρίῳ);
4. the brethren with Asyncritus, Phlegon, Hermes, Patrobas, and Hermas (v.14, καὶ τοὺς σὺν αὐτοῖς ἀδελφούς); and
5. the saints who are with Philologus, Julia, Nereus and his sister, and Olympas (v.15, καὶ τοὺς σὺν αὐτοῖς πάντας ἁγίους).

The list also contains several family connections. There are probably three husband and wife teams: Priscilla and Aquila (v.3); Andronicus and Junia (v.7); and Philologus and Julia (v.15).[21] Those listed with the latter pair are possibly their children Nereus,[22] his sister, and Olympas their brother (v.15). Tryphaena and Tryphosa (v.12) were probably twin sisters. Rufus and his mother (v.13) also make a family pairing.

One of the most interesting sets of family connections is found in Andronicus and Junia (v.7) and Herodion (v.11), whom Paul lists as his fellow-kinsmen (συγγενεῖς), as he does Lucius, Jason, and Sosipater, who are with Paul as he writes (v.21). Unfortunately these connections are

---

19 Cf. Bauckham, *Gospel Women*, 112–113, noting an *inclusio* between 8:2-3 and 24:10. Commentaries regularly list Joanna as one of Luke's sources.
20 See Bolt, 'What Actually Happened on Resurrection Morning?'. 'Prominent among the apostles' may therefore indicate she was associated with ministry of Jesus and with the women who reported the empty tomb; see further, Bauckham, 'Joanna the Apostle', 166–186. In this case, her association with Mary wife of Cleopas (v.6) actively continued.
21 For husband and wife teams as doctors, see *NewDocs* 2 #2, p.17; in the purple trade, *NewDocs* 2 #3.
22 Ilan, *Lexicon*, provides no listing for Nereus. If it is a Jewish person, the name may be related to Neriyah, the name of Baruch's father (Jer 32:12), and of Zechora's father (2 Chron 36:5), but the LXX renders this name Νηρίας or Νηρεῖος.

commonly obscured by taking Paul's language in a metaphorical sense, as if these six people were also Jews (usually supported by a cross reference to Rom 9:3).[23] Certainly, other familial terms are used metaphorically for relationships within the Christian community both in the New Testament itself and in later Christian Papyri.[24] However, given the blood-ties that also existed within Christian communities the metaphorical use should not be assumed too quickly in either set of sources, unless they demonstrably do not pertain.[25]

Noting that Paul refrains from referring to other Jews in his list in this way (Priscilla and Aquila, v.3; Rufus and his mother, v.13; perhaps Mary, v.6), some have read the term literally of Paul's blood-relatives.[26] This suits the predominant wider usage[27] and especially that of the NT elsewhere, where συγγενής is always used of kin, that is, a smaller group than someone's racial connections (Mark 6:4; Luke 1:58; 14:12; 21:16; John 18:26; Acts 10:24; cf. συγγένεια: Luke 1:61; Acts 7:3 = Gen 12:1; Acts 7:14)—such as Paul's sister and nephew (Acts 23:16), who apparently lived in Jerusalem. As for Romans 9:3, it adds even

---

23 E.g. Edmundson, *Church in Rome*, 25; Sanday & Headlam, *Romans*, 423, who refer to 9:3, and argue that it would be 'most improbable' for Paul to have so many relatives in Rome and Macedonia (v.21)—an argument rendered otiose by the present hypothesis; Cranfield, *Romans* 2, 788, referring to 9:3, where he claims the 'meaning is clear'. For the English translations, see n.26 below.

24 Cf. discussion at *NewDocs* 1, #18 for relational terms used for non blood-relatives more widely than the Christian sphere; cf. *NewDocs* 6, #21; 25; *NewDocs* 8, #15 p. 171; *NewDocs* 10, #28. The metaphorical use is, of course, present in NT with 'brothers', when Paul called himself father (1 Cor 4:15), or pictures himself as mother (1 Thess 2:7), and in Rom 16:13 when he claims Rufus' mother as his own. Despite such usage being 'clearly a loose use of familial titles to indicate "respect and affection"' (Llewellyn, *NewDocs* 6, #21, p. 158 n. 178), it cannot demand that blood-ties are never present, as they demonstrably were within the early Christian movement.

25 Editors of letters in the Christian papyri can sometimes opt for metaphor when the terms seem to refer to blood-relations, see e.g. *NewDocs* 1, #84. For a particularly clear example of the alternative, see the 4th c. letter in which Horigenes greets fourteen brothers, five sisters, two mothers, and one father, which suggests that he applied the familial terms 'to members of the same community or group of believers', *NewDocs* 10, #29, p.173; for another clear loose use of these terms, see *NewDocs* 6, #21, p. 158 n. 178.

26 Bauckham, *Gospel Women*, 170, notes Ellis, 'Paul and his Co-Workers', 186; Lagrange, *St Paul*, 366. The classic stream of English translation has 'kinsmen' (AV, RV, ASV, NASB, ESV; 'relatives': NRSV), whereas the more recent vary this to 'fellow Jews' (NIV); 'fellow countrymen' (HCSB); or 'compatriots' (NET). Bauckham prefers 'fellow Jews', even though he acknowledges this is an unusual use and that other Jews in the chapter do not get this designation.

27 LSJ does not list any racial usage; BDAG supports a racial reading at Rom 9:3 only with Josephus *B.J.* 7.262, *A.J.* 12.338, which are at best unclear, but more likely referring to actual relatives; some of the examples in *TDNT* possibly refer to non-blood relatives.

greater poignancy to his argument if Paul mentions his grief over his own unbelieving blood-relatives, even if, by metonymy, they also stand for the wider Jewish race. In addition, to speak more generally of Jewish Christians, Paul uses other terms, such as 'the saints' (ἅγιοι), as he does twice in Romans 16 (vv. 2, 15).[28]

A further strange feature of this list is that it is saturated with affection between Paul and those named, built on fond memories of shared experiences. Phoebe (v.1) is his patron (προστάτις); Priscilla and Aquila once risked their lives for him (v.3); Epaenetus, Stachys, and Persis are described as beloved (ἀγαπητός; v.5b, 9, 12b);[29] Apelles as approved (τὸν δόκιμον, v.10); the mother of Rufus he calls his own (v.13). On the usual reading, how could Paul have developed such intimacy with so many in the congregation(s) at Rome, a city which he had never visited? And why didn't he have a similar affectionate list in any other letter—especially perhaps that to the Corinthians, amongst whom he spent over eighteen months (Acts 18:11)?

Since he had not visited Rome previously (Rom 1:8–13), the relationship Paul shared with the people on this list must have been forged in the East. This is consistent with the list referring explicitly only to Eastern locations (Cenchrea, v.1; presumably the churches of v.4; Asia, v.5). The usual view therefore requires all these individuals to have made their way to Rome subsequent to their previous dealings with the apostle, and that Paul would know of their presence in the Roman congregation(s).

It is significant that these mutually affectionate relationships did not simply arise out of random past experiences, but out of their previous involvement with the apostle in the work of the gospel in the Eastern realms. Phoebe (vv.1–2) is a benefactor to many and to Paul, and so to his gospel work; Priscilla and Aquila, and Urbanus (vv.3, 9) are called co-workers—a loaded term (συνεργός) used for special members of his

---

28 See Robinson, *Assembling*, Chapters 1–13.
29 For examples and discussion of 'beloved brothers', see *NewDocs* 4 #124. Esthlades, a Greek soldier, requests his parents to look after his sisters, Pelops, Stachys, and Senathyris. White, *Light*, Letter 43 = SelPap I 101 (=WChr 10) 130 B.C.E.

team.³⁰ Priscilla and Aquila are to be thanked by all the Gentile churches (v.4). Epaenetus is the first convert in Asia (v.5b). Mary (v.6), Tryphaena and Tryphosa (v.12a), and Persis are all women commended for working hard in the Lord, using a word (κοπιάω) associated with missionary labours.³¹ Apelles (v.10) is approved (δόκιμος), perhaps through trials associated with the mission. Andronicus and Junia have not only been Paul's fellow prisoners³² (v.7; like Aristarchus, Col 4:10, and Epaphras, Philem 23), but they were in Christ before him, which dates their conversion back to the earliest Palestinian phase of the gospel mission (ie between A.D. 33 and 34, within months of Paul's, rather than years), possibly as members of the Synagogue of the Freedmen (Acts 6:9).³³ Rufus and his mother, if related to Simon of Cyrene, also date back to the earliest days (v.18) and probably also to that synagogue. Perhaps their special bond even arose during his first two weeks of troublesome mission in Jerusalem (Acts 9:26–30; Gal 1:18–19), when she, like Barnabas, may have assisted him, or perhaps in Antioch, if members of this family were numbered amongst the Cyrenians who were part of the original mission team to that city (Acts 11:20; 13:1).

With this missional background, the relationship enjoyed between these exiles from the East and the apostle to the Gentiles does not require them to be members of the Roman congregation. On the hypothesis being tested here, they would be well-known to Paul because, after already being actively engaged in the East, they have now been sent as his mission team to Rome, along with his letter, prior to his imminent arrival.

---

30 Priscilla and Aquila (Rom 16:3); Urbanus (Rom 16:9); Timothy (Rom 16:21; 1 Thess 3:2; 2 Cor 1:19, 24); Titus (2 Cor 8:23); Apollos (1 Cor 3:9); Silas (2 Cor 1:19, 24); Clement and others (Phil 4:3); Epaphroditus (Phil 2:25); Aristarchus, Mark, Jesus/Justus, Epaphras, Luke, Demas (Col 4:11, 12, 14; Philem24); Philemon (Philem 2).
31 Harnack, 'κοπιᾶν', followed by Mathew, *Women*, 109.
32 Bauckham, *Gospel Women*, 171 n.263, notes that some take this as a reference to an Ephesian imprisonment; 'but since Andronicus & Junia were members of the early Jerusalem church, an earlier period is more likely: perhaps during the early mission to Antioch (Dodd, *Romans*, 241) or even perhaps during Paul's first missionary enterprise in Arabia (Nabatea), where Junia & Andronicus might have gone because of their Nabataean connections (if Andronicus is Chuza)'.
33 Edmundson, *Church in Rome*, 26: 'their conversion dated back at least as far as the days of St Stephen's activity', suggesting that they possibly belonged to the Synagogue of the Libertines (Acts 6:9). For Paul's conversion in A.D. 33 (or 31) see Robinson, *Redating*, 37. Mathew, *Women*, 105, 107, with Paul's conversion in A.D. 34, suggests that they may have been witnesses of the resurrection, visitors from Rome at Pentecost (Acts 2:10), or members of the Jerusalem Church (Acts 6:1; 11:19).

But is this hypothesis consistent with the actual language of the chapter?

2. The Vocabulary of Greeting
a. The Commendation of Phoebe (vv.1–2)

In Romans 16, Paul uses two sets of verbs with respect to the various people he mentions. As he opens (Rom 16:1–2), he commends (συνίστημι) Phoebe, in order that the Romans might 'welcome her' and 'stand by her' in her every need (ἵνα αὐτὴν προσδέξησθε ... καὶ παραστῆτε αὐτῇ ...). Even though brief, this is commonly recognized to be a 'letter of recommendation' for Phoebe.[34]

Clearly, Phoebe has come from Paul, arrived in Rome, and Paul is urging the Roman Christians to receive her warmly and give her every assistance.[35] Although many have sought to explain her role as 'deacon' and 'benefactor' internally, with respect to the congregation at Cenchreae, clearly the Romans are meeting her in a role that has brought her from her congregation to theirs. Since διάκονος could aptly be used of this external role, the term itself cannot be used to deny that Phoebe is portrayed here as an itinerant missionary,[36] when, on face value this is exactly how she seems to be depicted. As with other 'apostles of the churches' (2 Cor 8:23; cf. 1 Cor 12:28), she was sent by her home congregation as their 'servant', doing the work of the gospel as part of Paul's missionary team. Similarly, her role as προστάτις, 'benefactor', need not be confined to hospitality she showed at Cenchreae, for it aptly describes 'missionary patronage'.[37] Just as Joanna, Mary, and Susanna travelled with Jesus and supported his ministry (Luke 8:1–3), so too Phoebe travelled with,

---

34 Mathew, *Women*, 4, 66.
35 Cf. *NewDocs* 1, #21, a letter requesting the recipient to deal kindly with the sailor who brings the letter, as a favour for the sender: 'Such letters introducing the bearer to someone elsewhere are of a kind with letters of recommendation alluded to in the NT (Acts 18.27; 2 Cor 3:11; Rom 16:1; Col 4:10) and used by Christians' (p.65). The tone of patron-client is most noticeable in Philemon, where Paul plays the role of patron.
36 *Contra* Mathew, *Women*, 66–74, and Ellis, 'Paul and his Coworkers', 7–10 ('the essential factor seems to be ministry not movement').
37 *Contra* Mathew, *Women*, 81–83, despite her noting Jewett's term 'missionary patronage'. See also *NewDocs* 4, p.242; and Kearsley, '#3. Women'.

and supported, Paul's missionary team to Rome.

Clearly, Phoebe was not already in Rome, but she has just arrived in Rome on a mission with the apostle behind her, and so he commends the Romans to welcome and support her in that mission. All this is usually recognized. What is not noticed, however, is that, in terms of 'point of view', these opening verses fix the eyes of Paul's Roman readers not upon themselves, but upon Phoebe who has just arrived amongst them. On the usual explanation of this chapter, Paul immediately switches from commending someone who comes from him to Rome (vv.1–2), to sending his own greetings to those who are already resident there (vv.3–15). But having fixed the congregation's eyes on his messenger, contextually, when he goes on to list the others (vv.3–15), does he break the Romans' point of view to turn their eyes on themselves (and if so, what is the clear marker that he does so?), or is he sustaining the same point of view as he turns their eyes on those arriving with Phoebe?

Apart from the introduction of a new verb (ἀσπάζομαι), there is little to indicate such a shift in point of view. According to the hypothesis being tested, the people in this list have also come from Paul, in company with Phoebe, engaged in the same mission. Even though Paul now switches from commendation to the language of greeting, he is effectively doing exactly the same thing in verses 3–15 as he did with Phoebe in verses 1–2. He is calling upon the Roman believers to warmly receive and support the mission team that has arrived with Phoebe, by greeting them by name.

b. The Borderline of Human Encounter

The vocabulary of greeting is the language of human encounter. As with other greeting terms, the verb ἀσπάζομαι is used in the moment when one person comes into the proximity of another, whether face to face, or through the medium of a letter, or even that of a gravestone. The language of greeting refers to what takes place along the boundary line when people come together, whether to travelers meeting on a journey (Luke 10:4; compare Mark 9:15), or when someone arrives (Matt 10:12; Luke 1:40; Acts 18:22, 21:7, 19, 25:13), or even when someone departs (Acts 20:1).

Although the occasional terse letter may get down to business without wasting time on a greeting,[38] in the vast majority of cases, greetings are found both at the beginning and at the end of ancient letters, both inside and outside the NT.[39]

i. Conventional Opening Greetings: χαίρειν

In terms of language, outside the NT the opening greeting is usually χαίρειν—a form of 'I rejoice'—, which receives a suitably archaic feel when translated with something like, 'Hail!'.[40] As the opening greetings in the letters of the NT contain expansions,[41] so too those of the papyri letters often add such things as best wishes for the health of the recipient, or the hope that they may not be afflicted by the evil eye.[42]

Although χαίρειν is found in the NT,[43] it is usually not the preferred language of the NT writers themselves, but the conventional language of greeting being reported by them about others. This is so for the imperative form, χαῖρε (Matt 26:49; Luke 1:28; Matt. 27:29, Mark 15:18, John 19:3), and for the infinitive form (χαίρειν) more usual in the papyri letters (Acts 23:26; 2 John 10-11).

It is likely that the apostle Paul is responsible for gently but powerfully revolutionizing the conventional greeting to deliver a profoundly Christian form, as χαίρειν became χάριν. Retaining a familiar sound, Paul's new greeting was loaded with the grace of God displayed in Jesus

---

38 See the angry letter from Zoilos to Diogenes; *NewDocs* 4, #17. Even at his tersest in Galatians, Paul still adds his usual Christian greeting (1:3), albeit in an unelaborated form.
39 Noted by Mathew, *Women*, 22-28.
40 This greeting is ubiquitous; e.g. *NewDocs* 1, #15, #16, #17, #18, #20, #21, #63; *NewDocs* 2, #20, #21 (Nos. 5, 6a, 6b, 7a, 7b), #103; *NewDocs* 4, #15, #16, #18, #124; *NewDocs* 8, p.21, p.24, #32, #33; *NewDocs* 9, #14, #20; *NewDocs* 10, #19, #28, #29. It appears in the earliest Christian letter, *NewDocs* 6, #25 (end I/early II)—note that this is earlier than the third century *P.Bas.* 2.43, recently claimed to be the earliest; Whelan, 'World's Oldest Christian Letter'. The regular greeting χαίρειν also appears on gravestones, acting as the deceased person's final correspondence with the world, by addressing those who pass by their eternal resting place; E.g. *NewDocs* 2, #16; *NewDocs* 4, #13.
41 See O'Brien, *Introductory Thanksgivings*.
42 For wishes for health, e.g. *NewDocs* 1, #15: χαίρειν καὶ διὰ παντὸς ὑγιαίνειν. For wishes against the evil eye, most frequently in relation to children, see: *NewDocs* 1, #85: l.4 ἀσπάζωμαι τὰ ἀβάσκαντά σου τέκνα, 'I greet your children – may they be immune from the evil eye'; *NewDocs* 3, #1: ἀβάσκαντα, examples listed in index p.52; *NewDocs* 3, #2: Greet most noble Alexandros, and his Sarapio and Theon and Aristokleia—may the evil eye not touch them!—and Aristokleia's children; Wishes against the evil eye can also be found in final greetings, e.g. *NewDocs* 2, #103 l.16, and p.176; *NewDocs* 1, #24, p.70.
43 That is, as a greeting. Of course, χαίρω occurs frequently in its meaning of 'I rejoice'.

Christ, with the addition of the conventional Jewish greeting, 'peace', now enriched by God's ancient promises of peace being fulfilled in Christ (Rom 1:7, cf. 16:20; 1 Cor 1:3; 2 Cor 1:2; Gal 1:3; Eph 1:2; Phil 1:2; Col 1:2; 1 Thess 1:1; 2 Thess 1:2; 1 Tim 1:2; 2 Tim 1:2; Titus 1:4; Philem 3). Once the revolution began with Paul's letters, the other New Testament letter-writers followed suit (1 Peter 1:2; 2 Peter 1:2; 2 John 3; Rev 1:4)—even if the conventional greeting persisted in the letters of ordinary Christians for centuries.[44]

The two cases in which χαίρειν is used not in report, but as the native language of a New Testament writer, can be explained by the fact that these greeting were penned prior to the Pauline revolution in Christian greeting conventions—in the letter from the Jerusalem Council (Acts 15:23), written late in the year 48,[45] and the letter of James (1:1), written about the same time.[46]

ii. Conventional Concluding Greetings: ἀσπάζ-

The papyri letters also used other words to convey greetings,[47] and any one letter may contain a mixture of vocabulary. Although some of these words, such as the frequent προσαγόρευαι,[48] are not used in the NT letters, ἀσπάζομαι, the term found repeatedly in Romans 16, is common to both the papyri letters and the NT. As in Romans 16, the papyri tend to use this word not in opening greetings, but in final greetings. As in

---

44 e.g. *NewDocs* 1, #83, late III/ early IV, unknown; a letter from a Christian (?) farmer to his patron. Perhaps it is because his patron is not a Christian that the conventional form is used. *NewDocs* 8, #15: Christian letters, late III or early IV, Panopolis?, ll.4, 17 χαίρειν. The greeting χαίρειν began to disappear about the 4th c. A.D.; cf. *NewDocs* 8, #15, p.171.
45 For a discussion of the dating of the Council working backwards from 'the most reliable [external] fixed point' for NT chronology, derived from the Gallio inscription; see Robinson, *Redating*, 35.
46 James played a key role in the Jerusalem Council. He already had a prominent position in Jerusalem when Paul visited in ca. 35 (Gal 1:19), and certainly by ca. 42 or 44 when Peter was under threat (Acts 12:17); see Robinson, *Redating*, 138. In chapter 5, Robinson argues that, on balance, James could date to early 48, or 47, listing the 'surprisingly persistent support' for this early date for James (pp. 138–139).
47 For alternatives for directly greeting with χαίρειν, see *NewDocs* 7, p.48.
48 E.g. *NewDocs* 1, #19: Προσαγόρευαι ὡς ἀπ' ἐμοῦ, 'Greet as from me'. The author then lists several people. See also *NewDocs* 1, #20, Anatolios to his brother Neilos. This verb is used only once in the NT, in its sense of 'address': Heb. 5:10 προσαγορευθεὶς ὑπὸ τοῦ θεοῦ ἀρχιερεὺς κατὰ τὴν τάξιν Μελχισέδεκ. After noting how common ἀσπάζομαι is in the papyri, Horsley notes that it is 'the regular New Testament equivalent'; *NewDocs* 1, #21, p.66.

the papyri, both indicative and imperative forms occur in Romans 16.[49]

The indicative form functions to pass greetings from those on the author's side over to the recipients. It is quite regularly found in the papyri[50] and NT letters (1 Cor 16:19, 19, 20; 2 Cor 13:12; Phil 4:21b, 22; Col 4:10–11, 12, 14; Philem 23), and it is used when Timothy, Lucius, Jason, Sosipater, Tertius, Gaius and his church, Erastus, and Quartus send their greetings at the end of Romans 16 (vv.21–24).[51]

However, to test the present hypothesis, it is the imperative which needs further discussion. At its most basic, the imperative throws the onus for a response over to those on the recipient side. It tells them, 'Greet!'. But the mood itself does not indicate anything about those to be greeted, for its function is a little more complex.

It can be used to pass greetings from a first person to a second person, that is, from the author to people at the recipient end. In comparison to its frequency in the papyri letters,[52]—with Romans 16 off the table for a moment—this usage is surprisingly rare in the New Testament, which furnishes four examples at the most (Heb 13:24a; 2 Tim 4:19; Phil 4:21; 3 John 15—although, if the hypothesis of this essay is correct, even this brief number may be whittled down, as we shall see below. This is, of course, the usual way that the imperatives of Rom 16:3–15 have been read, namely, that they pass greetings from sender to recipient.

However, the imperative is also capable of a different nuance. Rather than inflexibly indicating that the sender is greeting the recipient, the imperative can also be used to pass greetings from a first person to a third person by way of a second person.

One of the most obvious examples of this grammar is the instruction to 'greet one another with a holy kiss', found in Romans 16:16, three

---

49 Ἀσπάσασθε 2nd plural aorist middle imperative 16x (vv. 3, 5, 6, 7, 8, 9, 10, 10, 11, 11, 12, 12, 13, 14, 15, 16a); Ἀσπάζονται 3rd plural present middle indicative 1x (v.16b); Ἀσπάζεται 3rd singular present middle indicative 3x (vv.21, 23, 24); ἀσπάζομαι 1st singular mid indicative 1x (v.22).
50 E.g. *NewDocs* 3, #1, l.10: 'Gaia greets (ἀσπάζετ[αι) you as do her children | and her husband'. *NewDocs* 1, #16, l.20: 'all the gods here greet (ἀσπάζονται) you'; *NewDocs* 2, #103, 'We greet (ἀσπάζωμει) our sister'. See also *NewDocs* 2, #21 No. 6b l.39.
51 Cf. *NewDocs* 10, #29, in which the writer greets multiple recipients, repeating the verb each time, in the first person singular indicative.
52 The imperative is usually singular (ἄσπασε), given that letters are commonly addressed to an individual recipient; e.g. *NewDocs* 2, #21 Nos. 5, 6a. But this would properly change to the plural, if this suits the plurality of recipients.

times elsewhere in Paul (1 Thess 5:26; 1 Cor 16:20; 2 Cor 13:12), and once in 1 Peter (5:14).[53] In this instance, the imperative instructs the recipients to do something internally amongst themselves. Although it may have later become a feature of congregational worship, presumably it arose in the context of the greetings' usual borderline of encounter, whether arrival or departure. The form itself, of course, cannot indicate whether those present are to use a holy kiss to greet those who have been there for a while, such as the usual Roman congregation, or those just arriving, such as a mission team from Paul.

Apart from the instruction to holy kissing, it has not proven easy to find other examples of this usage of the imperative. Of course, even if this were a solitary instance it would be all that is required to demonstrate that a grammatical possibility was also part of actual linguistic usage. But other examples of this usage of the imperative can be cited, such as when a patron requests the protection of a sailor, one of his clients, which is a first person seeking action for a third person by way of a second person—even if the verb here is not one of greeting.[54] The 'letters of commendation' provide the same syntactical analogy along with a closer lexical analogy, for they 'commend' the courier as part of a request that they be received, just as Paul commends (συνίστημι) Phoebe in Rom 16:1–2.[55] But, again, although an exact analogy for presumed circumstances, it is not strictly the greeting language.

However, the best analogy, in terms of both grammar and lexeme is

---

53 Rom 16:16   Ἀσπάσασθε ἀλλήλους ἐν φιλήματι ἁγίῳ.
    1 Cor 16:20b: Ἀσπάσασθε ἀλλήλους ἐν φιλήματι ἁγίῳ.
    2 Cor. 13:12   ἀσπάσασθε ἀλλήλους ἐν ἁγίῳ φιλήματι. ἀσπάζονται ὑμᾶς οἱ ἅγιοι πάντες.
    1Th. 5:26   Ἀσπάσασθε τοὺς ἀδελφοὺς πάντας ἐν φιλήματι ἁγίῳ.
    1 Peter 5:14   ἀσπάσασθε ἀλλήλους ἐν φιλήματι ἀγάπης.

   Cranfield, *Romans* 2.795, notes Justin, *1 Apology*, 65, as the earliest clear reference to the kiss being part of the worship, and Tertullian's kiss of peace.
54 *NewDocs* 1, #21.
55 Rom. 16:1–2 is frequently deemed a 'letter of commendation'; see Mathew, *Women*, 4, 35–36, noting that this is 'widely accepted', 66. See the discussion in *NewDocs* 8, #15 of Christian letters of recommendation, calling upon recipients to 'receive in peace' (προσδέσασθαι ἐν εἰρήνῃ), even adding 'through whom I and those with me greet you and those with you'. Letters of recommendation were 'written to an established formula', albeit with variation, attested in nine papyri, p.170; 'it would appear that the individuals who are recommended carried the letters with them on their journeys and presented them to the local churches as need demanded, e.g. food and accommodation each night. The purpose of the journeys is not stated' (p.170).

actually found in Paul himself. In the interchange at the end of his letter to his co-worker Titus, Paul provides a three-part greeting (Titus 3:15):

> ¹⁵ All those who are with me greet you (ἀσπάζονταί).
> Greet (ἄσπασαι) those who love us in the faith.
> Grace be with all of you.

Firstly, in the indicative usual to such greetings, Paul passes greetings from those present with him to Titus (v. 15a, Ἀσπάζονταί σε οἱ μετ' ἐμοῦ πάντες; cf. Rom 16:21–24). Lastly, Paul himself directly greets the recipients of his letter, Titus and his company, using a variant of his usual Christian prayer for grace, 'grace be with you all' (15c, Ἡ χάρις μετὰ πάντων ὑμῶν).

But what should be made of the imperative in the middle sentence (15b)? This is clearly Paul requesting a second party, Titus (ἄσπασαι is a singular imperative, and in a personal letter addressed to just one man), to greet some third parties, namely 'those who love us in the faith' (τοὺς φιλοῦντας ἡμᾶς ἐν πίστει), who are present in the same location as Titus, that is, at the recipient's end of the transaction.

This is a direct analogy with the vocabulary, the grammar and also with the situation being hypothesized for Romans 16. Even though this is an instruction to an individual appropriately utilizing the singular imperative, the same usage of the plural imperative could be applied to a group of people, i.e., a first party could address a group of second parties, in order to instruct them to greet some third parties. The grammar therefore allows the possibility that by using the plural imperatives in Romans 16, Paul is not himself greeting the Roman Christians, but he is calling upon them to greet some third parties, namely, his mission team arriving with Phoebe carrying the apostle's letter.

Mathew's analysis has demonstrated that the second person imperative functions rhetorically to forge a 'web of mutual interaction' by calling upon the recipients to greet others, who are commended by the sender—not merely on behalf of the sender (making it an equivalent of the first person),[56] but as if entirely on their own initiative.[57] She notes that this further implies that 'the parties who are to be greeted are not a part of the congregation to whom the letter was addressed'.[58] But rather than proposing that these parties are 'specific persons who belonged to other house churches in the capital city', it is historically much simpler if these persons are those arriving with Phoebe from the apostle Paul.

3. Return to the Hypothesis: What is Happening in Romans 16?

a. Summary

The hypothesis proposes a situation in Rome, in which a team from Paul has arrived, under a patron (Phoebe), and under the additional leadership of two of Paul's experienced co-workers who are already familiar with Rome (Priscilla and Aquila). The letter outlining Paul's gospel is read out, and, as it comes to a conclusion, Paul now commends his patron and introduces his mission team, by requesting the Romans greet them one by one.

b. Phoebe ...

The first person we meet in the Chapter is Phoebe. Her lengthy description shows she is a Christian ('our sister', τὴν ἀδελφὴν ἡμῶν),[59] a deacon of (not in) the church in Cenchreae (διάκονον τῆς ἐκκλησίας τῆς ἐν Κεγχρεαῖς),[60] and, significantly, that she has become a 'patroness' (προστάτις), for many, including Paul himself (αὐτὴ προστάτις πολλῶν ἐγενήθη καὶ ἐμοῦ αὐτοῦ). Since this term may suggest she was 'a person of some wealth and position', and a Patronus was 'the legal representative

---

56 Mathew, *Women*, 32–33, 39, disagreeing with Gamble, *Textual History*, 92–93.
57 Mathew, *Women*, (drawing upon Weima, *Neglected Endings*), 1, 14–15, 26, 31–32, 39–40, 160, and elsewhere.
58 Mathew, *Women*, 32ff. (citing Weima, *Neglected Endings*, 108); cf. 40.
59 Bauckham, *Gospel Women*, 214–215, notes that it is not clear ἀδελφός/ ἀδελφή means Christian worker *per se* when applied to individuals.
60 Cenchreae: *NewDocs* 4, #37: 'Acts 18:18, Rom 16:1 constitute two of the only five literary testimonia known from Kenchreai, one of the two important ports for Corinth, about 9 km from the ancient city'. For archaeology: Scranton, *Kenchreai*.

of the foreigner',[61] it may well be that Phoebe has come to Rome to use her status for the advantage of the Pauline mission. Certainly Paul requests that she be given every assistance in her work, which suggests that her work aligns with his.[62]

Although Phoebe is only known from her pre-eminent place in this list of greetings, for centuries she has been presumed to be the bearer of Paul's letter to the Romans,[63] which is at least one of the ways she expressed her patronage of Paul. She comes to Rome from the apostle to the Gentiles as his patroness, bearing a letter which is the paramount expression of his gospel, forming a vanguard of his own imminent arrival on his way to preach the gospel in Spain (see Rom 1:11–15; 15:23–33).

c. ... and Friends?

Even if she had come to Rome on private business, it is unlikely that Phoebe would have travelled alone.[64] It is even more unlikely that she would arrive as a singular representative of the mission to the Gentiles. From the beginning, Christ's mission was conducted in company, whether in pairs (e.g. Luke 10:1), through the twelve, the wider circle of disciples (e.g. Luke 8:1–3), or the Pauline circle. According to Eusebius (*HE* III.37.2), for centuries the pattern of the historic Christian mission was the same as that reflected in the Pastoral Epistles: the apostolic word was taught by the apostolic delegates (such as Titus and Timothy), who, before moving on, then appointed elders in every place, so that the deposit of truth could be handed on further.

This regular missional pattern raises the question, who were the others who accompanied Phoebe on her missionary journey? The

---

61 Sanday & Headlam, *Romans*, 418. Mathew, *Women*, 5–6, notes that she is not necessarily wealthy.
62 If the hypothesis in this essay proves true, then it negates the view of Mathew, *Women*, 90–92 (following Fiorenza), that Priscilla and Aquila worked independently of Paul and differed in mission strategy.
63 Luther; Cranfield, *Romans* 2.780: 'highly probable'; Sanday & Headlam, *Romans*, 416; *NewDocs* 7, 27, 51, 56: Sending a letter involves sending a courier, but the letter is really to endorse the message and so the messenger, not merely the couriers. Because she is commended, Phoebe is probably the courier; see also *NewDocs* 8, 171.
64 See Stanton, 'Accommodation', who notes that parties of travellers would have included slaves, for example, even if not specifically mentioned.

hypothesis of this paper suggests that they were the people listed in verses 3–15. After commending Phoebe, the patroness, Paul asks the Romans to greet the rest of the mission team having just arrived with her.

4. Two Potential Objections to the Hypothesis
a. The Roman Character of the Names

Drawing on observations from Bishop Lightfoot, some commentators have made a lot of the Roman character of the names on this list.[65] Many of these names occur with a high frequency in inscriptions from Rome, and several names are found amongst the slaves and freedmen of the imperial household.[66] Archaeological discoveries suggest that Priscilla may have had Roman connections, perhaps mentioned prior to her husband because of her pre-eminence in social status gained through her connection to a prominent Roman household.[67] If this is so, of course, it would give good reasons why Priscilla and Aquila lived in Rome prior to the time they first met Paul (see Acts 18:2), and good reasons for them to return.

However, the fact that a person bears a name with Roman connections cannot determine their location, whether in general, or, in particular with respect to Romans 16. Most of the names of those greeted are, in fact, Greek, and the six Latin names (Aquila, Junia, Ampliatus, Urbanus, Rufus, Julia) are by no means solely attested in Rome. Despite bearing names that are especially frequent in Rome, Ampliatus and

---

65   Sanday & Headlam, *Romans*, xciv, refer to Lightfoot on Phil. 4:22, who illustrates Romans 16 names from an inscription from the imperial household's columbarium, and slaves in the household. Cf. Cranfield, *Romans* 2; Lampe, 'Roman Christians'; Edmundson, *Church in Rome*, 26: Aristobulus and Narcissus: freedmen or slaves; Aristobulus: perhaps the grandson of Herod the Great who made his permanent home in Rome (Joseph. AJ 20.1.2; BJ 2.11.6). cf. 'Herodion, my kinsmen'; claiming, 'Narcissus can be scarcely other than the freedman and favourite of Claudius'. He was put to death 3 years before, but his slaves and dependents retain his name. Perhaps part of Caesar's household, of which there were about 6000 names found in the inscriptions.

66   Cf. Edmundson, *Church in Rome*, 25, for example: 'A study of the names enables us to draw the conclusion that the Roman Christians mainly belonged to the class of Greek-speaking freedmen and slaves', with 'a large proportion Orientals'.

67   See discussion in Sanday & Headlam, *Romans*, 418–420; briefly, Lampe, 'Prisca'.

Urbanus are known to Paul from the East,[68] as are Rufus and Junia.

When it comes to names, status is similar to geography. The presence of a name amongst slaves, even if frequent, cannot determine that it always designated a slave or freedman. Perhaps Persis (v.12b) was a slave who acquired a name based on her ethnicity, but this is not certain, neither is it certain Julia was a freedwoman.[69] The honorific name Asyncritus (v.14) may suggest someone of servile status, the name earned from good service, but clearly some who bore it were not slaves.[70] Similarly for the sisters Tryphaena and Tryphosa (v.12). Despite Tryphaena being frequently attested from Rome and attached to slaves, in at least two cases it is borne by Roman citizens, and is well-attested elsewhere.[71] Roman names were taken by those from the East, including Jews.[72] In themselves, the names of Romans 16 can tell us nothing about the location of their bearer when Paul was writing.

---

68 Wiefel, 'Jewish Community', 112.
69 For slaves named by ethnic origin, see *NewDocs* 4 #94, p.178, referring to Joppa, Ioudaios, Zmyrna/Smyrna, Syra/Syrion. For Persis (v.12), Mathew, *Women*, 110, suggests the name may be Gentile or Jewish, 'a typical name for a feminine slave, a name found six times in the Roman epigraphic and literary sources' (drawing upon Lampe, 'Persis'); Lampe, 'Julia'.
70 *NewDocs* 2, #85: an honorific inscription, imperial date, from Ankara, for a man who held various posts, including phylarch, ἀσψνκρίτως |[κ]αὶ μεγαλοπρεπῶς 'incomparably and magnificently'. Two further instances come from Rome dated I² and 250–350, and six other incomplete names possibly Asynkritos. Not always servile, see *P.Oxy* 12 (1916) 1413.21–22; *P.Lips.* 1 (1906) 98 col. 1, l.2.
71 *NewDocs* 3, #81: MM provides several papyri examples; Solin, *GPR* 2.783–784, 'provides over 60 examples from Rome alone, not one of which is indubitably of free status'; ranging from Augustus to IV¹, but the bulk are from I A.D.; *NewDocs* mentions in addition one from Lydia, three from Egypt from the Ptolemaic period; *NewDocs* 4, #94 p.178 refers to Reilly's catalogue of 3,250 slave names derived from manumission texts from Greece and the Aegean islands from V B.C. to III A.D., which includes Tryphaina (3014–15); *NewDocs* 5, p.144, adds five more epigraphical instances of Tryphaina, two being Roman citizens; in *NewDocs* 9, #20 one of the addressees is Tryphaena.

NewDocs 3, #9: a dated inscription from Lydia, A.D. 96/97 refers to a Tryphosa married to Theophilos. Horsley comments, p.39, 'no papyrus attestations are known to me, though there are a good number of inscriptions. MM, s.v., note several from Magnesia, and the new text printed here provides a further Asian Minor example. Solin, *GPR* 2.787–788, collects 33 from Rome (including the NT Tryphosa, Rom 16:12); nearly all of the 13 for whom status can reasonably be determined (freed or servile) occur within the period I–II'; *NewDocs* 5, p.143, adds eleven more epigraphical instances of Tryphosa from Asia Minor, one being a Roman citizen.
72 Cf. Ilan, *Lexicon*. The picture is further complicated by the fact that Greeks may have taken Latin names without having Roman citizenship, and manumitted slaves may have acquired citizenship; see, briefly, Judge, 'Greek Names'. He notes the 'tantalizing questions' raised by the fact that '30 of the 91 personal names in the Pauline connection are of Latin derivation'.

b. Addressing household groups

The second potential objection to the hypothesis concerns the several groups mentioned amongst the greetings, who are already associated with various households. To list them again:

1. The church associated with the household of Priscilla and Aquila (v.5, τὴν κατ' οἶκον αὐτῶν ἐκκλησίαν);
2. those who are out of the people of Aristobulus (v.10b, τοὺς ἐκ τῶν Ἀριστοβούλου);
3. those who are out of the people of Narcissus, in the Lord (v.11b, τοὺς ἐκ τῶν Ναρκίσσου τοὺς ὄντας ἐν κυρίῳ);[73]
4. the brethren with Asyncritus, Phlegon, Hermes, Patrobas, and Hermas (v.14, καὶ τοὺς σὺν αὐτοῖς ἀδελφούς); and
5. the saints who are with Philologus, Julia, Nereus and his sister, and Olympas (v.15, καὶ τοὺς σὺν αὐτοῖς πάντας ἁγίους).

Perhaps this is the most serious piece of evidence that threatens the hypothesis being tested here, for if the five groups represent households physically residing in Rome, then the hypothesis fails.

Both the papyri and the NT itself certainly have letters in which greetings are either sent from or to whole households.[74] Following the greeting (v.5) to the church taken to be meeting in Priscilla and Aquila's 'home' (HCSB) or 'house' (ESV), interpreters commonly imagine that several other Roman house-churches are in view,[75] even though translations regularly and correctly render the expressions in verses 10–11 relationally ('households'; 'family'; etc), where 'house' (οἶκος) does not appear.[76]

The Greek οἶκος was the fundamental unit of society. It was 'a co-resident group, many (though not all) of whose members were kin or *affines* (related by marriage)', but they also 'included many non-kin members,

---

73 Ilan, *Lexicon*, III.338, lists two possible Jews with this Greek name, a father and son, from a sarcophagus, in Asia, 2nd–3rd c., one the husband, the other the son, of Mariam (CIJ 779).
74 E.g. *NewDocs* 4, #123: 'My husband greets you warmly; and do pray for him. My whole household greets you too (l.25 ἀσπ[άζ]ετέ σε δὲ καὶ ὅλος ὁ οἶκός | μου)'.
75 Sanday & Headlam, *Romans*, 420, note that there is no evidence before the third century for special church buildings, whereas the early Christians met in houses of some size, such as the house of Mary, mother of John (Acts 12:2).
76 For another NT analogy, see Phil 4:22 οἱ ἐκ τῆς Καίσαρος οἰκίας.

of lower, non-citizen status' such as slaves and freedmen or women and perhaps lodgers during their sojourn.⁷⁷ Similarly, the Roman *familia* has a range of meanings:

> the physical household; the persons comprising a household (e.g. patron and freedman); a body of persons united by a common legal tie such as all kin subject to a living *paterfamilias*, or a body more loosely connected such as all agnatically related kin; a body of slaves, or slaves and sons; and all blood descendants of an original family founder.⁷⁸

It was thoroughly regular, even after the death of the master of a household, that the group of people known by his name could continue to be called 'those of his house'. How much more while he was still alive, but away from home; or when they were away from home, but still to be designated as belonging to their master's household?

Surely this explanation also holds for those belonging to the various Christian groups. The physical house in which a group may have congregated was not as significant as the group itself,⁷⁹ which congregated as households within houses large enough to hold them. Those from the Jerusalem Church, scattered through persecution, were still known as 'the church', even when not gathered together (Acts 9:31).⁸⁰ The church which met in the actual house of Nympha (Col 4:15) would be associated with her name, even when they were not meeting, but were elsewhere, perhaps engaging in a common activity such as the work of the gospel.

One such example is the household of Stephanas. As Paul closed his first (surviving) letter to the Corinthians, he mentioned that those in this household (τὴν οἰκίαν Στεφανᾶ) were 'the first converts in Achaia' and that they were devoted to the service of the Lord's people, and the Corinthians ought to submit themselves to such people who join in the work and labour at it (1 Cor 16:15–18; cf.1:16). But Paul then reveals

---

77 Foxhall, 'Household, Greek', 729.
78 Bradley, 'Household, Roman', 730; see also Treggia, 'Family, Roman', 586.
79 Cf. the use of οἶκος + gen = for a 'household', 'family' (1 Tim 3:4), rather than a building: e.g. of David (with allusion to 2 Sam 7; Luke 1:69; 1:27; Acts 7:49); of Israel (Acts 2:36; 7:42; Heb 8:8, 10); of Judah (Heb 8:8); of Jacob (Acts 7:46); of God (1 Tim 3:15; cf. 5:4; Heb 3:6; 1 Peter 4:17); of Noah (Heb 11:7).
80 Robinson, *Assembling*, 131, 216–217, 222.

that Stephanas, as well as Fortunatus, and Achaicus (presumably members of this household), have arrived to be with him. Their support of the apostle and his mission has led to this household —or at least several members of it—now being on the move.

Turning to the church associated with Priscilla and Aquila (Rom 16:5), the language (κατ' οἶκον) does not, in fact, highlight their meeting in a physical structure. κατά is the language of association: this group had become designated 'according to the household of Priscilla and Aquila'. The same expression is found for the church associated with Priscilla and Aquila at the end of 1 Corinthians (1 Cor 16:19: σὺν τῇ κατ' οἶκον αὐτῶν ἐκκλησίᾳ), just after the mention of the household of Stephanas, when they were with Paul, sending their greetings to the Corinthians. They seem to be a second 'house church', now on the move.

Rather than insisting that this couple had a church meeting in their home wherever they were (which they may have done), whether Corinth, Ephesus, or Rome,[81] the language also allows for the interesting possibility that the group of people who originally assembled in the home of this highly mobile couple in Corinth, then joined them in their missionary endeavours. They would retain the same label whether they were meeting at the time or not. They would have retained the title if, like those of the household of Stephanas, they were so committed to the Pauline mission that they were now a group on the move. The expression used for both groups would be an equivalent to 'Paul and his entourage' (οἱ περὶ Παῦλον, Acts 13:13).[82] And, given this possibility, what if their proven dedication to the gospel work in the east, then led them to remain under the leadership of Priscilla and Aquila to become part of the mission team that, under the patronage of Phoebe, was then sent to Rome?

5. Four Potential Parallels?

There are four other potential NT parallels to the greetings of Romans 16, which serve to strengthen the likelihood of the hypothesis being true—two of which may also arise from a similar situation.

---

81 So, e.g. Mathew, *Women*, 90–92.
82 Stanton, 'Accommodation', 230, or 'Paul's team'.

1. Even though the vocabulary is different, there may be a close parallel to the situation being proposed here in Paul's instruction to the Colossians to welcome Mark should he come to them (Col 4:10, ἐὰν ἔλθῃ πρὸς ὑμᾶς, δέξασθε αὐτόν). Since Mark's arrival is still future, it is appropriate for Paul to urge the Colossians to welcome him, when he eventually arrives. However, on the occasion when they did so, they would greet him (ἀσπάζομαι) as the initial stage of their welcome. One could therefore imagine that if Paul directed his instructions to that specific moment of initial encounter, he would use the imperative ἀσπάσασθε, as in Romans 16.

2. There may also be a further analogy in the enigmatic closing verse of 3 John (v 15), which uses the same vocabulary as Romans 16. Here the greetings flow to Gaius from the friends (ἀσπάζονταί σε οἱ φίλοι), and Gaius is likewise instructed to greet the friends (ἀσπάζου τοὺς φίλους κατ' ὄνομα). Some English translators attempt to clarify the confusion they feel by adding 'the friends here' and 'the friends there' (NIV 2011, TNIV, NRSV, NET), thus separating the two groups of friends in view. But there is nothing in the text to indicate location, and if it is the same group of friends, this may be an exact parallel to the situation proposed for Romans 16, with John commending the friends who have arrived with his letter, and requesting that Gaius returns their greetings as they arrive. Whereas John uses a general expression 'by name' (κατ' ὄνομα), also found in the papyri,[83] in Romans 16 Paul goes further by articulating the names of his mission team for the Romans to use.

3. 2 Tim 4:19 might reveal a similar situation:

   Ἄσπασαι Πρίσκαν καὶ Ἀκύλαν καὶ τὸν Ὀνησιφόρου οἶκον.
   If a similar situation is reflected here, then Timothy is receiving Prisca and Aquila, and the household of Onesiphorus, also now on the move for the sake of the Gentile mission. Only known from this verse and 2 Tim 1:16, Onesiphorus is the one who expected to find Paul in Rome, but when he could not—as suggested by Reicke—, he then travelled across the Mediterranean to assist him during his imprisonment at

---

[83] See examples in note 2, above.

Caesarea.[84] Like others of sufficient means to travel across the empire, he would be accompanied by an entourage, those from his household. On this hypothesis, this greeting would reflect the situation that, having found the apostle, he and his household then accompanied Priscilla and Aquila to Ephesus, bearing Paul's letter to Timothy who was at or near that city.[85]

4. Hebrews 13:24–25

Heb. 13:24 Ἀσπάσασθε πάντας τοὺς ἡγουμένους ὑμῶν καὶ πάντας τοὺς ἁγίους.
ἀσπάζονται ὑμᾶς οἱ ἀπὸ τῆς Ἰταλίας.
[25]ἡ χάρις μετὰ πάντων ὑμῶν.

Hebrews 13:24 may reflect a similar situation as being proposed for Romans 16. The final clause is clearly a greeting from the author to the recipients (v.25, cf. Titus 3:15c). This is preceded by a greeting from 'those from Italy' who are with the author, to the recipients, using the indicative form, ἀσπάζονται. But what of the imperative, preceding both these greetings? Once again, it may well be that the leaders of the Hebrews' community are returning home after having been with the author, carrying his letter, and now accompanied by some Jewish Christians (πάντας τοὺς ἁγίους), most probably those from the Jerusalem church.[86] Whether the letter is directed to Rome, or to Palestine, the dating and occasion may well need reconfiguring, if the hypothesis of this article reflects historical reality—especially if 'those from Italy' sending greetings are Priscilla and Aquila.[87]

---

84 Reicke, 'The Chronology of the Pastoral Epistles', 115–116; accepted by Robinson, *Redating*, 73–76.
85 Reicke, 'Colossians', 434, notes that Timothy may have been active at Troas in Mysia, northwest of Ephesus (cf. 2 Tim 4:13).
86 For 'the saints' as the Jerusalem Church, see Robinson, *Assembling*, 153–154.
87 So Montefiore, *Hebrews*, ad loc. Robinson, *Redating*, 206–207: 'the most natural supposition to be drawn from the message, that the letter was sent to Rome, is the one, I believe, that yields the most fruitful results'. On the other hand, the earliest tradition that we have—from Chrysostom—, locates the recipients 'in Jerusalem and Palestine', and 'a Palestinian destination has become all the more probable since the discovery of the Dead Sea Scrolls'; Hughes, *Hebrews*, 11, 18, 19.

6. Some Further Reinforcements and Implications

As an integral part of the letter (assumed here), Romans 16 needs to be factored in to discussions of Romans' situation, date, purpose, and so on. If the hypothesis tested here has merit, then it has the potential for reconfiguring these discussions accordingly. But it also has wider implications. Just like Ellis was sure that 'a clarification of [Paul's associates'] role may serve to illuminate the structure of the early Christian mission',[88] so too the clarification of the relationship with the apostle enjoyed by persons in Romans 16 illuminates that mission.

This section draws upon suggestions—mostly previously advanced and known for a long time—that seek to integrate the broader available data on the assumption of the coherence of the early Christian movement, especially in view of the fact that it originated with a small group of people which then expanded its membership through natural networks. Because the rationalistic criticism that has plagued New Testament studies for centuries has maximised diversity and demanded certainty, it has often too quickly dismissed such possibilities as 'conjecture', or even 'speculation', as if coherence is not a necessary and natural part of a burgeoning movement and conjecture is not a fundamental and necessary part of empirical historical inquiry. The principle of 'realistic coherence' allows for historical possibilities to be tabled and duly considered, as the empirical data are brought together.

a. The Apostle and his Companions

As is true of any human movement including the Christian movement at any stage of history, it is clear that the earliest Christian movement was anchored in the historical reality of people who were already bound together by bonds of friendship and blood. As with Acts (23:16), Romans 16 reveals that this was also true of the apostle Paul. Those listed as Paul's relatives (Andronicus and Junia, v.7; Herodion, v.11; Lucius, Jason & Sosipater, v.21) reveal some further significant potential connections.

---

88 Ellis, 'Paul and his Coworkers', 3.

Two relatives with him at the point of origin (v.21) are Jason of Thessalonica (Acts 17:5–9),[89] and Lucius, who should probably be identified both with Lucius of Cyrene (Acts 13:1) and with Luke, the physician and travelling companion of Paul and the writer of the third Gospel.[90]

Through Junia/Joanna (v.7) and Herodion (v.11), Paul appears to also be linked by blood to the Herods, which is reinforced by Luke's statement that Manaen was τε Ἡρῴδου τοῦ τετραάρχου σύντροφος καὶ Σαῦλος 'brought up with both Herod the Tetrarch and Paul' (Acts 13:1). Junia (Joanna), certainly, and Herodion, possibly, could bear witness to some of Jesus' Galilean ministry, as well as his journey to Jerusalem and his last days.

If Andronicus is the name chosen by Joanna's Chuza as his presentation to the Graeco-Roman world, since he was a Nabatean it would be the Jewess Junia/Joanna who would be related to Paul. Already known to be connected with the household of Herod Antipas (Luke 8:1–3),

---

89 This would indicate that Paul's visit to Thessalonica was, at least in part, determined by his own family connections. Cf. Paul and Barnabas exploiting Barnabas' Cypriot connections (Acts 13:4–7), before the family links of Sergius Paulus possibly led them to Psidian Antioch (Acts 13:13–14); see *NewDocs* 9, p.26; Stanton, 'Accommodation', 230: 'he seems to have advised Barnabas and Paul to go directly from Paphos to Pisidian Antioch, where his family was based. He would surely have arranged accommodation for them there. In response Saul adopted the name Paul (13:9)' (with Mitchell).

90 So Sanday & Headlam, *Romans*, 432; summarily dismissed by Cranfield, *Romans* 2, 805. Although recognising that the identification of Luke the evangelist with Lucius of Rom. 16:21 was noted by Origen (*In Rom. Comm.* 10, 39) and hinted at by Ephraem Syrus, Cadbury initially argued there was no early identification of Luke and Lucius of Cyrene ('Tradition', 247). However, after becoming aware of the Armenian commentary of Ephrem Syrus (published in 1921), he drew attention to the comment on Acts 12:25–13:1: 'But Saul and Barnabas, who carried food for the saints in Jerusalem, returned with John who was called Mark and so did Luke of Cyrene. But both these are evangelists and wrote before the discipleship of Paul, and therefore he used to repeat everywhere from their gospel'. Noting 'his identification of Luke with the Cyrenian is made on the basis of tradition or else independently', Cadbury ('Lucius', 494) agreed that it is as good as any other conjecture—although Harnack, Deissmann, and Ramsay supported the identification with more positive historical arguments. The identification with Luke has often been dismissed by the argument that the two names are fundamentally different, not only because of the differences in spelling (Λουκᾶς; Λούκιος), but because Luke could not be an abbreviation of Lucius. However, despite being so often ignored, the evidence that falsifies this argument has been available since Ramsay's 1915 publication of inscriptions from Pisidia; Cadbury, 'Lucius', 491; Ford, 'St. Luke'. For another spelling variation for Lucius, as Λούκις, see *NewDocs* 2, #49 (Buresch, *Aus Lydien*, No. 35). If Lucius = Luke, then Ellis, 'Paul and his Coworkers', 3 and n.4, was mistaken to exclude Lucius from consideration amongst Paul's coworkers on the grounds that he (along with Manaen, Simeon Niger, Gaius of Macedonia, Philip the Evangelist) are mentioned only in Acts, not in Paul's own letters.

if she can also be identified with the Joanna mentioned on an ossuary which turned up in 1983,[91] she would be the daughter of Jonathan (Acts 4:6)[92] and granddaughter of Theophilus, who was another son of Annas and the High Priest who succeeded his brother-in-law Caiaphas (A.D. 37–41; Josephus, *A.J.* 19.297 [19.6.2]).[93] In this case, Joanna/Junia would be the grandniece of Caiaphas and Paul would also be somehow in the family circle of the High Priest who presided over Christ's death and supplied Paul with his license to persecute the earliest believers (cf. Acts 8:1; 9:1–2; 22:4–5; 26:10, 12; Gal 1:13–14).

Even though it may be hard to specify the details precisely, Romans 16 also alludes to events that formed part of Paul's early biography that go otherwise unrecorded: Phoebe's previous benefactions (v.2); Priscilla and Aquila risking their lives for Paul (v.4); his role in Epaenetus' conversion (v.5b); Mary's hard work for the Romans (v.6); his imprisonment with Andronicus and Junia, converted prior to Paul (v.7); and his experience with Rufus' mother (v.13).

The list also reveals his close links to the Jerusalem church and to some of the key witnesses to the final events of Jesus' life (Mary, v.6; Junia, 7; Rufus and his mother, v.13; the saints, v.15).

It is abundantly clear both from his own letters and from Acts, that Paul travelled with companions. This is not only further confirmed by Romans 16, but on the hypothesis advanced here, Paul travelled both with already well-connected individuals and already established groups[94]—some known from elsewhere in the New Testament, but

91 Barag & Flusser, 'The Ossuary of Yehoḥanah', 39 n.1, 41. It was reported as coming from the village of ḥizma, 7 km NNE of Jerusalem. See also the discussion in Evans, *Jesus and the Ossuaries*, 104–112.
92 John is clarified by Codex Bezae and the Old Latin: Jonathas. Alternatively, Hengel & Schwemer, *Paul Between Damascus and Antioch*, 250 n.1309, identify the Jonathan of Acts 4:6 with the Jonathan, son of Theophilus, recorded in the inscription under discussion—mistakenly citing Barag & Flusser in support.
93 Steinmann, *From Abraham to Paul*, 328, estimates his arrival in the summer of A.D. 41. It is generally agreed that Agrippa I removed Theophilus after he arrived to take control of Judea in A.D. 41, although Schwartz, *Agrippa I*, 11–14, argues for the dismissal in A.D. 38. VanderKam, *From Joshua to Caiaphas*, 440–443, refutes Schwartz's arguments. Jonathan was probably installed between mid December A.D. 36 and mid-January A.D. 37, when Vitellius visited Jerusalem to dismiss Pilate; Smallwood, 'High Priests and Politics', 22; see also her 'Date of the Dismissal'.
94 Cf. Stanton, 'Accommodation', who notes that Paul's team could normally consist of nine or more persons. If the hypothesis here is correct, the number that travelled with Phoebe on the mission to Rome was more than triple the usual.

some only through this cameo at the end of Romans.

In the greetings sent from those with Paul at origin (vv.21–23): Timothy is one of his well-known co-workers; Jason (Acts 17:5–9), Erastus (Acts 19:22; 2 Tim 4:20), and Sosipater (Acts 20:4, = Sopater) are known associates; Tertius, the amanuensis, and Quartus are otherwise unknown.[95] It is likely that Gaius is also otherwise known, although the name was a common and not very defining Roman praenomen, and the New Testament occurrences may refer to more than one person associated with different places (Acts 19:29 [Macedonia]; 20:4 [Derbe]; 1 Cor 1:14 [Corinth]; 3 John 1 [elsewhere]).[96] The collocation between Erastus and Gaius, both elsewhere associated with Corinth (2 Tim 4:20; 1 Cor 1:14),[97] usually adds to the argument that the letter was written from that city.[98]

Alongside the commendations of individual members of his mission team, Paul also requests the Romans to welcome already established groups, whether husband and wife teams (Priscilla and Aquila, v.3; Andronicus and Junia, v.7), other family groups (Tryphaena and Tryphosa, v.12; Rufus and mother, v.13; Philologus and family, v.14), or members of household churches and other groups now on the move for mission (that of Priscilla and Aquila, v.5; Aristobulus, v.10b; Narcissus, v.11; Asyncritus and the others, v.14). Even the individuals are probably backed by the churches from which they originated and which they now represent, whether Gentile (Phoebe, vv.1–2; Priscilla and Aquila, v.4; Epaenetus, v.5), or the congregation(s) in Jerusalem (Mary, v.6; Andronicus and Junia, v.7; Rufus and mother, v.13; the saints, v.15).

As well as reflecting the links of friendship, family, and common activity (fellowship) that are characteristic of the early Jesus movement, if the people of Romans 16 are the members of Paul's mission team to

---

95 Are these two numerically named brothers, and are they perhaps related to Secundus (Acts 20:4); and/or —as suggested by Souter (Cadbury, 'Lucius', 490 n.3)—to Erastus.
96 Cadbury, 'Lucius', 490 n.5., who also suggests that other New Testament characters, such as Epaphroditus, could conceivably have had Gaius as a praenomen (p.491); as could Titius Justus (Acts 18:7), who has also been suggested to be the Gaius of Rom 16:23 (cf. Cranfield, *Romans* 2, 807, referring to Ramsay, Goodspeed, and Bruce).
97 E.g. Cadbury, 'Lucius', 490 n.5; Sanday & Headlam, *Romans*, 432; Cranfield, *Romans* 2, 806–807. Erastus has also been identified with the Corinthian 'commissioner of public works' mentioned in a first century inscription; Cadbury, 'Erastus'.
98 E.g. Sanday & Headlam, *Romans*, xxxvii; Robinson, *Redating*, 55.

Rome, they also illustrate what is evident elsewhere, that like Paul himself, his associates were also frequently mobile. They had become 'homeless' (cf. 1 Cor 4:11, ἀστατοῦμεν) for the sake of the gospel mission.

Just like Jesus sent a vanguard ahead of him to already engage in the gospel work even prior to his arrival (e.g. Luke 10:1–11), Paul also adopted the same pattern by sending his delegates ahead of him (e.g. 1 Cor 4:17; 2 Cor 8:18, 22; 12:17; Col 4:8; Eph 6:21–22; Col 4:7–9; Philem 10, 22; 1 Thess 3:2, 5; 2 Tim 4:12. Cf. Heb 13:23). No doubt given the significance of the mission to Rome, as Paul makes plans to come himself, Romans 16 shows that he sent a very large team to begin the work in the meantime.

It was a team of people who had already proven themselves in the work of the gospel elsewhere, as the descriptions of the various persons indicate. It was also well-connected to the historical events at the beginning of the Jesus movement. Just like Jerusalem church members formed the bridgehead to the earliest Gentile congregation at Antioch (Acts 11:20), now more members of the Jerusalem congregations are part of the team to Rome. A large number of women are on the team, but more significant than their sex is their proven track record of working hard (κοπιάω) for the gospel of Christ. Three in particular were of paramount importance because of their connection to the foundational events of the Christian movement and its gospel.

The wife of Simon of Cyrene—and one of their sons, Rufus—(v.13; Mark 15:21), was personally connected to the man who was pressed to carry Christ's cross and no doubt converted by the experience. Mary (v.6), the wife of Cleopas, could bear testimony to the tomb of Christ being found empty by her and her two companions on resurrection morning. Junia/Joanna (v.7) could also testify to having been involved with those women at the report back to the apostles.[99] Building on the

---

99 See Bolt, 'What Really Happened?'. Given the point of view apparent in Luke 24:10–12 Luke himself (cf. Rom 16:21) could also have been at the report-back.

previous visit to Rome from some of their number (cf. Rom 15:20),[100] the Jerusalem church now sends representatives to the capital as part of Paul's mission—including these three significant witnesses of Jesus' crucifixion and resurrection.

Alongside those from the foundational Jerusalem congregation(s), the team to Rome also had those who had been there at the beginning of the gentile mission. Epaenetus was the first convert from Asia (v.5), Priscilla and Aquila must have been close to the first from Rome. The members of the various house groups could also testify to the embrace of the gospel in their own locality, and to its ongoing progress. Through such people 'all the churches of Christ' (a formula unique to Romans) in the east could send their greetings to those in Rome (v.16c; cf. vv.1, 4), to reinforce what had already happened at one end of the empire, as Paul's Gentile-oriented gospel movement now arrived at the other end, reaching the capital at last.

---

[100] There were other members of the Jerusalem Church linked with Rome: Peter, Silvanus/Silas, and John Mark (1 Peter 5:13); see Robinson, *Redating*, 150–151. Peter and Mark were probably in Rome as early as A.D. 42; see (Acts 12:1–4, 17; Eusebius, *Hist.* 3.39.15; Irenaeus, *Adv.Haer.* 3.1.2). According to Jerome's Latin translation of Eusebius' *Chronicle*, Peter's visit was in the second year of Claudius (A.D. 42). Had Mary also been there before (cf. v.6, 'who worked very hard for you'). If correct, the hypothesis of this essay would further reinforce, Bauckham's observation that, 'the church in Rome is an example of an extremely important Christian community whose origins had nothing to do with the Pauline mission, but probably much to do with the Jerusalem Church. Its links with Jerusalem seem to have remained close (Rom 16:7, 13; 1 Peter 5:12–13)'; *James*, 18.

Bibliography

Barag, D., & D. Flusser, 'The Ossuary of Yehoḥanah Granddaughter of the High Priest Theophilus', *Israel Exploration Journal* 36.1/2 (1986), 39–44.

Bradley, K.R. 'Household, Roman', in S. Hornblower & A. Spawforth (eds.), *Oxford Classical Dictionary* (Oxford: Oxford University Press, ³2003 [1949]), 730.

Bauckham, R. *Gospel Women. Studies of the Named Women in the Gospels* (Grand Rapids: Eerdmans, 2002).

Bauckham, R. *James. Wisdom of James, Disciple of Jesus the Sage* (London & New York: Routledge, 1999).

Bolt, P.G. 'What Actually Happened on Resurrection Morning? A Clear and Simple Account', *Journal of Gospels and Acts Research* 2 (2018), 86–100.

Cadbury, H.J. 'Erastus of Corinth', *JBL* 50 (1931), 42–58.

Cadbury, H.J. 'Lucius of Cyrene', F.J. Foakes Jackson & K. Lake (eds.), *The Beginnings of Christianity. Part 1: The Acts of the Apostles.* Vol. 5: *Additional Notes* (London: Macmillan, 1933), 489–495.

Cadbury, H.J. 'The Tradition', in F.J. Foakes Jackson & K. Lake (eds.), *The Beginnings of Christianity. Part 1: The Acts of the Apostles. Vol. 2: Prolegomena II: Criticism* (London: Macmillan, 1922), 209–264.

Cranfield, C.E.B. *The Epistle to the Romans* 2 (ICC; 2 vols.; Edinburgh: T.&T. Clark, 1979).

Dodd, C. H. *The Epistle of Paul to the Romans* (MNTC; London/Glasgow: Fontana, 1960 [1932]).

Edmundson, G. *The Church in Rome in the First Century* (London: Longmans, Green & Co, 1913).

Ellis, E.E. 'Paul and his Co-Workers', in E.E. Ellis, *Prophecy and Hermeneutics in Early Christianity. New Testament Essays* (WUNT 18; Tübingen: Mohr Siebeck, 1978; reprinted: Grand Rapids: Eerdmans, 1980), 3–22.

Evans, C.A. *Jesus and the Ossuaries: What Jewish Burial Practices Reveal about the Beginning of Christianity* (Waco, TX: Baylor University Press, 2003).

Evans, C.A.	'Excavating Caiaphas, Pilate, and Simon of Cyrene: Assessing the Literary and Archaological Evidence', in J.H. Charlesworth (ed.), *Jesus and Archaeology* (Grand Rapids & Cambridge: Eerdmans, 2006), 323-340.
Ford, R.C.	'St. Luke and Lucius of Cyrene', *ExpT* 32.5 (1921), 219-220.
Foxhall, L.	'Household, Greek', in S. Hornblower & A. Spawforth (eds.), *Oxford Classical Dictionary* (Oxford: Oxford University Press, ³2003 [1949]), 729-730.
Gamble, H.Y.	*The Textual History of the Letter to The Romans: A Study in Textual and Literary Criticism* (Studies and Documents, 42; Grand Rapids: Eerdmans, 1977).
von Harnack, A.	'κοπιᾶν (Οἱ Κοπιῶντες) im früchristlichen Sprachgebrauch', *ZNW* 27 (1928), 1-10.
Hengel, M., & A.M. Schwemer,	*Paul Between Damascus and Antioch. The Unknown Years* (J. Bowden, trans.; London & Louisville: SCM & Westminster John Knox, 1997).
Hughes, P.E.	*A Commentary on the Epistle to the Hebrews* (Grand Rapids: Eerdmans, 1977).
Ilan, T.	*Lexicon of Jewish Names in Late Antiquity*. Part I: *Palestine 330 BCE-200 CE* (Texts & Studies in Ancient Judaism 91; Tübingen: Mohr Siebeck, 2002).
Ilan, T.	*Lexicon of Jewish Names in Late Antiquity*. Part II: *Palestine 200-650* (Texts & Studies in Ancient Judaism 148; Tübingen: Mohr Siebeck, 2012).
Ilan, T. & T. Ziem	*Lexicon of Jewish Names in Late Antiquity*. Part III: *The Western Diaspora 330 BCE-650 CE* (Texts & Studies in Ancient Judaism 126; Tübingen: Mohr Siebeck, 2008).
Ilan, T. & K. Hünefeld	*Lexicon of Jewish Names in Late Antiquity*. Part IV: *The Eastern Diaspora 330 BCE-650 CE* (Texts & Studies in Ancient Judaism 141; Tübingen: Mohr Siebeck, 2011).
Ilan, T.	'Notes on the Distribution of Jewish Women's Names in Palestine in the Second Temple and Mishnaic Periods', *JJS* 40 (1989), 186-200.
Judge, E.A.	'#26. The Names of Jewish Women', *NewDocs* 10, 156-158.
Judge, E.A.	'#84. Greek Names of Latin Origin', *NewDocs* 2, pp.106-108

Kearsley, R.A.	'#3. Women in Public Life', *NewDocs* 6, 24–27.
Lagrange, M J.	*St Paul: Épitre aux Romains* (Ebib; Paris: Gabalda, 1931).
Lampe, P.	'The Roman Christians of Romans 16', in K.P. Donfried (ed.), *The Romans Debate* (Grand Rapids: Baker Academic, 1991 [revised]), 216–230.
Lampe, P.	'Persis', 'Prisca', *ABD* 5 (1992) 244; 467–468; 'Julia', 'Junias', *ABD* 3 (1992), 1125, 1127.
Letronne, M.	'Sur les noms grecs de Cléophas et de Cléoas (ΚΛΕΟΦΑΣ et ΚΛΕΟΠΑΣ)', *Revue Archéologique* 1.2 (1844–45), 485–491.
Llewelyn, S.R.	'#12. The Development of the Codex', *NewDocs* 8, 249–256,
Mathew, S.	*Women in the Greetings of Rom 16.1–16: A Study of Mutuality and Women's Ministry in the Letter to the Romans* (Library of New Testament studies, 471; London: Bloomsbury T&T Clark, 2013).
Montefiore, H.	*Epistle to the Hebrews* (BNTC; London: Black, 1964).
NewDocs	
1.	G.H.R. Horsley (ed.), *New Documents Illustrating Early Christianity. A Review of the Greek Inscriptions and Papyri published in 1976* (Macquarie University: Ancient History Documentary Research Centre, 1981).
2.	G.H.R. Horsley (ed.), *New Documents Illustrating Early Christianity, 2. A Review of the Greek Inscriptions and Papyri published in 1977* (Macquarie University: Ancient History Documentary Research Centre, 1982).
3.	G.H.R. Horsley (ed.), *New Documents Illustrating Early Christianity, 3. A Review of the Greek Inscriptions and Papyri published in 1978* (Macquarie University: Ancient History Documentary Research Centre, 1983).
4.	G.H.R. Horsley (ed.), *New Documents Illustrating Early Christianity, 4. A Review of the Greek Inscriptions and Papyri published in 1979* (Macquarie University: Ancient History Documentary Research Centre, 1987).
5.	G.H.R. Horsley (ed.), *New Documents Illustrating Early Christianity, 5. Linguistic Essays* (Macquarie University: Ancient History Documentary Research Centre, 1989).

6.	S.R. Llewelyn (ed.), with R.A. Kearsley, *New Documents Illustrating Early Christianity*, 6. *A Review of the Greek Inscriptions and Papyri published in 1980–81* (Macquarie University: Ancient History Documentary Research Centre, 1992).
7.	S.R. Llewelyn (ed.), with R.A. Kearsley, *New Documents Illustrating Early Christianity*, 7. *A Review of the Greek Inscriptions and Papyri published in 1982–83* (Macquarie University: Ancient History Documentary Research Centre, 1994).
8.	S.R Llewelyn (ed.), *New Documents Illustrating Early Christianity* 8. *A Review of the Greek Inscriptions and Papyri published 1984–1985* (Grand Rapids & Macquarie University: Eerdmans & Ancient History Documentary Research Centre, 1997).
9.	S.R. Llewelyn (ed.), *New Documents Illustrating Early Christianity*, 9. *A Review of the Greek Inscriptions and Papyri published in 1986–87* (Grand Rapids & Macquarie University: Eerdmans & Ancient History Documentary Research Centre, 2002).
10.	S.R. Llewelyn & J.R. Harrison (eds.), with E.J. Bridge, *New Documents Illustrating Early Christianity*, 10. *A Review of Greek and Other Inscriptions and Papyri published between 1988 and 1992* (Grand Rapids & Macquarie University: Eerdmans & Ancient History Documentary Research Centre, 2012).
O'Brien, P.T.	*Introductory Thanksgivings in the Letters of Paul* (NovTSup 49; Leiden: Brill, 1977).
Pixner, B.	*Paths of the Messiah and Sites of the Early Church from Galilee to Jerusalem* (R. Riesner, ed.; K. Meyrick, S. & M. Randall, transls.; San Francisco: Ignatius Press, 2010 [German: 1991]).
Reicke, B.	'The Historical Setting of Colossians', *RevExp* 70 (1973), 429–438. Republished in *Re-examining Paul's Letters. The History of the Pauline Correspondence* (D.P. Moessner & I. Reicke, eds.; Harrisburg: Trinity Press International, 2001), 121–130.

Reicke, B.   'The Chronology of the Pastoral Epistles', in *Re-examining Paul's Letters. The History of the Pauline Correspondence* (D.P. Moessner & I. Reicke, eds.; Harrisburg: Trinity Press International, 2001), 105–120. Originally published as 'Chronologie der Pastoralbriefe', *TLZ* 101 (1976), 82–94.

Reilly, L.C.   *Slaves in Ancient Greece. Slaves from Greek Manumission Inscriptions* (Chicago: Ares, 1978).

Robinson, D.W.B.   *Donald Robinson. Selected Works.* Vol. 1: *Assembling God's People* (P.G. Bolt & M.D. Thompson, eds.; Camperdown, NSW: Australian Church Record/ Moore College, 2008).

Robinson, J.A.T.   *Redating the New Testament* (London: SCM, 1976; Reprint: Wipf & Stock, 2000).

Sanday, W.S. & A.C. Headlam,   *The Epistle to the Romans* (ICC; Edinburgh: T.&T. Clark, ^{4}1900 [1895]).

Schwartz, D.R.   *Agrippa I: The Last King of Judea* (Tübingen: Mohr Siebeck, 1990).

Scranton, R., et al.   *Kenchreai. Eastern Port of Corinth. 1. Topography and Architecture* (Leiden: Brill, 1978).

Smallwood, E.M.   'High Priests and Politics in Roman Palestine', *JTS* 13.1 (1962), 14–34.

Smallwood, E.M.   'The Date of the Dismissal of Pontius Pilate from Judaea', *JJS* 5 (1954), 12–21.

Stanton, G.   'Accommodation for Paul's Entourage', *NovT* 60.3 (2018), 227–246.

Steinmann, A.E.   *From Abraham to Paul. A Biblical Chronology* (St Louis: Concordia, 2011).

Treggia, S.M.   'Family, Roman', in S. Hornblower & A. Spawforth (eds.), *Oxford Classical Dictionary* (Oxford: Oxford University Press, ^{3}2003 [1949]), 586.

VanderKam, J.C.   *From Joshua to Caiaphas: High Priests after the Exile* (Minneapolis & Assen: Fortress & Van Gorcum, 2004).

Weima, J.A.D.   *Neglected Endings: The Significance Of The Pauline Letter Closings* (JSNTSup 101; Sheffield: Sheffield Academic Press, 1994).

Wenham, J.	*Easter Enigma: Are the Resurrection Accounts in Conflict?* (Grand Rapids, MI: Baker, ²1992 [1984]; Reprint: Eugene, Or.: Wipf & Stock, 2005).
Whelan, E.	'World's Oldest Christian Letter Found On 3rd Century Egyptian Papyrus', *Ancient Origins* 12/7/2019. www.ancient-origins.net/news-history-archaeology/christian-letter-0012278.
White, J.L.	*Light from Ancient Letters* (Philadelphia: Fortress, 1978).
Wiefel, W.	'The Jewish Community in Ancient Rome and the Origins of Roman Christianity', in K.P. Donfried (ed.), *The Romans Debate* (Minneapolis: Augsburg, 1977), 100–119.
Winter, B.W.	*Roman Wives, Roman Widows: the Appearance of the New Woman and the Pauline Communities* (Grand Rapids: Eerdmans, 2003).

CHAPTER 14

Phoebe in and around Romans: The Weight of Marginal Reception

Alan H. Cadwallader

Phoebe of Cenchreae has been overshadowed in some commentary in recent years by the elevation of the importance of Tertius, the secretary who intrudes himself into the letter at its conclusion (Rom 16:22).[1] However, the Greek manuscripts of Romans do not prefigure this contemporary accent. Tertius barely scrapes a mention in the subscripts to the letter and marginal commentary (usually sifted from the writings of church literati such as John Chrysostom) underscore not his skill but rather that the function is uplifted by Paul's appropriation. By contrast, Phoebe's preeminent position in the list of salutations and the special commendation she receives (Rom 16:1–2) seem to have elicited marked attention. She is given particular notice in subscripts, marginal glosses and formal commentary (and catenae) attached to the central text of the epistle. This chapter explores the reception of Phoebe in the manuscripts that transmit the text of our knowledge of her. The array of material returns us to an appreciation of her considerable importance in Paul's epistolary and missionary purposes.

---

1 See Cadwallader, 'Tertius in the Margins'.

1. Randolph Richards and the Subscript Role of Tertius and Phoebe in Romans

In his highly influential monograph, Randolph Richards allowed that there was one other possible claimant to the role of secretary for the writing out of Romans besides the famous Tertius of Rom 16:22. That 'pretender' was Phoebe of Cenchreae. In the body of Richards' argument promoting Tertius as the exemplar of secretarial creativity, Phoebe rather was the beneficiary of Tertius' construction of the letter of recommendation.[2] Phoebe was credited only (and briefly) with bearing the letter to the Romans.[3] Phoebe is apparently of such little relevance to the letter that she gains no entry in the indices of Richards' two works on the secretary and somehow manages to be completely overlooked when he admits the importance of the letter carrier.[4] Anything else was confined to a footnote, where Richards supplied a reference to a subscription, long made part of the text of the letter to the Romans in the KJV though, there, usually marked with a ¶.[5] He relies on the text of NA26 for the subscription 'found in most minuscules'. He initially took the reading ἐπιστολὴ πρὸς Ῥωμαίους ἐγράφη διὰ Φοίβης as a claim that she had been the secretary of the letter, pointing out that this 'actually contradicts the testimony of the letter itself' and, in any case, derives from 'unquestionably late' manuscripts that 'have no link to authentic tradition'.[6] He opted for the 'discerning alteration' of minuscule 337,[7] though this is not explicated. NA26 provided the reading and numbering of this variant in the wording of the subscript—'the letter to the

---

2   The role of Tertius became considerably exposited in Richards' later work, *Paul and First-Century Letter Writing*, 205–206. The work of Ian Elmer substantially depends on that of Richards, though he accents the communal dimensions in the activity of the construction of a 'Pauline' letter. See Elmer, 'I, Tertius. Secretary or Co-author of Romans'; 'Setting the Record Straight at Galatia', 25–28; 'The Pauline letters as community documents'.
3   Richards, *Secretary*, 170, 171.
4   Richards, *Secretary*, 7–10, 71–73; *Paul and First-Century Letter Writing*, 77.
5   The KJV included a subscript to Romans, 'Written to the Romans from Corinthus, and sent by Phebe servant of the Church at Cenchrea'. Subscripts usually concluded the Pauline letters in the KJV, though came under increasing criticism in nineteenth-century moves for revision. William Sanday, a contributor to the popular Ellicott's New Testament Commentary, tersely noted that 'The subscription in its present form hardly dates back beyond the ninth century'; 'The Epistle of Paul the Apostle to the Romans', in Ellicott, *A New Testament Commentary*, 2.272.
6   Richards, *Secretary*, 172 n.203.
7   Fitzmyer, *Romans*, 755, makes a similar value judgement: 'MS 337 finally gets it straight'.

Romans was written by (ἐγράφη διά) Tertius but sent via (ἐπέμπθη διά) Phoebe'.[8]

In fact, the provided minuscule number is incorrect.[9] A confusion reigns as regards which manuscript(s) carries this subscript variation. Both Augustin Scholz and Constantin von Tischendorf listed the reading, but their forebears, Johan Wettstein, John Mill and Johann Griesbach did not. Scholz and Tischendorf listed the supporting manuscript for Tertius's presence in the subscript as minuscule 133. But Scholz followed by Tischendorf had noted four different manuscripts as 133.[10] His numbering system was based on an index of manuscripts he consulted for each section of the Greek New Testament, not on a number which had been immutably assigned to a particular minuscule. Scholz was governed more by the actual holding entity, a standard approach in the eighteenth and nineteenth centuries.[11] Thus, minuscule 133 for his work on the Gospels, Scholz identified as the eleventh century Vatican Gr. 363.[12] But this particular manuscript (that is, Vatican Gr. 363) also contains the Pauline corpus. Its subscript to Romans is one of the most common forms of subscript, Πρὸς Ῥωμαίους ἐγράφη ἀπὸ Κορίνθου διὰ Φοίβης τῆς διακόνου. However, Kurt Aland does not include the Scholz-Tischendorf manuscript 133= Vatican Gr. 363 in his list of the four manuscripts previously given as 133,[13] precisely because Gregory's standardization of manuscript numbers operated on the New Testament sections *after the Gospels*.[14] Accordingly, Vatican Gr. 363 remained with the number 133.[15] Similarly, Scholz's 133 for Acts also contained the Pauline epistles. The catalogue mark was more

---

8   In this carefully expanded subscription, there may be some legacy of the earlier documentary expression that identifies the carrier within the letter, that is ἔπεμψά σοι διὰ x. See, for example, P.Oxy. 113.
9   The error was repeated in N27, 28.
10 Scholz, *Novum Testamentum Graece*, 1.lxiv; 2.xvi, xxix; compare Gregory, *Textkritik des Neuen Testamentes*, 1.276, 300, 322. Gregory was responsible for pulling together the manuscripts and their numbers used by Tischendorf in his *Editio Octava*.
11 See Scrivener, *A Plain Introduction to the Criticism of the New Testament*, 1.391, who accents that the arrangement of the manuscripts is 'according to the countries where they are and the owners to whom they belong'.
12 Scholz, *Novum Testamentum Graece*, LXIV.
13 Aland, *Kurzgefasste Liste*, 325.
14 K. & B. Aland, *The Text of the New Testament*, 39.
15 Aland, *Kurzgefasste Liste*, 422.

precisely identified by Frederick Scrivener as manuscript C. vi. 19,[16] at the Biblioteca Nazionale in Turin. Aland's *Kurzgefasste Liste*, accords it the Gregory number 611[17] and dated it to the twelfth century. Its reading cannot be checked because the manuscript was one of the many items destroyed in a devastating fire in 1904.[18]

Our particular interest lies in the manuscript 133 that Scholz used for the Pauline corpus. This is the twelfth century Bibliotheque nationale de Français Ms Grec 56. This is given the Gregory(-Aland) number 337.[19] The manuscript has a longer subscript, but still without mention of Tertius: Ἡ πρὸς Ῥωμαίους ἐγράφη ἀπὸ Κορίνθου διὰ Φοίβης τῆς διακόνου τῆς ἐν Κεγχρεαῖς. To my knowledge, the only manuscript that specifies Tertius as the writer of the letter in its subscript is minuscule 18 (= BnF Grec 47), dated to the fourteenth century. I have no explanation for this confusion, except the possibility of a typographical error, given that this manuscript was given the number 132 by Scholz-Tischendorf. If this is the case, then the mistake has been simply reiterated without further checking of readings.[20]

The suspicion therefore is that some ambiguity had attached to the wording of the plentiful subscription(s) that contained some version of ἔγραψα διὰ Φοιβῆς—at least an ambiguity in the scribal world behind these late minuscules. A similar distinction between the roles of Tertius and Phoebe is found two centuries earlier (c. 1116 CE) in the writing of the Byzantine imperial courtier and theologian, Nicetas Seides. He taught, 'The epistle to the Romans was written from Corinth by the hand of Tertius, with Paul dictating to him, and was sent through Phoebe the deacon to Rome, during the time when Claudius drove out all the Jews.'[21]

16 Scrivener, *A Plain Introduction*, 1.294.
17 Aland, *Kurzgefasste Liste*, 325, 428.
18 This did not prevent Bruce Metzger listing it in his 'Supplementary Lists of Greek Manuscripts' in *A Textual Commentary*, 694, doubtless on the basis of citation in earlier editions of the Greek New Testament. Compare Aland, *Kurzgefasste Liste*, 93, 428.
19 Aland, *Kurzgefasste Liste*, 325.
20 One wonders whether this misnumbering applies across the Pauline corpus or merely for the subscript to Romans.
21 <Ἡ> πρὸς Ῥωμαίους ἐπιστολὴ ἐγράφη ἀπὸ Κορίνθου διὰ χειρὸς Τερτίου <Παύλου>, ὑπαγορεύσαντος αὐτῷ ἀπεστάλη δὲ διὰ Φοίβης τῆς διακόνου εἰς Ῥώμην, καθ' ὃν χρόνον Κλαύδιος ἀπήλασε πάντας ἀπὸ Ῥώμης τοὺς Ἰουδαίους. Simotas, Νικήτα Σεΐδου, 23.19–23 (p. 286); see also ll. 30–31.

In a separate essay, Richards returned in greater erudition to the use of γράφω διά in 1 Pet 5:12 in order to test the meaning and function of the phrase. In spite of how he had read the stock (KJV) subscription to Romans as indicating Phoebe as secretary, he had, in the same monograph, argued that the form of expression in the subscript probably refers to the letter carrier'.[22] His later research made this more certain in his estimation, as well as providing the opportunity to correct the earlier misdirection.[23] Richards claims that γράφω διά τινος is a literary formula that indicates the letter bearer rather than the letter secretary.[24] The formula had to be strictly circumscribed so as to remove some claimants from consideration, including the reference to Barsabbas and Silas in Acts 15:23.[25] One is left with three secular papyri that support the phrase,[26] a thin number to substantiate the claim to 'a literary formula'. Nevertheless, Richards concludes that γράφω διά τινος only identifies the letter carrier, and that 'the expanded superscription for Romans found in the majority text' clearly indicates Phoebe as the letter-carrier, not the secretary.[27]

It should be noted that, because of Richards' tight control on the acceptable combination of words, other uses of διά in a secretarial context are not investigated. This interpretative stricture may have secured an absolutism in the resulting conclusion that a wider sensitivity to the evidence may want to qualify. So, for example, in the census record preserved in *P. Mich*. III 178, dated to the early second century, the preposition is used in a phrase that clearly refers to secretaries, since, after the name following διά, γραμματέως is added. So, for example, lines 28–9 read: κατακεχώρ(ικα) Αὐ(νῆς) Αὐνεί(ους) λ[αο]γρ(άφος) διὰ Ἐπιμάχο(υ) γρ(αμματέως), 'I, Aunes, son of Aunes, registration officer, have recorded it through Epimachos, secretary'.[28] Here κατακεχώρικα is simply a more technically apt term for the bureaucratic task at hand than ἔγραψα. It may therefore be more circumspect in the face of the evidence to suggest

---

22 Richards, *Secretary*, 73.
23 Richards, 'Silvanus', 426.
24 Richards, 'Silvanus', 424.
25 Richards, 'Silvanus', 426.
26 *P. Fay.* 123; *P. Oxy.* 937; *BGU* 1 33.
27 Richards, 'Silvanus', 426.
28 Translation from Parkin & Pomeroy, *Roman Social History*, 130.

that context rather than a tightly defined formula is the determinant. Indeed the intrusion of ἐμοῦ into the supposed formula in *P.Berol.* inv. 17490 (δι' ἐμοῦ Ἱερημίου ἐγρ[άφη]) is much more likely to refer to a secretary than a carrier personally identifying himself in the letter.[29]

The testing of Richards' valuable research given above is not intended to dispute the *status quo* and suggest that Phoebe was the secretary for Paul's letter to the Romans, rather than the self-promoted Tertius of Rom 16:22. Rather it raises the issue of how Phoebe's importance in relation to the letter is to be understood. It proffers an invitation to explore some matters further, especially regarding the reception and appreciation of Phoebe as witnessed in the manuscripts of the text of Romans. The subscriptions attest a very different weighting given to Phoebe compared to the importance and standing that Richards delivered to Tertius. It seems that commentators from John Chrysostom to Nicetas Seides saw in Tertius nothing more than a transcriber of Paul's dictation, though honoured by that task.[30] A couple of writers added him as the second bishop of Iconium,[31] and Nicetas Seides includes him as one of the 'fellow-travellers' (presumably of Christians generally or of Paul's band).[32] The service of Paul shape the limited marginal comments about Tertius found in New Testament manuscripts. So, for example, minuscules 1933 and 1878 (both eleventh century) have ἀντὶ μεγάλου τέθεικεν ἐπαίνου τὸ εἶναι ὑπογραφέα Παύλου ('To be a secretary for Paul was indeed great praise') as their only observation about Tertius. Occasionally the problem of Tertius appearing to cultivate his own praise is addressed. Chrysostom provided the benchmark, if this received comment at all. Tertius, so the text was construed, was not after his own honour but rather that a warm love might accrue to him for his

---

29 See Poethke, 'Misthosis-vertrag über fischereirechte aus Aphrodite', 554.
30 'This is no small honour, to be a secretary for Paul' (Οὐ μικρὸν καὶ τοῦτο ἐγκώμιον ὑπογραφέα εἶναι Παύλου); Chrysostom, *Homilies on the Epistle to the Romans* (PG 60.677 §756; repeated in the catenae: see Cramer, *Catenae Graecorum*, 4.527; compare his *Homilies on the Epistle to the Galatians* (PG 61.678 §727). Cf. 'He was also one of those considered worthy to enjoy the apostolic teaching ...' (Εἷς ἦν καὶ οὗτος τῶν τῆς ἀποστολικῆς διδασκαλίας ἠξιωμένων); Theodoret, *Commentary on the Fourteen Letters of S. Paul* (PG 82.224D).
31 Epiphanius, 'Index discipulorum, item μα' (T. Schermann, *Prophetarum vitae fabulosae* [Leipzig: Teubner, 1907], 123, l. 6; *Vitae Prophetarum* index item μζ' (Schermann, *Prophetarum vitae*, 140, l.10). This became thoroughly entrenched in Byzantine synaxaria.
32 Simotas, Νικήτα Σεΐδου, 23.31 (p. 287).

ministry, cementing inter-city relations between those 'in the Lord'.[33] The nicety is a fine one but is taken one step further in a minuscule of Paul's letters that attaches a comment to each major phrase. In the thirteenth century minuscule, 1973, the scribe begins with a Chrysostom-inspired negation of Tertius's self-serving but then provides a variation on Chrysostom's theme, making Tertius's own construction of letters an act of love: ἀλλ' ἵνα πλεῖν ἀγαπη θῆ ὑπ' αὐτῶν, ὡς διακονίας τοῖς πρὸς αὐτοῦ γράμμασιν ('... but rather that love be set over them all, as over a ministry in the letter-forms from him').[34] These attachments to the text proper of Romans found in the manuscripts of Paul's letter, appear to be the sum total of the notice of Tertius. By contrast, the notice given to Phoebe is markedly more prolix and apparent.

2. Phoebe in the Manuscript Subscriptions to the Letter to the Romans

The following are the Greek subscripts to Romans that I have collated from a combination of the apparatuses of Scholz, Tischendorf (updated to their GA number) and NA[26-28] and a selection of individual manuscripts available online through the Institut für Neutestamentliche Textforschung, the Centre for the Study of New Testament Manuscripts, the Bibliothèque nationale de Français, the British Library, the National Library of Greece and the Leimonos Monastery on the island of Lesbos. In the list, no distinction is made between uncial and minuscule letters[35] abbreviations have been expanded; extra diacritical marks (e.g. diaresis) have been omitted; lection, liturgical and stichometrical notations are not included; ink colour changes are not noted. In some manuscripts, an introduction (ὑπόθεσις) is given which notes that the letter to the Romans was written from Corinth; this can sometimes 'replace' the

---

33 Πλὴν οὐκ ἵνα ἑαυτὸν ἐγκωμιάσῃ ... ἀλλ' ἵνα θερμὴν ἐπισπάσηται παρ' αὐτῶν τὴν ἀγάπην ἀπὸ τῆς διακονίας; Chrysostom *Homilies on Romans* (PG 60.677 §756).
34 My awkward translation is an effort to capture the semantic distinction in 'letters'. I have yet to find another example of this interpretation.
35 Sometimes in minuscule manuscripts, the subscript is written in uncial letters (eg. 458).

same/similar note in a subscript.[36] Finally, it should be noted that the list, whilst extensive, makes no claim to complete coverage, either in the manuscripts supporting any particular subscript or in the diversity of expressions in available subscripts.

No subscript[37] 010 (F), 5, 38, 57, 76, 131, 308, 312, 319, 365, 456, 465, 620, 629, 630, 876, 1505, 1611, 1762, 1765, 1873, 2344, 2746, 2892

Πρὸς Ῥωμαίους 01 (ℵ), 02 (A), 03ᶜ (Bᶜ + ἐγράφη ἀπὸ Κορίνθουᶜ²), 04 (C), 06 (Dᴾ + ἐγράφη ἀπὸ Κορίνθουᶜ), 1, 14, 30, 35, 41, 49, 135

Πρὸς Ῥωμαίους ἐτελέσθη (+ ad romanos explicit) 012 (G)

Πρὸς Ῥωμαίους ἐγράφη ἀπὸ Κορίνθου Dᵖᶜ³⁸ 2110³⁹

Πρὸς Ῥωμαίους ἐγράφη ἀπὸ Κορίνθου διὰ Φοίβης τῆς διακόνου 6, 43, 82, 88, 90, 110, 133, 181, 203, 216, 325, 339, 398, 458, 462, 466*, 506, 517, 605, 623, 627, 642, 910 (Κορινθίους!), 920, 1175, 1243, 1244, 1424 (first subscript),[40] 1720, 2464, 2484, Lesb. Leim. 55

Πρὸς Ῥωμαίους ἐγράφη ἀπὸ Κορίνθου διὰ Φοίβης διακόνου 62, 80

Πρὸς Ῥωμαίους ἐπιστολὴ ἐγράφη ἀπὸ Κορίνθου διὰ Φοίβης τῆς διακόνου 049

Πρὸς Ῥωμαίους ἐπιστολὴ ἐγράφη ἀπὸ Κορίνθου διὰ Φοίβης τῆς διακόνου τῆς ἐν Κεγχρεαῖς ἐκκλησίας 1875

Πρός Ῥωμαίους ἐγράφη ἀπὸ Κορίνθου διὰ Φοίβης τῆς διακόνου τῆς ἐν Κεγχρεαῖς ἐκκλησίας 10, 101, 109, 110, 111, 177, 241, 250, 454, 460, 466, 469, 498, 602, 603, 618, 1244ᶜ, 1878, 1907, 1923, 1924, 1927, 1932, 1933

Πρός Ῥωμαίους ἐγράφη ἀπὸ Κορίνθου διὰ Φοίβης τῆς διακόνου ἢ τῆς ἐν Κεγχρεαῖς ἐκκλησίας 911

---

36 See, for example, Codex 056. It became common for Corinth to be named as the place from which the letter came in both introduction and subscript (see, for example, 367, 676).
37 Fragments of the Pauline corpus that contain no sequence from the end of one letter to the beginning of the next are excluded.
38 The addition/correction to the Greek subscript appears to be fostered by the Latin subscript which, from the same hand, reads *epistula Pauli apostoli scribens a Corinthum*.
39 Minuscule 2110 includes the number of stichoi apparently as part of the subscript.
40 The first subscript is written in uncial letters; the second uses minuscule letters.

Πρός τοὺς Ῥωμαίους ἐγράφη ἀπὸ Κορίνθου διὰ Φοίβης τῆς διακόνου τῆς ἐν Κεγχρεαῖς ἐκκλησίας 1911[41]

Ἡ πρὸς Ῥωμαίους ἐγράφη ἀπὸ Κορίνθου διὰ Φοίβης τῆς διακόνου 796c (part margin)

Ἡ πρὸς Ῥωμαίους ἐγράφη ἀπὸ Κορίνθου διὰ Φοίβης τῆς διακόνου τῆς ἐν Κεγχρεαῖς 337

Ἡ πρὸς Ῥωμαίους ἐγράφη ἀπὸ Κορίνθου διὰ Φοίβης τῆς διακόνου τῆς ἐν Κεγχρεαῖς ἐκκλησίας 384

Ἡ πρὸς Ῥωμαίους ἐπιστολὴ ἐγράφη ἀπὸ Κορίνθου διὰ Φοίβης τῆς διακόνου 97, 2652

Ἡ πρὸς Ῥωμαίους ἐπιστολὴ ἐγράφη ἀπὸ Κορίνθου διὰ Φοίβης τῆς διακόνου τῆς ἐν Κεχρεαῖς [sic] ἐκκλησίας 641

Ἡ πρὸς Ῥωμαίους αὕτη[42] ἐπιστολὴ ἐγράφη ἀπὸ Κορίνθου διὰ Φοίβης διακόνου 3

Ἡ πρὸς Ῥωμαίους αὕτη ἐπιστολὴ ἐγράφη ἀπὸ Κορίνθου διὰ Φοίβης τῆς διακόνου Lesb. Leim 195

Ἡ πρὸς Ῥωμαίους αὕτη ἐπιστολὴ ἐγράφη ἀπὸ Κορίνθου διὰ Φοίβης τῆς διακόνου τῆς ἐν Κεγχρεαῖς ἐκκλησίας 385

Αὕτη ἡ πρὸς Ῥωμαίους ἐγράφη διὰ Φοίβης τῆς διακόνου ἀπὸ Κορίνθου 808

Αὕτη ἡ ἐπιστολὴ ἐγράφη ἀπὸ Κορίνθου διὰ Φοίβης τῆς διακόνου τῆς ἐν Κεγχρεαῖς ἐκκλησίας 314, 424, 913, 1830, 1956, 2125

ἐγράφη ἀπὸ Κορίνθου 2138

ἐγράφη διὰ Φοίβης ἀπὸ Κορίνθου 201, 614, 757, 801

ἐγράφη ἀπὸ Κορίνθου διὰ Φοίβης τῆς διακόνου 69, 81, 122, 457, 676, 1761, 1894 (second subscript), Lesb. Leim. 132

ἐγράφη ἀπὸ Κορίνθου διὰ Φοίβης διακόνου 436

---

41 This minuscule is thought to be a handwritten transcript of the first edition of Erasmus' Greek new Testament.
42 This has been rendered with a soft aspirant.

ἐγράφη ἀπὸ Κορίνθου διὰ Φοίβης τῆς διακόνου τῆς ἐν Κεγχρεαῖς ἐκκλησίας (91 second subscript, margin)

ἐγράφη ἡ πρὸς Ῥωμαίους ἐπιστολὴ διὰ Τερτίου ἐπέμφθη δὲ διὰ Φοίβης ἀπὸ Κορίνθου 18

Παύλου ἐπιστολὴ πρὸς Ῥωμαίους 044 (Ψ)

Παύλου ἀποστόλου ἐπιστολὴ πρὸς Ῥωμαίους ἐγράφη ἀπὸ Κορίνθου διὰ Φοίβης τῆς διακόνου 104

Παύλου ἀποστόλου ἐπιστολὴ πρὸς Ῥωμαίους ἐγράφη ἀπὸ Κορίνθου διὰ Φοίβης διακόνου 88

Τοῦ ἁγίου καὶ πανευφήμου ἀποστόλου Παύλου ἐπιστολὴ πρὸς Ῥωμαίους ἐγράφη ἀπὸ Κορίνθου διὰ Φοίβης τῆς διακόνου 020 (L)

τελός 61

τελὸς τῆς πρὸς Ῥωμαίους 876 (margin)

τελὸς τῆς πρὸς Ῥωμαίους ἐπιστολῆς 94, 1367, 1827, 1828, 1894 (first subscript)

τελὸς σὺν θῶι τῆς πρὸς Ῥωμαίους ἐπιστολῆς 91 (first subscript)

τελὸς τῆς πρὸς Ῥωμαίους ἐπιστολῆς ἥτις ἐγράφη ἀπὸ Κορίνθου διὰ Φοίβης τῆς διακόνου 794

τελὸς τῆς πρὸς Ῥωμαίους ἐπιστολῆς ἥτις ἐγράφη ἀπὸ Κορίνθου διὰ Φοίβης διακόνου 42, 51, 912, 1739, 2279

τελὸς τῆς πρὸς Ῥωμαίους ἐπιστολῆς ἥτις ἐγράφη ἀπὸ Κορίνθου διὰ Φοίβης τῆς διακόνου 223, 367

τελὸς τῆς πρὸς Ῥωμαίους ἐπιστολῆς ἐγράφη ἀπὸ Κορίνθου διὰ Φοίβης τῆς διακόνου NLG 122

τελὸς τῆς πρὸς Ῥωμαίους ἐπιστολῆς ἐγράφη δὲ ἀπὸ Κορίνθου διὰ Φοίβης τῆς διακόνου 496, 1315

τελὸς τῆς πρὸς Ῥωμαίους ἐπιστολῆς ἐγράφη δὲ ἀπὸ Κορίνθου διὰ Φοίβης τῆς διακόνου BnF Grec 222

τελὸς τῆς πρὸς Ῥωμαίους ἐπιστολῆς τοῦ ἁγίου καὶ πανευφήμου ἀποστόλου Παύλου 1424 (second subscript) τέλος τῆς ἐπιστολῆς Παύλου τοῦ ἀποστόλου τῆς πρὸς Ῥωμαίους· ἢ καὶ ἐγράφη ἀπὸ Κορίνθου διὰ Φοίβης τῆς διακόνου καὶ ἀπεστέλλη εἰς Ῥώμην· πρὸς ἐπιστήριγμα 451.

The total number of Greek subscripts to Romans listed here is forty-two,[43] substantially more than the seven varieties provided by Bruce Metzger,[44] or the twelve/thirteen from Scholz and Tischendorf,[45] even allowing that some variations are so slight (for example, the presence or absence of an article) that they can be grouped together (as has been done peripherally in some editions of the Greek New Testament). Some arbitrary decision-making was made for the compilation. The τέλός of minuscule 61 was included (even though a sixteenth century manuscript) because it was added after a space under the central column of the main text rather than in a right or left-hand margin as would be usual for a lexical mark; and it appears to be related to a series of expansions built on the τέλός, from the brief marginal subscript of minuscule 876 (twelfth century) to the lengthier embellishment of minuscule 451 (eleventh century). At the same time the long (ten line) addition to the end of Romans 16:24 in Codex 056 appears less a subscript than a catenous comment on the importance of Timothy (v.21) in Paul's work; it is separated from the end of the epistle by a superscript τέλός at the end of v.24.[46]

The forty-two different options in the Greek subscripts to the letter to the Romans suggests that there was a greater freedom in their wording than for the text of the letter, in spite of the inclusion (of one form) of the subscript in the King James Version and the suggestion that this is the reading of the 'Majority Text'.[47] Although the subscripts for the Pauline letters are sometimes sourced to the work of Euthalius, bishop of Sulca in Egypt, in the fifth century,[48] the variety cannot, at

---

43 Manuscripts without a subscript are not included in this number.
44 Metzger, *A Textual Commentary*, 477.
45 Scholz, *Novum Testamentum Graece*, 2.203; Tischendorf, *Novum Testamentum* 8, 2.457.
46 It is worth noting that minuscule 1505 has the potential to throw into greater confusion the discussion of Paul's secretary for Romans. The minuscule has a small drawing of Paul dictating to Timothy as his amanuensis. The accompanying explanatory gloss identifies that text as 'the epistle to the Romans'. This must await a later time for a more detailed examination.
47 Richards, 'Silvanus', 426.
48 See Willard, *A Critical Study of the Euthalian Apparatus*.

this stage, be traced in any sense of a chronological progression, linear development or common source—the absence of any subscript or the repetition of the incipit runs through early and late manuscripts, even if the fuller subscript detailing Phoebe's relationship to the text gains few instances among the uncial manuscripts. Even then, those uncial manuscripts are later (so, 020, ninth century; 049, ninth century).[49] The Latin versions tend to be less inventive and more terse,[50] though a full list has yet to be compiled.

These subscripts to Romans seem initially to have begun as a simple reading aid, signaling a break between the end of the letter and the beginning of the next. For those manuscripts across a number of centuries that resisted any subscript, a break between Romans and First Corinthians was nevertheless achieved by an ornamental line (for example, 131), sometimes provided in red ink (for example, 757), sometimes little more than a small ornament to complete the line ending in the 'Amen' of 16:27 (for example, 76) and sometimes a tailored reduction of lines into a triangle, culminating in the 'Amen' (for example, 57). At other times, the main indication of a break was simply a notice of the approach of First Corinthians—an incipit, a summary of the argument (the ὑπόθεσις) and/or a list of kephalaia for the opening of the Corinthian correspondence (for example, 1611). Sometimes these embroideries were combined with the subscripts, highlighting them; again, colour (usually red) might be used for both. At other times the subscript was added in right, left or top margins rather than centrally following the text (as, for example, in 796).

This functional aid also carried a compact didactic intent. A wad of information was added that was informed by elements in the letter itself (epistle, Romans, Corinth-Cenchreae, Phoebe, letter purpose), by hagiographical devotion (the adulation of Paul), liturgical and lectionary

---

49   This would appear to confirm Sanday's judgment above but it needs to be acknowledged that the sixth-century Codex 015 (Coislinianus), though fragmentary and not containing Romans, does include subscripts after endings of letters that are extant in the manuscript (for example, Hebrews).

50   So, for example, *explicit epistula ad Romanos* 51(gig), 61(a), 95, 629(lat); *Explicit Pauli apostoli epistula ad Romanos* 62; *epistula Pauli apostoli scribens a Corinthum* D^p(lat).

marks joining with the subscript (τελός).⁵¹ Sometimes, also, the subscript is directly followed by the stichoi count for the letter (for example NLG 122).⁵² In a few instances, the scribe's awareness of multiple subscripts witnesses two distinct subscripts added (for example, 91, 1894). The variety in the subscripts accompanies the variety in the endings to Romans, following 16:23, 24 or 27 and in one case (88) after v.25, a truncation of the disputed 'longer' ending to Romans.⁵³

Whilst Phoebe is not included in every form of subscript, she is the most frequently named person. She appears in 32 of the 42 subscript options, compared to six for Paul and one for Tertius. She can be connected generally with Corinth or more specifically with Cenchreae or more narrowly still with the church at Cenchreae. Of the various credentials provided in the letter of recommendation in 16:1–2 (ἀδέλφη, προστάτις), it is the identification as deacon (διάκονος) that stands out.⁵⁴ Other commendations of bearers in the New Testament note that the bearer is a brother (1 Peter 5:12; cf 1 Cor 16:3). In only one subscript variation is she identified by name alone (201, 614, 757, 801), and in no subscript is she identified as deaconess (διακόνισσα) even though the term appears to have entered church usage (as a distinctive / separate office for women) in the fourth century.⁵⁵ Even then (in the fourth century), Phoebe *as deacon* exercised a powerful hold on the imagination of

---

51 Some of these elements (for example, Corinth as the place of writing of the letter) can be traced as far back as Theodoret of Cyrrhus (*PG* 82:42B, 124:549B), though it is clear that he deduces this from the reference to Phoebe of Cenchreae, claiming Cenchreae as 'a great village of Corinth' (κώμη τίς ἐστι' τῆς Κορινθίας μεγίστη). See Cramer, *Catenae Graecorum patrum in Novum Testamentum*, 4.517. Blomkvist, *Euthalian Traditions*, 149, notes that the 'Marcionite' prologue supplied Athens as the letter's provenance.
52 NLG=National Library of Greece. The stichoi for this manuscript of Romans (as also 049, 122, 177, 181, 398, 436 among a number) is given as Ϡ'Κ that is, 920 lines. 025 has the stichoi as Ϡ'Ν, that is, 950 lines.
53 On the variety in the endings to Romans, see Gamble, *Textual History*.
54 Compare Osiek, '*Diakonos* and *prostasis*', 364, 367; McCabe, 'A Reexamination of Phoebe'.
55 *Apostolic Constitutions* 3.7; compare however Pliny, *Ep* 10.96. See Marucci, 'The "Diaconate" of Phoebe', 4–5. It should be noted however that the *Inscriptiones Christianae Graecae* database contains four instances that a given *terminus a quo* before the fourth century (*ICG* 439, 473, 748, 1241) even though the date range for each instance is extremely wide (two to four hundred years). See http://www.epigraph.topoi.org/ (accessed December 2018). I have found one instance (minuscule 1973) where, in the commentary, Phoebe is identified as a διακονίξ, the only instance of this word that I know.

some Christians.[56] Recent insistence by (male) commentators to retain the term 'deaconess' is misleading,[57] even though the feminine article is used. However, in a number of subscripts the word is anarthrous, suggesting either that the subscript was conformed to the exactitude of the text of Rom 16:1 or that there was an emphasis on Phoebe as a member of the diaconate—the retrojection of later church solidification of the office.

One might speculate about the reason(s) for the emphasis on Phoebe as deacon rather than as sister or benefactor. Certainly 'deacon' acquired a specific significance in ecclesial structures. But the particular functions of the 'deacon' seem to aggregate around two accents: one, as agent of another and two, as a spokesperson or reader in an ecclesial or other setting.[58] Certainly, the descriptor occurring in Paul's commendation chosen for the subscript, when it does occur (thirty different subscripts), is 'deacon', not 'sister' or 'benefactor', though it would be unwise to insulate these terms from one another. It does suggest that 'deacon' has a particular nuance in relation to the letter and its dispatch to the Christians in Rome and is not confined to a function or office at Cenchreae, even though Theodoret seems to lock the title into the church there. He asserted that, though the place was a village, the Christian community there had grown so large that even [!] a woman was made a deacon.[59] Such an interpretation does not adequately explain the emphasis on deacon in the subscript. Accordingly, even with the qualifications I have given to Richards's narrow constraints on the phrase ἐγράφη διά, I am in agreement with him that the letter was carried by Phoebe from its place of writing (Corinth or Cenchreae) to the Christian assemblies at Rome. This, in the emphatic majority of the subscripts, was a diaconal service. The subscripts are divided in their brief intimation over whether this diaconal service was to Paul, to the Christ followers in Rome, or as a ministry coming from the church at

---

56 An epitaph for a woman named Sophia calls her 'a second Phoebe' and names her as 'deacon' (*IG* III 3527). See *NewDocs* 4.239–41 for analysis.
57 See, for example, Esler, *Conflict and Identity in Romans*, 117. Note the critique offered by Mathew, *Women in the Greetings*, 71–2.
58 See Jewett, *Romans*, 944.
59 Καὶ τοσοῦτον ἦν τῆς τῶν Κεγχρεῶν Ἐκκλησίας τὸ σύστημα, ὡς καὶ γυναῖκα διάκονον ἔχειν. Theodoret, *Commentary* 14.2 (PG 82.219D–220A).

Cenchreae represented by Phoebe as their deacon.[60]

Here, the work of Cavan Concannon is helpful because it redirects attention from the ideas written in the text of a Pauline letter to 'the logistical practicalities, financial costs and social and institutional networks that had to be navigated to get a few sheets [sic!] of papyrus from one place to another'.[61] Here, Phoebe's diaconal services clearly rely upon the resources she can bring to ensure the remit—resources that include travel, modes of transportation and accommodation, networks of connectivity, let alone the sheer cost of the materials necessary for the pre-production and production of a scroll (rather than a few sheets!) of the length of Romans. This last might not have been covered by Phoebe's munificence but Paul's accent on her benefaction to himself as well as others is highly suggestive not merely of hospitality in her house but the provision of necessary equipment for the promotion of his mission.[62] Robert Jewett suggests she covered the costs of the secretary, Tertius.[63] In this sense, though unmentioned in the subscripts, the recognition of Phoebe as προστάτις undergirds her role and function (and office?) as διάκονος if, as contemporary commentators and ancient subscripts assert, she carried the letter to the communities at Rome.[64] As Concannon emphasizes, the work of a letter required a serious consideration—'a mental map'—of all the primary factors that actually are 'more fundamental' to the cultivation of communication and connection than simply inking a piece of persuasion onto papyrus.[65]

At the same time, the letter itself is a clear indication that this conveyance was no mere serendipitous conjunction of Paul's intent and the

---

60 On this last possibility, see Stegemann, 'Coexistence and Transformation', 17 n.80.
61 Concannon, 'Intercity Travel', 344.
62 Female benefactors were a ready attraction for proposals for support. See Friesen, 'Junia Theodora of Corinth'. This qualifies the work of Winter, *Roman Wives, Roman Widows*, 183–210.
63 Jewett, *Romans*, 22, 947–8.
64 Compare the suggestion that Phoebe's function has undergirded her leadership position as in the church at Cenchreae: Mathew, *Women in the Greetings*, 78–9; Agosto, 'Paul and Commendation', 1.160–161. The sheer recognition of Phoebe as bearer of the letter to Rome pushes her diaconal benefaction beyond the community of Christ-followers probably meeting in her house at Cenchreae. Agosto suggests that her benefaction might also have been extended to the communities of Christ-followers in Rome (p.162).
65 Concannon, 'Intercity Travel', 344, 346.

opportunity provided by Phoebe's travel.[66] Firstly, it includes the letter of recommendation that places Phoebe at the head of a list that signals connectivity. It should be remembered that for all the work compiling letters of recommendation as *comparanda*,[67] the vast majority of letters do not contain them. The presence of a ἐπιστολὴ συστατική is a marker of the importance of the matters contained within the longer letter. Secondly, that encompassing letter is no usual letter, even allowing that its length might find some broad comparison in the ancient world.[68] Stanley Stowers argues that the level of sophistication demanded by Paul's letter to the Romans generates a general perception of the recipients.[69] This more specialized audience was also configured by reference to household management and leadership, settings in which the literacy required to appropriate and disseminate Paul's ideas would be located. Here, Stowers allows Phoebe as one such head of household. Accordingly, the mere carriage of such an important, erudite document as Romans indicated it likely was a sophistication in which Phoebe shared, particularly given the interplay of patronage that the letter of commendation entertains. As writer of the letter of commendation, Paul acts as Phoebe's patron; but part of the praise strengthening that commendation underscores that Paul was beneficiary of Phoebe's patronage. There is a measure of mutuality operating here which adds an edge to how the third term, ἀδελφή, is to be understood. Here, another marginal comment occurring in a small number of manuscripts is significant.

---

66 The suggestion that Phoebe was a business-women travelling to Rome because of commercial interests (and thus affording Paul the opportunity to convey the letter) seems to have arisen in the medieval period. The thirteenth-century Dominican master, Humbert of Romans, refers to Phoebe as going to Rome on business and cites a marginal 'gloss' in his manuscript of Romans as his authority; see Tugwell, *Early Dominicans*, 305 §492. See Whelan, 'Amica Pauli', 82 n.38; Osiek, '*Diakonos* and *Prostatis*', *passim*.

67 Keyes, 'The Greek Letter of Introduction'; Kim, *Form and Structure*, 145–238; Treu, 'Christliche Empfehlungs-Schemabriefe'; Weima, *Neglected Endings*, 150–51, 227–28; Blumell, 'A Second-Century AD Letter of Introduction'; Agosto, 'Paul and Commendation', *passim*.

68 Arzt-Grabner, 'Papyrologie', notes that *P. Ammon* 1.3 roughly matches the length of Galatians— still some way from the extent of Romans, but suggestive.

69 Stowers, 'The Social Formations of Paul and His Romans', 84–85.

3. Phoebe as Sister to Paul

The structural function of subscripts in marking the end of the letter has meant that, in the vast majority of cases, the subscripts are easy to recognise. Only occasionally does an explanatory addition cloud the simple 'line' under the letter to the Romans (as in the case of Codex 056). But many manuscripts, most especially the minuscules, frequently make use of the bare, receptive margins to add elements that were never part of the original text of the letter. These range from the esoteric hermeneia of Codex Bezae to the fully developed and ascribed catenae of Codex Monacensis that formed the basis of Cramer's early publication of New Testament catenae (for Romans).[70] But the definitional boundaries of gloss, comment, commentary and catenae are sometimes difficult to draw with precision.[71] Chains of comments that follow after the name of some learned divine such as John Chrysostom are readily categorised as 'catenae'. Manuscripts such as 1973, which gives clauses and lines of text followed by an (anonymous) interpretation, can be classified as 'commentary' or 'text and commentary'. But texts that have diples or numbers placed throughout the lines of text, aligning to an identical mark in the margins, with a comment following, frequently provide a relatively standardized excerpt from some divine's homiletic commentary on Romans (such as Theodoret, Chrysostom, Pseudo-Oecumenius) though maintaining anonymity. Minuscules 1933 and 1878 are clearly arranged to support both the text of Romans and a relatively standardized commentary. The commentary in the former case, is regarded as so important that the numbers are given in gold letters, both above the word eliciting comment and in the margin marking the onset of the comment on the particular word or phrase. Karl Staab adjudged 1933 (=BnF Grec 223) to provide variant readings from Ps-Oecumenius,[72] though none of the comments on Rom 16:1–2 are to be found in his sweep of eleven authors gleaned for marginal commentary.[73] He does not include 1878 from St Catherine's monastery (=Sinai Grec 281).

---

70   Cramer, *Catenae Graecorum patrum in Novum Testamentum* Vol. 4; see also Staab, *Die Pauluskatenen*.
71   See Houghton & Parker, 'Introduction', 2–3.
72   Staab, *Die Pauluskatenen*, 148–50.
73   Staab, *Pauluskommentare*.

The comments show a number of instances that depart from the usual text of Ps-Oecumenius's commentary and yet frequently agree with one another in their departures. At the same time, they are not averse to differing from one another in their comments, even though the family resemblance is strong (most especially in the items marked with numbers that call forth comment). So it appears that, even though there was some hold over the interpretative comments provided, there was at the same time, some tolerance of variation.

For both these minuscules, Romans 16:1–2 attracts five comments marked in relation to the same words: συνίστημι, ἐν κυρίῳ, παραστῆτε, ἐγενήθη/προστάτις,[74] ἐμοῦ. There is considerable overlap in the comments made, though minuscule 1878 contains additional material. By contrast, Tertius, in both manuscripts, gains one short comment, as we have already noted above. Space prevents examination of the detail and variety of the commentaries / catenae on Phoebe. We await with eager anticipation the results of the project on the catenae and commentaries on the Pauline corpus, headed by Hugh Houghton at Birmingham.

However, there is one concluding remark in the first comment that compels a consideration of the reference to Phoebe as sister, in the overall context of the letter of recommendation. It appears to be more an ejaculatory remark—except that the same comment appears in the margins of more than one manuscript. In addition to 1933 and 1878, I have found virtually an identical conclusion to the same opening comment for Rom 16:1–2 in 94, 250, 920, 1907 and an oddly positioned instance in 2007. That comment is, τὶ δὲ ἶσον τοῦ εἶναι παύλου ἀδελφήν. The reading τὶ δαί occurs in 250 and 1933, whilst τὶ δέ is found in 94, 920, 1878, 1907 and 2007. Δαί often mistakenly renders δέ.[75] In this last manuscript (2007), it is found at the end of the letter at 16:24. The elative remark concludes a longer comment usually attached to the opening συνίστημι. The full context is thus:

---

74 Although the identified word commencing the numbered, marginal comment is different between the two manuscripts, the actual comment is the same: Μέγας ὁ ἔπαινος. καὶ ἱκανὸς αὐτοῖς προτρέψασθαι. ('Great is the praise! And it is fitting to urge this on them'.)
75 LSJ sv δαί.

ὄρα δια πόσων αὐτὴν σεμμύνει· τῶι πρώτης μνῆσθναι· τῶι ἀδελφὴν καλέται. τί δὲ ἴσον τοῦ εἶναι παύλου ἀδελφήν.[76]

'See through how many ways he exalts her; for one, he remembers her first of all; for another he calls her sister. What equality indeed from being a sister of Paul!'.

Until the final comment, this exposition, a little freely, follows Chrysostom (not Oecumenius) but Chrysostom moves to the value assessment οὐ μικρὸν δὲ Παύλου κληθῆναι ἀδελφήν, 'It is no little thing to be called the sister of Paul'. Chrysostom does not use ἴσον, though he is familiar with the expression τὶ δὲ ἴσον elsewhere,[77] and he moves on to accent her as 'deacon'.[78] It seems that, in the course of the transmission of his rhetorical flourish, οὐ μικρὸν δέ, has flowered into a full-scale affirmation, τὶ δὲ ἴσον.

There are some minuscules that seem to record a liturgical heading for the opening of Romans 16 and add the vocative ἀδελφοί, changing the accent to 'Brothers, I commend to you Phoebe'.[79] This shifts the focus of relationship from Paul to the general Christian community, thus restraining her exalted position from too close an identification with the blessed apostle. It must be acknowledged that both the minuscule comment and Chrysostom's interpretation tie Phoebe's eminence to the status already held by Paul and conferred by him to her. Nevertheless, it is the Pauline status which Phoebe is allocated, at least in the judgement of Chrysostom and these marginal commentaries on the text of Romans appearing in a number of minuscules.

John White has noted, 'Either Paul calls attention to the apostolic character of his letter or he recommends the messenger who carries the letter, but he does not refer to both on the same occasion'.[80] The former is missing in Romans. This therefore makes Phoebe into Paul's *parousia*.

---

76 There is a secondary comment in smaller hand-writing given in 1878 that accents that the greetings that follow are given to both men and women,
77 Chrysostom, *Quod regulares feminae* 12.14.
78 This is picked up in minuscule 94, the only one of the group gathered here not to conclude with the elative statement.
79 See, for example, 367, 911, 913, 2746.
80 White, *Light from Ancient Letters*, 219. White relies on the seminal essay of Funk, 'The Apostolic *parousia*'.

Her being sister is not merely a standard 'comradeship' among the Christ-followers.[81] It is specifically tied to Paul and his purpose in the intent of transmitting a letter to the Romans. This eminent position is recognised in the comments transcribed along with the text of the letter itself.

4. Conclusion

The marginal additions adorning the text of Romans in ancient manuscripts of the New Testament have shown considerable sensitivity to the nuances worked into the mention of Phoebe of Cenchreae. Certainly, both subscript and commentary have privileged her position far above that of Tertius. There is retained a memory and experience that the carriage of letters, most especially one of the stature of the letter to the Romans, was no mean task. In fact, the sheer bearing of the letter marked out a special relationship between the author and the one accepting the task of delivery. Peter Head has questioned whether the step from one kind of delivery to another, that is, from the carriage to the performance, can be made.[82] However, given the status accorded to Phoebe not only in the letter to the Romans itself, but also in the comments that the history of reception has preserved, there is no question that Phoebe held the standing necessary to read out and explain the long and difficult text. As far as later perception of Roman Christians was concerned, Phoebe held a similar position to that of the fictionalized Seneca, who not only delivered a copy of Paul's letters to the emperor Nero; he delivered them orally as well.[83] But that discussion is one for a later opportunity.

---

81   Against, for example, the line of traditional interpretation as found in Jewett, *Romans*, 944.
82   See Head, 'Named Letter-Carriers'; "'Witnesses between You and Us'"; compare Jewett, *Romans*, 23.
83   *Epistles of Paul and Seneca* §7.

Bibliography

Agosto, E. 'Paul and Commendation', in *Paul in the Greco-Roman World: A Handbook, Volume 1* (J. P. Sampley, ed.; 2 vols.; London: T&T Clark, 2016), 143–168.

Aland, K. *Kurzgefasste Liste der griechischen Handschriften des Neuen Testaments. Vol 1. Gesamtübersicht* (Berlin: de Gruyter, 1963).

Aland, K. & B. *The Text of the New Testament* (E.F. Rhodes, transl.; Grand Rapids: Eerdmans, 1987).

Arzt-Grabner, P. 'Papyrologie und Neutestamnetliche Wissenschaft: Einige Beispiele aus neueren Papyruseditionen', in P. Arzt-Grabner & C.M. Kreinecker (eds.), *Light from the East. Papyrologische Kommentare zum Neuen Testament* (Wiesbaden: Harrassowitz, 2010), 11–26.

Blomkvist, Vemund *Euthalian Traditions: Text, Translation and Commentary* (Berlin: de Gruyter, 2012).

Blumell, L.H. 'A Second-Century AD Letter of Introduction in the Washington State University Collection', *Tyche* 26 (2011), 33–40.

Cadwallader, A.H. 'Tertius in the Margins: A Critical Appraisal of the Secretary Hypothesis', *New Testament Studies* 64 (2018), 378–396.

Concannon, C. 'Economic Aspects of Intercity Travel among the Pauline Assemblies', in T.R. Blanton IV and R. Pickett (ed.), *Paul and Economics: A Handbook* (Minneapolis: Fortress, 2017), 333–360.

Cramer, J. *Catenae Graecorum patrum in Novum Testamentum* (8 vols.; Oxford: E Typographeo academico, 1844).

Ellicott, C.J. (ed.) *A New Testament Commentary for English Readers* (Vol. II) (London: Cassell, 1901).

Elmer, I. 'I, Tertius. Secretary or Co-author of Romans', *ABR* 56 (2008), 45–60.

Elmer, I. 'Setting the Record Straight at Galatia', in W. Mayer & B. Neil (eds.), *Religious Conflict from Early Christianity to the Rise of Islam* (Berlin/Boston: de Gruyter, 2013), 21–37.

Elmer, I.	'The Pauline letters as Community Documents', in B. Neil & P. Allen (eds.), *Collecting Early Christian Letters. From the Apostle Paul to Late Antiquity* (Cambridge: Cambridge University Press, 2015), 37–53.
Esler, P.	*Conflict and Identity in Romans* (Minneapolis: Fortress Press, 2003).
Fitzmyer, J.A.	*Romans* (Anchor Bible 33; New York: Doubleday, 1993).
Friesen, S.J.	'Junia Theodora of Corinth: Gendered Inequalities in the Early Empire', in S.J. Friesen, S.A. James & D.N. Schowalter (eds.), *Corinth in Contrast* (Leiden: Brill, 2013), 203–226.
Funk, Robert W.	'The Apostolic *parousia*: Form and Significance', in W.R. Farmer, C.F.D. Moule, & R.R. Niebuhr (eds.), *Christian History and Interpretation: Studies Presented to John Knox* (Cambridge: Cambridge University Press, 1967), 249–268.
Gamble, H.	*The Textual History of the Letter to the Romans: A Study in Textual and Literary Criticism* (Grand Rapids: Eerdmans, 1977).
Gregory, C.	*Textkritik des Neuen Testamentes* (3 vols.; Leipzig: Hinrichs, 1900–1909).
Head, P.	'Named Letter-Carriers among the Oxyrhynchus Papyri', *Journal for the Study of the New Testament* 31 (2009), 279–299.
Head, P.	'"Witnesses between You and Us": The Role of the Letter-Carriers in 1 Clement', in Daniel M. Gurtner, Juan Hernández Jr., & Paul Foster (eds.), *Studies on the Text of the New Testament and Early Christianity: Essays in Honour of Michael W. Hol* (Boston: Brill, 2015), 477–493.
Houghton, H.A.G., & D.C. Parker	'An Introduction to Greek New Testament Commentaries with a Preliminary Checklist of New Testament Catena Manuscripts', in H.A.G. Houghton (ed.), *Commentaries, Catenae and Biblical Tradition* (TS 13; Piscataway: Gorgias, 2016), 1–35.
Jewett, R.	*Romans: A Commentary* (Hermeneia; Philadelphia: Fortress, 2006).
Keyes, C.W.	'The Greek Letter of Introduction', *American Journal of Philology* 56 (1935), 28–44.

Kim, C.-H.	*Form and Structure of the Familiar Letter of Recommendation* (Missoula: SBL, 1972).
Marucci, C.	'The "Diaconate" of Phoebe (Rom 16:1–2) According to Modern Exegesis', in P. Zagano (ed.), *Women Deacons? Essays with Answers* (Collegeville: Liturgical Press, 2016), 1–12.
Mathew, S.	*Women in the Greetings of Romans 16:1–16: A Study of Mutuality and Women's Ministry in the Letter to the Romans* (London: T&T Clark, 2013).
McCabe, E.A.	'A Reexamination of Phoebe as Diakonos and Prostasis: Exposing the Inaccuracies of English Translations', in E.A. McCabe (ed.), *Women in the Biblical World: A Survey of Old and New Testament Perspectives* (Lanham: University Press of America, 2009), 99–116.
Metzger, Bruce	*A Textual Commentary on the Greek Testament* (Stuttgart: Deutsche Bibelgesellschaft, 1994 2nd ed.).
Osiek, C.	'*Diakonos* and *prostasis*: Women's Patronage in Early Christianity', *Harvard Theological Studies* 61 (2005), 347–370.
Parkin, T.G. & A.J. Pomeroy, (eds.)	*Roman Social History: A Sourcebook* (London: Routledge, 2007).
Poethke, Günther	'Misthosis-vertrag über fischereirechte aus Aphrodite', in H. Melaerts (ed.), *Papyri in honorem Johannis Bingen octogenarii (P. Bingen)* (Leuven: Peeters, 2000), 551–554.
Richards, E.R.	*The Secretary in the Letters of Paul* (Tübingen: J. C. B. Mohr, 1991).
Richards, E.R.	'Silvanus was not Peter's Secretary: Theological Bias in interpreting διὰ Σιλουανοῦ... ἔγραψα in 1 Peter 5:12', *Journal of the Evangelical Theological Society* 43.3 (2000), 417–432.
Richards, E.R.	*Paul and First-Century Letter Writing. Secretaries, Composition and Collection* (Downers Grove: IVP, 2004).
Scholz, J.M.A.	*Novum Testamentum Graece* (2 vols.; Leipzig: Fleischer, 1830).
Scrivener, F.	*A Plain Introduction to the Criticism of the New Testament* (E. Miller, ed.; 2 vols.; London: George Bell, 1894 4th ed.).
Simotas, N.	Νικήτα Σεΐδου Σύνοψις τῆς Ἁγίας Γραφῆς (Analecta Vlatadon 42; Thessaonica: Patriarchal Institute for Patristic Studies, 1984).

Staab, K.	*Die Pauluskatenen nach den handschriftlichen Quellen untersucht* (Rome: PBI, 1926).
Staab, K.	*Pauluskommentare aus der Griechischen Kirche: aus Katenenhandschriften gesammelt und herausgegeben* (Munster: Aschendorff, 1933).
Stegemann, E.W.	'Coexistence and Transformation: Reading the Politics of Identity in Romans in an Imperial Context', in K. Ehrensperger & B.J. Tucker (ed.), *Reading Paul in Context: Explorations in Identity Formation* (London/New York: T&T Clark, 2010), 3–23.
Stowers, S.K.	'The Social Formations of Paul and His Romans: Synagogues, Churches, and Ockham's Razor', in S.A. Harvey, N. DesRosiers, S.L. Lander, J. Pastis, & D. Ullucci (eds.), *A Most Reliable Witness: Essays in Honor of Ross Shepard Kraemer* (Brown Judaic Studies 358; Providence: Brown University, 2015), 77–88.
Treu, K.	'Christliche Empfehlungs-Schemabriefe auf Papyrus', in *Zetesis. Album amicorum, door vrienden en collega's aangeboden aan E. de Strycker* (Antwerp: De Nederlandsche boekhandel, 1973), 629–636.
Tugwell, S., (ed.)	*Early Dominicans: Selected Writings* (Classics of Western Spirituality; Mahwah: Paulist Press, 1982).
Weima, Jeffrey A.D.	*Neglected Endings: The Significance of the Pauline Letter Closings* (Sheffield: Sheffield Academic Press, 1994).
Whelan, C.F.	'Amica Pauli: The Role of Phoebe in the Early Church', *Journal for the Study of the New Testament* 49 (1993), 67–85.
White, John L.	*Light from Ancient Letters* (Philadelphia: Fortress, 1986).
Willard, L.C.	*A Critical Study of the Euthalian Apparatus* (New York: de Gruyter, 2009).
Winter, B.W.	*Roman Wives, Roman Widows: The Appearance of New Women and the Pauline Communities* (Grand Rapids: Eerdmans, 2003).

PART 5

The Theological, Social and Philosophical Legacy of Romans: From Augustine to Agamben

CHAPTER 15

The Legacy of Paul's Epistle to the Romans: From Augustine To Agamben

Peter G. Bolt, James R. Harrison, and Peter Laughlin

Prolegomena

In this chapter Paul's legacy is examined against the backdrop of expositions of Romans from the Patristic (Augustine), Reformed (Martin Luther, John Calvin) and Neo-orthodox traditions (Karl Barth). Because of the limited extent of this foray into the reception history of Romans,[1] many commentators have necessarily been omitted from the discussion. The figures who could have been mentioned belong to (a) the Patristic period (Origen, Ambrosiaster, John Chrysostom, Pelagius, Theodore of Mopsuestia, Theodoret of Cyprus),[2] (b) the Medieval age (Thomas Aquinas, Peter Abelard, William of St Thierry, Peter Lombard, Nicholas of Lyra),[3] (c) the Reformation era (Philip Melanchthon, Peter

---

1 For an excellent coverage spanning Marcion to E. P. Sanders, see Thiselton, *Discovering Romans*, 32–52.
2 Origen, *Romans*; Ambrosiaster, *Romans*; Chrysostom, *Romans*; Pelagius, *Romans*; David, *Theodore of Mopsuestia's Commentary on Romans*; Theodoret of Cyprus, *Commentary* 1.42–157.
3 Aquinas, *Epistolae ad Romanos*; Abelard, *Romans*; St Thierry, *Romans*. For Peter Lombard's introduction to Romans and Nicholas of Lyra's commentaries on Romans 9, 10, 11, 13, 15, and 16, see Levy, Krey, & Ryan, *The Letter to the Romans*. For discussion of Aquinas, see Boguslawski, *Aquinas' Commentary*. For discussion of the medieval commentators on Romans more generally, see Campbell, Hawkins, & Schildgen, *Medieval Readings of Romans*.

Martyr Vermigli),[4] and (d) twentieth century Neo-orthodoxy (Emil Brunner).[5] Erasmus and John Colet—Renaissance humanists contemporary with the Protestant reformers—could also have been investigated, but space restrictions have dictated otherwise.[6] At the outset, it is also worth noting that whatever differences may have existed between Catholics and Protestants over the epistle to the Romans during the Reformation period, these have disappeared since the Second Vatican Council (1959). The use of the same critical methods by Catholics and Protestants in analysing the biblical texts have spawned the same exegetical results.[7] Moreover, the nub of the debate between Catholics and Protestants at the beginning of the Reformation was Luther's ninety five theses, as opposed to the theological legacy of Romans, no matter how much the epistle initiated Luther's breakthrough theological insights and subsequently undergirded Reformation thought and ecclesiastical practice.

What has dictated our choices for discussion? Augustine's two *unfinished* writings on Romans—a work of propositions and a commentary—have been selected because they have been little discussed as works themselves in modern scholarship.[8] Furthermore, they articulate views which Augustine later abandoned as his theology matured. Therefore, they possess an intrinsic interest because of their transitional status in Augustine's thought. They are also intriguing because, in the context of contemporary Romans scholarship, they articulate the glimmerings of modern debates and methodological approaches. Last, the vast size of and the complexity of analysis undertaken in Augustine's corpus means that he has a 'multitude of perspectives on any issue'.[9] In sum, a limited foray into Augustine's writings on Romans is required

---

4   Melanchthon, *Commentary on Romans*; Vermigli, *Predestination and Sanctification*. For discussion of Peter Martyr Vermigli, see Chapter 16 in this volume.
5   Brunner, *Romans*.
6   Erasmus, *Paraphrases on Romans*; Erasmus, *Annotations on Romans*; Colet, *Romans*.
7   Note, for example, the commentaries of Viard, *Épître aux Romans*; Fitzmyer, *Romans*; Byrne, *Romans*; Matera, *Romans*. For a useful discussion of the wide range of critical methodologies available for the interpretation of Romans, see Thiselton, *Discovering Romans*, 7–31.
8   For translations, see Fredriksen, *Augustine on Romans*. For English discussion, see Souter, *Earliest Latin Commentaries*, 143–204; Fredriksen, *Augustine's Early Interpretation of Paul*, 119–73; Gorday, *Argument of the Epistle to the Romans*, 203–77.
9   Gorday, *Argument of the Epistle to the Romans*, 203.

because 'one has to survey his entire literary production in order to create a complete picture of his exegesis of that epistle'.[10] This means that we will be not analysing *De Diversis Quaestionibus ad Simplicianum*, written in A.D. 396–397, where his views on Romans shifted somewhat and became the bedrock for his theological approach to the epistle thenceforth.[11] In the case of Luther, Calvin and Barth, the reason for our choice is more readily apparent: each figure is a towering figure in studies of the exegetical and hermeneutical legacy of Romans.

Unusually for reception history studies of Romans, the modern European philosophers (Jacob Taubes, Alain Badiou, Giorgio Agamben) will also feature in our discussion of the legacy of the epistle.[12] Crucially for our study, these continental thinkers have recognised the pivotal importance of Romans for the western intellectual tradition, in contrast to other philosophers who have dismissed its significance. Furthermore, they have highlighted the strategic significance of particular emphases in the epistle, with a view to ameliorating the homogenised society of late capitalism and overcoming the sense of existential threat hanging over western democracies. The fact that these European philosophers do not subscribe to the Christian faith and, intriguingly, came to differing conclusions among themselves about the precise contribution of Romans, makes their positive assessments all the more intriguing. With this perspective established, a final assessment of the legacy of Romans in the western intellectual tradition will be undertaken.[13]

---

10 Gorday, *Argument of the Epistle to the Romans*, 203.
11 Gorday, *Argument of the Epistle to the Romans*, 204–05.
12 Thiselton, *Discovering Romans*, for example, bypasses the European philosophers in his study of the reception history of Romans.
13 The author of each section below is indicated in a footnote, with the Prolegomena and Part A written by James R. Harrison.

PART A: AUGUSTINE AND THE LEGACY OF ROMANS

Augustine's *Propositions* and *Commentary on Romans*: Context, Significance, and Subsequent Retractions

Both the *Propositions from the Epistle to the Romans* (*Expositio Quarundam Propositionum ex Epistola ad Romanos*)[14] and the *Unfinished Commentary on the Epistle to the Romans* (*Epistolae ad Romanos Inchoata Expositio*) were written in A.D. 394–396.[15] Upon becoming a priest in A.D. 391, Augustine met with the Christian believers at Carthage and ministered to them by answering their various questions on Romans, a text that they had found especially puzzling.[16] He wrote down his answers upon their request, with the result that the text of the rewritten lecture notes, the *Propositions*, was completed during in the fall of A.D. 394. Augustine's formal *Unfinished Commentary* on Romans was commenced in the same period, but Augustine was sidetracked by an exegetical issue.[17] Upon returning to his exposition, Augustine was 'discouraged by the magnitude and labour of this task'[18] and never returned to finish the commentary.[19]

Fredriksen comments that much of Augustine's exegetical work during this period is generated by his preoccupation with the Manichees, having been converted himself from the heretical error of Manicheism. We see this preoccupation explicitly in the *Propositions* ('this is the error

---

14 Two other compositions, based around the *quaestio*-form, are devoted to the exegesis of Romans: *De Diversis Quaestionibus* 83 and *De Diversis Quaestionibus ad Simplicianum*. See Gorday, *Argument of the Epistle to the Romans*, 219–20, who notes (p.204): 'Augustine's interpretation of Romans has a massive consistency that never underwent *substantial* change after he wrote the *De Diversis Quaestionibus ad Simplicianum* in 396–97'.
15 English scholarship on the work is thin. A masterful discussion is found in Fredriksen, *Augustine's Early Interpretation of Paul*, 119–73, followed by the insightful coverage of Gorday, *Argument of the Epistle to the Romans*, 203–77, and the still helpful older work of Souter, *Earliest Latin Commentaries*, 143–204. Breytenbach, 'Romans as Paul's Legacy', 276–78, makes some perceptive comments on how Augustine understood Christ's death.
16 *Retr.* 1.23 (22) and 26 (5), cited by Fredriksen, *Augustine's Early Interpretation of Paul*, 120 n. 5.
17 *Retr.* 1.25 (24), cited by Fredriksen, *Augustine's Early Interpretation of Paul*, 120 n. 6.
18 *Retr.* 1.25 (24), cited by Fredriksen, *Augustine's Early Interpretation of Paul*, 120 n. 7.
19 On the sources available to Augustine for his *Unfinished Commentary* and *Propositions*, see Gorday, *Argument of the Epistle to the Romans*, 207–20; Fredriksen, *Augustine's Early Interpretation of Paul*, 114–18. Gorday concludes (p. 220): 'Augustine clearly uses some of the work of his forebears, but is genuinely original and creative in the systematic rigor and consistency with which he applies these insights. Furthermore, in offering his understanding of the gratuity of salvation in the letter to Simplician he takes a decisive step beyond his predecessors'.

of the Manichees': *Propp.* 53), whereas, in the case of the *Unfinished Commentary*, the Manichees are implicitly identified and condemned by the false doctrine with which they were associated.[20] Either way, Augustine so emphasises the freedom of the will in response to their threat that it becomes a liability in his subsequent engagement with the Pelagian error.[21] Other heretical movements are also polemicised against in the *Unfinished Commentary* by reference to their false teaching: specifically, the Modalists (*Inch. Ex.* 15.13), Subordinationists (*Inch. Ex.* 15.14), Monatists (*Inch. Ex.* 15.15), Donatists (*Inch. Ex.* 15.15), and Novationists (*Inch. Ex.* 16.3-4). In what follows, we will concentrate upon Augustine's exposition of the four ages in the *Propositions*, considering some of the limitations of Augustine's understanding of divine grace, the atoning work of Christ, and his Christology in his development as a theologian and exegete at this early stage. Augustine's subsequent departures from what he had written in these two early works on Romans will be briefly referred to in the *Rectractiones*.

In discussing Romans 3:20 ('For no flesh will be justified before him by the Law, for through the Law comes knowledge of sin': *Propp.* 13–18.1), Augustine sets out the four stages in the development of salvation history and of the individual:

> Such statements must be read with great care, so that the Apostle seems neither to condemn the Law nor to take away man's free will. Therefore, let us distinguish these *four stages of man*: *prior to the Law; under the Law; under grace; and in peace*. Prior to the Law we pursue fleshly concupiscence; under the Law, we are pulled by it; under grace, we neither pursue nor are pulled by it; in peace, there is no concupiscence of the flesh .... Therefore *prior to the Law* we do not struggle, because not only do we lust and sin, but we even assent to sin. *Under*

---

20 *Inch. Ex.* 15.14: 'Further, they pretend that this very same Holy Spirit, which the Lord had promised to send to his disciples, had come not on the fiftieth day after the Lord's resurrection, as the *Acts of the Apostles* testifies (Acts 2:1–4), but only after some three hundred years in the form of a man'. *Propp.* = *Propositions from the Epistles to the Romans.*
21 Thus, as Fredriksen, *Augustine's Early Interpretation of Paul*, 121 n. 9, correctly notes, Augustine apologises in the *Retractiones* for both works on Romans and throughout provides reinterpretations of the epistle.

the Law we struggle but we are overcome. We admit that we do evil, and by that admission that we really do not want to do it, but because we still lack grace we are overwhelmed. In this stage we learn how low we lie, and when we want to rise and yet we fall, we are more the gravely afflicted ... Therefore let the man lying low, when he realises that he cannot rise by himself, implore the aid of the Liberator. For *then comes grace*, which pardons earlier sins and aids the struggling one, adds charity to justice, and takes away fear. When this happens, even though certain fleshy desires fight against our spirit when we are in this life, to lead us into sin, nonetheless our spirit resists them and ceases to sin ... Thus here he [Apostle] shows we still have desires but, by not obeying them, that we do not allow sin to reign in us. But these desires arise from the mortality of the flesh, which we bear from the first sin of the first man, whence we are born fleshly. Thus they will not cease save at the resurrection of the body, when we will have merited that transformation promised to us. Then *there will be perfect peace*, when we have been established in *the fourth stage*.[22]

A series of observations and questions emerge from the passage above. First, as Fredriksen has emphasised,[23] Augustine has modified his former division of history into six periods, corresponding to the six days of creation in Genesis (*de gen. c. Man.* 1.23–24.42), to a new formulation here involving four stages. But why does Augustine revert to a 'four ages' paradigm and not to the traditional Jewish apocalyptic division of the present evil age from the age to come, though now eschatologically reformulated by Paul in Romans 5:12–21 under the motifs of the reign of Sin and Death over against the reign of Grace in Christ? I suspect that Augustine has implicitly pivoted his understanding of the linear progression of salvation history in Romans, culminating in the resurrection age, over against the Hesiodic construct of the eternal cycle of the decline and rejuvenation of history, symbolised by the

---

22 Augustine, *Propp.* 13–18.1–4, 7–8, 10–11. Elsewhere Augustine refers again to the 'second of the four stages of man' (*Propp.* 30.3), the 'third stage' (35.1), and 'the fourth of those four stages' (51.1).
23 Fredriksen, *Augustine's Early Interpretation of Paul*, 121–22.

deteriorating value of the metals in the four Graeco-Roman ages (Gold, Silver, Bronze, and Iron: Hesiod, *Op.* 109–201). Here we see Augustine the apologist and exegete at his very best.

Second, why does Augustine so heavily emphasise the importance of humanity still having the ability to exercise their free will at the outset of our passage, a theme to which he routinely returns in the *Propositions*?[24] There is little doubt that Augustine is contrasting his belief in free will with the fatalism of the Manichees who deny that evil originates with free will. By contrast, in *Propp.* 60–61, Augustine argues that under grace (*sub gratia*) the believer 'is never free from the power of evil until the body is transformed by the resurrection and one arrives in the final stage in complete peace (*in pace*)'.[25] Notwithstanding, in *Propp.* 44.3 Augustine claims that with the aid of God's liberating grace, one 'might cease to sin', a fourth-century A.D. presaging of the later Wesleyan perfectionism. But, as noted, this Augustinian overemphasis on free will later play into the hands of the Pelagians who asserted that even the wicked could do good by their own free will.[26]

Third, what elements of doctrine in the *Propositions* does Augustine later retract as his theology develops? Two examples will suffice. Augustine, in his discussion of Romans 7:15–16 in *Propp.* 44.1–2, sees the passage as referring to the man 'under Law, prior to grace'. In other words, the paradigmatic 'I' refers to pre-conversion humanity in general. However, in *Retractiones* 1.23.1, Augustine admits that the words 'could be understood even of the Apostle himself'.[27] In this shift of perspective, Augustine opened up the possibility for Reformed thought to propose that Romans 7:14ff might refer to the believer's struggle against sin in the present age, as opposed to being a description of pre-conversion humanity. Again, to cite another example, Augustine had posited the idea that divine mercy was only granted to those whose repentance was foreseen by God, thereby earning their salvation through the meritorious act of a freely willed faith (*Propp.* 55.4; 60.11; 62.15; though, *pace*, see 20.2). However, Augustine would later modify this view in

---

24 Augustine, *Propp.* 13–18.1; 44.3; 60.2; 62.3–4.
25 Breytenbach, 'Romans as Paul's Legacy', 277.
26 See Evans, 'Neither a Pelagian nor a Manichee'.
27 Souter, *Earliest Latin Commentaries*, 186.

Retractiones 1.23.3–4 and in *Inch. Ex.* 9.6,[28] moving away from the meritorious implications of what he had said to a more fully grace-based construct.

Fourth, what other elements of Augustine's theology remain doctrinally and exegetically deficient in their development in the *Propositions*? One clear exegetical example is Augustine's blinkered restriction of the cosmic groaning in Romans 8:22–25 to humanity alone, lest it smacked of a widespread Manichaean error: 'We should not think that this implies a sorrowing and sighing of trees and vegetables and stones and other suchlike creatures—for this is the error of the Manichees' (*Propp.* 53.2).[29] Such a conclusion on Augustine's part, however, has been roundly rejected by modern exegetes who, in setting the passage in its Jewish apocalyptic creation context, correctly see it as referring to all creation and not just humanity.[30] In terms of a doctrinal example, Fredriksen has drawn attention to the limitations of Augustine's exegesis of Romans 8:3–4 (*Propp.* 48.1–8), observing that

> His view of the incarnation is free of the complication of theodicy, or of a doctrine of atonement. Christ is still primarily the divine *paedagogos*, pointing out to men by his example the correct ordering of priorities, eternal goods before temporal, in order to secure the happy life.[31]

We now turn to several cases of Augustinian exegesis that presage modern debates in terms of their methodology and preoccupations: to what extent was Augustine ahead of his age as a biblical interpreter?

---

28   Souter, *Earliest Latin Commentaries*, 188.
29   Fredriksen, *Augustine's Early Interpretation of Paul*, 145, writes: 'Augustine neutralises the passage in the face of Manichean pantheism'.
30   See Hahne, *Corruption and Redemption of Creation*.
31   Fredriksen, *Augustine's Early Interpretation of Paul*, 147.

Augustine's *Propositions* and *Commentary on Romans*: Resonances with the Modern Pauline Scholarship and Its Methodologies

Not unexpectedly, Augustine's expositions of Romans reflect certain pre-critical positions, such as accepting the Pauline authorship of Hebrews,[32] reflecting the majority view of the Apostolic Fathers in the Greek East from the second century A.D. onwards, over against the outright rejection of Pauline authorship in the modern era. Furthermore, Augustine's exegesis employs traditional methods such as allegory, as his exposition of Romans 7:2 amply illustrates,[33] though Paul and the Gospel writers adopt it as an interpretative methodology (Gal 4:23–31; Matt 13:36–43; Mark 4:13–20). However, other aspects of Augustine's writings on Romans have a disconcertingly modern ring in his exegetical observations, airing conclusions that methodologically anticipate several modern approaches to Pauline studies across several disciplines. Three examples will suffice.

First, Augustine interprets the evidence of Romans in the context of the literature of Second Temple Judaism, While the evidence for Augustine's engagement with its literature is slender in terms of its scope on the propositions and commentary,[34] it is nonetheless especially perceptive in its concentration upon the *Wisdom of Solomon (Sap.)* in reference to Romans 1:18 (*Sap.* 13.9),[35] 1:28 (*Sap.* 2.12),[36] 2:5 (*Sap.* 12.18).[37] Modern New Testament scholars have long since noted the striking parallels between Wisdom 13–14 and Romans 1:18–31 (Rom 1:10, 21, 22, 26, 29; *Sap.* 12:24; 13:1, 5, 8; 12:24; 14:24, 17).[38] Marked similarities also exist between Romans 9 and Wisdom 12 and 15 (Rom 9:10, 11, 22; *Sap.* 12:12, 20; 15:7).[39] As much as Augustine perceptively

---

32 Augustine, *Inch. Ex.* 11.3, 19.1.
33 Augustine (*Propp.* 35) says of Romans 7:2: 'therefore he makes this triple analogy—the soul symbolised by the wife, the passions of sin by the husband, and the Law by the law of the husband'.
34 In addition to the Wisdom of Solomon discussed below, note the reference to Ecclesiasticus in *Propp.* 4 (*Ecclis.* 10.15).
35 Augustine, *Propp.* 3.
36 Augustine, *Propp.* 6.
37 Augustine, *Propp.* 9.
38 See Metzger, *Introduction to the Apocrypha*, 158–59.
39 Metzger, *Introduction to the Apocrypha*, 160–61.

draws legitimate parallels in thought between Paul and the literature of Second Temple Judaism, Augustine is nevertheless careful to highlight what is distinctive between the apostle's thought and the *Wisdom of Solomon*. In contrasting Romans 1:18 with *Sap*. 13.9, Augustine draws this distinction between both texts in discussing the Gentile rejection of God:

> Those whom Solomon reproved had failed to know the creator though his creation; but those whom the apostle reproved knew (*cognoverunt*) but did not give thanks (*sed gratias non egerunt*) and, claiming to be wise, actually became fools and fell into idolatry.[40]

In other words, the pseudonymous author of the *Wisdom of Solomon* views Gentile sin as primarily noetic, whereas the apostle Paul, drawing upon the benefaction ideology of the Graeco-Roman world,[41] identifies sin as an inexplicable case of ingratitude towards the generous Benefactor and Creator of the world. Augustine correctly identifies the substantial difference in world-view between each author regarding sin, notwithstanding their similarities elsewhere. His methodological caution should have been a warning to the later nineteenth century Religionsgeschichtliche Schule scholars, who too often emphasised what was common between ancient cultural comparanda and the New Testament corpus at the expense of what was distinctive.

Second, Augustine notes similarities between the prophetic expectations associated with the Julian house of Augustus and those aroused by the prophecies of the Old Testament Scriptures regarding Jesus Christ. Notably in this regard, Paul had pointed to the advent of the anointed Messiah-King whose descent, according to the flesh, was through the house of David (Rom 1:3).[42] As Augustine writes in relation to the text:

> This sort of thing is said even about the Sibyl, which I would not readily credit were it not for one of the poets, the greatest in the Roman language. The poet, before describing the

---

40 Augustine, *Propp*. 3.
41 See Harrison, *Paul's Language of Grace*, 242–49.
42 Augustine, *Inch. Ex.* 3.3 (=Unfinished Commentary on the Epistle to the Romans).

renewal of the world in a way which seems to harmonise and accord well with the kingdom of our lord Jesus Christ, prefaced a verse saying

> The last age prophesied by the Cumaean Song has now come.[43]
>
> (Vergil, *Eclogues* 4.4)

However, referring to Romans 1:3b, Augustine qualifies the scope and implications of his 'Empire theology' when he observes that Paul's crucial addition of the phrase, 'in the Holy Scriptures' (Rom 1:3b), was intended 'to show that the writings of the Gentiles, so very full of superstitious idolatry, ought not be considered holy just because they say something about Christ'.[44] The imperial prophetic heritage is thereby designated as inferior because of its idolatrous intent. Elsewhere Augustine implicitly critiques the inflated claims of the imperial cult when he says: '... we urge them as much as we can to acknowledge Christ and through him God the Father; we urge them to fight for the *true, the highest* Emperor'.[45] Here we see, contrary to modern claims, that some of the church Fathers interacted with the imperial cult apologetically, demoting the Roman ruler to merely being a servant of God and deeming him insignificant in comparison to heavenly Emperor.[46]

Third, Augustine draws attention to Paul's daring substitution of a new salutation for the traditional secular epistolary greeting in the papyri. The conventional greeting of *chairein*—literally, 'May you have joy,' but routinely translated 'Greetings'—was replaced by Paul with his new salutation of 'grace' and 'peace':

> Only the salutation remains to complete the customary opening of a letter, like 'X to Y, greetings', Instead of saying 'greetings,' Paul says, 'Grace to you and peace from God our Father and the Lord Jesus Christ' ... Grace then is from God the

---

43 Augustine, *Inch. Ex.* 3.3.
44 Augustine, *Inch. Ex.* 3.3.
45 Augustine, *Inch. Ex.* 15.4, my emphasis.
46 For scholarship on the imperial context of Romans and Paul more generally, see Elliott, *The Arrogance of the Nations*; Harrison, *Paul and the Imperial Authorities*; Harrison, *Reading Romans with Roman Eyes*; Bird, *An Anomalous Jew*, 204–55.

Father and the Lord Jesus Christ, by which our sins, which had turned us from God, are remitted; and from them also is this peace, whereby we are reconciled to God.[47]

Here Augustine draws methodologically upon the stereotyped greetings of the documentary papyri in order to illustrate how the arrival of the gospel had not only changed centuries of epistolary convention,[48] but also it allowed Paul from the very beginning to highlight the centrality of grace in his theology in each of his epistles—and, indeed, in the theology of Augustine himself. This subtle change reflected in the conventional epistolary salutations of Paul's letters (Rom 1:7; 1 Cor 1:3; 2 Cor 1:2; Gal 1:3; Eph 1:2; Phil 1:2; Col 1:2; 1 Thess 1:1; 2 Thess 1:2; cf. 1 Tim 1:2; 2 Tim 1:2; Titus 1:4) heralded the collision between the classical worldview of social relations, based upon reciprocity rituals and the hierarchies of status, and the emergence of the new community of the early believers based upon God's impartial extension of grace and peace to the undeserving, a feature also routinely reinforced by Paul for his readers at letter's end (1 Cor 16:24; 2 Cor 13:14; Gal 6:18; Eph 6:23–24; Phil 1:23; Col 4:18b; 1 Thess 5:28; 2 Thess 3:18; Phlm 25; cf. Rom 15:23). This change adds weight to another social novelty of Paul's correspondence: his complex letter-essays are written to groups, whereas the mundane and superficial communications of the epistolary papyri are confined to communications between individuals.

Conclusion

Fredriksen is correct in saying that we must resist reading the early theology of the *Propositions* and *Unfinished Commentary* in light of the more sophisticated theology of Augustine's later works. Only then will we interpret these earlier writings in a methodologically cautious and respectful way.[49] It will also allow us to track Augustine's trajectory as a theologian and exegete with greater sensitivity and accuracy.

---

47 Augustine, *Inch. Ex.* 8.1.
48 See the excellent comparison of the papyrus letter *BGU* 27 and Paul's letter to Philemon in Roetzel, *The Letters of Paul*, 69–84.
49 Fredriksen, *Augustine's Early Interpretation of Paul*, 170–71.

Last, Augustine reveals, unbeknown to him, glimmerings of trends in Romans scholarship that would be taken up in the full light of late twentieth and early twenty-first century scholarship. Augustine's skill and prescience as an exegete often transcended the insights of his contemporaries, challenging moderns to remember that we stand on the shoulders of the greats of the past, as opposed to naively assuming that modern scholarship is the source of all innovation in Romans studies.

PART B: LUTHER AND THE LEGACY OF ROMANS[50]

Luther on Romans

Luther's deep engagement with the Scriptures can be traced at least to his time as a young Augustinian monk in the cloister at Erfurt. He recalled many times later in life that upon entering the monastery he was lent a Bible bound in red leather which became his constant companion.[51] Over the coming months he devoured it, committing large portions of Scripture to memory which made him somewhat of an oddity within the cloister.[52] However, Luther's love and mastery of the Scriptures caught the eye of Johannes von Staupitz, the Vicar-General of the Augustinians and Dean of theology at the university of Wittenberg. Under Staupitz's direction, Luther would permanently leave Erfurt for Wittenberg in 1511 and once his doctorate was complete he commenced his role as Professor of Biblical Studies in 1513, a position he would hold for the rest of his life.[53]

By all accounts Luther was a brilliant teacher and the university swelled with new students who came from far and wide to hear his 'spellbinding' lectures.[54] What attracted the students was Luther's dedication to allowing the Scriptures to speak for themselves. This notion of engaging the biblical text directly was somewhat of a novelty at the time as the

---

50 This section is written by Peter Laughlin.
51 Mansch & Peters, *Martin Luther*, 27.
52 Usingen, one of the senior monks, warned Luther from reading the Bible too much as it was 'the cause of all disturbances'. In any case, it was commonly thought that the ancient writers had already distilled all that needed to be known. Mansch and Peters, *Martin Luther*, 27.
53 Metaxas, *Martin Luther*, 52–53.
54 Metaxas, *Martin Luther*, 74.

common practice was to mediate Scripture through Aristotle and the work of the scholastics such as Duns Scotus and Peter Lombard. Luther was, of course, very familiar with the latter, having already obtained a degree in *Sententiarius*, but he increasingly found that Scholasticism obfuscated the biblical text rather than revealing it. If the Word was to be heard, which was an idea that would take firm root in Luther's heart, one must prayerfully and deliberately engage with the text of Scripture directly.[55] So whilst adhering at this time to the standard medieval hermeneutical framework (known as *quadriga*[56]), Luther nonetheless emphasised the importance of *revelation* to the understanding of spiritual truth. Interpretation was not based on intellectual analysis alone but upon the attending presence of God which therefore demanded of the student a prayerful and contrite attitude.[57]

During this early period in which Luther lectured through the Psalms, he spent much time meditating on the meaning of the righteousness of God, a theme he frequently encountered during his exegesis. It is almost impossible to overstate just how crucial a theological theme this proved to be. Luther was himself keenly aware that within (what we now know as) medieval piety the Christian life was an 'anxious pilgrimage'.[58] The search for righteousness was full of unresolved tensions with the fear of judgement offset by such penitential practices as confession, self-abasing disciplines, saintly intercessions and good works. But there was never any certainty that one had done enough to favourably tip the balance of the ledger. During his time at Erfurt, Luther had done all that was possible to put himself into the right before God. But God's perfect righteousness eluded him and despite his vigorous monastic efforts he was haunted by his failure to live up to the divine standard. His early, and now infamous breakdown at the point of elevating his

---

55 According to Ebeling, 'New Hermeneutics', 37, Luther's approach to the Scriptures is 'unparalleled in the surrounding historical milieu'.
56 This was a fourfold scheme for establishing the sense of Scripture. There was the literal sense and then three forms of spiritual sense: the allegorical, the tropological or moral, and the anagogical. The literal or historical sense was the most fundamental and the three spiritual senses were subordinate to it. For an extensive discussion, McGrath, *Luther's Theology of the Cross*, 76–80.
57 See discussion in Metaxas, *Martin Luther*, 76–77.
58 Santrac, 'Legacy', 1.

first mass reveals a man who feared the wrath of God against what he rightly judged as his own unworthiness.

This understanding of the demands of God's righteousness was a significant early contributor to Luther's own *Anfechtungen,* a condition that would plague him in various ways for much of his life.[59] The problem for Luther was that the talisman the Church offered to ward off this anxiety (tasks such as penance, confession, good works and the like) proved to be of no real comfort. There was never any way of knowing when one's eternal ledger moved out of the red and into the black. As he reflected much later, the result of this uncertainty was that he 'did not love—in fact, [he] hated—that righteous God who punished sinners, if not with silent blasphemy, then certainly with great murmuring'.[60] What was Luther to do? There was only one thing that could be done. Pound ever harder on Scripture until the truth was at last broken free.

But as McGrath has shown, by the conclusion of his lectures on the Psalter in 1514 Luther still held to an understanding of justification that sat well within the medieval theological system. Justification was the result of God honouring his covenant to redeem those who had done what was required in order to receive grace. As McGrath summarises, 'All that was required of man [to be justified] was that he humbled himself before God, in order that he might receive the gift of grace which God would then bestow upon him'.[61] That is, justification for Luther was still dependent *quod in se est*—on each person fulfilling 'what lies within him'. The theological breakthrough of justification *sola fide* would have to await Luther's so called 'tower experience' and his deep exegetical work on Romans.

---

59 The term is difficult to translate into English and contains both objective and subjective elements. Objectively Luther used the term to describe the spiritual attacks he felt from the devil and his forces, but subjectively it arose in the guise of depression and anxiety. Even though it plagued him, Luther welcomed it as if it came from the very hand of God as it propelled him to seek the truth with all his being.
60 Preface to collected works (1545); Luther, *Luther's Works*.
61 McGrath, *Luther's Theology of the Cross*, 92.

Luther and the Epistle to the Romans

Luther began lecturing on Romans on November 3, 1515 and concluded on September 7, 1516.[62] Commencing at 6am each Monday and Friday throughout the three semesters, Luther would teach through his notes, which by the time he concluded consisted of 28 sheets of glosses and 123 sheets of *scholia* or commentary.[63] The lectures demonstrate a substantive development in both his approach to interpreting Scripture and in his understanding of the righteousness of God. That such a development is possible in what is a relatively short period of time, demonstrates just how invested and focused Luther's study of the Scriptures were. His was no idle curiosity. His deep yearning for grace and the Church's ungodly leveraging of people's fears required a vigorous commitment to (re)discover the transforming power of the gospel.[64] Thus, it is difficult to overestimate the importance of these months for Luther's later life and ministry. Certainly, without the time spent preparing and delivering these lectures it is unlikely that Luther would have posted his 95 theses on All Saints Day in 1517. While it was Tetzel's preaching of indulgences which catalysed the action, it was the time spent with Romans that grounded Luther with the unshakeable confidence that faith itself negated the need for such practices entirely.

This confidence would increasingly develop as Luther spent time praying, preaching and teaching through Romans. As he reflected in his later Table Talks, 'I did not learn my theology all at once, but I had to search deeper for it, where my temptations [*Anfechtungen*] took me'.[65] This search had a profound impact upon Luther's hermeneutical approach for he moved away from the fourfold *quadriga* and developed a historical-Christological interpretation that was to be the core of his

---

62 He did not lecture on Romans again. Melanchthon took up responsibility for the class in 1518.
63 Glosses were comments within the margins and between the lines of the text that Luther had specially printed for the use of his students. Scholia consisted of longer commentary on selected passages and it was these that were turned into his Romans 'Commentary'.
64 In the midst of these lectures, Luther was writing very critical comments about the Holy Father himself. 'The pope and the priests who are so generous in granting indulgences for the temporal support of churches are cruel above all cruelty if they are not even more generous or at least equally so in their concern for God and the salvation of souls', *LW*, 25:409.
65 WA TR 1, 146. Cited in George, *Theology of the Reformers*, 60–61.

teaching and preaching in the years to come.⁶⁶ In the gloss to Romans 1:3, Luther states this approach up front: 'Here the door is thrown open wide for the understanding of Holy Scripture, that is, that everything must be understood in relation to Christ'.⁶⁷ This renewed Christological focus grounded Luther's exegetical method and gave him a way to apply the biblical text to the believer. For what is true of Christ is also true of the believer who is found 'in Christ'.⁶⁸

What was clear to him by this time was that any human attempt to obtain righteousness was doomed to failure. He opens his lectures by saying rather bluntly that 'the chief purpose of this letter is to break down, to pluck up, and to destroy all wisdom and righteousness of the flesh'.⁶⁹ There is then, an immediate and decisive focus of his lectures against the notion that humanity can do anything to deserve or acquire through effort a level of righteousness of its own (a 'righteousness of the flesh'). And here we begin to see a departure from the earlier idea that righteousness is dependent *quod in se est*. In fact, Luther goes so far as to suggest that any reliance on one's self—even a simple claim of appropriate humility is nothing but Pelagianism.⁷⁰ Indeed, he goes on to say in the same *scholia* (Romans 1:1):

> God does not want to redeem us through our own, but through external, righteousness and wisdom; not through one that comes from us and grows in us, but through one that comes to us from the outside; not through one that originates here on earth, but through one that comes from heaven. Therefore, we must be taught a righteousness that comes completely from the outside and is foreign.⁷¹

---

66 Luther's earlier work on the Psalter was thoroughly Christological but this emphasis saw a decisive exegetical shift in his Romans lectures. Indeed, by the time of his lecturing on Galatians (1517), Luther could boldly say that he no longer used the *Quadriga* because the Apostles didn't use it. See WA 2.550; 8.552, cited in Eaghll, *Martin Luther and the God Who Acts*, 45.
67 LW 25: 4 (n. 4).
68 General introduction to Luther, *Lectures on Romans*, xxxiii.
69 LW 25:135.
70 LW 25:497.
71 LW 25:136.

This idea of a righteousness that comes from the outside and is foreign is also described as a righteousness that is 'alien' to us. It is the righteousness that comes to us from Christ, but more than that, it is the righteousness of Christ himself that through the grace of God is extended to the humble believer. As he concludes in his discussion on Romans 3:26, '[T]he righteousness of God is a term which describes that by which He makes us righteous, just as the wisdom of God is that by which He makes us wise'.[72]

This was essentially the gospel message writ large. God's abundant grace overwhelms humanity's darkest sins. This was the insight that enabled Luther to understand ultimately what Paul meant in Romans 1:17: 'the righteousness of God that is revealed in the gospel from faith to faith'. In his lectures on Romans, Luther's treatment of this verse is very brief, consisting of the exposition of two phrases only: 'the righteousness of God is revealed' and 'from faith to faith'. But even in this brief exegesis the seeds of his full-flowered understanding are evident for he comments that according to God, righteousness precedes works and thus [good] works are the results of righteousness and not their cause. The logical conclusion to this understanding would be fully birthed as he continued to pound upon this verse even after completing his lectures. In what has become known as his 'tower experience' Luther made his discovery that would inevitably 'topple heaven and consume earth by fire':[73]

> At last, as I meditated day and night on the relation of the words 'the righteousness of God is revealed in it, as it is written, the righteous person shall live by faith', I began to understand that 'righteousness of God' as that by which the righteous person lives by the gift of God (faith); and this sentence 'the righteousness of God is revealed', to refer to a passive righteousness, by which the merciful God justifies us by faith, as it is written, 'the righteous person lives by faith'. This immediately made me feel

---

72 LW 25:249.
73 The tower experience is so called because the Cloaca Tower at the Black Cloister in Wittenberg was where Luther had his study and it was where he did his biblical exegesis. The words are from Luther's preface to his Latin works. LW 34:336.

as though I had been born again, and as though I had entered through open gates into paradise itself. From that moment, I saw the whole face of Scripture in a new light ... And now, where I had once hated the phrase, 'the righteousness of God', I began to love and extol it as the sweetest of phrases, so that this passage in Paul became the very gate of paradise to me.[74]

And having entered into paradise, Luther would find the strength to stand firm against the might and power of the church of Rome.

Conclusion

Luther continued to read, reflect and preach on Romans throughout his life. The letter influenced his understanding of civil obedience, his attitude to Judaism and most crucially his practice of the Christian life. He saw the letter as the 'purest Gospel', which contained that 'power which comes from God' (Rom 1:16)—a power that engenders faith simply through hearing the Word.[75] 'If', he once wrote, 'you were to ask a Christian what his task is and by what he is worthy of the name Christian, there could be no other response than hearing the Word of God, that is faith. Ears are the only organs of the Christian'.[76] So along with Luther, may we all have ears to hear.

---

74 LW 34:336.
75 Preface to Luther, *Commentary on Romans*, xiii.
76 WA 4, 9. As cited in George, *Theology of the Reformers*, 54.

PART C: CALVIN, BARTH AND THE LEGACY OF ROMANS

Brevity and Bombshells: Calvin and Barth on Romans[77]

Both Calvin and Barth wrote commentaries on Romans that have rightly been recognized as groundbreaking. This section explores the place of their exegetical work on Romans within their wider theological contribution. It briefly examines the key features of their method, despite the reticence of both men to be self-conscious about such matters. Barth's debt to Calvin is strong and clear and as he dares to push his master even further, Calvin's brevity becomes Barth's bombshell.

The Brevity of John Calvin

After lecturing on Romans at Geneva between Autumn 1536 and his ejection from the city just after Easter 1538, John Calvin (1509–1564) was persuaded to take a position in Strasbourg, which had become an intellectual centre of the Reformation. While he lectured in Jean Sturm's newly opened humanist High School, he also completed the first edition of his *Commentaries on the Epistle of St Paul to the Romans*.[78] It was dedicated 18 October 1539 and published early in 1540,[79] to be followed a decade later (in 1551) by a second edition in an edition on all the epistles, and a third edition expanding on that of 1540 arrived 1556.[80] His exposition is 'organized around the theme of the mercy of God in Christ as the central meaning of the gospel,'[81] an argument centering on justification by faith.[82]

---

77 This section is written by Peter G. Bolt.
78 Wendel, *Calvin*, 56–61; Parker, *Commentaries*, 9.
79 Parker, *Commentaries*, 5.
80 Demson, 'John Calvin', 138.
81 Demson, 'John Calvin', 137.
82 See Santmire, 'Justification'.

Table 1: Calvin's commentaries, first editions:[83]

Year	Book
1532	Seneca, *De Clementia*
1540	Romans
1542	Jude (French)
1546	1 Corinthians
1547	2 Corinthians (French; Latin, 1548)
1548	Galatians, Ephesians, Philippians, Colossians
1548	1 & 2 Timothy
1549	Hebrews
1550	1 & 2 Thessalonians, Philemon
1550	Titus (French)
1550	James (French)
1551	The Pauline Epistles, including Hebrews
1551	Epistles of Peter, John, James, Jude
1551	Isaiah
1552	Acts (part 1)
1553	John
1554	Acts (part 2)
1555	Harmony of Matthew, Mark, Luke
1554	Genesis
1557	Psalms
1563	Exodus to Deuteronomy
1564	Joshua

83 Based upon the annotated list of editions in Parker, *Commentaries*, 153–68; and the list in de Greef, 'Calvin's Writings', 44–45. Latin editions unless indicated otherwise. These are those he wrote himself, apart from the *praelectiones*, published from notes of others who heard his lectures: Hosea (1557), Minor Prophets (1559, 1560), Daniel (1561, 1562), Jeremiah and Lamentations (1563, 1565), Ezekiel 1–20:44 (1565). On Calvin's publication history, see also Holder, 'Calvin as Commentator', at 226–37.

The *Commentaries on Romans* was 'the first and one of the most welcome of a long and brilliant series of exegetical works'[84] on the Bible (see Table 1), but it was not his first published commentary. In 1532, at the age of twenty-two[85] and prior to his sudden conversion to Reformation teaching during his twenty-fourth year,[86] working with the text of Seneca's *De Clementia*, Calvin demonstrated his aptitude as a Humanist in several ways, not least in his method. Although conversant with classical antiquity and the Church Fathers, Erasmus, and a range of French and Italian Humanists, his focus was on the text, which he elucidated by referring to philology, grammar, logic, rhetorical figures, and comparisons from antiquity.[87] Even after his conversion 'Calvin remained always more or less the humanist he had been in 1532'.[88] Whereas Valla and Erasmus had begun to use such methods on the New Testament, 'it was Calvin who first made it the very basis of his exegesis and in doing so founded the modern science of exegesis'.[89] His experience commentating on Seneca

> no doubt revealed to him, if he was not aware of it before, that he possessed in abundance the qualities that make a genuine commentator—attentiveness to the author's speech, the grasp of the total meaning of a passage and its relation to the component parts, and the ability to communicate what he has himself heard. There was, then, nothing surprising in his desire to make use of these gifts in the elucidation of the Scriptures.[90]

Unlike his predecessors, he avoided extracting τόποι or *loci*, i.e. its definitive concepts, and providing excurses. Instead, 'the understanding of the total meaning is reached by a continuous exegesis and exposition

---

84 Wendel, *Calvin*, 61.
85 Wendel, *Calvin*, 28, puts his age at 23, however, to be more precise, it was published in April 1532 (Battles & Hugo, *Calvin's Commentary on Seneca's* De Clementia, 3), just before his 23rd birthday on 10 July.
86 Wendel, *Calvin*, 33, 37–45. He places Calvin's conversion after 23 Aug 1533, but probably shortly before May 1534 (pp. 39–40, 42). Calvin himself calls it sudden (*Commentary on the Psalms* [1557], 10b, 22; Wendel, *Calvin*, 37, 38; See also Battles, 'Introduction', xxx.
87 Wendel, *Calvin*, 31.
88 Wendel, *Calvin*, 33, who deals with Calvin's Christian humanism on pp.27–37.
89 Wendel, *Calvin*, 31.
90 Parker, *Commentaries*, 26–27.

of the language'—exactly as seen later in his biblical commentaries.[91] When he took the skills he honed on Seneca into his work on Romans, he began a new way of commentating on Scripture, even surpassing that of his immediate Reformation predecessors Bullinger and Bucer.

His commentary on Romans was ground-breaking, but it was not the first. Despite his English Translator, John Owen, complaining that he had few to draw on in comparison to later generations,[92] Calvin himself appreciated the 'many Commentaries by the ancients, and many by modern writers' on the Epistle.[93] He particularly noted those of Melanchthon, Bullinger, and Bucer, the three who 'represented a distinctive literary tradition and had imposed this tradition on the commentary, so that Protestant commentaries bade fair to becoming set in a pattern'.[94] In fact, initially he was deterred from commencing his own work on Paul's great epistle through fear that he 'incur the imputation of presumption by applying my hand to a work which had been executed by so many illustrious workmen'.[95] But he realised he had something to offer after all: *perspicua brevitas.*

In the 'Epistle Dedicatory' to Simon Grynaeus (dated 18 October 1539), Professor of Greek in Basel and one of Calvin's closest friends, Calvin shows that he 'had been deeply pondering the problems which face a commentator'.[96] Three years earlier (early 1535 to Feb 1536), the two men used to discuss together 'technical problems of exposition',[97] agreeing that the 'chief excellency of an expounder' was 'lucid brevity', something lacking in those who were 'more copious and diffused in their explanations of Scripture' (most probably referring to Bucer).

---

91 Parker, *Commentaries*, 49; cf. Holder, 'Pauline Epistles', 237–45.
92 Owen, 'Translator's Preface'. Mentioning Origen, Jerome, Chrystostom, Augustine, Theodoret, Oecumenius, Theophylact, Luther, Zwingli, Melanchthon, Owen regards the first complete commentary as that of Bullinger, with Bucer providing a second.
93 Calvin, 'Epistle Dedicatory'.
94 Parker, *Commentaries*, 27, explaining the method of each: Melanchthon: 29–36; Bullinger: 36–42; Bucer: 42–48.
95 Calvin, 'Epistle Dedicatory'.
96 Cranfield, *Romans*, 1.39. Apart from scattered remarks elsewhere, this dedicatory letter is one of the two places Calvin is self-conscious about method, the other being his *Preface to the Homilies of Chrysostom*—a preface to a volume he never completed; see Thompson, 'Calvin as a Biblical Interpreter', 60–64. Beyond these two explicit statements from Calvin, Thompson also attempts to analyse Calvin's method from his practice.
97 Parker, *Commentaries*, 6.

This was the principle Calvin sought to apply in his commentary on Romans.

Calvin's commitment to 'lucid brevity' shaped him as a 'humble' commentator, for his *Romans*:

> display[s] to an outstanding degree that humility before the text which is shared to some degree by every commentator on a historical document who is of any worth, the humility which seeks, not to master and manipulate, but to understand and to elucidate.
>
> This humility lies behind his quest for 'perspicua brevitas', his patient detailed exegesis, his refusal to shirk difficulties and his respect for the natural meaning of the text; it prevents him from imagining that his own exegesis can claim finality and makes him ready to leave some questions undecided; it emboldens him to dare to stand alone among commentators, where respect for the text seems to him to require it, and at the same time makes him set before himself a high standard of scholarly courtesy.[98]

Calvin displayed an 'un-humanistic reticence on intention and method' in his commentaries on both Seneca and the Bible, '[his] understanding of the total meaning [being] reached by a continuous exegesis and exposition of the language'.[99] As his dedication to Grynaeus makes clear, for him method is only a means to the end of explaining Scripture, but he is convinced of his own method. Brevity was 'one of the foremost aims of the Renaissance' and he associates perspicuity with 'simplicity', i.e. 'what is easily understood', using the two to criticize his three predecessors. Trying to squeeze both commentary and *loci* into one book, Bucer suffered from prolixity and obscurity. Although Calvin criticized Melanchthon for partiality, he followed him in separating the two tasks into two separate volumes.[100]

When he was in Strasbourg, Calvin was working on both the

---

98   Cranfield, *Romans*, 1.40.
99   Parker, *Commentaries*, 49.
100 Parker, *Commentaries*, 50–52.

Institutes and *Romans* at the same time. Although he is famous for his *Institutes*, his work as a 'systematic theologian' must be understood alongside his work as a biblical commentator, for that is how he intended them. Despite the frequent charge that he was a man of only one book, captured by 'the old cry of *Calvinus homo unius libri*', 'Calvin wrote commentaries on almost every book of the New Testament [and] is commonly accepted as one of the greatest commentators, not only of the sixteenth, but of any century'.[101] The *Institutes* were part of his strategy to enable the commentaries to display their 'lucid brevity'.

When first published in 1536, the *Institutes* 'looked like an elaborated catechism', a 'guidebook',[102] but by August 1539, the revised edition 'was now a copious manual of dogmatic theology'.[103] Written and published at exactly the same time, the revised *Institutes*—even if Calvin considered further refinement still necessary—and *Romans* can be regarded as 'the mature result of Calvin's labours upon the principal epistle of St Paul the Apostle'.[104] Both need to be read together, and both were aids to reading Scripture[105]—and, in fact, it is his work on Romans that provides the 'theological substructure' for the *Institutes*.[106]

Calvin's treatment of justification by faith, one of the central axioms of the Reformation, provides a parade example of how Calvin's exegetical work needs to be read alongside the 'systematic'. Despite declaring justification by faith to be the 'main hinge on which religion turns' and 'the sum of all piety' (*Inst.* 3.11.1; 3.15.7), interpreters have noted the

---

101 Parker, *Commentaries*, 1–2.
102 De Graaf, 'Writings', 42.
103 Wendel, *Calvin*, 61.
104 Citation from P. Barth, in Wendel, *Calvin*, 115. The 1539 *Institutes* were influenced by Melanchthon's *loci communes* (1535), which were influenced by Paul's Romans; de Graaf, 'Writings', 43.
105 De Greef, 'Calvin's Writings', 43; cf. Holder, 'Pauline Epistles', 232–35.
106 Hansen, 'Door and Passageway', 87. Ehrensperger's critique of Hansen's article ('Structure or Door', 96), that 'Calvin's perception of Romans' should be viewed in the light of 'the hermeneutical presuppositions of the Reformers' agenda', which had already prioritized justification by faith and so viewed Romans as an exposition of this doctrine, creates a chicken-and-egg scenario. For, despite Stendahl and his wake—and as Ehrensperger herself acknowledges (p. 97)—, the Reformers themselves would say that they rediscovered the priority of this doctrine from reading Romans. The breadth of Calvin's influences from the Classics, the Church Fathers and other humanists (see, amongst others, Wendel, *Calvin*, 31; Holder, 'Pauline Epistles', 245–47), as well as his clear independence of thought, ought to place a strong question mark over attempts to simply make him a puppet to his Reformation contemporaries.

relatively minor place the doctrine holds in the *Institutes*. This can be explained because his Romans commentary, published in the same period as his 1539 revision, contains 'a comprehensive doctrine of justification which has largely been overlooked'.[107]

When John Calvin published the second edition of his famous *Institutes of the Christian Religion* in 1539, he conceived it as a forerunner and servant of any commentaries on Scripture yet to fall from his pen.

> If, after this road has, as it were, been paved, I shall publish any interpretations of Scripture, I shall always condense them, because I shall have no need to undertake long doctrinal discussions, and to digress into commonplaces (*loci communes*). In this way the godly reader will be spared great annoyance and boredom, provided he approach Scripture armed with a knowledge of the present work, as a necessary tool.[108]

The French edition (1541) similarly spoke of the mutual value of *Institutes* and commentary:

> I can at least promise that it can be a key to open a way for all children of God into a good and right understanding of Holy Scripture. Thus, if henceforth our Lord gives me the means and opportunity of writing some commentaries, I shall use the greatest possible brevity, because there will be no need for long digressions, seeing that I have here treated at length almost all the articles pertaining to Christianity.[109]

Even at this early stage he planned to write a series of commentaries.[110] In January 1551 in his dedication of his *Commentary on the Canonical Epistles* to Edward VI of England, he recalled that, whilst laboring hard in Geneva he had decided to devote the rest of his life to writing

---

107 Santmire, 'Justification', 294.
108 See Calvin, 'John Calvin to the Reader (1559)', *Institutes* [McNeil], vol. 1, 5.
109 See Calvin, 'Subject Matter of the Present Work (1560)', *Institutes* [McNeil], vol. 1, 7.
110 Parker, *Commentaries*, 10, notes that he offered a set of commentaries on the Pauline epistles to the publisher Rihelius of Strasbourg in 1539. Because Rihelius did not have Hebrew type no Hebrew words could be discussed in *Romans* or *1 Corinthians*, which was one of the reasons Calvin later shifted to a Genevan printer, John Girard (p.16).

commentaries. Whereas many of his other writings were occasional, pressed upon him by the needs of the moment, 'the commentaries were planned and deliberate from an early period of his life'[111] and the preface to 1539 *Institutes*, announced that 'the Commentary on the Epistle to the Romans will afford an example of what I purpose; so I can let it speak for itself instead of giving a prospectus'. Unfortunately, the press of political and pastoral work, and his move back to Geneva, meant '*Romans* remained for years as the solitary pledge of an unredeemed promise'.[112] But, seeing the potential displayed in it, his friends constantly urged him to further expositional work and after taking a decade to produce only *Romans* and *1 Corinthians*, once *2 Corinthians* appeared (1547), 'the rest of the Pauline Commentaries followed at a speed that moved Beza to professional admiration'[113] and by July 1555, the publication of the *Harmony on the Synoptic Gospels* brought his work on the New Testament to an end, having 'expounded every book except II and III John and Revelation'.[114] As he switched his focus to his Old Testament commentaries, unlike those on the New, Isaiah was dictated,[115] and the rest were taken down from his lectures by his three secretaries, then arranged and read back to Calvin for correction and supplementation.[116]

But it all began with *Romans*.[117] Like the *Institutes*, it also needed revision and when the collected edition was published in January 1551, 'the earlier ones, especially *Romans*, were altered considerably'— with appreciation being expressed especially for his treatment of the hebraisms that Erasmus had failed to explain properly.[118] But Calvin's commentary-writing journey illustrates his claim that the book of

---

111 Parker, *Commentaries*, 4.
112 Parker, *Commentaries*, 12.
113 Parker, *Commentaries*, 16. Whereas *Romans* had been written by hand, he was later greatly assisted by the provision of secretaries (p. 20).
114 Parker, *Commentaries*, 25. His aversion to Revelation is well-known; cf. Wendel, *Calvin*, 285.
115 Parker, *Commentaries*, 20.
116 Parker, *Commentaries*, 22.
117 For an excellent discussion of the place of the letter of Romans in Calvin's hermeneutic, see Hansen, 'Door and Passageway'.
118 Parker, *Commentaries*, 19–20, referring to remarks from Ambrose Moiban of Bratislava, a former student of Reuchlin. For the humanists, 'a mastery of Latin alone was no longer enough to make one a respectable scholar: Greek and Hebrew were also required'; Thompson, 'Biblical Interpreter', 58.

Romans opens up all the Scriptures[119] and all of the Scriptures point to Christ as the revelation of the Father.[120] In keeping with this scriptural Christocentricity,[121] the book of Romans outlines the key aspects of the gospel of Jesus Christ: justification by faith through the mercy of God.

> for having begun with the proof of his Apostleship, he then comes to the Gospel with the view of recommending it; and as this necessarily draws with it the subject of faith, he glides into that, being led by the chain of words as by the hand: and thus he enters on the main subject of the whole Epistle justification by faith; in treating which he is engaged to the end of the fifth chapter. The subject then of these chapters may be stated thus— man's only righteousness is through the mercy of God in Christ, which being offered by the Gospel is apprehended by faith.[122]

The Bombshell of Karl Barth

In 1919, Karl Barth (1886–1968), the 33 year-old pastor of Safenwil, published his commentary on the Epistle to the Romans. Although written with 'a joyful sense of discovery', Barth called the commentary 'no more than a preliminary undertaking',[123] and by 1921 a totally revised second edition 'fell like a bomb on the playground of the theologians'.[124]

---

119 'Romans opens up all of Scriptures. when any one understands this Epistle, he has a passage opened to him to the understanding of the whole Scripture'; Calvin, *Calvin's Commentaries (Complete)*, paragraph 78559.
120 'God has willed to reveal himself in the incarnate Christ, so also does Christ make himself known in his living word', Wendel, *Calvin*, 155, noting that, for Calvin: 'Jesus Christ is at the centre of the whole of the Bible, of which he is the vivifying spirit, since God, hidden from sinful man, has been revealed only in Jesus Christ, and it is the Bible that bears witness to that revelation'.
121 As Kraus, 'Calvin's Exegetical Principles', 17–18, observes, reading the Scriptures with the 'scope of Christ', i.e. 'with the purpose of finding Christ in it', Calvin was 'more strictly oriented to history' than Luther and his Christological interpretation of OT 'looked to the future for the fulfilment of promises and prophecies, and his New Testament commentaries have as the determinative factor for exegesis a movement toward Christ, a movement that is always based on the conviction that the clarity of sacred Scripture is grounded in Christ alone'.
122 Calvin, *Calvin's Commentaries (Complete)*, paragraph 78570.
123 Barth, 'Preface to the First Edition', in *Romans* [Hoskyns], 2.
124 The famous 'bomb' comment is from Karl Adam, writing in the Roman Catholic monthly, *Das Hochland*. However, Barth himself supplied the image (not in the first edition) when he described the resurrection of Christ (on Rom. 1:4), as 'the crater made at the percussion point of an exploding shell', *Romans* [Hoskyns], 29.

The reaction of the English-speaking world was somewhat delayed and muted, having to wait for Hoskyns' 1933 translation of the sixth German edition. Although not as productive a commentator as Calvin, Barth also published commentaries on several portions of the New Testament, before, as last in the series, he returned to where he began in *A Shorter Commentary on Romans* (1956). Despite its significance as 'a turning-point in the history of theology', Barth's first attempt had 'very serious deficiencies as an exposition of Romans', and even Barth himself acknowledged its weaknesses, and, with his characteristic humour, he summed up its impact by quoting Shakespeare: 'Well roared, Lion'.[125] In Cranfield's estimation, as a product of his mature theological thinking, Barth's *Shorter Commentary*, 'while it is only brief and does not give much help in matters of detail, is [...] extraordinarily perceptive and suggestive. The exposition of Romans 8 may be mentioned as specially illuminating'.[126]

The reasons for Barth's bomb-blast among the theologians were no doubt many, but in large measure it arose from his method. In the preface to the much re-written second edition, Barth replied to the accusation that his first edition showed that he was 'an enemy of historical criticism'. Barth denied this at length, saying that historical criticism has its place, even if he *had* issued a strong protest against the 'scientific exegesis' of his day:

> My complaint is that recent commentators confine themselves to an interpretation of the text which seems to me to be no commentary at all, but merely the first step towards a commentary.[127]

In keeping with proper scientific method, which dictates that a method of study needs to be consonant with the object of study,[128] he then

---

125 Cranfield, *Romans*, I.42, referring to *CD* 2.1, 635, where Barth cites Demetrius from *A Midsummer Night's Dream*, Act 5.1.272.
126 Cranfield, *Romans*, I.43.
127 *Romans* [Hoskyns], 6.
128 See further, Torrance, *Reality and Evangelical Theology*, 30: 'Each science—theological science and natural science—operates in accordance with the nature of the realities it is investigating and the field structures that characterize it, and in accordance with its own distinctive objective'. Cf. Burnett, *Theological Exegesis*, 97.

suggests that 'the critical historian needs to be more critical':

> Criticism (κρίνειν) applied to historical documents means for me the measuring of words and phrases by the standard of that about which the documents are speaking—unless indeed the whole be nonsense [. ...] When an investigation is rightly conducted, boulders composed of fortuitous or incidental or merely historical conceptions ought to disappear almost entirely. The Word ought to be exposed in the words.[129]

Although Barth often surpasses Calvin as he reconfigures him—which often involves forcibly extracting the master from the straight-jacket of later Reformed theology[130]—his debt to the sixteenth-century reformer is both acknowledged and clear.

Just as Calvin's *Institutes* and commentaries are meant to mutually illuminate God's great act of mercy in Jesus Christ to bring about assurance through justification by faith, so, too, Barth's obvious contribution to theology, especially through his magisterial *Church Dogmatics*, needs to be set alongside his life-time work as a biblical exegete[131]—even if this is regularly ignored by his interpreters.[132] As with Calvin before him, perhaps it does more justice to the two aspects of Barth's scholarly work to recognize him as a *biblical* theologian.

Barth's influences on Biblical Theology are numerous and varied. He had an indirect influence on the American Biblical Theology Movement of the 50s and 60s, since his son Markus, who stood positively disposed

---

129 *Romans* [Hoskyns], 8.
130 For a discussion of the long debate about 'Calvin against or for the Calvinists', see Trueman, 'Calvin and Calvinism'. Over against that debate, it is important to note that Barth's critique is not that Calvin was some kind of normative authority by which 'post-Calvinists' ought to be judged, but (to provide one example, from his discussion about the Bible as the word of God) that later developments 'failed to take the newly opened road [...] and then it obviously took a different and mistaken way' (*CD* 1.2, 522–523) and 'prevented whole generations and innumerable individual theologians and believers from seeing the true, spiritual biblical and Reformation meaning of the statement, causing them to go past Luther and Calvin and even Paul in order to accompany Voetius and Calov' (*CD* 1.2, 526).
131 See the overview of his exegetical work in Burnett, *Theological Exegesis*, 23–31.
132 For a brief attempt to explore the contribution of his exegetical writings in relation to the interrelation of the Trinity to the Christian community in to his theology, see Bolt, 'The Interruption of Grace'. For *Romans*, see 91–94.

towards his father's theology,[133] was one of its foremost advocates.[134] Karl Barth's influence is also apparent through others associated with Biblical Theology, such as Hans Frei and Brevard Childs.[135] In fact, it has been claimed that his 1921 Commentary on Romans 'cleared the ground for his own version of "biblical theology"', with the declaration that criticism needs to be even more critical,[136] and Walter Brueggemann goes so far as to credit Barth with 'the re-creation of the possibility of a biblical theology'.[137]

His shaping as a biblical theologian can be traced through a sketch of his academic career—which was launched by the bomb-shell of his commentary on *Romans*. In his first teaching post at Göttingen (1921–1925), he taught historical theology for three hours and, at his own initiative, New Testament exegesis for one (teaching courses on Ephesians, James, 1 Corinthians 15, 1 John, Philippians, Colossians, and the Sermon on the Mount). While holding the combined chair in Dogmatics and New Testament Exegesis at Münster (1925 to 1930), he lectured on the Gospel of John, Philippians, Colossians, and James. At Bonn (1930 to 1935), he repeated his lectures on James, Philippians, John, and the Sermon on the Mount, and after he moved to Basle in 1935 he continued exegetical lectures on Colossians, 1 Peter, and again he turned to Romans. All told, Barth spent more than twenty years of his academic life teaching New Testament exegesis. He himself published his famous commentary on *Romans*, another on *1 Corinthians*, and one on *Philippians*. Some of his other exegetical lectures were published with his agreement, and more

---

133 S. E. Barth, 'Markus Barth and Karl Barth', 1: 'In his work, [Markus] did not consider himself a successor or even a competitor to his famous father, Karl Barth. Rather, he thought of himself as a "friend", realizing a familiar nearness of love and respect'.
134 'But as [Karl Barth's] representative in Scotland was said to be Tom Torrance, so his representative in America was with us not only in spirit but in the flesh, living, breathing, teaching among us, in the person of his son Markus Barth', Dickinson, 'Markus Barth and Biblical Theology', 96 and 98; cf. Gowan, 'In Memory of Markus Barth', 94: 'The presence of Rylaarsdam, Harrelson, and [Markus] Barth on the faculty during the late 50's made Chicago a place where Biblical Theology was taken seriously'.
135 On Shead's classification, Barth is influential, not in the 'neutral' biblical theology of Gabler/Barr, but in the 'confessing' biblical theology, as represented by Ebeling/Childs; Shead, *A Mouth Full of Fire*, 24–25.
136 Dickinson, 'Markus Barth', 98 and 99.
137 Brueggemann, *Theology of the Old Testament*, 18.

continue to be published up to the present time.¹³⁸

Even his writings as a Systematician are heavily exegetical. As the volumes of *Church Dogmatics* emerged, they became increasingly exegetical—the post-War volumes containing more than twice the exegesis than their pre-War companions,¹³⁹ with the final count showing that *Church Dogmatics* contains over 1500 biblical references, and more than 2000 examples of detailed exegesis.¹⁴⁰ According to Richard Burnett, 'No theologian since John Calvin has been more committed to biblical exegesis than Karl Barth', and, despite it being largely ignored, 'his entire theological enterprise stands or falls on the basis of his exegesis'.¹⁴¹ Amongst that exegesis, Romans remains strongly represented, so that Cranfield's landmark commentary for the English-speaking world could draw attention to 'the considerable sections of very valuable Romans exegesis in the *Church Dogmatics*'.¹⁴²

Fundamental to his method, Barth proposed his own break with Lessing's 'wide ugly ditch' between the contemporary world and the world of the first century—with implications for the other consequent divides between biblical and theological studies, and between the academy and the church. His exegesis of Scripture aimed at exposing the Word in the words, and required the interpreter to participate in the subject-matter of the text, which was God.¹⁴³ By so doing, the ditch is crossed from the other side, as the Word of God creates its own hearer.¹⁴⁴ Here he explicitly follows Calvin, in his 'theological exegesis'.

138 McCormack, 'Significance', v–vi.
139 Burnett, *Theological Exegesis*, 31, drawing upon Baxter, 'Barth—A Truly Biblical Theologian?', whose statistics are elaborated in her unpublished PhD thesis, *Movement from Exegesis to Dogmatics*, 445–65.
140 Burnett, *Theological Exegesis*, 9.
141 Burnett, *Theological Exegesis*, 9, 10. And yet, 'no other modern theologian has even come close to producing the amount of exegesis he produced, yet the significance of Barth's achievement as a biblical exegete continues to be assessed' (p. 9). Burnett suggests that because his has been regarded as a 'virtuoso performance', it has made no real impact upon biblical studies (p. 10).
142 Cranfield, *Romans*, 1.43 n. 4.
143 See, for example, Burnett, *Theological Exegesis*, 108–9. Whereas the Enlightenment historical-critical method was the dominant paradigm, driving a resultant strong wedge between the academy and the church, 'Karl Barth's early exegetical studies challenged such a divorce between church and academy or between the Bible and theology. In fact, it was Barth's Romans commentary that offered the first serious academic challenge to such a disjunction', Condie, '"Of God"', 50, referring to Treier, *Introducing Theological Interpretation*, 14–20.
144 Burnett, *Theological Exegesis*, 260, citing *CD* 1.1, 148–49; Bolt, 'Interruption', 90–91.

How energetically Calvin, having first established what stands in the text, sets himself to re-think the whole material and to wrestle with it, till the walls which separate the sixteenth century from the first become transparent! Paul speaks, and the man of the sixteenth century hears. The conversation between the original record and the reader moves round the subject-matter, until a distinction between yesterday and to-day becomes impossible.[145]

But, as with Calvin before him, Barth was impatient with discussions about method and hermeneutics, preferring instead to get on with the task of explaining the Bible and allowing the results to commend the method by which they were achieved.[146] Because of this impatience with hermeneutical discussion, the prevailing view has been that Barth did not have any hermeneutical principles, but his method of exegesis was simply *ad hoc*, as he addressed the various texts under his gaze.[147] However, since 2001 this view has been overturned by Richard Burnett's careful examination of Barth's work, especially through an examination of the six draft prefaces to the first edition of his Romans commentary which have only become available for study since 1985.[148]

Barth broke with his former liberalism in or about the summer of 1915. On February 6, 1917, he gave an address at Leutwil, entitled, 'the New World of the Bible',[149] shortly before he published the first edition of *Romans* to be quickly followed by the revised second edition in 1921,

---

145 *Romans* [Hoskyns], 7.
146 'In Barth's view, hermeneutical discussions had an unfortunate tendency to distract attention from the concrete practice of interpreting biblical texts. Exegesis, he thought, must have priority over hermeneutics. If, on the basis of a concrete engagement with biblical texts, one could then say something about the "hermeneutical principles" that have emerged in the actual practice of exegesis, well and good', McCormack, 'Significance', xv.
147 According to McCormack, 'Significance', vii n.3, Burnett's work has shown that 'Barth operated exegetically with clear hermeneutical "principles" and was not the *ad hoc* exegete defended by representatives of the so-called "Yale School"'.
148 Burnett, *Theological Exegesis*, 8. In this volume the draft Prefaces are published in English for the first time (Appendix 2), as well as an explanation of their historical background (Appendix 1). They were first published in Barth, *Gesamtausgabe. Der Römerbrief (Erste Fassung) 1919*. For a brief overview of all the prefaces, including the drafts, see Oakes, *Reading Karl Barth*, Chapter 3.
149 For the English translation, see 'The Strange, New World of the Bible', although we should note that 'strange' appears in Barth's original address neither in the title nor the contents.

dropping like a bomb. His major theological life-work commenced at Göttingen in 1924, with *Unterricht in der christlichen Religion*—first published in German 1990, and in English in 1991 as *The Göttingen Dogmatics*—, and the *Church Dogmatics* began to appear from 1932 and continued through to the end of his days. Despite the prevailing opinion to the contrary, Burnett has shown that across the length of this trajectory Barth had four clear hermeneutical principles that emerged almost from the beginning, continued to mark his 'theological exegesis', and are certainly evident in his work on Romans.[150]

1. *Barth's first and most fundamental principle is to interpret the Bible 'sachlicher, inhaltlicher, wesentlicher': 'more in accordance with its subject-matter, content, and substance'.*[151]
The interpreter needs to deal with 'the Subject-Matter'. Although Barth from time to time varies in his description of what this Subject-Matter is—whether 'infinite qualitative difference', God, or Revelation, or Jesus Christ—, it basically amounts to the same thing.[152] The Bible's Subject-Matter is God, or God as he has revealed himself culminating in Jesus Christ. Barth did not arrive at this conclusion 'as a result of abstract thinking or as a consequence of any philosophical inquiry […] it came from reading the Bible'.[153]

Although accused of being an enemy of historical criticism, Barth was, instead, simply trying to avoid the dualism of a 'double-entry book-keeping' approach to exegesis. Rather than approaching 'what is there' in the Scriptures in two stages, firstly according to the grammatical and literary and historical sense, and then according to theology, he urged that these senses could not be interpreted separately and need to be interpreted together.[154]

Barth urged that the whole must be read in the light of the parts, and the parts in the light of the whole.[155] To do justice to the text of Scripture, the interpreter must have a sense of what the whole text is

---

150 For the first two, see also Bolt, 'Interruption', 89–91.
151 Burnett, *Theological Exegesis*, Chapter 3.
152 McCormack, 'Significance', xvii.
153 Burnett, *Theological Exegesis*, 73.
154 Burnett, *Theological Exegesis*, 84.
155 Burnett, *Theological Exegesis*, 78–84.

about, and to interpret by reference to the whole is what Barth later referred to as 'the universal rule of interpretation' (*CD* 1.2, 493).[156] In fact, there is no possibility of rightly interpreting the parts without considering the whole.[157] Here he is talking about the whole of the Bible, but even more importantly, since God is the Subject Matter of the Bible, 'the whole' is God himself. As with Calvin but far more consistently, here is the exegetical basis for his Christocentricity.

2. Barth's second principle alerts the interpreter to the need to enter into the meaning of the Bible.[158]

Although this is a very complex thought in Barth, the basic notion of the need for the participation of the interpreter is easy enough to grasp. Against the insistence that objectivity was a necessary part of being scientific, Barth urged the necessity of the interpreter's participation. Being truly scientific means being faithful to the object under investigation,[159] and when it came to the Bible, that object was God, who is always a living Subject who addresses human beings as their God. As for Calvin, words are not signs, windows to meaning, but 'the text is the place where the expositor encounters his author'.[160] God Himself was the 'living context' of the Scriptures, who 'continues to be an agent of revelation',[161] and it is only as the interpreter enters into the experience of this living context that the true significance of the events narrated in the Scriptures can be truly grasped,[162] and Revelation discloses the meaning of history.[163] We can only take from the Bible what we have ears to hear.[164] In order for the Scriptures to be properly heard, *they must be received as God's message to us.*

---

156 Burnett, *Theological Exegesis*, 79.
157 Burnett, *Theological Exegesis*, 83.
158 Burnett, *Theological Exegesis*, Chapter 4.
159 Burnett, *Theological Exegesis*, 97.
160 Parker, *Commentaries*, 56.
161 Condie, '"Of God"', 51.
162 Burnett, *Theological Exegesis*, 109. Participation presupposes a living context which requires openness to the possibility that what was once true will always be true and what was once a serious matter is still serious today.
163 Burnett, *Theological Exegesis*, 107–8. 'We *can* participate in Christ, we *can* also understand Geschichte'. The key is the notion of simultaneity, which he identifies as revelation, Jesus Christ, which means the difference between the past and present is not significant.
164 Burnett, *Theological Exegesis*, 115.

3. *As his third principle, Barth urged that the interpreter must deal with the Subject Matter and enter into the meaning of the Bible, with more attention and love.*[165]
Barth believed that the 'scientific exegesis' of his day had been inattentive and loveless with respect to the meaning of the Bible.[166] To enter the meaning of the Bible with more attention and love requires the primary difference of standing *with* the author through the process of interpreting, that is, 'taking his words in earnest', not smiling sympathetically beside him but really standing on his side and looking in the directions his words pointed, participating with the author in the subject matter. In other words, rather than a hermeneutics of suspicion and mistrust, he proposed approaching an author with a relationship of love and trust; not as a source, but as a sign; not as an object, but as a witness.[167]

4. *As his fourth principle, Barth urged the interpreter to read more in accordance with the meaning of the Bible itself.*[168]
Prior to 1915, the Bible had no clear meaning to Barth. It was a cacophony of disparate voices, and he had no concern for its actual words.[169] But after he made his break with liberalism, he said 'the language and content are one'.[170] Even though the relationship between the Word and the words of the Bible is indirect, it is impossible to separate the words of the Bible from its actual content. This gives rise to the need to interpret the Bible according to the meaning of the Bible itself, for the Bible bears witness to God. This demonstrates the capacity of revelation to bear witness to itself through human language.[171] It also explains why the art of the commentator is basically to paraphrase Paul,[172] for the commentator is obliged to say the same thing, but in relevant, contemporary language, in a way that reflects the immediate implications of the

---

165 Burnett, *Theological Exegesis*, Chapter 6.
166 Burnett, *Theological Exegesis*, 125.
167 Burnett, *Theological Exegesis*, 126.
168 Burnett, *Theological Exegesis*, Chapter 6.
169 Burnett, *Theological Exegesis*, 221–23.
170 Burnett, *Theological Exegesis*, 279, 283 (= Barth, *Gesamtausgabe. Der Römerbrief,* 584, 590).
171 Burnett, *Theological Exegesis*, 228.
172 Bolt, 'Interruption', 90; Condie, '"Of God"', 55, 'Barth himself believed that he was simply restating what Paul had said in his epistle'.

text for the thought world of the present, not addressing everything, but certainly addressing those things which lie 'directly in the path of Paul's words'.[173] For Barth, 'if we are to read and understand and expound Holy Scripture as the Word of God, it will always have to be a matter of taking the road which Scripture itself lays down for us' (*CD* 1.2, 505–506).

This explains why Barth's commentaries do not always read like the verse by verse explanation found more regularly in commentaries. He commentates on the text *as Scripture*, or even better, as *the address of God to its readers*. This may not be the usual stance of the biblical commentator,[174] but Barth insisted it ought to be their proper task.[175] 'For Barth, the key task of the theologian is not to explain the text, but to speak it. The responsibility is to place God's revelation before the reader or hearer so that the intent and significance of the word of God might be heard',[176] in order that the reader might be led to astonishment and wonder.[177]

Conclusion

Neither Calvin or Barth were Protestant versions of Aquinas, 'seeking to construct a system of theology'.[178] Although both made major contributions to dogmatic theology, Calvin through the *Institutes* and Barth through *Church Dogmatics*, both were pre-eminently biblical theologians whose exegetical work was both basic and integral to their theological work. For both, Paul's letter to the Romans was a pathway into all of Scripture and into the central message of the Christian gospel. For both, their commentaries on Romans therefore hold a special place in the history of interpretation. Whether in brevity, or in bombshell, these two sought to speak Paul's words to their own day, because in his words those of any and every day can hear the Word of God, and that is a word of mercy for us all. How astonishing!

173 Burnett, *Theological Exegesis*, 247–48.
174 See, for example, the comparison made between Barth and Rosner/Ciampa's commentaries on 1 Corinthians in Condie, "'Of God'", 46–50.
175 See, for example, the preface to the English Translation, *Romans* [Hoskyns], ix.
176 Condie, "'Of God'", 36, speaking of *The Resurrection of the Dead*.
177 Condie, "'Of God'", 45–46. For the importance of 'wonder' in theological existence, see Barth, *Evangelical Theology*, Chapter 6.
178 Parker, *Commentaries*, 2 (on Calvin).

PART D: PHILOSOPHERS AND THE LEGACY OF ROMANS[179]

St Paul, the Epistle to the Romans, and the Modern European Philosophers

Ever since K. Stendahl's famous study which asserted that Pauline scholarship has been beguiled by the introspective conscience of the West,[180] interests in New Testament scholarship in the late 20th century have moved away from individualistic portraits of Paul's theology to a more socially oriented construct, including the 'New Perspective', 'Paul and Empire', among others. Wills sums up the legacy of the 'introspective' tradition of Pauline scholarship in the West in this manner:

> The heart of the problem is this. Paul entered the bloodstream of Western civilization mainly through one artery, the vein carrying a consciousness of sin, of guilt, of the tortured conscience. This is the Paul we came to know through the brilliant self-examinations of Augustine and Luther, of Calvin and Pascal and Kierkegaard.[181]

The strong interest in the political dimension of Paul's thought that has emerged from this shift away from the 'introspective' Paul has found support in the late twentieth century onwards from an unexpected quarter. Modern philosophers, claiming no personal commitment to Paul's gospel, have found political perspectives in the apostle's thought that remain valuable for the Western intellectual tradition. However, the precise reason for this intense interest in Paul on the part of European philosophers in particular is harder to identify.[182] M. Lilla, in a review

---

179 This section is extracted from Harrison, 'Judging the Legacy of Paul', 30–42.
180 Stendahl, 'The Apostle Paul and the *Introspective* Conscience of the West'.
181 Wills, *What Paul Meant*, 172.
182 On Paul and modern European philosophers, there is an explosion of literature: Blanton, *Displacing Christian Origins*; Blanton, *A Materialism for the Masses*; Odell-Scott, *Reading Romans*; Caputo & Alcoff, *St. Paul among the Philosophers*; Welborn, "'Extraction from the Mortal Site'"; Welborn, *Paul's Summons to Messianic Life*; Barclay, 'Paul and the Philosophers'; Harink, *Paul, Philosophy, and the Theopolitical Vision*; Milbank, Žižek, & Davis, *Paul's New Moment*; Blanton & de Vries, *Paul and the Philosophers*; Frick, *Paul in the Grip of the Philosophers*; J. Brejdak, *The Thorn in the Flesh*; van der Heiden, van Kooten, & Cimino, *Saint Paul and Philosophy*; Tofighi, *Construction of the European Self*; Dickinson, *Continental Philosophy and Theology*; Løland, *The Reception of Paul*.

essay discussing the works of seven continental philosophers, proposes rather provocatively this generic explanation:

> These authors, and probably many of their readers, belong to the cult of political romanticism that longs to live life on more dramatic terms than those offered by bourgeois society, to break out and feel the hot pulse of passion, to upset the petty laws and conventions that crush the human spirit. We recognize this longing and know how it has shaped modern consciousness and politics, often at great cost. But its patron saint is not Paul of Tarsus. It is Emma Bovary.[183]

More likely than Lilla's 'romanticism' as an explanation for the European philosophers' interest in Paul is the suggestion that these philosophers are intensely aware of 'the threat that hangs over the present moment'[184] and are disquieted by the 'reigning models of liberal democracy and secular power'.[185] In other words, these philosophers, contrary to Lilla, are not 'armchair intellectuals', rather they are deeply engaged in a conversation about the political decline of the West, each of whom represents the perspective of the 'renascent left-wing of European political thought'.[186] They find in the apostle Paul a valuable (and unexpected) dialogue partner regarding the political pathway ahead. In what follows we will briefly examine the interpretations of the apostle Paul offered by Jacob Taubes, Alain Badiou, and Giorgio Agamben, noting the assessments of their work by several New Testament scholars. Although Badiou does not concentrate upon Romans with the same intensity that Taubes and Agamben do, he nevertheless appeals to Romans for his construct of

---

183 Lilla, 'A New, Political Saint Paul?'. By contrast, Tofighi, *Paul's Letters and the Construction of the European Self*, 7, writes regarding Paul and the modern European philosophers: 'The Jewish Messiah on the cross was a paradox that shattered his messianic followers exactly as the modern technology and science ruined the Europeans' belief in supernatural redemption. For the modern, literally God-forsaken humanity, the best model was a God-forsaken apostle, who after his enlightening vision could no longer care about circumcision or dietary laws', Lilla and Tofighi divorce the continental philosophers from their sociological, political and philosophical currents, resorting instead to generic assumptions about their motivations. By contrast, note the contextualised discussion of Badiou, *Saint Paul*, 4–15.
184 Welborn, *Paul's Summons to Messianic Life*, xii. See Welborn for a full exposition on what the 'dehumanising' elements of the current 'threat' is.
185 Britt, 'The Schmittian Messiah', 263.
186 See Svenungsson, 'Law and Liberation', 68.

Paul's thought. Due to space constraints, two other famous European philosophers and interpreters of Paul, Stanislas Breton and Slavoj Žižek, will be omitted from the discussion.[187]

Jacob Taubes

We commence with the Swiss Jewish philosopher, Jacob Taubes (1923–1987), who concentrates on the epistle to the Romans in his interpretation of Paul. The 1993 German publication of his book, *The Political Theology of Paul*, emanated from a series of taped lectures delivered in Heidelberg shortly before his death in 1987.[188] Before its publication, Taubes had depicted Paul as the founder of a new movement, transitioning 'Christianity' from apocalypticism to Gnosticism.[189] With the failure of the advent of Jesus' *parousia* and the eschatological fulfilment of the law, Paul interiorises the messianic expectation, thereby avoiding the tragedy of the Jewish insurrection against Rome. But, as Taubes argues, Paul's new spiritual movement had 'to found a new empire in the world, being the revolutionary substitute for the Roman Empire'.[190]

In his discussion of Romans, Jacob Taubes, on the basis of Romans 1:1–7, proposes that Paul's epistle represents 'a literature of protest against the flourishing cult of the emperor'.[191] Whereas Judaism was a *religio licita*, Paul faces potential opposition from his fellow Jews and (possibly) the Jewish believers at Jerusalem because of his provocative delivery of the Jerusalem collection from the Gentile churches (Rom 15:30–33). However, Paul's new community is covenantal, consisting of God-fearers and Gentiles, who are justified in Christ without

---

187 See Breton, *A Radical Philosophy* and Žižek, *The Puppet and the Dwarf*. Breton approaches Paul from the viewpoint of epistemology and ontology. For appreciative reviews, see Seesengood, 'Review of Stanislas Breton', and Blanton, 'Dispossessed Life'. On Žižek, see Løland, *The Reception of Paul the Apostle*.
188 Taubes, *The Political Theology of Paul*. For discussions of Taubes: Brejdak, *The Thorn in the Flesh*, 159–65; Terpstra, 'The Management of Distinctives'; Terpstra and de Wit, '"No Spiritual Investment in the World As It Is"'; Terpstra, '"God's Love for His Enemies"'; Welborn, *Paul's Summons to Messianic Life*, 2–3; Tofighi, *Paul's Letters*, 31–37.
189 I am indebted here to Terpstra, '"God's Love for His Enemies"', 190–91.
190 Terpstra, '"God's Love for His Enemies"', 191.
191 Taubes, *The Political Theology of Paul*, 12–16, at 16.

circumcision because of their incorporation in Abraham's justifying faith (Gen 15:6; Rom 4:3).[192] Consequently, this new covenantal community, without official legitimation from the Roman authorities, has been legitimised by the sovereign power of the electing God (Rom 9–11).[193] Therefore, like the Jews, Paul's new covenanters do not have to participate in the emperor cult but instead function as a 'subterranean society,'[194] possessing its own 'supra-ethnic *imperium*'.[195] Furthermore, the legitimisation of the new covenantal community comes from life in the pneumatic community in the messianic age as opposed to the law, whether Jewish or Roman.[196] Thus the authority of Jerusalem and Rome is relativised by the fourfold 'as if' in 1 Corinthians 7:29–31, which, Taubes argues,[197] is pertinent not only for believers living in a 'world' that is 'passing away' (7:31b) but also for believers living under the 'night' of the Roman Empire which is similarly transient (Rom 13:11–14). Finally, 'the Law of Moses (Jerusalem) and the Law of the Emperor (Rome) should not be resisted by creating another law, be it that of a revolutionary or a reactionary power, but by overcoming the law—through love' (cf. Rom 13:8–18).[198] Hence Paul contests the dual 'love' commandment of Jesus, opting instead for the one 'love' command.[199] In this contestation we see the emergence of a 'new universalism' based on the 'new order of "faith"'.[200] It is 'faith in' as opposed to the propositional 'faith that' which is *'the center of messianic logic'*.[201]

While New Testament scholars have noted that Taubes was one of the first scholars who in the 1980's highlighted the political nature of Paul's thought in a Roman imperial context, his position underestimates the subtlety of Paul's rhetorical strategy in Romans 13. The apostle strips

---

192 Taubes, *The Political Theology of Paul*, 17–21, at 20; also 49.
193 Taubes, *The Political Theology of Paul*, 23–41, 48–49. Taubes is here indebted to the discussion of 'sovereign power' in the state of exception in Schmitt, *Political Theology*. See Taubes, *The Political Theology of Paul*, s.v. 'Index of Names, Schmitt, Carl', esp. 64–70.
194 Taubes, *The Political Theology of Paul*, 54.
195 Davies, *Theology of Transformation*.
196 Taubes, *The Political Theology of Paul*, 41–43.
197 Taubes, *The Political Theology of Paul*, 55–56.
198 Terpstra, '"God's Love for His Enemies"', 196. See Taubes, *The Political Theology of Paul*, 52–54.
199 Taubes, *The Political Theology of Paul*, 52–53.
200 Davies, *Theology of Transformation*.
201 Taubes, *The Political Theology of Paul*, 7, original emphasis.

the Roman ruler of all his honorific accolades, demoting him in Old Testament manner to God's 'servant,' while encouraging believers nevertheless to honour him and, in the case of the more 'wealthy' believers in the house and tenement churches at Rome, to act as benefactors as opportunity demanded.[202]

Alain Badiou

In contrast to the antinominian approach of Taubes, it has been argued that Alain Badiou and Slavoj Žižek are 'creators of a militant subjectivity,'[203] Brejdak observes that Badiou reduces the religious dimensions of Paul's epistles into a social sphere and from there progresses to ontological concerns.[204] The portrait that emerges in his 1997 French monograph, translated into English in 2003,[205] is a radical Paul who rejects the status quo.[206]

Badiou, formerly a Maoist, constructed his portrait of Paul in the context of post-holocaust politics, the radical right-wing political parties in post-war France, and the ethics of late capitalism. He argues that both Marshal Philippe Pétain, the 'zealous servant of the Nazi occupier' of the puppet state Vichy France, and Jean-Marie Le Pen, the founder of the right-wing National Front party in 1972, discriminated against and persecuted 'arbitrarily those people designated as the non-French.'[207] Moreover, late capitalism homogenises society, stripping people of their singularity,[208] while cultural fragmentation further marginalises various people groups.[209] What emerged is the 'uniform dictatorship

---

202 See Harrison, *Paul and the Imperial Authorities*, 271–323.
203 Dickinson, *Continental Philosophy*, 8. For discussions of Badiou's Paul, see Bell, 'Badiou's Faith and Paul's Gospel'; Welborn, '"Extraction from the Mortal Site"'; Barclay, 'Paul and the Philosophers'; Olfert, 'Luther's Behemot'; Klassen & Marshall, 'Saint as Cipher'; Brejdak, *The Thorn in the Flesh*, 85–88; Delahaye, 'The Philosophers' Paul', 85–88; Tofighi, *Construction of the European Self*, 80–84.
204 Brejdak, *The Thorn in the Flesh*, 167.
205 Badiou, *Saint Paul*. For a helpful interview of Badiou, see Miller, 'An Interview with Alain Badiou'.
206 Delahaye, 'The Philosophers' Paul', 92–93.
207 Badiou, *Saint Paul*, 8.
208 Badiou, *Saint Paul*, 9–10.
209 Badiou, *Saint Paul*, 10.

of modernity,'[210] which is, in Badiou's estimation, 'organically *without truth*'.[211] This 'communitarization of the public sphere' as meant the abandonment of 'all universal principle'.[212]

Over against this portrait of Western culture, Badiou pivots Galatians 3:28 ('There is neither Jew nor Greek, slave nor free, male nor female, for you are all one in Christ Jesus'), the unity characteristic of the God who shows no partiality (Rom 2:10).[213] Distinctions between people, the weapon of oppressive governments, count for nothing in Paul's politics.[214] The declaration of the abolition of any difference between Jew and Greek 'establishes Christianity's potential universality'.[215] For Badiou, Paul is 'one of the very first theoreticians of the universal,'[216] or, differently put in light of 1 Corinthians 2:1–5, the '*antiphilosophical theoretician* of universality' (Rom 10:12).[217]

Central to Paul's universality is the apostle's declaration of the Truth Event, by which Badiou means the post-eventual Truth of Christ's resurrection that arose out of the eventual site of Israel and her Scriptures.[218] Brejdak correctly notes that Badiou's so-called Truth Event is only a *secularised* version of the resurrection.[219] Badiou declares the resurrection to be a 'fable'[220] and is accordingly dismissed as a-historical or non-historical,[221] being neither 'falsifiable or demonstrable'.[222] Significantly, however, 'the Christ event is nothing but resurrection,'[223] with suffering playing no role in Paul's apologetic or in Christ's death because it possesses no redemptive function.[224] Christ's death is only the occasion for the divine intervention of the resurrection,[225] functioning as a

210 Badiou, *Saint Paul*, 11.
211 Badiou, *Saint Paul*, 11. Original emphasis.
212 Badiou, *Saint Paul*, 9.
213 Badiou, *Saint Paul*, 9.
214 Badiou, *Saint Paul*, 14.
215 Badiou, *Saint Paul*, 57.
216 Badiou, *Saint Paul*, 108.
217 Badiou, *Saint Paul*, 108; cf. 27–28. Original emphasis.
218 Badiou, *Saint Paul*, 17–18.
219 Brejdak, *The Thorn in the Flesh*, 168.
220 Badiou, *Saint Paul*, 58.
221 Badiou, *Saint Paul*, 61.
222 Badiou, *Saint Paul*, 45.
223 Badiou, *Saint Paul*, 73.
224 Badiou, *Saint Paul*, 66–68.
225 Badiou, *Saint Paul*, 69–70.

condition of immanence,[226] and setting up '*an immanentization of the spirit*.'[227] Succinctly put, 'This is what Paul is about: not the cult of death but the foundation of a universal "yes"'.[228]

Why, then, is the resurrection the pivotal event that provides 'the basis for a universalism'?[229] First, 'the resurrected Son filiates all humanity,'[230] establishing the equality of human beings before each other. Set over all alterities (Jew/Greek, slave/free, male/female) is sameness and equality.[231] Second, the 'gratuitousness of the Christ-event' has 'universal address'.[232] Because the character of the resurrection event is δωρεάν ("freely" given: Rom 3:24a), it provides 'the essential link between the "for all" of the universal and the "without cause"'.[233]

Initially, New Testament scholars have been slow to respond to the appearance of Badiou's suggestive work of philosophy, but responses have gathered momentum over recent years. First, D. Martin argues that while there are elements of universality in Romans as far as the inclusion of the Gentiles into God's covenantal family by faith, the Gentiles are nonetheless grafted into the ethnic nation of Israel: the priority of Israel remains, as the presence of 'remnant' theology in Romans also underscores.[234] Second, D. B. Boyarin points to the dehistoricising agenda of Badiou, commenting that 'something is lost when Paul is read in a way so disrespecting of time, place, and circumstance, simply repeating Paul's own gesture as if indicative of the non-being of ethnicity, gender and class'.[235] Third, L. L. Welborn has argued that Badiou is wrong in discounting the death of Christ and elevating his resurrection by contrast: this overlooks Paul's deep engagement with the social consequences of death in his theology, especially given the reign of death in

---

226 Badiou, *Saint Paul*, 70.
227 Badiou, *Saint Paul*, 69. Original emphasis.
228 Badiou, *Saint Paul*, 72.
229 Badiou, *Saint Paul*, 73.
230 Badiou, *Saint Paul*, 59.
231 Badiou, *Saint Paul*, 109.
232 Badiou, *Saint Paul*, 75.
233 Badiou, *Saint Paul*, 77.
234 Martin, 'The Promise of Teleology', 101–103. Similarly, Fredriksen, 'Historical Integrity', 71.
235 Boyarin, 'Paul among the Antiphilosophers', 120.

Neronian Rome.[236] Fourth, J. M. G. Barclay, while endorsing Badiou's emphasis on Paul's universalism and its link to unconditioned grace, argues that Badiou's de-theologising of key Pauline terms (e.g. 'faith', 'grace'), his de-historicising of history, and, agreeing with Welborn, his cutting asunder the death of Christ from his resurrection are deficiencies in Badiou's approach.[237] Fifth, Badiou, in divorcing the death of Christ from his resurrection, misses out on the powerful interplay between 'dying and rising' in Christ present throughout Pauline theology, which embraces the past, present, and future of the believer's corporate existence in the Body of Christ. It explains the paradoxical interplay between power and weakness which characterises the new age in Christ before its culmination in the Parousia.

Last, Judge argues that 'experimental proof' is one of Paul's more significant legacies in the Western intellectual tradition:[238] Badiou has miscalculated in asserting that the resurrection—for Paul the ground of the believer's epistemological and soteriological surety (1 Cor 15:1–11)—is neither falsifiable nor demonstrable. In conclusion, while philosophers cannot reasonably be expected be historians, Badiou's dismissal of the historical context and Jewish bedrock of Paul's letters for more universal concerns fails to do justice to the radical content of the universalism that the apostle does in fact advocate.

Giorgio Agamben

Giogio Agamben's commentary on Romans, in contrast to Jacob Taubes' Talmud and liturgy-referenced monograph, offers little engagement with the cultural and historical context of the epistle.[239] Nevertheless, Agamben's scholarship is characterised by an insightful historical,

---

236 Welborn, '"Extraction from the Mortal Site"'. More generally, see Harrison, 'Paul and the Social Relations of Death'.
237 Barclay, 'Paul and the Philosophers'.
238 See Judge, 'Experimental Proof in Paul'.
239 Agamben, *The Time That Remains*. For discussion of Agamben on Romans, see Britt, 'The Schmittian Messiah'; Welborn, *Paul's Summons to Messianic Life*, 14–17; Cimino, 'Agamben's Political Messianism'; Brejdak, *The Thorn in the Flesh*, 191–202; Delahaye, 'The Philosophers' Paul'; Delahaye, 'About *chronos* and *kairos*'; Svenungsson, 'Law and Liberation'.

philological, and philosophical analysis of Paul's text.[240] Significantly, Agamben dedicates his commentary to Jacob Taubes, whose monograph represents in his view 'an important turning point' in the interpretation of Paul.[241] As noted, Taubes had highlighted how Paul's understanding of the 'messianic event' had modified Jesus' own reference to the double 'love' command by replacing it with a single 'love' command (Rom 13:8–10).[242] The *pneuma* of the messianic kingdom had infused Paul's covenantal community so that its alternative 'empire' of love could now be established within the Roman Empire. Agamben likewise takes up the challenge of Taubes' messianic focus, but he does so by concentrating on the issue of *kairos* in Romans (3:26; 8:18; 11:5; 13:11).

Notably, Agamben rejects Badiou's understanding of a 'universalising' Paul. Rather than founding a new religion, Paul is better located in his Jewish messianic context.[243] Agamben distils his reservations about Badiou's case for universalism with these words:

> For Paul it is not a matter of 'tolerating' or getting past differences in order to pinpoint a sameness or universal lurking beyond. This is not a transcendent principle through which differences may be perceived—such a perspective of transcendence is not available to Paul. Rather, this 'transcendental' involves an operation that divides the divisions of the law themselves and renders them inoperative, without even reaching any final ground. No universal man, no Christian can be found in the depths of Jew and Greek, neither as a principal or as an end. [244]

Why did Agamben decide to write a commentary on Romans? It was written in order to restore the epistle 'to the status of the fundamental

---

240 Cimino, 'Agamben's Political Messianism', 102, 104.
241 Agamben, *The Time That Remains*, 3.
242 Agamben, *The Time That Remains*, 108, argues that because Christ is the *telos* of the Mosaic law, the law is fulfilled and recapitulated in love (Rom 13:8–10).
243 Agamben, *The Time That Remains*, 2, observes: 'The restoration of Paul to his messianic context therefore suggests, above all, that we attempt to understand the meaning and internal form of the time he defines as *ho nyn kairos*, the "time of the now"'. On the notion of the 'messianic ruptures of the "everyday"' in continental philosophy, see Tofighi, *Paul's Letters and the Construction of the European Self*, 40–57.
244 Agamben, *The Time That Remains*, 52–53.

messianic text of the western tradition'[245] and 'to interpret messianic time as a paradigm of historical time'.[246] How does Agamben unveil Paul's understanding of *kairos* in the epistle and depict its relation to '*messianic* time' over against *chronos*?[247]

Surprisingly, Agamben does not start with the evidence of Romans but rather adopts the same hermeneutical strategy as Jacob Taubes. Messianic *kairos* is viewed through the lens of First Corinthians 7:29 ('remaining time') and its adjoining pericopes (7:17–22, 29–32).[248] For Agamben, this represents 'the messianic situation par excellence'[249] and provides the best avenue for exploring Paul's apostolic 'calling' or 'vocation' (Rom 1:1: *klêtos*).[250] In this regard, the critical phrase which Agamben isolates in 1 Corinthians 7 is *hōs mê* ('as not': 7:29–31). Paul sets forth the idea that 'the messianic vocation relativizes the meaning and importance of our worldly identities: the followers of the Messiah are urged to live *as though* the actual legal relationships that define their lives no longer have any significance.'[251] The messianic community 'is literally all *klê*seis, all messianic vocations,' having no specific content other than living as the '*as not*' community, and is freed from its worldly identities ('circumcised/uncircumcised; free/slave; man/woman').[252]

Agamben also refers to Paul's 'remnant' theology in Romans as having an important political legacy in western thought.[253] In contrast to our antiquated notions of people and democracy, Agamben claims that 'the (messianic) people is neither the all nor the part, neither the majority nor the minority'.[254] But how may concerted political action be achieved when one considers the existential threat, noted above,

---

245 Agamben, *The Time That Remains*, 1.
246 Agamben, *The Time That Remains*, 3.
247 On *kairos* and *chronos*, see Agamben, *The Time That Remains*, 68–72. Agamben argues that Parousia refers to the 'Pauline decomposition of messianic presence' (pp. 70–71). He claims that a 'uni-dual structure of the messianic event' exists, consisting of 'two heterogeneous zones', *kairos* and *chronos*, which are co-extensive. However, they cannot be supplemented by a second messianic event, i.e. the traditionally conceived Parousia of Christian doctrine (p.70).
248 Agamben, *The Time That Remains*, 19–27.
249 Agamben, *The Time That Remains*, 5–6.
250 Agamben, *The Time That Remains*, 19–43.
251 Britt, 'The Schmittian Messiah', 70.
252 Agamben, *The Time That Remains*, 22–23, 26.
253 On the 'remnant' in Agamben, see Delahaye, 'About *chronos* and *kairos*', 88–89.
254 Agamben, *The Time That Remains*, 57.

hanging over western democracies? The idea of the 'remnant', Agamben proposes, shows how politics should work in messianic time, in a manner analogous to the Marxist proletariat: 'The remnant is the figure, or the substantiality assumed by the people in a decisive moment, and as such is the only real political subject'.[255]

In terms of traditional Jewish categories for understanding Paul in Romans, the vocation of 'prophet' (*nabi*) does not do justice to his apostolic *klêsis* and the messianic 'now' of his message.[256] Nor is apocalyptic to be confused with Paul's messianic *kairos*[257] because 'the Messiah has already arrived, the messianic event has already arrived'.[258] Agamben, to be sure, seems to subscribe to traditional notions of the *already* and *not yet* dynamic of salvation.[259] But, in terms of Paul's *nun kairos*, Agamben concludes that 'messianic time is the time we need to make time end; the time that is left to us'.[260]

Presumably, given what Agamben has already said, messianic time is advanced when the 'remnant' people acts decisively in politics or experiences freedom from worldly identities. But, as Welborn correctly notes,[261] Agamben portrays the messianic community as dwelling 'in a zone of absolute indiscernibility between imminence and transcendence'.[262] So what does political action really mean in Agamben's indeterminate state of messianic living? Wherein does true identity, political or communal, reside, in the present or in the future? Agamben is very clear on the latter issue: there is no 'new identity' in the messianic vocation.[263] Agamben does allow for the 'power-weakness' dialectic (1 Cor 1:27; 2 Cor 12:9–10) in describing the operations of messianic *dynamis*.[264] How this works out in terms of the revolutionary potential of the

---

255 Agamben, *The Time That Remains*, 57.
256 Agamben, *The Time That Remains*, 60–61.
257 Agamben, *The Time That Remains*, 64.
258 Agamben, *The Time That Remains*, 71.
259 Agamben, *The Time That Remains*, 69.
260 Agamben, *The Time That Remains*, 67.
261 See Welborn's excellent discussion of Agamben's philosophical limitations in *Paul's Summons to Messianic Life*, 66–67.
262 Agamben, *The Time That Remains*, 25.
263 Agamben, *The Time That Remains*, 26.
264 Agamben, *The Time That Remains*, 97.

new community is politically and socially unclear.[265] The 'power' and 'weakness' dynamic is not locked into the soteriological identity markers of the new age that Paul mentions (e.g. 2 Cor 4:10–12; 12:9–10; 13:4). Perhaps Svenungsson best sums up the what might be considered the clear parameters of Agamben's position: 'Redemption, according to Agamben's reading of Paul, is not about a sudden apocalyptic break that puts an end to this world. Rather, it is a matter of transforming history from within by relativizing the standards of justice set by this world in the name of a higher justice'.[266]

L. L. Welborn has incisively analysed Romans 13:8–14 and its messianic summons in light of the contributions of Agamben and Badiou to the political theology of Paul. Welborn agrees with Agamben that Romans 13:11–14 cannot be understood in light of the traditional apocalyptic eschatology about the Parousia of Jesus.[267] Rather Paul was summoning Roman auditors out of their slumber during the Neronian reign of death at Rome to act as a messianic community, but not in the indiscernible mode of existence that Agamben advocates. Rather, drawing upon Badiou's insights, Welborn forcefully argues that Paul calls Christ's messianic community to recognise the Other, transitioning from *chronos* to *kairos*, and undermining the obligation engendered by imperial patronage through a renewed sense of mutuality to all and equality before all. Welborn encapsulates Paul's understanding of the messianic awakening with these words:

> The awakened self is a militant, armed for struggle against the powers of darkness that had once enthralled him and that still hypnotize others. And the awakened self participates in a collective consciousness, bound to others by the love that led the Messiah to die for all.[268]

---

265 Welborn, *Paul's Summons to Messianic Life*, 66, states: 'The problem is that Agamben's notion of the collective subjectivity to which Paul summons seems to be devoid of content, that is, of identity: the worldly vocations are never replaced by a new vocation'.
266 Svenungsson, 'Law and Liberation', 70.
267 See Welborn's clear warning to his readers regarding his position on the Parousia in the preface, *Paul's Summons to Messianic Life*, xvi–xvii.
268 Welborn, *Paul's Summons to Messianic Life*, 53.

There is little doubt that Welborn has analysed with great insight the dehumanising character of Neronian Rome from which lethal slumber Paul is summoning the messianic community, as well as adeptly incorporating the conflicting portraits of Paul provided by Badiou and Agamben into his exegesis of Romans 13:11–14.[269] Welborn has made a powerful philosophical and historical contribution to Pauline scholarship in grappling with Paul's messianic summons in Romans 13, underscoring in his discussion how fruitfully the European philosophers have grappled with the legacy of Paul's thought today in western democracies.

However, Paul's awareness of the culture of death and violence at Neronian Rome, as I have argued elsewhere,[270] is perhaps more appropriately located under 'the reign of death' terminology in Romans 5 (vv. 14, 17, 21) rather than, as Welborn proposes, the 'night' and 'slumber' motifs of 13:11. Although the Parousia is not explicitly mentioned in Romans in the same direct way as the Thessalonian epistles (1 Thess 1:9–10; 4:13–18),[271] there are sufficient implicit glimmerings of its presence elsewhere in Romans (2:5, 16 [cf. Acts 17:31]; 8:24–25; 11:26b) to give pause to rejecting outright the presence of any apocalyptic eschatology in Romans 13:11–12.[272] Last, as noted, the Neronian 'night' and 'slumber' of the messianic community in Romans 13:11–12 needs to brought into further dialogue with Paul's honorific and benefaction culture in 13:1–7, directed as it was towards securing the commendation of the sword-wielding imperial authorities (13:4; cf. 8:35). How does each *pericope*, Romans 13:1–10 and 13:11–14, intersect and inform each other? If vv. 11–12 are announcing in apocalyptic imagery the coming eschatological judgement of the Parousia, as traditional exegesis posits, then Paul's pointedness in alluding to the imminent collapse of the Neronian regime, characterised by violence and death, is extremely bold. This is especially so when one remembers that the apostle simultaneously encourages Roman believers to seek, in traditional Jewish fashion (Jer 29:7), the welfare of the city and its authorities in vv. 1–7.

---

269 Welborn, *Paul's Summons to Messianic Life*, 23–36.
270 Harrison, 'Paul and the Social Relations of Death'.
271 Middendorf, *Romans 9–16*, 134, observes that Romans 13:11–14 'most closely aligns' with 1 Thess 5:1–10.
272 The apocalyptic eschatology underlying the passage is set out in Jewett, *Romans*, 822–24.

Conclusion

There is little doubt that the European philosophers have engaged Paul appreciatively from within the methodologies and frameworks of their discipline, but in so doing, have raised acute questions regarding the political legacy of Paul's thought amidst the ongoing convulsions of western democracies and late capitalism. Pauline theologians, exegetes, and historians need to heed the apostle's messianic summons.

PART E: WHAT IS THE LEGACY OF ROMANS TODAY?

Romans and the Western Intellectual Tradition[273]

In speaking about legacy of Romans in the western intellectual tradition, we have highlighted the epistle's contribution to Patristic, Reformed, and Neo-orthodox thought, moving from church to society in its application, and back from late capitalistic society to the church again in the case of the twentieth and twenty-first European philosophers.[274] What we have not shown is the collision of the alternative social vision of Romans with the dominant values of Augustan and Neronian society.[275] This conflict between the classical tradition and Paul's apocalyptic gospel of grace in Romans still reverberates today in the unresolved ideological tensions that characterise the complex social and political fabric of the West.[276] Several suggestions, by no means exhaustive, will be made about the impact of Paul's gospel in Romans over against the values of the Roman cultural and political tradition.[277]

First, in contrast to the later Christian rulers of Roman empire, Paul refused to perpetuate the iconographic stereotypes that demeaned the barbarian. Paul's understanding of his indebtedness to Greek and barbarian (Rom 1:14) not only relativised the cultural and ethnic divide but traded conceptually, to some degree, on Roman practices of reciprocity

---

273　This section is written by James R. Harrison.
274　See Chapter 1 in this volume.
275　The four paragraphs below are adapted from Harrison, *Reading Romans with Roman Eyes*, Chapter 10.
276　See Judge, *Paul and the Conflict of Cultures*.
277　See also Harrison, *Paul and the Imperial Authorities*, 97–323.

in accommodating the barbarian tribes of the Latin West.[278] Instead, Paul places believers under a perpetual debt of love towards those inside and outside the Body of Christ (Rom 13:8–10), no matter their status or ethnicity. By placing believers in a position of accountability towards humanity in general, the apostle scuttled the Stoic notion of *autarkeia* ("self-sufficiency") and the Greek love of autonomy. Accountability, based on Christ's love and cruciform service, provided a different conception of moral accountability, both in the private and civic spheres, to that found in Cicero's *De Officiis*.

Second, in terms of the Graeco-Roman benefaction system, Paul interacted implicitly with the imperial propaganda about the overflowing grace of Augustus and Nero by skilfully employing its benefaction terminology and by emphasising highpoints in the age of grace in ways reminiscent of the imperial honorific inscriptions.[279] However, the apostle radically diminished the significance of the Julio-Claudian contribution to their clients by highlighting the unparalleled and vastly superior soteriological benefaction of Christ, unleashing the reign of grace under which his dependents were now securely placed. The 'Great Man' in history has been deposed by, paradoxically, an impoverished and dishonoured Benefactor (Rom 5:6–8; 2 Cor 8:9).[280] The divinely gifted Body of Christ functions in a manner different to the local associations in antiquity by virtue of its radical rejection of status, the interdependence and giftedness of each member, the contribution made by each member to corporate growth in Christ, and, last, the undiscriminating allocation of beneficence to insiders and outsiders.

Third, of special interest for our generation is how Paul nominated 'covetousness' as a pivotal expression of the Flesh, which Sin had suborned for its own enslaving purposes, and against which the restraining power of the Mosaic Law was powerless (Rom 7:8a: ἐπιθυμία; cf. πλεονεξία: 1:29). Not only was the rapacity of the Roman empire in consuming resources well situated under this dynamic,[281] but so is the consumerism of the Western world which has wreaked vast ecological

---

278   See Harrison, 'Paul's "Indebtedness" to the Barbarian'.
279   See Harrison, *Paul's Language of Grace*.
280   See Harrison, *Paul and the Ancient Celebrity Circuit*; Judge, 'Changing Ideals of the Great Man'.
281   See Harrison, *Reading Romans with Roman Eyes*, Chapter 6.

damage and species extinction through its insatiable desire for more and more, as well impoverishing the Third World. The 'groaning' creation has its own expectation of eschatological delivery in the history of salvation (Rom 8:18–25). We are called to die to our unrestrained consumerism and, as an expression of the newness of the Spirit and our slavery to Christ's righteousness, work to alleviate the human-imposed suffering of God's good earth.

Fourth, Paul works with considerable subtlety in undermining the corrosive effects of Julio-Claudian social values upon the alternative lifestyle that he was advocating for the house and tenement churches at Rome. Where the social values of Roman society could be endorsed, such as the positive expressions of the honour and reciprocity system (Rom 13:1–7), Paul does so without reservation: but he reconfigures their social operation through the prism of the gospel of the crucified Christ. Alternatively, he subverts other values and replaces them with Septuagint-based and Christ-centred values. In the case of Augustus' *Res Gestae*, it is tempting to speculate that Paul wanted to loosen the grip of Augustan values in Roman hearts by articulating a new social vision of the life lived under Christ and its radical impact upon social relations in the Body of Christ.[282] In particular, Paul's dismantling of Graeco-Roman boasting culture (Rom 3:27–28; cf. 2 Cor 11:16–12:10) led to the establishment of humility as a desirable value in the West (Rom 12:3b, 16b). Presumably Paul had hoped that Romans might influence civil society more generally, as believers, in their mission to outsiders, became not only agents of Christ's redemptive grace to individuals, families, and people groups, but also were compassionate models of the alternative set of human relationships lived out in Christ's servant and benefaction communities in the city. In so doing by means of the epistle to the Romans, the apostle launched forces which would inevitably shape the western intellectual tradition, challenging the values both of the Classical tradition and its Roman heirs.

---

282 See Harrison, 'Augustan Rome and the Body of Christ'.

Bibliography

Abelard, Peter	*Commentary on the Epistle to the Romans* (Fathers of the Church Medieval Continuation, 12; Stephen R. Cartwright, transl.; Washington: Catholic University of America Press, 2011).
Agamben, Giorgio	*The Time That Remains: A Commentary on the Letter to Romans* (Stanford: Stanford University Press, 2005; Italian orig. 2000).
Ambrosiaster	*Ambrosiaster's Commentary on the Pauline Epistles: Romans* (Writings from the Greco-Roman World, 41; Theodore S. de Bruyn, ed.; Atlanta: SBL Press, 2017).
Aquinas, Thomas	*Epistolae ad Romanos Inchoata Expositio* and *Expositio Quarundum Propositionum ex Epistolae ad Romanos*, in *Augustine on Romans* (Paula Fredriksen Landes, transl; Atlanta: SBL Press, 1982).
Badiou, A.	*Saint Paul: The Foundation of Universalism* (Stanford: Stanford University Press, 2003: Fr. orig. 1997).
Barclay, John M.G.	'Paul and the Philosophers: Alain Badiou and the Event', *New Blackfriars* 91.1032 (2010), 171–84.
Barth, K.	'The Strange, New World within the Bible', *The Word of God and the Word of Man* (D. Horton, transl.; Gloucester, Mass.: Peter Smith, 1978), 28–50.
Barth, K.	*Evangelical Theology: An Introduction* (Edinburgh: T&T Clark, 1963).
Barth, K.	*A Shorter Commentary on Romans* (London: SCM, 1959 [German: 1956]).
Barth, K.	*Church Dogmatics* 1.1: *The Doctrine of the Word of God* (Edinburgh; T&T Clark, 1936, 1975, 1980).
Barth, K.	*Church Dogmatics* 1.2: *The Doctrine of the Word of God* (Edinburgh; T&T Clark, 1956).
Barth, K.	*Church Dogmatics* 2.1: *The Doctrine of God* (Edinburgh; T&T Clark, 1957).
Barth, K.	*The Resurrection of the Dead* (H. J. Stenning, transl.; London: Hodder and Stoughton, 1933).

Barth, K.	*The Epistle to the Romans* (E. C. Hoskyns, transl.; Oxford: Oxford University Press, 1933 [German: ⁶1929]).
Barth, K.	*Epistle to the Philippians. 40th Anniversary Edition* (J. W. Leitch, transl.; Louisville: Westminster John Knox, 2002 [German: 1927]).
Barth, K.	*Gesamtausgabe. Der Römerbrief (Erste Fassung) 1919* (H. von Schmidt, hrsg.; Zürich: Theologischer Verlag, 1985).
Barth, S. E.	'Markus Barth and Karl Barth', *Letter from the Karl Barth-Archives* 3 (10 May, 2001), 1–2. http://pages.unibas.ch/karlbarth/dok_letter3.html.
Battles, F. L., and A. M. Hugo	*Calvin's Commentary on Seneca's* De Clementia *with Introduction, Translation, and Notes* (Leiden: E. J. Brill, 1969).
Battles, F. L.	'Introduction', in J. Calvin, *The Institutes of the Christian Religion*. (LCL 20–21; 2 Vols.; J. T. McNeill, ed.; F. L. Battles, transl.; Philadelphia: Westminster, 1960), I.xxix–lxxi.
Baxter, C.	'Barth—A Truly Biblical Theologian?', *TynB* 38 (1987), 3–27.
Baxter, C.	*The Movement from Exegesis to Dogmatics in the Theology of Karl Barth* (Unpublished PhD thesis, Durham University, 1981).
Bell, D.M., Jr.	'Badiou's Faith and Paul's Gospel', *Angelaki: Journal of Theoretical Humanities* 12.1 (2007), 97–111.
Bird, Michael F.	*An Anomalous Jew: Paul Among the Jews, Greek, and Romans* (Grand Rapids: Eerdmans, 2016).
Blanton, Ward	'Dispossessed Life: Introduction to Breton's Paul', in S. Breton, *A Radical Philosophy of St Paul* (New York: Columbia University Press, 2011; French orig. 1988), 1–29.
Blanton, Ward	*Displacing Christian Origins: Philosophy, Secularity, and the New Testament* (Chicago: University of Chicago Press, 2007).
Blanton, Ward	*A Materialism for the Masses: Saint Paul and the Philosophy of Undying Life* (New York: Columbia University Press, 2014).
Blanton, Ward, & Hent de Vries, (eds.)	*Paul and the Philosophers* (New York: Fordham University Press, 2013).

Boguslawski, Steven C.   *Aquinas' Commentary on Romans 9–11* (Unpublished PhD diss., Yale University, 1999).

Bolt, P. G.   'The Interruption of Grace and the Formation of Christian Community: Soundings in Barth's Earliest Exegetical Writings', in M. P. Jensen (ed.), *The Church of the Triune God. Understanding God's Work in his People Today* (Fs. Robert C. Doyle; Sydney South: Aquila, 2013), 87–105.

Boyarin, Daniel   'Paul among the Antiphilosophers; or, Saul among the Sophists', in J.D. Caputo & I. M. Alcoff (eds.), *St. Paul among the Philosophers* (Bloomington & Indianapolis: Indiana University Press, 2009), 109–140.

Brejdak, Jaromir   *The Thorn in the Flesh: The Thought of the Apostle Paul in Modern Philosophy* (Zürich: LIT, 2017).

Breton, Stanislas   *A Radical Philosophy of St Paul* (New York: Columbia University Press, 2011; French orig. 1988).

Breytenbach, Cilliers   'The Letter to the Romans as Paul's Legacy to Theology: Reception in Exposition', *Stellenbosch Theological Journal* 3.2 (2017), 269–97.

Britt, Brian   'The Schmittian Messiah in Agamben's *The Time That Remains*', *Critical Enquiry* 36 (2010), 262–87.

Brueggemann, Walter   *Theology of the Old Testament: Testimony, Dispute, Advocacy* (Minneapolis: Fortress, 1997).

Brunner, Emil   *The Letter to the Romans* (London: Lutterworth Press, 1959; orig. *Der Römerbrief*, Kessel: J. G. Oncken Verlag, 1938).

Burnett, R. E.   *Karl Barth's Theological Exegesis. The Hermeneutical Principles of the* Römerbrief *Period* (Grand Rapids: Eerdmans, 2004; [J. C. B. Mohr, 2001]).

Byrne, Brendan   *Romans* (Sacrina Pagina 6; Collegeville: Michael Glazier/ Liturgical Press, 1996).

Calvin, J.   *Calvin's Commentaries (Complete)* (John King, transl.; Edinburgh: Calvin Translation Society, 1847). Accordance electronic edition.

Calvin, J.   *The Institutes of the Christian Religion.* (LCL 20–21; 2 Vols.; J. T. McNeill, ed.; F. L. Battles, transl.; Philadelphia: Westminster, 1960).

Campbell, William S., Peter S. Hawkins, & Brenda D. Schildgen (eds.) *Medieval Readings of Romans* (London & New York: T&T Clark, 2007).

Caputo, J. D., & I. M. Alcoff *St. Paul among the Philosophers* (Bloomington & Indianapolis: Indiana University Press, 2009).

Chrysostom, St John *Homilies on Romans* (Brookline: Holy Cross Orthodox Press, 2013).

Cimino, A. 'Agamben's Political Messianism in "The Time That Remains"', *International Journal of Philosophy and Theology* 77.3 (2016), 102–18.

Colet, John *An Exposition of St. Paul's Epistle to the Romans, Delivered as Lectures in the University of Oxford about the Year 1497* (J. H. Lupton, transl.; London: Bell and Daldy, 1873).

Condie, K. G. '"Of God": Karl Barth and the Coherence of 1 Corinthians', in B.S. Rosner (ed.), *The Wisdom of the Cross: Exploring 1 Corinthians* (Nottingham: IVP [Apollos], 2011), 32–56.

Cranfield, C. E. B. *The Epistle to the Romans. Vol. 1: Romans I–VIII* (2 vols.; ICC; Edinburgh: T&T Clark, 1975).

David, Charles D. *Theodore of Mopsuestia's Commentary on Romans: An Annotated Translation* (Unpublished PhD diss.; The Southern Baptist Theological Seminary, Louisville, 1992).

Davies, Oliver *Theology of Transformation: Faith, Freedom, and the Christian Act* (Oxford: Oxford University Press, 2013).

De Greef, W. 'Calvin's Writings', in D. K. McKim (ed.), *The Cambridge Companion to John Calvin* (Cambridge: Cambridge University Press, 2004), 41–57.

Delahaye, E. 'About *chronos* and *kairos*: On Agamben's interpretation of Pauline Temporality through Heidegger', *International Journal of Philosophy and Theology* 77.3 (2016), 85–101.

Delahaye, E. 'The Philosophers' Paul: A Radically Subversive Thinker', in G.-J. van der Heiden, G. van Kooten, & A. Cimino (eds.), *Saint Paul and Philosophy: The Consonance of Ancient and Modern Thought* (Berlin & Boston: De Gruyter, 2017), 81–93.

Demson, D.	'John Calvin', in J.P. Greenman & T. Larsen (eds.), *Reading Romans through the Centuries: From the Early Church to Karl Barth* (Grand Rapids: Brazos, 2005), 137–48.
Dickinson, C.	'Markus Barth and Biblical Theology: A Personal Review', *HBT* 17.2 (1995), 96–116.
Dickinson, Colby	*Continental Philosophy and Theology* (Leiden: Brill, 2018).
Eaghll, Tenzan	*Martin Luther and the God Who Acts: Finding Common Ground in the Current Debates on Justification* (Unpublished MA thesis, Department of Religious Studies, University of Calgary, 2010).
Ebeling, Gerhard	'New Hermeneutics and the Early Luther', *Theology Today* 21.1 (1964), 34–46.
Ehrensperger, K.	'Structure or Door: Romans as Key to Reading Scripture: Response to Gary Neal Hansen', in K. Ehrensperger & R.W. Holder (eds.), *Reformation Readings of Romans* (Edinburgh: T&T Clark, 2008), 95–97.
Elliott, Neil	*The Arrogance of the Nations: Reading Romans in the Shadow of Empire* (Minneapolis: Fortress Press, 2008).
Erasmus, Desiderius	*Paraphrases on Romans* [(1517)] *and Galatians* (Collected Works of Erasmus, 42; Robert D. Payne, Albert Rabil, & Warren S. Smith, transls.; Toronto: University of Toronto Press, 1984).
Erasmus, Desiderius	*Annotations on Romans (1516/1535)* (Collected Works of Erasmus, 56; Robert D. Payne, transl.; Toronto: University of Toronto Press, 1994).
Evans, Gillian R.	'Neither a Pelagian nor a Manichee', *Vigiliae Christianae* 35.3 (1981), 232–44.
Fitzmyer, Joseph A.	*Romans: A New Translation with Introduction and Commentary* (Anchor Bible 33; London: Geoffrey Chapman, 1992).
Fredriksen, Paula	*Augustine's Early Interpretation of Paul* (unpublished PhD diss., Princeton University, 1979).
Fredriksen, Paula	*Augustine on Romans: Propositions from the Epistle to the Romans Unfinished Commentary on the Epistle to the Romans* (Texts and Translations, 23; Chico: SBL Press, 1982).

Fredriksen, Paula 'Historical Integrity, Interpretive Freedom: The Philosopher's Paul', in J.D. Caputo & I.M. Alcoff (eds.), *St. Paul among the Philosophers* (Bloomington & Indianapolis: Indiana University Press, 2009), 61–73.

Frick, Peter (ed.) *Paul in the Grip of the Philosophers: The Apostle and Contemporary Continental Philosophy* (Minneapolis: Fortress, 2013).

George, Timothy *Theology of the Reformers* (Nashville: Broadman Press, 1988).

Gorday, Peter J. *The Place of Chapters 9–11 in the Argument of the Epistle to the Romans: A Study of the Romans Exegesis of Origen, John Chrysostom and Augustine* (Unpublished PhD thesis, Vanderbilt University, 1980).

Gowan, D. E. 'In Memory of Markus Barth: A Personal Note', *HBT* 17.2 (1995), 93–95.

Hahne, H.A. *The Corruption and Redemption of Creation: Nature in Romans 8:19–22 and Jewish Apocalyptic Literature* (LNTS 336; London: T&T Clark, 2006).

Hansen, G.N. 'Door and Passageway: Calvin's Use of Romans as Hermeneutical and Theological Guide', in K. Ehrensperger & R.W. Holder (eds.), *Reformation Readings of Romans* (Edinburgh: T&T Clark, 2008), 77–94.

Harink, Douglas (ed.) *Paul, Philosophy, and the Theopolitical Vision: Critical Engagements with Agamben, Badiou, Žižek, and Others* (Eugene, Or.: Cascade, 2010).

Harrison, James R. 'Judging the Legacy of Paul', in E. A. Judge, *Paul and the Conflict of Cultures: The Legacy of His Thought Today* (James R. Harrison, ed.; Eugene: Cascade, 2019), 30–42.

Harrison, James R. *Paul's Language of Grace in Its Graeco-Roman Context* (WUNT II 172; Tübingen: Mohr Siebeck, 2003; rpt. Eugene, Or.: Wipf and Stock, 2017).

Harrison, James R. *Paul and the Imperial Authorities at Thessalonica and Rome: A Study in the Conflict of Ideology* (WUNT 273; Tübingen: Mohr Siebeck, 2011).

Harrison, James R. 'Paul and the Social Relations of Death at Rome (Rom 5:14, 17, 21)', in Stanley E. Porter (ed.), *Paul and His Social Relations. Pauline Studies: Volume VII* (Leiden: Brill, 2012), 85–123.

Harrison, James R. 'Paul's "Indebtedness" to the Barbarian (Rom 1:14) in Latin West Perspective', *Novum Testamentum* 55.4 (2013), 311–48.

Harrison, James R. 'Augustan Rome and the Body of Christ: A Comparison of the Social Vision of the *Res Gestae* and Paul's Letter to the Romans', *Harvard Theological Review* 106.1 (2013), 1–36.

Harrison, James R. *Paul and the Ancient Celebrity Circuit: The Cross and Moral Transformation* (Tübingen: Mohr Siebeck, forthcoming).

Harrison, James R. *Reading Romans with Roman Eyes: Studies on the Social Perspective of Paul* (Minneapolis: Lexington/Fortress, forthcoming).

Holder, R.W. 'Calvin as Commentator on the Pauline Epistles', in D.K. McKim (ed.), *Calvin and the Bible* (Cambridge: Cambridge University Press, 2006), 224–55.

Jewett, R. *Romans* (Hermeneia; Minneapolis: Fortress, 2007).

Judge, E. A. *Paul and the Conflict of Cultures: The Legacy of His Thought Today* (James R. Harrison, ed.; Eugene, Or.: Cascade, 2019).

Judge, E. A. 'Experimental Proof in Paul', *Paul and the Conflict of Cultures: The Legacy of His Thought Today* (James R. Harrison, ed.; Eugene, Or.: Cascade, 2019), 106–121.

Judge, E. A. 'Changing Ideals of the Great Man', *Paul and the Conflict of Cultures: The Legacy of His Thought Today* (James R. Harrison, ed.; Eugene, Or.: Cascade, 2019), 122–37.

Klassen, P.E., & J.W. Marshall 'Saint as Cipher: Paul, Badiou, and the Politics of Ritual Repudiation', *History of Religions* 51.4 (2012), 344–63.

Kraus, H.-J. 'Calvin's Exegetical Principles', *Interpretation* 31 (1977), 8–18 (German: 1968).

Levy, Ian, Philip Krey, & Thomas Ryan, (transls. & eds.) *The Letter to the Romans: The Bible in Medieval Tradition* (Grand Rapids: Eerdmans, 2013).

Lilla, Mark	'A New, Political Saint Paul?', *The New York Review of Books* 55.16 (October 23, 2008), 1–9.
Løland, O. J.	*The Reception of Paul the Apostle in the Works of Slavoj Žižek* (Cham: Palgrave Macmillan, 2018).
Luther, Martin	*Commentary on Romans* (J. Theodore Mueller, ed.; Grand Rapids: Kregel Publications, 1954).
Luther, Martin	*Luther's Works* (American Edition; 55 vols.; Jaroslav Pelikan & Helmut T. Lehman, eds.; St. Louis: Concordia, 1955–1986). Citation: *LW* followed by volume: page numbers.
Luther, Martin	*Lectures on Romans* (Wilhelm Pauck, ed.; Louisville: Westminster John Knox Press, 1961).
McCormack, B.	'The Significance of Karl Barth's Theological Exegesis of Philippians', in K. Barth, *Epistle to the Philippians. 40th Anniversary Edition* (J. W. Leitch, transl.; Louisville: Westminster John Knox, 2002 [German: 1927]), v–xxv.
McGrath, Alister	*Luther's Theology of the Cross* (Oxford: Blackwell Publishers, 1985).
Mansch, Larry D., & Curtis H. Peters	*Martin Luther: The Life and Lessons* (Jefferson: McFarland & Company, Inc., 2016).
Martin, Dale B.	'The Promise of Teleology, the Constraints of Epistemology, and Universal Vision in Paul', in J.D. Caputo & I. M. Alcoff (eds.), *St. Paul among the Philosophers* (Bloomington & Indianapolis: Indiana University Press, 2009), 91–108.
Matera, Frank J.	*Romans* (Paideia; Grand Rapids: Baker Academic, 2010).
Melanchthon, Philip	*Commentary on Romans* (St Louis: Concordia Publishing House, 1992).
Metaxas, Eric	*Martin Luther: The Man Who Rediscovered God and Changed the World* (New York: Viking, 2017).
Metzger, Bruce M.	*An Introduction to the Apocrypha* (New York: Oxford University Press, 1957).
Middendorf, M.P.	*Romans 9–16* (St Louis: Concordia Publishing House, 2013).
Milbank, John, Slavoj Žižek, & Creston Davis	*Paul's New Moment: Continental Philosophy and the Future of Christian Theology* (Grand Rapids: Brazos, 2010).

Miller, A.S.	'An Interview with Alain Badiou: "Universal Truths and the Question of Religion"', *Journal of Philosophy and Scripture* 3.1 (2005), 20–24.
Oakes, K.	*Reading Karl Barth: A Companion to Karl Barth's Epistle to the Romans* (Eugene, Or.: Cascade, 2011).
Odell-Scott, David W.	*Reading Romans with Contemporary Philosophers and Theologians* (New York: T&T Clark, 2007).
Olfert, Ryan J.	'Luther's Behomet: The Politics of Grace between Paul and Badiou', *Studies in Religion* 40.1 (2011), 45–62.
Origen	*Commentary on the Epistle to the Romans* (Fathers of the Church 103–104, 2 vols.; Thomas P. Scheck, trans.; Washington: The Catholic University of America Press, 2001–2002).
Owen, J.	'Translator's Preface', John Calvin, *Calvin's Commentaries (Complete)* (Edinburgh: Calvin Translation Society, 1847). Accordance electronic edition.
Parker, T. H. L.	*Calvin's New Testament Commentaries* (London: SCM, 1971).
Pelagius	*Pelagius's Commentary on St. Paul's Epistle to the Romans* (Oxford Early Christian Studies; Theodore de Bruyn, transl.; Oxford: Clarendon Press, 1993).
Roetzel, Calvin J.	*The Letters of Paul: Conversations in Context* (Louisville: John Knox Press, 2015, 6th edition).
Santmire, H. P.	'Justification in Calvin's 1540 Romans Commentary', *Church History* 33.3 (1964), 294–313.
Santrac, Aleksandar S.	'The Legacy of Martin Luther's *Sola Fide*', *In die Skriflig* 51.1 (2017), 1–7. https://doi.org/ 10.4102/ids.v51i1.2275.
Schmitt, Carl	*Political Theology: Four Chapters on the Concept of Sovereignty* (Chicago: University of Chicago Press, 2005; German rev. ed. 1934).
Seesengood, Robert P.	'Review of Stanislas Breton, *A Radical Philosophy of St Paul*', *The Bible and Critical Theory* 9.1–2 (2013), 130–36.
Shead, A. G.	*A Mouth Full of Fire. The Word of God in the Words of Jeremiah* (NSBT 29; Nottingham: IVP, 2012).

Souter, A. *The Earliest Latin Commentaries of the Epistles of St Paul: A Study* (Oxford: Clarendon Press, 1927).

Stendahl, Krister 'The Apostle Paul and the *Introspective* Conscience of the West', *HTR* 56 (1963), 199–215.

St Thierry, William of *Exposition on the Epistle to the* Romans (Cistercian Fathers Series 27; J. B. Hasbrouck, transl.; Kalamazoo: Cistercian Publications, 1980).

Svenungsson, Jayne 'Law and Liberation: Critical Notes on Agamben's Political Messianism', *European Judaism* 50.1 (2017), 68–77.

Taubes, Jacob *The Political Theology of Paul* (Stanford: Stanford University Press, 2004; German orig. 1993).

Terpstra, M. '"God's Love for His Enemies": Jacob Taubes' Conversation with Carl Schmitt on Paul', *Bijdragen, International Journal in Philosophy and Theology* 70 (2009), 185–206.

Terpstra, M. 'The Management of Distinctives: Jacob Taubes on Paul's Political Theology', in G.-J. van der Heiden, G. van Kooten, & A. Cimino (eds.), *Saint Paul and Philosophy: The Consonance of Ancient and Modern Thought* (Berlin & Boston: De Gruyter, 2017), 251–68.

Terpstra, Marin, & Theo de Wit, '"No Spiritual Investment in the World As It Is": Jacob Taubes's Negative Political Theology', in I.N. Bulhof & L.T. Kate (eds.), *Flight of the Gods: Philosophical Perspectives on Negative Theology* (New York: Fordham University Press, 2000), 320–53.

Theodoret of Cyprus *Commentary on the Letters of St Paul.* Volume 1 (Brookline: Holy Cross Press, 2001).

Thiselton, Anthony C. *Discovering Romans: Content, Interpretation, Reception* (London: SPCK, 2016).

Thompson, J. L. 'Calvin as a Biblical Interpreter', in D. K. McKim (ed.), *The Cambridge Companion to John Calvin* (Cambridge: Cambridge University Press, 2004), 58–73.

Tofighi, Fatima *Paul's Letters and the Construction of the European Self* (London & New York: Bloomsbury/T&T Clark, 2017).

Torrance, T. F. *Reality and Evangelical Theology: The Realism of Christian Revelation* (Downers Grove, Ill.: IVP, 1982).

Treier, D. J.	*Introducing Theological Interpretation of Scripture: Recovering a Christian Practice* (Grand Rapids: Baker Academic, 2012).
Trueman, C. R.	'Calvin and Calvinism', in D.K. McKim (ed.), *The Cambridge Companion to John Calvin* (Cambridge: Cambridge University Press, 2004), 225–44.
Vermigli, Peter Martyr	*Predestination and Sanctification: Two Theological Loci* (The Peter Martyr Library Volume 8; Frank A. James III, transl. & ed.; Kirksville: Truman State University Press, 2003).
Van der Heiden, Gert Jan, George Henry van Kooten, & Antonio Cimino	*Saint Paul and Philosophy: The Consonance of Ancient and Modern Thought* (Berlin and Boston: De Gruyter, 2017).
Viard, A.	*Saint Paul, Épitre aux Romans* (Sources Bibliques; Paris: Librairie Lecroffre, 1973).
Welborn, L. L.	'"Extraction from the Mortal Site": Badiou on the Resurrection in Paul', *New Testament Studies* 55 (2009) 295–314.
Welborn, L. L.	'Jacob Taubes—Paulinist, Messianist', in P. Frick (ed.), *Paul in the Grip of the Philosophers: The Apostle and Contemporary Continental Philosophy* (Minneapolis: Fortress, 2013), 69–90.
Welborn, L. L.	*Paul's Summons to Messianic Life: Political Theology and the Coming Awakening* (New York: Columbia University Press, 2015).
Wendel, F.	*Calvin The Origins and Development of his Religious Thought* (P. Mairet, transl.; London: Collins, 1963, 1980 [French: 1950]).
Wills, Garry	*What Paul Meant* (New York: Viking Penguin, 2006).
Žižek, Slavoj	*The Puppet and the Dwarf: The Perverse Core of Christianity* (Cambridge, Mass.: MIT Press, 2003).

CHAPTER 16

Locus on Justification in Vermigli's Commentary on Romans

Jin Heung Kim

St. Paul's epistle to the Romans is often called as 'the book of the Reformation' because of its doctrine of justification by faith alone. Peter Martyr Vermigli (1499–1562), one of the most learned scholars in the sixteenth century, lectured on Romans not only in Italy but also in the Protestant cities. His commentary on Romans (1558) had considerable influence, especially in the Reformed camp. In Vermigli's locus on justification from the commentary, this essay finds a typical Reformed approach to the doctrine and thereby identifies some characteristic features of Reformed tradition.

This article has three parts. First, a general introduction to Vermigli and his work of locus on justification will be undertaken. A brief introduction to Vermigli and his historical significance, which includes a survey on his engagement with Romans, and a description of his 'Locus on Justification'. The second part presents an analysis of Vermigli's Reformed doctrine of justification and, the final section evaluates the significance and influence of his doctrine of justification. The discussion will show that the most outstanding feature in Vermigli's discussion of justification is his consistent application of the fundamental principle of the Reformation, *sola scriptura*.

1. Peter Martyr Vermigli and Romans

1.1. *Vermigli as Codifier of the Reformed Theology*

On the oil painting portrait of Vermigli, drawn by Henrik Hondius (1540), a succinct summary of Vermigli's life and work in various countries is carved in Latin words: *Tuscia te pepulit. Germania et Anglia fovit. Martyr quem extinctam, nunc tegit Helvetia.* Peter Martyr Vermigli, an Italian theologian and abbot, worked diligently to establish not only renewal and revitalisation in the Roman Catholic churches of the Italian cities but also in the Reformed Protestant churches in Strasbourg, Oxford, and Zurich. He is not so famous in the estimation of today's scholars and theologians, but the historical significance of this learned Reformer was well acknowledged by his contemporaries. For example, Joseph Justus Scaliger (1540–1609), professor at Geneva and Leiden and himself an influential leader of the Reformed circle in his times, considered Vermigli as one of the two greatest contemporary leaders, together with John Calvin:

> The two most excellent theologians of our times are John Calvin and Peter Martyr, the former has dealt with the Holy Scriptures as they ought to be dealt with—with sincerity, purity, and simplicity, without any scholastic subtleties ... Peter Martyr, because it seemed to fall to him to engage the Sophists, he has overcome them sophistically, and struck them down with their own weapons.[1]

Vermigli had an equal authority to that of Calvin, according to Scaliger, and, especially in theological controversies with the Roman Catholic theologians, Vermigli was considered the very best of the contemporary Reformed theologians. About his doctrine of Lord's Supper, Calvin said admiringly of Vermigli's most extensive Eucharistic treatise *Defensio* (1559) that 'by this work Vermigli left nothing more to be done on this matter'.[2]

Vermigli played a significant role in establishing Reformed theology, and is chiefly remembered for his contributions to the doctrines of

---

[1] McLelland, 'Translator's Introduction', xxvii.
[2] Donnelly, 'Instruction', xiii.

Predestination and the Lord's Supper. Concerning the Reformed doctrine of predestination, Alister McGrath evaluates that the influence of Vermigli's doctrine of predestination outweighs that of Calvin in the later Calvinist discussion.[3] Furthermore, this very learned Italian scholar is now evaluated by Richard Muller as one of the four codifiers of the Reformed tradition.[4] Therefore, considering this high evaluation of his historical significance in the history of Reformed theology, Vermigli's commentary on Romans and his 'locus on justification' deserve attention. His work on this doctrine enables some characteristic features of the Reformed doctrine of justification to be identified.

1.2. *Vermigli and Romans*

Animated by the conviction that the Church should be reformed by patristic and Scriptural studies, scholars undertook significant studies on St. Paul's letters across Western Europe, even before the Reformation. John Colet in England, Lefèvre d'Étaples in France, Cisneros in Spain, and Gasparo Contarini in Italy. Each of these men were noteworthy commentators of a high scholarly calibre on Paul's letters.[5] Possibly under the influence of such 'Paulism before Luther' or 'pre-Lutheran Paulism' in Italy, especially thanks to Contarini, Vermigli had already studied and lectured Romans in his Italian period.[6] This letter of St. Paul converted an Italian abbot—who was extremely learned in Scholasticism, Humanism, and resurgent Augustinianism[7]—into a convinced Protestant scholar. After his defection to the Protestant camp, Vermigli devoted himself everywhere in his travels to the promotion of the cause of the Reformation through his lectures on this letter.

During his Naples period as the abbot of San Pietro ad Aram (1537–1540), Vermigli had close association with the Valdesian group, a humanist and spiritual circle led by Juan Valdès. Through this fellowship Vermigli became acquainted with the various Reformers' writings

---

3   McGrath, *A Life of John Calvin*, 207.
4   Muller, *Christ and the Decree*, 67, referring to Calvin, Bullinger, W. Musculus, and Vermigli.
5   McNair, *Peter Martyr in Italy*, 150.
6   James, 'Romans Commentary', 306.
7   James, 'Peter Martyr Vermigli. At the Crossroads', 63.

and finally accepted the doctrine of justification by faith alone.⁸ Here in Naples Vermigli gave his first lecture on Romans, which is not extant, but known from a testimony from one of his pupils. In Lucca (1541–1542), Vermigli, as prior of San Frediano, lectured on Romans for the second time to his students in the unique academy that he established there: the so-called 'the first and last reformed theological college in pre-Tridentine Italy'.⁹ Girolamo Zanchi, one of the 18 students of this college who had followed Vermgili in crossing the Alps, testified that he had heard Vermigli's lecture on Romans in Lucca.¹⁰ Like the first lecture in Naples, however, there is no extant writing of Vermigli about this second lecture on Romans.

In his first Strasbourg period (1542–1547), after he crossed over the Alps for religious freedom, for the third time Vermigli lectured on Romans (1545–1546) at the Senior School. According to a young French student Hubert de Bapasme, in a letter dated 10 March 1546, Vermigli was lecturing the twelfth chapter of the Pauline epistle.¹¹ But still there is no extant manuscript on this lecture by Vermigli. In his Oxford period (1547–1553), as Regius Professor, Vermigli chose Romans for his second series of lectures at the university. Vermigli's choice of Romans was closely connected to his mission in England: by means of the doctrine of *sola fide*, which Romans taught so clearly in Vermigli's view, he wanted to improve influence and quality of the Reformation movement in England. Vermigli's daily lectures on Romans at Oxford University during this period provided the content for his commentary on Romans, which was eventually published in Basel in 1558. Moreover, the Two Loci on Predestination and Justification also had their origins in the academic debates at the university.¹²

---

8   Di Gangi, *Peter Martyr Vermigli*, 41.
9   McNair, *Peter Martyr in Italy*, 221. James, 'Peter Martyr Vermigli, 1499–1562', 199.
10 James, 'Translator's Introduction', xx.
11 James, 'Translator's Introduction', xx.
12 Methuen, 'Oxford: Reading Scripture in the University', 90–91. As regius professor, Vermigli was obliged to lead the biweekly theological debates.

1.3. Vermigli's Commentary on Romans

Among the various commentaries on Romans in the sixteenth century Reformation, Vermigli's commentary on Romans is remarkable in terms of the extraordinary academic background of the author. He was a first-class Reformed theologian with a profound knowledge of Roman Catholicism, Patristics, Christian Humanism, and the Old and New Testaments. Edmund Grindal, bishop of London, evaluated highly the quality of Vermigli as a theological scholar in a letter to Sir William Cecil: 'no man alive is more fit than Peter Martyr... for he is better versed in old doctors, councils, and ecclesiastical histories than any Roman doctor of Christendom'.[13] According to this evaluation, Vermigli's commentary on Romans is not just one of the same kind, but a particular work based on his comprehensive knowledge of Christian faith, old and new. In this regard, it is significant that Klaus Sturm, in his study on Vergmili's early understanding of justification in the first period in Strasbourg (1543–1547), evaluated Vermigli's doctrine of justification as 'Reformkatholic'.[14]

In the preface, Vermigli mentioned the obligation that he felt to publish his own commentary on Romans, in addition to those already published by Luther, Melanchthon, Bucer and Calvin. In Oxford, he helped Archbishop Cranmer to make a theological alliance with the continental Reformers in opposition to the anti–Reformation decisions of the Council of Trent. Vermigli's lectures and commentary on Romans were in this regard his theological response to the Tridentine doctrine of justification.[15] So his commentary on Romans was not merely a rite of passage for a significant reformer, but rather a mature vindication of the fundamental doctrine of the Reformation. Among his Biblical writings, Vermigli's commentary on Romans was the most influential, as we can see in the eight editions published between 1558–1613.

---

13 James, 'Peter Martyr Vermigli, 1499–1562', 201.
14 Sturm, *Die Theologie Peter Martyr Vermiglis*, 69.
15 James, *De Justificatione*, 274–275.

2. Vermigli's Doctrine of Justification

In his commentaries on the Scriptural books, Vermigli often included various *loci*, where he concentrated on specific theological or ethical topics. The *Loci* method was developed and applied to the hermeneutic method in the sixteenth century by Christian humanism and the Reformation.[16] Vermigli's posthumous systematic theological work was also compiled in this method and so named the *Loci communes* of Peter Martyr Vermigli.[17] While he presented many *loci* in other commentaries, Vermigli wrote only two *loci* in his Romans commentary: a locus on predestination after the exegesis on chapter 9, and a locus on justification after chapter 11. This shows the extraordinary significance of the two topics in his understanding of Romans. His discussion of the two *loci* in Romans had considerable significance for and influence within Reformed theology. Indeed, in regards to the doctrine of double predestination, his commentary on Romans contributed substantially to the colour of Zurich theology, with the result that it became typically 'Reformed'. Also in regard to the doctrine of justification, it helped to maintain the comprehensive character of the Reformed view, in contrast to the Lutheran development of a strictly forensic concept of Justification. These two theological loci were also included in all the editions of Vermigli's *Loci communes* from the publication of the London edition (1576).[18]

2.1. Locus on Justification

The 'Locus on Justification' in his commentary on Romans provides Vermigli's most comprehensive doctrine of justification. This was because Vermigli believed that this Pauline epistle more clearly taught the doctrine than any other Scriptural book.[19]

---

16 Amos, 'Exegesis and Theological Method', 182.
17 See McLelland, 'A Literary History of the Loci Communes', 486.
18 Vermigli, *Predestination and Justification*, xliii–xliv.
19 James, *De Justificatione*, 276.

2.1.1. *Contour of Locus of Justification*

Vermigli's 'Locus on Justification' is composed of three propositions: (1) Justification is not by works; in other words, good works cannot justify us; (2) Justification is by faith; and (3) Justification is by faith *alone*. To establish these three statements 'with reasons from Holy Scripture' and to defend them from the opposition and railings of his adversaries is Vermigli's purpose in argument.[20] The first proposition covers almost half of the whole *locus*, while the third falls short of 8 percent. So it is very easy to see where Vermigli's argument is focused. That the bulk of the material is assigned to the first proposition is due to his careful refutation of the criticism that good works are destroyed by it: 'justification is not by works'.

2.1.2. Vermigli's Argument for the First Proposition

The 'Scriptural and patristic testimonies' comprise an outstanding feature in his argument for the first proposition. Vermigli employs Scriptural testimonies first from Romans, then from Paul's other letters, and finally from several books from the Old and New Testaments. Proof from Paul's letter to Romans is prominent in his argument, evidenced by the fact that Vermigli cites various statements from every chapter of Romans, ranging from the first chapter to the fourteenth.[21] All these testimonies from Romans, according to Vermigli, 'clearly show that he agrees with Paul in all points, and does not depart from Paul's doctrine of justification in any way'.[22] Among the other Pauline letters, testimonies from Galatians are by far the most frequent in number. From there, Vermigli continues to appeal to the Scriptural testimonies from the Gospels, a few non–Pauline epistles, and some books of the Old Testament such as Job, Psalms, and Isaiah. On the basis of these Scriptural testimonies, Vermigli proceeds to consider the various objections to his proposition, such as (1) Moral and Ceremonial Works of the Law, (2) Good Works of Fallen Believers, (3) Good Works of

---

20 Vermigli, *Predestination and Justification*, 96.
21 Vermigli, *Predestination and Justification*, 97–106. Five different verses are cited from chapter 8, showing the importance of this chapter to Vermigli.
22 Vermigli, *Predestination and Justification*, 97.

Unbelievers, (4) Good Works and Common Grace, (5) Good Works and Merit, (6) Preparatory Works, (7) Good Works of the Function of the Law, and (8) Additional Objections from the Scripture. So, very impressively in terms of the sweep of the argument, objections from 8 categories are dealt with comprehensively.[23] This part of Vermigli's discussion, therefore, provides an extensive and complete defence of the Reformed doctrine of justification over against all kinds of objections already raised against the classic Reformation doctrine. Again, in this refutation of the various objections, Vermigli's appeal to the Scriptural testimonies is remarkable: he refutes all these objections by recourse to Romans and other Pauline letters by relentlessly highlighting the importance of *sola Scriptura*.

In this way Vermigli discloses the weakness of his opponents' arguments in their Biblical foundation, and then proceeds to deal with the 'Proof from the Church Fathers and Councils'.[24] Here, his purpose is to confirm the following three theses, which are crucial in his defence of the *sola gratia* principle: (1) All Works before Justification Are Sins; (2) Justification is through Grace; and (3) Good Works are the Fruit of Justification.[25] And in this connection, Church Fathers such as Basil, Gregory of Nazianzus, Augustine, Chrysostom, Ambrose, Cyprian, and Origen, are used as the secondary authorities in support of his doctrine of justification. All these patristic testimonies are in agreement with the Scriptural teaching, which is the first and ultimate criterion for Vermigli. Proof from Church Councils is added in the same way: 'We ought to receive and reverence only those councils that have kept their doctrine within the rule of the Holy Scriptures'.[26] By comparing the Tridentine doctrine of justification with the canons of the Council of Milevis (in North Africa, 402) and the Second Council of Orange (529), Vermigli clearly shows the importance of a Biblical approach to the traditional authorities. In terms of Vermigli's Scriptural and patristic evidences, the Tridentine position was nothing else than Pelagianism: 'But when our men of Trent speak they pretend to distinguish themselves from the

---

23 Vermigli, *Predestination and Justification*, 115–143.
24 Vermigli, *Predestination and Justification*, 143–160.
25 Vermigli, *Predestination and Justification*, 143–144.
26 Vermigli, *Predestination and Justification*, 152.

Pelagians, yet they can never prove it. They say they do not deny grace, but in fact they put forward a kind of grace that the Pelagians would never have denied'.[27]

2.1.3. Vermigli's Arguments for the Second and the Third Propositions

In his discussion of the second proposition 'Justification is by faith', the procedure is almost the same: first by Scriptural and then by patristic testimonies. In dealing with the objections to this proposition, however, he concentrates on Albert Pighius, a Dutch theologian, whom Vermigli introduces as the Achilles (i.e. hero) of Roman Catholicism regarding the doctrine of Justification.[28] Again by means of Scriptural and patristic testimonies, Vermigli carefully refuted Pighius' arguments that faith can be separated from justification:

> First, we deny that faith can be separated from justification. Although Pighius says this is not repugnant to the nature and definition of faith, we do not admit it, for against that opinion are the Holy Scriptures, a proper understanding of the definition of faith, and the fathers.[29]

Vermigli contrasted the patristic authorities such as Irenaeus, Tertullian, Cyprian, Origen, Chrysostom (11 times, second to Augustine), Jerome, Ambrose, Augustine (18 times), Cyril, Leo I, Gregory the Great, with Pighius' authority. He also appealed to the Council of Mainz, which was held under the supervision of Charlemagne. By these patristic testimonies, Vermigli clearly shows that Pighius (and the other Roman Catholic theologians) cannot accept the Reformational doctrine of *sola fide* and *sola gratia*: 'But this is something our Pighius cannot accept, for he derides us every time we say that faith is acquired by the grace and the inward working of the Holy Spirit'.[30] It is noteworthy in his

---

27 Vermigli, *Predestination and Justification*, 158.
28 Vermigli, *Predestination and Justification*, 172. 'We will begin with Pighius because our adversaries have him for their Achilles and think that by his subtle acumen he has penetrated into the secret mysteries of the truth'.
29 Vermigli, *Predestination and Justification*, 173.
30 Vermigli, *Predestination and Justification*, 208.

refutation of Pighius that Vermigli also rejected the authority of the Prince of Christian Humanism, Erasmus of Rotterdam.[31]

In the third proposition 'Justification is by Faith *Alone*', Vermigli's target is Richard Smith, his predecessor to the regius professorship in Oxford. Smith criticised the Protestant addition of the word 'only' to the faith. By analysing the Biblical usage of term '*gratis*', Vermigli rejected Smith's argument:

> But this sharp-witted man, so well exercised in the concordance of the Bible, should have remembered that this word *gratis* signifies 'without a cause' or 'without reward and price'; therefore we rightly say that justification comes by faith alone (*sola fide*), because it is said to be given freely (*gratis*).[32]

Vermigli was convinced that all the Scriptures prove that we are justified by faith only, even if this word 'only' is not mentioned in the Scriptures. Again, in this argument, in addition to the Scriptural testimonies, Vermigli appealed to patristic testimonies not only from the famous Fathers but also from not so well-known Greek Fathers.[33] As noted before in regards to Vermigli's argumentation elsewhere, his profound Scriptural and patristic knowledge undergirds his argument of the third proposition. Vermigli's use of the Church Fathers represents a typical example of how the Reformed theologians in the 16th century understood the fundamental principle of *sola scriptura* and applied it to the cause of the Reformed Protestantism.

By his Scriptural and patristic treatment of the three propositions, therefore, Vermigli achieved his purpose in the Locus on Justification: namely, that the doctrine of justification is the 'head, fountain, and mainstay' of all religion and therefore 'we should be more sure and certain of this above all'.[34]

---

31 Vermigli, *Predestination and Justification*, 176–177. Vermigli rejects Erasmus in this matter, because 'his reason is very weak and it is false'.
32 Vermigli, *Predestination and Justification*, 219.
33 He cites such famous Fathers as Origen, Cyril, Basil, Hilary of Poitier, Ambrose, and also not well known Greek Fathers like Hesychius, Phocius patriarch of Constantinople, Acacius of Berea, and even the medieval theologian Bernard of Clairvaux; *Predestination and Justification*, 228–230.
34 Vermigli, *Predestination and Justification*, 96–97.

2.2. Notable Features of Vermigli's Doctrine of Justification

2.2.1. Typical Protestant Doctrine of Justification

In his use of the terms 'forensic' and 'imputation', Vermigli demonstrates a typical Protestant viewpoint in his doctrine of justification. In his explanation of justification, he made use of the Latin word *'forense'*, thereby demonstrating that he understood justification first of all as a legal matter. According to Vermigli, the crucial matter in justification relates to the righteous Divine Judge: that is, how God can reach a verdict of 'not guilty' to the legal guilt inherited by all Adam's descendants.[35] He explains this legal process by the concept of *duplex imputatio*, by which the righteousness of Christ is imputed to the sinners, and, at the same time, the sins are not imputed to the sinners themselves, because of Christ's personal appropriation of their punishment for sin on the cross. This concept of twofold imputation is almost the same as Luther's concept of the 'blessed exchange between Christ and His bride' in his early writing *On Christian Freedom* (1520). The twofold legal benefit is given to the believers, according to Vermigli, as the result of the twofold imputation: forgiveness of sins as well as new relationship to the Divine Judge. Vermigli emphasized this new relationship with God more than the mere legal remission, when he said that the 'chief and principal part' of forgiveness of our sins is 'that we are received into the favour of God'. F.A. James interprets this new relationship as something like 'adoption', which adds a 'relational' aspect to Vermigli's doctrine of justification. So the forgiveness exercised by the Divine Judge is not of the same kind as King David's forgiveness of Absalom, where a full restoration of the broken relationship does not occur (2 Sam. 14:32).

Vermigli's concept of the twofold imputation inevitably led to the concept of 'the righteousness outside of us' (*iustitia extra nos*). That is to say, the forensic notion of justification is not the inherent grace (*gratia inhaerens*) which makes an actual transformation of the sinners from inside. Vermigli consistently interpreted the term *iustificatio* not as making sinners actually righteous but as declaring them righteous. In this regard, he demonstrates fundamental agreement with Luther and

---

35 For this paragraph, James, 'Peter Martyr Vermigli, 1499–1562', 202.

Calvin in the rejection of the Roman Catholic semi-Pelagianism in the doctrine of justification. It is noteworthy that Vermigli never made use of Luther's famous idiom *simul iustus et peccator* in his writings,[36] however what the idiom represents is nevertheless clearly seen in his commentary on Romans: 'every Christian is both fully a sinner in himself and fully righteous in Christ'.[37]

2.2.2. The Threefold Justification

On the one hand, Vermigli shows us his fundamental accord with the other Reformers by his legal concept of justification, but, on the other hand, by his 'threefold justification' concept Vermigli declares his distinct 'Reformed' understanding of justification. 'Threefold Justification' means that regeneration, justification, and sanctification could be distinguished in concept, but they should never be separated from one another in the application of redemption. In his commentary on Romans 1:17 we can find a clear explanation of the concept:

> God declares his *righteousness or goodness* towards us by three things chiefly. First, he receives us into favour, forgiving us our sins: not imputing death to us for those sins we commit, but on the contrary, imputes to us instead the obedience and holiness of Christ. Second, he kindles in our heart a desire to live uprightly, he renews our will, illuminates our reason and makes us prone to live virtuously, although before we abhorred that which was just and honest. Third he gives us pure and chaste conduct good actions and a sincere life.[38]

Here we see that Vermigli regarded imputation as 'justification in a narrow sense', while he joined the other two elements in his concept of Biblical justification. Also in regards to Romans 3:21, Vermigli explained the concept thus:

---

36 Donnelly, *Calvinism and Scholasticism*, 154. According to Donnelly, this paradoxical expression is foreign to Vermigli's mentality, and also does not square with Vermigli's understanding of justification by faith alone. Donnelly seems to suggest this omission as a proof of Roman Catholic nuances that Vermigli retained even after he became a Protestant.
37 'Peter Martyr Vermigli, 1499–1562', 203.
38 James, 'Romans Commentary', 312.

> The righteousness of God, as I have declared in other places, is threefold. The first is that we are received into favour through Christ and our sins forgiven and the righteousness of Christ is imputed to us. The second righteousness follows this, namely that through the help of the Holy Spirit, our mind is reformed and we are inwardly renewed by grace. Third, holy and godly works follow.[39]

In his lectures on Genesis in Strasbourg, and on 1 Corinthians and Romans in Oxford, Vermigli consistently asserted the distinct but inseparable connection between the three elements in his doctrine of justification. It is noteworthy that Vermigli added 'regeneration' to the conventional emphasis on the close relationship between justification and sanctification. In this regard, Vermigli presented the two ways by which God gives righteousness to us: first, by imputation (*iustitia extra nobis*), second, by the renewing power of Holy Spirit within us (*iustita in nobis*). Here, regeneration is considered as the beginning of the second way, while sanctification is the result of it. This threefold justification concept is the fruit of Vermigli's extensive studies on the doctrine of justification by the Scriptural and patristic testimonies.

Vermigli's threefold justification had a strong ethical orientation in the sense that it could contradict the Roman Catholic denunciation of '*sola gratia, sola fide*' as a pretext for licentiousness. According to Vermigli's understanding, justification in its forensic sense, based upon the imputed righteousness of Christ, necessarily accompanies the regenerating work of the Holy Spirit, which makes the moral change of the sinner's soul, leading thereby to sanctification. Vermigli was convinced that justification, correctly understood by the Scriptural teaching, should be directly connected with piety. Today, voices that worry about the abuse of justification in an extreme forensic sense are often heard in Reformed and Presbyterian churches. Those who have concerns about its abuse put emphasis upon the balanced teaching that exists in the relation between justification and sanctification in the Reformed soteriology.

---

39 James, 'Romans Commentary', 312.

However, Vermigli as one of the codifiers of the Reformed tradition, had long before already put an even stronger emphasis upon the ethical orientation in this matter. Much stronger is his conviction that justification without regeneration and without the sanctification of the Holy Spirit is not Scriptural justification! According to his threefold justification, redemption from the *massa perditionis* cannot be achieved merely by forensic justification. The gospel message of the holistic redemption requires the ethical change of the sinners by the redemptive work of the Holy Spirit.

Compared with developments elsewhere in the Lutheran camp, Vermigli's threefold justification can be evaluated as a distinct 'Reformed' feature. In reaction to the *anathemas* of the Council of Trent, Lutheran theologians such as Johannes Agricola, Andreas Osiander, Nicholaus von Amsdorf, adopted an extreme forensic concept of justification. They defied the necessity of sermons on the Law, inclined towards anti-nomianism, and even denounced 'good works' as harmful to *sola fide*. Most of the Lutheran theologians felt sympathetic to the Arminian cause during the Synod of Dort (1616–1619) because they felt that the Remonstrants were defending the Lutheran cause.[40] In the Reformed camp, however, Vermigli's threefold justification significantly contributed to the Biblical balance between forensic and relational righteousness, in the same way that Calvin had in his final edition of the *Institutes* (1559). Both Vermigli and Calvin firmly confessed the fundamental forensic understanding of justification, while at the same time consistently emphasizing the sanctification inseparably connected to legal justification.

2.2.3. *Doctrine of Justification and* Sola Scriptura *Principle*

The most characteristic feature in Vermigli's discussion of justification is his consistent application of the fundamental principle of *sola scriptura*. The purpose in his discussion of the first proposition clearly shows it: 'I will rehearse in due order the explanations Paul has in the letter to the Romans. By this it may be easily understood that I agree with him in all

---

40 Praamsma, *De kerk van alle tijden*, 213–214.

points, nor do I depart from his doctrine in any way'.[41] So he displayed detailed proof from Romans, and other New and Old Testament books, in support of his doctrine as well as in refutation of his opponents. Vermigli believed in the illumination of the Holy Spirit, without which one cannot accept the Scriptural testimonies, no matter how many they are. So he added a significant remark to the Scriptural testimonies: 'Although I could bring many more reasons to confirm this proposition (indeed an almost infinite number), yet these I have already brought are enough, and I will refrain from others. For those who are not persuaded by these reasons will not be affected by any others'.[42] By this remark, Vermigli expressed the conviction that the doctrine of *sola fide*, which (according to him) is directly connected with *soli Deo gloria*, cannot be attained by any human persuasion, but only by the gracious work of the Holy Spirit through the testimonies of Scripture. So he tried his best to show what the whole Scripture said about justification consistently, and expected the persuasive power of the Holy Spirit.

Also in his use of secondary authorities, Vermigli consistently applied the principle of *sola scriptura*. In his commentary on Romans, Vermigli made abundant use of the patristic and conciliar authorities, but he considered them only as a 'secondary' authority, not as authoritative themselves. They are rather 'sources' (*fontes*) which could be authoritative as far as they are in line with the Scriptural teaching. As one of the best patrologists of his times, Vermigli could criticize and refute effectively his opponents' appeals to the patristic and conciliar authorities. His sarcasm that they should be called patrologians (*patrologi*) rather than theologians (*theologi*), because they could not appeal to the Scripture but only to the Fathers and the councils,[43] betrays the fundamental significance of the *sola scriptura* principle in his argument of justification. For Vermigli, the ultimate criterion or authority in the theological discussion is the Word of God, and only under this principal authority could all other sources be properly used as authoritative.

---

41 Vermigli, *Predestination and Justification*, 97.
42 Vermigli, *Predestination and Justification*, 115.
43 Vermigli, *Predestination and Justification*, 143. 'Now we have certain adversaries who judge little or nothing at all on the basis of Scripture, but measure all their religion by fathers and councils, so much that they can be called *patrologi* rather than *theologi*'.

Vermigli's use of the Fathers, councils, and the Schoolmen can be regarded as selective for his overall support of his argument, as was the case with Calvin.[44] However, his application of the *sola scriptura* principle was consistent and it functioned not as an exclusive criterion. By the 'Rule of Patristics' that he suggested as the ten hermeneutic principles for the right understanding of the Fathers,[45] Vermigli could embrace the various secondary authorities harmoniously. Church Fathers, the councils, and the Schoolmen are evaluated as 'authoritative' in so far as they are sustained by the singular authority of the Scripture. In this sense the authority of the Scripture is really unique or '*sola*' for Vermigli, as opposed to arbitrary and selective.[46] He applied this 'Rule for Patristics' regularly in his other polemical writings as well as in his Two Loci on Romans. Thus Zwingli's pioneering work to establish the principle of *sola scriptura* by the time of the Bern Theses (1528)[47] brought forth plentiful fruit in Vermigli's application of the principle to the patristic sources. Vermigli's masterly treatment of the various patristic writings by his classifying skill is best displayed in his Eucharistic treatises.[48]

3. Significance and Influence of Vermigli's Doctrine of Justification

3.1. 'Union with Christ'

As mentioned above, Vermigli was evaluated together with Calvin as the two leading theologians in the Reformed camp. We can find a further significant feature of characteristic Reformed doctrine of justification in the common idea of 'Union with Christ'. This concept is regarded as the key idea to understand Calvin's thought on the relation between justification and sanctification.[49] Also for Vermigli, this concept is the 'dynamic' of his theology, which plays an important role not only in

---

44 Lane, *John Calvin*, 53. Calvin was 'not seeking to give a balanced detached assessment of the fathers, but was appealing to them for support'.
45 Vermigli, *The Oxford Treatise and Disputation on the Eucharist 1549*, 76–79.
46 Kim, *Scripturae et Patrum Testimoniis*, 247–248.
47 See Backus, *The Disputation of Baden*.
48 For Vermigli's application of this principle to the patristic sources, see Kim, *Scripturae et Patrum Testimoniis*. His utilisation of 'Evaluation, De-valuation, and Relativization-Appropriation' is outstanding in his handling of the Fathers, the Scholastics, and the Councils.
49 McGrath, *Iustitia Dei*, 224.

his doctrine of justification but also in his Eucharistic teaching. In this regard McLelland summarised the main bases of Vermigli's theology as follows:

> *First*, faith means union with Christ. Justification has substance in the realm of being as well as of knowledge. Sanctification means the increase of this union, but always deriving from the ongoing union from the side of Christ. *Second*, this growth has as its nourishment the Word of God as the 'chief food of the soul'. It is Christ Himself who grows in the believer, by the continual apprehension of His Person. *Third*, this apprehension is dependent upon the effective action of the Holy Spirit, who uses earthly elements as signs through and from which He raises up the mind and soul to grasp the Risen Man, Jesus Christ.[50]

This displays the fundamental agreement between the two theologians about the significance of the 'union with Christ' concept in Reformed soteriology. These two codifiers of the Reformed tradition put strong emphasis upon the crucial role of the Holy Spirit, who applies the redemption accomplished by Jesus Christ to the elect by the inseparably connected works of justification and sanctification. About this concept, Vermigli sent letters to Calvin and Beza in May 1553, describing his threefold union with Christ—first, natural or incarnation union; second, spiritual union or unison of similarity; third, mystical union.[51] Calvin responded to this with wholehearted agreement: 'Were I teaching any other person, I should follow up this subject more diffusely; in addressing you, I have glanced at it briefly, with the simple view of showing you that we entirely agree in sentiment'.[52] On the basis of this common understanding of 'union with Christ', the two codifiers concurred in emphasising the inseparable connection between justification and sanctification.

In this way, Vermigli and Calvin affirmed the fundamental 'forensic' aspect of justification and at the same time never lost the Scriptural

---

50   McLelland, *The Visible Words of* God, 160.
51   Fesco, 'Peter Martyr Vermigli on Union with Christ and Justification', 42–43.
52   Calvin to Martyr, 8/8/1555, 352.

emphasis on the sanctifying work of the Holy Spirit. To declare righteous and to make righteous are distinct but are never separable for the two Reformed theologians. While the Zurich theologian consistently underlined this by the threefold justification, the Genevan theologian emphasized the same by the so-called 'twofold acceptance' of us by God. According to this concept, God accepts first our 'person' and then our 'work', but both only thanks to God's mercy toward us. The second acceptance (of our work) depends on the first, and the accepted work of ours is the fruit of the Holy Spirit's inner sanctifying work in us.[53] By this concept of 'twofold acceptance', Calvin could harmonize the Scriptural testimonies that promise the reward for the law-keeping good works with the doctrine of *sola gratia*. It was not, however, intended to weaken the forensic understanding of justification of Reformed theology. Rather, Calvin wanted to put much stronger emphasis upon the close relation between forensic and relational aspects in the Reformed doctrine of justification.[54] Therefore for the other Reformed theologians, who followed the pioneering works by Vermigli and Calvin, 'the faith in justification' is alive, that is to say, 'to prove itself by the fruits of good work'. This ought to be remembered in today's Reformed and Presbyterian churches, where the forensic aspect of justification is so exaggerated and abused that the relational aspect (sanctification) is almost forgotten in the understanding of the principles of *sola fide, sola gratia*.

3.2. *A Comparison with Martin Bucer's 'Twofold Righteousness'*

There seems to be a striking similarity between Vermigli's 'threefold' justification and Martin Bucer's 'twofold' justification concepts. Since the First Strasbourg period, Bucer's influence upon Vermigli is undeniable, as we can see from the latter's remark:

> I would dare to assert that I always left that table more learned because I was always hearing something about which I had never before reflected very precisely or about which I had been

---

53 Venema, *Accepted and Renewed in Christ*, 165.
54 Baschera, 'Independent Yet Harmonious', 53.

unsatisfied ... Behold dear brothers, there are truly holy bishops in our time on earth or rather in the Church of Christ!'[55]

In this regard, there is an opinion that Bucer's twofold justification is the most important source for Vermigli's threefold justification. Especially in this connection the Regensburg Book (1541) is mentioned, which represents an ecumenical effort between the Protestant and the Roman Catholic Churches. Bucer was the major contributor to the writing of the book from the Protestant side. On the doctrine of justification, the fifth article of this book confessed the twofold concept of 'imputed' and 'inherent' justice, which played an important role in making an agreement on the doctrine from both sides.[56] When Vermigli was Prior of San Frediano in Lucca (1542), he got firsthand information about the process of ecumenical debates in Regensburg from Cardinal Contarini, who stayed at San Frediano upon returning from the unsuccessful meeting with the Protestants. So Vermigli was aware of the twofold justification concept from the Roman Catholic viewpoint already in his Italian period, and later in Strasbourg he could get the Protestant understanding of the same concept from Bucer.[57]

Although Bucer's concept of the twofold justification may have influenced Vermigli, Vermigli's originality is nevertheless clear in his

---

55 Vermigli, 'To All the Faithfull of the Church of Lucca Called to Be Saints', in *Life, Letters, and Sermons*, 97.
56 Baschera, 'Independent Yet Harmonious', 55. In spite of the historical agreement in the doctrine of justification, which even Calvin approved as substantially consistent with Protestant doctrine, the Colloquy of Regensburg (1541) itself was not successful because of fundamental differences over the doctrines of the Lord's Supper and Church.
57 Especially in regards to the 'inherent' justice in terms of imputation, however, the interpretations were different between Bucer and Gropper, the Roman Catholic theologian who co-authored the 'Regensburg Book'. While Bucer defined imputed righteousness as the only formal cause and regarded inherent justice as the consequent process of becoming righteous, Gropper emphasized incorporation with Christ in his doctrine of justification by the idiom 'to the extent that we are grafted into Christ, on that account we are righteous'. Such incorporation with Christ took place mainly through the sacraments. So Gropper's viewpoint remains within the traditional Roman Catholic standpoint, the so-called 'transformational-sacramental' framework. See Lugioyo, *Martin Bucer's Doctrine of Justification*, 104. Unlike Gropper, Bucer did not consider so-called 'double justification' as 'separate judgements', first by faith and then by works. God's goodwill is the only foundation for the salvation of the sinners, according to Bucer, who conceives the believers as always in the midst of the spiritual conflicts between spirit and flesh. So, his doctrine of justification includes the works love, but the priority of imputed righteousness is clear and distinct: 'God's verdict creates the reality it declares' (pp. 101–102).

threefold justification concept. For example, in his use of the term 'habitus' for the explanation of the inherent righteousness, we can see his distinctive thought. Employing this term in his explanation of the relation between forensic justification (imputation) and sanctification, Vermigli showed a different approach to the topic. The 'inherent' righteousness is, according to Vermigli, the inner renovation that the imputed righteousness gives rise to in the lives of the saints. As the result of this renovation, the good works follow, which can please God. When these good works are repeated consistently in the believer's life, a certain character (habitus) is shaped, which Vermigli calls inherent righteousness. It is neither imputed nor infused, but is acquired by the saints' good works and holy behaviours. By this kind of argument, Vermigli put emphasis upon the peculiar feature of sanctification, which is inseparably related to justification.[58] In his commentary on 1 Corinthians, Vermigli summarised this understanding of the twofold righteousness:

> We possess a twofold righteousness. One is imputed to us by God; through it we are truly justified, not earning it by good works, but apprehending it by faith. The second righteousness inheres in us and consists of faith, hope, and love, as well as of all good works which, however, never entail a perfect, but only an inchoative obedience to the law. This inchoative obedience does not consist but in the effort to act in conformity with the law, as far as we can.[59]

We can see that the Heidelberg Catechism represents the same idea of this codifier of the Reformed theology: Q & A 114: 'But can those converted to God obey these commandments perfectly? No. In this life even the holiest have only a small beginning of this obedience. Nevertheless, with all seriousness of purpose, they do begin to live according to all, not only some, of God's commandments'.[60]

---

58 Vermigli's concept of *habitus* should not be confused with that of Thomas Aquinas, for whom inherent or habitual righteousness is infused and can be regarded as the ground of the righteousness by itself, while Vermigli never accepts the idea that inherent righteousness could be recognized as our merit before the Divine Judge. See Baschera, 'Independent Yet Harmonious', 53–54.
59 Vermigli, *In Corinthios*, fol.357, cited from Baschera, 'Independent Yet Harmonious', 54.
60 Klooster, *Our Only Comfort*, 2.1030.

3.3. Continuous Influence and Significance of Vermigli's Doctrine of Justification

As mentioned above, Luther's dynamic understanding between justification and sanctification in his *On Christian Liberty* (1520) had suffered considerable change in his own section of the Reformation since the Council of Trent. The Lutheran theologians put more and more emphasis upon forensic justification, while the codifiers of the Reformed theology, Calvin and Vermigli, continued to stress the unity of justification and sanctification, which displayed a strong ethical concept of justification.[61] Together with Calvin's final edition of the *Institutes* (1559), Vermigli's *Two Loci* (1558) most vividly represented the continuity of this Reformed characteristic feature in the doctrine of justification.

The balanced viewpoint of Reformed theology about the close relation between justification and sanctification, with a strong emphasis on ethical orientation, continued through the Heidelberg Catechism (1563) and the Westminster Larger Catechism (1648)[62] and still appears in today's Reformed dogmatics. The concept of *ordo salutis*, which was first suggested by the Lutheran theologian Jacob Carpov (1737), was either critically accepted (by G.I. Williamson) or rejected (by G.G. Berkouwer) in the Reformed camp. One of the important reasons for this is that the order of salvation seems to distinguish sanctification from justification not only in logical sense but also in serial order. As one can see in the diagram of G.I. Williamson,[63] sanctification begins only after justification and adoption, and, furthermore, it seems that justification and adoption are not to be affected by sanctification. The second diagram 'Way of Salvation' by A.A. Hoekema[64] represents more clearly Vermigli's Reformed concept of threefold justification:

---

61 James, 'Romans Commentary', 315.
62 Vos, *The Westminster Larger Catechism*, xi–xii. According to W.R. Godfrey, who wrote an instruction to this work, 'questions 70–77 provide an excellent statement of the Reformation doctrines of justification and sanctification', providing 'an especially full and rich exposition of the Ten Commandments' and accordingly 'highly moralistic' so that 'no work of the kind offers a more suggestive and helpful treatment of the ethical and social teachings of the New Testament'.
63 Williamson, *The Shorter Catechism*. Vol. 1, Appendix B. Of course, Williamson himself does not understand the 'order' of salvation as sequel in time, but many Presbyterian pastors did understand the diagram without the Reformed emphasis on the inseparable relationship between justification and sanctification.
64 Hoekeman, *Saved by Grace*, 16.

with regeneration as the beginning of new life, justification and sanctification go hand in hand with continuous conversion (repentance and faith) and perseverance. By this diagram Hoekema insisted that the various aspects in the way of salvation ought not to be understood as a serial and in consecutive order but rather as a simultaneous and continuous process. In this sense, Hoekema's diagram should be considered a typical example of the continuous influence of the Reformed doctrine of justification.

THE ORDER OF SALVATION

A man is walking down the road to hell.
1. He is effectually called.
2. He is converted (by faith and repentance).
3...4. He is instantly justified and adopted.
5. He is gradually sanctified, during the rest of his life.
6. He dies.
7. His soul goes to heaven.
8. His body enters the grave.
9. At the resurrection of the last day, body and soul together enter into
10. Glory.

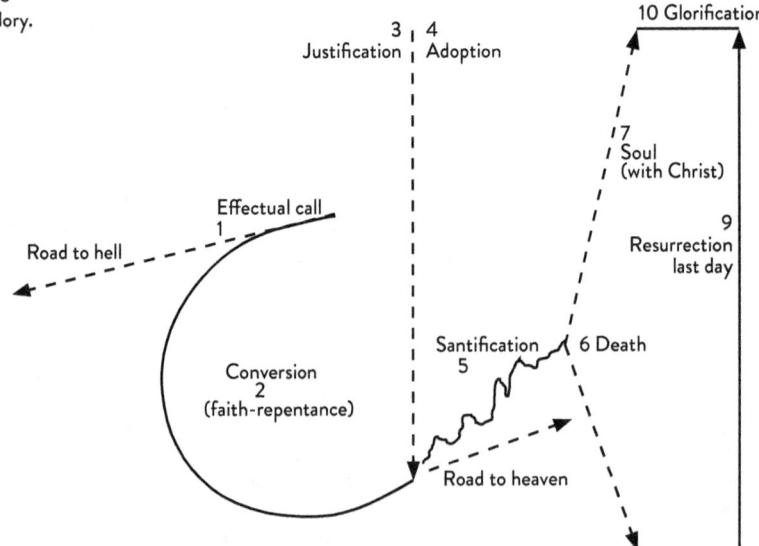

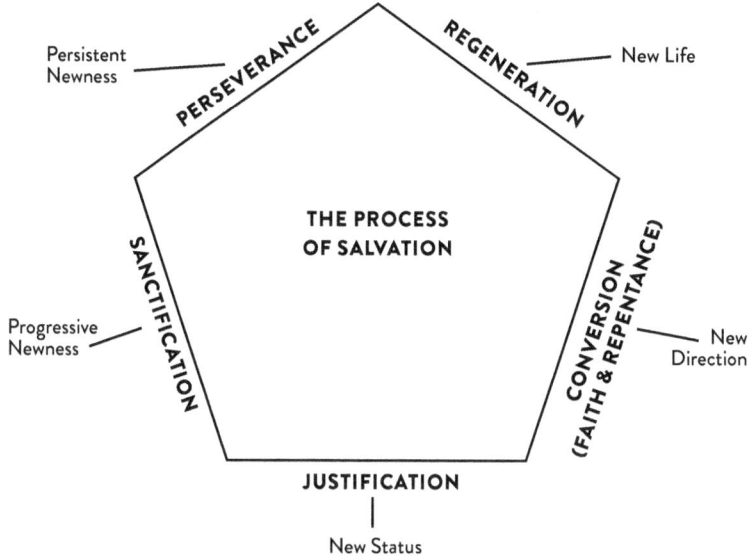

When considered against the 'New Perspective' on Paul, Vermigli's Reformed doctrine of justification, especially his threefold justification concept, is significant, because this 'new' perspective is not all that different from Gropper's understanding of the double justification in the Regensburg Book. A crucial common point is the 'neutralisation' of imputation by the emphasis on the inherent righteousness, either by the sacraments or by the good works of the saints. 'Not imputation but sanctification'—this is why the writers of the New Perspective can enjoy widespread popularity even among the orthodox Presbyterian and Reformed Christians. A long history of the exploitation of sola gratia in 'extreme forensic sense' makes the descendants of the Reformed tradition feel balanced because of the strong emphasis on the new perspective upon the holy life. Neglect of the holy life in practice may indeed be a serious problem in today's Christian life, however, the Reformed doctrine of imputation cannot be blamed for this negligence! The New Perspective criticizes this very doctrine, which is evaluated as an 'irreducible core of a genuine Protestant doctrine of justification'.[65] That is to say, the core of the Reformation doctrine of justification is

---

65 James, 'Romans Commentary', 317.

now under attack. But, already in the sixteenth century, Vermigli had answered the question about the Scriptural relationship between justification and sanctification in a masterly way. His threefold justification did justice to the fundamental role of imputed righteousness and at the same time it never lost the significance of regeneration and sanctification in the lifelong process of the saints' experience of salvation. In this respect Vermgili's 'Locus on Justification' is one of the masterpieces of the Reformational treatments of the doctrine, supported by the convincing Scriptural and patristic testimonies (scripturae et patrum testimoniis). His doctrine of justification can still help us to understand the New Perspective doctrine of the 'double justification' properly from the Scriptural and Reformed viewpoint.

Bibliography

1. Primary Sources

Calvin, J., to P. Martyr, 8/8/1555, in G.C. Gorham (ed.), *Gleanings of a Few Scattered Ears During the Time of the Reformation in England and the Times Immediately Succeeding: 1533–88* (London: Bell and Daldy, 1857), 349–352. https://babel.hathitrust.org.

Vermigli, Peter Martyr *Life, Letters and Sermons* (Peter Martyr Library, 5; J.P. Donnelly, ed.; Kirksville: Sixteenth Century Essays & Studies, 1999).

Vermigli, Peter Martyr *Predestination and Justification: Two Theological Loci* (Kirksville: Sixteenth Century Essays & Studies, 2003).

Vermigli, Peter Martyr *The Oxford Treatise and Disputation on the Eucharist 1549* (Kirksville: Sixteenth Century Essays & Studies, 2000).

2. Secondary Sources

Amos, N.S. 'Exegesis and Theological Method', in T. Kirby, E. Campi, & F.A. James III (eds.) *A Companion to Peter Martyr Vermigli* (Leiden: Brill, 2009), 175–193.

Backus, Irena	*The Disputation of Baden, 1526 and Berne, 1528: Neutralizing the Early Church* (Princeton: Princeton Theological Seminary, 1993). *Studies in Reformed Theology and History,* 1.1 (1993), 1067–4268.
Baschera, L.	'Independent Yet Harmonious: Some Remarks on the Relationship between Theology of Peter Martyr Vermigli (1499–1562) and John Calvin', *Church History and Religious Culture* 91.1–2 (2011), 43–57.
Di Gangi, M.D.	*Peter Martyr Vermigli 1499–1562: Renaissance Man, Reformation Master* (Lanham: University Press of America, 1993).
Donnelly, J.P.	'Instruction', in P.M. Vermigli, *Dialogue on the Two Natures in Christ* (Peter Martyr Library, 2; Kirksville, MO: Sixteenth Century Essays & Studies, 1995), lx–xxv.
Donnelly, J.P.	*Calvinism and Scholasticism in Vermigli's Doctrine of Man and Grace* (Leiden: E.J. Brill, 1976).
Fesco, J.V.	'Peter Martyr Vermigli on Union with Christ and Justification', *The Reformed Theological Review* 70:1 (2011), 37–57.
Hoekema, A.A.	*Saved by Grace* (Grand Rapids: Eerdmans, 1994).
James, F.A., III	'Romans Commentary: Justification and Sanctification', in T. Kirby, E. Campi, & F.A. James III (eds.), *A Companion to Peter Martyr Vermigli* (Leiden: Brill, 2009), 305–317.
James, F.A., III	'Translator's Introduction', in P.M. Vermigli, *Predestination and Justification: Two Theological Loci* (Peter Martyr Library, 8; Kirksville: Sixteenth Century Essays & Studies, 2003), xv–xliv.
James, F.A., III	'Peter Martyr Vermigli, 1499–1562', in C. Lindberg (ed.), *The Reformation Theologians: An Introduction to Theology in the Early Modern Period* (Oxford: Blackwell, 2002), 198–212.
James, F.A., III	*De Justificatione: The Evolution of Peter Martyr Vermigli's Doctrine of Justification* (Unpublished Doctoral Dissertation, Westminster Theological Seminary, 2000).

James, F.A., III — 'Peter Martyr Vermigli: At the Crossroads of Late Medieval Scholasticism, Christian Humanism and Resurgent Augustinianism', in C. Trueman & R. Clark (eds.), *Protestant Scholasticism: Essays in Reassessment* (Carlisle: Paternoster, 1999), 62–78.

Kim, Jin Heung — *Scripturae et Patrum Testimoniis: The Function of the Church Father and the Medievals in Peter Martyr Vermigli's Two Eucharistic Treatises: Tractatio and Dialogus* (Apeldoorn: Instituut voor Reformatieonderzoek, 2009).

Klooster, F.H. — *Our Only Comfort: A Comprehensive Commentary on the Heidelberg Catechism*, Vol. 2 (Grand Rapids: Faith Alive, 2001).

Lane, A.N.S. — *John Calvin: Student of the Church Fathers* (Grand Rapids: Baker Books, 1999).

Lugioyo, Brian — *Martin Bucer's Doctrine of Justification: Reformation Theology and Early Modern Irenicism* (Oxford: Oxford University Press, 2010).

McGrath, A.E. — *A Life of John Calvin: A Study in Shaping of Western Culture* (Oxford: Blackwell, 1990).

McGrath, A.E. — *Iustitia Dei: A History of the Christian Doctrine of Justification* (Cambridge: Cambridge University Press, 1998).

McLelland, J.C. — 'A Literary History of the Loci Communes', in T. Kirby, E. Campi, & F.A. James III (eds.) *A Companion to Peter Martyr Vermigli* (Leiden: Brill, 2009), 479–494.

McLelland, J.C. — 'Translator's Introduction', in *Philosophical Works of Peter Martyr Vermigli* (Peter Martyr Library, 4; Kirksville: Sixteenth Century Essays & Studies, 1966), xix–xli.

McLelland, J.C. — *The Visible Words of God: An Exposition of the Sacramental Theology of Peter Martyr Vermigli: 1500–1562* (Edinburgh: Oliver & Boyd, 1957).

McNair, Philip — *Peter Martyr in Italy: An Anatomy of Apostasy* (Oxford: Clarendon Press, 1967).

Methuen, C. — 'Oxford: Reading Scripture in the University', in T. Kirby, E. Campi, and F.A. James III (eds.), *A Companion to Peter Martyr Vermigli* (Leiden: Brill, 2009), 71–93.

Muller, Richard A.	*Christ and the Decree. Christology and Predestination in Reformed Theology from Calvin to Perkins* (Eerdmans: Baker Academic, rpt. orig. 1986).
Praamsma, L.	*De kerk van alle tijden: verkenningen in het landschap van de kerkgeschiednis* 4 delen (Franeker: Uitgeverij T. Wever B.V., 1980).
Sturm, K.	*Die Theologie Peter Martyr Vermiglis während seines ersten Aufenthalts in Straßburg 1542–1547* (Neukirchen: Neukirchener Verlag, 1971).
Venema, Cornelis P.	*Accepted and Renewed in Christ: The 'Twofold Grace of God' and the Interpretation of Calvin's Theology* (Göttingen: Vandenhoeck & Ruprecht, 2007).
Vos. J.	*The Westminster Larger Catechism, A Commentary* (G.I. Williamson, ed.; Phillipsburg: P&R Publishing, 2002).
Williamson, G.I.	*The Shorter Catechism. Vol. 1: Questions 1–38* (Phillipsburg: Presbyterian and Reformed Publishing Co., 1970).

PART 6

A Personal Reflection on the Legacy of Romans

CHAPTER 17

On First Looking into Paul's Romans and Why Roman Catholics Need To Do It More

Michele Connolly

Introduction

This is one of those 'true confession' kind of essays.

The true confession I have to make is that as an undergraduate Theology student I feared studying a course on Romans. As someone who had grown up Catholic in a New South Wales rural environment, I had only ever encountered Romans occasionally and only in a very shallow way. I had never read Romans, intimidated by its reputation as the Epistle that our Protestant brothers and sisters seemed to claim in a very particular way. In my small reading as an undergraduate biblical student, while studying a Pauline survey course that covered everything *except* Romans, I had noticed that whenever a scholar wanted to say something conclusive and erudite about anything Paul wrote, they went to Romans. It seemed to carry an enormous weight of authority which silenced all arguments.

What's more, I noticed in this small amount of research—in which I read a number of Protestant scholars (but without any sense at all of the subtle differences there might be between them)—that they dealt with quite complex and subtle theological ideas, named with abstract nouns ending in 'ation', 'ism', or 'ness'. These words were not part of my Catholic religious vocabulary so that it was as though I had strayed into a foreign land where I did not know the culture or the language. 'Justification', just to name one fairly prominent word was only ever used in my hyphenated world with the prefix 'self' and was never a good thing. The same could be said for 'righteousness'. 'Sanctification', was another word which in my ... well, I had heard of that but in a context redolent of incense and Latin hymns and a fair amount of 'offering up' and 'making sacrifices'. But I didn't know that it was extremely important to be clear about which of 'justification' and 'sanctification' is the basis for the other and what relation they both bear to 'election'. Not to mention 'predestination', which I then discovered sometime later could be considered to be either single or double! And that one's salvation, which I had thought I knew about, could apparently hinge on the position one took on the relationship between all these matters.

So perhaps it is not surprising that, signing up for a course unit on Galatians and Romans, I feared the sheer intellectual effort of entering into this mighty theological enterprise and that somehow I would be required to defend my Catholic faith against the mighty edifice of studies on Romans by all those towering European scholars like Bultmann and Käsemann and Barth.

Who knew that, as it turned out, reading Käsemann on Abraham's faith in Romans 4, I would come to love his comment on Paul's view of God so much that I would learn it off by heart:

> Unlike the idols, the Father of Jesus works with poor, perishable material and always and most profoundly for and with the dead.[1]

I suspect that I may have been feeling somewhat poor and perishable at the time when I read this statement, and so it struck a chord with me. And so, I began to discover that despite 'righteousness', 'justification' and 'predestination', all the complex dynamisms of salvation, Paul in Romans was dealing with the human condition. For a one-time English literature teacher, I began to think of Romans as Paul's *King Lear* or Milton's 'Paradise Lost' and began to think that I could glimpse some intelligible shape in this mammoth and daunting letter.

---

1   Käsemann, *Perspectives on Paul*, 92.

Studying Romans as an Undergraduate

I will say that I *had* learned something in the Pauline survey course unit which I had done previously, that gave me a bit of a 'leg-up' into Romans. I had really been taken by the idea put forward by the Catholic scholar, Jerome Murphy-O'Connor, OP, who, in his work on Paul's Corinthian correspondence, argued that Paul as a Christian believer came to see that before Christ we were all spiritual troglodytes. That is, we were all religiously, cave-dwellers, virtually sub-human. Murphy-O'Connor writes that for Paul, 'If the truly human are those who have actuated the capacity for creative love that is built into their being, then those who fail to actuate this potentiality are non-human, or sub-human'.[2] Seeing the human predicament in this way, Paul believed that 'to move from the sub-human state of "death" to "life" the person has to be the recipient of the creative love of Christ, and that possibility is grasped only by those who exercise that same creativity for the benefit of others'.

This role of creative love in restoring God's Creation exercised by Jesus of Nazareth, crucified and acclaimed as the risen Lord and Messiah, was something that Paul as a Pharisee would have rejected vehemently, with the same intense passion with which he could stand by and approve of a riotous crowd stoning Stephen to death (see Acts 7:58–8:3). But once Paul had been captured by Christ, once he had been confronted by the Risen Lord, and had come to know the experience of living now, not his old life so driven by striving zealously and exhaustingly for holiness, but a life in which it was Christ who lived in him (Gal 2:20) —well, this was a new man. This Paul could say that his old life, even his greatest spiritual treasures were so much σκύβαλα (*skubala*), 'rubbish' to be discarded and thrown out (Phil 3:8). This new Paul would say 'Christ loved me and gave himself for me' (Gal 2:20).

In the last line or two, I have been following the coat-tails of another Catholic scholar, Brendan Byrne. Byrne's book *Reckoning with Romans*, published in the late 80s, when I was a theology undergraduate student, helped me to make sense of Paul's letter.[3] Byrne says in his Foreword to

---

2 Murphy-O'Connor, *Becoming Human Together*, 65.
3 Byrne, *Reckoning with Romans*. Byrne followed this book with a major commentary on Romans and a further treatment of Galatians and Romans together in one volume. See Byrne, *Romans and Galatians and Romans*.

Reckoning with Romans that in an effort to understand Paul from within his own thought world, he would attend carefully to Paul's language, focusing on words such as 'gospel', 'salvation', 'glory' and so forth. I found that it was the clear, and psychologically realistic way (without in any way resorting to psycho-babble) in which he explained 'flesh', 'spirit' and 'mind' and the way he lined up the *dramatis personae* (without in any way being histrionic) of the great struggle between Flesh, Sin, Law and Death on the one hand and Spirit, Christ, Freedom / Grace, and Life on the other, all fought out on the battle ground of the human person, that made the whole conceptual chess game become a recognizably human enterprise. Romans was talking about what it was to be human, about what Byrne labelled 'The Fatal Tension' when discussing Romans 7:14–26. This fatal tension operated between the desire in the human being to be at one with God and the opposing, seductive lure of being independent, answering only to oneself, effectively becoming one's own idol. This was the human being writ large in relationship with God, set within the scope of the destiny of God's Creation.

What's more, Romans spelled out theologically how in his death and resurrection, understood against the dramatic—even violent—backdrop of apocalyptic eschatology, Jesus took on the worst that Sin and Death could do. Sin and Death could have been fascinating in the way Milton's Satan was, except for the fact that Paul made clear in what an evil fashion Sin exploited the 'flesh' tendency in me to respond very poorly to 'Law', no matter how good or true that Law was. Reading Byrne's *Reckoning*, I came to see how all this sat within God's embrace and was resolved in the unimaginable glory of the resurrection—which was not just for Jesus but was also for me! Not just for me, but for all of us, for all of God's creation, standing on 'tippy toe', aching for God's true children to be revealed, so that the fatal tension of impossibility of being at rights with God was resolved and a new possibility for living emerged. This was for me, truly, a revelation. I had never heard the Christian life put quite that way before.

Romans' Vision of a New Possibility for Living

In particular, it was the sense of the *possibility* of living on a different basis—now out of a different mindset because of my daring to believe in the radical shift in reality that resurrection means—that offered a new vista to me. It is for this reason that I titled this presentation 'On First Looking Into Paul's Romans'. Just in case my poetic allusion escapes anyone, let me read the young John Keats' poem, 'On First Looking into Chapman's Homer', which names my sense of having come upon a new, vast and world-opening vista.

> ### On First Looking into Chapman's Homer[4]
> Much have I travell'd in the realms of gold,
> And many goodly states and kingdoms seen;
> Round many western islands have I been
> Which bards in fealty to Apollo hold.
> Oft of one wide expanse had I been told
> That deep-brow'd Homer ruled as his demesne;
> Yet did I never breathe its pure serene
> Till I heard Chapman speak out loud and bold:
> Then felt I like some watcher of the skies
> When a new planet swims into his ken;
> Or like stout Cortez when with eagle eye
> He star'd at the Pacific—and all his men
> Look'd at each other with a wild surmise—
> Silent, upon a peak in Darien.
>   JOHN KEATS

It may seem a bit dramatic, but as someone who had never encountered the ideas Paul spells out in Romans I did feel as though I had glimpsed an entirely new land with vast space within it.

I was ready to read Romans, I think, because I had scrambled somehow, untidily, in a previous academic course, up the foothills of Galatians and already had caught a glimpse of the new horizon at that spot in Galatians 5 where Paul names the works of the flesh and the fruits of the spirit. The contrasting metaphor of 'works' and 'fruits'

---

4 See Dame Helen Gardner, *The New Oxford Book of English Verse, 1250–1950*, 602.

already spoke of two different dynamics. All those 'works' were things I could at least imagine doing, with no assistance from anyone. For the record, I hadn't resorted to idolatry or sorcery (Gal 5:20) but I knew enough about other 'works of the flesh' such as 'enmities, strife, jealousy, anger and quarrels' (Gal 5:20) to be able to recognize myself. What Romans explained more fully than in Galatians was that on account of the devious exploitation of the frailty of my 'flesh' condition by Sin, provoking me through the Law, I was significantly disadvantaged, precariously situated, far too easily prone to acting contrary to God's Law. It was no excuse, but at the same time it was certainly no wonder if I were no better than 'the first Adam'. On the other hand, I knew how challenging it was to live in a sustained way, the 'love, joy, peace, patience, kindness, generosity, faithfulness,[23] gentleness, and self-control' listed in Galatians 5:22–23. But the clue and the hope were in the fact that Paul called them 'the fruits of the Spirit'. It was not *I* who would produce these but the Spirit in me would make these fruits grow in me as I allowed the Risen Lord to operate in my life. Attempting to produce these characteristic features of the good person, of the Christian, by my own grim determination and ferocious application, was simply not sustainable. How well I knew—indeed, my hunch is, we all know—Paul's cry 'Wretched [wo]man that I am! Who will rescue me from this body of death?' (Rom 7:24).

And I found it really and effectively consoling that in Romans, Paul immediately responds to this human predicament with the clarification: 'Thanks be to God through Jesus Christ our Lord! So then, with my mind I am a slave to the law of God, but with my flesh I am a slave to the law of sin. (Rom 7:24–25)'. I think I am resonating with what Paul means here because, to go back to Galatians, I found that being relieved of the obligation to produce solely out of my own resources, 'patience, kindness, generosity' produced a strange kind of freedom —indeed, an almost devil-may-care freedom about the need to 'be good'. I have no capacity to chart the intricate, interweaving, dynamic boundary between the ocean of God's grace offered and the landmass of my response to it. Suffice it to say that I then began to find that if I recognized what God knows, namely my 'flesh' condition, from within which God has acted decisively in Christ, and allow God's grace to produce the fruit of kindness, what God does is to provide me with lots of opportunities for kindness to be enacted!! And generosity! And gentleness!! And patience, above all!! To the strictly empirical external observer, my achievements on any these beautiful features of the Christian believer may not have changed a whit from when I was pursuing them on my own steam, but from within myself I have felt less grim, less anxious, more able to tolerate my own frailty, hopefully more tolerant of that of others, but also more able to relax and let God work towards the horizon that only God knows and only God can reach.

The Benefits to Catholics of Encounter with Romans

So, why should Catholics look into Romans more often? My thesis is simple—Romans is an untapped source offering Catholics a language they rarely use to talk about God's engagement with our world, reconciling us to God in the life, death and resurrection of Jesus of Nazareth, God's Messiah. Paul's way of talking about God's act of reconciliation of the world to Godself enables us to see that while God has a vast cosmic vision for Creation, God is also present to us lovingly in our everyday lives, urging us to live the realities of resurrection into the world.

Catholics do read Romans formally, in public liturgy. Romans is read at the Catholic Eucharistic Liturgy both on Sundays in Year A of the three year cycle and during the week in Year I of the 2-year daily cycle. The table in Appendix A shows what is and is not read. At first glance we see that the challenging chapters 2 and 7 are not used on Sundays—presumably because they would be too difficult to preach on in the 10–12 minute homily that is the norm in the Catholic Sunday liturgy. Otherwise, either the opening statements or the conclusions of most chapters are read, with a great focus on Romans 5 and the major part of chapter 8. Most of chapter 12 is avoided, except for the programmatic first two verses; the difficult verses about obeying governing authorities at the beginning of chapter 13 are omitted as are the fascinating verses at the beginning of chapter 16. Nevertheless, as a core of Romans, the selection people hear on Sundays introduces them to the major structures and argument of the letter.

If we add what people hear if they attend the daily Eucharist, then in year I, weeks 28–31, typically in about November, they hear Romans' argument extended. Some sections are repeated from the Sunday readings, while some gaps are filled. Rom 2:1–10 is heard and the final 9 verses (18–25) of Rom 7. All of Rom 8 is read, a considerable part of Chapter 12 and the early verses of Romans 16, except for that troublesome reference in the first two verses to Phoebe, deacon of Cenchreae!

The problem with Catholics is that although we do hear a substantial amount of Romans read across the liturgical cycle, we very rarely hear a homily on it and it is not the language with which we discuss our religious lives, either as individuals or as members of church and society. I have never in my life heard a *series* of homilies on Romans in a Catholic parish church. I have heard a few homilies here and there that focused mostly on the reading from one of Paul's letters, but never anything sustained over a series of weeks. I have lived in Australian country towns large and small, the cities of Melbourne and Sydney and have lived for a number of years in the USA, in Chicago and Berkeley. I think the Americans might preach on Paul a bit more than Australians do, but the Catholic tendency is for the Sunday homily to focus on the Gospel. The reasons are obvious enough: we always have a Gospel reading, for it's mostly a narrative about Jesus that is easy for the congregation to relate to and for the preacher to find some homiletic material to work with. The casualty is the formation of Catholic people in understanding in a Pauline way what God is doing in the world in Christ.

I believe that if Catholics heard more of Paul's letter to the Romans and understood what he was trying to achieve, the immense human and religious issues he was dealing with, they would benefit from having an enlarged horizon for their faith. They would gain a clearer sense of the Jewish context of the life of Jesus of Nazareth, by encountering what Ben Witherington III calls Paul's 'narrative thought world'.[5] That is, Paul writes his theology out of a sense of God acting in history, as told in the sacred scriptures of the Jewish people, the Old Testament. In Romans, we encounter some of the major figures of this narrative of God's encounter with the world. Adam, the first of all of us, is the symbol of the choice to favour the flesh condition in turning against God, thus setting in train the drama of God's action to reconcile human

---

5   See Witherington III, *Paul's Narrative Thought World*.

beings to Godself through Christ. We hear the story of Abraham whose paradigmatic act of faith in the God who 'gives life to the dead and calls into existence that which is not' (Rom 4:17), puts him at rights with God and establishes Abraham as the pattern by which we, believing in the resurrection of Jesus, are also put at rights with God.

The effect of Abraham's faith, Romans explains, was not just for Abraham but was for all of us who exercise the same 'right-making' faith as Abraham did. In our case it is not that we trust that, out of a situation of death, God will produce through us a great progeny. Rather, for us, the situation of death is first that of Jesus of Nazareth crucified and, second, our own spiritually deathly state. We share in Abraham's act of faith when we trust both that God raised Jesus from the dead and that God will also raise us with Jesus. Enacting this faith in the creative, restorative power and will of God, we are 'reckoned as righteous' as Abraham was.

I have suggested that in the realm of personal spirituality and Christian living, Paul can set people free from a limiting understanding of their relationship with God. I would say that Paul's apocalyptic eschatology, which of course we have to interpret for our own context, can help us deal with the sense many people have, that we are constructing from within God's beautiful creation a world of new, previously unknown evils. We need a theological way to talk about the faceless, inaccessible exploitation of globalisation that makes some so wealthy and others so mired in poverty, giving rise amongst other things, to terrorism. We need to talk about the way our faith in God relates to the grave dangers of global warming, which must lie behind the extreme weather events around the planet and which feature with increasing frequency in our news bulletins. Romans 8 can help us address anew these issues being raised now by the strongly emerging new discipline of ecotheology.

Apart from understanding that God is with us in the events of our world and the hope that rises from such understanding, Paul offers excitement. When people understand that Paul is the first writer in the New Testament to put into language the earliest experience of living faith in the resurrection of Jesus, then they can catch a sense of the transforming encounter with the Risen Lord that turned Paul's own life around. They can catch the enormous sense of wonder that I think Paul had, that he was living in a moment in which God had acted decisively in the world. They can get the sense of something irrepressibly fresh and new, something incorruptible because it arises out of the very creative core of God's own self, acting now in the world, for a purpose. Catholics right now in many places of the world could do with a new vision of hope. They could do with an encounter with God's word as Paul offers it, which suggests hope. The ordinary Catholic in the pew has had too much of an encounter with the reality of corruption in our very midst, that casts serious doubt on the 'already' and challenges the hopes of the 'not yet' in Paul's 'already but not yet' apocalyptic view of reality.

Reading Paul, hearing him preached, people can, above all, be reminded of the resurrection. It is my hunch, from sitting in the pews these many years, that not many Catholics have the resurrection at the forefront of their consciousness. They know we celebrate it each year at the Easter triduum. And, of course, it is the living breath of every liturgy we pray. But the Catholic focus tends to be on Jesus, his divinity and his ministry of healing and preaching here among us. We know that Jesus' ministry led to this death and resurrection but we could benefit from reflecting more specifically on this fundamental basis of our faith and hope.

Conclusion

To some extent I have caricatured my own religious tradition in its reception of Paul in regular liturgical practice, but I hope I have not done so unfairly. Whenever I get the chance to teach Paul I urge anybody who will teach or preach, but especially those who will preach, to think of preaching regularly on Paul. I believe that if Paul's letters, especially Romans, were to be focused on more specifically in regular Catholic worship and language, Catholics would find themselves thinking through, in a language new to them and thus in a fresh way, the central mysteries of our faith. In particular, if we were to think about the resurrection of Jesus, which was not for his sake only but for our sake as well, we would encounter the core energy of our faith. We would have a fresh sense of being at rights with God. It could be like standing on a previously unknown mountain peak in Darien. And that would be a good thing.

Appendix A
Romans Texts Read in the Roman Catholic Lectionary

Sundays and Major Feasts, Year A	**Weekday Masses, Year I**
Rom 1:1–7	Rom 1:1–7
	Rom 1:16–25
	Rom 2:1–11
Rom 3:21–25, 28	Rom 3:21–30
	Rom 4:1–8
	Rom 4:13, 16–18
Rom 4:18–25	Rom 4:20–25
Rom 5:1–2, 5–8	
Rom 5:1–5	
Rom 5:5b–11	
Rom 5:6–11	
Rom 5:12–15	
Rom 5:12–19 or 5:12, 17–19	Rom 5:12, 15b, 17–19, 20b–21
Rom 6:3–11	
Rom 6:3–4, 8–11	
	Rom 6:12–18
	Rom 6:19–23
	Rom 7:18–25a
Rom 8:8–11	Rom 8:1–11
Rom 8:8–17	Rom 8:12–17
Rom 8:9, 11–13	
Rom 8:14–17	
Rom 8:18–23	Rom 8:18–25
Rom 8:22–27	
Rom 8:26–27	Rom 8:26–30
Rom 8:28–30	
Rom 8:31b–34	Rom 8:31b–39
Rom 8:35, 37–39	
Rom 9:1–5	Rom 9:1–5

Sundays and Major Feasts, Year A	Weekday Masses, Year I
Rom 10:8–13	
	Rom 11:1–2a, 11–12, 25–29
Rom 11:13–15, 29–32	Rom 11:29–36
Rom 11:33–36	
Rom 12:1–2	
	Rom 12:5–16ab
Rom 13:8–10	Rom 13:8–10
Rom 13:11–14	
Rom 14:7–9	Rom 14:7–12
Rom 15:4–9	
	Rom 15:14–21
	Rom 16:3–9, 16, 22–27
Rom 16:25–27	

Bibliography

Byrne, B.	*Galatians and Romans* (Collegeville: Liturgical Press, 2010).
Byrne, B.	*Reckoning with Romans: A Contemporary Reading of Paul's Gospel* (Wilmington: Michael Glazier, 1986).
Byrne, B.	*Romans* (Collegeville: Liturgical Press, 1996).
Gardner, H., (ed.)	*The New Oxford Book of English Verse, 1250–1950* (Oxford: Oxford University Press, 1972).
Käsemann, E.	*Perspectives on Paul* (Margaret Kohl, transl; London: SCM, 1971).
Murphy-O'Connor, J.	*Becoming Human Together* (Dublin: Veritas, 1978).

www.ingramcontent.com/pod-product-compliance
Lightning Source LLC
Chambersburg PA
CBHW071327080526
44587CB00017B/2755